SECOND EDITION

HOMESTEADING

A BACKYARD GUIDE TO:
GROWING YOUR OWN FOOD • CANNING
KEEPING CHICKENS • GENERATING YOUR OWN ENERGY
CRAFTING • HERBAL MEDICINE • AND MORE

EDITED BY
ABIGAIL R. GEHRING

Skyhorse Publishing

Skyhorse Publishing books may be purchased in bulk at special discounts for sales promotion, corporate gifts, fund-raising, or educational purposes. Special editions can also be created to specifications. For details, contact the Special Sales Department, Skyhorse Publishing, 307 West 36th Street, 11th Floor, New York, NY 10018 or info@skyhorsepublishing.com.

Skyhorse® and Skyhorse Publishing® are registered trademarks of Skyhorse Publishing, Inc.®, a Delaware corporation.

www.skyhorsepublishing.com

10 9 8 7 6 5

Library of Congress Cataloging-in-Publication Data is available on file.

Print ISBN: 978-1-62914-366-8
Ebook ISBN: 978-1-62914-990-5

Printed in China

Contents

Acknowledgments

"I would maintain that thanks are the highest form of thought, and that gratitude is happiness doubled by wonder."

—*G. K. Chesterton*

This book was a team effort and it is something of an injustice that only one name appears on the cover. I am hugely grateful for all the people who used their time, skills, and creativity to bring it together.

Thanks to Tony Lyons for entrusting me with another exciting and challenging project, and for all his support along the way, and to Ann Treistman for her encouragement, ideas, and editorial guidance. Julie Matysik, this book wouldn't have gotten done if it weren't for the hours and hours you spent researching, compiling information, organizing, and writing—thank you. Bill Wolfsthal, Kathleen Go, and Adam Bozarth—I continue to be grateful for your marketing, editing, and designing skills, and for helping to make this work we do so fulfilling. Jessie Shiers, thanks for your close copyeditor's eye and useful comments. Thanks also to Janike Ruginis, Heather Chapman, Loren Yandoc, Erika Meller, and Matt Messmer for your willingness to jump in and help at any moment. To the many people who offered their thoughts, experiences, and expertise, I am truly grateful.

Finally, thanks to my family for being supportive even as I spent portions of so many evenings, weekends, and holidays with my eyes glued to the computer screen. Tim Lawrence, I am more and more amazed by your many talents. Thank you for not only encouraging me but for willingly doing so many excellent drawings to illustrate the words in these pages. We make a good team.

Introduction

"There is something in every one of you that waits and listens for the sound of the genuine in yourself. It is the only true guide you will ever have. And if you cannot hear it, you will all of your life spend your days on the ends of strings that somebody else pulls."

—Howard Thurman

Homesteading is about creating a lifestyle that is first of all genuine. It's about learning to recognize your needs—including energy, food, financial, and health needs—and finding out how they can be met creatively and responsibly. In order to harness your own energy for heat or electricity, you first have to face the facts about how much energy you use versus how much you actually need, and then assess your environment and resources to determine the best method for meeting those needs. Before buying chicks or any other animal to raise, be honest with yourself about the time you have to invest in caring for them. If you want a garden, there's no reason not to have one—but think about how large a plot you can manage before you start digging up dirt. Homesteading is different for every individual or family. Sometimes being genuine means letting go—at least temporarily—of grandiose schemes for acres of land, a home that is completely off the grid, and a barn full of animals. It could mean simply shopping at the local farmers' market for your produce, or making candles to light in the evenings to conserve electricity. If you live in an urban apartment, maybe you can plant vegetables on your roof, or start a community garden in a park or at a school.

This book is meant for everyone who has a desire to be a responsible steward of our natural resources, whether living in the heart of the city or on a hundred acres of farmland in rural Vermont. It's meant to give you inspiration, information, and the basic directions you need to take a few steps closer to a healthier, happier, and more responsible lifestyle. From sprouting seeds to making a solar water heater to handcrafting paper to brewing herbal teas, you'll find more ideas than you'll ever be able to put into practice in one lifetime. In this updated edition you'll also find new gems, including an appendix to help you identify trees, constellations, and birds.

Even if you only try one of the projects here, you'll have learned something new and experienced a different way of being, which hopefully you'll find enriching. Most importantly, you'll have had an opportunity to learn something about yourself and what homesteading means to you.

—Abigail R. Gehring

Part One

The Home Garden

"My green thumb came only as a result of the mistakes I made while learning to see things from the plant's point of view."

—H. Fred Ale

Creating a garden—whether it's a single tomato plant in a pot on your windowsill or a full acre chock-full of flowers and veggies—takes imagination, hard work, a bit of planning, patience, and a willingness to take risks. There are some factors you can control, like the condition of the soil you bury your seeds in, the time of year you start planting, and what plants you put where. But there will always be situations you can't predict; you might get a frost in June, an old discarded pumpkin seed might sprout up in the middle of your magnolias, or the cat could knock your basil plant off the counter to its demise on the kitchen floor. This element of surprise is one of the joys and challenges of gardening. If you can learn to skillfully navigate the factors in your control and accept the unpredictable circumstances with patience and a sense of humor, you'll have mastered a great life lesson. The following pages are meant to help you with that first part: gaining the knowledge and insight you need to give your garden the best chance of thriving. From understanding a plant's basic needs, to properly preparing soil, to protecting against weeds and harmful insects, this section covers all the gardening basics. Beyond that, you'll find information on growing plants without soil, tips for keeping your garden organic, and inspiration for gardening in urban environments. There is little in life as rewarding as enjoying a salad composed entirely of things you've picked from your own garden. But gardening is also about the process: If you can learn to love the feel of the dirt between your fingers, the burn in your muscles as you dig, and the quiet, slow way in which sprouts reach toward the sun, no moment of your labor will have been a waste, regardless of the end results.

Planning a Garden

Basic Plant Requirements

Before you start a garden, it's helpful to understand what plants need to thrive. Some plants, like dandelions, are tolerant of a wide variety of conditions, while others, such as orchids, have very specific requirements in order to grow successfully. Before spending time, effort, and money attempting to grow a new plant in a garden, do some research to learn about the conditions that a particular plant needs to grow properly.

Environmental factors play a key role in the proper growth of plants. Some of the essential factors that influence this natural process are as follows:

1. Length of Day

The amount of time between sunrise and sunset is the most critical factor in regulating vegetative growth, blooming, flower development, and the initiation of dormancy. Plants utilize increasing day length as a cue to promote their growth in spring, while decreasing day length in fall prompts them to prepare for the impending cold weather. Many plants require specific day length conditions in order to bloom and flower.

2. Light

Light is the energy source for all plants. Cloudy, rainy days or any shade cast by nearby plants and structures can significantly reduce the amount of light available to the plant. In addition, plants adapted to thrive in shady spaces cannot tolerate full sunlight. In general, plants will only survive where adequate sunlight reaches them at levels they are able to tolerate.

▲ Some gardens require more planning than others. Flower gardens can be carefully arranged to create patterns or to contain a specific range of colors, or they can be more casual, as this garden is. However, always keep in mind a plant's specific environmental needs before choosing a place for it.

Planning a Garden

3. Temperature

Plants grow best within an optimal range of temperatures. This temperature range may vary drastically depending on the plant species. Some plants thrive in environments where the temperature range is quite wide; others can only survive within a very narrow temperature variance. Plants can only survive where temperatures allow them to carry on life-sustaining chemical reactions.

4. Cold

Plants differ by species in their ability to survive cold temperatures. Temperatures below 60°F injure some tropical plants. Conversely, arctic species can tolerate temperatures well below zero. The ability of a plant to withstand cold is a function of the degree of dormancy present in the plant, its water status, and its general health. Exposure to wind, bright sunlight, or rapidly changing temperatures can also compromise a plant's tolerance to the cold.

5. Heat

A plant's ability to tolerate heat also varies widely from species to species. Many plants that evolved to grow in arid, tropical regions are naturally very heat tolerant, while sub-arctic and alpine plants show very little tolerance for heat.

▼ Feeling the soil can give you a sense of how nutrient-rich it is. Dark, crumbly, soft soil is usually full of nutrients. However, determining the pH requires a soil test (see page 13).

▲ Some plants, like cacti, thrive in hot, dry conditions.

6. Water

Different types of plants have different water needs. Some plants can tolerate drought during the summer but need winter rains to flourish. Other plants need a consistent supply of moisture to grow well. Careful attention to a plant's need for supplemental water can help you to select plants that need a minimum of irrigation to perform well in your garden. If you have poorly drained, chronically wet soil, you can select garden plants that naturally grow in bogs, marshlands, and other wet places.

7. Soil pH

A plant root's ability to take up certain nutrients depends on the pH—a measure of the acidity or alkalinity—of your soil. Most plants grow best in soils that have a pH between 6.0 and 7.0. Ericaceous plants, such as azaleas and blueberries, need acidic soils with a pH below 6.0 to grow well. Lime can be used to raise the soil's pH, and materials containing sulfates, such as aluminum sulfate and iron sulfate, can be used to lower the pH. The solubility of many trace elements is controlled by pH, and plants can only use the soluble forms of these important micronutrients.

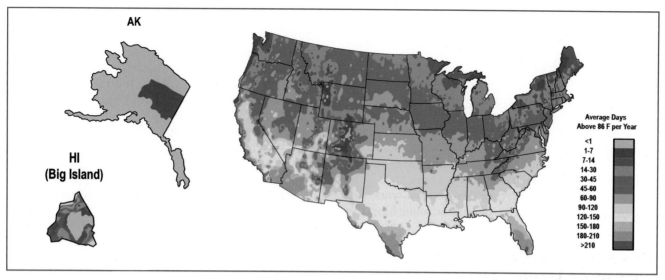

▲ This map shows the average number of days each year that an area experiences temperatures over 86 degrees ("heat days"). Zone 1 has less than one heat day and Zone 12 has more than 210 heat days. Most plants begin to suffer when it gets any hotter than 86 degrees, though different plants have different levels of tolerance.

A Basic Plant Glossary

Here is some terminology commonly used in reference to plants and gardening:

annual—a plant that completes its life cycle in one year or season.

arboretum—a landscaped space where trees, shrubs, and herbaceous plants are cultivated for scientific study or educational purposes, and to foster appreciation of plants.

axil—the area between a leaf and the stem from which the leaf arises.

bract—a leaflike structure that grows below a flower or cluster of flowers and is often colorful. Colored bracts attract pollinators, and are often mistaken for petals. Poinsettia and flowering dogwood are examples of plants with prominent bracts.

cold hardy—capable of withstanding cold weather conditions.

conifers—plants that predate true, flowering plants in evolution; conifers lack true flowers and produce separate male and female strobili, or cones. Some conifers, such as yews, have fruits enclosed in a fleshy seed covering.

cultivar—a cultivated variety of a plant selected for a feature that distinguishes it from the species from which it was selected.

deciduous—having leaves that fall off or are shed seasonally to avoid adverse weather conditions, such as cold or drought.

herbaceous—having little or no woody tissue. Most perennials or annuals are herbaceous.

hybrid—a plant, or group of plants, that results from the interbreeding of two distinct cultivars, varieties, species, or genera.

inflorescence—a floral axis that contains many individual flowers in a specific arrangement; also known as a flower cluster.

native plant—a plant that lives or grows naturally in a particular region without direct or indirect human intervention.

panicle—a pyramidal, loosely branched flower cluster; a panicle is a type of inflorescence.

perennial—a plant that persists for several years, usually dying back to a perennial crown during the winter and initiating new growth each spring

shrub—a low-growing, woody plant, usually less than 15 feet tall, that often has multiple stems and may have a suckering growth habit (the tendency to sprout from the root system).

taxonomy—the study of the general principles of scientific classification, especially the orderly classification of plants and animals according to their presumed natural relationships.

tree—a woody perennial plant having a single, usually elongated main stem, or trunk, with few or no branches on its lower part.

wildflower—a herbaceous plant that is native to a given area and is representative of unselected forms of its species.

woody plant—a plant with persistent woody parts that do not die back in adverse conditions. Most woody plants are trees or shrubs.

Selecting a Site for Your Garden

Selecting a site for your garden is the first step in growing the vegetables, fruits, and herbs that you want. You do not need a large space to grow a significant amount. Creating a garden that is about 25 feet squared should be sufficient for a family. It is important that you don't start off with a space that is too large—it is better to start small and then work your way up if you find that gardening is something that you truly enjoy.

Five Factors to Consider When Choosing a Garden Site

1. Sunlight

Sunlight is crucial for the growth of vegetables and other plants. For your garden to grow, your plants will need at least six hours of direct sunlight per day. To make sure your garden receives an ample amount of sunlight, don't select a garden site that will be in the shade of trees, shrubs, houses, or other structures. Certain vegetables, such as broccoli and spinach, grow just fine in shadier spots, so if your garden does receive some shade, plant those types of vegetables in the shadier areas. However, on a whole, if your garden does not receive at least six hours of intense sunlight per day, it will not grow as efficiently or successfully.

2. Proximity

Another consideration is how close you place your garden to your home. If your garden is closer to your house and easy to reach, you will most likely use it more often—and to its fullest potential. Having a garden close to your home will help you to pick your vegetables and fruit at their peak ripeness, allowing you access to an abundance of fresh produce on a regular basis. Weeding, watering, and controlling pests are all more likely to be attended to if your garden is situated near your home. Overall, gardens placed closer to the home will receive more attention and thus be healthier and more productive.

3. Soil Quality

Contrary to some beliefs, you do not need perfect soil to start and grow a productive garden. However, it is best to have soil that is fertile, full of organic materials that provide nutrients to the plant roots, and easy to dig and till. Loose, well-drained soil is ideal for growing a good garden. If there is a section of your yard where water does not easily drain after a good, soaking rain, it is best not to plant your garden in that area, as the excess water will most likely drown your garden plants. Furthermore, soils that are of a clay or sandy consistency are not as effective in growing plants. To make these types of soils more nutrient-rich and fertile, add in organic materials (such as compost or manure) to improve their quality.

4. Water Availability

Water is vital to keeping your garden green, healthy, and productive. A successful garden needs around 1 inch of water per week to thrive. Rain and irrigation systems

▲ A garden of about 25 feet squared should be adequate to produce enough vegetables for a family of four to six to enjoy.

▲ If you don't have enough space for a full garden, you can plant in flowerpots or other containers. Potted plants are especially convenient because you can move them around to get more light or to make watering easier.

▼ Gloves, a trowel, and a watering can are some of the most basic tools you should have on hand for gardening.

are effective in maintaining this 1-inch-per-week quota. Situating your garden near a spigot or hose is ideal, allowing you to keep the soil moist and your plants happy.

5. Elevation

Make sure your garden is not located in an area where air cannot circulate and where frost quickly forms. Placing your garden in a low-lying area, such as at the base of a slope, should be avoided, as these lower areas do not warm as quickly in the spring, and frost forms quickly during the spring and fall because the cold air collects in these areas. Your garden should, if at all possible, be elevated slightly, on ground that is higher up. This way, your garden plants will be less likely to be affected by frost and you'll be able to start your garden growing earlier in the spring and harvest well into the fall.

Some Other Things to Consider

When planning out your garden, it is useful to sketch a diagram of what you want your garden to look like. What sorts of plants to you want to grow? Do you want a garden purely for growing vegetables or do you want to mix in some fruits, herbs, and wildflowers? Choosing the appropriate plants to grow next to each other will help your garden grow well and will provide you with ample produce throughout the growing season (see the charts on page 10).

When planting a garden, be sure to have access to many types of tools. You'll need a spade or digging fork for digging holes for seeds or seedlings (or, if the soil is loose enough, you can just use your hands). You'll also need a trowel, rake, or hoe to smooth over the garden surface. A measuring stick is helpful when spacing your plants or seeds (if you don't have a measuring stick, you can use a precut string to measure). If you are planting seedlings or established plants, you may need stakes and string to tie them up (so they don't fall over in inclement weather or when they start producing fruit or vegetables). Finally, if you are interested in installing an irrigation system for your garden, you will need to buy the appropriate materials for this purpose.

Companion Planting

Plants have natural substances built into their structures that repel or attract certain insects and can have an effect on the growth rate and even the flavor of the other plants around them. Thus, some plants aid each other's growth when planted in close proximity and others inhibit each other. Smart companion planting will help your garden remain healthy, beautiful, and in harmony, while deterring certain insect pests and other factors that could be potentially detrimental to your garden plants.

These charts list various types of garden vegetables, herbs, and flowers and their respective companion and "enemy" plants.

Vegetables

Type	Companion plant(s)	Avoid
Asparagus	Tomatoes, parsley, basil	Onion, garlic, potatoes
Beans	Eggplant	Tomatoes, onion, kales
Beets	Mint	Runner beans
Broccoli	Onion, garlic, leeks	Tomatoes, peppers, mustard
Cabbage	Onion, garlic, leeks	Tomatoes, peppers, beans
Carrot	Leeks, beans	Radish
Celery	Daisies, snapdragons	Corn, aster flower
Corn	Legumes, squash, cucumber	Tomatoes, celery
Cucumber	Radishes, beets, carrots	Tomatoes
Eggplant	Marigolds, mint	Runner beans
Leeks	Carrots	Legumes
Lettuce	Radish, carrots	Celery, cabbage, parsley
Melon	Pumpkin, squash	None
Peppers	Tomatoes	Beans, cabbage, kales
Onion	Carrots	Peas, beans
Peas	Beans, corn	Onion, garlic
Potato	Horseradish	Tomatoes, cucumber
Tomatoes	Carrots, celery, parsley	Corn, peas, potato, kales

Herbs

Type	Companion Plant(s)	Avoid
Basil	Chamomile, anise	Sage
Chamomile	Basil, cabbage	Other herbs (it will become oily)
Cilantro	Beans, peas	None
Chives	Carrots	Peas, beans
Dill	Cabbage, cucumber	Tomatoes, carrots
Fennel	Dill	Everything else
Garlic	Cucumber, peas, lettuce	None
Oregano	Basil, peppers	None
Peppermint	Broccoli, cabbage	None
Rosemary	Sage, beans, carrots	None
Sage	Rosemary, beans	None
Summer savory	Onion, green beans	None

Flowers

Types	Companion Plant(s)	Avoid
Geraniums	Roses, tomatoes	None
Marigolds	Tomatoes, peppers, most plants	None
Petunias	Squash, asparagus	None
Sunflowers	Corn, tomatoes	None
Tansies	Roses, cucumber, squash	None

Plants for the Shade

It is best to situate your garden in an area that receives at least six hours of direct sunlight per day—especially if you want to grow vegetables or fruits. However, if the only part of your yard suitable for gardening is blocked by partial or full shade (or part of your sunlit garden receives partial shade during the day), you can still grow plenty of things in these areas—you just need to select plants that grow best in these types of environments. It is a good idea, either when buying seedlings from your local nursery or planting your own seeds, to read the accompanying label or packet or do a little research before planting to make sure your plants will thrive in a shadier environment.

Flowering plants that do well in partial and full shade:
- Bee balm
- Bellflower
- Bleeding heart
- Cardinal flower
- Coleus
- Columbine
- Daylily
- Dichondra
- Fern
- Forget-me-not
- Globe daisy
- Golden bleeding heart
- Impatiens
- Leopardbane
- Lily of the valley
- Meadow rue
- Pansy
- Periwinkle
- Persian violet
- Primrose
- Rue anemone
- Snapdragon
- Sweet alyssum
- Thyme

▲ Beets like cool weather and do well in shady areas with rich soil. Plant beets at least 1 inch deep and 2 inches part. Weed regularly to ensure strong root development.

Vegetable plants that can grow in partial shade:
- Arugula
- Beans
- Beets
- Broccoli
- Brussels sprouts
- Cauliflower
- Endive
- Kale
- Leaf lettuce
- Peas
- Radish
- Spinach
- Swiss chard

▲ Bee balm does well in partial shade. Its bright color and sweet nectar have a tendency to attract bees and humming birds.

▲ Spinach and other green, leafy vegetables tend to do well in shady areas. Just be sure they get enough water; trees or other shade-producing canopies can also block rainfall.

Improving Your Soil

When gardening, it is essential to have nutrient-rich, fertile soil in order to grow the best and healthiest plants—plants that will supply you with quality fruits, vegetables, and flowers. Sometimes, soil loses its fertility (or has minimum fertility based on the region in which you live), and so measures must be taken to improve your soil and, subsequently, your garden.

Soil Quality Indicators

Soil quality is an assessment of how well soil performs all of its functions now and how those functions are being preserved for future use. The quality of soil cannot just be determined by measuring row or garden yield, water quality, or any other single outcome, nor can it be measured directly. Thus, it is important to look at specific indicators to better understand the properties of soil. Plants can provide us with clues about how well the soil is functioning—whether a plant is growing and producing quality fruits and vegetables or failing to yield such things is a good indicator of the quality of the soil it's growing in.

Indicators are measurable properties of soil or plants that provide clues about how well the soil can function. Indicators can be physical, chemical, and biological properties, processes, or characteristics of soils. They can also be visual features of plants.

Useful indicators of soil quality:
- are easy to measure
- measure changes in soil functions
- encompass chemical, biological, and physical properties
- are accessible to many users
- are sensitive to variations in climate and management

Indicators can be assessed by qualitative or quantitative techniques, such as soil tests. After measurements are collected, they can be evaluated by looking for patterns and comparing results to measurements taken at a different time.

Examples of soil quality indicators:

1. Soil Organic Matter

Promotes soil fertility, structure, stability, nutrient retention, and helps combat soil erosion.

2. Physical Indicators

These include soil structure, depth, infiltration and bulk density, and water hold capacity. Quality soil will retain and transport water and nutrients effectively;

▼ Good soil is usually dark, moist, and dense.

it will provide habitat for microbes; it will promote compaction and water movement; and, it will be porous and easy to work with.

3. Chemical Indicators

These include pH, electrical conductivity, and extractable nutrients. Quality soil will be at its threshold for plant, microbial, biological, and chemical activity; it will also have plant nutrients that are readily available.

4. Biological Indicator

These include microbial biomass, mineralizable nitrogen, and soil respiration. Quality soil is a good repository for nitrogen and other basic nutrients for prosperous plant growth; it has a high soil productivity and nitrogen supply; and there is a good amount of microbial activity.

Soil and Plant Nutrients

Nutrient Management

There are 20 nutrients that all plants require. Six of the most important nutrients, called macronutrients, are: calcium, magnesium, nitrogen, phosphorous, potassium, and sulfur. Of these, nitrogen, phosphorus, and potassium are essential to healthy plant growth and so are required in relatively large amounts. Nitrogen is associated with lush vegetative growth, phosphorus is required for flowering and fruiting, and potassium is necessary for durability and disease resistance. Calcium, sulfur, and magnesium are also required in comparatively large quantities and aid in the overall health of plants.

The other nutrients, referred to as micronutrients, are required in very small amounts. These include such elements as copper, zinc, iron, and boron. *While both macro- and micronutrients are required for good plant growth, over-application of these nutrients can be as detrimental to the plant as a nutrient deficiency.* Over-application of plant nutrients may not only impair plant growth, but may also contaminate groundwater by penetrating through the soil or may pollute surface waters.

Soil Testing

Testing your soil for nutrients and pH is important in order to provide your plants with the proper balance of nutrients (while avoiding over-application). If you are establishing a new lawn or garden, a soil test is strongly recommended. The cost of soil testing is minor in comparison to the cost of plant materials and labor. Correcting a problem before planting is much simpler and cheaper than afterwards.

Once your garden is established, continue to take periodic soil samples. While many people routinely lime their soil, this can raise the pH of the soil too high. Likewise, since many fertilizers tend to lower the soil's pH, it may drop below desirable levels after

▲ This electronic soil tester runs on one AA battery and gives pH, nutrient, and moisture level readings within minutes.

several years, depending on fertilization and other soil factors, so occasional testing is strongly encouraged.

Home tests for pH, nitrogen, phosphorus, and potassium are available from most garden centers. While these may give you a general idea of the nutrients in your soil, they are not as reliable as tests performed by the Cooperative Extension Service at land grant universities. University and other commercial testing services will provide more detail, and you can request special tests for micronutrients if you suspect a problem. In addition to the analysis of nutrients in your soil, these services often provide recommendations for the application of nutrients or how best to adjust the pH of your soil.

The test for soil pH is very simple. pH is a measure of how acidic or alkaline your soil is. A pH of 7 is considered neutral. Below 7 is acidic and above 7 is alkaline. Because pH greatly influences plant nutrients, adjusting the pH will often correct a nutrient problem. At a high pH, several of the micronutrients become less available for plant uptake. Iron deficiency is a common problem, even at a neutral pH, for such plants as rhododendrons and blueberries. At a very low soil pH, other micronutrients may be too available to the plant, resulting in toxicity.

Phosphorus and potassium are tested regularly by commercial testing labs. While there are soil tests for nitrogen, these may be less reliable. Nitrogen is present in the soil in several forms that can change rapidly. Therefore, a precise analysis of nitrogen is

Steps for Taking a Soil Test

1. If you intend to send your sample to the land grant university in your state, contact the local Cooperative Extension Service for information and sample bags. If you intend to send your sample to a private testing lab, contact them for specific details about submitting a sample.
2. Follow the directions carefully for submitting the sample. The following are general guidelines for taking a soil sample:
   - Sample when the soil is moist but not wet.
   - Obtain a clean pail or similar container.
   - Clear away the surface litter or grass.
   - With a spade or soil auger, dig a small amount of soil to a depth of 6 inches.
   - Place the soil in the clean pail.
   - Repeat until the required number of samples has been collected.
   - Mix the samples together thoroughly.
   - From the mixture, take the sample that will be sent for analysis.
   - Send immediately. Do not dry before sending.
3. If you are using a home soil testing kit, follow the above steps for taking your sample. Follow the directions in the test kit carefully so you receive the most accurate reading possible.

more difficult to obtain. Most university soil test labs do not routinely test for nitrogen. Home testing kits often contain a test for nitrogen that may give you a general, though not necessarily completely accurate, idea of the presence of nitrogen in your garden soil.

Organic matter is often part of a soil test. Organic matter has a large influence on soil structure and so is highly desirable for your garden soil. Good soil structure improves aeration, water movement, and retention. This encourages increased microbial activity and root growth, both of which influence the availability of nutrients for plant growth. Soils high in organic matter tend to have a greater supply of plant nutrients compared to many soils low in organic matter. Organic matter tends to bind up some soil pesticides, reducing their effectiveness, and so this should be taken into consideration if you are planning to apply pesticides to your garden.

Tests for micronutrients are usually not performed unless there is reason to suspect a problem. Certain plants have greater requirements for specific micronutrients and may show deficiency symptoms if those nutrients are not readily available. (See charts on pages 16 and 67.)

▲ To determine the various layers of your soil, called your "soil profile," a core sample can be taken. This requires a boring machine, which will insert a hollow core rod, or "probe" like these shown here deep into the ground to extract soil. The layers will be distinguishable by the change in soil color. Several core samples can be mixed together for a more accurate soil test.

Enriching Your Soil

Organic and Commercial Fertilizers and Returning Nutrients to Your Soil

Once you have the results of the soil test, you can add nutrients or soil amendments as needed to alter the pH. If you need to raise the soil's pH, use lime. Lime is most effective when it is mixed into the soil; therefore, it is best to apply before planting (if you apply lime in the fall, it has a better chance of correcting any soil acidity problems for the next growing season). For large areas, rototilling is most effective. For small areas or around plants, working the lime into the soil with a spade or cultivator is preferable. When working around plants, be careful not to dig too deeply or roughly so that you damage plant roots. Depending on the form of lime and the soil conditions, the change in pH may be gradual. It may take several months before a significant change is noted. Soils high in organic matter and clay tend to take larger amounts of lime to change the pH than do sandy soils.

If you need to lower the pH significantly, especially for plants such as rhododendrons, you can use aluminum sulfate. In all cases, follow the soil test or manufacturer's recommended rates of application. Again, mixing well into the soil is recommended.

There are numerous choices for providing nitrogen, phosphorus, and potassium, the nutrients your plants need to thrive. Nitrogen (N) is needed for healthy, green growth and regulation of other nutrients. Phosphorus (P) helps roots and seeds properly develop and resist disease. Potassium (K) is also important in root development and disease resistance. If your soil is of adequate fertility, applying compost may be the best method of introducing additional nutrients. While compost is relatively low in nutrients compared to commercial fertilizers, it is especially beneficial in improving the condition of the soil and is nontoxic. By keeping the soil loose, compost allows plant roots to grow well throughout the soil, helping them to extract nutrients from a larger area. A loose soil enriched with compost is also an excellent habitat for earthworms and other beneficial soil microorganisms that are essential for releasing nutrients for plant use. The nutrients from compost are also released slowly, so there is no concern about "burning" the plant with an over-application of synthetic fertilizer.

Manure is also an excellent source of plant nutrients and is an organic matter. Manure should be composted before applying, as fresh manure may be too strong and can injure plants. Be careful when composting manure. If left in the open, exposed to rain, nutrients may leach out of the manure and the runoff can contaminate nearby waterways. Store the manure away from wells and any waterways and make sure that any runoff is confined or slowly released into a vegetated area. Improperly applied manure

◀ After rototilling or mixing in the fertilizer with a spade, you may wish to rake out the soil to make it smooth and well-aerated.

▲ For potted plants, you can apply fertilizer around the edge of the pot if needed, but try to avoid direct contact between the plant's roots, leaves, or stem and the fertilizer.

8 to 12 inches. If adding to existing plants, work carefully around the plants so as not to harm the existing roots.

Green manures are another source of organic matter and plant nutrients. Green manures are crops that are grown and then tilled into the soil. As they break down, nitrogen and other plant nutrients become available. These manures may also provide additional benefits of reducing soil erosion. Green manures, such as rye and oats, are often planted in the fall after the crops have been harvested. In the spring, these are tilled under before planting.

With all organic sources of nitrogen, whether compost or manure, the nitrogen must be changed to an inorganic form before the plants can use it. Therefore, it is important to have well-drained, aerated soils that provide the favorable habitat for the soil microorganisms responsible for these conversions.

There are also numerous sources of commercial fertilizers that supply nitrogen, phosphorus, and potassium, though it is preferable to use organic fertilizers, such as compost and manures. However, if you choose to use a commercial fertilizer, it is important to know how to read the amount of nutrients contained in each bag. The first number on the fertilizer analysis is the percentage of nitrogen; the second number is phosphorus; and the third number is the potassium content. A fertilizer that has a 10-20-10 analysis contains twice as much of each of the nutrients as a 5-10-5. How much of each nutrient you need depends on your soil test results and the plants you are fertilizing.

As was mentioned before, nitrogen stimulates vegetative growth while phosphorus stimulates flowering. Too much nitrogen can inhibit flowering and fruit production. For many flowers and vegetables, a fertilizer higher in phosphorus than nitrogen is preferred, such

also can be a source of pollution. If you are not composting your own manure, you can purchase some at your local garden store. For best results, work composted manure into the soil around the plants or in your garden before planting.

If preparing a bed before planting, compost and manure may be worked into the soil to a depth of

Soil Test Reading	What to Do
High pH	Your soil is alkaline. To lower pH, add elemental sulfur, gypsum, or cottonseed meal. Sulfur can take several months to lower your soil's pH, as it must first convert to sulfuric acid with the help of the soil's bacteria.
Low pH	Your soil is too acidic. Add lime or wood ashes.
Low nitrogen	Add manure, horn or hoof meal, cottonseed meal, fish meal, or dried blood.
High nitrogen	Your soil may be over-fertilized. Water the soil frequently and don't add any fertilizer.
Low phosphorus	Add cottonseed meal, bonemeal, fish meal, rock phosphate, dried blood, or wood ashes.
High phosphorous	Your soil may be over-fertilized. Avoid adding phosphorous-rich materials and grow lots of plants to use up the excess.
Low potassium	Add potash, wood ashes, manure, dried seaweed, fish meal, or cottonseed meal.
High potassium	Continue to fertilize with nitrogen and phosphorous-rich soil additions, but avoid potassium-rich fertilizers for at least two years.
Poor drainage or too much drainage	If your soil is a heavy, clay-like consistency, it won't drain well. If it's too sandy, it won't absorb nutrients as it should. Mix in peat moss or compost to achieve a better texture.

as a 5-10-5. For lawns, nitrogen is usually required in greater amounts, so a fertilizer with a greater amount of nitrogen is more beneficial.

Fertilizer Application

Commercial fertilizers are normally applied as a dry, granular material or mixed with water and poured onto the garden. If using granular materials, avoid spilling on sidewalks and driveways because these materials are water soluble and can cause pollution problems if rinsed into storm sewers. Granular fertilizers are a type of salt, and if applied too heavily, they have the capability of burning the plants. If using a liquid fertilizer, apply directly to or around the base of each plant and try to contain it within the garden only.

To decrease the potential for pollution and to gain the greatest benefits from fertilizer, whether it's a commercial variety, compost, or other organic materials, apply it when the plants have the greatest need for the nutrients. Plants that are not actively growing do not have a high requirement for nutrients; thus, nutrients applied to dormant plants, or plants growing slowly due to cool temperatures, are more likely to be wasted. While light applications of nitrogen may be recommended for lawns in the fall, generally, nitrogen fertilizers should not be applied to most plants in the fall in regions of the country that experience

cold winters. Since nitrogen encourages vegetative growth, if it is applied in the fall it may reduce the plant's ability to harden properly for winter.

In some gardens, you can reduce fertilizer use by applying it around the individual plants rather than broadcasting it across the entire garden. Much of the phosphorus in fertilizer becomes unavailable to the plants once spread on the soil. For better plant uptake, apply the fertilizer in a band near the plant. Do not apply directly to the plant or in contact with the roots, as it may burn and damage the plant and its root system.

A Cheap Way to Fertilize

To save money while still providing your lawn and garden with extra nutrients, simply mow your lawn on a regular basis and leaving the grass clippings to decompose on the lawn, or spread them around your garden to decompose into the soil. Annually, this will provide nutrients equivalent to one or two fertilizer applications and it is a completely organic means of boosting a soil's nutrient content.

▲ The fertilizer in this garden has only been applied to the garden rows.

How to Properly Apply Fertilizer to Your Garden

- Apply fertilizer when the soil is moist, and then water lightly. This will help the fertilizer move into the root zone where its nutrients are available to the plants, rather than staying on top of the soil where it can be blown or washed away.
- Watch the weather. Avoid applying fertilizer immediately before a heavy rain system is predicted to arrive. Too much rain (or sprinkler water) will take the nutrients away from the lawn's root zone and could move the fertilizer into another water system, contaminating it.
- Use the minimum amount of fertilizer necessary and apply it in small, frequent applications. An application of two pounds of fertilizer, five times per year, is better than five pounds of fertilizer twice a year.
- If you are spreading the fertilizer by hand in your garden, wear gardening gloves and be sure not to damage the plant or roots around which you are fertilizing.

Rules of Thumb for Proper Fertilizer Use

It is best to apply fertilizer before or at the time of planting. Fertilizers can either be spread over a large area or confined to garden rows, depending on the condition of your soil and the types of plants you will be growing. After spreading, till the fertilizer into the soil about 3 to 4 inches deep. Only spread about one half of the fertilizer this way and then dispatch the rest 3 inches to the sides of each row and also a little below each seed or established plant. This method, minus the spreader, is used when applying fertilizer to specific rows or plants by hand.

Composting in Your Backyard

Composting is nature's own way of recycling yard and household wastes by converting them into valuable fertilizer, soil organic matter, and a source of plant nutrients. The result of this controlled decomposition of organic matter—a dark, crumbly, earthy-smelling material—works wonders on all kinds of soil by providing vital nutrients and contributing to good aeration and moisture-holding capacity, to help plants grow and look better.

Composting can be as simple or as involved as you would like, depending on how much yard waste you have, how fast you want results, and the effort you are willing to invest. Because all organic matter eventually decomposes, composting speeds up the process

▲ The calcium in eggshells encourages cell growth in plants. You can even mix crushed eggshells directly into the soil around tomatoes, zucchini, squash, and peppers to prevent blossom end rot. Eggshells also help deter slugs, snails, and cutworm.

by providing an ideal environment for bacteria and other decomposing microorganisms. The composting season coincides with the growing season, when conditions are favorable for plant growth, so those same conditions work well for biological activity in the compost pile. However, since compost generates heat, the process may continue later into the fall or winter. The final product—called humus or compost—looks and feels like fertile garden soil.

Compost Preparation

While a multitude of organisms, fungi, and bacteria is involved in the overall process, there are four basic ingredients for composting: nitrogen, carbon, water, and air.

A wide range of materials may be composted because anything that was once alive will naturally decompose. The starting materials for composting, commonly referred to as feed stocks, include leaves, grass clippings, straw, vegetable and fruit scraps, coffee grounds, livestock manure, sawdust, and shredded paper. However, some materials that should always be avoided include diseased plants, dead animals, noxious weeds, meat scraps that may attract animals, and dog or cat manure, which can carry disease. Since adding kitchen wastes to compost may attract flies and insects, make a hole in the center of your pile and bury the waste.

Common Composting Materials

Cardboard	Vegetable scraps
Coffee grounds	Weeds without seed
Corn cobs	heads
Corn stalks	Wood chips
Food scraps	Woody brush
Grass clippings	
Hedge trimmings	**Avoid using:**
Livestock manure	Bread and grains
Newspapers	Cooking oil
Plant stalks	Dairy products
Pine needles	Dead animals
Old potting soil	Diseased plant mate-
Sawdust	rial
Seaweed	Dog or cat manure
Shredded paper	Grease or oily foods
Straw	Meat or fish scraps
Tea bags	Noxious or invasive
Telephone books	weeds
Tree leaves and twigs	Weeds with seed heads

---

pile so it has many air passages. The air in the pile is usually used up faster than the moisture, and extremes of sun or rain can adversely affect this balance, so the materials must be turned or mixed up often with a pitchfork, rake, or other garden tool to add air that will sustain high temperatures, control odor, and yield faster decomposition.

Over time, you'll see that the microorganisms will break down the organic material. Bacteria are the first to break down plant tissue and are the most numerous and effective compost makers in your compost pile. Fungi and protozoans soon join the bacteria and, later in the cycle, centipedes, millipedes, beetles, sow bugs, nematodes, worms, and numerous others complete the composting process. With the right ingredients and favorable weather conditions, you can have a finished compost pile in a few weeks.

How to Make Your Own Backyard Composting Heap

1. Choose a level, well-drained site, preferably near your garden.
2. Decide whether you will be using a bin after checking on any local or state regulations for composting in urban areas, as some communities require

▲ Most of your household food waste can be composted. Avoid composting meat scraps, dairy products, grains, or very greasy foods.

For best results, you will want an even ratio of green, or wet, material, which is high in nitrogen, and brown, or dry, material, which is high in carbon. Simply layer or mix landscape trimmings and grass clippings, for example, with dried leaves and twigs in a pile or enclosure. If there is not a good supply of nitrogen-rich material, a handful of general lawn fertilizer or barnyard manure will help even out the ratio.

Though rain provides the moisture, you may need to water the pile in dry weather or cover it in extremely wet weather. The microorganisms, which are small forms of plant and animal life, in the compost pile function best when the materials are as damp as a wrung-out sponge—not saturated with water. A moisture content of 40 to 60 percent is preferable. To test for adequate moisture, reach into your compost pile, grab a handful of material, and squeeze it. If a few drops of water come out, it probably has enough moisture. If it doesn't, add water by putting a hose into the pile so that you aren't just wetting the top, or, better yet, water the pile as you turn it.

Air is the only part that cannot be added in excess. For proper aeration, you'll need to punch holes in the

▼ As your compost begins to break down, you may notice gases escaping from the pile.

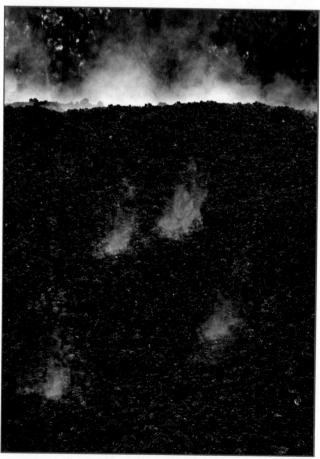

rodent-proof bins. There are numerous styles of compost bins available, depending on your needs, ranging from a moveable bin formed by wire mesh to a more substantial wooden structure consisting of several compartments. You can also easily make your own bin using chicken wire or scrap wood. While a bin will help contain the pile, it is not absolutely necessary, as you can build your pile directly on the ground. To help with aeration, you may want to place some woody material on the ground where you will build your pile.

3. Ensure that your pile will have a minimum dimension of 3 feet all around, but is no taller than 5 feet, as not enough air will reach the microorganisms at the center if it is too tall. If you don't have this amount at one time, simply stockpile your materials until a sufficient quantity is available for proper mixing. When composting is completed, the total volume of the original materials is usually reduced by 30 to 50 percent.

4. Build your pile by using either alternating equal layers of high-carbon and high-nitrogen material or by mixing equal parts of both together and then heaping it into a pile. If you choose to alternate layers, make each layer 2 to 4 inches thick. Some composters find that mixing the two together is more effective than layering. Adding a few shovels of soil will also help get the pile off to a good start because soil adds commonly found, decomposing organisms to your compost.

5. Keep the pile moist but not wet. Soggy piles encourage the growth of organisms that can live without oxygen and cause unpleasant odors.

6. Punch holes in the sides of the pile for aeration. The pile will heat up and then begin to cool. The most efficient decomposing bacteria thrive in temperatures between 110 and 160 degrees Fahrenheit. You can track this with a compost thermometer, or you can simply reach into the pile to determine if it is uncomfortably hot to the touch. At these temperatures, the pile kills most weed seeds and plant diseases. However, studies have shown that compost produced at these temperatures has less ability to suppress diseases in the soil, since these temperatures may kill some of the beneficial bacteria necessary to suppress disease.

8. Check your bin regularly during the composting season to assure optimum moisture and aeration are present in the material being composted.

9. Move materials from the center to the outside of the pile and vice versa. Turn every day or two and you should get compost in less than four weeks. Turning every other week will make compost in one to three months. Finished compost will smell sweet and be cool and crumbly to the touch.

Other Types of Composting

Cold or Slow Composting

Cold composting allows you to just pile organic material on the ground or in a bin. This method requires no maintenance, but it will take several months to a year or more for the pile to decompose, though the process is faster in warmer climates than in cooler areas. Cold composting works well if you are short on time needed to tend to the compost pile at least every other day, have little yard waste, and are not in a hurry to use the compost.

For this method, add yard waste as it accumulates. To speed up the process, shred or chop the materials by running over small piles of trimmings with your lawn mower, because the more surface area the microorganisms have to feed on, the faster the materials will break down.

Cold composting has been shown to be better at suppressing soilborne diseases than hot composting and also leaves more non-decomposed bits of material, which can be screened out if desired. However, because of the low temperatures achieved during decomposition, weed seeds and disease-causing organisms may not be destroyed.

Vermicomposting

Vermicomposting uses worms to compost. This takes up very little space and can be done year-round in a basement or garage. It is an excellent way to dispose of kitchen wastes.

▲ Any large bucket can be turned into a compost barrel. You can cut out a piece of the barrel for easy access to the compost, as shown here, or simply access the compost through the lid. Drilling holes in the sides and lids of the bucket will increase air circulation and speed up the process. Leave your bucket in the sun and shake it, roll it, or stir the contents regularly.

▼ Grass clippings and other plant debris can all be added to your compost pile. Note, however, that weeds can germinate again in your compost and thus end up back in your garden.

Here's how to make your own vermicomposting pile:

1. Obtain a plastic storage bin. One bin measuring 1 foot by 2 feet by 3½ feet will be enough to meet the needs of a family of six.

2. Drill 8 to 10 holes about ¼ inch in diameter in the bottom of the bin for drainage.

3. Line the bottom of the bin with a fine nylon mesh to keep the worms from escaping.

4. Put a tray underneath to catch the drainage.

5. Rip newspaper into pieces to use as bedding and pour water over the strips until they are thoroughly moist. Place these shredded bits on one side of your bin. Do not let them dry out.

6. Add worms to your bin. It's best to have about two pounds of worms (roughly 2,000 worms) per one pound of food waste. You may want to start with less food waste and increase the amount as your worm population grows. Redworms are recommended for best composting, but other species can be used. Redworms are the common, small worms found in most gardens and lawns. You can collect them from under a pile of mulch or order them from a garden catalog.

7. Provide worms with food wastes such as vegetable peelings. Do not add fat or meat products. Limit their feed, as too much at once may cause the material to rot.

8. Keep the bin in a dark location away from extreme temperatures.

9. Wait about three months and you'll see that the worms have changed the bedding and food wastes into compost. At this time, open your bin in a bright

▲ Worms will filter your organic waste through their systems and turn it into nutrient-rich humus.

light and the worms will burrow into the bedding. Add fresh bedding and more food to the other side of the bin. The worms should migrate to the new food supply.

10. Scoop out the finished compost and apply to your plants or save to use in the spring.

Common Problems

Composting is not an exact science. Experience will tell you what works best for you. If you notice that nothing is happening, you may need to add more nitrogen, water, or air, chip or grind the materials, or adjust the size of the pile.

If the pile is too hot, you probably have too much nitrogen and need to add additional carbon materials to reduce the heating.

A bad smell may indicate not enough air or too much moisture. Simply turn the pile or add dry materials to the wet pile to get rid of the odor.

Planting Your Garden

Once you've chosen a spot for your garden (as well as the size you want to make your garden bed), and

▼ Some plugs are biodegradable so that you can insert them directly into the garden bed, rather than having to transplant them.

prepared the soil with compost or other fertilizer, it's time to start planting. Seeds are very inexpensive at your local garden center, or you can browse through seed catalogs and order seeds that will do well in your area. Alternately, you can start with bedding plants (or seedlings) available at nurseries and garden centers.

Read the instructions on the back of the seed package or on the plastic tag in your plant pot. You may have to ask experts when to plant the seeds if this information is not stated on the back of the package. Some seeds (such as tomatoes) should be started indoors, in small pots or seed trays, before the last frost, and only transplanted outdoors when the weather warms up. For established plants or seedlings, be sure to plant as directed on the plant tag or consult your local nursery about the best planting times.

Seedlings

If you live in a cooler region with a shorter growing period, you will want to start some of your plants indoors. To do this, obtain plug flats (trays separated into many small cups or "cells") or make your own small planters by poking holes in the bottom of paper cups. Fill the cups two-thirds full with potting soil or composted soil. Bury the seed at the recommended depth, according to the instructions on the package.

Uses for Compost

Compost contains nutrients, but it is not a substitute for fertilizers. Compost holds nutrients in the soil until plants can use them, loosens and aerates clay soils, and retains water in sandy soils.

To use as a soil amendment, mix 2 to 5 inches of compost into vegetable and flower gardens each year before planting. In a potting mixture, add one part compost to two parts commercial potting soil, or make your own mixture by using equal parts of compost and sand, or Perlite.

As a mulch, spread an inch or two of compost around annual flowers and vegetables, and up to 6 inches around trees and shrubs. Studies have shown that compost used as mulch, or mixed with the top 1-inch layer of soil, can help prevent some plant diseases, including some of those that cause damping of seedlings.

As a top dressing, mix finely sifted compost with sand and sprinkle evenly over lawns.

▼ You can grow seedlings in any wood, metal, or plastic container that is at least 3 inches deep. Egg cartons work very well if you don't have access to regular plug flats. Just punch holes in the bottom for drainage.

Seeds can be sprouted and eaten on sandwiches, salads, or stirfries any time of the year. They are delicious and full of vitamins and proteins. Mung bean, soybean, alfalfa, wheat, corn, barley, mustard, clover, chickpeas, radish, and lentils all make good sprouts. Find seeds for sprouting from your local health food store or use dried peas, beans, or lentils from the grocery store. Never use seeds intended for planting unless you've harvested the seeds yourself—commercially available planting seeds are often treated with a poisonous chemical fungicide.

To grow sprouts, thoroughly rinse and strain the seeds, then soak overnight in cool water. You'll need about four times as much water as you have seeds. Drain the seeds and place them in a wide-mouthed bowl or on a cookie sheet with a lip. Sprinkle with water to keep the seeds slightly damp. You may wish to place the seeds on a damp paper towel to better hold in the moisture. Keep the seeds at 60 to 80 degrees F and rinse twice a day, returning them to their bowl or tray after. Once sprouts are 1 to 1 ½ inches long (generally after 3 to 5 days), they are ready to eat.

◄ Radish sprouts are delicious on their own or in sandwiches or salads

Tamp down the soil lightly and water. Keep the seedlings in a warm, well-lit place, such as the kitchen, to encourage germination.

Once the weather begins to warm up and you are fairly certain you won't be getting any more frosts (you can contact your local extension office to find out the last "frost free" date for your area) you can begin to acclimate your seedlings to the great outdoors. First place them in a partially shady spot outdoors that is protected from strong wind. After a couple of days, move them into direct sunlight, and then finally transplant them to the garden.

Recommended plants to start as seedlings

Crop [s] small seed [l] large seed (planting cell size)	Weeks before transplanting	Seed planting depth (inches)	Transplant spacing	
			Within row	between row
Broccoli [s]	(1)	4–6	¼–½'	8–10"
Cabbage [s]	(1)	4–6	¼–½'	18–24"
Cucumber [l]	(2)	4–5	½'	2'
Eggplant [s]	(2)	8	¼'	18"
Herbs [s]	(1)	4	¼'	4–6"
Lettuce [s]	(2)	4–5	¼'	12"
Melon [l]	(3)	4–5	¼'	2–3'
Onion [s]	(8–12)	8	¼'	4"
Pepper [s]	(2)	8	¼'	12–18"
Pumpkin [l]	(3)	2–4	1'	5–6'
Summer squash [l]	(3)	2–4	¾–1'	18"
Tomato [s]	(3)	8	¼'	18"–24"
Watermelon [l]	(3)	4–5	½–¾'	3–4'
Winter squash [l]	(3)	2–4	1	3–4'

23

How to Best Water Your Soil

After your seeds or seedlings are planted, the next step is to water your soil. Different soil types have different watering needs. You don't need to be a soil scientist to know how to water your soil properly. Here are some tips that can help to make your soil moist and primed for gardening:

1. Loosen the soil around plants so water and nutrients can be quickly absorbed.

2. Use a 1- to 2-inch protective layer of mulch on the soil surface above the root area. Cultivating and mulching help reduce evaporation and soil erosion.

3. Water your plants at the appropriate time of day. Early morning or night is the best time for watering, as evaporation is less likely to occur at these times. Do not water your plants when it is extremely windy outside. Wind will prevent the water from reaching the soil where you want it to go.

▲ A gentle spray will soak into the soil without damaging the plants. The thin layer of mulch will help to keep the water from evaporating too quickly.

Types of Soil and Their Water Retention

Knowing the type of soil you are planting in will help you best understand how to properly water and grow your garden plants. Three common types of soil and their various abilities to absorb water are listed below:

Clay soil: To make this type of soil more loamy, add organic materials, such as compost, peat moss, and well-rotted leaves, in the spring before growing and also in the fall after harvesting your vegetables and fruits. Adding these organic materials allows this type of soil to hold more nutrients for healthy plant growth. Till or spade to help loosen the soil.

Since clay soil absorbs water very slowly, water only as fast as the soil can absorb the water.

Sandy soil: As with clay soil, adding organic materials in the spring and fall will help supplement the sandy soil and promote better plant growth and water absorption.

Left on its own (with no added organic matter) the water will run through sandy soil so quickly that plants won't be able to absorb it through their roots and will fail to grow and thrive.

Loam soil: This is the best kind of soil for gardening. It's a combination of sand, silt, and clay. Loamy soil is fertile, deep, easily crumbles, and is made up of organic matter. It will help promote the growth of quality fruits and vegetables, as well as flowers and other plants.

Loam absorbs water readily and stores it for plants to use. Water as frequently as the soil needs to maintain its moisture and to promote plant growth.

▲ A good old-fashioned watering can is great for small gardens and potted plants.

◀ Sandy soil is usually lighter in color and won't easily clump together in your hands. It needs organic matter and plenty of water to be suitable for growing.

Conserving Water

Wise use of water for hydrating your garden and lawn not only helps protect the environment, but saves money and also provides optimum growing conditions for your plants. There are simple ways of reducing the amount of water used for irrigation, such as growing xeriphytic species (plants that are adapted to dry conditions), mulching, adding water-retaining organic matter to the soil, and installing windbreaks and fences to slow winds and reduce evapotranspiration.

You can conserve water by watering your plants and lawn in the early morning, before the sun is too intense. This helps reduce the amount of water lost due to evaporation. Installing rain gutters and collecting water from downspouts—in collection bins such as rain barrels—also helps reduce water use.

How Plants Use Water

Water is a critical component of photosynthesis, the process by which plants manufacture their own food from carbon dioxide and water in the presence of light. Water is one of the many factors that can limit plant growth. Other important factors include nutrients, temperature, and amount and duration of sunlight.

Plants take in carbon dioxide through their stomata—microscopic openings on the undersides of the leaves. The stomata are also the place where water is lost, in a process called transpiration. Transpiration, along with evaporation from the soil's surface, accounts for most of the moisture lost from the soil and subsequently from the plants.

When there is a lack of water in the plant tissue, the stomata close to try to limit excessive water loss. If the tissues lose too much water, the plant will wilt. Plants adapted to dry conditions have developed certain characteristics that support numerous mechanisms for reducing water loss—they typically have narrow, hairy leaves and thick, fleshy stems and leaves. Pines, hemlocks, and junipers are also well-adapted to survive extended periods of dry conditions—an environmental factor they encounter each winter when the frozen soil prevents the uptake of water. Cacti, which have thick stems and leaves reduced to spines, are the best example of plants well-adapted to extremely dry environments.

▲ Heath flowers are well-adapted to dry environments and make a very attractive ground cover.

Choosing Plants for Low Water Use

You are not limited to cacti, succulents, or narrow-leafed evergreens when selecting plants adapted to low water requirements. Many plants growing in humid environments are well-adapted to low levels of soil moisture. Numerous plants found growing in coastal or mountainous regions have developed mechanisms for dealing with extremely sandy, excessively well-drained soils or rocky, cold soils in which moisture is limited for months at a time. Try alfalfa, aloe, artichokes, asparagus, blue hibiscus, chives, columbine, eucalyptus, garlic, germander, lamb's ear, lavender, ornamental grasses, prairie turnip, rosemary, sage, sedum, shrub roses, thyme, yarrow, yucca, and verbena.

▲ Even very dry areas can be made attractive with tasteful placement of grasses, yarrow, and similar plants.

Trickle Irrigation Systems

Trickle irrigation and drip irrigation systems help reduce water use and successfully meet the needs of most plants. With these systems, very small amounts of water are supplied to the bases of the plants. Since the water is applied directly to the soil—rather than onto the plant—evaporation from the leaf surfaces is reduced, thus allowing more water to effectively reach the roots. In these types of systems, the water is not wasted by being spread all over the garden; rather, it is applied directly to the appropriate source.

▲ A simple trickle irrigation system.

Installing Irrigation Systems

An irrigation system can be easy to install, and there are many different products available for home irrigation systems. The simplest system consists of a soaker hose that is laid out around the plants and connected to an outdoor spigot. No installation is required, and the hose can be moved as needed to water the entire garden.

A slightly more sophisticated system is a slotted pipe system. Here are the steps needed to install this type of irrigation system in your garden:

1. Sketch the layout of your garden so you know what materials you will need. If you intend to water a vegetable garden, you may want one pipe next to every row or one pipe between every two rows.
2. Depending on the layout and type of garden, purchase the required lengths of pipe. You will need a length of solid pipe for the width of your garden, and perforated pipes that are the length of your lateral rows (and remember to buy one pipe for each row or two).
3. Measure the distances between rows and cut the solid pipe to the proper lengths.
4. Place T-connectors between the pieces of solid pipe.
5. In the approximate center of the solid pipe, place a T-connector to which a hose connector will be fitted.
6. Cut the perforated pipe to the length of the rows.
7. Attach the perforated pipes to the T-connectors so that the perforations are facing downward. Cap the end of the pipe.

8. Connect a garden hose to the hose connector on the solid pipe. Adjust the pressure of the water flowing from the spigot until the water slowly emerges from each of the perforated pipes.

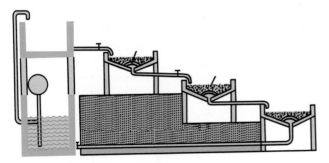

▲ A slotted pipe irrigation system.

Rain Barrels

Another very efficient and easy way to conserve water—and save money—is to buy or make your own rain barrel. A rain barrel is a large bin that is placed beneath a downspout and that collects rainwater runoff from a roof. The water collected in the rain barrel can then be routed through a garden hose and used to water your garden and lawn.

Rain barrels can be purchased from specialty home and garden stores, but a simple rain barrel is also quite easy to make. Here are simple instructions on how to make your own rain barrel.

Instructions

1. Obtain a suitable plastic barrel, a large plastic trashcan with a lid, or a wooden barrel (e.g., a wine barrel) that has not been stored dry for too many seasons, since it can start to leak. Good

How to Make a Simple Rain Barrel

Things You'll Need

- A clean, plastic barrel; tall trash can with lid; or a wooden barrel that does not leak (a 55-gallon plastic drum or barrel does a very good job at holding rainwater)
- Two hose bibs (a valve with a fitting for a garden hose on one end and a flange with a short pipe sticking out of it at the other end)
- Garden hose
- Plywood and paint (if your barrel doesn't already have a top)
- Window screen
- Wood screws
- Vegetable oil
- A drill
- A hacksaw
- A screwdriver

places to find plastic barrels include suppliers of dairy products, metal plating companies, and bulk food suppliers. Just be sure that nothing toxic or harmful to plants and animals (including you!) was stored in the barrel. A wine barrel can be obtained through a winery. Barrels that allow less light to penetrate through will eliminate the risk of algae growth and the establishment of other microorganisms.

2. Once you have your barrel, find a location for it under or near one of your home's downspouts. For the barrel to fit, you will probably need to shorten the downspout by a few feet. You can do this by removing the screws or rivets located at a joint of the downspout, or by simply cutting off the last few feet with a hacksaw or other

▲ Rain barrels can be made from any large bucket. It is especially convenient to have a spigot coming from the bottom of the bucket so you can fill smaller containers with water as needed.

cutter. If your barrel will not be able to fit underneath the downspout, you can purchase a flexible downspout at your local home improvement store. These flexible tubes will direct the water from the downspout into the barrel. An alternate, and aesthetically appealing, option is to use a rain chain—a large, metal chain that water can run down.

3. Create a level, stable platform for your rain barrel to sit on by raking the dirt under the spout, adding gravel to smooth out lawn bumps, or using bricks or concrete blocks to make a low platform. Keep in mind that a barrel full of water is very heavy, so if you decide to build a platform, make sure it is sturdy enough to hold such heavy weight.

4. If your barrel has a solid top, you'll need to make a good-sized hole in it for the downspout to pour into. You can do this using a hole-cutting attachment on a power drill or by drilling a series of smaller holes close together and then cutting out the remaining material with a hacksaw blade or a scroll saw.

5. Mosquitoes are drawn to standing water, so to reduce the risk of breeding these insects, and to also keep debris from entering the barrel, fasten a piece of window screen to the underside of the top so it covers the entire hole.

6. Next, drill a hole so the hose bib you'll attach to the side of the barrel fits snugly. Place the hose bib as close to the bottom of the barrel as possible, so you'll have access to the maximum amount of water in the barrel. Attach the hose bib using screws driven into the barrel. You'll probably need to apply some caulking, plumber's putty, or silicon sealant around the joint between the barrel and the hose bib to prevent

leaks, depending on the type of hardware you're using and how snug it fits in the hole you drilled.

7. Attach a second hose bib to the side of the barrel near the top, to act as an overflow drain. Attach a short piece of garden hose to this hose bib and route it to a flowerbed, lawn, or another nearby area that won't be damaged by some running water if your barrel gets too full (or, if you want

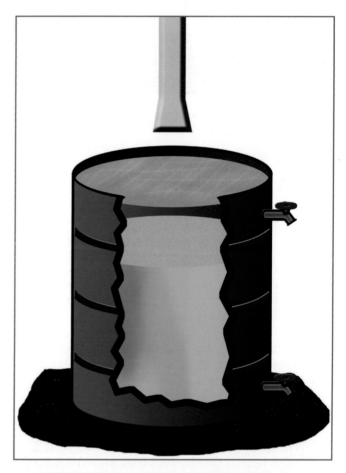

Things to Consider

• Put some water in the barrel from a garden hose once everything is in place and any sealants have had time to thoroughly dry. The first good downpour is not the time to find out there's a leak in your barrel.

• If you don't own the property on which you are thinking of installing a rain barrel, be sure to get permission before altering the downspouts.

• If your barrel doesn't already have a solid top, cover it securely with a circle of painted plywood, an old trashcan lid screwed to the walls of the barrel, or a heavy tarp secured over the top of the barrel with bungee cords. This will protect children and small animals from falling into the barrel and drowning.

• As stated before, stagnant water is an excellent breeding ground for mosquitoes, so it would be a good idea to take additional steps to keep them out of your barrel by sealing all the openings into the barrel with caulk or putty. You might also consider adding enough non-toxic oil (such as vegetable cooking oil) to the barrel to form a film on top of the water that will prevent mosquito larvae from hatching.

Always double check to make sure the barrel you're using (particularly if it is from a food distribution center or other recycled source) did not contain pesticides, industrial chemicals, weed killers, or other toxins or biological materials that could be harmful to you, your plants, or the environment. If you are concerned about this, it is best to purchase a new barrel or trashcan so there is no doubt about its safety.

to have a second rain barrel for excess water, you can attach it to another hose bib on a second barrel. If you are chaining multiple barrels together, one of them should have a hose attached to drain off the overflow.

8. Attach a garden hose to the lower hose bib and open the valve to allow collected rain water to flow to your plants. The lower bib can also be used to connect multiple rain barrels together for a larger water reservoir.

9. Consider using a drip irrigation system in conjunction with the rain barrels. Rain barrels don't achieve anything near the pressure of city water supplies, so you won't be able to use microsprinkler attachments, and you will need to use button attachments that are intended to deliver four times the amount of city-supplied water you need.

10. Now, wait for a heavy downpour and start enjoying your rain barrel!

Mary Maddox and her husband and children maintain a full vegetable garden and raise chickens, ducks, turkeys, and a goose on less than half an acre of land. They describe their experiences and share tips on their blog, "The Yardstead," www.yardstead.com.

My husband, children, and I live in a small town in North Florida. Like most of our neighbors we live on a little less than ½ acre lot. We dream of becoming homesteaders on 10 to 15 acres but until that dream becomes reality, we do what we can on our small plot. We currently maintain a 30 x 30-ft. vegetable garden, and keep chickens, ducks, turkeys, and a goose. These birds only require 3–4 sq. ft. per bird and are easy to care for in an appropriate-sized pen.

We keep between 10 and 20 chickens most of the time in a 72 sq. ft. pen, with an adjoining 200 sq. ft. pen for a few ducks, turkeys, and a goose. We supply our family, friends, and neighbors with fresh eggs year-round and put a few chickens in the freezer as well. We recently were given a rooster by one of our neighbors, and our hens have hatched their first babies this spring.

We try to keep something growing in the garden all year-round. Each year we are able to grow enough squash and zucchini to eat fresh all spring and summer and put enough away in the freezer to last through the winter. We also grow enough onions and garlic most years to meet all our needs and share with our friends and family. We dabble in other vegetables and grow a variety of gourds on our fence line each year.

We have landscaped the yard with mostly edible plants and trees. Our backyard shade is provided by a pecan, mulberry, persimmon, and other trees. We have chosen some native shrubs, like the pineapple guava, that also produces edible flowers and fruit. We keep several dwarf citrus as potted plants that can be moved in and out of the house depending on our winter temperatures each year. Last fall we planted a few small sugarcane. These clumps of sugarcane will be mostly for our children to enjoy in late summer each year.

We try to garden and care for our animals and yard with an emphasis on permaculture, and we follow organic practices as much as possible. All of the yard waste and food waste we produce go first to the chickens and other birds who love to eat table scraps as well as grass clippings and the like. They eat what they like, and the leftovers along with the rich droppings are raked out occasionally and added to the compost pile. This provides us a constant supply of rich compost, which is the fertilizer we use in the garden. We also let some chickens roam the garden after the plants have grown to 8–10 inches in height. They do an excellent job of keeping the garden pest-free by eating every bug they can find.

We love teaching our children about gardening and caring for animals, and we all enjoy a healthy sense of self-reliance. We share our produce as much as possible and also try to share as much knowledge as possible with anyone who is interested.

Mulching in Your Garden and Yard

Mulching is one of the simplest and most beneficial practices you can use in your garden. Mulch is simply a protective layer of material that is spread on top of the soil to enrich the soil, prevent weed growth, and help provide a better growing environment for your garden plants and flowers.

Mulches can either be organic—such as grass clippings, bark chips, compost, ground corncobs, chopped cornstalks, leaves, manure, newspaper, peanut shells, peat moss, pine needles, sawdust, straw, and wood shavings—or inorganic—such as stones, brick chips, and plastic. Both organic and inorganic mulches have numerous benefits, including:

1. Protecting the soil from erosion
2. Reducing compaction from the impact of heavy rains
3. Conserving moisture, thus reducing the need for frequent watering

Common Organic Mulching Materials	
Bark chips	Newspaper
Chopped cornstalks	Peanut shells
Compost	Peat moss
Grass clippings	Pine needles
Ground corncobs	Sawdust
Hay	Straw
Leaves	Wood shavings
Manure	

4. Maintaining a more even soil temperature
5. Preventing weed growth
6. Keeping fruits and vegetables clean
7. Keeping feet clean and allowing access to the garden even when it's damp
8. Providing a "finished" look to the garden

Organic mulches also have the benefit of improving the condition of the soil. As these mulches slowly decompose, they provide organic matter to help keep the soil loose. This improves root growth, increases

▲ Wood chips or shavings are some of the most common forms of mulch.

the infiltration of water, improves the water-holding capacity of the soil, provides a source of plant nutrients, and establishes an ideal environment for earthworms and other beneficial soil organisms.

While inorganic mulches have their place in certain landscapes, they lack the soil-improving properties of organic mulches. Inorganic mulches may be difficult to remove if you decide to change your garden plans at a later date.

▲ A trowel and hand fork are helpful for mulching small areas around and between plants.

▲ Mulch can be neat and attractive, especially if kept from spilling into your yard with a row or circle of stones.

Where to Find Mulch Materials

You can find mulch materials right in your own back-yard. They include:

1. Lawn clippings.

These make an excellent mulch in the vegetable garden if spread immediately to avoid heating and rotting. The fine texture allows them to be spread easily, even around small plants.

2. Newspaper.

As a mulch, newspaper works especially well to control weeds. Save your own newspapers and only use the text pages, or those with black ink, as color dyes may be harmful to soil microflora and fauna if composted and used. Use three or four sheets together, anchored with grass clippings or other mulch material to prevent them from blowing away.

3. Leaves.

Leaf mold, or the decomposed remains of leaves, gives the forest floor its absorbent, spongy structure. Collect leaves in the fall and chop with a lawnmower or shredder. Compost leaves over winter, as some studies have indicated that freshly chopped leaves may inhibit the growth of certain crops.

4. Compost.

The mixture makes wonderful mulch—if you have a large supply—as it not only improves the soil structure but also provides an excellent source of plant nutrients.

5. Bark chips and composted bark mulch.

These materials are available at garden centers and are sometimes used with landscape fabric or plastic that is spread atop the soil and beneath the mulch to provide additional protection against weeds. However, the barrier between the soil and the mulch also prevents any improvement in the soil condition and makes planting additional plants more difficult. Without the barrier, bark mulch makes a neat finish to the garden bed and will eventually improve the condition of the soil. It may last for one to three years or more, depending on the size of the chips or how well-composted the bark mulch is. Smaller chips are easier to spread, especially around small plants.

6. Hay and straw.

These work well in the vegetable garden, although they may harbor weed seeds.

7. Seaweed mulch, ground corncobs, and pine needles.

Depending on where you live, these materials may be readily available and can also be used as mulch.

However, pine needles tend to increase the acidity of the soil, so they work best around acid-loving plants, such as rhododendrons and blueberries.

When choosing a mulch material, think of your primary objective. Newspaper and grass clippings are great for weed control, while bark mulch gives a perfect, finishing touch to a front-yard perennial garden. If you're looking for a cheap solution, consider using materials found in your own yard or see if your community offers chipped wood or compost to its residents.

If you want the mulch to stay in place for several years around shrubs, for example, you might want to consider using inorganic mulches. While they will not provide organic matter to the soil, they will be more or less permanent.

When to Apply Mulch

Time of application depends on what you hope to achieve by mulching. Mulches, by providing an insulating barrier between the soil and the air, moderate the soil temperature. This means that a mulched soil in the summer will be cooler than an adjacent, unmulched soil; while in the winter, the mulched soil may not freeze as deeply. However, since mulch acts as an insulating layer, mulched soils tend to warm up more slowly in the spring and cool down more slowly in the fall than unmulched soils.

If you are using mulches in your garden, it is best to apply or add additional mulch after the soil has warmed up in the spring. Organic mulches reduce the soil temperature by 8 to 10 degrees Fahrenheit during the summer, so if they are applied to cold garden soils, the soil will warm up more slowly and delay plant growth.

Mulches used to help moderate winter temperatures can be applied late in the fall after the ground has frozen, but before the coldest temperatures arrive. Applying mulches before the ground has frozen may attract rodents looking for a warm over-wintering site. Delayed applications of mulch should prevent this problem.

Mulches used to protect plants over the winter should be composed of loose material, such as straw, hay, or pine boughs that will help insulate the plants without compacting under the weight of snow and ice. One of the benefits of winter applications is the reduction in the freezing and thawing of the soil in the late winter and early spring. These repeated cycles of freezing at night and then thawing in the warmth of the sun cause many small or shallow-rooted plants to heave out of the soil. This leaves their root systems exposed and results in injury, or death, of the plant. Mulching helps prevent these rapid fluctuations in soil temperature and reduces the chances of heaving.

▲ Gather fallen leaves in the fall and compost them or use them in large plastic bags as extra house insulation over the winter. Come spring, the decomposed leaves will be ready for mulch.

General Mulching Guidelines

Mulch is measured in cubic feet, so, if you have an area measuring 10 feet by 10 feet, and you wish to apply 3 inches (¼ foot) of mulch, you would need 25 cubic feet to do the job correctly.

While some mulch can come from recycled material in your own yard, it can also be purchased bagged or in bulk from a garden center. Buying in bulk may be cheaper if you need a large volume and have a way to haul it. Bagged mulch is often easier to handle, especially for smaller projects, as most bagged mulch comes in 3-cubic-foot bags.

To start, remove any weeds. Begin mulching by spreading the materials in your garden, being careful not to apply mulch to the plants themselves. Leave an inch or so of space next to the plants to help prevent diseases from flourishing in times of excess humidity.

How Much Do I Apply?

The amount of mulch to apply to your garden depends on the mulching material used. Spread bark mulch and wood chips 2 to 4 inches deep, keeping it an inch or two away from tree trunks.

Scatter chopped and composted leaves 3 to 4 inches deep. If using dry leaves, apply about 6 inches.

Grass clippings, if spread too thick, tend to compact and rot, becoming slimy and smelly. They should be applied 2 to 3 inches deep, and additional layers should be added as clippings decompose. Make sure not to use clippings from lawns treated with herbicides.

Sheets of newspaper should only be ¼ inch thick and covered lightly with grass clippings or other mulch material to anchor them. If other mulch materials are not available, cover the edges of the newspaper with soil.

If using compost, apply 3 to 4 inches deep, as it's an excellent material for enriching the soil.

Organic Gardening

"Organically grown" food is food grown and processed using no synthetic fertilizers or pesticides. Pesticides derived from natural sources (such as biological pesticides—compost and manure) may be used in producing organically grown food.

Organic gardeners grow the healthiest, highest-quality foods and flowers—all without the addition of chemical fertilizers, pesticides, or herbicides. Organic gardening methods are healthier, environmentally friendly, safe for animals and humans, and are generally less expensive, since you are working with natural materials. It is easy to grow and harvest organic foods in your backyard garden and typically, organic gardens are easier to maintain than gardens that rely on chemical and unnatural components to help them grow effectively.

Organic production is neither simply the avoidance of conventional chemical inputs, nor is it the substitution of natural inputs for synthetic ones. Organic farmers apply techniques first used thousands of years ago, such as crop rotations and the use of composted animal manures and green manure crops, in ways that are economically sustainable in today's world.

Organic farming entails:

- Use of cover crops, green manures, animal manures, and crop rotations to fertilize the soil, maximize biological activity, and maintain long-term soil health
- Use of biological control, crop rotations, and other techniques to manage weeds, insects, and diseases
- An emphasis on biodiversity of the agricultural system and the surrounding environment
- Reduction of external and off-farm inputs and elimination of synthetic pesticides and fertilizers and other materials, such as hormones and antibiotics
- A focus on renewable resources, soil and water conservation, and management practices that restore, maintain, and enhance ecological balance

▲ A row of lettuce thrives in the compost-fertilized soil.

How to Start Your Own Organic Garden

Step One:
Choose a Site for Your Garden

1. Think small, at least at first. A small garden takes less work and materials than a large one. If done well, a 4 x 4-foot garden will yield enough vegetables and fruit for you and your family to enjoy.

2. Be careful not to over-plant your garden. You do not want to end up with too many vegetables that will end up over-ripening or rotting in your garden.

3. You can even start a garden in a window box if you are unsure of your time and dedication to a larger bed.

▼ Your garden can be as small or large as your space allows, but be sure to start with a size you can manage.

Step Two: Make a Compost Pile

Compost is the main ingredient for creating and maintaining rich, fertile soil. You can use most organic materials to make compost that will provide your soil with essential nutrients. To start a compost pile, all you need are fallen leaves, weeds, grass clippings, and other vegetation that is in your yard. (See pages 18–22 for more details on how to make compost.)

Step Three: Add Soil

To have a thriving organic garden, you must have excellent soil. Adding organic material (such as that in your compost pile) to your existing soil will only make it better. Soil containing copious amounts of organic material is very good for your garden. Organically rich soil:

- Nourishes your plants without any chemicals, keeping them natural
- Is easy to use when planting seeds or seedlings, and it also allows for weeds to be more easily picked
- Is softer than chemically treated soil, so the roots of your plants can spread and grow deeper
- Helps water and air find the roots

Step Four: Weed Control

Weeds are invasive to your garden plants and thus must be removed in order for your organic garden to grow efficiently. Common weeds that can invade your garden are ivy, mint, and dandelions.

Using a sharp hoe, go over each area of exposed soil frequently to keep weeds from sprouting. Also, plucking off the green portions of weeds will deprive them of the nutrients they need to survive.

Gently pull out weeds by hand to remove their root systems and to stop continued growth. Be careful when weeding around established plants so you don't uproot them as well.

Mulch unplanted areas of your garden so that weeds will be less likely to grow. You can find organic mulches, such as wood chips and grass clippings, at your local garden store. These mulches will not only discourage weed growth but will also eventually break down and help enrich the soil. Mulching also helps regulate soil temperatures and helps in conserving water by decreasing evaporation. (See pages 30–33 for more on mulching.)

▲ A hand fork can be useful in digging up tough roots of pesky weeds.

Things to Consider

- "Organic" means that you don't use any kinds of materials, such as paper or cardboard, that contain chemicals, and especially not fertilizer or pesticides. Make sure that these products do not find their way into your garden or compost pile.
- If you are adding grass clippings to your compost pile, make sure they don't come from a lawn that has been treated with chemical fertilizer.
- If you don't want to start a compost pile, simply add leaves and grass clippings directly to your garden bed. This will act like a mulch, deter weeds from growing, and will eventually break down to help return nutrients to your soil.
- If you find insects attacking your plants, the best way to control them is by picking them off by hand. Also practice crop rotation (planting different types of plants in a given area from year to year), which might reduce your pest problem. For some insects, just a strong stream of water is effective in removing them from your plants.
- Shy away from using bark mulch. It robs nitrogen from the soil as it decomposes and can also attract termites.

Step Five:
Be Careful of Lawn Fertilizers

If you have a lawn and your organic garden is situated in it, be mindful that any chemicals you place on your lawn may find their way into your organic garden. Therefore, refrain from fertilizing your lawn with chemicals and, if you wish to return nutrients to your grass, simply let your cut grass clippings remain in the yard to decompose naturally and enrich the soil beneath.

Start Your Own Vegetable Garden

If you want to start your own vegetable garden, just follow these simple steps and you'll be on your way to growing your own yummy vegetables—right in your own backyard.

Steps to Making Your Own Vegetable Garden

1. Select a site for your garden.

- Vegetables grow best in well-drained, fertile soil (loamy soils are the best).
- Some vegetables can cope with shady conditions, but most prefer a site with a good amount of sunshine—at least six hours a day of direct sunlight.

▲ After soil is tilled it should be loose and free from weeds or root systems.

2. Remove all weeds in your selected spot and dispose of them.

If you are using compost to supplement your garden soil, do not put the weeds on the compost heap, as they may germinate once again and cause more weed growth among your vegetable plants.

3. Prepare the soil by tilling it.

This will break up large soil clumps and allow you to see and remove pesky weed roots. This would also be the appropriate time to add organic materials (such as compost) to the existing soil to help make it more fertile. The tools used for tilling will depend on the size of your garden. Some examples are:

- Shovel and turning fork—using these tools is hard work, requiring strong upper body strength.
- Rotary tiller—this will help cut up weed roots and mix the soil.

▲ You can often grow two crops of cabbage or other green leafy vegetables in one growing season if you start the garden early enough.

▲ A shovel is perfectly adequate for turning over soil in a small garden.

▲ For very small seeds, such as carrot seeds, you can sprinkle 15 to 20 seeds per inch in a shallow channel. To make the row straight, tie a string to two small sticks and drive each stick into the ground on either side of your garden so that the string is taut. Use a hoe to dig a shallow channel in the string's shadow.

4. Begin planting.

If you would like straight rows in your garden, a guide can be made from two wooden stakes and a bit of rope. Vegetables can be grown from seeds or transplanted.

- If your garden has problems with pests such as slugs, it's best to transplant older plants, as they are more likely to survive attacks from these organisms.
- Transplanting works well for vegetables like tomatoes and onions, which usually need a head start to mature within a shorter growing season. These can be germinated indoors on seed trays on a windowsill before the growing season begins.

5. Follow these basic steps to grow vegetables from seeds:

- Information on when and how deep to plant vegetable seeds is usually printed on seed packages

▲ Seeds should be planted at a depth of twice their width. If the seed is ¼ inch wide, it should be planted ½ inch below the surface.

▼ Tomato plants will grow best if begun as seedlings indoors and then transplanted into your garden well after the last frost.

or on various websites. You can also contact your local nursery or garden center to inquire after this information.

- Measure the width of the seed to determine how deep it should be planted. Take the width and multiply by 2. That is how deep the seed should be placed in the hole. As a general rule, the larger the seed, the deeper it should be planted.

6. **Water the plants and seeds well to ensure a good start.**

Make sure they receive water at least every other day, especially if there is no rain in the forecast.

Things to Consider

- In the early days of a vegetable garden, all your plants are vulnerable to attack by insects and animals. It is best to plant multiples of the same plant to ensure that some survive. Placing netting and fences around your garden can help keep out certain animal pests. Coffee grains or slug traps filled with beer will also help protect your plants against insect pests.
- If sowing seed straight onto your bed, be sure to obtain a photograph of what your seedlings will look like so you don't mistake the growing plant for a weed.
- Weeding early on is very important to the overall success of your garden. Weeds steal water, nutrients, and light from your vegetables, which will stunt their growth and make it more difficult for them to thrive.

Start Your Own Flower Garden

Flower gardens are easy to grow and will beautify your lawn or backyard. Just follow the steps below.

Step One:
Start with a Small Garden

Gardening takes a lot of work, and so for the beginner gardener, tackling a large garden can be overwhelming. Start with a small flowerbed around 25 square feet. This will provide you with room for about 20 to 30 plants—enough room for three types of annuals and two types of perennials. As your gardening experience grows, so can the size of your garden!

If you would like to start even smaller, you can always begin your first flower garden in a container, or create a border from treated wood or bricks and stones around your existing bed. That way, when you are ready to expand your garden, all you need to do is remove the temporary border and you'll be all set. Even a small container filled with a few different types of plants can be a wonderful addition to any yard.

Step Two:
Plan Your Flower Garden

Draw up a plan of how you'd like your garden to look, and then dig a flowerbed to fit that plan. Planning your garden before gathering the seeds or plants and beginning the digging can give you a clearer sense of how your garden will be organized and can facilitate the planting process.

Step Three:
Choose a Spot for Your Garden

It is important, when choosing where your flower garden will be located, that you consider an area that receives at least six hours of direct sunlight per day, as this will be adequate for a large variety of garden plants. Be careful that you will not be digging into utility lines or pipes, and that you place your garden

▲ Flower gardens do not need to be as carefully organized as vegetable gardens. Experiment with different color combinations and flower varieties. In general, it's best to put taller plants toward the center or back of your garden so that the shorter flowers will still be visible.

at least a short distance away from fences or other structures.

If you live in a part of the country that is quite hot, it might be beneficial for your flowers to be placed in an area that gets some shade during the hot afternoon sun. Placing your garden on the east side of your home will help your flowers flourish. If your garden will get more than six hours of sunlight per day, it would be wise to choose flowers that thrive in hot, sunny spaces, and make sure to water them frequently.

It is also important to choose a spot that has good, fertile soil in which your flowers can grow. Try to avoid any areas with rocky, shallow soil or where water collects and pools. Make sure your garden is away from large trees and shrubs, as these plants will compete with your flowers for water and nutrients. If you are concerned that your soil may not contain enough nutrients for your flowers to grow properly, you can have a soil test done, which will tell you the pH of the soil. Depending on the results, you can then adjust the types of nutrients needed in your soil by adding organic materials or certain types of fertilizers.

▲ Some flowers, like lilies, do best if started in pots and then transplanted into your garden.

Step Four: Start Digging

Now that you have a site picked out, mark out the boundaries with a hose or string. Remove the sod and any weed roots that may re-grow. Use your spade or garden fork to dig up the bed at least 8 to 12 inches deep, removing any rocks or debris you come across.

▼ Echinacea is beautiful as well as useful for medicinal purposes. It grows best in sunny areas. Plant in early spring for summer blooming, or about two months before the first frost for flowers the next year.

▲ Bright, fragrant flowers will attract butterflies to your garden.

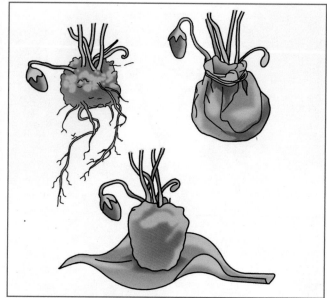

Once your bed is dug, level it and break up the soil with a rake. Add compost or manure if the soil is not fertile. If your soil is sandy, adding peat moss or grass clippings will help it hold more water. Work any additions into the top 6 inches of soil.

Step Five:
Purchase Your Seeds or Plants

Once you've chosen which types of flowers you'd like to grow in your garden, visit your local garden store or nursery and pick out already-established plants or packaged seeds. Follow the planting instructions on the plant tabs or seed packets. The smaller plants should be situated in the front of the bed. Once your plants or seeds are in their holes, pack in the soil around them. Make sure to leave ample space between your seeds or plants for them to grow and spread out (most labels and packets will alert you to how large your flower should be expected to grow, so you can adjust the spacing as needed).

Step Six:
Water Your Flower Garden

After your plants or seeds are first put into the ground, be sure they get a thorough watering. Continue to check your garden to see whether or not the soil is drying out. If so, give your garden a good soaking with the garden hose or watering can. The amount of water your garden needs is dependent on the climate you live in, the exposure to the sun, and how much rain your area has received.

Step Seven: Your Flowers

Once your flowers begin to bloom, feel free to cut them and display the beautiful blooms in your home. Pruning your flower garden (cutting the dead or dying blooms off the plant) will help certain plants to re-bloom. Also, if you have plants that are becoming top

▲ To transplant flowers from one growing location to another, dig up the plant, being careful not to damage the root system. Wrap the root ball in a large leaf or a cloth and tie at the top around the steps to keep the roots from drying out. Leaf wrappings do not need to be removed before replanting. Be sure to water the plant thoroughly after planting it in its new location.

heavy, support them with a stake and some string so you can enjoy their blossoms to the fullest.

Things to Consider

- Annuals are plants that you need to replant every year. They are often inexpensive, and many have brightly colored flowers. Annuals can be

▲ Garden centers or farm stands often sell flowers that are started in flats or plugs. Because the root systems are already established, they are easier to grow and create an instantly attractive garden.

rewarding for beginner gardeners, as they take little effort and provide lovely color to your garden. The following season, you'll need to replant or start over from seed.

- Perennials last from one year to the next. They, too, will require annual maintenance but not yearly replanting. Perennials may require division, support, and extra care during winter months. Perennials may also need their old blooms and stems pruned and cut back every so often.
- Healthy, happy plants tend to be less susceptible to pests and diseases. It is easier to practice prevention rather than curing existing problems. Do your best to give your plants good soil, nutrients, and appropriate moisture, and choose plants that are well-suited to your climate. This way, your garden will be more likely to grow to its maximum potential and your plants will be strong and healthy.

Barrel Plant Holder

If you have some perennials you want to display in your yard away from your flower garden, you can create a planter out of an old barrel. This plant holder is made by sawing an old barrel (wooden or metal) into two pieces and mounting it on short or tall legs—whichever design fits better in your yard. You can choose to either paint it or leave it natural. Filling the planter with good-quality soil and compost and planting an array of multi-colored flowers into the barrel planter will brighten up your yard all summer long. If you do not want to mount the barrel on legs, it can be placed on the ground on a smooth and level surface where it won't easily tip over.

◀ A fence can be set up around your garden to keep out deer and other wild animals. See pages 262–266 for fence construction ideas.

Wooden Window Box

Planting perennial flowers and cascading plants in window boxes is the perfect way to brighten up the front exterior of your home. Making a simple wooden window box to hold your flowers and plants is quite easy. These boxes can be made from pre-existing wooden boxes (such as fruit crates) or you can make your own out of simple boards. Whatever method you choose, make sure the boards are stout enough to hold the brads firmly.

The size of your window will ultimately determine the size of your box, but this plan calls for a box roughly 21 x 7 x 7 inches. You can decorate your boxes with waterproof paint or you can nail strips of wood or sticks to the panels. Make sure to cut a few holes in the bottom of the box to allow for water drainage. The window box can be kept in position by two metal angle-pieces screwed to the wood sill and to the back of the box.

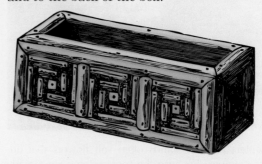

Rustic Plant Stand

If you'd like to incorporate a rustic, natural-looking plant stand in your garden or on your patio or deck, one can easily be made from a preexisting wooden box or by nailing boards together. This box should be mounted on legs. To make the legs, saw the piece of wood meant for the leg in half to a length from the top equal to the depth of the box. Then, cross-cut and remove one half. The corner of the box can then be inserted in the middle of the crosscut and the leg nailed to the side of the box.

The plant stand can be decorated to suit your needs and preference. You can nail smaller, alternating twigs or cut branches around the stand to give it a more natural feel or you can simply paint it a soothing, natural color and place it in your yard.

Planting Trees

Trees in your yard can become home to many different types of wildlife. Trees also reduce your cooling costs by providing shade, help clean the air, add beauty and color, provide shelter from the wind and the sun, and add value to your home.

Choosing a Tree

Choosing a tree should be a well-thought-out decision. Tree planting can be a significant investment, both in money and time. Selecting the proper tree for your yard can provide you with years of enjoyment, as well as significantly increase the value of your property. However, a tree that is inappropriate for your property can be a constant maintenance problem, or even a danger to your and others' safety. Before you decide to purchase a tree, take advantage of the many references on gardening at local libraries, universities, arboretums, native plant and gardening clubs, and nurseries. Some questions to consider in selecting a tree include:

1. What purpose will this tree serve?

Trees can serve numerous landscape functions, including beautification, screening of sights and sounds, shade and energy conservation, and wildlife habitat.

2. Is the species appropriate for your area?

Reliable nurseries will not sell plants that are not suitable for your area. However, some mass marketers have trees and shrubs that are not fitted for the environment in which they are sold. Even if a tree is hardy, it may not flower consistently from year to

▼ Fruit trees provide sweet-smelling flowers in the spring and fruit in the fall.

▲ Full-grown trees create a shade-producing canopy of branches and leaves. Shade can be a good addition to your property, but be sure you don't plant trees in an area where you want a garden that requires full sun.

year if the environmental factors are not conducive for it to do so. If you are buying a tree for its spring flowers and fall fruits, consider climate when deciding which species of tree to plant.

- Be aware of microclimates. Microclimates are localized areas where weather conditions may vary from the norm. A very sheltered yard may support vegetation not normally adapted to the region. On the other hand, a north-facing slope may be significantly cooler or windier than surrounding areas, and survival of normally adapted plants may be limited.
- Select trees native to your area. These trees will be more tolerant of local weather and soil conditions, enhance natural biodiversity in your neighborhood, and be more beneficial to wildlife than many non-native trees. Avoid exotic trees that can invade other areas, crowd out native plants, and harm natural ecosystems.

3. How big will it get?

When planting a small tree, it is often difficult to imagine that in 20 years it will most likely be shading your entire yard. Unfortunately, many trees are planted and later removed when the tree grows beyond the dimensions of the property.

Certain insects and diseases can cause serious problems for some desirable species in certain regions. Depending on the pest, control of the problem may be difficult and the pest may significantly reduce the attractiveness, if not the life expectancy, of the tree. Other species, such as the silver maple, are known to have weak wood that is susceptible to damage in ice storms or heavy winds. All these factors should be kept in mind, as controlling pests or dealing with tree limbs that have snapped in foul weather can be expensive and potentially damaging.

7. How common is this species in your neighborhood or town?

Some species are over-planted. Increasing the natural diversity in your area will provide habitat for wildlife and help limit the opportunity for a single pest to destroy large numbers of trees.

8. Is the tree evergreen or deciduous?

Evergreen trees will provide cover and shade year-round. They may also be more effective as wind and noise barriers. On the other hand, deciduous trees will give you summer shade but allow the winter sun to shine in. If planting a deciduous tree, keep these heating and cooling factors in mind when placing the tree in your yard.

Placement of Trees

Proper placement of trees is critical for your enjoyment and for their long-term survival. Check with local authorities about regulations pertaining to placement of trees in your area. Some communities have ordinances restricting placement of trees within a specified distance from a street, sidewalk, streetlight, or other city utilities.

Before planting your tree, consider the tree's potential maximum size. Ask yourself these simple questions:

1. When the tree nears maturity, will it be too close to your or a neighbor's house? An evergreen tree planted on your north side may block the winter sun from your next-door neighbor.

4. What is the average life expectancy of the tree?

Some trees can live for hundreds of years. Others are considered "short-lived" and may live for only 20 to 30 years. Many short-lived trees tend to be smaller, ornamental species. Short-lived species should not necessarily be ruled out when considering plantings, as they may have other desirable characteristics, such as size, shape, tolerance of shade, or fruit, that would be useful in the landscape. These species may also fill a void in a young landscape and can be removed as other larger, longer-lived species mature.

5. Does it have any particular ornamental value, such as leaf color or flowers and fruits?

Some species provide beautiful displays of color for short periods in the spring or fall. Other species may have foliage that is reddish or variegated and can add color in your yard year-round. Trees bearing fruits or nuts can provide an excellent source of food for many species of wildlife.

6. Does it have any particular insect, disease, or other problem that may reduce its usefulness in the future?

2. Will it provide too much shade for your vegetable and flower gardens? Most vegetables and many flowers require considerable amounts of sun. If you intend to grow these plants in your yard, consider how the placement of trees will affect these gardens.

3. Will the tree obstruct any driveways or sidewalks?

4. Will it cause problems for buried or overhead power lines and utility pipes?

Once you have taken these questions into consideration and have bought the perfect tree for your yard, it is time to start digging!

Planting a Tree

A properly planted and maintained tree will grow faster and live longer than one that is incorrectly planted. Trees can be planted almost any time of the year, as long as the ground is not frozen. Late summer or early fall is the optimum time to plant trees in many areas. By planting during these times, the tree

▲ B&B trees are dug from a nursery, wrapped in burlap, and kept in the nursery for an additional period of time, giving the roots opportunity to regenerate. B&B plants can be quite large.

Things You'll Need
• Tree
• Shovel
• Watering can or garden hose
• Measuring stick
• Mulch
• Optional: scissors or knife to cut the burlap or container, stakes, and supporting wires

---

has a chance to establish new roots before winter arrives and the ground freezes. When spring comes, the tree is then ready to grow. Another feasible time for planting trees is late winter or early spring. Planting in hot summer weather should be avoided if possible as the heat may cause the young tree to wilt. Planting in frozen soil during the winter is very difficult and is tough on tree roots. When the tree is dormant and the ground is frozen, there is no opportunity for the new roots to begin growing.

Trees can be purchased as container-grown, balled and burlapped (B&B), or bare root. Generally, container-grown are the easiest to plant and successfully establish in any season, including summer. With container-grown stock, the plant has been growing in a container for a period of time. When planting container-grown trees, little damage is done to the roots as the plant is transferred to the soil. Container-grown trees range in size from very small plants in gallon pots up to large trees in huge pots.

Bare root trees are usually extremely small plants. Because there is no soil around the roots, they must be planted when they are dormant to avoid drying out, and the roots must be kept moist until planted. Frequently, bare root trees are offered by seed and nursery mail order catalogs, or in the wholesale trade. Many state-operated nurseries and local conservation districts also sell bare root stock in bulk quantities for only a few cents per plant. Bare root plants are usually offered in the early spring and should be planted as soon as possible.

Be sure to carefully follow the planting instructions that come with your tree. If specific instructions are not available, here are some general tree-planting guidelines:

1. Before starting any digging, call your local utility companies to identify the location of any underground wires or lines. In the U.S., you can call 811 to have your utility lines marked for free.

2. Dig a hole twice as wide as, and slightly shallower than, the root ball. Roughen the sides and bottom of the hole with a pick or shovel so that the roots can easily penetrate the soil.

3. With a potted tree, gently remove the tree from the container. To do this, lay the tree on its side with the

▲ Burlap wraps do not need to be removed before planting your tree. They will decompose in the soil with time.

container end near the planting hole. Hit the bottom and sides of the container until the root ball is loosened. If roots are growing in a circular pattern around the root ball, slice through the roots on a couple of sides of the root ball. With trees wrapped in burlap, remove the string or wire that holds the burlap to the root crown; it is not necessary to remove the burlap completely. Plastic wraps must be completely removed. Gently separate circling roots on the root ball. Shorten exceptionally long roots and guide the shortened roots downward and outward. Root tips die quickly when exposed to light and air, so complete this step as quickly as possible.

4. Place the root ball in the hole. Leave the top of the root ball (where the roots end and the trunk begins) ½ to 1 inch above the surrounding soil, making sure not to cover it unless the roots are exposed. For bare root plants, make a mound of soil in the middle of the hole and spread plant roots out evenly over the mound. Do not set the tree too deep into the hole.

5. As you add soil to fill in around the tree, lightly tap the soil to collapse air pockets, or add water to help settle the soil. Form a temporary water basin around the base of the tree to encourage water penetration, and be sure to water the tree thoroughly after planting. A tree with a dry root ball cannot absorb water; if the root ball is extremely dry, allow water to trickle into the soil by placing the hose at the trunk of the tree.

6. Place mulch around the tree. A circle of mulch, 3 feet in diameter, is common.

7. Depending on the size of the tree and the site conditions, staking the tree in place may be beneficial. Staking supports the tree until the roots are well-established to properly anchor it. Staking should allow for some movement of the tree on windy days. After trees are established, remove all supporting wires. If these are not removed, they can girdle the tree, cut into the trunk, and eventually kill the tree.

Pruning

Usually, pruning is not needed on newly planted trees. As the tree grows, lower branches may be pruned to provide clearance above the ground, or to remove dead or damaged limbs or suckers that sprout from the trunk. Sometimes larger trees need pruning to allow more light to enter the canopy. Small branches can be removed easily with pruners. Large branches should be removed with a pruning saw. All cuts should be vertical. This will allow the tree to heal quickly without the use of any artificial sealants. Major pruning should be done in late winter or early spring. At this time, the tree is more likely to "bleed," as sap is rising through the plant. This is actually healthy and will help prevent invasion by many disease-carrying organisms.

Under no circumstance should trees be topped (topping is chopping off large top tree branches). Not only does this practice ruin the natural shape of the tree, but it also increases its susceptibility to diseases and results in very narrow crotch angles (the angle between the trunk and the side branch). Narrow crotch angles are weaker than wide ones and more susceptible to damage from wind and ice. If a large tree requires major reduction in height or size, contact a professionally trained arborist.

Maintenance

For the first year or two, especially after a week or so of especially hot or dry weather, watch your tree closely for signs of moisture stress. If you see any leaf wilting or hard, caked soil, water the tree well and slowly enough to allow the water to soak in. This will encourage deep root growth. Keep the area under the tree mulched.

Some species of evergreen trees may need protection against winter sun and wind. A thorough watering in the fall before the ground freezes is recommended.

Fertilization is usually not needed for newly planted trees. Depending on the soil and growing conditions, fertilizer may be beneficial at a later time.

Young trees need protection against rodents, frost cracks, sunscald, lawn mowers, and weed whackers. In the winter months, mice and rabbits frequently girdle small trees by chewing away the bark at the snow level. Since the tissues that transport nutrients in the tree are located just under the bark, a girdled tree often dies in the spring when growth resumes. Weed whackers are also a common cause of girdling.

To prevent girdling, use plastic guards, which are inexpensive and easy to control.

Frost cracking is caused by the sunny side of the tree expanding at a different rate than the colder, shaded side. This can cause large splits in the trunk. To prevent this, wrap young trees with paper tree wrap, starting from the base and wrapping up to the bottom branches. Sunscald can occur when a young tree is suddenly moved from a shady spot into direct sunlight. Light-colored tree wraps can be used to protect the trunk from sunscald.

Final Thoughts

Trees are natural windbreaks, slowing the wind and providing shelter and food for wildlife. Trees can help protect livestock, gardens, and larger crops. They also help prevent dust particles from adding to smog over urban areas. Tree plantings are key components of an effective conservation system and can provide your yard with beauty; shade; and rich, natural resources.

Container Gardening

An alternative to growing vegetables, flowers, and herbs in a traditional garden is to grow them in containers. While the amount that can be grown in a container is certainly limited, container gardens work well for tomatoes, peppers, cucumbers, herbs, salad greens, and many flowering annuals. Choose vegetable varieties that have been specifically bred for container growing. You can obtain this information online or at your garden center. Container gardening also brings birds and butterflies right to your doorstep. Hanging baskets of fuchsia or pots of snapdragons are frequently visited by hummingbirds, allowing for up-close observation.

Container gardening is an excellent method of growing vegetables, herbs, and flowers, especially if you do not have adequate outdoor space for a full garden bed. A container garden can be placed anywhere—on the patio, balcony, rooftop, or windowsill. Vegetables such as leaf lettuce, radishes, small tomatoes, and baby carrots can all be grown successfully in pots.

How to Grow Vegetables in a Container Garden

Here are some simple steps to follow for growing vegetables in containers.

1. Choose a sunny area for your container plants. Your plants will need at least five to six hours of sunlight a day. Some plants, such as cucumbers, may need more.

Select plants that are suitable for container growing. Usually their name will have words such as "patio," "bush," "dwarf," "toy," or "miniature" in them. Peppers, onions, and carrots are also good choices.

2. Choose a planter that is at least 5 gallons, unless the plant is very small. Poke holes in the bottom if they don't already exist; the soil must be able to drain to prevent the roots from rotting. Avoid terracotta or dark-colored pots as they tend to dry out quickly.

3. Fill your container with potting soil. Good potting soil will have a mixture of peat moss and vermiculite. You can make your own potting soil using composted soil (see pages 18–22). Read the directions on the seed packet or label to determine how deep to plant your seeds.

4. Check the moisture of the soil frequently. You don't want the soil to become muddy, but the soil should always feel damp to the touch. Do not wait until the plant is wilting to water it—at that point, it may be too late.

▲ You only need a few simple tools for container gardening.

• You may wish to line your container with porous materials such as shredded newspaper or rags to keep the soil from washing out. Be sure the soil can still drain easily.

Things to Consider

• Follow normal planting schedules for your climate when determining when to plant your container garden.

How to Grow Herbs in a Container

Herbs will thrive in containers if cared for properly. And if you keep them near your kitchen, you can easily snip off pieces to use in cooking. Here's how to start your own herb container garden:

1. If your container doesn't already have holes in the bottom, poke several to allow the soil to drain. Pour gravel into the container until it is about a quarter of the way full. This will help the water drain out and help to keep the soil from washing out.

2. Fill your container three-quarters of the way with potting soil or a soil-based compost.

3. It's best to use seedlings when planting herbs in containers. Tease the roots slightly, gently spreading them apart with your fingertips. This will encourage them to spread once planted. Place each herb into the pot and cover the root base with soil. Place herbs that will grow taller in the center of your container, and the smaller ones around the edges. Leave about four square inches of space between each seedling.

4. As you gently press in soil between the plants, leave an inch or so between the container's top and the soil. You don't want the container to overflow when you water the herbs.

5. Cut the tops off the taller herb plants to encourage them to grow faster and to produce more leaves.

6. Pour water into the container until it begins to leak out the bottom. Most herbs like to dry out between watering, and over-watering can cause some herbs to rot and die, so water only every few days unless the plants are in a very hot place.

Things to Consider

- Growing several kinds of herbs together helps the plants to thrive. A few exceptions to this rule are oregano, lemon balm, and tea balm. These herbs should be planted on their own because they will overtake the other herbs in your container.
- You may wish to choose your herbs according to color to create attractive arrangements for your home. Any of the following herbs will grow well in containers:
- Silver herbs: artemsias, curry plans, santolinas
- Golden herbs: lemon thyme, calendula, nasturtium, sage, lemon balm
- Blue herbs: borage, hyssop, rosemary, catnip
- Green herbs: basil, mint, marjoram, thyme, parsley, chives, tarragon
- Pink and purple herbs: oregano (the flowers) are pink, lavender
- If you decide to transplant your herbs in the summer months, they will grow quite well outdoors and will give you a larger harvest.

▲ It's easiest to grow herbs from seedlings like these, though you can certainly grow them from seeds, too.

▲ Cinder blocks or simple wooden planters made of scrap wood can make inexpensive container gardens.

How to Grow Flowers from Seeds in a Container

1. Cover the drainage hole in the bottom of the pot with a flat stone. This will keep the soil from trickling out when the plant is watered.

2. Fill the container with soil. The container should be filled almost to the top and for the best results, use potting soil from your local nursery or garden center.

3. Make holes for the seeds. Refer to the seed packet to see how deep to make the holes. Always save the seed packet for future reference—it most likely has helpful directions about thinning young plants.

4. Place a seed in each hole. Pat the soil gently on top of each seed.

5. Use a light mist to water your seeds, making sure that the soil is only moist and not soaked.

6. Make sure your seeds get the correct amount of sunlight. Refer to the seed packet for the adequate amount of sunlight each seedling needs.

7. Watch your seeds grow. Most seeds take 3 to 17 days to sprout. Once the plants start sprouting, be sure to pull out plants that are too close together so the remaining plants will have enough space to establish good root systems.

8. Remember to water and feed your container plants. Keep the soil moist so your plants can grow. And in no time at all, you should have wonderful flowers growing in your container garden.

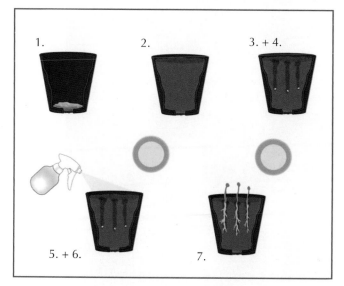

▲ Growing flowers from seeds.

Preserving Your Container Plants

As fall approaches, frost will soon descend on your container plants and can ultimately destroy your garden. Container plants are particularly susceptible to frost damage, especially if you are growing tropical plants, perennials, and hardy woody plants in a single container garden. There are many ways that you can preserve and maintain your container garden plants throughout the winter season.

Preservation techniques will vary depending on the plants in your container garden. Tropical plants can be over-wintered using methods replicating a dry season, forcing the plant into dormancy; hardy perennials and woody shrubs need a cold dormancy to grow in the spring, so they must stay outside; cacti and succulents prefer their winters warm and dry and must be brought inside, while many annuals can be propagated by stem cuttings or can just be repotted and maintained inside.

Preserving Tropical Bulbs and Tubers

Many tropical plants, such as cannas, elephant ears, and angel's trumpets can be saved from an untimely death by over-wintering them in a dark corner or sunny window of your home, depending on the type of plant. A lot of bulbous and tuberous tropical plants have a natural dry season (analogous to our winter) when their leafy parts die off, leaving the bulb behind. Don't throw the bulbs away. After heavy frosts turn the aboveground plant parts to mush, cut the damaged foliage off about 4 inches above the thickened bulb. Then, dig them up and remove all excess soil from the roots. At this point, you can determine if the clump needs dividing. If it needs dividing, be sure to dust all cut surfaces with a sulfur-based fungicide made for bulbs to prevent the wounds from rotting. Cut the roots back to 1 inch from the bulb and leave to dry out evenly. Rotten bulbs or roots need to be thrown away so infection doesn't spread to the healthy bulbs.

A bulb's or tuber's drying time can last up to two weeks if it is sitting on something absorbent like newspaper and located somewhere shaded and dry—preferably around 50°F—such as a garage or basement. Once clean and dry, bulbs should be stored all winter in damp (not soggy) milled peat moss. This prevents the bulbs from drying out any further, which could cause them to die. Many gardeners don't have a perfectly cool basement or garage to keep bulbs dormant. Alternative methods for dry storage include a dark closet with the door cracked for circulation, a cabinet, or underneath a bed in a cardboard box with a few holes punched for airflow. The important thing to keep in mind is that the bulb needs to be kept on the dry side, in the dark, and moderately warm.

If a bulb was grown as a single specimen in its own pot, the entire pot can be placed in a garage that stays above 50°F or a cool basement and allowed to dry out completely. Cut all aboveground plant parts flush with the soil and don't water until the outside temperatures stabilize above 60°F. Often, bulbs break dormancy unexpectedly in this dry pot method. If this happens, pots can be moved to a sunny location near a window and watered sparingly until they can be placed outside. The emerging leaves will be stunted, but once outside, the plant will replace any spindly leaves with lush, new ones.

Annuals

Many herbaceous annuals can also be saved for the following year. By rooting stem cuttings in water on a sunny windowsill, plants like impatiens, coleus, sweet potato vine cultivars, and purple heart can be held over winter until needed in the spring. Otherwise, the plants can be cut back by half, potted in a peat-based, soilless mix, and placed on a sunny windowsill. With a wide assortment of "annuals" available on the market, some research is required to determine which annuals can be over-wintered successfully. True annuals (such as basils, cockscomb, and zinnias)—regardless of any treatment given—will go to seed and die when brought inside.

Cacti and Succulents

If you planted a mixed dry container this year and want to retain any of the plants for next year, they should be removed from the main container and re-potted into a high-sand-content soil mix for cacti and succulents. Keep them near a sunny window and water when dry. Many succulents and cacti do well indoors, either in a heated garage or a moderately sunny corner of a living room.

As with other tropical plants, succulents also need time to adjust to sunnier conditions in the spring. Move them to a shady spot outside when temperatures have stabilized above 60°F and then gradually introduce them to brighter conditions.

Hardy Perennials, Shrubs, and Vines

Hardy perennials, woody shrubs, and vines needn't be thrown away when it's time to get rid of accent containers. Crack-resistant, four-season containers can house perennials and woody shrubs year-round. Below is a list of specific perennials and woody plants that do well in both hot and cold weather, indoors and out:

- Shade perennials, like coral bells, lenten rose, assorted hardy ferns, and Japanese forest grass are great for all weather containers.
- Sun-loving perennials, such as sedges, some salvias, purple coneflower, daylily, spiderwort, and bee blossom are also very hardy and do well in year-round containers. Interplant them with cool growing plants, like kale, pansies, and Swiss chard, for fall and spring interest.
- Woody shrubs and vines—many of which have great foliage interest with four-season appeal—are ideal for container gardens. Red-twigged dogwood cultivars, clematis vine cultivars, and dwarf crape myrtle cultivars are great container additions that can stay outdoors year-round.

If the container has to be removed, hardy perennials and woody shrubs can be temporarily planted in the ground and mulched. Dig them from the garden in the spring, if you wish, and replant into a container. Or, leave them in their garden spot and start over with fresh ideas and new plant material for your container garden.

Sustainable Plants and Money in Your Pocket

Over-wintering is a great form of sustainable plant conservation achieved simply and effectively by adhering to each plant's cultural and environmental needs. With careful planning and storage techniques, you'll save money as well as plant material. The beauty and interest you've created in this season's well-grown container garden can also provide enjoyment for years to come.

▼ You can make container gardens out of almost anything.

Rooftop Gardens

If you live in an urban area and don't have a lawn, that does not mean you cannot have a garden. Whether you live in an apartment building or own your own home without yard space, you can grow your very own garden, right on your roof!

Is Your Roof Suitable for a Rooftop Garden?

Theoretically, any roof surface can be greened—even sloped or curved roofs can support a layer of sod or wildflowers. However, if the angle of your roof is over 30 degrees you should consult with a specialist. Very slanted roofs make it difficult to keep the soil in place until the plant's roots take hold. Certainly, a flat roof, approximating level ground conditions is the easiest on which to grow a garden, though a slight slant can be helpful in allowing drainage.

Also consider how much weight your roof can bear. A simple, lightweight rooftop garden will weigh between 13 and 30 pounds per square foot. Add to this your own weight—or that of anyone who will be tending or enjoying the garden—gardening tools, and, if you live in a colder climate, the additional weight of snow in the winter.

Benefits of Rooftop Gardening

- Create more outdoor green space within your urban environment.
- Grow your own fresh vegetables—even in the city.
- Improve air quality and reduce CO_2 emissions.
- Help delay stormwater runoff.
- Give additional insulation to building roofs.
- Reduce noise.

Will a Rooftop Garden Cause Water Leakage or Other Damage?

No. In fact, planting beds or surfaces are often used to protect and insulate roofs. However, you should take some precautions to protect your roof:

1. Cover your roof with a layer of waterproof material, such as a heavy-duty pond liner. You may want to place an old rug on top of the waterproof material to help it stay in place and to give additional support to the materials on top.

▲ Rooftop gardens are becoming more popular in urban areas around the world.

How to Make a Rooftop Garden

Preparation

1. Before you begin, find out if it is possible and legal to create a garden on your roof. You don't want to spend lots of time and money preparing for a garden and then find out that it is prohibited.

2. Make sure that the roof is able to hold the weight of a rooftop garden. If so, figure out how much weight it can hold. Remember this when making the garden and use lighter containers and soil as needed.

▲ You can use container plants on your rooftop rather than laying a garden directly on the roof. However, still be sure that your roof is sturdy enough to hold the pots and the people who will be tending them.

Setting Up the Garden

1. Install your waterproof, protective drainage, and filter layers, as described earlier. If your roof is angled, you may want to place a wooden frame around the edges of the roof to keep the layers from sliding off. Be sure to use rot-resistant wood and cut outlets into the frame to allow excess water to drain away. Layer pebbles around the outlets to aid drainage and to keep vegetation from clogging them.

2. Add soil to your garden. It should be 1–4 inches thick and will be best if it's a mix of ¾ inorganic soil (crushed brick or a similar granular material) and ¼ organic compost.

Planting and Maintaining the Garden

1. Start planting. You can plant seeds, seedlings, or transplant mature plants. Choose plants that are wind-resistant and won't need a great deal of maintenance. Sedums make excellent rooftop plants as they require very little attention once planted, are hardy, and are attractive throughout most of the year. Most vegetables can be grown in-season on rooftops, though the wind will make taller vegetables (like corn or beans) difficult to grow. If your roof is slanted, plant drought-resistant plant varieties near the peak, as they'll get less water.

2. Water your garden immediately after planting, and then regularly throughout the growing season, unless rain does the work for you.

2. Place a protective drainage layer on top of the waterproof material. Otherwise, shovels, shoe heels, or dropped tools could puncture the roof. Use a coarse material such as gravel, pumice, or expanded shale.

3. Place a filter layer on top of the drainage layer to keep soil in place so that it won't clog up your drainage. A lightweight polyester geotextile (an inexpensive, non-woven fabric found at most home improvement stores) is ideal for this. Note that if your roof has an angle of over 10 degrees, only install the filter layer around the edges of the roof as it can increase slippage.

4. Using movable planters or containers, modular walkways and surfacing treatment, and compartmentalized planting beds will make it easier to fix leaks should they appear.

Things to Consider

1. If you live in a very hot area, you may want to build small wooden platforms to elevate your plants above the hot rooftop. This will help increase the ventilation around the plants.

2. When determining the strength of your roof, remember that large pots full of water and soil will be very heavy, and if the roof is not strong enough, your garden could cause structural damage.

3. You can use pots or other containers on your rooftop rather than making a full garden bed. You should still first find out how much weight your roof can hold and choose lightweight containers.

4. Consider adding a fence or railing around your roof, especially if children will be helping in the garden.

Terracing

Terraces can create several mini-gardens in your backyard. On steep slopes, terracing can make planting a garden possible. Terraces also prevent erosion by shortening a long slope into a series of shorter, more level steps. This allows heavy rains to soak into the soil rather than to run off and cause erosion and poor plant growth.

Materials Needed for Terraces

Numerous materials are available for building terraces. Treated wood is often used in terrace building and has several advantages: It is easy to work with, it blends well with plants and the surrounding environment, and it is often less expensive than other materials. There are many types of treated wood available for terracing—railroad ties and landscaping timbers are just two examples. These materials will last for years, which is crucial if you are hoping to keep your terraced garden intact for any length of time. There has been some concern about using these treated materials around plants, but studies by Texas A&M University and the Southwest Research Institute concluded that these materials are not harmful to gardens or people when used as recommended.

Other materials for terraces include bricks, rocks, concrete blocks, and similar masonry materials. Some masonry materials are made specifically for walls and terraces and can be more easily installed by a homeowner than other materials. These include fieldstone and brick. One drawback is that most stone or masonry products tend to be more expensive than wood, so if you are looking to save money, treated wood will make a sufficient terrace wall.

How High Should the Terrace Walls Be?

The steepness of the slope on which you wish to garden often dictates the appropriate height of the terrace wall. Make the terraces in your yard high enough so the land between them is fairly level. Be sure the terrace material is strong enough and anchored well to stay in place through freezing and thawing, and during heavy rainstorms. Do not underestimate the

▼ Terraces help prevent erosion and encourage vegetation on sloped ground.

pressure of waterlogged soil behind a wall—it can be enormous and will cause improperly constructed walls to bulge or collapse.

Many communities have building codes for walls and terraces. Large projects will most likely need the expertise of a professional landscaper to make sure the walls can stand up to water pressure in the soil. Large terraces also need to be built with adequate drainage and tied back into the slope properly. Because of the expertise and equipment required to do this correctly, you will probably want to restrict terraces you build on your own to no more than a foot or two high.

Building Your Own Terrace

The safest way to build a terrace is by using the cut and fill method. With this method, little soil is disturbed, giving you protection from erosion should a sudden storm occur while the work is in progress. This method will also require little, if any, additional soil. Here are the steps needed to build your own terrace:

1. Contact your utility companies to identify the location of any buried utility lines and pipes before starting to dig.

2. Determine the rise and run of your slope. The rise is the vertical distance from the bottom of the slope to the top. The run is the horizontal distance between the top and the bottom. This will allow you to determine how many terraces you will need. For example, if your run is 20 feet and the rise is 8 feet, and you want each bed to be 5 feet wide, you will need four beds. The rise of each bed will be 2 feet.

3. Start building the beds at the bottom of your slope. You will need to dig a trench in which to place your first tier. The depth and width of the trench will vary depending on how tall the terrace will be and the specific building materials you are using. Follow the manufacturer's instructions carefully when using masonry products, as many of these have limits on the number of tiers or the height that can be safely built. If you are using landscape timbers and your terrace is low (less than 2 feet), you only need to bury the timber to about half its thickness or less. The width of the trench should be slightly wider than your timber. Make sure the bottom of the trench is firmly packed

▲ Neat rows of green plants line this terraced hill, which would otherwise likely be barren.

and completely level, and then place your timbers into the trench.

4. For the sides of your terrace, dig a trench into the slope. The bottom of this trench must be level with the bottom of the first trench. When the depth of the trench is one inch greater than the thickness of your timber, you have reached the back of the terrace and can stop digging.

5. Cut a piece of timber to the correct length and place it into the trench.

6. Drill holes through your timbers and pound long spikes, or pipes, through the holes and into the ground. A minimum of 18 inches of pipe length is recommended, and longer pipes may be needed in higher terraces for added stability.

7. Place the next tier of timbers on top of the first, overlapping the corners and joints. Pound a spike through both tiers to fuse them together.

8. Move the soil from the back of the bed to the front of the bed until the surface is level. Add another tier as needed.

9. Repeat, starting with step 2, to create the remaining terraces. In continuously connected terrace systems, the first timber of the second tier will also be the back wall of your first terrace.

10. The back wall of the last bed will be level with its front wall.

11. When finished, you can start to plant and mulch your terraced garden.

Other Ways to Make Use of Slopes in Your Yard

If terraces are beyond the limits of your time or money, you may want to consider other options for backyard slopes. If you have a slope that is hard to mow, consider using groundcovers on the slope rather than grass. There are many plants adapted to a wide range of light and moisture conditions that require little care (and do not need mowing) and provide soil erosion protection. These include:

· Juniper
· Wintercreeper
· Periwinkle
· Cotoneaster
· Potentilla
· Heathers and heaths

Strip-cropping is another way to deal with long slopes in your yard. Rather than terracing to make garden beds level, plant perennial beds and strips of grass across the slope. Once established, many perennials are effective in reducing erosion. Adding mulch also helps reduce erosion. If erosion does occur, it will be basically limited to the gardened area. The grass strips will act as filters to catch much of the soil that may run off the beds. Grass strips should be wide enough to mow easily, and wide enough to effectively reduce erosion.

▲ Heather grows wild in many areas but can also be planted on your hillsides to help prevent erosion.

▲ Periwinkles require little maintenance, spread quickly, and will grow easily on a slope in your yard.

Raised Beds

If you live in an area where the soil is wet (preventing a good vegetable garden from growing the spring), find it difficult to bend over to plant and cultivate your vegetables or flowers, or if you just want a different look to your backyard garden, consider building a raised bed.

A raised bed is an interesting and affordable way to garden. It creates an ideal environment for growing vegetables, since the soil concentration can be closely monitored and, as it is raised above the ground, it reduces the compaction of plants from people walking on the soil.

Raised beds are typically 2 to 6 feet wide and as long as needed. In most cases, a raised bed consists of a "frame" that is filled in with nutrient-rich soil (including compost or organic fertilizers) and is then planted with a variety of vegetables or flowers, depending on the gardener's preference. By controlling the bed's construction and the soil mixture that goes into the bed, a gardener can effectively reduce the amount of weeds that will grow in the garden.

When planting seeds or young sprouts in a raised bed, it is best to space the plants equally from each other on all sides. This will ensure that the leaves will be touching once the plant is mature, thus saving space and reducing the soil's moisture loss.

▲ Raised beds make neat, attractive gardens and make it easy to monitor the condition of the soil.

How to Make a Raised Bed

Step One: Plan Out Your Raised Bed

1. Think about how you'd like your raised bed to look, and then design the shape. A raised bed is not

Things You'll Need

- Forms for your raised bed (consider using 4 x 4-inch posts cut to 24 inches in height for corners, and 2 x 12-inch boards for the sides)
- Nails or screws
- Hammer or screwdriver
- Plastic liner (to act as a weed barrier at the bottom of your bed)
- Shovel
- Compost, or composting manure
- Soil (either potting soil or soil from another part of your yard)
- Rake (to smooth out the soil once in the bed)
- Seeds or young plants
- Optional: PVC piping and greenhouse plastic (to convert your raised bed to a greenhouse)

extremely complicated, and all you need to do is build an open-top and open-bottom box (if you are ambitious, you can create a raised bed in the shape of a circle, hexagon, or star). The main purpose of this box is to hold soil.

2. Make a drawing of your raised bed, measure your available garden space, and add those measurements to your drawing. This will allow you to determine how much material is needed. Generally, your bed should be at least 24 inches in height.

3. Decide what kind of material you want to use for your raised bed. You can use lumber, plastic, synthetic wood, railroad ties, bricks, rocks, or a number of other items to hold the dirt. Using lumber is the easiest and most efficient method.

4. Gather your supplies.

Step Two: Build Your Raised Bed

1. Make sure your bed will be situated in a place that gets plenty of sunlight. Carefully assess your placement, as your raised bed will be fairly permanent.

2. Connect the sides of your bed together (with either screws or nails) to form the desired shape of your bed. If you are using lumber, you can use 4 x 4-inch posts to serve as the corners of your bed, and then nail or screw the sides to these corner posts. By doing so, you will increase the strength of the structure and ensure that the dirt will stay inside.

3. Cut a piece of gardening plastic to fit inside your raised bed, and lay it out in the appropriate location. This will significantly reduce the amount of weeds growing in your garden.

4. Place your frame over the gardening plastic (this might take two people).

Step Three: Start Planting

1. Add some compost into the bottom of the bed and then layer potting soil on top of the compost. If you have soil from other parts of your yard, feel free to use that in addition to the compost and potting soil. Plan to fill at least ⅓ of your raised bed with compost or composted manure (available from nurseries or garden centers in 40-pound bags).

2. Mix in dry organic fertilizers (like wood ash, bone meal, and blood meal) while building your bed. Follow the package instructions for how best to mix it in.

3. Decide what you want to plant. Some people like to grow flowers in their raised beds; others prefer to grow vegetables. If you do want to grow food, raised beds are excellent choices for salad greens, carrots, onions, radishes, beets, and other root crops.

Things to Consider

1. To save money, try to dig up and use soil from your yard. Potting soil can be expensive, and yard soil is just as effective when mixed with compost.

2. Be creative when building your raised planting bed. You can construct a great raised bed out of recycled goods or old lumber.

3. You can convert your raised bed into a greenhouse. Just add hoops to your bed by bending and connecting PVC pipe over the bed. Then clip greenhouse plastic to the PVC pipes, and you have your own greenhouse.

4. Make sure to water your raised bed often. Because it is above ground, your raised bed will not retain water as well as the soil in the ground. If you keep your bed narrow, it will help conserve water.

5. Decorate or illuminate your raised bed to make it a focal point in your yard.

6. If you use lumber to construct your raised bed, keep a watch out for termites.

7. Beware of old, pressure-treated lumber, as it may contain arsenic and could potentially leak into the root systems of any vegetables you might grow in your raised bed. Newer, pressure-treated lumber should not contain these toxic chemicals.

Growing Plants without Soil

Plants grown in soilless cultures still need the basic requirements of plant growth, such as temperature, light (if indoors, use a heat lamp and set the container near or on a windowsill), water, oxygen (you can produce good airflow by using a small, rotating fan indoors), carbon dioxide, and mineral nutrients (derived from solutions). But plants grown without soil have their roots either free-floating in a nutrient-rich solution or bedded in a soil-like medium, such as sand, gravel, brick shards, Perlite, or rockwool. These plants do not have to exert as much energy to gather nutrients from the soil and thus they grow more quickly and, usually, more productively.

▲ Lettuce is especially well-suited to hydroponics systems.

Types of Soilless Systems

There are two main types of soilless cultures that can be used to grow plants and vegetables. The first is a water culture, in which plants are supplied with mineral nutrients directly from the water solution. The second, called aggregate culture or "sand culture," uses an aggregate (such as sand, gravel, or Perlite) as soil to provide an anchoring support for the plant roots. Both types of hydroponics are effective in growing soilless plants and in providing essential nutrients for healthy and productive plant growth.

Water Culture

The main advantage of using a water culture system is that a significant part of the nutrient solution is always in contact with the plants' roots. This provides an adequate amount of water and nutrients. The main challenges of this system are providing sufficient air supply for the roots and providing the roots with proper support and anchorage.

The Benefits and Drawbacks of Growing Plants in a Hydroponics System

Hydroponics is the method of growing plants in a container filled with a nutrient-rich bath (water with special fertilizer) and no soil.

Benefits:
- Plants can be grown in areas where normal plant agriculture is difficult (such as deserts and other arid places, or cities).
- Most terrestrial plants will grow in a hydroponics system.
- There is minimal weed growth.
- The system takes up less space than soil system.
- It conserves water.
- No fear of contaminated runoff from garden fertilizers.

- There is less labor and cost involved.
- Certain seasonal plants can be raised during any season.
- The quality of produce is generally consistent.
- Old nutrient solution can be used to water houseplants.

Drawbacks:
- Can cause salmonella to grow due to the wet and confined conditions.
- More difficult to grow root vegetables, such as carrots and potatoes.
- If nutrient solution is not regularly changed, plants can become nutrient deficient and thus not grow or produce.

▲ In this type of hydroponics system, a dripper releases the nutrient solution into the top layer of piping. It then flows in a steady stream down through the other layers of piping.

Materials Needed to Make Your Own Water Culture

A large water culture system will need either a wood or concrete tank 6 to 18 inches deep and 2 to 3 feet wide. If you use a wooden container, be sure there are no knots in the wood and seal the tank with non-creosote or tar asphalt.

For small water culture systems, which are recommended for beginners, glass jars, earthenware crocks, or plastic buckets will suffice as your holding tanks. If your container is transparent, be sure to paint the outside of the container with black paint to keep the light out (and to keep algae from growing inside your system). Keep a narrow, vertical strip unpainted in order to see the level of the nutrient solution inside your container.

The plant bed should be 3 or more inches deep and large enough to cover the container or tank. To support the weight of the litter (where your seeds or seedlings are placed), cover the bottom of the bed with chicken wire and then fill the bed with litter (wood shavings, sphagnum moss, peat, or other organic materials that do not easily decay). If you are starting your plants from seeds, germinate the seeds in a bed of sand and then transplant to the water culture bed, keeping the bed moist until the plants get their roots down into the nutrient solution.

Aeration

A difficulty in using water culture is keeping the solution properly aerated. It is important to keep enough space between the seed bed and the nutrient solution so the plant's roots can receive proper oxygen. To make sure that air can easily flow into the container, either prop up the seed bed slightly to allow air flow or drill a hole in your container just above the highest solution level.

Install an aquarium pump in your water culture system to ensure sufficient oxygen reaching the plant roots. Just make sure that the water is not agitated too much or the roots may be damaged. You can also use an air stone or perforated pipe to gently introduce air flow into your container.

Water Supply

Your hydroponics system needs an adequate supply of fresh water to maintain healthy plant life. Make sure that the natural minerals in your water are not going to adversely affect your hydroponics plants. If there is too much sodium in your water (usually an effect of softened water), it could become toxic to your plants. In general, the minerals in water are not harmful to the growth of your plants.

Nutrient Solution

You may add nutrient solution by hand, by a gravity-feed system, or mechanically. In smaller water culture systems, mixing the nutrient solution in a small container and adding it by hand, as needed, is typically adequate.

If you are using a larger setup, a gravity-feed system will work quite well. In this type of system, the nutrient solution is mixed in a vat and then tapped from the vat into your container as needed. You can use a plastic container or larger earthenware jar as the vat.

A pump can also be used to supply your system with adequate nutrient solution. You can insert the pump into the vat and then transfer the solution to your hydroponics system.

When your plants are young, it is important to keep the space between your seed bed and the nutrient

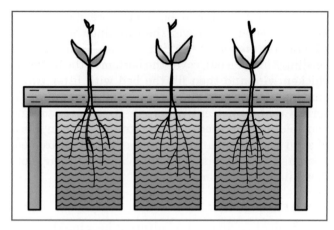

▲ In a water culture system, the roots are always in contact with the nutrient solution.

Things You'll Need

- External pump
- Air line or tubing
- Air stones
- Waterproof bin, bucket, or fish tank to use as a reserve
- Styrofoam
- Net pots
- Type of growing medium, such as rockwool or grow rocks
- Hydroponics nutrients, such as grow formula, bloom formula, supplements, and pH
- Black spray paint (this is only required if the reservoir is transparent)
- Knife, box cutter, or scissors
- Tape measure

solution small (that way, the young plant roots can reach the nutrients). As your plants grow, the amount of space between the bed and solution should increase (but do this slowly and keep the level rather consistent).

If the temperature is rather high and there is increased evaporation, it is important to keep the roots at the correct level in the water and change the nutrient solution every day, if needed.

Drain your container every two weeks and then renew the nutrient solution from your vat or by hand. This must be done in a short amount of time so the roots do not dry out.

Transplanting

When transplanting your seedlings, it's important that you are careful with the tiny root systems. Gently work the roots through the support netting and down into the nutrient solution. Then fill in the support netting with litter to help the plant remain upright.

How to Build a Simple, Homemade Hydroponics System

Steps to Building Your Hydroponics System:

1. Find a container to use as a reservoir, such as a fish tank, a bin, or a bucket of some sort. The reservoir should be painted black if it is not lightproof

(or covered with a thick, black trash bag if you want to reuse the tank at some point), and allowed to dry before moving on to the next step. Allowing light to enter the reservoir will promote the growth of algae. It is a good idea to use a reservoir that is the same dimensions (length and width) from top to bottom.

2. Using a knife or sharp object, score a line on the tank (scratch off some paint in a straight line from top to bottom). This will be your water level meter, which will let you see how much water is in the reservoir and will give you a more accurate and convenient view of the nutrient solution level in your tank.

3. Use a tape measure to determine the length and width of your reservoir. Measure the inside of the reservoir from one end to the other. Once you have the dimensions, cut the Styrofoam ¼ inch smaller than the size of the reservoir. For example, if your dimensions are 36 x 20 inches, you should cut the Styrofoam to 35 ¾ x 19 ¾ inches. The Styrofoam should fit nicely in the reservoir, with just enough room to adjust to

▼ A simple hydroponics system.

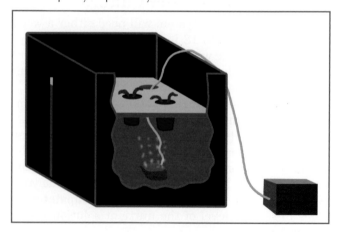

any water level changes. If the reservoir tapers off at the bottom (the bottom is smaller in dimension than the top) the floater (Styrofoam) should be 2 to 4 inches smaller than the reservoir, or more if necessary.

4. Do not place the Styrofoam in the reservoir yet. First, you need to cut holes for the net pots. Put the net pots on the Styrofoam where you want to place each plant. Using a pen or pencil, trace around the bottom of each net pot. Use a knife or box cutter to follow the trace lines and cut the holes for pots. On one end of the Styrofoam, cut a small hole for the air line to run into the reservoir.

5. The number of plants you can grow will depend on the size of the garden you build and the types of crops you want to grow. Remember to space plants appropriately so that each receives ample amounts of light.

6. The pump you choose must be strong enough to provide enough oxygen to sustain plant life. Ask for advice choosing a pump at your local hydroponics supply store or garden center.

7. Connect the air line to the pump and attach the air stone to the free end. The air line should be long enough to travel from the pump into the bottom of the reservoir, or at least float in the middle of the tank so the oxygen bubbles can get to the plant roots. It also must be the right size for the pump you choose. Most pumps will come with the correct size air line. To determine the tank's capacity, use a one-gallon bucket or bottle and fill the reservoir. Remember to count how many gallons it takes to fill the reservoir and you will know the correct capacity of your tank.

Setting Up Your Hydroponics System

1. Fill the reservoir with the nutrient solution.
2. Place the Styrofoam into the reservoir.
3. Run the air line through the designated hole or notch.
4. Fill the net pots with growing medium and place one plant in each pot.

5. Put the net pots into the designated holes in the Styrofoam.
6. Plug in the pump, turn it on, and start growing with your fully functional, homemade hydroponics system.

Aggregate Culture

Aggregate culture systems utilize different mediums that act in place of soil to stabilize the plant and its roots. The aggregate in the container is flooded with the nutrient solution. The advantage of this type of system is that there is not as much trouble with aerating the roots. Also, aggregate culture systems allow for the easy transplantation of seedlings into the aggregate medium and it is less expensive.

Materials Needed for an Aggregate Culture System

The container should be watertight to conserve the nutrient solution. Large tanks can be made of concrete or wood, and smaller operations can effectively be done in glass jars, earthenware containers, or plastic buckets. Make sure to paint transparent containers black.

Aggregate materials may differ greatly, depending on what type you choose to use. Silica sand (well washed) is one of the best materials that can be used. Any other type of coarse-textured sand is also effective, but make sure it does not contain lime. Sand holds moisture quite well and it allows for easy transplantation. A mixture of sand and gravel together is also an effective aggregate. Other materials, such as peat moss, vermiculite, wood shavings, and coco peat, are also good aggregates. You can find aggregate materials at your local garden center, home center, or garden-supply house.

▼ A simple aggregate culture system.

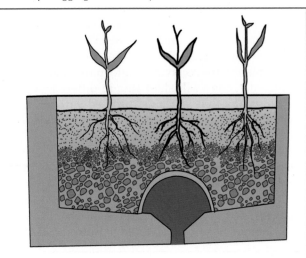

Things to Consider

- A homemade hydroponics system like this is not ideal for large-scale production of plants or for commercial usage. This particular system does not offer a way to conveniently change the nutrient solution. An extra container would be required to hold the floater while you change the solution.

- Lettuce, watercress, tomatoes, cucumbers, and herbs grow especially well hydroponically.

Aeration

Aggregate culture systems allow much easier aeration than water culture systems. Draining and refilling the container with nutrient solution helps the air to move in and out of the aggregate material. This brings a fresh supply of oxygen to the plant roots.

Water Supply

The same water requirements are needed for this type of hydroponics system as for a water culture system. Minerals in the water tend to collect in the aggregate material, so it's a good idea to flush the material with fresh water every few weeks.

Nutrient Solution

The simplest way of adding the nutrient solution to aggregate cultures is to pour it over the aggregates by hand. You may also use a manual gravity-feed system with buckets or vats. Attach the vat to the bottom of the container with a flexible hose, raise the vat to flood the container, and lower it to drain it. Cover the vat to prevent evaporation and replenish it with new nutrient solution once every two weeks.

A gravity drip-feed system also works well and helps reduce the amount of work you do. Place the vat higher than the container, and then control the solution drip so it is just fast enough to keep the aggregate moist.

It is important that the nutrient solution is added and drained or raised and lowered at least once a day. In hotter weather, the aggregate material may need more wetting with the solution. Make sure that the material is not drying out the roots. Drenching the aggregate with solution often will not harm the plants but letting the roots dry out could have detrimental effects.

Always replace your nutrient solution after two weeks. Not replacing the solution will cause salts and harmful fertilizer residues to build up, which may ultimately damage your plants.

Planting

You may use either seedlings or rooted cuttings in an aggregate culture system. The aggregate should be flooded and solution drained before planting to create a moist, compacted seed bed. Seeds may also be planted directly into the aggregate material. Do not plant the seeds too deep, and flood the container frequently with water to keep the aggregate moist. Once the seedlings have germinated, you may start using the nutrient solution.

If you are transplanting seedlings from a germination bed, make sure they have germinated in soilless material, as any soil left on the roots may cause them to rot and may hamper them in obtaining nutrients from the solution.

Pre-mixed Chemicals

Many of the essential nutrients needed for hydroponic plant growth are now available already mixed in their correct proportions. You may find these solutions in catalogs or from garden-supply stores. They are typically inexpensive and only small quantities are needed to help your plants grow strong and healthy. Always follow the directions on the container when using pre-mixed chemicals.

Making Your Own Solution

In the event that you want to make your own nutrient solution, here is a formula for a solution that will provide all the major elements required for your plants to grow.

Salt	Grade	Nutrients	Amt. for 25 gallons of solution
Potassium phosphate	Technical	Potassium, phosphorus	½ ounce (1 Tbsp)
Potassium nitrate	Fertilizer	Potassium, nitrogen	2 ounces (4 Tbsp of powdered salt)
Calcium nitrate	Fertilizer	Calcium, nitrogen	3 ounces (7 Tbsp)
Magnesium sulfate	Fertilizer	Magnesium, sulfur	1½ ounces (4 Tbsp)

Making Nutrient Solutions

For plants to grow properly, they must receive nitrogen, phosphorous, potassium, calcium, magnesium, sulfur, iron, manganese, boron, zinc, copper, molybdenum, and chlorine. There is a wide range of nutrient solutions that can be used. If your plants are receiving inadequate amounts of nutrients, they will show this in different ways. This means that you must proceed with caution when selecting and adding the minerals that will be present in your nutrient solution.

It is important to have pure nutrient materials when preparing the solution. Using fertilizer-grade chemicals is always the best route to go, as it is cheapest. Make sure the containers are closed and not exposed to air. Evaporated solutions increase the amount of salt which could harm your plants.

You can obtain all of these chemicals from garden-supply stores or drugstores.

After all the chemicals have been mixed into the solution, check the pH of the solution. A pH of 7.0 is neutral; anything below 7.0 is acidic and anything above is alkaline. Certain plants grow best in certain pHs. Plants that grow well at a lower pH (between 4.5 and 5.5) are azaleas, buttercups, gardenias, and roses; plants that grow well at a neutral pH are potatoes, zinnias, and pumpkins; most plants grow best in a slightly acidic pH (between 5.5 and 6.5).

To determine the pH of your solution, use a pH indicator (these are usually paper strips). The strip will change color when placed in different levels of pH. If you find your pH level to be above your desired range, you can bring it down by adding dilute sulfuric acid in small quantities using an eyedropper. Keep retesting until you reach your desired pH level.

Plant Nutrient Deficiencies

When plants are lacking nutrients, they typically display these deficiencies outwardly. Following is a list of symptoms that might occur if a plant is lacking a certain type of nutrient. If your plants display any of these symptoms, it is imperative that the level of that particular nutrient be increased.

Deficient Nutrient	Symptoms
Boron	Tip of the shoot dies; stems and petioles are brittle
Calcium	Tip of the shoot dies; tips of the young leaves die; tips of the leaves are hooked
Iron	New upper leaves turn yellow between the veins; edges and tips of leaves may die
Magnesium	Lower leaves are yellow between the veins; leaf margins curl up or down; leaves die
Manganese	New upper leaves have dead spots; leaf might appear netted
Nitrogen	Leaves are small and light green; lower leaves are lighter than upper leaves; weak stalks
Phosphorous	Dark-green foliage; lower leaves are yellow between the veins; purplish color on leaves
Potassium	Lower leaves might be mottled; dead areas near tips of leaves; yellowing at leaf margins and toward the center
Sulfur	Light-green upper leaves; leaf veins are lighter than surrounding area

▲ Nutrient deficiencies and their symptoms.

◄ Aggregate culture is especially useful in urban areas where quality soil is not readily available. If the only spot you have for a garden is outside your window, you should still be able to grow a variety of flowers, vegetables, or herbs.

Pest and Disease Management

Pest management can be one of the greatest challenges to the home gardener. Yard pests include weeds, insects, diseases, and some species of wildlife. Weeds are plants that are growing out of place. Insect pests include an enormous number of species from tiny thrips that are nearly invisible to the naked eye, to the large larvae of the tomato hornworm. Plant diseases are caused by fungi, bacteria, viruses, and other organisms—some of which are only now being classified. Poor plant nutrition and misuse of pesticides also can cause injury to plants. Slugs, mites, and many species of wildlife, such as rabbits, deer, and crows can be extremely destructive as well.

Identify the Problem

Careful identification of the problem is essential before taking measures to control the issue in your garden. Some insect damage may at first appear to be a disease, especially if no visible insects are present. Nutrient problems may also mimic diseases. Herbicide damage, resulting from misapplication of chemicals, can also be mistaken for other problems. Learning about different types of garden pests is the first step in keeping your plants healthy and productive.

Insects and Mites

All insects have six legs, but other than that they are extremely different depending on the species. Some insects include such organisms as beetles, flies, bees,

▲ A Japanese beetle eats holes in a leaf.

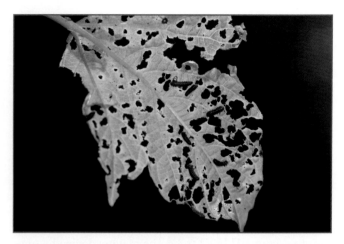

▲ Leaf damage from Japanese beetles.

ants, moths, and butterflies. Mites and spiders have eight legs—they are not, in fact, insects but will be treated as such for the purposes of this section.

Insects damage plants in several ways. The most visible damage caused by insects is chewed plant leaves and flowers. Many pests are visible and can be readily identified, including the Japanese beetle, Colorado potato beetle, and numerous species of caterpillars such as tent caterpillars and tomato hornworms. Other chewing insects, however, such as cutworms (which are caterpillars) come out at night to eat, and burrow into the soil during the day. These are much harder to identify but should be considered likely culprits if young plants seem to disappear overnight or are found cut off at ground level.

Sucking insects are extremely common in gardens and can be very damaging to your vegetable plants and flowers. The most known of these insects are leafhoppers, aphids, mealy bugs, thrips, and mites. These insects insert their mouthparts into the plant tissues and suck out the plant juices. They also may carry diseases that they spread from plant to plant as they move about the yard. You may suspect that these insects are present if you notice misshapen plant leaves or flower petals. Often the younger leaves will appear curled or puckered. Flowers developing from the buds may only partially develop if they've been sucked by these bugs. Look on the undersides of the leaves—that is where many insects tend to gather.

Other insects cause damage to plants by boring into stems, fruits, and leaves, possibly disrupting the plant's ability to transport water. They also create opportunities for disease organisms to attack the plants. You may suspect the presence of boring insects if you see small accumulations of sawdustlike material on plant stems or fruits. Common examples of boring insects include squash vine borers and corn borers.

Integrated Pest Management (IPM)

It is difficult, if not impossible, to prevent all pest problems in your garden every year. If your best prevention efforts have not been entirely successful, you may need to use some control methods. Integrated pest management (IPM) relies on several techniques to keep pests at acceptable population levels without excessive use of chemical controls. The basic principles of IPM include monitoring (scouting), determining tolerable injury levels (thresholds), and applying appropriate strategies and tactics to solve the pest issue. Unlike other methods of pest control where pesticides are applied on a rigid schedule, IPM applies only those controls that are needed, when they are needed, to control pests that will cause more than a tolerable level of damage to the plant.

Monitoring

Monitoring is essential for a successful IPM program. Check your plants regularly. Look for signs of damage from insects and diseases as well as indications of adequate fertility and moisture. Early identification of potential problems is essential.

There are thousands of insects in a garden, many of which are harmless or even beneficial to the plants. Proper identification is needed before control strategies can be adopted. It is important to recognize the different stages of insect development for several reasons. The caterpillar eating your plants may be the larvae of the butterfly you were trying to attract. Any small larvae with six spots on its back is probably a young ladybug, a very beneficial insect.

Thresholds

It is not necessary to kill every insect, weed, or disease organism invading your garden in order to maintain

▲ Certain kinds of worms and beetles will leave damaging holes in your plants.

the plants' health. When dealing with garden pests, an economic threshold comes into play and is the point where the damage caused by the pest exceeds the cost of control. In a home garden, this can be difficult to determine. What you are growing and how you intend to use it will determine how much damage you are willing to tolerate. Remember that larger plants, especially those close to harvest, can tolerate more damage than a tiny seedling. A few flea beetles on a radish seedling may warrant control, whereas numerous Japanese beetles eating the leaves of beans close to harvest may not.

If the threshold level for control has been exceeded, you may need to employ control strategies. Effective and safe strategies can be discussed with your local Cooperative Extension Service, garden centers, or nurseries.

Mechanical/Physical Control Strategies

Many insects can simply be removed by hand. This method is definitely preferable if only a few, large insects are causing the problem. Simply remove the insect from the plant and drop it into a container of soapy water or vegetable oil. Be aware that some insects have prickly spines or excrete oily substances that can cause injury to humans. Use caution when handling unfamiliar insects. Wear gloves or remove insects with tweezers.

Many insects can be removed from plants by spraying water from a hose or sprayer. Small vacuums can also be used to suck up insects. Traps can be used effectively for some insects as well. These come in a variety of styles depending on the insect to be caught. Many traps rely on the use of pheromones—naturally occurring chemicals produced by the insects and used to attract the opposite sex during mating. They are extremely specific for each species and, therefore, will not harm beneficial species. One caution with traps is that they may actually draw more insects into your yard, so don't place them directly into your garden. Other traps (such as yellow and blue sticky cards) are more generic and will attract numerous species. Different insects are attracted to different colors of these traps. Sticky cards also can be used effectively to monitor insect pests.

Other Pest Controls

Diatomaceous earth, a powderlike dust made of tiny marine organisms called diatoms, can be used to reduce damage from soft-bodied insects and slugs. Spread this material on the soil—it is sharp and cuts or irritates these soft organisms. It is harmless to other organisms. Put out shallow dishes of beer to trap slugs.

Pest and Disease Management

Biological Controls

Biological controls are nature's way of regulating pest populations. Biological controls rely on predators and parasites to keep organisms under control. Many of our present pest problems result from the loss of predator species and other biological control factors.

Some biological controls include birds and bats that eat insects. A single bat can eat up to 600 mosquitoes an hour. Many bird species eat insect pests on trees and in the garden.

Chemical Controls

When using biological controls, be very careful with pesticides. Most common pesticides are broad spectrum, which means that they kill a wide variety of organisms. Spray applications of insecticides are likely to kill numerous beneficial insects as well as the pests. Herbicides applied to weed species may drift in the wind or vaporize in the heat of the day and injure non-targeted plants. Runoff of pesticides can pollute water. Many pesticides are toxic to humans as well as pets and small animals that may enter your yard. Try to avoid using these types of pesticides at all costs—and if you do use them, read the labels carefully and avoid spraying them on windy days.

▲ Cutworms.

Some common, non-toxic household substances are as effective as many toxic pesticides. A few drops of dishwashing detergent mixed with water and sprayed on plants is extremely effective in controlling many soft-bodied insects, such as aphids and whiteflies. Crushed garlic mixed with water may control certain insects. A baking soda solution has been shown to help control some fungal diseases on roses.

Beneficial Insects that Help Control Pest Populations

Insect	Pest Controlled
Green lacewings	Aphids, mealy bugs, thrips, and spider mites
Ladybugs	Aphids and Colorado potato beetles
Praying mantises	Almost any insect
Ground beetles	Caterpillars that attack trees and shrubs
Seedhead weevils and other beetles	Weeds

Natural Pest Repellants

Pest	Repellant
Ant	Mint, tansy, or pennyroyal
Aphids	Mint, garlic, chives, coriander, or anise
Bean leaf beetle	Potato, onion, or turnip
Codling moth	Common oleander
Colorado potato bug	Green beans, coriander, or nasturtium
Cucumber beetle	Radish or tansy
Flea beetle	Garlic, onion, or mint
Imported cabbage worm	Mint, sage, rosemary, or hyssop
Japanese beetle	Garlic, larkspur, tansy, rue, or geranium
Leaf hopper	Geranium or petunia
Mice	Onion
Root knot nematodes	French marigolds
Slugs	Prostrate rosemary or wormwood
Spider mites	Onion, garlic, cloves, or chives
Squash bug	Radish, marigolds, tansy, or nasturtium
Stink bug	Radish
Thrips	Marigolds
Tomato hornworm	Marigolds, sage, or borage
Whitefly	Marigolds or nasturtium

▼ Aphids.

Alternatives to Pesticides and Chemicals

When used incorrectly, pesticides can pollute water. They also kill beneficial as well as harmful insects. Natural alternatives prevent both of these events from occurring and save you money. Consider using natural alternatives for chemical pesticides: Non-detergent insecticidal soaps, garlic, hot pepper spray, 1 teaspoon of liquid soap in a gallon of water, used dishwater, or a forceful stream of water from a hose all work to dislodge insects from your garden plants.

Another solution is to also consider using plants that naturally repel insects. These plants have their own chemical defense systems, and when planted among flowers and vegetables, they help keep unwanted insects away.

Plant Diseases

Plant disease identification is extremely difficult. In some cases, only laboratory analysis can conclusively identify some diseases. Disease organisms injure plants in several ways: Some attack leaf surfaces and limit the plant's ability to carry on photosynthesis; others produce substances that clog plant tissues that transport water and nutrients; still other disease organisms produce toxins that kill the plant or replace plant tissue with their own.

Symptoms that are associated with plant diseases may include the presence of mushroomlike growths on trunks of trees; leaves with a grayish, mildewed appearance; spots on leaves, flowers, and fruits; sudden wilting or death of a plant or branch; sap exuding from branches or trunks of trees; and stunted growth.

Misapplication of pesticides and nutrients, air pollutants, and other environmental conditions—such as flooding and freezing—can also mimic some disease problems. Yellowing or reddening of leaves and stunted growth may indicate a nutritional problem. Leaf curling or misshapen growth may be a result of herbicide application.

Pest and Disease Management Practices

Preventing pests should be your first goal when growing a garden, although it is unlikely that you will be able to avoid all pest problems because some plant seeds and disease organisms may lay dormant in the soil for years.

Diseases need three elements to become established in plants: the disease organism, a susceptible species, and the proper environmental conditions. Some disease organisms can live in the soil for years; other organisms are carried in infected plant material that falls to the ground. Some disease organisms are carried by insects. Good sanitation will help limit some problems with disease. Choosing resistant varieties of plants also prevents many diseases from occurring. Rotating annual plants in a garden can also prevent some diseases.

Plants that have adequate, but not excessive, nutrients are better able to resist attacks from both diseases and insects. Excessive rates of nitrogen often result in extremely succulent vegetative growth and can make plants more susceptible to insect and disease problems, as well as decreasing their winter hardiness. Proper watering and spacing of plants limits the spread of some diseases and provides good

▲ Powdery mildew leaf disease.

aeration around plants, so diseases that fester in standing water cannot multiply. Trickle irrigation, where water is applied to the soil and not the plant leaves, may be helpful.

Removal of diseased material certainly limits the spread of some diseases. It is important to clean up litter dropped from diseased plants. Prune diseased branches on trees and shrubs to allow for more air circulation. When pruning diseased trees and shrubs, disinfect your pruners between cuts with a solution of chlorine bleach to avoid spreading the disease from plant to plant. Also try to control insects that may carry diseases to your plants.

You can make your own natural fungicide by combining 5 teaspoons each of baking soda and hydrogen peroxide with a gallon of water. Spray on your infected plants. Milk diluted with water is also an effective fungicide, due to the potassium phosphate in it, which boosts a plant's immune system. The more diluted the solution, the more frequently you'll need to spray the plant.

Attracting Birds, Butterflies, and Bees to Your Garden

A wonderful part of having a garden is the wildlife it attracts. The types of trees, shrubs, vines, plants, and flowers you choose for your garden and yard affect the types of wildlife that will visit. Whether you are looking to attract birds, butterflies, or bees to your garden, here are some specific types of plants that will bring these creatures to your yard.

Plant Species for Birds

Following is a list of trees, shrubs, and vines that will attract various birds to your yard and garden. Be sure to check with your local nursery to find out which plants are most suitable for your area.

Trees:
- American beech
- American holly
- Balsam fir
- Crab apple
- Flowering dogwood
- Oak

Shrubs:
- Common juniper
- Hollies
- Sumacs
- Viburnums

Vines:
- Strawberry
- Trumpet honeysuckle
- Virginia creeper
- Wild grape

Flowers and Nectar Plants for Hummingbirds, Butterflies, and Bees

To attract hummingbirds, butterflies, and bees to your garden, consider planting these nectar-producing shrubs and flowers. Again, check with your local nursery to make sure these plants are suitable for your geographic area. Some common nectar plants are:

- Aster
- Azalea
- Butterfly bush
- Clover and other legumes
- Columbine
- Coneflower
- Honeysuckle
- Lupine
- Milkweeds
- Zinnia

▲ A Kingfisher sits on the branch of a crab apple tree.

Harvesting Your Garden

It is essential, to get the best freshness, flavor, and nutritional benefits from your garden vegetables and fruits, to harvest them at the appropriate time. The vegetable's stage of maturity and the time of day at which it is harvested are essential for good-tasting and nutritious produce. Overripe vegetables and fruits will be stringy and coarse. When possible, harvest your vegetables during the cool part of the morning. If you are going to can and preserve your vegetables and fruits, do so as soon as possible. Or, if this process must be delayed, cool the vegetables in ice water or crushed ice and store them in the refrigerator. Here are some brief guidelines for harvesting various types of common garden produce:

Asparagus—Harvest the spears when they are at least 6 to 8 inches tall by snapping or cutting them at ground level. A few spears may be harvested the second year after crowns are set out. A full harvest season will last four to six weeks during the third growing season.

▼ Don't cut asparagus below the soil as it could damage other buds on the crown that would otherwise send up new spears.

Beans, snap—Harvest before the seeds develop in the pod. Beans are ready to pick if they snap easily when bent in half.

Beans, lima—Harvest when the pods first start to bulge with the enlarged seeds. Pods must still be green, not yellowish.

Broccoli—Harvest the dark green, compact cluster, or head, while the buds are shut tight, before any

▼ If you have an overabundance of snap peas, blanch them for 1 to 2 minutes, drain, dunk them in ice water, drain again, and freeze in airtight plastic bags.

▼ Dried corn can be made into cornmeal by removing the kernels from the husk and grinding them in a food processor.

yellow flowers appear. Smaller side shoots will develop later, providing a continuous harvest.

Brussels sprouts—Harvest the lower sprouts (small heads) when they are about 1 to 1 ½ inches in diameter by twisting them off. Removing the lower leaves along the stem will help to hasten the plant's maturity.

Cabbage—Harvest when the heads feel hard and solid.

Cantaloupe—Harvest when the stem slips easily from the fruit with a gentle tug. Another indicator of ripeness is when the netting on the skin becomes rounded and the flesh between the netting turns from a green to a tan color.

Carrots—Harvest when the roots are ¾ to 1 inch in diameter. The largest roots generally have darker tops.

Cauliflower—When preparing to harvest, exclude sunlight when the curds (heads) are 1 to 2 inches in diameter by loosely tying the outer leaves together above the curd with a string or rubber band. This process is known as blanching. Harvest the curds when they are 4 to 6 inches in diameter but still compact, white, and smooth. The head should be ready 10 to 15 days after tying the leaves.

Collards—Harvest older, lower leaves when they reach a length of 8 to 12 inches. New leaves will grow as long as the central growing point remains, providing a continuous harvest. Whole plants may be harvested and cooked if desired.

Corn, sweet—The silks begin to turn brown and dry out as the ears mature. Check a few ears for maturity by opening the top of the ear and pressing a few kernels with your thumbnail. If the exuded liquid is milky rather than clear, the ear is ready for harvesting. Cooking a few ears is also a good way to test for maturity.

Cucumbers—Harvest when the fruits are 6 to 8 inches in length. Harvest when the color is deep green and before yellow color appears. Pick four to five times per week to encourage continuous production. Leaving mature cucumbers on the vine will stop the production of the entire plant.

Eggplant—Harvest when the fruits are 4 to 5 inches in diameter and their color is a glossy, purplish black. The fruit is getting too ripe when the color starts to dull or become bronzed. Because the stem is woody, cut—do not pull—the fruit from the plant. A short stem should remain on each fruit.

Kale—Harvest by twisting off the outer, older leaves when they reach a length of 8 to 10 inches and are medium green in color. Heavy, dark green leaves are overripe and are likely to be tough and bitter. New leaves will grow, providing a continuous harvest.

Lettuce—Harvest the older, outer leaves from leaf lettuce as soon as they are 4 to 6 inches long. Harvest heading types when the heads are moderately firm and before seed stalks form.

Mustard—Harvest the leaves and leaf stems when they are 6 to 8 inches long; new leaves will provide a continuous harvest until they become too strong in flavor and tough in texture, due to temperature extremes.

Okra—Harvest young, tender pods when they are 2 to 3 inches long. Pick the okra at least every other day during the peak growing season. Overripe pods become woody and are too tough to eat.

Onions—Harvest when the tops fall over and begin to turn yellow. Dig up the onions and allow them

to dry out in the open sun for a few days to toughen the skin. Then remove the dried soil by brushing the onions lightly. Cut the stem, leaving 2 to 3 inches attached, and store in a net-type bag in a cool, dry place.

Peas—Harvest regular peas when the pods are well rounded; edible-pod varieties should be harvested when the seeds are fully developed but still fresh and bright green. Pods are getting too old when they lose their brightness and turn light or yellowish green.

Peppers—Harvest sweet peppers with a sharp knife when the fruits are firm, crisp, and full size. Green peppers will turn red if left on the plant. Allow hot peppers to attain their bright red color and full flavor while attached to the vine; then cut them and hang them to dry.

Potatoes (Irish)—Harvest the tubers when the plants begin to dry and die down. Store the tubers in a cool, high-humidity location with good ventilation, such as the basement or crawl space of your house. Avoid exposing the tubers to light, as greening, which denotes the presence of dangerous alkaloids, will occur even with small amounts of light.

Pumpkins—Harvest pumpkins and winter squash before the first frost. After the vines dry up, the fruit color darkens and the skin surface resists puncture from your thumbnail. Avoid bruising or scratching the fruit while handling it. Leave a 3- to 4-inch portion of the stem attached to the fruit and store it in a cool, dry location with good ventilation.

Radishes—Harvest when the roots are ½ to 1½ inches in diameter. The shoulders of radish roots often appear through the soil surface when they are mature. If left in the ground too long, the radishes will become tough and woody.

Rutabagas—Harvest when the roots are about 3 inches in diameter. The roots may be stored in the ground and used as needed, if properly mulched.

Spinach—Harvest by cutting all the leaves off at the base of the plant when they are 4 to 6 inches long. New leaves will grow, providing additional harvests.

Squash, summer—Harvest when the fruit is soft, tender, and 6 to 8 inches long. The skin color often changes to a dark, glossy green or yellow, depending on the variety. Pick every two to three days to encourage continued production.

Sweet potatoes—Harvest the roots when they are large enough for use before the first frost. Avoid bruising or scratching the potatoes during handling. Ideal storage conditions are at a temperature of 55 degrees Fahrenheit and a relative humidity of 85 percent. The basement or crawl space of a house may suffice.

Swiss chard—Harvest by breaking off the developed outer leaves 1 inch above the soil. New leaves will grow, providing a continuous harvest.

Tomatoes—Harvest the fruits at the most appealing stage of ripeness, when they are bright red. The flavor is best at room temperature, but ripe fruit may be held in the refrigerator at 45 to 50 degrees Fahrenheit for 7 to 10 days.

Turnips—Harvest the roots when they are 2 to 3 inches in diameter but before heavy fall frosts occur. The tops may be used as salad greens when the leaves are 3 to 5 inches long.

Watermelons—Harvest when the watermelon produces a dull thud rather than a sharp, metallic sound when thumped—this means the fruit is ripe. Other ripeness indicators are a deep yellow rather than a white color where the melon touches the ground; brown tendrils on the stem near the fruit; and a rough, slightly ridged feel to the skin surface.

Community Gardens

A community garden is considered any piece of land that many people garden. These gardens can be located in urban areas, out in the country, or even in the suburbs, and they grow everything from flowers to vegetables to herbs—anything that the community members want to produce. Community gardens help promote the growing of fresh food, have a positive impact on neighborhoods by cleaning up vacant lots, educate youth about gardening and working together as a community. Whether the garden is just one plot or many individual gardens in a specified area, a community garden is a wonderful way to reach out to fellow neighbors while growing fresh foods wherever you live.

10 Steps to Beginning Your Own Community Garden

The following steps are adapted from the American Community Garden Association.

1. Organize a meeting for all those interested. Determine whether a garden is really needed and wanted, what kind it should be (vegetable, flower, or a combination, and organic or not), whom it will involve, and who benefits. Invite neighbors, tenants, community organizations, gardening and horticultural societies, and building superintendents (if it is at an apartment building).

▲ A gardener transplants flowers from a pot in his home to a community garden.

2. Establish a planning committee. This group can be made up of people who feel committed to the creation of the garden and who have the time to devote to it, at least in the initial stages. Choose well-organized people as garden coordinators and form committees to tackle specific tasks such as funding and partnerships, youth activities, construction, and communication.

3. Compile all of your resources. Do a community asset assessment. What skills and resources already exist in the community that can aid in the garden's creation? Contact local municipal planners about possible sites, as well as horticultural societies and other local sources of information and assistance. Look within your community for people with experience in landscaping and gardening.

4. Look for a sponsor. Some gardens "self-support" through membership dues, but for many, a sponsor is essential for donations of tools, seeds, or money. Churches, schools, private businesses, or parks and recreation departments are all possible sponsors.

5. Choose a site for your garden. Consider the amount of daily sunshine (vegetables need at least six hours a day), availability of water, and soil testing for possible pollutants. Find out who owns the land. Can the gardeners get a lease agreement for at least three years? Will public liability insurance be necessary?

6. Prepare and develop the chosen site. In most cases, the land will need considerable preparation for planting. Organize volunteer work crews to clean it, gather materials, and decide on the design and plot arrangement.

7. Organize the layout of the garden. Members must decide how many plots are available and how they will be assigned. Allow space for storing tools and making compost, and allot room for pathways between each plot. Plant flowers or shrubs around the garden's edges to promote goodwill with non-gardening neighbors, pedestrians, and municipal authorities.

8. Plan a garden just for kids. Consider creating a special garden for the children of the community—including them is essential. Children are not as interested in the size of the harvest but rather in the process of gardening. A separate area set aside for them allows them to explore the garden at their own speed and can be a valuable learning tool.

9. Draft rules and put them in writing. The gardeners themselves devise the best ground rules. We are more willing to comply with rules that we have had a hand in creating. Ground rules help gardeners to know what is expected of them. Think of it as a code of behavior. Some examples of issues that are best dealt with by agreed-upon rules are: What kinds of dues will members pay? How will the money be used? How are plots assigned? Will gardeners share tools, meet regularly, and handle basic maintenance?

10. Keep members involved with one another. Good communication ensures a strong community garden with active participation by all. Some ways to do this are: form a telephone tree, create an e-mail list, install a rainproof bulletin board in the garden, and have regular community celebrations. Community gardens are all about creating and strengthening communities.

Tools Needed to Create and Maintain a Community Garden

When purchasing tools for your community garden, buy high-quality tools. These will last longer and are an investment that will benefit your garden and those working in it for years to come. Every community garden should be equipped with these 10 essential tools:

Fork: You can't dig and divide perennials without a heavy-duty fork.

Gloves: Leather gloves hold up best. If you have roses, get a pair that is thick enough to resist thorn pricks.

Hand fork or cultivator: A hand fork helps cultivate soil, chop up clumps, and work fertilizer and compost into the soil. A hand fork is necessary for cultivating in closely planted beds.

Hand pruners: There are different types and sizes of pruners depending on the type and size of the job. Hand pruners are for cutting small diameters, up to the thickness of your little finger.

Hoe: A long-handled hoe is key to keeping weeds out of your garden.

Hose: This is the fastest way to transport lots of water to your garden plants. Consider using drip irrigation hoses or tape to apply a steady stream of water to your plants.

Shovels and spades: There are several different types and shapes of shovels and spades, each with its own purpose. There are also different types of handles for either—a D shape, a T shape, or none at all. A shovel is a requisite tool for planting large perennials, shrubs, and trees; breaking ground; and moving soil, leaves, and just about anything else. The sharper the blade, the better.

Trowel: A well-made trowel is your most important tool. From container gardening to large beds, a trowel will help you get your plants into the soil.

Watering can: A watering can creates a fine, even stream of water that delivers with a gentleness that won't wash seedlings or sprouting seeds out of their soil.

Wheelbarrow: Wheelbarrows come in all different sizes (and prices). They are indispensable for hauling soil, compost, plants, mulch, hoses, tools, and everything else you'll need to make your garden a success.

Things to Consider

There are many things that need to be considered when you create your own community garden. Remember that community gardens take a lot of work and foresight in order for them to be successful and beneficial for all those involved.

The Organization of the Garden

Will your garden establish rules and conditions for membership—such as residence, dues, and agreement with any drafted rules and regulations? It is important to know who will be able to use the garden and who will not. Furthermore, deciding how the garden will be parceled out is another key topic to discuss before beginning your community garden. Will the plots be assigned by family size or need? Will some plots be bigger to accommodate larger families? Will your garden incorporate children's plots as well?

Insurance

It is becoming increasingly difficult to obtain leases from landowners without liability insurance. Garden insurance is a new thing for many insurance carriers, and their underwriters are reluctant to cover community gardens. It helps if you know what you want out of your community garden before you start talking to insurance agents. Two tips: Work with an agent from a firm that deals with many different carriers (so you can get the best policy for your needs), and you will probably have better success with someone local who has already done this type of policy or who works with social service agencies in the area. Shop around until you find a policy that fits the needs of your community garden and its users.

Set Up a Garden Association

Many garden groups are organized very informally and operate successfully. Leaders rise to the occasion to propose ideas and carry out tasks. However, as the workload expands, many groups choose a more formal structure for their organization.

A structured program is a conscious, planned effort to create a system so that each person can participate fully and the group can perform effectively. It's vital that the leadership be responsive to the members and their needs.

If your group is new, have several planning meetings to discuss your program and organization. Try out suggestions raised at these meetings, and after a few months of operation, you'll be in a better position to develop bylaws or organizational guidelines. A community garden project should be kept as simple as possible.

Creating Bylaws

Bylaws are rules that govern the internal affairs of an organization. Check out bylaws from other community garden organizations when creating your own.

Bylaws cover these topics:
- The full name of the organization and address
- The organizing members and their addresses
- The purpose, goal, and philosophy of the organization
- Membership eligibility and dues
- Timeline for regular meetings of the committee
- How the bylaws can be rescinded or amended
- Maintenance and cleanup of the community garden
- A hold harmless clause: "We the undersigned members of the [name] garden group hereby agree to hold harmless [name landowner] from and against any damage, loss, liability, claim, demand, suit, cost, and expense directly or indirectly resulting from, arising out of or in connection with the use of the [name] garden by the garden group, its successors, assigns, employees, agents, and invitees."

Sample Guidelines and Rules for Garden Members

Here are some sample guidelines community garden members may need to follow:
- I will pay a fee of $___ to help cover garden expenses.
- I will have something planted in the garden by [date] and keep it planted all summer long.
- If I must abandon my plot for any reason, I will notify the garden leadership.
- I will keep weeds at a minimum and maintain the areas immediately surrounding my plot.
- If my plot becomes unkempt, I understand I will be given one week's notice to clean it up. At that time, it will be reassigned or tilled in.
- I will keep trash and litter out of the plot, as well as adjacent pathways and fences.

10 Benefits of Creating a Community Garden

1. Improves the quality of life for people using the garden.
2. Provides a pathway for neighborhood and community development and promotes inter-generational and cross-cultural connections.
3. Stimulates social interaction and reduces crime.
4. Encourages self-reliance.
5. Beautifies neighborhoods and preserves green space.
6. Reduces family food budgets while providing nutritious foods for families in the community.
7. Conserves resources.
8. Creates an opportunity for recreation, exercise, therapy, and education.
9. Creates income opportunities and economic development.
10. Reduces city heat from streets and parking lots.

- I will participate in the fall cleanup of the garden.
- I will plant tall crops where they will not shade neighboring plots.
- I will pick only my own crops unless given permission by another plot user.
- I will not use fertilizers, insecticides, or weed repellents that will in any way affect other plots.
- I understand that neither the garden group nor owners of the land are responsible for my actions. I therefore agree to hold harmless the garden group and owners of the land for any liability, damage, loss, or claim that occurs in connection with use of the garden by me or any of my guests.

Preventing Vandalism of Your Community Garden

Vandalism is a common fear among community gardeners. Try to deter vandalism by following these simple, preventative methods:

- Make a sign for the garden. Let people know that the garden is a community project.
- Put up fences around your garden. Fences can be of almost any material. They serve as much to mark possession of a property as to prevent entry.
- Invite everyone in the neighborhood to participate in the garden project from the very beginning. If you exclude people, they may become potential vandals.

- Plant raspberries, roses, or other thorny plants along the fence as a barrier to anyone trying to climb the fence.
- Make friends with neighbors whose windows overlook the garden. Trade them flowers and vegetables for a protective eye.
- Harvest all ripe fruit and vegetables on a daily basis to prevent the temptation of outsiders to harvest your crops.
- Plant a "vandal's garden" at the entrance. Mark it with a sign: "If you must take food, please take it from here."

People Problems and Solutions

Angry neighbors and bad gardeners pose problems for a community garden. Neighbors may complain to municipal governments about messy, unkempt gardens or rowdy behavior; most gardens cannot afford poor relations with neighbors, local politicians, or potential sponsors. Therefore, choose bylaws carefully so you have procedures to follow when members fail to keep their plots clean and up to code. A well-organized garden with strong leadership and committed members can overcome almost any obstacle.

School Gardens

A school garden provides children with an ideal outdoor classroom. Within a single visit to a garden, a student can record plant growth, study decomposition while turning a compost pile, and learn more about plants, nature, and the outdoors in general. Gardens also provide students with opportunities to make healthier food choices, learn about nutrient cycles, and develop a deeper appreciation for the environment, community, and each other. While school gardens are typically used for science classes, they can also teach children about the history of their community (what their town was like hundreds of years ago and what people did to farm food), and be incorporated into math curriculum and other school subjects.

How to Start a School Garden

School gardens do not need to start on a grand scale. In fact, individual classrooms can grow their very own container gardens by just planting seeds in small pots, watering them daily, placing them in a sunny corner of the room, and watching the seedlings grow. However, if there is space for a larger, outdoor garden, this is the ideal place to teach children about working as a community, about plant and vegetables, and responsibility. A school garden should eventually become a permanent addition to the school and be maintained year-round.

When starting a school garden, it is important to find someone to coordinate the garden program. This is the perfect way to get parents involved in the school's garden. Establish a volunteer garden committee and assign certain parents particular tasks in the planning, upkeep (even during the summer months when school is generally not in session), and funding for the school's garden.

It is important, so the garden is not neglected, to plan particular classroom activities and lessons that will incorporate the garden and its plants. Assigning students various jobs that relate to the garden will be a wonderful way of introducing them to gardening as well as responsibility and community.

After all the initial planning is done, it is time to choose a spot for the school garden. A place in the lawn that receives plenty of sunlight and that will be close enough to the building for easy access is ideal. It should also be near an outdoor spigot so the plants can be easily watered. If there is enough space, it might be beneficial to have a garden shed, where gardening gloves, tools, buckets, hoses, and other items can be stored for use in the garden. Once you have chosen your spot, it's time to start digging and planting!

Both new and established gardens benefit from the use of compost and mulch. Many schools purchase compost when they initially establish their garden, and then they start making their own compost—which is a wonderful science lesson for students as well. You can use grass clippings, yard trimmings, rotten vegetables, and even food scraps from the cafeteria or students' lunches to build and maintain your compost pile. While some schools choose to make compost piles in the garden, others compost with worm boxes right in the classroom!

Depending on funding and the needs and desires of the school, these gardens can become quite elaborate, with fences, ponds, trellises, trees and shrubs, and other structures. However, all a school garden truly needs is a little bit of dirt and a few plants (preferably an assortment of vegetables, fruit, and wildflowers) that students can study and even eat. Whether the school garden is established only for one class or grade level, or if it is going to be available to everyone at the school, is a factor that will determine the types of plants and the size of the overall garden.

Whether big or small, complex or simple, school gardens provide a wonderful, enriching learning experience for children and their parents alike.

Farmers' Markets

Farmers' markets are an integral part of the urban–farm linkage and have continued to rise in popularity, mostly due to growing consumer interest in obtaining fresh products directly from the farm. Farmers' markets allow consumers to have access to locally grown, farm-fresh produce, enable farmers the opportunity to develop a personal relationship with their customers, and cultivate consumer loyalty with the farmers who grow the produce. Direct marketing of farm products through farmers' markets continues to be an important sales outlet for agricultural producers nationwide. Today, there are more than 4,600 farmers' markets operating throughout the nation.

Who Benefits from Farmers' Markets?

- Small farm operators: Those with less than $250,000 in annual receipts who work and manage their own operations meet this definition (94 percent of all farms).
- Farmers and consumers: Farmers have direct access to markets to supplement farm income. Consumers have access to locally grown, farm-fresh produce and the opportunity to personally interact with the farmer who grows the produce.
- The community: Many urban communities—where fresh, nutritious foods are scarce—gain easy access to quality food. Farmers' markets also help to promote nutrition education, wholesome eating habits, and better food preparation, as well as boosting the community's economy.

Getting Involved in a Farmers' Market

A farmers' market is a great place for new gardeners to learn what sorts of produce customers want, and it also promotes wonderful community relationships between the growers and the buyers. If you have a well-established garden, and know a few other people who also have fruits, vegetables, and even garden flowers to spare, you may want to consider organizing and implementing your own local farmers' market (if your town or city already has an established farmers' market, you may want to go visit it one day and ask the farmers how you could join, or contact your local Cooperative Extension Service for more information). Joining existing farmers' markets may require that you pay an annual fee, and your produce may also be subject to inspection and other rules established by the market's organization or the local government.

Establishing a farmers' market is not simply setting up a stand in front of your home and selling your vegetables—though you can certainly do this if you

become a member, where the market will be located (preferably in a place with ample parking, good visibility, and cover in case of bad weather), and when and for how long the market will be open to the public. It is also a good idea to discuss how the produce should be priced and make sure you are following all local and state regulations.

Ideally, it is beneficial for your market's vendors and the community to gather support and involvement from local farmers in your area. That way, your garden vegetable and fruit stand will be supplemented with other locally grown produce and crops from farms, which will draw more people to your market.

Once your farmers' market is up and running, it is important to maintain a good rapport with the community. Be friendly when customers come to your stand, and make sure that you are offering quality products for them to purchase. Price your vegetables and fruits fairly and make your displays pleasing to the eye, luring customers to your stall. Make sure your produce is clearly marked with the name and price, so your customers will have no doubt as to what they are buying. Make your stall as personal as possible, and always, always interact with the customer. In this way, you'll begin to build relationships with your community members and hopefully continue to draw in business for yourself and the other vendors in the farmers' market.

If you are looking to find a local farmers' market near you (either to try to join or just to visit), here is a link to a Web site that offers extensive listings for farmers' markets by state: http://apps.ams.usda .gov/ farmersmarkets.

prefer. A farmers' market must have a small group of people who are all looking to sell their produce and garden harvests. It is important, before planning even begins, to hold a meeting and discuss the feasibility of your venture. Is there other local competition that might impede on your market's success? Are there enough people and enough produce to make a farmers' market profitable and sustainable? What kind of monetary cost will be incurred by establishing a farmers' market? It is also a good idea to think about how you can sponsor your market—such as through members, nonprofit organizations, or the chamber of commerce. If at all possible, it is best to try to get your entire neighborhood and local government involved and promote the idea of fresh, home-grown fruits and vegetables that will be available to the community through the establishment of a farmers' market.

Once you've decided that you want to go ahead with your plan, you should establish rules for your market. Such rules and regulations should determine if there will be a board of directors, who will be responsible for the overall management of the market, who can

Part Two

Pantry

"The greatest delight the fields and woods minister is the suggestion of an occult relation between man and the vegetable. I am not alone and unacknowledged. They nod to me and I to them."

—*Ralph Waldo Emerson*

One of the greatest pleasures of self-sufficiency is preparing, preserving, and eating your own food. After the hard work of planting and tending your gardens, or raising animals for eggs, milk, or meat, your kitchen will become a laboratory where you can create wonderful foods from the fruits of your labor to enjoy or to share. With a little preparation, your pantry can become a treasure trove of canned and dried foods, ready to draw from all winter long. There is something distinctly rewarding about running out to the garden to pick salad makings in the summer, or reaching into the cupboard for a new jar of strawberry jam in the middle of the winter. It's a gift more and more people are finding time to accept, as the quality of supermarket offerings seems to plummet and a new awareness of the benefits of locally grown food sweeps across rural and urban areas alike. If you don't have the space or time to grow or produce your own food, there are farmers' markets springing up all over where you can find fresh, delicious produce, meats, baked goods, and dairy products to enjoy on your own or to inspire a festive dinner party. Whether you go to the garden, the pantry, or the market for your food, remember the work that went into its growth and preparation and you will begin to see food not only as a necessity and a pleasure, but also as a great gift.

Eating Well

Why Eat Organically Grown Food?

Organically grown produce is becoming more and more readily available, regardless of where you live. If you grow your own fruits and vegetables or have ready access to a farmers' market, eating organically may be cheaper than purchasing commercially grown produce at the supermarket. Though organic foods bought at a grocery store may be 10 to 50 percent more expensive than their traditionally grown companions, the benefits are often worth the cost. Here are just a few of many reasons to eat organically grown produce:

- Improved taste. Tests comparing various gardening methods have shown that fruit grown organically has a higher natural sugar content, firmer flesh, and is less apt to bruise easily. Do your own taste test and you'll easily tell the difference!
- Fewer health risks. Pesticides have been linked to cancer and other diseases.
- Help support smaller farms. Most organic farms are small, family-owned endeavors. By purchasing organic produce, you'll be helping them survive and thrive.
- Help the environment. According to the EPA (Environmental Protection Agency), agriculture is responsible for 70 percent of the pollution in the United States' streams and rivers. Organic farmers don't use the synthetic pesticides and fertilizers that cause this pollution.
- Better nutrition. Higher levels of lycopene, polyphenols, and flavonols have been found in organically produced fruits and vegetables. Phytonutrients (many of which are antioxidants involved in the plant's own defense system) may be higher in organic produce because crops rely more on their own defenses in the absence of regular applications of chemical pesticides.

Why Eat Locally Grown Food?

Even if you grow the majority of your own produce, you may want to supplement your menu with food from other sources. When doing so, there are lots of great reasons to choose foods grown near where you live. Here are a few:

- Support the local economy. According to a study by the New Economics Foundation in London, a dollar spent locally generates twice as much income for the local economy.
- Fresher food. Produce you buy at the supermarket has likely been in transit for several days or even weeks, and during that time it's been declining in flavor and nutrition. Produce you buy from a farmers' market or local farm stand was likely picked the same day.
- Help the environment. By eating food grown locally, you're cutting down on the number of miles it had to travel to get to you, thus lowering fuel emissions.
- Stay attuned to the seasons. Eating locally means that you may not get asparagus in October or sweet potatoes in April, but those foods will not be at their best quality in those months anyway. You'll get more nutritious, better-tasting food if you eat it at its growing peak. You'll also feel more connected to the natural seasonal rhythms.
- Encourage variety. By supporting the local farmers, you give them the opportunity to try less common or heirloom varieties that wouldn't travel as well, produce as high a yield, or have the shelf life of most supermarket varieties.

Food Co-ops

What Are the Different Types of Food Co-ops?

Typically, there are two types of food co-ops: the co-op grocery store and the buying club. Each is owned and run by members but they do vary in their structure and number of members.

Co-op Grocery Store

Co-op grocery stores are basically regular grocery stores that are member-owned and -operated and provide low-cost, healthy foods to members and often to the public as well. There are around 500 co-op grocery stores in the United States alone.

Buying Club

A buying club consists of a small group of people (friends, neighbors, families, or colleagues) who get together and buy food in bulk from a co-op distributor (a co-op warehouse or natural foods distributor) or from local farms. By ordering in bulk, the members are able to save money on grocery items. The members of the buying club share the responsibilities of collecting money from the other members, placing orders with the distributor, picking up the orders from the drop-off site, and distributing the food to the individual members or families.

What Is a Food Co-op?

Food co-ops are non-profit, democratic, and member-owned businesses that provide low-cost organic or natural foods to members and, in some cases, non-members.

Since food co-ops are established and operated by members, each member has a voice regarding what types of foods will be sold, maintenance issues, and management of the stores. Food co-ops are democratically run, so each member has one vote in any type of election. Members generally elect a board of directors to oversee the everyday running of the co-op and to hire staff.

How Do You Become a Food Co-op Member?

To become a member of a food co-op, you must pay a small initial fee and then typically invest a certain amount of money into the co-op to purchase a share. Sometimes members can accumulate more shares (by paying an annual fee, for example). Members can also help run the co-op by volunteering their time. Members reap the benefits of their membership by having access to discounted prices on food products. However, if you decide not to become a member, some food co-ops still allow non-members to shop at their stores without the membership discount.

How Do You Become a Buying Club Member?

If you are looking to join a buying club in your area, it is best to contact your regional co-op distributor and ask them for information on local buying clubs. Check out the websites of local distributors to see if they have links to buying clubs near you. Or ask friends and neighbors if they're aware of any buying clubs that are active in your area.

How Do You Start Your Own Food Co-op?

Here are some steps you need to follow to establish your own food co-op:

1. Invite potential members to meet and discuss the start-up of a food co-op. Identify how a food co-op may help the finances of the members.
2. Hold a meeting in which potential members vote to continue the process of forming a co-op and then select a committee for this purpose.
3. Determine how often the co-op will be used by the potential members.
4. Discuss the results of any surveys at another meeting and then vote to see if the plans should proceed.
5. Do a needs analysis (determine what the members will need in order to establish a food co-op).
6. Hold a meeting to discuss the outcome of the needs analysis and vote (anonymously) on whether or not to proceed with the co-op.
7. Develop a business plan for the co-op and decide the financial contribution needed to start the co-op.
8. At another meeting, have members vote on the business plan and if members want to continue, decide on whether or not to keep the committee members.
9. Prepare all legal documents and incorporate.
10. Hold a meeting for all potential members to review and accept the bylaws (terms of operation, responsibilities of members, and board of directors). Hold an election for the board of directors.
11. At the first board of directors meeting, elect officers and assign them certain responsibilities in carrying out the business plan.
12. Hold a membership drive—try to recruit new members to the food co-op.
13. Pool monetary resources and create a loan application package.
14. Employ a manager for the co-op store.
15. Find a building or storefront to house the co-op.
16. Start your business!

Example of bylaws for a food co-op:
- Establish membership requirements.
- Formulate the rights and responsibilities of all members and the board of directors.
- Stipulate the grounds for member expulsion.
- Establish rules for calling and implementing membership meetings.
- Determine how members will vote.
- Provide election procedures for board members and officers.
- Specify the number of board members and officers and how long their terms in office will be and what sort of compensation they will be awarded.
- Establish what time and where meetings will be held.
- Specify the co-op's fiscal year dates.
- Provide information on the distribution of net earnings.
- Include any other rules of management for the co-op.

How Do You Start Your Own Buying Club?

To start your own buying club, you will need to collect a group of people (preferably more than five households). If no one in your new group has any experience with organizing a buying club, it may be beneficial for you to temporarily join a buying club to see how it works. Once you are confident in your understanding of a buying club, it's time to begin!

1. Find a co-op distributor's (wholesaler's) pricing guide to share with the others in your buying club, so you all have an understanding of the products

▲ Fruits displayed at a food co-op.

available and the savings from which you'll benefit. If you'll be buying from local farms, discuss pricing and bulk discounts with the farmers.

2. Have a meeting and invite all those who are interested in joining your buying club. Emphasize that a buying club requires its members to share in all responsibilities—from placing orders to picking up deliveries to collecting the money—and that they will all reap the benefits of obtaining great organic and natural foods at wholesale prices.

3. Establish an organizational committee. Discuss areas such as coordination, price guide distribution, orders, potential delivery location, what supplies will be needed, bookkeeping, and how to orient new members.

4. Draw up any membership requirements you think necessary.

5. Brainstorm possible delivery sites, such as churches, firehouses, or other public buildings. Your optimal site should be able to accommodate a large truck and have long hours of operation. Make sure you will have enough space at the site to go through the products and distribute them accordingly.

6. Develop a name for your buying club and fill out a membership application with the co-op distributor of your choice. You should receive some sort of confirmation, complete with order deadlines, date of delivery, and a simple orientation to the buying club.

7. Start enjoying your healthy foods for lower prices!

▲ Vegetables packaged for distribution.

Food Co-ops and Distributors by State

Alabama

Grow Alabama
2301 Finley Boulevard
Birmingham, Alabama 35202
(205) 991-0042
info@growalabama.com
www.growalabama.com

Alaska

Organic Alaska
3404 Willow Street
Anchorage, Alaska 99517
(907) 306-3931
organic@alaska.com
www.organicalaska.com

Arizona

Food Conspiracy Co-op
412 North 4th Avenue
Tucson, Arizona 85705
(520) 624-4821
www.foodconspiracy.org

Arkansas

Ozark Natural Foods Co-op
1554 North College Avenue
Fayetteville, Arkansas 72703
(479) 521-7558
www.ozarknaturalfoods.com

California

Briar Patch Community Market
290 Sierra College Dr, Ste A
Grass Valley, California 95945
(530) 272-5333
info@briarpatch.coop
www.briarpatch.coop

Co-opportunity Natural Foods
1525 Broadway
Santa Monica, California 90404
(310) 451-8902
service@coopportunity.com
www.coopportunity.com

Davis Food Co-op
620 G Street
Davis, California 95616
(530) 758-2667
www.davisfood.coop

Isla Vista Food Co-op
6575 Seville Road
Isla Vista, California 93117
(805) 968-1401
gm@islavistafood.coop
www.islavistafood.coop

Kresge Food Co-op
600 Kresge Court
Kresge College UCSC
Santa Cruz, California 95064
(831) 426-1506
www.kresge.ucsc.edu/activities/coops/food-coop
   .html

North Coast Co-op, Arcata
811 I Street
Arcata, California 95521
(707) 822-5947
co-oparc@northcoastco-op.com
www.northcoastco-op.com

North Coast Co-op, Eureka
25 4th Street
Eureka, California 95501
(707) 443-6027
www.northcoastco-op.com

Ocean Beach People's Organic Food Market
4765 Voltaire Street
San Diego, California 92107
(619) 224-1387
www.obpeoplesfood.coop

Other Avenues Community Food Store
3930 Judah Street
San Francisco, California 94122
(415) 661-7475
info@otheravenues.org
www.otheravenues.org

Quincy Natural Foods Co-op
269 Main Street
Quincy, California 95971
(530) 283-3528
www.qnf.coop

Rainbow Grocery Co-op
1745 Folsom Street
San Francisco, California 94103
(415) 863-0620
general@rainbow.coop
www.rainbow.coop

Sacramento Natural Foods Co-op
1900 Alhambra Boulevard
Sacramento, California 95816
(916) 455-2667
www.sacfoodcoop.com

Santa Rosa Community Market & Café
1899 Mendocino Avenue
Santa Rosa, California 95401
(707) 546-1806
www.srcommunitymarket.com

Ukiah Natural Foods
721 South State Street
Ukiah, California 95482
(707) 462-4778
www.ukiahcoop.com

Colorado

Fort Collins Food Co-op
250 East Mountain Avenue
Fort Collins, Colorado 80524
(970) 484-7448
info@ftcfood.coop
www.ftcfoodcoop.com

High Plains Food Co-op
5655 South Yosemite Street,
Suite 400
Greenwoods Village,
Colorado 80111
(785) 626-3640
info@highplainsfood.org
http://highplainsfood.org

Connecticut

Willimantic Food Co-op
91 Valley Street
Willimantic, Connecticut 06226
(860) 456-3611
www.willimanticfood.coop

Delaware

Newark Natural Foods Cooperative
280 East Main Street, Market East Plaza
Newark, Delaware 19711
(302) 368-5894
www.newarknaturalfoods.com

Florida

Ever'man Cooperative
315 West Garden Street
Pensacola, Florida 32502
(850) 438-0402
info@everman.org
www.everman.org

Homegrown Organic Local Food Co-op
2310 North Orange Avenue
Orlando, Florida 32804
(407) 895-5559
info@homegrowncoop.org
www.homegrowncoop.org

Sunseed Food Co-op, Inc.
6615 North Atlantic Avenue
Cape Canaveral, Florida 32920
(321) 784-0930
www.sunseedfoodcoop.com

Georgia

Daily Groceries Food Co-op
523 Prince Avenue
Athens, Georgia 30601
(706) 548-1732
info@dailygroceries.org
www.dailygroceries.org

Life Grocery Natural Food Co-op & Café
1453 Roswell Road
Marietta, Georgia 30062
(770) 977-9583
www.lifegrocery.com

Sevananda Food Co-op
467 Moreland Avenue NE
Atlanta, Georgia 30307
(404) 681-2831
info@sevananda.com
www.sevananda.coop

Hawaii

Kokua Market Natural Foods Co-op
2643 South King Street
Honolulu, Hawaii 96826
(808) 941-1922
info@kokua.coop
www.kokua.coop

Idaho

Boise Consumer Co-op
888 West Fort Street
Boise, Idaho 83702
(208) 472-4500
www.boisecoop.com

Moscow Food Co-op
121 East 5th Street
Moscow, Idaho 83843
(208) 882-8537
www.moscowfood.coop

Illinois

Common Ground Food Co-op
300 South Broadway Suite 166
Urbana, Illinois 61801
(217) 352-3347
info@commonground.coop
www.commonground.coop

Duck Soup Co-op
129 East Hillcrest Drive
DeKalb, Illinois 60115
(815) 756-7044
ducksoupcoopgm@gmail.com
www.ducksoupcoop.com

Neighborhood Co-op Grocery
1815 West Main Street
Carbondale, Illinois 62901
(618) 529-3533
info@neighborhood.coop
www.neighborhood.coop

South Suburban Food Co-op
208 Forest Boulevard
Park Forest, Illinois 60466
(708) 747-2256
info@southsuburbanfoodcoop.com
www.southsuburbanfoodcoop.com

Stone Soup Ashland
4637 North Ashland Avenue
Chicago, Illinois 60640
(773) 669-7687
www.stonesoupcoop.org

West Central Illinois Food Cooperative
176 North Farnham Street
Galesburg, Illinois 61401

Indiana

Bloomingfoods Kirkwood
419 East Kirkwood Avenue
Bloomington, Indiana 47408
(812) 336-5300
www.bloomingfoods.coop

Bloomingfoods East
3220 East Third Street
Bloomington, Indiana 47401
(812) 336-5400
www.bloomingfoods.coop

Bloomingfoods Near West Side
316 West Sixth Street
Bloomington, Indiana 47404
(812) 333-7312
www.bloomingfoods.coop

Clear Creek Food Co-op
710 East Main Street
Richmond, Indiana 47374
(765) 939-4390

Lost River Market & Deli
26 Library Street
Paoli, Indiana 47454
(812) 723-3735
www.lostrivercoop.com

Maple City Market
314 South Main Street
Goshen, Indiana 46526
(574) 534-2355
info@maplecitymarket.com
www.maplecitymarket.com

River City Food Co-op
116 Washington Avenue
Evansville, Indiana 47713
(812) 401-7301
www.rivercityfoodcoop.org

Three Rivers Food Co-op's Natural Grocery
1612 Sherman Boulevard
Fort Wayne, Indiana 46808
(260) 424-8812
gm@3riversfood.coop
www.3riversfood.coop

Iowa

New Pioneer Co-Op Coralville
1101 2nd Street
Coralville, Iowa 52241
(319) 358-5513
www.newpi.com

New Pioneer Co-op Iowa City
22 South Van Buren Street
Iowa City, Iowa 52240
(319) 338-9441
www.newpi.com

Oneota Community Food Co-op
312 West Water Street
Decorah, Iowa 52101
(563) 382-4666
customerservice@oneotacoop.com
http://oneotatestsite.com

Wheatsfield Cooperative Grocery
413 Northwestern Avenue
Ames, Iowa 50010
(515) 232-4094
shop@wheatsfield.coop
www.wheatsfield.coop

Kansas

Community Market & Deli
901 Iowa Street
Lawrence, Kansas 66044
(785) 843-8544
themerc@themerc.coop
www.themerc.coop

Prairieland Market
138 South 4th
Salinas, Kansas 67401
(785) 827-5877

Southeast Kansas Buying Club
11th & Walnut
Independence, Kansas 67301
(620) 205-7095
http://seksbuyingclub.wordpress.com

Topeka Natural Food Coop
503 Southwest Washburn Avenue
Topeka, Kansas 66606
(785) 235-2309
http://topekafoodcoop.wordpress.com

Kentucky

Good Foods Market & Café
455 Southland Drive
Lexington, Kentucky 40503
(859) 278-1813
goodfoods@goodfoods.coop
www.goodfoods.coop

Otherworld Food Co-op, Inc.
1865 Celina Road
Burkesville, Kentucky 42717
(270) 433-7400
otherworld@duo-county.com
www.duo-county.com/~otherworld

Louisiana

New Orleans Food Co-op
2372 St. Claude Avenue, Suite 110
New Orleans, Louisiana 70117
(504) 264-5579
www.nolafood.coop

Maine

Belfast Co-op
123 High Street
Belfast, Maine 04915
(207) 338-2532
www.belfast.coop

Blue Hill Co-op Community Market & Cafe
4 Ellsworth Road, P.O. Box 1133
Blue Hill, Maine 04614-1133
(207) 374-2165
info@bluehill.coop
http://bluehill.coop

Fare Share Market
443 Main Street
Norway, Maine 04268

(207) 743-9044
www.faresharecoop.org

Rising Tide Co-op
323 Main Street
Damariscotta, Maine 04543
(207) 563-5556
customercare@risingtide.coop
www.risingtide.coop

Maryland

Common Market Co-op
5728 Buckeystown Pike, Unit B1
Frederick, Maryland 21704
(301) 663-3416
www.commonmarket.coop

Glut Food Co-op
4005 34th Street
Mt. Rainier, Maryland 20712
(301) 779-1978
www.glut.org

Maryland Food Co-op
B-0203 Stamp Student Union
University of Maryland, College Park, Maryland
    20742
(301) 314-8089
http://thestamp.umd.edu/food/md_food_co-op

Takoma Park Silver Spring Co-op
201 Ethan Allen Avenue
Takoma Park, Maryland 20912
(301) 891-2667
www.tpss.coop

Massachusetts

Berkshire Co-op Market
42 Bridge Street
Great Barrington, Massachusetts 01230
(413) 528-9697
community@berkshire.coop
www.berkshirecoop.org

Green Fields Market
144 Main Street
Greenfield, Massachusetts 01301
(413) 773-9567
www.greenfieldsmarket.coop

Harvest Co-op Markets
580 Massachusetts Avenue
Cambridge, Massachusetts 02139
(617) 661-1580
www.harvest.coop

Harvest Co-op Markets
57 South Street
Jamaica Plain, Massachusetts 02130
(617) 524-1667
www.harvest.coop

River Valley Market
330 North King Street
Northampton, Massachusetts 01061
(413) 584-2665
info@rivervalleymarket.coop
www.rivervalleymarket.coop

Michigan

Brighton Food Cooperative
2715 West Coon Lake Road
Howell, Michigan 48843
(517) 546-4190
bfc@brightonfoodcoop.com
http://www.brightonfoodcoop.com

Dibbleville Food Cooperative
106 East Elizabeth Street
Fenton, Michigan 48430
(810) 629-1175
contact@dibbleville.com
www.dibbleville.com

East Lansing Food Co-op
4960 Northwind
East Lansing, Michigan 48823
(517) 337-1266
info@elfco.coop
www.elfco.coop

Grain Train Natural Food Market
220 East Mitchell Street
Petoskey, Michigan 49770
(231) 347-2381
www.graintrain.coop

Ionia Natural Food Co-op
6070 David Highway
Saranac, Michigan 48881
infc_mc@hotmail.com
https://www.facebook.com/IoniaNatrualFoodsCoop-
   erative/info

Keweenaw Food Co-op
1035 Ethel Avenue
Hancock, Michigan 49930

(906) 482-2030
info@keweenaw.coop
www.keweenaw.coop

Marquette Food Co-op
502 West Washington Street
Marquette, Michigan 49855
(906) 225-0671
info@marquettefood.coop
www.marquettefood.coop

Oryana Food Cooperative
260 East 10th Street
Traverse City, Michigan 49684
(231) 947-0191
www.oryana.coop

People's Food Co-op & Café Verde
216 North 4th Avenue
Ann Arbor, Michigan 48104
(734) 994-9174
info@peoplesfood.coop
www.peoplesfood.coop

People's Food Co-op of Kalamazoo
507 Harrison Street
Kalamazoo, Michigan 49007
(269) 342-5686
outreach@peoplesfoodco-op.org
www.peoplesfoodco-op.org

Simple Times Farm Market & Buying Club
9044 Gale Road
Goodrich, Michigan 48438
(810) 280-2143
www.simpletimesfarm.com

West Michigan Co-op
1475 Northeast Michigan Street
Grand Rapids, Michigan 49503
(616) 951-3287
help@wmcoop.com
www.westmichigancoop.com

Ypsilanti Food Co-op and River Street Bakery
312 North River Street
Ypsilanti, Michigan 48198
(734) 483-1520
info@ypsifoodcoop.org
www.ypsifoodcoop.org

Minnesota

Bluff Country Co-op
121 West 2nd Street
Winona, Minnesota 55987
(507) 452-1815
bccoop@bluff.coop
www.bluff.coop

Cook County Whole Foods Co-op
20 East 1st Street
Grand Marais, Minnesota 55604
(218) 387-2503
info@cookcounty.coop
www.cookcounty.coop

Crow Wing Food Co-op
720 Washington Street
Brainerd, Minnesota 56401
(218) 828-4600
cwfoodco-op@brainerd.net
www.crowwingcoop.com

Eastside Food Co-op
2551 Central Avenue
Minneapolis, Minnesota 55418
(612) 788-0950
luna@eastsidefood.coop
www.eastsidefood.coop

Hampden Park Food Co-op
928 Raymond Avenue
St. Paul, Minnesota 55114
(651) 646-6686
www.hampdenparkcoop.com

Harmony Food Co-op
302 Irvine Avenue
Bemidji, Minnesota 56601
(218) 751-2009
www.harmonycoop.com

Just Food Co-op
516 South Water Street
Northfield, Minnesota 55057
(507) 650-0106
www.justfood.coop

Lakewinds Natural Foods
435 Pond Promenade
Chanhassen, Minnesota 55317
(952) 697-3366
www.lakewinds.coop

Lakewinds Natural Foods
17501 Minnetonka Boulevard
Minnetonka, Minnesota 55345
(952) 473-0292
www.lakewinds.coop

Linden Hills Food Co-op
3815 Sunnyside Avenue
Minneapolis, Minnesota 55410
(612) 922-1159
info@lindenhills.coop
www.lindenhills.coop

Mississippi Market Food Co-op
622 Selby Avenue
St. Paul, Minnesota 55104
(651) 310-9499
info@msmarket.coop
www.msmarket.coop

Mississippi Market Natural Foods Co-op
1500 West 7th Street
St. Paul, Minnesota 55105
(651) 690-0507
info@msmarket.coop
www.msmarket.coop

Natural Harvest Whole Food Co-op
505 North 3rd Street
Virginia, Minnesota 55792
(218) 741-4663
www.naturalharvestfoodcoop.com

People's Food Co-op
519 1st Avenue Southwest
Rochester, Minnesota 55901
(507) 289-9061
www.pfc.coop

Pomme De Terre Food Co-op
613 Atlantic Avenue
Morris, Minnesota 56267
(320) 589-4332
www.pdtfoods.org

River Market Community Co-op
221 North Main Street
Stillwater, Minnesota 55082
(651) 439-0366
info@rivermarket.coop
www.rivermarket.coop

Seward Community Co-op
2823 East Franklin Avenue
Minneapolis, Minnesota 55404
(612) 338-2465
www.seward.coop

St. Peter Food Co-op & Deli
228 Mulberry Street
St. Peter, Minnesota 56082
(507) 934-4880
www.stpeterfood.coop

Valley Natural Foods Co-op
13750 County Road 11
Burnsville, Minnesota 55337
(952) 891-1212
info@valleynaturalfoods.com
www.valleynaturalfoods.com

Wedge Community Co-op
2105 Lyndale Avenue South
Minneapolis, Minnesota 55405
(612) 871-3993
www.wedge.coop

Whole Foods Co-op
610 East 4th Street
Duluth, Minnesota 55805
(218) 728-0884
info@wholefoods.coop
http://wholefoods.coop

Mississippi

Rainbow Co-op
2807 Old Canton Road
Jackson, Mississippi 39216
(601) 366-1602
www.rainbowcoop.org

Missouri

City Food Co-op
2639 Cherokee Street
St. Louis, Missouri 63118
(314) 771-7213
info@cityfoodcoopstl.com
www.cityfoodcoopstl.com

Montana

Community Food Co-op
908 West Main Street
Bozeman, Montana 59715
(406) 587-4039
info@bozo.coop
www.bozo.coop

Nebraska

Open Harvest Natural Foods Co-op
1618 South Street
Lincoln, Nebraska 68502
(402) 475-9069
harvest@openharvest.com
www.openharvest.com

Nevada

Great Basin Community Food Coop
240 Court Street
Reno, Nevada 89501
(775) 324-6133
info@greatbasinfood.coop
http://greatbasinfood.coop

New Hampshire

Concord Cooperative Market
24 South Main Street
Concord, New Hampshire 03301
(603) 225-6840
info@concordfoodcoop.coop
www.concordfoodcoop.coop

Co-op Community Food Market
43 Lyme Road
Hanover, New Hampshire 03755
(603) 643-2725
comment@coopfoodstore.com
www.coopfoodstore.com

Co-op Food Stores: Hanover
45 South Park Street
Hanover, New Hampshire 03755
(603) 643-2667
comment@coopfoodstore.com
www.coopfoodstore.com

Co-op Food Stores: Lebanon
12 Canterra Parkway
Lebanon, New Hampshire 03766
(603) 643-4889
comment@coopfoodstore.com
www.coopfoodstore.com

New Jersey

George Street Co-op
89 Morris Street
New Brunswick, New Jersey 08901
(732) 247-8280
www.georgestreetcoop.com

Purple Dragon Co-op
289 Washington Street
Glen Ridge, New Jersey 07028
(973) 429-0391
info@purpledragon.com
www.purpledragon.com

Sussex County Food Co-op
30 Moran Street
Newton, New Jersey 07860
(973) 579-1882
info@sussexcountyfoods.org
www.sussexcountyfoods.org

New Mexico

La Montañita Co-op and Food Market
226 West Coal Avenue
Gallup, New Mexico 87301
(505) 863-5383
http://lamontanita.coop

Silver City Food Co-op
520 North Bullard Street
Silver City, New Mexico 88061
(575) 388-2343
www.silvercityfoodcoop.com

New York

Abundance Cooperative Market
62 Marshall Street
Rochester, New York 14607
(585) 454-2667
www.abundance.coop

Flatbush Food Cooperative
1415 Cortelyou Road
Brooklyn, New York 11226
(718) 284-9717
info@flatbushfoodcoop.com
www.flatbushfoodcoop.com

4th Street Food Co-op
58 East 4th Street
New York, New York 10003-8914
(212) 674-3623
www.4thstreetfoodcoop.org

GreenStar Cooperative Market
701 West Buffalo Street
Ithaca, New York 14850
(607) 273-9392
www.greenstar.coop

High Falls Food Coop
1398 State Road 213
High Falls, New York 12440
(845) 687-7262
www.highfallsfoodcoop.com

Honest Weight Food Coop
100 Watervliet Ave
Albany, New York 12206
(518) 482-2667
www.honestweight.coop

Lexington Co-operative Market
807 Elmwood Avenue
Buffalo, New York 14222
(716) 866-2667
board@lexington.coop
www.lexington.coop

Park Slope Food Co-op
782 Union Street
Brooklyn, New York 11215
(718) 622-0560
www.foodcoop.com

Potsdam Consumer Co-op
24 Elm Street
Potsdam, New York 13676
(315) 265-4630
mail@potsdamcoop.com
www.potsdamcoop.com

Syracuse Real Food Co-op
618 Kensington Road
Syracuse, New York 13210
(315) 472-1385
www.syracuserealfood.coop

The Cambridge Food Co-op
1 West Main Street
Cambridge, New York 12816
(518) 677-5731
http://cambridgefoodcoop.com

North Carolina

Chatham Marketplace
480 Hillsboro Street, Suite 320
Pittsboro, North Carolina 27312
(919) 542-2643
mary@chathammarketplace.coop
www.chathammarketplace.coop

Company Shops Market
268 East Front Street
Burlington, North Carolina 27215

(336) 223-0390
info@companyshopsmarket.coop
www.companyshopsmarket.coop

Deep Roots Market
3728 Spring Garden Street
Greensboro, North Carolina 27407
(336) 292-9216
www.deeprootsmarket.com

French Broad Food Co-op
90 Biltmore Avenue
Asheville, North Carolina 28801
(828) 255-7650
info@frenchbroadfood.coop
www.frenchbroadfood.coop

Hendersonville Community Co-op
715 South Grove Street
Hendersonville, North Carolina 28792
(828) 693-0505
www.hendersonville.coop

Tidal Creek Cooperative Food Market
5329 Oleander Drive, Suite 100
Wilmington, North Carolina 28403
(910) 799-2667
mail@tidalcreek.coop
www.tidalcreek.coop

West Village Market & Deli
771 Haywood Road
Asheville, North Carolina 28806
(828) 225-4949
www.westvillagemarket.com

North Dakota

Amazing Grains Natural Food Market
214 De Mers Avenue
Grand Forks, North Dakota 58201
(701) 775-4542
www.amazinggrains.org

Ohio

Clintonville Community Market
200 Crestview Road
Columbus, Ohio 43202
(614) 261-3663
info@communitymarket.org
www.communitymarket.org

Kent Natural Foods Co-op
151 East Main Street
Kent, Ohio 44240
(330) 673-2878
http://kentnaturalfoods.org

Oregon

Ashland Food Co-op
237 North 1st Street
Ashland, Oregon 97520
(541) 482-2237
www.ashlandfood.coop

Astoria Cooperative
1355 Exchange Street
Astoria, Oregon 97103
(503) 325-0027
store@astoria.coop
www.astoria.coop/wp

Brookings Natural Food Co-op
630 Fleet Street
P.O. Box 8051
Brookings, Oregon 97415
(541) 469-9551

First Alternative Natural Foods Co-op
2855 Northwest Grant Avenue
Corvallis, Oregon 97330
(541) 452-3115
cs_north@firstalt.coop
www.firstalt.coop

First Alternative Natural Food Co-op
1007 Southeast 3rd Street
Corvallis, Oregon 97333
(541) 753-3115
cs_south@firstalt.coop
www.firstalt.coop

Food Front Cooperative Grocery
2375 Northwest Thurman Street
Portland, Oregon 97210
(503) 222-5658
info@foodfront.coop
http://foodfront.coop

Oceana Natural Foods Co-op
159 Southeast 2nd Street
Newport, Oregon 97365
(541) 265-8285
www.oceanafoods.org

People's Food Co-op
3029 Southeast 21st Avenue
Portland, Oregon 97202
(503) 232-9051
info@peoples.coop
www.peoples.coop

Pennsylvania

East End Food Co-op
7516 Meade Street
Pittsburgh, Pennsylvania 15208
(412) 242-3598
www.eastendfood.coop

Swarthmore Co-op
341 Dartmouth Avenue
Swarthmore, Pennsylvania 19081
(610) 543-9805
generalmanager@swarthmore.coop
www.swarthmore.coop

**Weavers Way Cooperative
  Association**
559 Carpenter Lane
Philadelphia, Pennsylvania 19119
(215) 843-2350
contact@weaversway.coop
www.weaversway.coop

Whole Foods Co-op
1341 West 26th & Brown Avenue
Erie, Pennsylvania 16508
(814) 456-0282
www.wholefoodscoop.org

Rhode Island

Alternative Food Co-op
357 Main Street
Wakefield, Rhode Island 02879
(401) 789-2240
www.alternativefoodcoop.com

South Carolina

Upstate Food Co-op
404 John Holiday Road
Six Mile, South Carolina 29682
(864) 868-3105
info@upstatefoodcoop.com
www.upstatefoodcoop.com

South Dakota

The Co-op Natural Foods
2504 South Duluth Avenue
Sioux Falls, South Dakota 57104
(605) 339-9506
www.coopnaturalfoods.com

Tennessee

Marketplace Buying Club Co-op
3511 Belmont Boulevard
Nashville, Tennessee 37214
www.marketplaceco-op.org

Morningside Buying Club
215 Morningside Lane
Liberty, Tennessee 37095
(615) 563-2353
www.morningsidefarm.com

Three Rivers Market
1100 North Central Street
Knoxville, Tennessee 37917
(865) 525-2069
info@threeriversmarket.coop
www.threeriversmarket.coop

Texas

Central City Co-op
2515 Waugh Drive
Houston, Texas 77006
info@centralcityco-op.com
www.centralcityco-op.com

Wheatsville Food Co-op
3101 Guadalupe Street
Austin, Texas 78704
(512) 478-2667
gm@wheatsville.com
www.wheatsville.com

Utah

The Community Food Co-op of Utah
1726 South 700 West
Salt Lake City, Utah 84104
(801) 746-7878
general@thecommunitycoop.org
https://thecommunitycoop.com

Vermont

Brattleboro Food Co-op
2 Main Street
Brattleboro, Vermont 05301
(802) 257-0236
adminbfc@sover.net
www.brattleborofoodcoop.com

City Market–Onion River Co-op
82 South Winooski Avenue
Burlington, Vermont 05401
(802) 861-9700
info@citymarket.coop
www.citymarket.coop

Hunger Mountain Co-op
623 Stone Cutters Way
Montpelier, Vermont 05602
(802) 223-8000
www.hungermountain.com

Putney Food Co-op
8 Carol Brown Way
Putney, Vermont 05346
(802) 387-5866
ptnycoop@sover.net
www.putneycoop.com

St. J. Food Co-op
490 Portland Street
St. Johnsbury, Vermont 05819
(802) 748-9498
info@stjfoodcoop.com
www.stjfoodcoop.com

Virginia

Eats Natural Foods Co-op
708A North Main Street
Blacksburg, Virginia 24060
(540) 552-2279
eatsnatural@gmail.com
www.eatsnaturalfoods.com

Healthy Foods Co-op
110 West Washington Street
Lexington, Virginia 24450
(540) 463-6954
healthyfoods@embarqmail.com
http://healthyfoodscoop.org

Roanoke Natural Foods Co-op
1319 Grandin Road Southwest
Roanoke, Virginia 24015
(540) 343-5652
info@roanokenaturalfoods.coop
www.roanokenaturalfoods.coop

Washington

Community Food Co-op
1220 North Forest Street
Bellingham, Washington 98225
(360) 734-8158
info@communityfood.coop
www.communityfood.coop

The Food Co-op
414 Kearney Street
Port Townsend, Washington 98368
(360) 385-2883
info@foodcoop.coop
www.foodcoop.coop

Madison Market/Central Co-op
1600 East Madison Street
Seattle, Washington 98122
(206) 329-1545
www.centralcoop.coop

Puget Consumers' Co-op–Fremont
600 North 34th Street
Seattle, Washington 98103
(206) 632-6811
www.pccnaturalmarkets.com

Puget Consumers' Co-op–Greenlake
7504 Aurora Avenue North
Seattle, Washington 98103
(206) 525-3586
www.pccnaturalmarkets.com

Puget Consumers' Co-op–Issaquah
1810 12th Avenue Northwest
Issaquah, Washington 98027
(425) 369-1222
issaquah.storems@pccsea.com
www.pccnaturalmarkets.com

Puget Consumers' Co-op–Kirkland
10718 Northeast 68th Street
Kirkland, Washington 98033
(425) 828-4622
www.pccnaturalmarkets.com

Puget Consumers' Co-op–Seward Park
5041 Wilson Avenue South
Seattle, Washington 98118
(206) 723-2720
www.pccnaturalmarkets.com

**Puget Consumers' Co-op–
    View Ridge**
6514 40th Street Northeast
Seattle, Washington 98115
(206) 526-7661
www.pccnaturalmarkets.com

**Puget Consumers' Co-op–
    West Seattle**
2749 California Avenue Southwest
Seattle, Washington 98116
(206) 937-8481
www.pccnaturalmarkets.com

Sno-Isle Natural Foods Co-op
2804 Grand Avenue
Everett, Washington 98201
(425) 259-3798
info@snoislefoods.coop
www.snoislefoods.coop

Yelm Food Co-op
17835 State Route 507
Yelm, Washington 98597
(360) 400-2210
yelmfoodcoop@gmail.com
http://yelmfarmersmarket.com

West Virginia

Mountain People's Market
1400 University Avenue
Morgantown, West Virginia 26505
(304) 291-6131
http://mountainpeoplescoop.com

Wisconsin

Basic Cooperative
1711 Lodge Drive
Janesville, Wisconsin 53545
(608) 754-3925
www.basicshealth.com

Food Co-ops

**Kickapoo Exchange
  Food Co-op**
209 Main Street
Gays Mills, Wisconsin 54631
(608) 735-4544
kickapooexchange@yahoo.com

Mega Pik N Save
1201 South Hastings Way
Eau Claire, Wisconsin 54701
(715) 839-5200
www.megafoods.com

Menomonie Market Food Co-op
521 2nd Street East
Menomonie, Wisconsin 54751
(715) 235-6533
info@mmfc.coop
www.mmfc.coop

Nature's Bakery Co-op
1019 Williams Street
Madison, Wisconsin 53703
(608) 257-3649
mail@naturesbakery.coop
www.naturesbakery.coop

Outpost Natural Foods Co-op
100 East Capital Drive
Milwaukee, Wisconsin 53212
(414) 961-2597
www.outpostnaturalfoods.coop

Outpost Natural Foods Co-op: Wauwatosa
7000 West State Street
Wauwatosa, Wisconsin 53213
(414) 778-2012

www.outpostnaturalfoods.coop

People's Food Co-op
315 South 5th Avenue
La Crosse, Wisconsin 54601
(608) 784-5798
www.pfc.coop

Riverwest Co-op Grocery & Café
733 North East Clarke Street
Milwaukee, Wisconsin 53212
(414) 264-7933
www.riverwestcoop.org

Viroqua Food Cooperative
609 North Main Street
Viroqua, Wisconsin 54665
(608) 637-7511
info@viroquafood.coop

Willy Street Co-op
1221 Williamson Street
Madison, Wisconsin 53703
(608) 251-6776
www.willystreet.coop

**Yahara River Grocery
  Cooperative**
229 East Main Street
Stoughton, Wisconsin 53589
(608) 877-0947
info@yaharagrocery.coop
www.yaharagrocery.coop

Canning

Introduction to Canning

On the next few pages, you will find descriptions of proper canning methods, with details on how canning works and why it is both safe and economical. Much of the information here is from the USDA, which has done extensive research on home canning and preserving. If you are new to home canning, read this section carefully as it will help to ensure success with the recipes that follow.

Whether you are a seasoned home canner or this is your first foray into food preservation, it is important to follow directions carefully. With some recipes it is okay to experiment with varied proportions or added ingredients, and with others it is important to stick to what's written. In many instances it is noted whether creative liberty is a good idea for a particular recipe, but if you are not sure, play it safe—otherwise you may end up with a jam that is too runny, a vegetable that is mushy, or a product that is spoiled. Take time to read the directions and prepare your foods and equipment adequately, and you will find that home canning is safe, economical, tremendously satisfying, and a great deal of fun!

Why Can Foods?

Canning is fun and a good way to preserve your precious produce. As more and more farmers' markets make their way into urban centers, city dwellers are also discovering how rewarding it is to make seasonal treats last all year-round. Besides the value of your labor, canning home-grown or locally grown food may

▲ Canned applesauce and peaches line this pantry's shelves.

save you half the cost of buying commercially canned food. And what makes a nicer, more thoughtful gift than a jar of homemade jam, tailored to match the recipient's favorite fruits and flavors?

The nutritional value of home canning is an added benefit. Many vegetables begin to lose their vitamins as soon as they are harvested. Nearly half the vitamins may be lost within a few days unless the fresh produce is kept cool or preserved. Within one to two weeks, even refrigerated produce loses half or more of certain vitamins. The heating process during canning destroys from one-third to one-half of vitamins A and C, thiamin, and riboflavin. Once canned, foods may lose from 5 percent to 20 percent of these sensitive vitamins each year. The amounts of other vitamins, however, are only slightly lower in canned compared with fresh food. If vegetables are handled properly and canned promptly after harvest, they can be more nutritious than fresh produce sold in local stores.

▼ Canned jams and nut butters.

Canning began in France, at the turn of the nineteenth century, when Napoleon Bonaparte was desperate for a way to keep his troops well-fed while on the march. In 1800, he decided to hold a contest, offering 12,000 francs to anyone who could devise a suitable method of food preservation. Nicolas François Appert, a French confectioner, rose to the challenge, considering that if wine could be preserved in bottles, perhaps food could be as well. He experimented until he was able to prove that heating food to boiling after it had been sealed in airtight glass bottles prevented the food from deteriorating. Interestingly, this all took place about 100 years before Louis Pasteur found that heat could destroy bacteria. Nearly 10 years after the contest began, Napoleon personally presented Nicolas with the cash reward.

The advantages of home canning are lost when you start with poor quality foods; when jars fail to seal properly; when food spoils; and when flavors, texture, color, and nutrients deteriorate during prolonged storage. The tips that follow explain many of these problems and recommend ways to minimize them.

How Canning Preserves Foods

The high percentage of water in most fresh foods makes them very perishable. They spoil or lose their quality for several reasons:

- Growth of undesirable microorganisms—bacteria, molds, and yeasts
- Activity of food enzymes
- Reactions with oxygen
- Moisture loss

Microorganisms live and multiply quickly on the surfaces of fresh food and on the inside of bruised, insect-damaged, and diseased food. Oxygen and enzymes are present throughout fresh food tissues.

▼ Green beans should be chopped into small pieces before canning.

▲ Peel potatoes before canning them.

Proper canning practices include:

- Carefully selecting and washing fresh food
- Peeling some fresh foods
- Hot packing many foods
- Adding acids (lemon juice, citric acid, or vinegar) to some foods
- Using acceptable jars and self-sealing lids
- Processing jars in a boiling-water or pressure canner for the correct amount of time

Collectively, these practices remove oxygen; destroy enzymes; prevent the growth of undesirable bacteria, yeasts, and molds; and help form a high vacuum in jars. High vacuums form tight seals, which keep liquid in and air and microorganisms out.

> A large stockpot with a lid can be used in place of a boiling-water canner for high-acid foods like tomatoes, pickles, apples, peaches, and jams. Simply place a rack inside the pot so that the jars do not rest directly on the bottom of the pot.

Canning Glossary

Acid foods—Foods that contain enough acid to result in a pH of 4.6 or lower. Includes most tomatoes; fermented and pickled vegetables; relishes; jams, jellies, and marmalades; and all fruits except figs. Acid foods may be processed in boiling water.

Ascorbic acid—The chemical name for vitamin C. Commonly used to prevent browning of peeled, light-colored fruits and vegetables.

Blancher—A 6- to 8-quart lidded pot designed with a fitted, perforated basket to hold food in boiling water or with a fitted rack to steam foods. Useful for loosening skins on fruits to be peeled or for heating foods to be hot packed.

Boiling-water canner—A large, standard-sized, lidded kettle with jar rack designed for heat-processing seven quarts or eight to nine pints in boiling water.

Botulism—An illness caused by eating a toxin produced by growth of *Clostridium botulinum* bacteria in moist, low-acid food containing less than 2 percent oxygen and stored between 40 and 120°F. Proper heat processing destroys this bacterium in canned food. Freezer temperatures inhibit its growth in frozen food. Low moisture controls its growth in dried food. High oxygen controls its growth in fresh foods.

Canning—A method of preserving food that employs heat processing in airtight, vacuum-sealed containers so that food can be safely stored at normal home temperatures.

Canning salt—Also called pickling salt. It is regular table salt without the anti-caking or iodine additives.

Citric acid—A form of acid that can be added to canned foods. It increases the acidity of low-acid foods and may improve their flavor.

Cold pack—Canning procedure in which jars are filled with raw food. "Raw pack" is the preferred term for describing this practice. "Cold pack" is often used incorrectly to refer to foods that are open-kettle canned or jars that are heat-processed in boiling water.

Enzymes—Proteins in food that accelerate many flavor, color, texture, and nutritional changes, especially when food is cut, sliced, crushed, bruised, or exposed to air. Proper blanching or hot-packing practices destroy enzymes and improve food quality.

Exhausting—Removing air from within and around food and from jars and canners. Exhausting or venting of pressure canners is necessary to prevent botulism in low-acid canned foods.

Headspace—The unfilled space above food or liquid in jars that allows for food expansion as jars are heated and for forming vacuums as jars cool.

Heat processing—Treatment of jars with sufficient heat to enable storing food at normal home temperatures.

Hermetic seal—An absolutely airtight container seal that prevents reentry of air or microorganisms into packaged foods.

Hot pack—Heating of raw food in boiling water or steam and filling it hot into jars.

Low-acid foods—Foods that contain very little acid and have a pH above 4.6. The acidity in these foods is insufficient to prevent the growth of botulism bacteria. Vegetables, some varieties of tomatoes, figs, all meats, fish, seafood, and some dairy products are low-acid foods. To control all risks of botulism, jars of these foods must be either heat processed in a pressure canner or acidified to a pH of 4.6 or lower before being processed in boiling water.

Microorganisms—Independent organisms of microscopic size, including bacteria, yeast, and mold. In a suitable environment, they grow rapidly and may divide or reproduce every 10 to 30 minutes. Therefore, they reach high populations very quickly. Microorganisms are sometimes intentionally added to ferment foods, make antibiotics, and for other reasons. Undesirable microorganisms cause disease and food spoilage.

Mold—A fungus-type microorganism whose growth on food is usually visible and colorful. Molds may grow on many foods, including acid foods like jams and jellies and canned fruits. Recommended heat processing and sealing practices prevent their growth on these foods.

Mycotoxins—Toxins produced by the growth of some molds on foods.

Open-kettle canning—A non-recommended canning method. Food is heat-processed in a covered kettle, filled while hot into sterile jars, and then sealed. Foods canned this way have low vacuums or too much air, which permits rapid loss of quality in foods. Also, these foods often spoil because they become recontaminated while the jars are being filled.

Pasteurization—Heating food to temperatures high enough to destroy disease-causing microorganisms.

pH—A measure of acidity or alkalinity. Values range from 0 to 14. A food is neutral when its pH is 7.0. Lower values are increasingly more acidic; higher values are increasingly more alkaline.

PSIG—Pounds per square inch of pressure as measured by a gauge.

Pressure canner—A specifically designed metal kettle with a lockable lid used for heat-processing low-acid food. These canners have jar racks, one or more safety devices, systems for exhausting air, and a way to measure or control pressure. Canners with 20- to 21-quart capacity are common. The minimum size of canner that should be used has a 16-quart capacity and can hold seven one-quart jars. Use of pressure saucepans with a capacity of less than 16 quarts is not recommended.

Raw pack—The practice of filling jars with raw, unheated food. Acceptable for canning low-acid foods, but allows more rapid quality losses in acid foods that are heat-processed in boiling water. Also called "cold pack."

Style of pack—Form of canned food, such as whole, sliced, piece, juice, or sauce. The term may also be used to specify whether food is filled raw or hot into jars.

Vacuum—A state of negative pressure that reflects how thoroughly air is removed from within a jar of processed food; the higher the vacuum, the less air left in the jar.

Proper Canning Practices

Growth of the bacterium *Clostridium botulinum* in canned food may cause botulism—a deadly form of food poisoning. These bacteria exist either as spores or as vegetative cells. The spores, which are comparable to plant seeds, can survive harmlessly in soil and water for many years. When ideal conditions exist for growth, the spores produce vegetative cells, which multiply rapidly and may produce a deadly toxin within three to four days in an environment consisting of:

- A moist, low-acid food;
- A temperature between 40 and 120°F; and
- Less than 2 percent oxygen.

Botulinum spores are on most fresh food surfaces. Because they grow only in the absence of air, they are harmless on fresh foods. Most bacteria, yeasts, and molds are difficult to remove from food surfaces. Washing fresh food reduces their numbers only slightly. Peeling root crops, underground stem crops, and tomatoes reduces their numbers greatly. Blanching also helps, but the vital controls are the method of canning and use of the recommended research-based processing times. These processing times ensure destruction of the largest expected number of heat-resistant microorganisms in home-canned foods.

Properly sterilized canned food will be free of spoilage if lids seal and jars are stored below 95°F. Storing jars at 50 to 70°F enhances retention of quality.

Food Acidity and Processing Methods

Whether food should be processed in a pressure canner or boiling-water canner to control botulism bacteria depends on the acidity in the food. Acidity may be natural, as in most fruits, or added, as in pickled food. Low-acid canned foods contain too little acidity to prevent the growth of these bacteria. Other foods may contain enough acidity to block their growth or to destroy them rapidly when heated. The term "pH" is a measure of acidity: the lower its value, the more acidic the food. The acidity level in foods can be increased by adding lemon juice, citric acid, or vinegar.

Low-acid foods have pH values higher than 4.6. They include red meats, seafood, poultry, milk, and all fresh vegetables except for most tomatoes. Most products that are mixtures of low-acid and acid foods also have pH values above 4.6 unless their ingredients include enough lemon juice, citric acid, or vinegar to make them acid foods. Acid foods have a pH of 4.6 or lower. They include fruits, pickles, sauerkraut, jams, jellies, marmalade, and fruit butters.

Although tomatoes usually are considered an acid food, some are now known to have pH values slightly above 4.6. Figs also have pH values slightly above 4.6. Therefore, if they are to be canned as acid foods, these products must be acidified to a pH of 4.6 or lower with lemon juice or citric acid. Properly acidified tomatoes and figs are acid foods and can be safely processed in a boiling-water canner.

Botulinum spores are very hard to destroy at boiling-water temperatures; the higher the canner temperature, the more easily they are destroyed. Therefore, all low-acid foods should be sterilized at temperatures of 240 to 250°F, attainable with pressure canners operated at 10 to 15 PSIG. (PSIG means pounds per square inch of pressure as measured by a gauge.) At these temperatures, the time needed to destroy bacteria in low-acid canned foods ranges from 20 to 100 minutes. The exact time depends on the kind of food being canned, the way it is packed into jars, and the size of jars. The time needed to safely process low-acid foods in boiling water ranges from 7 to 11 hours; the time needed to process acid foods in boiling water varies from 5 to 85 minutes.

Know Your Altitude

It is important to know your approximate elevation or altitude above sea level in order to determine a safe processing time for canned foods. Since the boiling temperature of liquid is lower at higher elevations, it is critical that additional time be given for the safe processing of foods at altitudes above sea level.

What Not to Do

Open-kettle canning and the processing of freshly filled jars in conventional ovens, microwave ovens, and dishwashers are not recommended because these practices do not prevent all risks of spoilage. Steam canners are not recommended because processing times for use with current models have not been adequately researched. Because steam canners may not heat foods in the same manner as boiling-water canners, their use with boiling-water processing times may result in spoilage. So-called canning powders are useless as preservatives and do not replace the need for proper heat processing.

It is not recommended that pressures in excess of 15 PSIG be applied when using new pressure-canning equipment.

Ensuring High-Quality Canned Foods

Examine food carefully for freshness and wholesomeness. Discard diseased and moldy food. Trim small diseased lesions or spots from food.

▲ Label your jars after processing with the contents and the date.

Can fruits and vegetables picked from your garden or purchased from nearby producers when the products are at their peak of quality—within 6 to 12 hours after harvest for most vegetables. However, apricots, nectarines, peaches, pears, and plums should be ripened one or more days between harvest and canning. If you must delay the canning of other fresh produce, keep it in a shady, cool place.

Fresh, home-slaughtered red meats and poultry should be chilled and canned without delay. Do not can meat from sickly or diseased animals. Put fish and seafood on ice after harvest, eviscerate immediately, and can them within two days.

Maintaining Color and Flavor in Canned Food

To maintain good natural color and flavor in stored canned food, you must:

- Remove oxygen from food tissues and jars,
- Quickly destroy the food enzymes, and
- Obtain high jar vacuums and airtight jar seals.

Follow these guidelines to ensure that your canned foods retain optimal colors and flavors during processing and storage:

- Use only high-quality foods that are at the proper maturity and are free of diseases and bruises.
- Use the hot-pack method, especially with acid foods to be processed in boiling water.
- Don't unnecessarily expose prepared foods to air; can them as soon as possible.
- While preparing a canner load of jars, keep peeled, halved, quartered, sliced, or diced apples, apricots, nectarines, peaches, and pears in a solution of 3 grams (3,000 milligrams) ascorbic acid to 1 gallon of cold water. This procedure is also useful in maintaining the natural color of mushrooms and potatoes and for preventing stem-end discoloration in cherries and grapes.

You can get ascorbic acid in several forms:

Pure powdered form—Seasonally available among canning supplies in supermarkets. One level teaspoon of pure powder weighs about 3 grams. Use 1 teaspoon per gallon of water as a treatment solution.

Vitamin C tablets—Economical and available year-round in many stores. Buy 500-milligram tablets;

crush and dissolve six tablets per gallon of water as a treatment solution.

Commercially prepared mixes of ascorbic and citric acid—Seasonally available among canning supplies in supermarkets. Sometimes citric acid powder is sold in supermarkets, but it is less effective in controlling discoloration. If you choose to use these products, follow the manufacturer's directions:

- Fill hot foods into jars and adjust headspace as specified in recipes.
- Tighten screw bands securely, but if you are especially strong, not as tightly as possible.
- Process and cool jars.
- Store the jars in a relatively cool, dark place, preferably between 50 and 70°F.
- Can no more food than you will use within a year.

Advantages of Hot Packing

Many fresh foods contain from 10 percent to more than 30 percent air. The length of time that food will last at premium quality depends on how much air is removed from the food before jars are sealed. The more air that is removed, the higher the quality of the canned product.

Raw packing is the practice of filling jars tightly with freshly prepared but unheated food. Such foods, especially fruit, will float in the jars. The entrapped air in and around the food may cause discoloration within two to three months of storage. Raw packing is more suitable for vegetables processed in a pressure canner.

Hot packing is the practice of heating freshly prepared food to boiling, simmering it three to five minutes, and promptly filling jars loosely with the boiled food. Hot packing is the best way to remove air and is the preferred pack style for foods processed in a boiling-water canner. At first, the color of hot-packed foods may appear no better than that of raw-packed foods, but within a short storage period, both color and flavor of hot-packed foods will be superior.

Whether food has been hot packed or raw packed, the juice, syrup, or water to be added to the foods should be heated to boiling before it is added to the jars. This practice helps to remove air from food tissues, shrinks food, helps keep the food from floating in the jars, increases vacuum in sealed jars, and improves shelf life. Preshrinking food allows you to add more food to each jar.

Controlling Headspace

The unfilled space above the food in a jar and below its lid is termed headspace. It is best to leave a ¼-inch headspace for jams and jellies, ½-inch for fruits and tomatoes to be processed in boiling water, and from 1 to 1¼ inches in low-acid foods to be processed in a pressure canner.

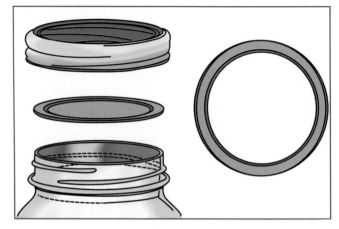

▲ A Mason jar, lid, screw band, and seal.

This space is needed for expansion of food as jars are processed and for forming vacuums in cooled jars. The extent of expansion is determined by the air content in the food and by the processing temperature. Air expands greatly when heated to high temperatures—the higher the temperature, the greater the expansion. Foods expand less than air when heated.

Jars and Lids

Food may be canned in glass jars or metal containers. Metal containers can be used only once. They require special sealing equipment and are much more costly than jars.

Mason-type jars designed for home canning are ideal for preserving food by pressure or boiling-water canning. Regular and wide-mouthed threaded Mason jars with self-sealing lids are the best choices. They are available in half-pint, pint, 1½-pint, and quart sizes. The standard jar mouth opening is about 2³/₈ inches. Wide-mouthed jars have openings of about 3 inches, making them more easily filled and emptied. Regular-mouthed decorative jelly jars are available in 8-ounce and 12-ounce sizes.

With careful use and handling, Mason jars may be reused many times, requiring only new lids each time. When lids are used properly, jar seals and vacuums are excellent.

Jar Cleaning

Before reuse, wash empty jars in hot water with detergent and rinse well by hand, or wash in a dishwasher. Rinse thoroughly, as detergent residue may cause unnatural flavors and colors. Scale or hard-water films on jars are easily removed by soaking jars for several hours in a solution containing 1 cup of vinegar (5 percent acid) per gallon of water.

Sterilization of Empty Jars

Use sterile jars for all jams, jellies, and pickled products processed less than 10 minutes. To sterilize empty jars, put them right side up on the rack in a boiling-water canner. Fill the canner and jars with hot (not boiling) water to 1 inch above the tops of the jars. Boil for 10 minutes. Remove and drain hot, sterilized jars one at a time. Save the hot water for processing filled jars. Fill jars with food, add lids, and tighten screw bands.

Empty jars used for vegetables, meats, and fruits to be processed in a pressure canner need not be sterilized beforehand. It is also unnecessary to sterilize jars for fruits, tomatoes, and pickled or fermented foods that will be processed 10 minutes or longer in a boiling-water canner.

Lid Selection, Preparation, and Use

The common self-sealing lid consists of a flat metal lid held in place by a metal screw band during processing. The flat lid is crimped around its bottom edge to form a trough, which is filled with a colored gasket material. When jars are processed, the lid gasket softens and flows slightly to cover the jar-sealing surface, yet allows air to escape from the jar. The gasket then forms an airtight seal as the jar cools. Gaskets in unused lids work well for at least five years from date of manufacture. The gasket material in older, unused lids may fail to seal on jars.

It is best to buy only the quantity of lids you will use in a year. To ensure a good seal, carefully follow the manufacturer's directions in preparing lids for use. Examine all metal lids carefully. Do not use old, dented, or deformed lids or lids with gaps or other defects in the sealing gasket.

After filling jars with food, release air bubbles by inserting a flat, plastic (not metal) spatula between the food and the jar. Slowly turn the jar and move the spatula up and down to allow air bubbles to escape. Adjust the headspace and then clean the jar rim (sealing surface) with a dampened paper towel. Place the lid, gasket down, onto the cleaned jar-sealing surface. Uncleaned jar-sealing surfaces may cause seal failures.

Then fit the metal screw band over the flat lid. Follow the manufacturer's guidelines enclosed with or on the box for tightening the jar lids properly:

- If screw bands are too tight, air cannot vent during processing, and food will discolor during storage. Overtightening also may cause lids to buckle and jars to break, especially with raw-packed, pressure-processed food.
- If screw bands are too loose, liquid may escape from jars during processing, seals may fail, and the food will need to be reprocessed.

Do not retighten lids after processing jars. As jars cool, the contents in the jar contract, pulling the self-sealing lid firmly against the jar to form a high vacuum. Screw bands are not needed on stored jars. They can be removed easily after jars are cooled.

When removed, washed, dried, and stored in a dry area, screw bands may be used many times. If left on stored jars, they become difficult to remove, often rust, and may not work properly again.

Selecting the Correct Processing Time

When food is canned in boiling water, more processing time is needed for most raw-packed foods and for quart jars than is needed for hot-packed foods and pint jars.

To destroy microorganisms in acid foods processed in a boiling-water canner, you must:

- Process jars for the correct number of minutes in boiling water.
- Cool the jars at room temperature.

To destroy microorganisms in low-acid foods processed with a pressure canner, you must:

- Process the jars for the correct number of minutes at 240°F (10 PSIG) or 250°F (15 PSIG).
- Allow canner to cool at room temperature until it is completely depressurized.

The food may spoil if you fail to use the proper processing times, fail to vent steam from canners properly, process at lower pressure than specified, process for fewer minutes than specified, or cool the canner with water.

Processing times for haft-pint and pint jars are the same, as are times for 1½-pint and quart jars. For some products, you have a choice of processing at 5, 10, or 15 PSIG. In these cases, choose the canner pressure (PSIG) you wish to use and match it with your pack style (raw or hot) and jar size to find the correct processing time.

Recommended Canners

There are two main types of canners for heat-processing home-canned food: boiling-water canners and pressure canners. Most are designed to hold seven

▲ A boiling water canner.

one-quart jars or eight to nine one-pint jars. Small pressure canners hold four one-quart jars; some large pressure canners hold 18 one-pint jars in two layers but hold only seven quart jars. Pressure saucepans with smaller volume capacities are not recommended for use in canning. Treat small pressure canners the same as standard larger canners; they should be vented using the typical venting procedures.

Low-acid foods must be processed in a pressure canner to be free of botulism risks. Although pressure canners also may be used for processing acid foods, boiling-water canners are recommended because they are faster. A pressure canner would require from 55 to 100 minutes to can a load of jars; the total time for canning most acid foods in boiling water varies from 25 to 60 minutes.

A boiling-water canner loaded with filled jars requires about 20 to 30 minutes of heating before its water begins to boil. A loaded pressure canner requires about 12 to 15 minutes of heating before it begins to vent, another 10 minutes to vent the canner, another 5 minutes to pressurize the canner, another 8 to 10 minutes to process the acid food, and, finally, another 20 to 60 minutes to cool the canner before removing jars.

Boiling-Water Canners

These canners are made of aluminum or porcelain-covered steel. They have removable perforated racks and fitted lids. The canner must be deep enough so that at least 1 inch of briskly boiling water will cover the tops of jars during processing. Some boiling-water canners do not have flat bottoms. A flat bottom must be used on an electric range. Either a flat or ridged bottom can be used on a gas burner. To ensure uniform processing of all jars with an electric range, the canner should be no more than 4 inches wider in diameter than the element on which it is heated.

Using a Boiling-Water Canner

Follow these steps for successful boiling-water canning:

1. Fill the canner halfway with water.
2. Preheat water to 140°F for raw-packed foods and to 180°F for hot-packed foods.
3. Load filled jars, fitted with lids, into the canner rack and use the handles to lower the rack into the water; or fill the canner, one jar at a time, with a jar lifter.
4. Add more boiling water, if needed, so the water level is at least 1 inch above jar tops.
5. Turn heat to its highest position until water boils vigorously.
6. Set a timer for the minutes required for processing the food.
7. Cover with the canner lid and lower the heat setting to maintain a gentle boil throughout the processing time.
8. Add more boiling water, if needed, to keep the water level above the jars.
9. When jars have been boiled for the recommended time, turn off the heat and remove the canner lid.
10. Using a jar lifter, remove the jars and place them on a towel, leaving at least 1 inch of space between the jars during cooling.

Pressure Canners

Pressure canners for use in the home have been extensively redesigned in recent years. Models made before the 1970s were heavy-walled kettles with clamp-on lids. They were fitted with a dial gauge, a vent port in the form of a petcock or counterweight, and a safety fuse. Modern pressure canners are lightweight, thin-walled kettles; most have turn-on lids. They have a jar rack, gasket, dial or weighted gauge, an automatic vent or cover lock, a vent port (steam vent) that is closed with a counterweight or weighted gauge, and a safety fuse.

Pressure does not destroy microorganisms, but high temperatures applied for a certain period of time do. The success of destroying all microorganisms capable of growing in canned food is based on the temperature obtained in pure steam, free of air, at sea level. At sea level, a canner operated at a gauge pressure of 10 pounds provides an internal temperature of 240°F.

Air trapped in a canner lowers the inside temperature and results in under-processing. The highest volume of air trapped in a canner occurs in processing raw-packed foods in dial-gauge canners. These canners do not vent air during processing. To be safe, all types of pressure canners must be vented 10 minutes before they are pressurized.

Canning

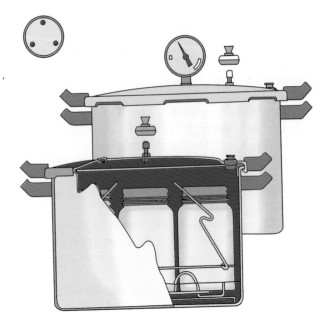

▲ A pressure canner.

To vent a canner, leave the vent port uncovered on newer models or manually open petcocks on some older models. Heating the filled canner with its lid locked into place boils water and generates steam that escapes through the petcock or vent port. When steam first escapes, set a timer for 10 minutes. After venting 10 minutes, close the petcock or place the counterweight or weighted gauge over the vent port to pressurize the canner.

Weighted-gauge models exhaust tiny amounts of air and steam each time their gauge rocks or jiggles during processing. The sound of the weight rocking or jiggling indicates that the canner is maintaining the recommended pressure and needs no further attention until the load has been processed for the set time. Weighted-gauge canners cannot correct precisely for higher altitudes, and at altitudes above 1,000 feet must be operated at a pressure of 15.

Check dial gauges for accuracy before use each year and replace if they read high by more than 1 pound at 5, 10, or 15 pounds of pressure. Low readings cause over-processing and may indicate that the accuracy of the gauge is unpredictable. If a gauge is consistently low, you may adjust the processing pressure. For example, if the directions call for 12 pounds of pressure and your dial gauge has tested 1 pound low, you can safely process at 11 pounds of pressure. If the gauge is more than 2 pounds low, it is unpredictable, and it is best to replace it. Gauges may be checked at most USDA county extension offices, which are located in every state across the country. To find one near you, visit www.csrees.usda.gov.

Handle gaskets of canner lids carefully and clean them according to the manufacturer's directions.

Nicked or dried gaskets will allow steam leaks during pressurization of canners. Gaskets of older canners may need to be lightly coated with vegetable oil once per year, but newer models are pre-lubricated. Check your canner's instructions.

Lid safety fuses are thin, metal inserts or rubber plugs designed to relieve excessive pressure from the canner. Do not pick at or scratch fuses while cleaning lids. Use only canners that have Underwriter's Laboratory (UL) approval to ensure their safety.

Replacement gauges and other parts for canners are often available at stores offering canner equipment or from canner manufacturers. To order parts, list canner model number and describe the parts needed.

Using a Pressure Canner

Follow these steps for successful pressure canning:

1. Put 2 to 3 inches of hot water in the canner. Place filled jars on the rack, using a jar lifter. Fasten canner lid securely.
2. Open petcock or leave weight off vent port. Heat at the highest setting until steam flows from the petcock or vent port.
3. Maintain high heat setting, exhaust steam 10 minutes, and then place weight on vent port or close petcock. The canner will pressurize during the next three to five minutes.
4. Start timing the process when the pressure reading on the dial gauge indicates that the

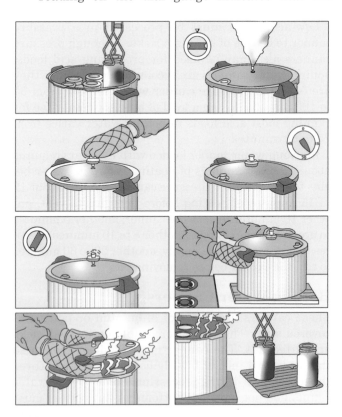

▲ Using a pressure canner.

recommended pressure has been reached or when the weighted gauge begins to jiggle or rock.

5. Regulate heat under the canner to maintain a steady pressure at or slightly above the correct gauge pressure. Quick and large pressure variations during processing may cause unnecessary liquid losses from jars. Weighted gauges on Mirro canners should jiggle about two or three times per minute. On Presto canners, they should rock slowly throughout the process.

When processing time is completed, turn off the heat, remove the canner from heat if possible, and let the canner depressurize. Do not force-cool the canner. If you cool it with cold running water in a sink or open the vent port before the canner depressurizes by itself, liquid will spurt from the jars, causing low liquid levels and jar seal failures. Force-cooling also may warp the canner lid of older model canners, causing steam leaks.

Depressurization of older models should be timed. Standard size heavy-walled canners require about 30 minutes when loaded with pints and 45 minutes with quarts. Newer thin-walled canners cool more rapidly and are equipped with vent locks. These canners are depressurized when their vent lock piston drops to a normal position:

1. After the vent port or petcock has been open for two minutes, unfasten the lid and carefully remove it. Lift the lid away from you so that the steam does not burn your face.

2. Remove jars with a lifter, and place on towel or cooling rack, if desired.

Cooling Jars

Cool the jars at room temperature for 12 to 24 hours. Jars may be cooled on racks or towels to minimize heat damage to counters. The food level and liquid volume of raw-packed jars will be noticeably lower after cooling because air is exhausted during processing, and food shrinks. If a jar loses excessive liquid during processing, do not open it to add more liquid. As long as the seal is good, the product is still usable.

Testing Jar Seals

After cooling jars for 12 to 24 hours, remove the screw bands and test seals with one of the following methods:

Method 1: Press the middle of the lid with a finger or thumb. If the lid springs up when you release your finger, the lid is unsealed and reprocessing will be necessary.

Method 2: Tap the lid with the bottom of a teaspoon. If it makes a dull sound, the lid is not sealed. If food is in contact with the underside of the lid, it will also cause a dull sound. If the jar lid is sealed correctly, it will make a ringing, high-pitched sound.

▲ Testing jar seals.

Method 3: Hold the jar at eye level and look across the lid. The lid should be concave (curved down slightly in the center). If center of the lid is either flat or bulging, it may not be sealed.

Reprocessing Unsealed Jars

If a jar fails to seal, remove the lid and check the jar-sealing surface for tiny nicks. If necessary, change the jar, add a new, properly prepared lid, and reprocess within 24 hours using the same processing time.

Another option is to adjust headspace in unsealed jars to 1½ inches and freeze jars and contents instead of reprocessing. However, make sure jars have straight sides. Freezing may crack jars with "shoulders."

Foods in single, unsealed jars could be stored in the refrigerator and consumed within several days.

Storing Canned Foods

If lids are tightly vacuum-sealed on cooled jars, remove screw bands, wash the lid and jar to remove food residue, then rinse and dry jars. Label and date the jars and store them in a clean, cool, dark, dry place. Do not store jars at temperatures above 95°F or near hot pipes, a range, a furnace, in an uninsulated attic, or in direct sunlight. Under these conditions, food will lose quality in a few weeks or months and may spoil. Dampness may corrode metal lids, break seals, and allow recontamination and spoilage.

Accidental freezing of canned foods will not cause spoilage unless jars become unsealed and re-contaminated. However, freezing and thawing may soften food. If jars must be stored where they may freeze, wrap them in newspapers, place them in heavy cartons, and cover them with more newspapers and blankets.

Identifying and Handling Spoiled Canned Food

Growth of spoilage bacteria and yeast produces gas, which pressurizes the food, swells lids, and breaks jar seals. As each stored jar is selected for use, examine its lid for tightness and vacuum. Lids with concave centers have good seals.

Next, while holding the jar upright at eye level, rotate the jar and examine its outside surface for streaks of dried food originating at the top of the jar. Look at the contents for rising air bubbles and unnatural color.

While opening the jar, smell for unnatural odors and look for spurting liquid and cotton-like mold growth (white, blue, black, or green) on the top food surface and underside of lid. Do not taste food from a stored jar you discover to have an unsealed lid or that otherwise shows signs of spoilage.

All suspect containers of spoiled, low-acid foods should be treated as having produced botulinum toxin and should be handled carefully as follows:

- If the suspect glass jars are unsealed, open, or leaking, they should be detoxified before disposal.
- If the suspect glass jars are sealed, remove lids and detoxify the entire jar, contents, and lids.

▲ You can cover lids with decorative cloth and ribbons to make an attractive gift.

Detoxification Process

Carefully place the suspect containers and lids on their sides in an eight-quart-volume or larger stockpot, pan, or boiling-water canner. Wash your hands thoroughly. Carefully add water to the pot. The water should completely cover the containers with a minimum of 1 inch of water above the containers. Avoid splashing the water. Place a lid on the pot and heat the water to boiling. Boil 30 minutes to ensure detoxifying the food and all container components. Cool and discard lids and food in the trash or bury in soil.

Thoroughly clean all counters, containers, and equipment including can opener, clothing, and hands that may have come in contact with the food or the containers. Discard any sponges or washcloths that were used in the cleanup. Place them in a plastic bag and discard in the trash.

Canned Foods for Special Diets

The cost of commercially canned, special diet food often prompts interest in preparing these products at home. Some low-sugar and low-salt foods may be easily and safely canned at home. However, it may take some experimentation to create a product with the desired color, flavor, and texture. Start with a small batch and then make appropriate adjustments before producing large quantities.

Canning without Sugar

In canning regular fruits without sugar, it is very important to select fully ripe but firm fruits of the best quality. It is generally best to can fruit in its own juice, but blends of unsweetened apple, pineapple, and white grape juice are also good for pouring over solid fruit pieces. Adjust headspaces and lids and use the processing recommendations for regular fruits. Add sugar substitutes, if desired, when serving.

▲ Canned fruits are perfect for use in baking.

Fruit

There's nothing quite like opening a jar of home-preserved strawberries in the middle of a winter snowstorm. It takes you right back to the warm, early-summer sunshine, the smell of the strawberry patch's damp earth, and the feel of the firm berries as you snipped them from the vines. Best of all, you get to indulge in the sweet, summery flavor even as the snow swirls outside the windows.

Preserving fruit is simple, safe, and it allows you to enjoy the fruits of your summer's labor all year-round. On the following pages, you will find reference charts for processing various fruits and fruit products in a dial-gauge pressure canner or a weighted-gauge pressure canner. The same information is also included with each recipe's directions. In some cases, a boiling-water canner will serve better; for these instances, directions for its use are offered instead.

Adding syrup to canned fruit helps to retain its flavor, color, and shape, although it does not prevent spoilage. To maintain the most natural flavor, use the Very Light Syrup listed in the table found on page 120. Many fruits that are typically packed in heavy syrup are just as good—and a lot better for you—when packed in lighter syrups. However, if you're preserving fruit that's on the sour side, like cherries or tart apples, you might want to splurge on one of the sweeter versions.

Process Times for Fruits and Fruit Products in a Dial-Gauge Pressure Canner*

Type of Fruit	Style of Pack	Jar Size	Process Time	Canner Pressure (PSI) at Altitudes of:			
				0–2,000 ft	2,001–4,000 ft	4,001–6,000 ft	6,001–8,000 ft
Applesauce	Hot	Pints	8 minutes	6 lbs	7 lbs	8 lbs	9 lbs
	Hot	Quarts	10 minutes	6 lbs	7 lbs	8 lbs	9 lbs
Apples, sliced	Hot	Pints or Quarts	8 minutes	6 lbs	7 lbs	8 lbs	9 lbs
Berries, whole	Hot	Pints or Quarts	8 minutes	6 lbs	7 lbs	8 lbs	9 lbs
	Raw	Pints	8 minutes	6 lbs	7 lbs	8 lbs	9 lbs
	Raw	Quarts	10 minutes	6 lbs	7 lbs	8 lbs	9 lbs
Cherries, sour or sweet	Hot	Pints	8 minutes	6 lbs	7 lbs	8 lbs	9 lbs
	Hot	Quarts	10 minutes	6 lbs	7 lbs	8 lbs	9 lbs
	Raw	Pints or Quarts	10 minutes	6 lbs	7 lbs	8 lbs	9 lbs
Fruit purées	Hot	Pints or Quarts	8 minutes	6 lbs	7 lbs	8 lbs	9 lbs
Grapefruit or orange sections	Hot	Pints or Quarts	8 minutes	6 lbs	7 lbs	8 lbs	9 lbs
	Raw	Pints	8 minutes	6 lbs	7 lbs	8 lbs	9 lbs
	Raw	Quarts	10 minutes	6 lbs	7 lbs	8 lbs	9 lbs
Peaches, apricots, or nectarines	Hot or Raw	Pints or Quarts	10 minutes	6 lbs	7 lbs	8 lbs	9 lbs
Pears	Hot	Pints or Quarts	10 minutes	6 lbs	7 lbs	8 lbs	9 lbs
Plums	Hot or Raw	Pints or Quarts	10 minutes	6 lbs	7 lbs	8 lbs	9 lbs
Rhubarb	Hot	Pints or Quarts	8 minutes	6 lbs	7 lbs	8 lbs	9 lbs

*After the process is complete, turn off the heat and remove the canner lid. Wait 5 to 10 minutes before removing jars.

Process Times for Fruits and Fruit Products in a Weighted-Gauge Pressure Canner*

Type of Fruit	Style of Pack	Jar Size	Process Time	Canner Pressure (PSI) at Altitudes of:	
				0–1,000 ft	Above 1,000 ft
Applesauce	Hot	Pints	8 minutes	5 lbs	10 lbs
	Hot	Quarts	10 minutes	5 lbs	10 lbs
Apples, sliced	Hot	Pints or Quarts	8 minutes	5 lbs	10 lbs
Berries, whole	Hot	Pints or Quarts	8 minutes	5 lbs	10 lbs
	Raw	Pints	8 minutes	5 lbs	10 lbs
	Raw	Quarts	10 minutes	5 lbs	10 lbs
Cherries, sour or sweet	Hot	Pints	8 minutes	5 lbs	10 lbs
	Hot	Quarts	10 minutes	5 lbs	10 lbs
	Raw	Pints or Quarts	10 minutes	5 lbs	10 lbs
Fruit purées	Hot	Pints or Quarts	8 minutes	5 lbs	10 lbs
Grapefruit or orange sections	Hot	Pints or Quarts	8 minutes	5 lbs	10 lbs
	Raw	Pints	8 minutes	5 lbs	10 lbs
	Raw	Quarts	10 minutes	5 lbs	10 lbs
Peaches, apricots, or nectarines	Hot or Raw	Pints or Quarts	10 minutes	5 lbs	10 lbs
Pears	Hot	Pints or Quarts	10 minutes	5 lbs	10 lbs
Plums	Hot or Raw	Pints or Quarts	10 minutes	5 lbs	10 lbs
Rhubarb	Hot	Pints or Quarts	8 minutes	5 lbs	10 lbs

*After the process is complete, turn off the heat and remove the canner lid. Wait 5 to 10 minutes before removing jars.

Syrups

Adding syrup to canned fruit helps to retain its flavor, color, and shape, although jars still need to be processed to prevent spoilage. Follow the chart on the right for syrups of varying sweetness. Light corn syrups or mild-flavored honey may be used to replace up to half the table sugar called for in syrups.

Directions
1. Bring water and sugar to a boil in a medium saucepan.
2. Pour over raw fruits in jars.

TIP

For hot packs, bring water and sugar to boil, add fruit, reheat to boil, and fill into jars immediately.

Sugar and Water in Syrup

Syrup Type	Approx. % Sugar	Measures of Water and Sugar				Fruits Commonly Packed in Syrup
		For 9-Pt Load*		For 7-Qt Load		
		Cups Water	Cups Sugar	Cups Water	Cups Sugar	
Very Light	10	6½	¾	10½	1¼	Approximates natural sugar levels in most fruits and adds the fewest calories.
Light	20	5¾	1½	9	2¼	Very sweet fruit. Try a small amount the first time to see if your family likes it.
Medium	30	5¼	2¼	8¼	3¾	Sweet apples, sweet cherries, berries, and grapes.
Heavy	40	5	3¼	7¾	5¼	Tart apples, apricots, sour cherries, gooseberries, nectarines, peaches, pears, plums.
Very Heavy	50	4¼	4¼	6½	6¾	Very sour fruit. Try a small amount the first time to see if your family likes it.

*This amount is also adequate for a four-quart load.

Apple Juice

The best apple juice is made from a blend of varieties. If you don't have your own apple press, try to buy fresh juice from a local cider maker within 24 hours after it has been pressed.

Directions

1. Refrigerate juice for 24 to 48 hours.
2. Without mixing, carefully pour off clear liquid and discard sediment. Strain the clear liquid through a paper coffee filter or double layers of damp cheesecloth.
3. Heat quickly in a saucepan, stirring occasionally, until juice begins to boil.
4. Fill immediately into sterile pint or quart jars or into clean, half-gallon jars, leaving ¼-inch headspace.
5. Adjust lids and process. See left for recommended times for a boiling-water canner.

Process Times for Apple Juice in a Boiling-Water Canner*

Style of Pack	Jar Size	Process Time at Altitudes of:		
		0–1,000 ft	1,001–6,000 ft	Above 6,000 ft
Hot	Pints or Quarts	5 min	10 min	15 min
	Half-gallons	10 min	15 min	20 min

*After the process is complete, turn off the heat and remove the canner lid. Wait five minutes before removing jars.

Apple Butter

The best apple varieties to use for apple butter include Jonathan, Winesap, Stayman, Golden Delicious, and Macintosh apples, but any of your favorite varieties will work. Don't bother to peel the apples, as you will strain the fruit before cooking it. This recipe will yield eight to nine pints.

Ingredients

8 lbs apples

2 cups cider

2 cups vinegar

2¼ cups white sugar

2¼ cups packed brown sugar

2 tbsp ground cinnamon

1 tbsp ground cloves

Directions

1. Wash, stem, quarter, and core apples.
2. Cook slowly in cider and vinegar until soft. Press fruit through a colander, food mill, or strainer.
3. Cook fruit pulp with sugar and spices, stirring frequently. To test for doneness, remove a spoonful and hold it away from steam for 2 minutes. If the butter remains mounded on

the spoon, it is done. If you're still not sure, spoon a small quantity onto a plate. When a rim of liquid does not separate around the edge of the butter, it is ready for canning.

4. Fill while hot into sterile half-pint or pint jars, leaving ¼-inch headspace. Quart jars need not be pre-sterilized.

Process Times for Apple Butter in a Boiling-Water Canner*

Style of Pack	Jar Size	Process Time at Altitudes of:		
		0–1,000 ft	1,001–6,000 ft	Above 6,000 ft
Hot	Half-pints or Pints	5 minutes	10 minutes	15 minutes
	Quarts	10 minutes	15 minutes	20 minutes

*After the process is complete, turn off the heat and remove the canner lid. Wait five minutes before removing jars.

Applesauce

Besides being delicious on its own or paired with dishes like pork chops or latkes, applesauce can be used as a butter substitute in many baked goods. Select apples that are sweet, juicy, and crisp. For a tart flavor, add one to two pounds of tart apples to each three pounds of sweeter fruit.

Quantity
1. An average of 21 pounds of apples is needed per canner load of seven quarts.
2. An average of 13½ pounds of apples is needed per canner load of nine pints.
3. A bushel weighs 48 pounds and yields 14 to 19 quarts of sauce—an average of three pounds per quart.

Directions
1. Wash, peel, and core apples. Slice apples into water containing a little lemon juice to prevent browning.
2. Place drained slices in an 8- to 10-quart pot. Add ½ cup water. Stirring occasionally to prevent burning, heat quickly until tender (5 to 20 minutes, depending on maturity and variety).
3. Press through a sieve or food mill, or skip the pressing step if you prefer chunky-style sauce. Sauce may be packed without sugar, but if desired, sweeten to taste (start with ⅛ cup sugar per quart of sauce).
4. Reheat sauce to boiling. Fill jars with hot sauce, leaving ½-inch headspace. Adjust lids and process.

Process Times for Applesauce in a Boiling-Water Canner*

Style of Pack	Jar Size	Process Time at Altitudes of:			
		0–1,000 ft	1,001–3,000 ft	3,001–6,000 ft	Above 6,000 ft
Hot	Pints	15 minutes	20 minutes	20 minutes	25 minutes
	Quarts	20 minutes	25 minutes	30 minutes	35 minutes

*After the process is complete, turn off the heat and remove the canner lid. Wait five minutes before removing jars.

Process Times for Applesauce in a Dial-Gauge Pressure Canner*

Style of Pack	Jar Size	Process Time	Canner Pressure (PSI) at Altitudes of:			
			0–2,000 ft	2,001–4,000 ft	4,001–6,000 ft	6,001–8,000 ft
Hot	Pints	8 minutes	6 lbs	7 lbs	8 lbs	9 lbs
	Quarts	10 minutes	6 lbs	7 lbs	8 lbs	9 lbs

*After the canner is completely depressurized, remove the weight from the vent port or open the petcock. Wait 10 minutes; then unfasten the lid and remove it carefully. Lift the lid with the underside away from you so that the steam coming out of the canner does not burn your face.

Process Times for Applesauce in a Weighted-Gauge Pressure Canner*

| Style of Pack | Jar Size | Process Time | Canner Pressure (PSI) at Altitudes of: | |
			0–1,000 ft	Above 1,000 ft
Hot	Pints	8 minutes	5 lbs	10 lbs
	Quarts	10 minutes	5 lbs	10 lbs

*After the canner is completely depressurized, remove the weight from the vent port or open the petcock. Wait 10 minutes, then unfasten the lid and remove it carefully. Lift the lid with the underside away from you so that the steam coming out of the canner does not burn your face.

Apricots, Halved or Sliced

Apricots are excellent in baked goods, stuffing, chutney, or on their own. Choose firm, well-colored, mature fruit for best results.

Quantity
- An average of 16 pounds is needed per canner load of seven quarts.
- An average of 10 pounds is needed per canner load of nine pints.
- A bushel weighs 50 pounds and yields 20 to 25 quarts—an average of 2¼ pounds per quart.

Directions
1. Dip fruit in boiling water for 30 to 60 seconds until skins loosen. Dip quickly in cold water and slip off skins.
2. Cut in half, remove pits, and slice if desired. To prevent darkening, keep peeled fruit in water with a little lemon juice.
3. Prepare and boil a very light, light, or medium syrup (see page 121) or pack apricots in water, apple juice, or white grape juice.

Process Times for Halved or Sliced Apricots in a Dial-Gauge Pressure Canner*

| Style of Pack | Jar Size | Process Time | Canner Pressure (PSI) at Altitudes of: | | | |
			0–2,000 ft	2,001–4,000 ft	4,001–6,000 ft	6,001–8,000 ft
Hot or Raw	Pints or Quarts	10 minutes	6 lbs	7 lbs	8 lbs	9 lbs

*After the process is complete, turn off the heat and remove the canner lid. Wait five minutes before removing jars.

Process Times for Halved or Sliced Apricots in a Weighted-Gauge Pressure Canner*

| Style of Pack | Jar Size | Process Time | Canner Pressure (PSI) at Altitudes of: | |
			0–1,000 ft	Above 1,000 ft
Hot or Raw	Pints or Quarts	10 minutes	5 lbs	10 lbs

*After the process is complete, turn off the heat and remove the canner lid. Wait five minutes before removing jars.

Berries, Whole

Preserved berries are perfect for use in pies, muffins, pancakes, or in poultry or pork dressings. Nearly every berry preserves well, including blackberries, blueberries, currants, dewberries, elderberries, gooseberries, huckleberries, loganberries, mulberries, and raspberries. Choose ripe, sweet berries with uniform color.

Quantity
- An average of 12 pounds is needed per canner load of seven quarts.
- An average of 8 pounds is needed per canner load of nine pints.
- A 24-quart crate weighs 36 pounds and yields 18 to 24 quarts—an average of 1¾ pounds per quart.

Directions
1. Wash 1 or 2 quarts of berries at a time. Drain, cap, and stem if necessary. For gooseberries, snip off heads and tails with scissors.
2. Prepare and boil preferred syrup, if desired (see page 121). Add ½ cup syrup, juice, or water to each clean jar.

Hot pack—(Best for blueberries, currants, elderberries, gooseberries, and huckleberries) Heat berries in boiling water for 30 seconds and drain. Fill jars and cover with hot juice, leaving ½-inch headspace.

▲ Choose ripe, fresh berries for canning.

Raw pack—Fill jars with any of the raw berries, shaking down gently while filling. Cover with hot syrup, juice, or water, leaving ½-inch headspace.

Recommended Process Times for Whole Berries in a Boiling-Water Canner*

Style of Pack	Jar Size	Process Time at Altitudes of:			
		0–1,000 ft	1,001–3,000 ft	3,001–6,000 ft	Above 6,000 ft
Hot	Pints or Quarts	15 minutes	20 minutes	20 minutes	25 minutes
Raw	Pints	15 minutes	20 minutes	20 minutes	25 minutes
	Quarts	20 minutes	25 minutes	30 minutes	35 minutes

*After the process is complete, turn off the heat and remove the canner lid. Wait five minutes before removing jars.

Process Times for Whole Berries in a Dial-Gauge Pressure Canner*

Style of Pack	Jar Size	Process Time	Canner Pressure (PSI) at Altitudes of:			
			0–2,000 ft	2,001–4,000 ft	4,001–6,000 ft	6,001–8,000 ft
Hot	Pints or Quarts	8 minutes	6 lbs	7 lbs	8 lbs	9 lbs
Raw	Pints	8 minutes	6 lbs	7 lbs	8 lbs	9 lbs
Raw	Quarts	10 minutes	6 lbs	7 lbs	8 lbs	9 lbs

*After the process is complete, turn off the heat and remove the canner lid. Wait five minutes before removing jars.

Process Times for Whole Berries in a Weighted-Gauge Pressure Canner*

Style of Pack	Jar Size	Process Time	Canner Pressure (PSI) at Altitudes of:	
			0–1,000 ft	Above 1,000 ft
Hot	Pints or Quarts	8 minutes	5 lbs	10 lbs
Raw	Pints	8 minutes	5 lbs	10 lbs
Raw	Quarts	10 minutes	5 lbs	10 lbs

*After the process is complete, turn off the heat and remove the canner lid. Wait five minutes before removing jars.

Berry Syrup

Juices from fresh or frozen blueberries, cherries, grapes, raspberries (black or red), and strawberries are easily made into toppings for use on ice cream and pastries. For an elegant finish to cheesecakes or pound cakes, drizzle a thin stream in a zigzag across the top just before serving. Berry syrups are also great additions to smoothies or milkshakes. This recipe makes about nine half-pints.

Directions

1. Select 6½ cups of fresh or frozen berries of your choice. Wash, cap, and stem berries and crush in a saucepan.
2. Heat to boiling and simmer until soft (5 to 10 minutes). Strain hot through a colander placed in a large pan and drain until cool enough to handle.
3. Strain the collected juice through a double layer of cheesecloth or jelly bag. Discard the dry pulp. The yield of the pressed juice should be about 4½ to 5 cups.
4. Combine the juice with 6¾ cups of sugar in a large saucepan, bring to a boil, and simmer 1 minute.
5. Fill into clean half-pint or pint jars, leaving ½-inch headspace. Adjust lids and process.

TIP To make syrup with whole berries, rather than crushed, save 1 or 2 cups of the fresh or frozen fruit, combine these with the sugar, and simmer until soft. Remove from heat, skim off foam, and fill into clean jars, following processing directions for regular berry syrup.

Process Times for Berry Syrup in a Boiling-Water Canner*

Style of Pack	Jar Size	Process Time at Altitudes of:		
		0–1,000 ft	1,001–6,000 ft	Above 6,000 ft
Hot	Half-pints or Pints	10 minutes	15 minutes	20 minutes

*After the process is complete, turn off the heat and remove the canner lid. Wait five minutes before removing jars.

Fruit Purées

Almost any fruit can be puréed for use as baby food, in sauces, or just as a nutritious snack. Puréed prunes and apples can be used as a butter replacement in many baked goods. Use this recipe for any fruit except figs and tomatoes.

Directions

1. Stem, wash, drain, peel, and remove pits if necessary. Measure fruit into large saucepan, crushing slightly if desired.
2. Add 1 cup hot water for each quart of fruit. Cook slowly until fruit is soft, stirring frequently. Press through sieve or food mill. If desired, add sugar to taste.
3. Reheat pulp to boil, or until sugar dissolves (if added). Fill hot into clean jars, leaving ¼-inch headspace. Adjust lids and process.

Process Times for Fruit Purées in a Boiling-Water Canner*

Style of Pack	Jar Size	Process Time at Altitudes of:		
		0–1,000 ft	1,001–6,000 ft	Above 6,000 ft
Hot	Pints or Quarts	15 minutes	20 minutes	25 minutes

*After the process is complete, turn off the heat and remove the canner lid. Wait five minutes before removing jars.

Process Times for Fruit Purées in a Dial-Gauge Pressure Canner*

Style of Pack	Jar Size	Process Time	Canner Pressure (PSI) at Altitudes of:			
			0–2,000 ft	2,001–4,000 ft	4,001–6,000 ft	6,001–8,000 ft
Hot	Pints or Quarts	8 minutes	6 lbs	7 lbs	8 lbs	9 lbs

*After the canner is completely depressurized, remove the weight from the vent port or open the petcock. Wait 10 minutes, then unfasten the lid and remove it carefully. Lift the lid with the underside away from you so that the steam coming out of the canner does not burn your face.

Process Times for Fruit Purées in a Weighted-Gauge Pressure Canner*

Style of Pack	Jar Size	Process Time (Min)	Canner Pressure (PSI) at Altitudes of:	
			0–1,000 ft	Above 1,000 ft
Hot	Pints or Quarts	8 minutes	5 lbs	10 lbs

*After the canner is completely depressurized, remove the weight from the vent port or open the petcock. Wait 10 minutes; then unfasten the lid and remove it carefully. Lift the lid with the underside away from you so that the steam coming out of the canner does not burn your face.

Grape Juice

Purple grapes are full of antioxidants and help to reduce the risk of heart disease, cancer, and Alzheimer's disease. For juice, select sweet, well-colored, firm, mature fruit.

Quantity

- An average of 24½ pounds is needed per canner load of seven quarts.
- An average of 16 pounds per canner load of nine pints.
- A lug weighs 26 pounds and yields seven to nine quarts of juice—an average of 3½ pounds per quart.

Directions

1. Wash and stem grapes. Place grapes in a saucepan and add boiling water to cover. Heat and simmer slowly until skin is soft.
2. Strain through a damp jelly bag or double layers of cheesecloth, and discard solids. Refrigerate juice for 24 to 48 hours.
3. Without mixing, carefully pour off clear liquid and save; discard sediment. If desired, strain through a paper coffee filter for a clearer juice.
4. Add juice to a saucepan and sweeten to taste. Heat and stir until sugar is dissolved. Continue heating with occasional stirring until juice begins to boil. Fill into jars immediately, leaving ¼-inch headspace. Adjust lids and process.

Process Times for Grape Juice in a Boiling-Water Canner*

Style of Pack	Jar Size	Process Time at Altitudes of:		
		0–1,000 ft	1,001–6,000 ft	Above 6,000 ft
Hot	Pints or Quarts	5 minutes	10 minutes	15 minutes
	Half-gallons	10 minutes	15 minutes	20 minutes

*After the process is complete, turn off the heat and remove the canner lid. Wait five minutes before removing jars.

Peaches, Halved or Sliced

Peaches are delicious in cobblers, crisps, and muffins, or grilled for a unique cake topping. Choose ripe, mature fruit with minimal bruising.

Quantity

- An average of 17½ pounds is needed per canner load of seven quarts.
- An average of 11 pounds is needed per canner load of nine pints.
- A bushel weighs 48 pounds and yields 16 to 24 quarts—an average of 2½ pounds per quart.

Directions

1. Dip fruit in boiling water for 30 to 60 seconds until skins loosen. Dip quickly in cold water and slip off skins. Cut in half, remove pits, and slice if desired. To prevent darkening, keep peeled fruit in ascorbic acid solution.
2. Prepare and boil a very light, light, or medium syrup or pack peaches in water, apple juice, or white grape juice. Raw packs make poor-quality peaches.

Hot pack—In a large saucepan, place drained fruit in syrup, water, or juice and bring to a boil. Fill jars with hot fruit and cooking liquid, leaving ½-inch headspace. Place halves in layers, cut side down.

Raw pack—Fill jars with raw fruit, cut side down, and add hot water, juice, or syrup, leaving ½-inch headspace.

3. Adjust lids and process.

Process Times for Halved or Sliced Peaches in a Boiling-Water Canner*

Style of Pack	Jar Size	Process Time at Altitudes of:			
		0–1,000 ft	1,001–3,000 ft	3,001–6,000 ft	Above 6,000 ft
Hot	Pints	20 minutes	25 minutes	30 minutes	35 minutes
	Quarts	25 minutes	30 minutes	35 minutes	40 minutes
Raw	Pints	25 minutes	30 minutes	35 minutes	40 minutes
	Quarts	30 minutes	35 minutes	40 minutes	45 minutes

*After the process is complete, turn off the heat and remove the canner lid. Wait five minutes before removing jars.

Process Times for Halved or Sliced Peaches in a Dial-Gauge Pressure Canner*

Style of Pack	Jar Size	Process Time	Canner Pressure (PSI) at Altitudes of:			
			0–2,000 ft	2,001–4,000 ft	4,001–6,000 ft	6,001–8,000 ft
Hot or Raw	Pints or Quarts	10 minutes	6 lbs	7 lbs	8 lbs	9 lbs

*After the canner is completely depressurized, remove the weight from the vent port or open the petcock. Wait 10 minutes; then unfasten the lid and remove it carefully. Lift the lid with the underside away from you so that the steam coming out of the canner does not burn your face.

Process Times for Halved or Sliced Peaches in a Weighted-Gauge Pressure Canner*

Style of Pack	Jar Size	Process Time	Canner Pressure (PSI) at Altitudes of:	
			0–1,000 ft	Above 1,000 ft
Hot or Raw	Pints or Quarts	10 minutes	5 lbs	10 lbs

*After the canner is completely depressurized, remove the weight from the vent port or open the petcock. Wait 10 minutes; then unfasten the lid and remove it carefully. Lift the lid with the underside away from you so that the steam coming out of the canner does not burn your face.

Pears, Halved

Choose ripe, mature fruit for best results. For a special treat, filled halved pears with a mixture of chopped dried apricots, pecans, brown sugar, and butter; bake or microwave until warm and serve with vanilla ice cream.

Quantity

- An average of 17½ pounds is needed per canner load of seven quarts.
- An average of 11 pounds is needed per canner load of nine pints.
- A bushel weighs 50 pounds and yields 16 to 25 quarts—an average of 2½ pounds per quart.

Directions

1. Wash and peel pears. Cut lengthwise in halves and remove core. A melon baller or metal measuring spoon works well for coring pears. To prevent discoloration, keep pears in water with a little lemon juice.
2. Prepare a very light, light, or medium syrup (see page 121) or use apple juice, white grape juice, or water. Raw packs make poor quality pears. Boil drained pears for five minutes in syrup, juice, or water. Fill jars with hot fruit and cooking liquid, leaving ½-inch headspace. Adjust lids and process.

Process Times for Halved Pears in a Boiling-Water Canner*

Style of Pack	Jar Size	Process Time at Altitudes of:			
		0–1,000 ft	1,001–3,000 ft	3,001–6,000 ft	Above 6,000 ft
Hot	Pints	20 minutes	25 minutes	30 minutes	35 minutes
	Quarts	25 minutes	30 minutes	35 minutes	40 minutes

*After the process is complete, turn off the heat and remove the canner lid. Wait five minutes before removing jars.

Process Times for Halved Pears in a Dial-Gauge Pressure Canner*

Style of Pack	Jar Size	Process Time	Canner Pressure (PSI) at Altitudes of:			
			0–2,000 ft	2,001–4,000 ft	4,001–6,000 ft	6,001–8,000 ft
Hot	Pints or Quarts	10 minutes	6 lbs	7 lbs	8 lbs	9 lbs

*After the canner is completely depressurized, remove the weight from the vent port or open the petcock. Wait 10 minutes; then unfasten the lid and remove it carefully. Lift the lid with the underside away from you so that the steam coming out of the canner does not burn your face.

Process Times for Halved Pears in a Weighted-Gauge Pressure Canner*

Style of Pack	Jar Size	Process Time	Canner Pressure (PSI) at Altitudes of:	
			0–1,000 ft	Above 1,000 ft
Hot	Pints or Quarts	10 minutes	5 lbs	10 lbs

*After the canner is completely depressurized, remove the weight from the vent port or open the petcock. Wait 10 minutes; then unfasten the lid and remove it carefully. Lift the lid with the underside away from you so that the steam coming out of the canner does not burn your face.

Rhubarb, Stewed

Rhubarb in the garden is a sure sign that spring has sprung and summer is well on its way. But why not enjoy rhubarb all year-round? The brilliant red stalks make it as appropriate for a holiday table as for an early summer feast. Rhubarb is also delicious in crisps, cobblers, or served hot over ice cream. Select young, tender, well-colored stalks from the spring or, if available, late fall crop.

Quantity

- An average of 10½ pounds is needed per canner load of seven quarts.
- An average of 7 pounds is needed per canner load of nine pints.
- A lug weighs 28 pounds and yields 14 to 28 quarts—an average of 1½ pounds per quart.

Directions

1. Trim off leaves. Wash stalks and cut into ½-inch to 1-inch pieces.
2. Place rhubarb in a large saucepan, and add ½ cup sugar for each quart of fruit. Let stand until juice appears. Heat gently to boiling. Fill jars without delay, leaving ½-inch headspace. Adjust lids and process.

Process Times for Stewed Rhubarb in a Boiling-Water Canner*

Style of Pack	Jar Size	Process Time at Altitudes of:		
		0–1,000 ft	1,001–6,000 ft	Above 6,000 ft
Hot	Pints or Quarts	15 minutes	20 minutes	25 minutes

*After the process is complete, turn off the heat and remove the canner lid. Wait five minutes before removing jars.

Process Times for Stewed Rhubarb in a Dial-Gauge Pressure Canner*

Style of Pack	Jar Size	Process Time	Canner Pressure (PSI) at Altitudes of:			
			0–2,000 ft	2,001–4,000 ft	4,001–6,000 ft	6,001–8,000 ft
Hot	Pints or Quarts	8 minutes	6 lbs	7 lbs	8 lbs	9 lbs

*After the canner is completely depressurized, remove the weight from the vent port or open the petcock. Wait 10 minutes; then unfasten the lid and remove it carefully. Lift the lid with the underside away from you so that the steam coming out of the canner does not burn your face.

Process Times for Stewed Rhubarb in a Weighted-Gauge Pressure Canner*

Style of Pack	Jar Size	Process Time	Canner Pressure (PSI) at Altitudes of:	
			0–1,000 ft	Above 1,000 ft
Hot	Pints or Quarts	8 minutes	5 lbs	10 lbs

*After the canner is completely depressurized, remove the weight from the vent port or open the petcock. Wait 10 minutes; then unfasten the lid and remove it carefully. Lift the lid with the underside away from you so that the steam coming out of the canner does not burn your face.

Canned Pie Fillings

Using a pre-made pie filling will cut your pie preparation time by more than half, but most commercially produced fillings are oozing with high fructose corn syrup and all manner of artificial coloring and flavoring. (Food coloring is not at all necessary, but if you're really concerned about how the inside of your pie will look, appropriate amounts are added to each recipe as an optional ingredient.) Making and preserving your own pie fillings means that you can use your own fresh ingredients and adjust the sweetness to your taste. Because some folks like their pies rich and sweet and others prefer a natural tart flavor, you might want to first make a single quart, make a pie with it, and see how you like it. Then you can adjust the sugar and spices in the recipe to suit your personal preferences before making a large batch. Experiment with combining fruits or adding different spices, but the amount of lemon juice should not be altered, as it aids in controlling the safety and storage stability of the fillings.

These recipes use Clear Jel (sometimes sold as Clear Jel A), a chemically modified cornstarch that produces excellent sauce consistency even after fillings are canned and baked. Look for brands of Clear Jel that are labeled non-GMO, and note that you do NOT want Instant Clear Jel for these recipes. By using Clear Jel, you can lower the sugar content of your fillings without sacrificing safety, flavor, or texture. (Note: Instant Clear Jel is not meant to be cooked and should not be used for these recipes. Sure-Gel is a natural fruit pectin and is not a suitable substitute for Clear Jel. Cornstarch, tapioca starch, or arrowroot starch can be used in place of Clear Jel, but the finished product is likely to be runny.) One pound of Clear Jel costs less than five dollars and is enough to make fillings for about 14 pies. It will keep for at least a year if stored in a cool, dry place. Clear Jel

is increasingly available among canning and freezing supplies in some stores. Alternately, you can order it by the pound at any of the following online stores:
- www.barryfarm.com
- www.kitchenkrafts.com
- www.theingredientstore.com

> **TIP** When using frozen cherries and blueberries, select unsweetened fruit. If sugar has been added, rinse it off while fruit is frozen. Thaw fruit, then collect, measure, and use juice from fruit to partially replace the water specified in the recipe.

Apple Pie Filling

Use firm, crisp apples, such as Stayman, Golden Delicious, or Rome varieties for the best results. If apples lack tartness, use an additional ¼ cup of lemon juice for each 6 quarts of slices. Ingredients are included for a one-quart (enough for one 8-inch pie) or a seven-quart recipe.

Ingredients

	1 Quart	7 Quarts
Blanched, sliced fresh apples	3½ cups	6 quarts
Granulated sugar	¾ cup + 2 tbsp	5½ cups
Clear Jel®	¼ cup	1½ cups
Cinnamon	¼ tsp	1 tbsp
Cold water	½ cup	2½ cups
Apple juice	¾ cup	5 cups
Bottled lemon juice	2 tbsp	¾ cup
Nutmeg (optional)	⅛ tsp	1 tsp

Directions

1. Wash, peel, and core apples. Prepare slices ½ inch wide and place in water containing a little lemon juice to prevent browning.
2. For fresh fruit, place 6 cups at a time in 1 gallon of boiling water. Boil each batch 1 minute after the water returns to a boil. Drain, but keep heated fruit in a covered bowl or pot.
3. Combine sugar, Clear Jel, and cinnamon in a large kettle with water and apple juice. Add nutmeg, if desired. Stir and cook on medium-high heat until mixture thickens and begins to bubble.
4. Add lemon juice and boil 1 minute, stirring constantly. Fold in drained apple slices immediately and fill jars with mixture without delay, leaving 1-inch headspace. Adjust lids and process immediately.

Process Times for Apple Pie Filling in a Boiling-Water Canner*

Style of Pack	Jar Size	Process Time at Altitudes of:			
		0–1,000 ft	1,001–3,000 ft	3,001–6,000 ft	Above 6,000 ft
Hot	Pints or Quarts	25 minutes	30 minutes	35 minutes	40 minutes

*After the process is complete, turn off the heat and remove the canner lid. Wait five minutes before removing jars.

Blueberry Pie Filling

Select fresh, ripe, and firm blueberries. Unsweetened frozen blueberries may be used. If sugar has been added, rinse it off while fruit is still frozen. Thaw fruit, then collect, measure, and use juice from fruit to partially replace the water specified in the recipe. Ingredients are included for a one-quart (enough for one 8-inch pie) or seven-quart recipe.

Ingredients

	1 Quart	7 Quarts
Fresh or thawed blueberries	3½ cups	6 quarts
Granulated sugar	¾ cup + 2 tbsp	6 cups
Clear Jel®	¼ cup + 1 tbsp	2¼ cups
Cold water	1 cup	7 cups
Bottled lemon juice	3½ cups	½ cup
Blue food coloring (optional)	3 drops	20 drops
Red food coloring (optional)	1 drop	7 drops

Directions

1. Wash and drain blueberries. Place 6 cups at a time in 1 gallon boiling water. Allow water to return to a boil and cook each batch for 1 minute. Drain but keep heated fruit in a covered bowl or pot.
2. Combine sugar and Clear Jel in a large kettle. Stir. Add water and food coloring if desired. Cook on medium-high heat until mixture thickens and begins to bubble.
3. Add lemon juice and boil 1 minute, stirring constantly. Fold in drained berries immediately and fill jars with mixture without delay, leaving 1-inch headspace. Adjust lids and process immediately.

Process Times for Blueberry Pie Filling in a Boiling-Water Canner*

Style of Pack	Jar Size	Process Time at Altitudes of:			
		0–1,000 ft	1,001–3,000 ft	3,001–6,000 ft	Above 6,000 ft
Hot	Pints or Quarts	30 minutes	35 minutes	40 minutes	45 minutes

*After the process is complete, turn off the heat and remove the canner lid. Wait five minutes before removing jars.

Cherry Pie Filling

Select fresh, very ripe, and firm cherries. Unsweetened frozen cherries may be used. If sugar has been added, rinse it off while the fruit is still frozen. Thaw fruit, then collect, measure, and use juice from fruit to partially replace the water specified in the recipe. Ingredients are included for a one-quart (enough for one 8-inch pie) or seven-quart recipe.

Ingredients

	1 Quart	7 Quarts
Fresh or thawed sour cherries	3⅓ cups	6 quarts
Granulated sugar	1 cup	7 cups
Clear Jel®	¼ cup + 1 tbsp	1¾ cups
Cold water	1⅓ cups	9⅓ cups
Bottled lemon juice	1 tbsp + 1 tsp	½ cup
Cinnamon (optional)	⅛ tsp	1 tsp
Almond extract (optional)	¼ tsp	2 tsp
Red food coloring (optional)	6 drops	¼ tsp

Directions

1. Rinse and pit fresh cherries, and hold in cold water. To prevent stem end from browning, use water with a little lemon juice. Place 6 cups at a time in 1 gallon boiling water. Boil each batch 1 minute after the water returns to a boil. Drain but keep heated fruit in a covered bowl or pot.
2. Combine sugar and Clear Jel in a large saucepan and add water. If desired, add cinnamon, almond extract, and food coloring. Stir mixture and cook over medium-high heat until mixture thickens and begins to bubble.
3. Add lemon juice and boil 1 minute, stirring constantly. Fold in drained cherries immediately and fill jars with mixture without delay, leaving 1-inch headspace. Adjust lids and process immediately.

Process Times for Cherry Pie Filling in a Boiling-Water Canner*

Style of Pack	Jar Size	Process Time at Altitudes of:			
		0–1,000 ft	1,001–3,000 ft	3,001–6,000 ft	Above 6,000 ft
Hot	Pints or Quarts	30 minutes	35 minutes	40 minutes	45 minutes

*After the process is complete, turn off the heat and remove the canner lid. Wait five minutes before removing jars.

Festive Mincemeat Pie Filling

Mincemeat pie originated as "Christmas Pie" in the eleventh century, when the English crusaders returned from the Holy Land bearing oriental spices. They added three of these spices—cinnamon, cloves, and nutmeg—to their meat pies to represent the three gifts that the magi brought to the Christ child. Mincemeat pies are traditionally small and are perfect paired with a mug of hot buttered rum. Walnuts or pecans can be used in place of meat if preferred. This recipe yields about seven quarts.

Ingredients

2 cups finely chopped suet
4 lbs ground beef or 4 lbs ground venison and 1 lb sausage
5 qts chopped apples
2 lbs dark, seedless raisins
1 lb white raisins
2 qts apple cider
2 tbsp ground cinnamon
2 tsp ground nutmeg
½ tsp cloves
5 cups sugar
2 tbsp salt

Directions

1. Cook suet and meat in water to avoid browning. Peel, core, and quarter apples. Put suet,

meat, and apples through food grinder using a medium blade.

2. Combine all ingredients in a large saucepan and simmer 1 hour or until slightly thickened. Stir often.

3. Fill jars with mixture without delay, leaving 1-inch headspace. Adjust lids and process.

Process Times for Festive Mincemeat Pie Filling in a Dial-Gauge Pressure Canner*

Style of Pack	Jar Size	Process Time	Canner Pressure (PSI) at Altitudes of:			
			0–2,000 ft	2,001–4,000 ft	4,001–6,000 ft	6,000–8,000 ft
Hot	Quarts	90 minutes	11 lbs	12 lbs	13 lbs	14 lbs

*After the canner is completely depressurized, remove the weight from the vent port or open the petcock. Wait 10 minutes, then unfasten the lid and remove it carefully. Lift the lid with the underside away from you so that the steam coming out of the canner does not burn your face.

Process Times for Festive Mincemeat Pie Filling in a Weighted-Gauge Pressure Canner*

Style of Pack	Jar Size	Process Time	Canner Pressure (PSI) at Altitudes of:	
			0–1,000 ft	Above 1,000 ft
Hot	Quarts	90 minutes	10 lbs	15 lbs

*After the canner is completely depressurized, remove the weight from the vent port or open the petcock. Wait 10 minutes, then unfasten the lid and remove it carefully. Lift the lid with the underside away from you so that the steam coming out of the canner does not burn your face.

Jams, Jellies, and Other Fruit Spreads

Homemade jams and jellies have lots more flavor than store-bought, over-processed varieties. The combinations of fruits and spices are limitless, so have fun experimenting with these recipes. If you can bear to part with your creations when you're all done, they make wonderful gifts for any occasion.

Pectin is what makes jams and jellies thicken and gel. Many fruits, such as crab apples, citrus fruits, sour plums, currants, quinces, green apples, or Concord grapes, have plenty of their own natural pectin, so there's no need to add more pectin to your recipes. You can use less sugar when you don't add pectin, but you will have to boil the fruit for longer. Still, the process is relatively simple and you don't have to worry about having store-bought pectin on hand.

To use fresh fruits with a low-pectin content or canned or frozen fruit juice, powdered or liquid pectin must be added for your jams and jellies to thicken and set properly. Jelly or jam made with added pectin requires less cooking and generally gives a larger yield. These products have more natural fruit flavors, too. In addition, using added pectin eliminates the need to test hot jellies and jams for proper gelling.

Beginning this section are descriptions of the differences between methods and tips for success with whichever you use.

> ### Making Jams and Jellies without Added Pectin
>
> If you are not sure if a fruit has enough of its own pectin, combine 1 tablespoon of rubbing alcohol with 1 tablespoon of extracted fruit juice in a small glass. Let stand 2 minutes. If the mixture forms into one solid mass, there's plenty of pectin. If you see several weak blobs, you need to add pectin or combine with another high-pectin fruit.

Jelly without Added Pectin

Making jelly without added pectin is not an exact science. You can add a little more or less sugar according to your taste, substitute honey for up to half of the sugar, or experiment with combining small amounts of low-pectin fruits with other high-pectin fruits. The Ingredients table below shows you the basics for common high-pectin fruits. Use it as a guideline as you experiment with other fruits.

As fruit ripens, its pectin content decreases, so use fruit that has recently been picked, and mix ¾ ripe

Canning

fruit with ¼ under-ripe. Cooking cores and peels along with the fruit will also increase the pectin level. Avoid using canned or frozen fruit as they contain very little pectin. Be sure to wash all fruit thoroughly before cooking. One pound of fruit should yield at least 1 cup of clear juice.

Ingredients

Fruit	Water to be Added per Pound of Fruit	Minutes to Simmer Fruit before Extracting Juice	Ingredients Added to Each Cup of Strained Juice		Yield from 4 Cups of Juice (Half-pints)
			Sugar (Cups)	Lemon Juice (Tsp)	
Apples	1 cup	20 to 25	¾	1½ (opt)	4 to 5
Black-berries	None or ¼ cup	5 to 10	¾ to 1	None	7 to 8
Crab apples	1 cup	20 to 25	1	None	4 to 5
Grapes	None or ¼ cup	5 to 10	¾ to 1	None	8 to 9
Plums	½ cup	15 to 20	¾	None	8 to 9

Directions

1. Crush soft fruits or berries; cut firmer fruits into small pieces (there is no need to peel or core the fruits, as cooking all the parts adds pectin).
2. Add water to fruits that require it, as listed in the Ingredients table above. Put fruit and water in large saucepan and bring to a boil. Then simmer according to the times in the chart until fruit is soft, while stirring to prevent scorching.

3. When fruit is tender, strain through a colander, then strain through a double layer of cheese-cloth or a jelly bag. Allow juice to drip through, using a stand or colander to hold the bag. Avoid pressing or squeezing the bag or cloth as it will cause cloudy jelly.

4. Using no more than 6 to 8 cups of extracted fruit juice at a time, measure fruit juice, sugar, and lemon juice according to the Ingredients table, and heat to boiling.

5. Stir until the sugar is dissolved. Boil over high heat to the jellying point. To test jelly for doneness, use one of the following methods:

Temperature test—Use a jelly or candy thermometer and boil until mixture reaches the following temperatures:

Sea Level	1,000 ft	2,000 ft	3,000 ft	4,000 ft	5,000 ft	6,000 ft
220°F	218°F	216°F	214°F	212°F	211°F	209°F

7,000 ft	8,000 ft
207°F	205°F

Sheet or spoon test—Dip a cool, metal spoon into the boiling jelly mixture. Raise the spoon about 12 inches above the pan (out of steam). Turn the spoon so the liquid runs off the side. The jelly is done when the syrup forms two drops that flow together and sheet or hang off the edge of the spoon.

6. Remove from heat and quickly skim off foam. Fill sterile jars with jelly. Use a measuring cup or ladle the jelly through a wide-mouthed funnel, leaving ¼-inch headspace. Adjust lids and process.

Process Times for Jelly without Added Pectin in a Boiling Water Canner*

Style of Pack	Jar Size	Process Time at Altitudes of:		
		0–1,000 ft	1,001–6,000 ft	Above 6,000 ft
Hot	Half-pints or pints	5 minutes	10 minutes	15 minutes

*After the process is complete, turn off the heat and remove the canner lid. Wait five minutes before removing jars.

Lemon Curd

Lemon curd is a rich, creamy spread that can be used on (or in) a variety of teatime treats—crumpets, scones, cake fillings, tartlets, or meringues are all enhanced by its tangy-sweet flavor. Follow the recipe carefully, as variances in ingredients, order, and temperatures may lead to a poor texture or flavor. For Lime Curd, use the same recipe but substitute 1 cup bottled lime juice and ¼ cup fresh lime zest for the lemon juice and zest. This recipe yields about three to four half-pints.

Ingredients
2½ cups superfine sugar*
½ cup lemon zest (freshly zested), optional
1 cup bottled lemon juice**
¾ cup unsalted butter, chilled, cut into approximately ¾-inch pieces
7 large egg yolks
4 large whole eggs

Directions
1. Wash 4 half-pint canning jars with warm, soapy water. Rinse well; keep hot until ready to fill. Prepare canning lids according to manufacturer's directions.
2. Fill boiling water canner with enough water to cover the filled jars by 1 to 2 inches. Use a thermometer to preheat the water to 180°F by the time filled jars are ready to be added. **Caution:** Do not heat the water in the canner to more than 180°F before jars are added. If the water in the canner is too hot when jars are added, the process time will not be long enough. The time it takes for the canner to reach boiling after the jars are added is expected to be 25 to 30 minutes for this product. Process time starts after the water in the canner comes to a full boil over the tops of the jars.
3. Combine the sugar and lemon zest in a small bowl, stir to mix, and set aside about 30 minutes. Pre-measure the lemon juice and prepare the chilled butter pieces.
4. Heat water in the bottom pan of a double boiler*** until it boils gently. The water should not boil vigorously or touch the bottom of the top double boiler pan or bowl in which the curd is to be cooked. Steam produced will be sufficient for the cooking process to occur.

If superfine sugar is not available, run granulated sugar through a grinder or food processor for 1 minute, let settle, and use in place of superfine sugar. Do not use powdered sugar.

** *Bottled lemon juice is used to standardize acidity. Fresh lemon juice can vary in acidity and is not recommended.*

*** *If a double boiler is not available, a substitute can be made with a large bowl or saucepan that can fit partway down into a saucepan of a smaller diameter. If the bottom pan has a larger diameter, the top bowl or pan should have a handle or handles that can rest on the rim of the lower pan.*

5. In the top of the double boiler, on the countertop or table, whisk the egg yolks and whole eggs together until thoroughly mixed. Slowly whisk in the sugar and zest, blending until well-mixed and smooth. Blend in the lemon juice and then add the butter pieces to the mixture.

6. Place the top of the double boiler over boiling water in the bottom pan. Stir gently but continuously with a silicone spatula or cooking spoon, to prevent the mixture from sticking to the bottom of the pan. Continue cooking until the mixture reaches a temperature of 170°F. Use a food thermometer to monitor the temperature.

7. Remove the double boiler pan from the stove and place on a protected surface, such as a dishcloth or towel on the countertop. Continue to stir gently until the curd thickens (about 5 minutes). Strain curd through a mesh strainer into a glass or stainless steel bowl; discard collected zest.

8. Fill hot, strained curd into the clean, hot half-pint jars, leaving ½-inch headspace. Remove air bubbles and adjust headspace if needed. Wipe rims of jars with a dampened, clean paper towel; apply two-piece metal canning lids. Process. Let cool, undisturbed, for 12 to 24 hours and check for seals.

Process Times for Lemon Curd in a Boiling-Water Canner*

Style of Pack	Jar Size	Process Time at Altitudes of:		
		0–1,000 ft	1,001–6,000 ft	Above 6,000 ft
Hot	Half-pints	15 minutes	20 minutes	25 minutes

*After the process is complete, turn off the heat and remove the canner lid. Wait five minutes before removing jars.

Jam without Added Pectin

Making jam is even easier than making jelly, as you don't have to strain the fruit. However, you'll want to be sure to remove all stems, skins, and pits. Be sure to wash and rinse all fruits thoroughly before cooking, but don't let them soak. For best flavor, use fully ripe fruit. Use the Ingredients table below as a guideline as you experiment with less common fruits.

Ingredients

Fruit	Quantity (Crushed)	Sugar	Lemon Juice	Yield (Half-pints)
Apricots	4 to 4 ½ cups	4 cups	2 tbsp	5 to 6
Berries*	4 cups	4 cups	None	3 to 4
Peaches	5 ½ to 6 cups	4 to 5 cups	2 tbsp	6 to 7

* Includes blackberries, boysenberries, dewberries, gooseberries, loganberries, raspberries, and strawberries.

1. Remove stems, skins, seeds, and pits; cut into pieces and crush. For berries, remove stems and blossoms and crush. Seedy berries may be put through a sieve or food mill. Measure crushed fruit into large saucepan using the ingredient quantities specified above.

2. Add sugar and bring to a boil while stirring rapidly and constantly. Continue to boil until mixture thickens. Use one of the following tests to determine when jams and jellies are ready to fill. Remember that the jam will thicken as it cools.

Temperature test—Use a jelly or candy thermometer and boil until mixture reaches the temperature for your altitude.

Sea Level	1,000 ft	2,000 ft	3,000 ft	4,000 ft	5,000 ft
220°F	218°F	216°F	214°F	212°F	211°F

6,000 ft	7,000 ft	8,000 ft
209°F	207°F	205°F

Refrigerator test—Remove the jam mixture from the heat. Pour a small amount of boiling jam on a cold plate and put it in the freezer compartment of a refrigerator for a few minutes. If the mixture gels, it is ready to fill.

---

3. Remove from heat and skim off foam quickly. Fill sterile jars with jam. Use a measuring cup or ladle the jam through a wide-mouthed funnel, leaving ¼-inch headspace. Adjust lids and process.

Process Times for Jams without Added Pectin in a Boiling-Water Canner*

Style of Pack	Jar Size	Process Time at Altitudes of:		
		0–1,000 ft	1,001–6,000 ft	Above 6,000 ft
Hot	Half-pints	5 minutes	10 minutes	15 minutes

*After the process is complete, turn off the heat and remove the canner lid. Wait five minutes before removing jars.

Jams and Jellies with Added Pectin

To use fresh fruits with a low-pectin content or canned or frozen fruit juice, powdered or liquid pectin must be added for your jams and jellies to thicken and set properly. Jelly or jam made with added pectin requires less cooking and generally gives a larger yield. These products have more natural fruit flavors, too. In addition, using added pectin eliminates the need to test hot jellies and jams for proper gelling.

Commercially produced pectin is a natural ingredient, usually made from apples and available at most grocery stores. There are several types of pectin now commonly available; liquid, powder, low-sugar, and no-sugar pectins each have their own advantages and downsides. Pomona's Universal Pectin® is a citrus pectin that allows you to make jams and jellies with little or no sugar. Because the order of combining ingredients depends on the type of pectin used, it is best to follow the common jam and jelly recipes that are included right on most pectin packages. However, if you want to try something a little different, follow one of the following recipes for mixed fruit and spiced fruit jams and jellies.

TIPS

- Adding ½ teaspoon of butter to the juice and pectin will reduce foaming. However, these may cause off-flavor in a long-term storage of jellies and jams.
- Purchase fresh fruit pectin each year. Old pectin may result in poor gels.
- Be sure to use Mason canning jars, self-sealing two-piece lids, and a five-minute process (corrected for altitude, as necessary) in boiling water.

Process Times for Jams and Jellies with Added Pectin in a Boiling-Water Canner*

Style of Pack	Jar Size	Process Time at Altitudes of:		
		0–1,000 ft	1,001–6,000 ft	Above 6,000 ft
Hot	Half-pints	5 minutes	10 minutes	15 minutes

*After the process is complete, turn off the heat and remove the canner lid. Wait five minutes before removing jars.

Pear-Apple Jam

This is a delicious jam perfect for making at the end of autumn, just before the frost gets the last apples. For a warming, spicy twist, add a teaspoon of fresh, grated ginger along with the cinnamon. This recipe yields seven to eight half-pints.

Ingredients
2 cups peeled, cored, and finely chopped pears (about 2 lbs)
1 cup peeled, cored, and finely chopped apples
¼ tsp ground cinnamon
6½ cups sugar
⅓ cup bottled lemon juice
6 oz liquid pectin

Directions
1. Peel, core, and slice apples and pears into a large saucepan and stir in cinnamon. Thoroughly mix sugar and lemon juice with fruits and bring to a boil over high heat, stirring constantly and crushing fruit with a potato masher as it softens.
2. Once boiling, immediately stir in pectin. Bring to a full rolling boil and boil hard 1 minute, stirring constantly.
3. Remove from heat, quickly skim off foam, and fill sterile jars, leaving ¼-inch headspace. Adjust lids and process.

Process Times for Pear-Apple Jam in a Boiling Water Canner*

Style of Pack	Jar Size	Process Time at Altitudes of:		
		0–1,000 ft	1,001–6,000 ft	Above 6,000 ft
Hot	Half-pints	5 minutes	10 minutes	15 minutes

*After the process is complete, turn off the heat and remove the canner lid. Wait five minutes before removing jars.

Strawberry-Rhubarb Jelly

Strawberry-rhubarb jelly will turn any ordinary piece of bread into a delightful treat. You can also spread it on shortcake or pound cake for a simple and unique dessert. This recipe yields about seven half-pints.

Ingredients
1½ lbs red stalks of rhubarb
1½ qts ripe strawberries
½ tsp butter or margarine to reduce foaming (optional)
6 cups sugar
6 oz liquid pectin

Directions
1. Wash and cut rhubarb into 1-inch pieces and blend or grind. Wash, stem, and crush strawberries, one layer at a time, in a saucepan. Place both fruits in a jelly bag or double layer of cheesecloth and gently squeeze juice into a large measuring cup or bowl.
2. Measure 3½ cups of juice into a large saucepan. Add butter and sugar, thoroughly mixing into juice. Bring to a boil over high heat, stirring constantly.
3. As soon as mixture begins to boil, stir in pectin. Bring to a full, rolling boil and boil hard 1 minute, stirring constantly. Remove from heat, quickly skim off foam, and fill sterile jars, leaving ¼-inch headspace. Adjust lids and process.

Process Times for Strawberry-Rhubarb Jelly in a Boiling-Water Canner*

Style of Pack	Jar Size	Process Time at Altitudes of:		
		0–1,000 ft	1,001–6,000 ft	Above 6,000 ft
Hot	Half-pints or pints	5 minutes	10 minutes	15 minutes

*After the process is complete, turn off the heat and remove the canner lid. Wait five minutes before removing jars.

Blueberry-Spice Jam

This is a summery treat that is delicious spread over waffles with a little butter. Using wild blueberries results in a stronger flavor, but cultivated blueberries also work well. This recipe yields about five half-pints.

Ingredients
2½ pints ripe blueberries
1 tbsp lemon juice
½ tsp ground nutmeg or cinnamon
¾ cup water

5½ cups sugar
1 box (1¾ oz) powdered pectin

Directions
1. Wash and thoroughly crush blueberries, adding one layer at a time, in a saucepan. Add lemon juice, spice, and water. Stir pectin and bring to a full, rolling boil over high heat, stirring frequently.
2. Add the sugar and return to a full, rolling boil. Boil hard for 1 minute, stirring constantly. Remove from heat, quickly skim off foam, and fill sterile jars, leaving ¼-inch headspace. Adjust lids and process.

Process Times for Blueberry-Spice Jam in a Boiling-Water Canner*

Style of Pack	Jar Size	Process Time at Altitudes of:		
		0–1,000 ft	1,001–6,000 ft	Above 6,000 ft
Hot	Half-pints or pints	5 minutes	10 minutes	15 minutes

*After the process is complete, turn off the heat and remove the canner lid. Wait five minutes before removing jars.

Grape-Plum Jelly

If you think peanut butter and jelly sandwiches are only for kids, try grape-plum jelly spread with a natural nut butter over a thick slice of whole wheat bread. You'll change your mind. This recipe yields about 10 half-pints.

Ingredients
3½ lbs ripe plums
3 lbs ripe Concord grapes
8½ cups sugar
1 cup water

½ tsp butter or margarine to reduce foaming (optional)

1 box (1¾ oz) powdered pectin

Directions

1. Wash and pit plums; do not peel. Thoroughly crush the plums and grapes, adding one layer at a time, in a saucepan with water. Bring to a boil, cover, and simmer 10 minutes.
2. Strain juice through a jelly bag or double layer of cheesecloth. Measure sugar and set aside. Combine 6½ cups of juice with butter and pectin in large saucepan. Bring to a hard boil over high heat, stirring constantly.
3. Add the sugar and return to a full, rolling boil. Boil hard for 1 minute, stirring constantly. Remove from heat, quickly skim off foam, and fill sterile jars, leaving ¼-inch headspace. Adjust lids and process.

Process Times for Grape-Plum Jelly in a Boiling-Water Canner*

Style of Pack	Jar Size	Process Time at Altitudes of:		
		0–1,000 ft	1,001–6,000 ft	Above 6,000 ft
Hot	Half-pints or pints	5 minutes	10 minutes	15 minutes

*After the process is complete, turn off the heat and remove the canner lid. Wait five minutes before removing jars.

Making Reduced-Sugar Fruit Spreads

A variety of fruit spreads may be made that are tasteful, yet lower in sugars and calories than regular jams and jellies. The most straightforward method is probably to buy low-sugar pectin and follow the directions on the package, but the following recipes show alternate methods of using gelatin or fruit pulp as thickening agents. Gelatin recipes should not be processed and should be refrigerated and used within four weeks.

Peach-Pineapple Spread

This recipe may be made with any combination of peaches, nectarines, apricots, and plums. You can use no sugar, up to two cups of sugar, or a combination of sugar and another sweetener (such as honey, Splenda, or agave nectar). Note that if you use aspartame, the spread may lose its sweetness within three to four weeks. Add cinnamon or star anise if desired. This recipe yields five to six half-pints.

Ingredients

4 cups drained peach pulp (follow directions below)

2 cups drained unsweetened crushed pineapple

¼ cup bottled lemon juice

2 cups sugar (optional)

Directions

1. Thoroughly wash 4 to 6 pounds of firm, ripe peaches. Drain well. Peel and remove pits. Grind fruit flesh with a medium or coarse blade, or crush with a fork (do not use a blender).
2. Place ground or crushed peach pulp in a 2-quart saucepan. Heat slowly to release juice, stirring constantly, until fruit is tender. Place cooked fruit in a jelly bag or strainer lined with four layers of cheesecloth. Allow juice to drip about 15 minutes. Save the juice for jelly or other uses.
3. Measure 4 cups of drained peach pulp for making spread. Combine the 4 cups of pulp, pineapple, and lemon juice in a 4-quart saucepan. Add up to 2 cups of sugar or other sweetener, if desired, and mix well.
4. Heat and boil gently for 10 to 15 minutes, stirring enough to prevent sticking. Fill jars quickly, leaving ¼-inch headspace. Adjust lids and process.

Process Times for Peach-Pineapple Spread in a Boiling-Water Canner*

Style of Pack	Jar Size	Process Time at Altitudes of:			
		0–1,000 ft	1,001–3,000 ft	3,001–6,000 ft	Above 6,000 ft
Hot	Half-pints	15 minutes	20 minutes	20 minutes	25 minutes
	Pints	20 minutes	25 minutes	30 minutes	35 minutes

*After the process is complete, turn off the heat and remove the canner lid. Wait five minutes before removing jars.

Refrigerated Apple Spread

This recipe uses gelatin as a thickener, so it does not require processing but it should be refrigerated and used within four weeks. For spiced apple jelly, add two sticks of cinnamon and four whole cloves to mixture before boiling. Remove both spices before adding the sweetener and food coloring (if desired). This recipe yields four half-pints.

Ingredients

2 tbsp unflavored gelatin powder

1 qt bottle unsweetened apple juice

2 tbsp bottled lemon juice

2 tbsp liquid low-calorie sweetener (e.g., sucralose, honey, or 1–2 tsp liquid stevia)

Ingredients

2 tbsp unflavored gelatin powder
1 bottle (24 oz) unsweetened grape juice
2 tbsp bottled lemon juice
2 tbsp liquid low-calorie sweetener (e.g., sucralose, honey, or
1–2 tsp liquid stevia)

Directions

1. In a saucepan, heat the gelatin in the grape and lemon juices until mixture is soft. Bring to a full, rolling boil to dissolve gelatin. Boil 1 minute and remove from heat. Stir in sweetener.
2. Fill jars quickly, leaving ¼-inch headspace. Adjust lids. Refrigerate (do not process or freeze).

Remaking Soft Jellies

Sometimes jelly just doesn't turn out right the first time. Jelly that is too soft can be used as a sweet sauce to drizzle over ice cream, cheesecake, or angel food cake, but it can also be re-cooked into the proper consistency.

To Remake with Powdered Pectin

1. Measure jelly to be re-cooked. Work with no more than 4 to 6 cups at a time. For each quart (4 cups) of jelly, mix ¼ cup sugar, ½ cup water, 2

Directions

1. In a saucepan, soften the gelatin in the apple and lemon juices. To dissolve gelatin, bring to a full, rolling boil and boil 2 minutes. Remove from heat.
2. Stir in sweetener and food coloring (if desired). Fill jars, leaving ¼-inch headspace. Adjust lids. Refrigerate (do not process or freeze).

Refrigerated Grape Spread

This is a simple, tasty recipe that doesn't require processing. Be sure to refrigerate and use within four weeks. This recipe makes three half-pints.

tablespoons bottled lemon juice, and 4 teaspoons powdered pectin. Bring to a boil while stirring.

2. Add jelly and bring to a rolling boil over high heat, stirring constantly. Boil hard for ½ minute. Remove from heat, quickly skim foam off jelly, and fill sterile jars, leaving ¼-inch headspace. Adjust new lids and process as recommended (see below).

To Remake with Liquid Pectin

1. Measure jelly to be re-cooked. Work with no more than 4 to 6 cups at a time. For each quart (4 cups) of jelly, measure into a bowl ¾ cup sugar, 2 tablespoons bottled lemon juice, and 2 tablespoons liquid pectin.

2. Bring jelly only to boil over high heat, while stirring. Remove from heat and quickly add the sugar, lemon juice, and pectin. Bring to a full, rolling boil, stirring constantly. Boil hard for 1 minute. Quickly skim off foam and fill sterile jars, leaving ¼-inch headspace. Adjust new lids and process as recommended (see below).

To Remake without Added Pectin

1. For each quart of jelly, add 2 tablespoons bottled lemon juice. Heat to boiling and continue to boil for 3 to 4 minutes.

2. To test jelly for doneness, use one of the following methods:

Temperature test—Use a jelly or candy thermometer and boil until mixture reaches the following temperatures at the altitudes below:

Sea Level	1,000 ft	2,000 ft	3,000 ft	4,000 ft	5,000 ft
220°F	218°F	216°F	214°F	212°F	211°F

6,000 ft	7,000 ft	8,000 ft
209°F	207°F	205°F

Sheet or spoon test—Dip a cool metal spoon into the boiling jelly mixture. Raise the spoon about 12 inches above the pan (out of steam). Turn the spoon so the liquid runs off the side. The jelly is done when the syrup forms two drops that flow together and sheet or hang off the edge of the spoon.

---

3. Remove from heat, quickly skim off foam, and fill sterile jars, leaving ¼-inch headspace. Adjust new lids and process.

Process Times for Remade Soft Jellies in a Boiling-Water Canner*

Style of Pack	Jar Size	Process Time at Altitudes of:		
		0–1,000 ft	1,001–6,000 ft	Above 6,000 ft
Hot	Half-pints or pints	5 minutes	10 minutes	15 minutes

*After the process is complete, turn off the heat and remove the canner lid. Wait five minutes before removing jars.

Vegetables, Pickles, and Tomatoes

Beans or Peas, Shelled or Dried (All Varieties)

Shelled or dried beans and peas are inexpensive and easy to buy or store in bulk, but they are not very convenient when it comes to preparing them to eat. Hydrating and canning beans or peas enable you to simply open a can and use them rather than waiting for them to soak. Sort and discard discolored seeds before rehydrating.

Quantity

- An average of five pounds is needed per canner load of seven quarts.
- An average of 3¼ pounds is needed per canner load of nine pints—an average of ¾ pounds per quart.

Directions

1. Place dried beans or peas in a large pot and cover with water. Soak 12 to 18 hours in a cool place. Drain water. To quickly hydrate beans, you may cover sorted and washed beans with boiling water in a saucepan. Boil 2 minutes, remove from heat, soak 1 hour, and drain.

2. Cover beans soaked by either method with fresh water and boil 30 minutes. Add ½ teaspoon of salt per pint or 1 teaspoon per quart to each jar, if desired. Fill jars with beans or peas and cooking water, leaving 1-inch headspace. Adjust lids and process.

Process Times for Beans or Peas in a Dial-Gauge Pressure Canner*

Style of Pack	Jar Size	Process Time	Canner Pressure (PSI) at Altitudes of:			
			0–2,000 ft	2,001–4,000 ft	4,001–6,000 ft	6,001–8,000 ft
Hot	Pints	75 minutes	11 lbs	12 lbs	13 lbs	14 lbs
	Quarts	90 minutes	11 lbs	12 lbs	13 lbs	14 lbs

*After the canner is completely depressurized, remove the weight from the vent port or open the petcock. Wait 10 minutes; then unfasten the lid and remove it carefully. Lift the lid with the underside away from you so that the steam coming out of the canner does not burn your face.

Process Times for Beans or Peas in a Weighted-Gauge Pressure Canner*

Style of pack	Jar Size	Process Time	Canner Pressure (PSI) at Altitudes of:	
			0–1,000 ft	Above 1,000 ft
Hot	Pints	75 minutes	10 lbs	15 lbs
	Quarts	90 minutes	10 lbs	15 lbs

*After the canner is completely depressurized, remove the weight from the vent port or open the petcock. Wait 10 minutes, then unfasten the lid and remove it carefully. Lift the lid with the underside away from you so that the steam coming out of the canner does not burn your face.

Baked Beans

Baked beans are an old New England favorite, but every cook has his or her favorite variation. Two recipes are included here, but feel free to alter them to your own taste.

Quantity
- An average of five pounds of beans is needed per canner load of seven quarts.
- An average of 3¼ pounds is needed per canner load of nine pints—an average of ¾ pounds per quart.

Directions
1. Sort and wash dry beans. Add 3 cups of water for each cup of dried beans. Boil 2 minutes, remove from heat, soak 1 hour, and drain.
2. Heat to boiling in fresh water, and save liquid for making sauce. Make your choice of the following sauces:

Tomato Sauce—Mix 1 quart tomato juice, 3 tablespoons sugar, 2 teaspoons salt, 1 tablespoon chopped onion, and ¼ teaspoon each of ground cloves, allspice, mace, and cayenne pepper. Heat to boiling. Add 3 quarts cooking liquid from beans and bring back to boiling.

Molasses Sauce—Mix 4 cups water or cooking liquid from beans, 3 tablespoons dark molasses, 1 tablespoon vinegar, 2 teaspoons salt, and ¾ teaspoon powdered dry mustard. Heat to boiling.

3. Place seven ¾-inch pieces of pork, ham, or bacon in an earthenware crock, a large casserole, or a pan. Add beans and enough molasses sauce to cover beans.

4. Cover and bake 4 to 5 hours at 350°F. Add water as needed—about every hour. Fill jars, leaving 1-inch headspace. Adjust lids and process.

Process Times for Baked Beans in a Dial-Gauge Pressure Canner*

Style of Pack	Jar Size	Process Time	Canner Pressure (PSI) at Altitudes of:			
			0–2,000 ft	2,001–4,000 ft	4,001–6,000 ft	6,001–8,000 ft
Hot	Pints	65 minutes	11 lbs	12 lbs	13 lbs	14 lbs
	Quarts	75 minutes	11 lbs	12 lbs	13 lbs	14 lbs

*After the canner is completely depressurized, remove the weight from the vent port or open the petcock. Wait 10 minutes, then unfasten the lid and remove it carefully. Lift the lid with the underside away from you so that the steam coming out of the canner does not burn your face.

Process Times for Baked Beans in a Weighted-Gauge Pressure Canner*

Style of pack	Jar Size	Process Time	Canner Pressure (PSI) at Altitudes of:	
			0–1,000 ft	Above 1,000 ft
Hot	Pints	65 minutes	10 lbs	15 lbs
	Quarts	75 minutes	10 lbs	15 lbs

*After the canner is completely depressurized, remove the weight from the vent port or open the petcock. Wait 10 minutes, then unfasten the lid and remove it carefully. Lift the lid with the underside away from you so that the steam coming out of the canner does not burn your face.

Green Beans

This process will work equally well for snap, Italian, or wax beans. Select filled but tender, crisp pods, removing any diseased or rusty pods.

Quantity

- An average of 14 pounds is needed per canner load of seven quarts.
- An average of nine pounds is needed per canner load of nine pints.
- A bushel weighs 30 pounds and yields 12 to 20 quarts—an average of 2 pounds per quart.

Directions

1. Wash beans and trim ends. Leave whole, or cut or break into 1-inch pieces.

Hot pack—Cover with boiling water; boil 5 minutes. Fill jars loosely, leaving 1-inch headspace.

Raw pack—Fill jars tightly with raw beans, leaving 1-inch headspace. Add 1 teaspoon of salt per quart to each jar, if desired. Add boiling water, leaving 1-inch headspace.

2. Adjust lids and process.

Process Times for Green Beans in a Dial-Gauge Pressure Canner*

Style of Pack	Jar Size	Process Time	Canner Pressure (PSI) at Altitudes of:			
			0–2,000 ft	2,001–4,000 ft	4,001–6,000 ft	6,001–8,000 ft
Hot or Raw	Pints	20 minutes	11 lbs	12 lbs	13 lbs	14 lbs
	Quarts	25 minutes	11 lbs	12 lbs	13 lbs	14 lbs

*After the canner is completely depressurized, remove the weight from the vent port or open the petcock. Wait 10 minutes, then unfasten the lid and remove it carefully. Lift the lid with the underside away from you so that the steam coming out of the canner does not burn your face.

Process Times for Green Beans in a Weighted-Gauge Pressure Canner*

Style of Pack	Jar Size	Process Time	Canner Pressure (PSI) at Altitudes of:	
			0–1,000 ft	Above 1,000 ft
Hot or Raw	Pints	20 minutes	10 lbs	15 lbs
	Quarts	25 minutes	10 lbs	15 lbs

*After the canner is completely depressurized, remove the weight from the vent port or open the petcock. Wait 10 minutes; then unfasten the lid and remove it carefully. Lift the lid with the underside away from you so that the steam coming out of the canner does not burn your face.

Beets

You can preserve beets whole, cubed, or sliced, according to your preference. Beets that are 1 to 2 inches in diameter are the best, as larger ones tend to be too fibrous.

Quantity
- An average of 21 pounds (without tops) is needed per canner load of seven quarts.
- An average of 13½ pounds is needed per canner load of nine pints.
- A bushel (without tops) weighs 52 pounds and yields 15 to 20 quarts—an average of three pounds per quart.

Directions
1. Trim off beet tops, leaving an inch of stem and roots to reduce bleeding of color. Scrub well. Cover with boiling water. Boil until skins slip off easily, about 15 to 25 minutes depending on size.
2. Cool, remove skins, and trim off stems and roots. Leave baby beets whole. Cut medium or large beets into ½-inch cubes or slices. Halve or quarter very large slices. Add 1 teaspoon of salt per quart to each jar, if desired.
3. Fill jars with hot beets and fresh hot water, leaving 1-inch headspace. Adjust lids and process.

Process Times for Beets in a Dial-Gauge Pressure Canner*

Style of Pack	Jar Size	Process Time	Canner Pressure (PSI) at Altitudes of:			
			0–2,000 ft	2,001–4,000 ft	4,001–6,000 ft	6,001–8,000 ft
Hot	Pints	30 minutes	11 lbs	12 lbs	13 lbs	14 lbs
	Quarts	35 minutes	11 lbs	12 lbs	13 lbs	14 lbs

*After the canner is completely depressurized, remove the weight from the vent port or open the petcock. Wait 10 minutes, then unfasten the lid and remove it carefully. Lift the lid with the underside away from you so that the steam coming out of the canner does not burn your face.

Process Times for Beets in a Weighted-Gauge Pressure Canner*

Style of Pack	Jar Size	Process Time	Canner Pressure (PSI) at Altitudes of:	
			0–1,000 ft	Above 1,000 ft
Hot or Raw	Pints	30 minutes	10 lbs	15 lbs
	Quarts	35 minutes	10 lbs	15 lbs

*After the canner is completely depressurized, remove the weight from the vent port or open the petcock. Wait 10 minutes; then unfasten the lid and remove it carefully. Lift the lid with the underside away from you so that the steam coming out of the canner does not burn your face.

Carrots

Carrots can be preserved sliced or diced according to your preference. Choose small carrots, preferably 1 to 1¼ inches in diameter, as larger ones are often too fibrous.

Quantity
- An average of 17½ pounds (without tops) is needed per canner load of seven quarts.
- An average of 11 pounds is needed per canner load of nine pints.
- A bushel (without tops) weighs 50 pounds and yields 17 to 25 quarts—an average of 2½ pounds per quart.

Directions

1. Wash, peel, and rewash carrots. Slice or dice.

Hot pack—Cover with boiling water; bring to boil and simmer for 5 minutes. Fill jars with carrots, leaving 1-inch headspace.

Raw pack—Fill jars tightly with raw carrots, leaving 1-inch headspace.

2. Add 1 teaspoon of salt per quart to the jar, if desired. Add hot cooking liquid or water, leaving 1-inch headspace. Adjust lids and process.

Process Times for Carrots in a Dial-Gauge Pressure Canner*

Style of Pack	Jar Size	Process Time	Canner Pressure (PSI) at Altitudes of:			
			0–2,000 ft	2,001–4,000 ft	4,001–6,000 ft	6,001–8,000 ft
Hot or Raw	Pints	25 minutes	11 lbs	12 lbs	13 lbs	14 lbs
	Quarts	30 minutes	11 lbs	12 lbs	13 lbs	14 lbs

*After the canner is completely depressurized, remove the weight from the vent port or open the petcock. Wait 10 minutes; then unfasten the lid and remove it carefully. Lift the lid with the underside away from you so that the steam coming out of the canner does not burn your face.

Process Times for Carrots in a Weighted-Gauge Pressure Canner*

Style of Pack	Jar Size	Process Time	Canner Pressure (PSI) at Altitudes of:	
			0–1,000 ft	Above 1,000 ft
Hot or Raw	Pints	25 minutes	10 lbs	15 lbs
	Quarts	30 minutes	10 lbs	15 lbs

*After the canner is completely depressurized, remove the weight from the vent port or open the petcock. Wait 10 minutes; then unfasten the lid and remove it carefully. Lift the lid with the underside away from you so that the steam coming out of the canner does not burn your face.

Corn, Cream Style

The creamy texture comes from scraping the corn-cobs thoroughly and including the juices and corn pieces with the kernels. If you want to add milk or cream, butter, or other ingredients, do so just before serving (do not add dairy products before canning). Select ears containing slightly immature kernels for this recipe.

Quantity

- An average of 20 pounds (in husks) of sweet corn is needed per canner load of nine pints.
- A bushel weighs 35 pounds and yields 12 to 20 pints—an average of 2¼ pounds per pint.

Directions

1. Husk corn, remove silk, and wash ears. Cut corn from cob at about the center of kernel. Scrape remaining corn from cobs with a table knife.

Hot pack—To each quart of corn and scrapings in a saucepan, add 2 cups of boiling water. Heat to boiling. Add ½ teaspoon salt to each jar, if desired. Fill pint jars with hot corn mixture, leaving 1-inch headspace.

Raw pack—Fill pint jars with raw corn, leaving 1-inch headspace. Do not shake or press down. Add ½ teaspoon salt to each jar, if desired. Add fresh boiling water, leaving 1-inch headspace.

2. Adjust lids and process.

Process Times for Cream-Style Corn in a Dial-Gauge Pressure Canner*

Style of pack	Jar Size	Process Time	Canner Pressure (PSI) at Altitudes of:			
			0–2,000 ft	2,001–4,000 ft	4,001–6,000 ft	6,001–8,000 ft
Hot	Pints	85 minutes	11 lbs	12 lbs	13 lbs	14 lbs
Raw	Pints	95 minutes	11 lbs	12 lbs	13 lbs	14 lbs

*After the canner is completely depressurized, remove the weight from the vent port or open the petcock. Wait 10 minutes; then unfasten the lid and remove it carefully. Lift the lid with the underside away from you so that the steam coming out of the canner does not burn your face.

Process Times for Cream-Style Corn in a Weighted-Gauge Pressure Canner*

Style of Pack	Jar Size	Process Time	Canner Pressure (PSI) at Altitudes of:	
			0–1,000 ft	Above 1,000 ft
Hot	Pints	85 minutes	10 lbs	15 lbs
Raw	Pints	95 minutes	10 lbs	15 lbs

*After the canner is completely depressurized, remove the weight from the vent port or open the petcock. Wait 10 minutes; then unfasten the lid and remove it carefully. Lift the lid with the underside away from you so that the steam coming out of the canner does not burn your face.

Corn, Whole Kernel

Select ears containing slightly immature kernels. Canning of some sweeter varieties or kernels that are too immature may cause browning. Try canning a small amount to test color and flavor before canning large quantities.

Quantity

- An average of 31½ pounds (in husks) of sweet corn is needed per canner load of seven quarts.
- An average of 20 pounds is needed per canner load of nine pints.
- A bushel weighs 35 pounds and yields 6 to 11 quarts—an average of 4½ pounds per quart.

Directions

1. Husk corn, remove silk, and wash. Blanch 3 minutes in boiling water. Cut corn from cob at about three-fourths the depth of kernel. Do not scrape cob, as it will create a creamy texture.

Hot pack—To each quart of kernels in a saucepan, add 1 cup of hot water, heat to boiling, and simmer 5 minutes. Add 1 teaspoon of salt per quart to each jar, if desired. Fill jars with corn and cooking liquid, leaving 1-inch headspace.

Raw pack—Fill jars with raw kernels, leaving 1-inch headspace. Do not shake or press down. Add 1 teaspoon of salt per quart to the jar, if desired.

2. Add fresh boiling water, leaving 1-inch headspace. Adjust lids and process.

Process Times for Whole Kernel Corn in a Dial-Gauge Pressure Canner*

Style of Pack	Jar Size	Process Time	Canner Pressure (PSI) at Altitudes of:			
			0–2,000 ft	2,001–4,000 ft	4,001–6,000 ft	6,001–8,000 ft
Hot or Raw	Pints	55 minutes	11 lbs	12 lbs	13 lbs	14 lbs
	Quarts	85 minutes	11 lbs	12 lbs	13 lbs	14 lbs

*After the canner is completely depressurized, remove the weight from the vent port or open the petcock. Wait 10 minutes; then unfasten the lid and remove it carefully. Lift the lid with the underside away from you so that the steam coming out of the canner does not burn your face.

Process Times for Whole Kernel Corn in a Weighted-Gauge Pressure Canner*

Style of Pack	Jar Size	Process Time	Canner Pressure (PSI) at Altitudes of:	
			0–1,000 ft	Above 1,000 ft
Hot or Raw	Pints	55 minutes	10 lbs	15 lbs
	Quarts	85 minutes	10 lbs	15 lbs

*After the canner is completely depressurized, remove the weight from the vent port or open the petcock. Wait 10 minutes; then unfasten the lid and remove it carefully. Lift the lid with the underside away from you so that the steam coming out of the canner does not burn your face.

Mixed Vegetables

Use mixed vegetables in soups, casseroles, pot pies, or as a quick side dish. You can change the suggested proportions or substitute other favorite vegetables, but avoid leafy greens, dried beans, cream-style corn, winter squash, and sweet potatoes as they will ruin the consistency of the other vegetables. This recipe yields about seven quarts.

Ingredients

6 cups sliced carrots
6 cups cut, whole-kernel sweet corn
6 cups cut green beans
6 cups shelled lima beans
4 cups diced or crushed tomatoes
4 cups diced zucchini

Directions

1. Carefully wash, peel, de-shell, and cut vegetables as necessary. Combine all vegetables in a large pot or kettle, and add enough water to cover pieces.
2. Add 1 teaspoon salt per quart to each jar, if desired. Boil 5 minutes and fill jars with hot pieces and liquid, leaving 1-inch headspace. Adjust lids and process.

Process Times for Mixed Vegetables in a Dial-Gauge Pressure Canner*

Style of Pack	Jar Size	Process Time	Canner Pressure (PSI) at Altitudes of:			
			0–2,000 ft	2,001–4,000 ft	4,001–6,000 ft	6,001–8,000 ft
Hot	Pints	75 minutes	11 lbs	12 lbs	13 lbs	14 lbs
	Quarts	90 minutes	11 lbs	12 lbs	13 lbs	14 lbs

*After the canner is completely depressurized, remove the weight from the vent port or open the petcock. Wait 10 minutes; then unfasten the lid and remove it carefully. Lift the lid with the underside away from you so that the steam coming out of the canner does not burn your face.

Process Times for Mixed Vegetables in a Weighted-Gauge Pressure Canner*

Style of Pack	Jar Size	Process Time	Canner Pressure (PSI) at Altitudes of:	
			0–1,000 ft	Above 1,000 ft
Hot	Pints	75 minutes	10 lbs	15 lbs
	Quarts	90 minutes	10 lbs	15 lbs

*After the canner is completely depressurized, remove the weight from the vent port or open the petcock. Wait 10 minutes; then unfasten the lid and remove it carefully. Lift the lid with the underside away from you so that the steam coming out of the canner does not burn your face.

Peas, Green or English, Shelled

Green and English peas preserve well when canned, but sugar snap and Chinese edible pods are better frozen. Select filled pods containing young, tender, sweet seeds, and discard any diseased pods.

Quantity

- An average of 31½ pounds (in pods) is needed per canner load of seven quarts.
- An average of 20 pounds is needed per canner load of nine pints.
- A bushel weighs 30 pounds and yields 5 to 10 quarts—an average of 4½ pounds per quart.

Directions

1. Shell and wash peas. Add 1 teaspoon of salt per quart to each jar, if desired.

Hot pack—Cover with boiling water. Bring to a boil in a saucepan, and boil 2 minutes. Fill jars loosely with hot peas, and add cooking liquid, leaving 1-inch headspace.

Raw pack—Fill jars with raw peas, and add boiling water, leaving 1-inch headspace. Do not shake or press down on peas.

2. Adjust lids and process.

Process Times for Peas in a Dial-Gauge Pressure Canner*

Style of Pack	Jar Size	Process Time	Canner Pressure (PSI) at Altitudes of:			
			0–2,000 ft	2,001–4,000 ft	4,001–6,000 ft	6,001–8,000 ft
Hot or Raw	Pints or Quarts	40 minutes	11 lbs	12 lbs	13 lbs	14 lbs

*After the canner is completely depressurized, remove the weight from the vent port or open the petcock. Wait 10 minutes; then unfasten the lid and remove it carefully. Lift the lid with the underside away from you so that the steam coming out of the canner does not burn your face.

Process Times for Peas in a Weighted-Gauge Pressure Canner*

Style of Pack	Jar Size	Process Time	Canner Pressure (PSI) at Altitudes of:	
			0–1,000 ft	Above 1,000 ft
Hot or Raw	Pints or Quarts	40 minutes	10 lbs	15 lbs

*After the canner is completely depressurized, remove the weight from the vent port or open the petcock. Wait 10 minutes; then unfasten the lid and remove it carefully. Lift the lid with the underside away from you so that the steam coming out of the canner does not burn your face.

Potatoes, Sweet

Sweet potatoes can be preserved whole, in chunks, or in slices, according to your preference. Choose small to medium-sized potatoes that are mature and not too fibrous. Can within one to two months after harvest.

Quantity
- An average of 17½ pounds is needed per canner load of seven quarts.
- An average of 11 pounds is needed per canner load of nine pints.
- A bushel weighs 50 pounds and yields 17 to 25 quarts—an average of 2½ pounds per quart.

Directions
1. Wash potatoes and boil or steam until partially soft (15 to 20 minutes). Remove skins. Cut medium potatoes, if needed, so that pieces are uniform in size. Do not mash or purée pieces.

2. Fill jars, leaving 1-inch headspace. Add 1 teaspoon salt per quart to each jar, if desired. Cover with your choice of fresh boiling water or syrup, leaving 1-inch headspace. Adjust lids and process.

Process Times for Sweet Potatoes in a Dial-Gauge Pressure Canner*

Style of Pack	Jar Size	Process Time	Canner Pressure (PSI) at Altitudes of:			
			0–2,000 ft	2,001–4,000 ft	4,001–6,000 ft	6,001–8,000 ft
Hot	Pints	65 minutes	11 lbs	12 lbs	13 lbs	14 lbs
	Quarts	90 minutes	11 lbs	12 lbs	13 lbs	14 lbs

*After the canner is completely depressurized, remove the weight from the vent port or open the petcock. Wait 10 minutes; then unfasten the lid and remove it carefully. Lift the lid with the underside away from you so that the steam coming out of the canner does not burn your face.

Process Times for Sweet Potatoes in a Weighted-Gauge Pressure Canner*

Style of Pack	Jar Size	Process Time	Canner Pressure (PSI) at Altitudes of:	
			0–1,000 ft	Above 1,000 ft
Hot	Pints	65 minutes	10 lbs	15 lbs
	Quarts	90 minutes	10 lbs	15 lbs

*After the canner is completely depressurized, remove the weight from the vent port or open the petcock. Wait 10 minutes; then unfasten the lid and remove it carefully. Lift the lid with the underside away from you so that the steam coming out of the canner does not burn your face.

Pumpkin and Winter Squash

Pumpkin and squash are great to have on hand for use in pies, soups, quick breads, or as side dishes.

They should have a hard rind and stringless, mature pulp. Small pumpkins (sugar or pie varieties) are best. Before using for pies, drain jars and strain or sieve pumpkin or squash cubes.

Quantity
- An average of 16 pounds is needed per canner load of seven quarts.
- An average of 10 pounds is needed per canner load of nine pints—an average of 2¼ pounds per quart.

Directions
1. Wash, remove seeds, cut into 1-inch-wide slices, and peel. Cut flesh into 1-inch cubes. Boil 2 minutes in water. Do not mash or purée.
2. Fill jars with cubes and cooking liquid, leaving 1-inch headspace. Adjust lids and process.

Process Times for Pumpkin and Winter Squash in a Dial-Gauge Pressure Canner*

| Style of Pack | Jar Size | Process Time | Canner Pressure (PSI) at Altitudes of: | | | |
			0–2,000 ft	2,001–4,000 ft	4,001–6,000 ft	6,001–8,000 ft
Hot	Pints	55 minutes	11 lbs	12 lbs	13 lbs	14 lbs
	Quarts	90 minutes	11 lbs	12 lbs	13 lbs	14 lbs

*After the canner is completely depressurized, remove the weight from the vent port or open the petcock. Wait 10 minutes; then unfasten the lid and remove it carefully. Lift the lid with the underside away from you so that the steam coming out of the canner does not burn your face.

Process Times for Pumpkin and Winter Squash in a Weighted-Gauge Pressure Canner*

| Style of Pack | Jar Size | Process Time | Canner Pressure (PSI) at Altitudes of: | |
			0–1,000 ft	Above 1,000 ft
Hot	Pints	55 minutes	10 lbs	15 lbs
	Quarts	90 minutes	10 lbs	15 lbs

*After the canner is completely depressurized, remove the weight from the vent port or open the petcock. Wait 10 minutes; then unfasten the lid and remove it carefully. Lift the lid with the underside away from you so that the steam coming out of the canner does not burn your face.

Succotash

To spice up this simple, satisfying dish, add a little paprika and celery salt before serving. It is also delicious made into a pot pie, with or without added chicken, turkey, or beef. This recipe yields seven quarts.

Ingredients
1 lb unhusked sweet corn or 3 qts cut whole kernels
14 lbs mature green podded lima beans or 4 qts shelled lima beans
2 qts crushed or whole tomatoes (optional)

Directions
1. Husk corn, remove silk, and wash. Blanch 3 minutes in boiling water. Cut corn from cob at about three-fourths the depth of kernel. Do not scrape cob, as it will create a creamy texture. Shell lima beans and wash thoroughly.

Hot pack—Combine all prepared vegetables in a large kettle with enough water to cover the pieces. Add 1 teaspoon salt to each quart jar, if desired. Boil gently 5 minutes and fill jars with pieces and cooking liquid, leaving 1-inch headspace.

Raw pack—Fill jars with equal parts of all prepared vegetables, leaving 1-inch headspace. Do not shake or press down pieces. Add 1 teaspoon salt to each quart jar, if desired. Add fresh boiling water, leaving 1-inch headspace.

2. Adjust lids and process.

Process Times for Succotash in a Dial-Gauge Pressure Canner*

| Style of Pack | Jar Size | Process Time | Canner Pressure (PSI) at Altitudes of: | | | |
			0–2,000 ft	2,001–4,000 ft	4,001–6,000 ft	6,001–8,000 ft
Hot or Raw	Pints	60 minutes	11 lbs	12 lbs	13 lbs	14 lbs
	Quarts	85 minutes	11 lbs	12 lbs	13 lbs	14 lbs

*After the canner is completely depressurized, remove the weight from the vent port or open the petcock. Wait 10 minutes; then unfasten the lid and remove it carefully. Lift the lid with the underside away from you so that the steam coming out of the canner does not burn your face.

Process Times for Succotash in a Weighted-Gauge Pressure Canner*

Style of Pack	Jar Size	Process Time	Canner Pressure (PSI) at Altitudes of:	
			0–1,000 ft	Above 1,000 ft
Hot or Raw	Pints	60 minutes	10 lbs	15 lbs
	Quarts	85 minutes	10 lbs	15 lbs

*After the canner is completely depressurized, remove the weight from the vent port or open the petcock. Wait 10 minutes; then unfasten the lid and remove it carefully. Lift the lid with the underside away from you so that the steam coming out of the canner does not burn your face.

Soups

Vegetable, dried bean or pea, meat, poultry, or seafood soups can all be canned. Add pasta, rice, or other grains to soup just prior to serving, as grains tend to get soggy when canned. If dried beans or peas are used, they *must* be fully rehydrated first. Dairy products should also be avoided in the canning process.

Directions
1. Select, wash, and prepare vegetables.
2. Cook vegetables. For each cup of dried beans or peas, add 3 cups of water, boil 2 minutes, remove from heat, soak 1 hour, and heat to boil. Drain and combine with meat broth, tomatoes, or water to cover. Boil 5 minutes.
3. Salt to taste, if desired. Fill jars halfway with solid mixture. Add remaining liquid, leaving 1-inch headspace. Adjust lids and process.

Process Times for Soups in a Dial-Gauge Pressure Canner*

Style of Pack	Jar Size	Process Time	Canner Pressure (PSI) at Altitudes of:			
			0–2,000 ft	2,001–4,000 ft	4,001–6,000 ft	6,001–8,000 ft
Hot	Pints	60** minutes	11 lbs	12 lbs	13 lbs	14 lbs
	Quarts	75** minutes	11 lbs	12 lbs	13 lbs	14 lbs
**Caution: Process 100 minutes if soup contains seafood.						

*After the canner is completely depressurized, remove the weight from the vent port or open the petcock. Wait 10 minutes; then unfasten the lid and remove it carefully. Lift the lid with the underside away from you so that the steam coming out of the canner does not burn your face.

Process Times for Soups in a Weighted-Gauge Pressure Canner*

Style of Pack	Jar Size	Process Time	Canner Pressure (PSI) at Altitudes of:	
			0–1,000 ft	Above 1,000 ft
Hot	Pints	60** minutes	10 lbs	15 lbs
	Quarts	75** minutes	10 lbs	15 lbs
**Caution: Process 100 minutes if soup contains seafood.				

*After the canner is completely depressurized, remove the weight from the vent port or open the petcock. Wait 10 minutes; then unfasten the lid and remove it carefully. Lift the lid with the underside away from you so that the steam coming out of the canner does not burn your face.

Meat Stock (Broth)

"Good broth will resurrect the dead," says a South American proverb. Bones contain calcium, magnesium, phosphorus, and other trace minerals, while cartilage and tendons hold glucosamine, which is important for joints and muscle health. When simmered for extended periods, these nutrients are released into the water and broken down into a form that our bodies can absorb. Not to mention that good broth is the secret to delicious risotto, reduction sauces, gravies, and dozens of other gourmet dishes.

Beef
1. Saw or crack fresh, trimmed beef bones to enhance extraction of flavor. Rinse bones and place in a large stockpot or kettle, cover bones with water, add pot cover, and simmer 3 to 4 hours.
2. Remove bones, cool broth, and pick off meat. Skim off fat, add meat removed from bones to broth, and reheat to boiling. Fill jars, leaving 1-inch headspace. Adjust lids and process.

Chicken or Turkey
1. Place large carcass bones in a large stockpot, add enough water to cover bones, cover pot, and simmer 30 to 45 minutes or until meat can be easily stripped from bones.
2. Remove bones and pieces, cool broth, strip meat, discard excess fat, and return meat to broth. Reheat to boiling and fill jars, leaving 1-inch headspace. Adjust lids and process.

Process Times for Meat Stock in a Dial-Gauge Pressure Canner*

Style of Pack	Jar Size	Process Time	Canner Pressure (PSI) at Altitudes of:			
			0–2,000 ft	2,001–4,000 ft	4,001–6,000 ft	6,001–8,000 ft
Hot	Pints	20 minutes	11 lbs	12 lbs	13 lbs	14 lbs
	Quarts	25 minutes	11 lbs	12 lbs	13 lbs	14 lbs

*After the canner is completely depressurized, remove the weight from the vent port or open the petcock. Wait 10 minutes; then unfasten the lid and remove it carefully. Lift the lid with the underside away from you so that the steam coming out of the canner does not burn your face.

Process Times for Meat Stock in a Weighted-Gauge Pressure Canner*

Style of Pack	Jar Size	Process Time	Canner Pressure (PSI) at Altitudes of:	
			0–1,000 ft	Above 1,000 ft
Hot	Pints	20 minutes	10 lbs	15 lbs
	Quarts	25 minutes	10 lbs	15 lbs

*After the canner is completely depressurized, remove the weight from the vent port or open the petcock. Wait 10 minutes; then unfasten the lid and remove it carefully. Lift the lid with the underside away from you so that the steam coming out of the canner does not burn your face.

Fermented Foods and Pickled Vegetables

Pickled vegetables play a vital role in Italian antipasto dishes, Chinese stir-fries, British piccalilli, and much of Russian and Finnish cuisine. And, of course, the Germans love their sauerkraut, kimchee is found on nearly every Korean dinner table, and many an American won't eat a sandwich without a good, strong dill pickle on the side.

Fermenting vegetables is not complicated, but you'll want to have the proper containers, covers, and weights ready before you begin. For containers, keep the following in mind:

- A one-gallon container is needed for each five pounds of fresh vegetables. Therefore, a five-gallon stone crock is of ideal size for fermenting about 25 pounds of fresh cabbage or cucumbers.
- Food-grade plastic and glass containers are excellent substitutes for stone crocks. Other one- to three-gallon non-food-grade plastic containers may be used if lined inside with a clean food-grade

plastic bag. **Caution: Be certain that foods contact only food-grade plastics. Do not use garbage bags or trash liners.**
- Fermenting sauerkraut in quart and half-gallon Mason jars is an acceptable practice, but may result in more spoilage losses.

Some vegetables, like cabbage and cucumbers, need to be kept 1 to 2 inches under brine while fermenting. If you find them floating to top of the container, here are some suggestions:

- After adding prepared vegetables and brine, insert a suitably sized dinner plate or glass pie plate inside the fermentation container. The plate must be slightly smaller than the container opening, yet large enough to cover most of the shredded cabbage or cucumbers.
- To keep the plate under the brine, weight it down with two to three sealed quart jars filled with water. Covering the container opening with a clean, heavy bath towel helps to prevent contamination from insects and molds while the vegetables are fermenting.
- Fine quality fermented vegetables are also obtained when the plate is weighted down with a very large, clean, plastic bag filled with three quarts of water containing 4½ tablespoons of salt. Be sure to seal the plastic bag. Freezer bags sold for packaging turkeys are suitable for use with five-gallon containers.

Be sure to wash the fermentation container, plate, and jars in hot, sudsy water, and rinse well with very hot water before use.

Dill Pickles

Feel free to alter the spices in this recipe, but stick to the same proportion of cucumbers, vinegar, and water. Check the label of your vinegar to be sure it contains 5 percent acetic acid. Fully fermented pickles may be stored in the original container for about four to six months, provided they are refrigerated and surface scum and molds are removed regularly, but canning is a better way to store fully fermented pickles.

Ingredients
Use the following quantities for each gallon capacity of your container:
4 lbs of 4-inch pickling cucumbers
2 tbsp dill seed or 4 to 5 heads fresh or dry dill weed
½ cup salt

¼ cup vinegar (5 percent acetic acid)

8 cups water and one or more of the following ingredients:

2 cloves garlic (optional)

2 dried red peppers (optional)

2 tsp whole mixed pickling spices (optional)

Directions

1. Wash cucumbers. Cut ¹⁄₁₆-inch slice off blossom end and discard. Leave ¼ inch of stem attached. Place half of dill and spices on bottom of a clean, suitable container (see page 149 for suggestions on containers, lids, and weights).

2. Add cucumbers, remaining dill, and spices. Dissolve salt in vinegar and water and pour over cucumbers. Add suitable cover and weight. Store where temperature is between 70 and 75°F for about 3 to 4 weeks while fermenting. Temperatures of 55 to 65°F are acceptable, but the fermentation will take 5 to 6 weeks. Avoid temperatures above 80°F, or pickles will become too soft during fermentation. Fermenting pickles cure slowly. Check the container several times a week and promptly remove surface scum or mold. **Caution: If the pickles become soft, slimy, or develop a disagreeable odor, discard them.**

3. Once fully fermented, pour the brine into a pan, heat slowly to a boil, and simmer 5 minutes. Filter brine through paper coffee filters to reduce cloudiness, if desired. Fill jars with pickles and hot brine, leaving ½-inch headspace. Adjust lids and process in a boiling water canner, or use the low-temperature pasteurization treatment described here:

Low-Temperature Pasteurization Treatment

The following treatment results in a better product texture but must be carefully managed to avoid possible spoilage.

1. Place jars in a canner filled halfway with warm (120 to 140°F) water. Then, add hot water to a level 1 inch above jars.

2. Heat the water enough to maintain 180 to 185°F water temperature for 30 minutes. Check with a candy or jelly thermometer to be certain that the water temperature is at least 180°F during the entire 30 minutes. Temperatures higher than 185°F may cause unnecessary softening of pickles.

Process Times for Dill Pickles in a Boiling-Water Canner*

Style of Pack	Jar Size	Process Time at Altitudes of:		
		0–1,000 ft	1,001–6,000 ft	Above 6,000 ft
Raw	Pints	10 minutes	15 minutes	20 minutes
	Quarts	15 minutes	20 minutes	25 minutes

*After the process is complete, turn off the heat and remove the canner lid. Wait five minutes before removing jars.

Sauerkraut

For the best sauerkraut, use firm heads of fresh cabbage. Shred cabbage and start kraut between 24 and 48 hours after harvest. This recipe yields about nine quarts.

Ingredients

25 lbs cabbage

¾ cup canning or pickling salt

Directions

1. Work with about 5 pounds of cabbage at a time. Discard outer leaves. Rinse heads under cold running water and drain. Cut heads in quarters and remove cores. Shred or slice to the thickness of a quarter.

2. Put cabbage in a suitable fermentation container (see page 149 for suggestions on containers, lids, and weights), and add 3 tablespoons of salt. Mix thoroughly, using clean hands. Pack firmly until salt draws juices from cabbage.

3. Repeat shredding, salting, and packing until all cabbage is in the container. Be sure it is deep enough so that its rim is at least 4 or 5 inches above the cabbage. If juice does not cover cabbage, add boiled and cooled brine (1½ tablespoons of salt per quart of water).

4. Add plate and weights; cover container with a clean bath towel. Store at 70 to 75°F while fermenting. At temperatures between 70 and 75°F, kraut will be fully fermented in about 3 to 4 weeks; at 60 to 65°F, fermentation may take 5 to 6 weeks. At temperatures lower than 60°F, kraut may not ferment. Above 75°F, kraut may become soft.

Note: If you weigh the cabbage down with a brine-filled bag, do not disturb the crock until normal fermentation is completed (when bubbling ceases). If you use jars as weight, you will have to check the kraut 2 to 3 times each week and remove scum if it forms. Fully fermented kraut may be kept tightly covered in the refrigerator for several months or it may be canned as follows:

Hot pack—Bring kraut and liquid slowly to a boil in a large kettle, stirring frequently. Remove from heat and fill jars rather firmly with kraut and juices, leaving ½-inch headspace.

Raw pack—Fill jars firmly with kraut and cover with juices, leaving ½-inch headspace.

5. Adjust lids and process.

Process Times for Sauerkraut in a Boiling-Water Canner*

Style of Pack	Jar Size	Process Time at Altitudes of:			
		0–1,000 ft	1,001–3,000 ft	3,001–6,000 ft	Above 6,000 ft
Hot	Pints	10 minutes	15 minutes	15 minutes	20 minutes
	Quarts	15 minutes	20 minutes	20 minutes	25 minutes
Raw	Pints	20 minutes	25 minutes	30 minutes	35 minutes
	Quarts	25 minutes	30 minutes	35 minutes	40 minutes

*After the process is complete, turn off the heat and remove the canner lid. Wait five minutes before removing jars.

Pickled Three-Bean Salad

This is a great side dish to bring to a summer picnic or potluck. Feel free to add or adjust spices to your taste. This recipe yields about five to six half-pints.

Ingredients
1½ cups cut and blanched green or yellow beans (prepared as below)
1½ cups canned, drained red kidney beans
1 cup canned, drained garbanzo beans
½ cup peeled and thinly sliced onion (about 1 medium onion)
½ cup trimmed and thinly sliced celery (1½ medium stalks)
½ cup sliced green peppers (½ medium pepper)
½ cup white vinegar (5 percent acetic acid)
¼ cup bottled lemon juice
¾ cup sugar
1¼ cups water
¼ cup oil
½ tsp canning or pickling salt

Directions
1. Wash and snap off ends of fresh beans. Cut or snap into 1- to 2-inch pieces. Blanch 3 minutes and cool immediately. Rinse kidney beans with tap water and drain again. Prepare and measure all other vegetables.
2. Combine vinegar, lemon juice, sugar, and water and bring to a boil. Remove from heat. Add oil and salt and mix well. Add beans, onions, celery, and green pepper to solution and bring to a simmer.

3. Marinate 12 to 14 hours in refrigerator, then heat entire mixture to a boil. Fill clean jars with solids. Add hot liquid, leaving ½-inch headspace. Adjust lids and process.

Process Times for Pickled Three-Bean Salad in a Boiling Water Canner*

Style of Pack	Jar Size	Process Time at Altitudes of:		
		0–1,000 ft	1,001–6,000 ft	Above 6,000 ft
Hot	Half-pints or Pints	15 minutes	20 minutes	25 minutes

Pickled Horseradish Sauce

Select horseradish roots that are firm and have no mold, soft spots, or green spots. Avoid roots that have begun to sprout. The pungency of fresh horseradish fades within one to two months, even when refrigerated, so make only small quantities at a time. This recipe yields about two half-pints.

Ingredients
2 cups (¾ lb) freshly grated horseradish
1 cup white vinegar (5 percent acetic acid)
½ tsp canning or pickling salt
¼ tsp powdered ascorbic acid

Directions
1. Wash horseradish roots thoroughly and peel off brown outer skin. Grate the peeled roots in a food processor or cut them into small cubes and put through a food grinder.
2. Combine ingredients and fill into sterile jars, leaving ¼-inch headspace. Seal jars tightly and store in a refrigerator.

Marinated Peppers

Any combination of bell, Hungarian, banana, or jalapeño peppers can be used in this recipe. Use more jalapeño peppers if you want your mix to be hot, but remember to wear rubber or plastic gloves while handling them or wash hands thoroughly with soap and water before touching your face. This recipe yields about nine half-pints.

Ingredients
4 lbs firm peppers
1 cup bottled lemon juice
2 cups white vinegar (5 percent acetic acid)
1 tbsp oregano leaves

1 cup olive or salad oil
½ cup chopped onions
2 tbsp prepared horseradish (optional)
2 cloves garlic, quartered (optional)
2¼ tsp salt (optional)

Directions

1. Select your favorite pepper. Peppers may be left whole or quartered. Wash, slash two to four slits in each pepper, and blanch in boiling water or blister to peel tough-skinned hot peppers. Blister peppers using one of the following methods:

Oven or broiler method—Place peppers in a hot oven (400°F) or broiler for 6 to 8 minutes or until skins blister.

Range-top method—Cover hot burner, either gas or electric, with heavy wire mesh. Place peppers on burner for several minutes until skins blister.

2. Allow peppers to cool. Place in pan and cover with a damp cloth. This will make peeling the peppers easier. After several minutes of cooling, peel each pepper. Flatten whole peppers.

3. Mix all remaining ingredients except garlic and salt in a saucepan and heat to boiling. Place ¼ garlic clove (optional) and ¼ teaspoon salt in each half-pint or ½ teaspoon per pint. Fill jars with peppers, and add hot, well-mixed oil/pickling solution over peppers, leaving ½-inch headspace. Adjust lids and process.

Process Times for Marinated Peppers in a Boiling-Water Canner*

Style of Pack	Jar Size	Process Time at Altitudes of:			
		0–1,000 ft	1,001–3,000 ft	3,001–6,000 ft	Above 6,000 ft
Raw	Half-pints and Pints	15 minutes	20 minutes	20 minutes	25 minutes

*After the process is complete, turn off the heat and remove the canner lid. Wait five minutes before removing jars.

Piccalilli

Piccalilli is a nice accompaniment to roasted or braised meats and is common in British and Indian meals. It can also be mixed with mayonnaise or crème fraîche as the basis of a French remoulade. This recipe yields nine half-pints.

Ingredients

6 cups chopped green tomatoes
1½ cups chopped sweet red peppers
1½ cups chopped green peppers
2¼ cups chopped onions
7½ cups chopped cabbage
½ cup canning or pickling salt
3 tbsp whole mixed pickling spice
4½ cups vinegar (5 percent acetic acid)
3 cups brown sugar

Directions

1. Wash, chop, and combine vegetables with salt. Cover with hot water and let stand 12 hours. Drain and press in a clean, white cloth to remove all possible liquid.

2. Tie spices loosely in a spice bag and add to combined vinegar and brown sugar and heat to a boil in a saucepan. Add vegetables and boil gently 30 minutes or until the volume of the mixture is reduced by one-half. Remove spice bag.

3. Fill hot sterile jars with hot mixture, leaving ½-inch headspace. Adjust lids and process.

Process Times for Piccalilli in a Boiling-Water Canner*

Style of Pack	Jar Size	Process Time at Altitudes of:		
		0–1,000 ft	1,001–6,000 ft	Above 6,000 ft
Hot	Half-pints or Pints	5 minutes	10 minutes	15 minutes

*After the process is complete, turn off the heat and remove the canner lid. Wait five minutes before removing jars.

Bread-and-Butter Pickles

These slightly sweet, spiced pickles will add flavor and crunch to any sandwich. If desired, slender (1 to 1½ inches in diameter) zucchini or yellow summer squash can be substituted for cucumbers. After processing and cooling, jars should be stored four to five weeks to develop ideal flavor. This recipe yields about eight pints.

Ingredients

6 lbs of 4- to 5-inch pickling cucumbers
8 cups thinly sliced onions (about 3 pounds)
½ cup canning or pickling salt
4 cups vinegar (5 percent acetic acid)
4½ cups sugar
2 tbsp mustard seed

1½ tbsp celery seed

1 tbsp ground turmeric

1 cup pickling lime (optional—for use in variation below for making firmer pickles)

Directions

1. Wash cucumbers. Cut ¹⁄₁₆ inch off blossom end and discard. Cut into ³⁄₁₆-inch slices. Combine cucumbers and onions in a large bowl. Add salt. Cover with 2 inches crushed or cubed ice. Refrigerate 3 to 4 hours, adding more ice as needed.
2. Combine remaining ingredients in a large pot. Boil 10 minutes. Drain cucumbers and onions, add to pot, and slowly reheat to boiling. Fill jars with slices and cooking syrup, leaving ½-inch headspace.
3. Adjust lids and process in boiling-water canner, or use the low-temperature pasteurization treatment described below:

Low-Temperature Pasteurization Treatment

The following treatment results in a better product texture but must be carefully managed to avoid possible spoilage.

1. Place jars in a canner filled halfway with warm (120 to 140°F) water. Then, add hot water to a level 1 inch above jars.
2. Heat the water enough to maintain 180 to 185°F water temperature for 30 minutes. Check with a candy or jelly thermometer to be certain that the water temperature is at least 180°F during the entire 30 minutes. Temperatures higher than 185°F may cause unnecessary softening of pickles.

Variation for firmer pickles: Wash cucumbers. Cut ¹⁄₁₆ inch off blossom end and discard. Cut into ³⁄₁₆-inch slices. Mix 1 cup pickling lime and ½ cup salt to 1 gallon water in a 2- to 3-gallon crock or enamelware container. Avoid inhaling lime dust while mixing the lime-water solution. Soak cucumber slices in lime water for 12 to 24 hours, stirring occasionally. Remove from lime solution, rinse, and resoak 1 hour in fresh cold water. Repeat the rinsing and soaking steps two more times. Handle carefully, as slices will be brittle. Drain well.

Process Times for Bread-and-Butter Pickles in a Boiling-Water Canner*

Style of Pack	Jar Size	Process Time at Altitudes of:		
		0–1,000 ft	1,001–6,000 ft	Above 6,000 ft
Hot	Pints or Quarts	10 minutes	15 minutes	20 minutes

*After the process is complete, turn off the heat and remove the canner lid. Wait five minutes before removing jars.

Quick Fresh-Pack Dill Pickles

For best results, pickle cucumbers within 24 hours of harvesting, or immediately after purchasing. This recipe yields seven to nine pints.

Ingredients

8 lbs of 3- to 5-inch pickling cucumbers

2 gallons water

1¼ to 1½ cups canning or pickling salt

1½ qts vinegar (5 percent acetic acid)

¼ cup sugar

2 to 2¼ quarts water

2 tbsp whole mixed pickling spice

3 to 5 tbsp whole mustard seed (2 tsp to 1 tsp per pint jar)

14 to 21 heads of fresh dill (1½ to 3 heads per pint jar) *or*

4½ to 7 tbsp dill seed (1-½ tsp to 1 tbsp per pint jar)

Directions

1. Wash cucumbers. Cut ¹⁄₁₆-inch slice off blossom end and discard, but leave ¼-inch of stem attached. Dissolve ¾ cup salt in 2 gallons water. Pour over cucumbers and let stand 12 hours. Drain.
2. Combine vinegar, ½ cup salt, sugar and 2 quarts water. Add mixed pickling spices tied in a clean white cloth. Heat to boiling. Fill jars with cucumbers. Add 1 tsp mustard seed and 1½ heads fresh dill per pint.
3. Cover with boiling pickling solution, leaving ½-inch headspace. Adjust lids and process.

Process Times for Quick Fresh-Pack Dill Pickles in a Boiling-Water Canner*

Style of Pack	Jar Size	Process Time at Altitudes of:		
		0–1,000 ft	1,001–6,000 ft	Above 6,000 ft
Raw	Pints	10 minutes	15 minutes	20 minutes
	Quarts	15 minutes	20 minutes	25 minutes

*After the process is complete, turn off the heat and remove the canner lid. Wait five minutes before removing jars.

Pickle Relish

A food processor will make quick work of chopping the vegetables in this recipe. Yields about nine pints.

Ingredients

3 qts chopped cucumbers

3 cups each of chopped sweet green and red peppers

1 cup chopped onions
¾ cup canning or pickling salt
4 cups ice
8 cups water
4 tsp each of mustard seed, turmeric, whole allspice, and whole cloves
2 cups sugar
6 cups white vinegar (5 percent acetic acid)

Directions

1. Add cucumbers, peppers, onions, salt, and ice to water and let stand 4 hours. Drain and re-cover vegetables with fresh ice water for another hour. Drain again.
2. Combine spices in a spice or cheesecloth bag. Add spices to sugar and vinegar. Heat to boiling and pour mixture over vegetables. Cover and refrigerate 24 hours.
3. Heat mixture to boiling and fill hot into clean jars, leaving ½-inch headspace. Adjust lids and process.

Process Times for Pickle Relish in a Boiling-Water Canner*

Style of Pack	Jar Size	Process Time at Altitudes of:		
		0–1,000 ft	1,001–6,000 ft	Above 6,000 ft
Hot	Half-pints or Pints	10 minutes	15 minutes	20 minutes

*After the process is complete, turn off the heat and remove the canner lid. Wait five minutes before removing jars.

Quick Sweet Pickles

Quick and simple to prepare, these are the sweet pickles to make when you're short on time. After processing and cooling, jars should be stored four to five weeks to develop ideal flavor. If desired, add two slices of raw whole onion to each jar before filling with cucumbers. This recipe yields about seven to nine pints.

Ingredients

8 lbs of 3- to 4-inch pickling cucumbers
⅓ cup canning or pickling salt
4½ cups sugar
3½ cups vinegar (5 percent acetic acid)
2 tsp celery seed
1 tbsp whole allspice
2 tbsp mustard seed
1 cup pickling lime (optional)

Directions

1. Wash cucumbers. Cut ¹⁄₁₆ inch off blossom end and discard, but leave ¼ inch of stem attached. Slice or cut in strips, if desired.
2. Place in bowl and sprinkle with salt. Cover with 2 inches of crushed or cubed ice. Refrigerate 3 to 4 hours. Add more ice as needed. Drain well.
3. Combine sugar, vinegar, celery seed, allspice, and mustard seed in 6-quart kettle. Heat to boiling.

Hot pack—Add cucumbers and heat slowly until vinegar solution returns to boil. Stir occasionally to make sure mixture heats evenly. Fill sterile jars, leaving ½-inch headspace.

Raw pack—Fill jars, leaving ½-inch headspace.

4. Add hot pickling syrup, leaving ½-inch headspace. Adjust lids and process.

Variation for firmer pickles: Wash cucumbers. Cut ¹⁄₁₆ inch off blossom end and discard, but leave ¼ inch of stem attached. Slice or strip cucumbers. Mix 1 cup pickling lime and ⅓ cup salt with 1 gallon water in a 2- to 3-gallon crock or enamelware container. **Caution: Avoid inhaling lime dust while mixing the lime-water solution.** Soak cucumber slices or strips in lime-water solution for 12 to 24 hours, stirring occasionally. Remove from lime solution, rinse, and soak 1 hour in fresh cold water. Repeat the rinsing and soaking two more times. Handle carefully, because slices or strips will be brittle. Drain well.

Process Times for Quick Sweet Pickles in a Boiling-Water Canner*

Style of Pack	Jar Size	Process Time at Altitudes of:		
		0–1,000 ft	1,001–6,000 ft	Above 6,000 ft
Hot	Pints or Quarts	5 minutes	10 minutes	15 minutes
Raw	Pints	10 minutes	15 minutes	20 minutes
	Quarts	15 minutes	20 minutes	25 minutes

*After the process is complete, turn off the heat and remove the canner lid. Wait five minutes before removing jars.

Reduced-Sodium Sliced Sweet Pickles

Whole allspice can be tricky to find. If it's not available at your local grocery store, it can be ordered at www.spicebarn.com or at www.gourmetsleuth .com. This recipe yields about four to five pints.

Ingredients

4 lbs (3- to 4-inch) pickling cucumbers
Canning syrup: 1²/₃ cups distilled white vinegar (5 percent acetic acid)
3 cups sugar
1 tbsp whole allspice
2¼ tsp celery seed
Brining solution: 1 qt distilled white vinegar (5 percent acetic acid)
1 tbsp canning or pickling salt
1 tbsp mustard seed
½ cup sugar

Directions

1. Wash cucumbers and cut ¹/₁₆-inch off blossom end, and discard. Cut cucumbers into ¼-inch slices. Combine all ingredients for canning syrup in a saucepan and bring to boiling. Keep syrup hot until used.
2. In a large kettle, mix the ingredients for the brining solution. Add the cut cucumbers, cover, and simmer until the cucumbers change color from bright to dull green (about 5 to 7 minutes). Drain the cucumber slices.
3. Fill jars, and cover with hot canning syrup leaving ½-inch headspace. Adjust lids and process.

Process Times for Reduced-Sodium Sliced Sweet Pickles in a Boiling-Water Canner*

Style of Pack	Jar Size	Process Time at Altitudes of:		
		0–1,000 ft	1,001–6,000 ft	Above 6,000 ft
Hot	Pints	10 minutes	15 minutes	20 minutes

*After the process is complete, turn off the heat and remove the canner lid. Wait five minutes before removing jars.

Tomatoes

Canned tomatoes should be a staple in every cook's pantry. They are easy to prepare and, when made with garden-fresh produce, make ordinary soups, pizza, or pastas into five-star meals. Be sure to select only disease-free, preferably vine-ripened, firm fruit. Do not can tomatoes from dead or frost-killed vines.

Green tomatoes are more acidic than ripened fruit and can be canned safely with the following recommendations:

- To ensure safe acidity in whole, crushed, or juiced tomatoes, add two tablespoons of bottled lemon juice or ½ teaspoon of citric acid per quart of tomatoes. For pints, use one tablespoon bottled lemon juice or ¼ teaspoon citric acid.
- Acid can be added directly to the jars before filling with product. Add sugar to offset acid taste, if desired. Four tablespoons of 5 percent acidity vinegar per quart may be used instead of lemon juice or citric acid. However, vinegar may cause undesirable flavor changes.
- Using a pressure canner will result in higher quality and more nutritious canned tomato products. If your pressure canner cannot be operated above 15 PSI, select a process time at a lower pressure.

Tomato Juice

Tomato juice is a good source of vitamin A and C and is tasty on its own or in a cocktail. It's also the secret ingredient in some very delicious cakes. If desired, add carrots, celery, and onions, or toss in a few jalapeños for a little kick.

Quantity

- An average of 23 pounds is needed per canner load of seven quarts, or an average of 14 pounds per canner load of nine pints.
- A bushel weighs 53 pounds and yields 15 to 18 quarts of juice—an average of 3¼ pounds per quart.

Directions

1. Wash tomatoes, remove stems, and trim off bruised or discolored portions. To prevent juice from separating, quickly cut about 1 pound of fruit into quarters and put directly into saucepan. Heat immediately to boiling while crushing.
2. Continue to slowly add and crush freshly cut tomato quarters to the boiling mixture. Make sure the mixture boils constantly and vigorously while you add the remaining tomatoes. Simmer 5 minutes after you add all pieces.
3. Press heated juice through a sieve or food mill to remove skins and seeds. Add bottled lemon juice or citric acid to jars (see page 112). Heat juice again to boiling.
4. Add 1 teaspoon of salt per quart to the jars, if desired. Fill jars with hot tomato juice, leaving ½-inch headspace. Adjust lids and process.

Process Times for Tomato Juice in a Boiling-Water Canner*

Style of Pack	Jar Size	Process Time at Altitudes of:			
		0–1,000 ft	1,001–3,000 ft	3,001–6,000 ft	Above 6,000 ft
Hot	Pints	35 minutes	40 minutes	45 minutes	50 minutes
	Quarts	40 minutes	45 minutes	50 minutes	55 minutes

*After the process is complete, turn off the heat and remove the canner lid. Wait five minutes before removing jars.

Process Times for Tomato Juice in a Dial-Gauge Pressure Canner*

Style of Pack	Jar Size	Process Time	Canner Gauge Pressure (PSI) at Altitudes of:			
			0–2,000 ft	2,001–4,000 ft	4,001–6,000 ft	6,001–8,000 ft
Hot	Pints or Quarts	20 minutes	6 lbs	7 lbs	8 lbs	9 lbs
		15 minutes	11 lbs	12 lbs	13 lbs	14 lbs

*After the canner is completely depressurized, remove the weight from the vent port or open the petcock. Wait 10 minutes; then unfasten the lid and remove it carefully. Lift the lid with the underside away from you so that the steam coming out of the canner does not burn your face.

Process Times for Tomato Juice in a Weighted-Gauge Pressure Canner*

Style of Pack	Jar Size	Process Time	Canner Gauge Pressure (PSI) at Altitudes of:	
			0–1,000 ft	Above 1,000 ft
Hot	Pints or Quarts	20 minutes	5 lbs	10 lbs
		15 minutes	10 lbs	15 lbs

Crushed Tomatoes with No Added Liquid

Crushed tomatoes are great for use in soups, stews, thick sauces, and casseroles. Simmer crushed tomatoes with kidney beans, chili powder, sautéed onions, and garlic to make an easy pot of chili.

Quantity

- An average of 22 pounds is needed per canner load of seven quarts.
- An average of 14 fresh pounds is needed per canner load of nine pints.
- A bushel weighs 53 pounds and yields 17 to 20 quarts of crushed tomatoes—an average of 2¾ pounds per quart.

Directions

1. Wash tomatoes and dip in boiling water for 30 to 60 seconds or until skins split. Then dip in cold water, slip off skins, and remove cores. Trim off any bruised or discolored portions and quarter.

2. Heat ¹/₆ of the quarters quickly in a large pot, crushing them with a wooden mallet or spoon as they are added to the pot. This will exude juice. Continue heating the tomatoes, stirring to prevent burning.

3. Once the tomatoes are boiling, gradually add remaining quartered tomatoes, stirring constantly. These remaining tomatoes do not need to be crushed; they will soften with heating and stirring. Continue until all tomatoes are added. Then boil gently 5 minutes.

4. Add bottled lemon juice or citric acid to jars (see page 112). Add 1 teaspoon of salt per quart to the jars, if desired. Fill jars immediately with hot tomatoes, leaving ½-inch headspace. Adjust lids and process.

Process Times for Crushed Tomatoes in a Dial-Gauge Pressure Canner*

Style of Pack	Jar Size	Process Time	Canner Gauge Pressure (PSI) at Altitudes of:			
			0–2,000 ft	2,001–4,000 ft	4,001–6,000 ft	6,001–8,000 ft
Hot	Pints or Quarts	20 minutes	6 lbs	7 lbs	8 lbs	9 lbs
		15 minutes	11 lbs	12 lbs	13 lbs	14 lbs

*After the canner is completely depressurized, remove the weight from the vent port or open the petcock. Wait 10 minutes; then unfasten the lid and remove it carefully. Lift the lid with the underside away from you so that the steam coming out of the canner does not burn your face.

Process Times for Crushed Tomatoes in a Weighted-Gauge Pressure Canner*

Style of Pack	Jar Size	Process Time	Canner Gauge Pressure (PSI) at Altitudes of:	
			0–1,000 ft	Above 1,000 ft
Hot	Pints or Quarts	20 minutes	5 lbs	10 lbs
		15 minutes	10 lbs	15 lbs

*After the canner is completely depressurized, remove the weight from the vent port or open the petcock. Wait 10 minutes; then unfasten the lid and remove it carefully. Lift the lid with the underside away from you so that the steam coming out of the canner does not burn your face.

Process Times for Crushed Tomatoes in a Boiling-Water Canner*

Style of Pack	Jar Size	Process Time at Altitudes of:			
		0–1,000 ft	1,001–3,000 ft	3,001–6,000 ft	Above 6,000 ft
Hot	Pints	35 minutes	40 minutes	45 minutes	50 minutes
	Quarts	45 minutes	50 minutes	55 minutes	60 minutes

*After the process is complete, turn off the heat and remove the canner lid. Wait five minutes before removing jars.

Tomato Sauce

This plain tomato sauce can be spiced up before using in soups or in pink or red sauces. The thicker you want your sauce, the more tomatoes you'll need.

Quantity

For thin sauce:
- An average of 35 pounds is needed per canner load of seven quarts.
- An average of 21 pounds is needed per canner load of nine pints.
- A bushel weighs 53 pounds and yields 10 to 12 quarts of sauce—an average of five pounds per quart.

For thick sauce:
- An average of 46 pounds is needed per canner load of seven quarts.
- An average of 28 pounds is needed per canner load of nine pints.
- A bushel weighs 53 pounds and yields seven to nine quarts of sauce—an average of 6½ pounds per quart.

Directions

1. Prepare and press as for making tomato juice (see page 155). Simmer in a large saucepan until sauce reaches desired consistency. Boil until volume is reduced by about one-third for thin sauce, or by one-half for thick sauce.

2. Add bottled lemon juice or citric acid to jars (see page 112). Add 1 teaspoon of salt per quart to the jars, if desired. Fill jars, leaving ¼-inch headspace. Adjust lids and process.

Process Times for Tomato Sauce in a Boiling-Water Canner*

Style of Pack	Jar Size	Process Time at Altitudes of:			
		0–1,000 ft	1,001–3,000 ft	3,001–6,000 ft	Above 6,000 ft
Hot	Pints	35 minutes	40 minutes	45 minutes	50 minutes
	Quarts	40 minutes	45 minutes	50 minutes	55 minutes

*After the process is complete, turn off the heat and remove the canner lid. Wait five minutes before removing jars.

Process Times for Tomato Sauce in a Dial-Gauge Pressure Canner*

Style of Pack	Jar Size	Process Time	Canner Gauge Pressure (PSI) at Altitudes of:			
			0–2,000 ft	2,001–4,000 ft	4,001–6,000 ft	6,001–8,000 ft
Hot	Pints or Quarts	20 minutes	6 lbs	7 lbs	8 lbs	9 lbs
		15 minutes	11 lbs	12 lbs	13 lbs	14 lbs

*After the canner is completely depressurized, remove the weight from the vent port or open the petcock. Wait 10 minutes; then unfasten the lid and remove it carefully. Lift the lid with the underside away from you so that the steam coming out of the canner does not burn your face.

Process Times for Tomato Sauce in a Weighted-Gauge Pressure Canner*

Style of Pack	Jar Size	Process Time	Canner Gauge Pressure (PSI) at Altitudes of:	
			0–1,000 ft	Above 1,000 ft
Hot	Pints or Quarts	20 minutes	5 lbs	10 lbs
		15 minutes	10 lbs	15 lbs

*After the canner is completely depressurized, remove the weight from the vent port or open the petcock. Wait 10 minutes; then unfasten the lid and remove it carefully. Lift the lid with the underside away from you so that the steam coming out of the canner does not burn your face.

Tomatoes, Whole or Halved, Packed in Water

Whole or halved tomatoes are used for scalloped tomatoes, savory pies (baked in a pastry crust with parmesan cheese, mayonnaise, and seasonings), or stewed tomatoes.

Quantity

- An average of 21 pounds is needed per canner load of seven quarts.
- An average of 13 pounds is needed per canner load of nine pints.
- A bushel weighs 53 pounds and yields 15 to 21 quarts—an average of three pounds per quart.

Directions

1. Wash tomatoes. Dip in boiling water for 30 to 60 seconds or until skins split; then dip in cold water. Slip off skins and remove cores. Leave whole or halve.
2. Add bottled lemon juice or citric acid to jars (see page 112). Add 1 teaspoon of salt per quart to the jars, if desired. For hot pack products, add enough water to cover the tomatoes and boil them gently for 5 minutes.
3. Fill jars with hot tomatoes or with raw peeled tomatoes. Add the hot cooking liquid to the hot pack, or hot water for raw pack to cover, leaving ½-inch headspace. Adjust lids and process.

Process Times for Water-Packed Whole Tomatoes in a Boiling-Water Canner*

Style of Pack	Jar Size	Process Time at Altitudes of:			
		0–1,000 ft	1,001–3,000 ft	3,001–6,000 ft	Above 6,000 ft
Hot or Raw	Pints	40 minutes	45 minutes	50 minutes	55 minutes
	Quarts	45 minutes	50 minutes	55 minutes	60 minutes

*After the process is complete, turn off the heat and remove the canner lid. Wait five minutes before removing jars.

Process Times for Water-Packed Whole Tomatoes in a Dial-Gauge Pressure Canner*

Style of Pack	Jar Size	Process Time	Canner Gauge Pressure (PSI) at Altitudes of:			
			0–2,000 ft	2,001–4,000 ft	4,001–6,000 ft	6,001–8,000 ft
Hot or Raw	Pints or Quarts	15 minutes	6 lbs	7 lbs	8 lbs	9 lbs
		10 minutes	11 lbs	12 lbs	13 lbs	14 lbs

*After the canner is completely depressurized, remove the weight from the vent port or open the petcock. Wait 10 minutes; then unfasten the lid and remove it carefully. Lift the lid with the underside away from you so that the steam coming out of the canner does not burn your face.

Process Times for Water-Packed Whole Tomatoes in a Weighted-Gauge Pressure Canner*

Style of Pack	Jar Size	Process Time	Canner Gauge Pressure (PSI) at Altitudes of:	
			0–1,000 ft	Above 1,000 ft
Hot or Raw	Pints or Quarts	15 minutes	5 lbs	10 lbs
		10 minutes	10 lbs	15 lbs

*After the canner is completely depressurized, remove the weight from the vent port or open the petcock. Wait 10 minutes; then unfasten the lid and remove it carefully. Lift the lid with the underside away from you so that the steam coming out of the canner does not burn your face.

Spaghetti Sauce without Meat

Homemade spaghetti sauce is like a completely different food than store-bought varieties—it tastes fresher, is more flavorful, and is far more nutritious. Adjust spices to taste, but do not increase proportions of onions, peppers, or mushrooms. This recipe yields about nine pints.

Ingredients
30 lbs tomatoes
1 cup chopped onions
5 cloves garlic, minced
1 cup chopped celery or green pepper
1 lb fresh mushrooms, sliced (optional)
4½ tsp salt
2 tbsp oregano
4 tbsp minced parsley
2 tsp black pepper
¼ cup brown sugar
¼ cup vegetable oil

Directions
1. Wash tomatoes and dip in boiling water for 30 to 60 seconds or until skins split. Dip in cold water and slip off skins. Remove cores and quarter tomatoes. Boil 20 minutes, uncovered, in large saucepan. Put through food mill or sieve.
2. Sauté onions, garlic, celery, or peppers, and mushrooms (if desired) in vegetable oil until tender. Combine sautéed vegetables and tomatoes and add spices, salt, and sugar. Bring to a boil.
3. Simmer uncovered, until thick enough for serving. Stir frequently to avoid burning. Fill jars, leaving 1-inch headspace. Adjust lids and process.

Process Times for Spaghetti Sauce without Meat in a Dial-Gauge Pressure Canner*

Style of Pack	Jar Size	Process Time	Canner Gauge Pressure (PSI) at Altitudes of:			
			0–2,000 ft	2,001–4,000 ft	4,001–6,000 ft	6,001–8,000 ft
Hot	Pints	20 minutes	11 lbs	12 lbs	13 lbs	14 lbs
	Quarts	25 minutes	11 lbs	12 lbs	13 lbs	14 lbs

*After the canner is completely depressurized, remove the weight from the vent port or open the petcock. Wait 10 minutes; then unfasten the lid and remove it carefully. Lift the lid with the underside away from you so that the steam coming out of the canner does not burn your face.

Process Times for Spaghetti Sauce without Meat in a Weighted-Gauge Pressure Canner*

Style of Pack	Jar Size	Process Time	Canner Gauge Pressure (PSI) at Altitudes of:	
			0–1,000 ft	Above 1,000 ft
Hot	Pints	20 minutes	10 lbs	15 lbs
	Quarts	25 minutes	10 lbs	15 lbs

*After the canner is completely depressurized, remove the weight from the vent port or open the petcock. Wait 10 minutes; then unfasten the lid and remove it carefully. Lift the lid with the underside away from you so that the steam coming out of the canner does not burn your face.

Tomato Ketchup

Ketchup forms the base of several condiments, including Thousand Island dressing, fry sauce, and barbecue sauce. And, of course, it's an American favorite in its own right. This recipe yields six to seven pints.

Ingredients
24 lbs ripe tomatoes
3 cups chopped onions
¾ tsp ground red pepper (cayenne)
4 tsp whole cloves
3 sticks cinnamon, crushed
1½ tsp whole allspice
3 tbsp celery seeds
3 cups cider vinegar (5 percent acetic acid)
1½ cups sugar
¼ cup salt

Directions
1. Wash tomatoes. Dip in boiling water for 30 to 60 seconds or until skins split. Dip in cold water. Slip off skins and remove cores. Quarter tomatoes into 4-gallon stockpot or a large kettle. Add onions and red pepper. Bring to boil and simmer 20 minutes, uncovered.
2. Combine remaining spices in a spice bag and add to vinegar in a 2-quart saucepan. Bring to boil. Turn off heat and let stand until tomato mixture has been cooked 20 minutes. Then, remove spice bag and combine vinegar and tomato mixture. Boil about 30 minutes.
3. Put boiled mixture through a food mill or sieve. Return to pot. Add sugar and salt, boil gently, and stir frequently until volume is reduced by one-half or until mixture rounds up on spoon without separation. Fill pint jars, leaving 1/8-inch headspace. Adjust lids and process.

Process Times for Tomato Ketchup in a Boiling-Water Canner*

		Process Time at Altitudes of:		
Style of Pack	Jar Size	0–1,000 ft	1,001–6,000 ft	Above 6,000 ft
Hot	Pints	15 minutes	20 minutes	25 minutes

*After the process is complete, turn off the heat and remove the canner lid. Wait five minutes before removing jars.

Chile Salsa (Hot Tomato-Pepper Sauce)

For fantastic nachos, cover corn chips with chile salsa, add shredded Monterey jack or cheddar cheese, bake under broiler for about five minutes, and serve with guacamole and sour cream. Be sure to wear rubber gloves while handling chiles or wash hands thoroughly with soap and water before touching your face. This recipe yields six to eight pints.

Ingredients
5 lbs tomatoes
2 lbs chile peppers
1 lb onions
1 cup vinegar (5 percent)
3 tsp salt
½ tsp pepper

Directions

1. Wash and dry chiles. Slit each pepper on its side to allow steam to escape. Peel peppers using one of the following methods:

   Oven or broiler method: Place chiles in oven (400°F) or broiler for 6 to 8 minutes until skins blister. Cool and slip off skins.

   Range-top method: Cover hot burner, either gas or electric, with heavy wire mesh. Place chiles on burner for several minutes until skins blister. Allow peppers to cool. Place in a pan and cover with a damp cloth. This will make peeling the peppers easier. After several minutes, peel each pepper.

2. Discard seeds and chop peppers. Wash tomatoes and dip in boiling water for 30 to 60 seconds or until skins split. Dip in cold water, slip off skins, and remove cores.

3. Coarsely chop tomatoes and combine chopped peppers, onions, and remaining ingredients in a large saucepan. Heat to boil, and simmer 10 minutes. Fill jars, leaving ½-inch headspace. Adjust lids and process.

Process Times for Chile Salsa in a Boiling-Water Canner*

		Process Time at Altitudes of:		
Style of Pack	Jar Size	0–1,000 ft	1,001–6,000 ft	Above 6,000 ft
Hot	Pints	15 minutes	20 minutes	25 minutes

*After the process is complete, turn off the heat and remove the canner lid. Wait five minutes before removing jars.

▲ Corn chips and homemade salsa make a great party snack.

▲ Add more or fewer chiles to make your salsa hotter or milder.

Drying and Freezing

Drying

Drying fruits, vegetables, herbs, and even meat is a great way to preserve foods for longer-term storage, especially if your pantry or freezer space is limited. Dried foods take up much less space than their fresh, frozen, or canned counterparts. Drying requires relatively little preparation time and is simple enough that kids will enjoy helping. Drying with a food dehydrator will ensure the fastest, safest, and best-quality results. However, you can also dry produce in the sunshine, in your oven, or strung up over a woodstove.

For more information on food drying, check out *So Easy to Preserve, 5th ed.* from the Cooperative Extension Service, the University of Georgia. Much of the information that follows is adapted from this excellent source.

▲ Orange slices dry on a food dehydrator tray.

Drying with a Food Dehydrator

Food dehydrators use electricity to produce heat and have a fan and vents for air circulation. Dehydrators are efficiently designed to dry foods fast at around 140°F. Look for food dehydrators in discount department stores, mail-order catalogs, the small appliance section of a department store, natural food stores, and seed or garden supply catalogs. Costs vary depending on features. Some models are expandable and additional trays can be purchased later. Twelve square feet of drying space dries about a half-bushel of produce.

Dehydrator Features to Look For

- Double-wall construction of metal or high-grade plastic. Wood is not recommended, because it is a fire hazard and is difficult to clean.
- Enclosed heating elements
- Countertop design
- An enclosed thermostat from 85 to 160°F
- Fan or blower
- Four to 10 open mesh trays made of sturdy, lightweight plastic for easy washing
- Underwriters Laboratory (UL) seal of approval
- A one-year guarantee
- Convenient service
- A dial for regulating temperature
- A timer. Often the completed drying time may occur during the night, and a timer turns the dehydrator off to prevent scorching.

Types of Dehydrators

There are two basic designs for dehydrators. One has horizontal air flow and the other has vertical air flow. In units with horizontal flow, the heating element and fan are located on the side of the unit. The major advantages of horizontal flow are: it reduces flavor mixture so several different foods can be dried at one time; all trays receive equal heat penetration; and juices or liquids do not drip down into the heating element. Vertical air flow dehydrators have the heating element and fan located at the base. If different foods are dried, flavors can mix and liquids can drip into the heating element.

Fruit Drying Procedures

Apples—Select mature, firm apples. Wash well. Pare, if desired, and core. Cut in rings or slices 1/8 to 1/4 inch thick or cut in quarters or eighths. Soak in ascorbic acid, vinegar, or lemon juice for 10 minutes. Remove from solution and drain well. Arrange in single layer on trays, pit side up. Dry until soft, pliable, and leathery; there should be no moist area in center when cut.

Apricots—Select firm, fully ripe fruit. Wash well. Cut in half and remove pit. Do not peel. Soak in ascorbic acid, vinegar, or lemon juice for 10 minutes. Remove from solution and drain well. Arrange in single layer on trays, pit side up with cavity popped up to expose more flesh to the air. Dry until soft, pliable, and leathery; there should be no moist area in center when cut.

Bananas—Select firm, ripe fruit. Peel. Cut in 1/8-inch slices. Soak in ascorbic acid, vinegar, or lemon juice for 10 minutes. Remove and drain well. Arrange in single layer on trays. Dry until tough and leathery.

Berries—Select firm, ripe fruit. Wash well. Leave whole or cut in half. Dip in boiling water 30 seconds to crack skins. Arrange on drying trays not more than two berries deep. Dry until hard and berries rattle when shaken on trays.

Cherries—Select fully ripe fruit. Wash well. Remove stems and pits. Dip whole cherries in boiling water 30 seconds to crack skins. Arrange in single layer on trays. Dry until tough, leathery, and slightly sticky.

Citrus peel—Select thick-skinned oranges with no signs of mold or decay and no color added to skin. Scrub oranges well with brush under cool running water. Thinly peel outer 1/16 to 1/8 inch of the peel; avoid white bitter part. Soak in ascorbic acid, vinegar, or lemon juice for 10 minutes. Remove from solution and drain well. Arrange in single layers on trays. Dry at 130°F for 1 to 2 hours, then at 120°F until crisp.

Figs—Select fully ripe fruit. Wash or clean well with damp towel. Peel dark-skinned varieties if desired. Leave whole if small or partly dried on tree; cut large figs in halves or slices. If drying whole figs, crack skins by dipping in boiling water for 30 seconds. For cut figs, soak in ascorbic acid, vinegar, or lemon juice for 10 minutes. Remove and drain well. Arrange in single layers on trays. Dry until leathery and pliable.

Grapes and black currants—Select seedless varieties. Wash, sort, and remove stems. Cut in half or leave whole. If drying whole, crack skins by dipping in boiling water for 30 seconds. If halved, dip in ascorbic acid or other antimicrobial solution for 10 minutes. Remove and drain well. Dry until pliable and leathery with no moist center.

Melons—Select mature, firm fruits that are heavy for their size; cantaloupe dries better than watermelon. Scrub outer surface well with brush under cool running water. Remove outer skin, any fibrous tissue, and seeds. Cut into 1/4- to 1/2-inch-thick slices. Soak in ascorbic acid, vinegar, or lemon juice for 10 minutes. Remove and drain well. Arrange in single layer on trays. Dry until leathery and pliable with no pockets of moisture.

Nectarines and peaches—Select ripe, firm fruit. Wash and peel. Cut in half and remove pit. Cut in quarters or slices if desired. Soak in ascorbic acid, vinegar, or lemon juice for 10 minutes. Remove and drain well. Arrange in single layer on trays, pit side up. Turn halves over when visible juice disappears. Dry until leathery and somewhat pliable.

Pears—Select ripe, firm fruit. Bartlett variety is recommended. Wash fruit well. Pare, if desired. Cut in half lengthwise and core. Cut in quarters, eighths, or slices 1/8 to 1/4 inch thick. Soak in ascorbic acid, vinegar, or lemon juice for 10 minutes. Remove and drain. Arrange in single layer on trays, pit side up. Dry until springy and suede-like with no pockets of moisture.

Plums and prunes—Wash well. Leave whole if small; cut large fruit into halves (pit removed) or slices. If left whole, crack skins in boiling water 1 to 2 minutes. If cut in half, dip in ascorbic acid or other antimicrobial solution for 10 minutes. Remove and drain. Arrange in single layer on trays, pit side up, cavity popped out. Dry until pliable and leathery; in whole prunes, pit should not slip when squeezed.

Fruit Leathers

Fruit leathers are a tasty and nutritious alternative to store-bought candies that are full of artificial sweeteners and preservatives. Blend the leftover fruit pulp from making jelly or use fresh, frozen, or drained canned fruit. Ripe or slightly overripe fruit works best.

Chances are the fruit leather will get eaten before it makes it into the cupboard, but it can keep up to one month at room temperature. For storage up to one year, place tightly wrapped rolls in the freezer.

Ingredients
2 cups fruit
2 tsp lemon juice or 1/8 tsp ascorbic acid (optional)
1/4 to 1/2 cup sugar, corn syrup, or honey (optional)

Directions
1. Wash fresh fruit or berries in cool water. Remove peel, seeds, and stem.

Spices, Flavors, and Garnishes

To add interest to your fruit leathers, include spices, flavorings, or garnishes.

- **Spices to try**—Allspice, cinnamon, cloves, coriander, ginger, mace, mint, nutmeg, or pumpkin pie spice. Use sparingly; start with 1/8 teaspoon for each 2 cups of purée.
- **Flavorings to try**—Almond extract, lemon juice, lemon peel, lime juice, lime peel, orange extract, orange juice, orange peel, or vanilla extract. Use sparingly; try 1/8 to 1/4 teaspoon for each 2 cups of purée.
- **Delicious additions to try**—Shredded coconut, chopped dates, other dried chopped fruits, granola, miniature marshmallows, chopped nuts, chopped raisins, poppy seeds, sesame seeds, or sunflower seeds.
  - **Fillings to try**—Melted chocolate, softened cream cheese, cheese spreads, jam, preserves, marmalade, marshmallow cream, or peanut butter. Spread one or more of these on the leather after it is dried and then roll. Store in refrigerator.

2. Cut fruit into chunks. Use 2 cups of fruit for each 13 x 15-inch inch fruit leather. Purée fruit until smooth.
3. Add 2 teaspoons of lemon juice or 1/8 teaspoon ascorbic acid (375 mg) for each 2 cups light-colored fruit to prevent darkening.

Hints:

- Applesauce can be dried alone or added to any fresh fruit purée as an extender; it decreases tartness and makes the leather smoother and more pliable.
- To dry fruit in the oven, a 13 x 15-inch cookie pan with edges works well. Line pan with plastic wrap, being careful to smooth out wrinkles. Do not use waxed paper or aluminum foil.

4. Optional: To sweeten, add corn syrup, honey, or sugar. Corn syrup or honey is best for longer storage because these sweeteners prevent crystals. Sugar is fine for immediate use or short storage. Use 1/4 to 1/2 cup sugar, corn syrup, or honey for each 2 cups of fruit. Avoid aspartame sweeteners as they may lose sweetness during drying.
5. Pour the leather. Fruit leathers can be poured into a single large sheet (13 x 15 inches) or into several smaller sizes. Spread purée evenly, about 1/8 inch thick, onto drying tray. Avoid pouring purée too close to the edge of the cookie sheet.
6. Dry the leather. Dry fruit leathers at 140°F. Leather dries from the outside edge toward the center. Larger fruit leathers take longer to dry. Approximate drying times are 6 to 8 hours in a dehydrator, up to 18 hours in an oven, and 1 to 2 days in the sun. Test for dryness by touching center of leather; no indentation should be evident. While warm, peel from plastic and roll, allow to cool, and rewrap the roll in plastic. Cookie cutters can be used to cut out shapes that children will enjoy. Roll, and wrap in plastic.

Vegetable Leathers

Pumpkin, mixed vegetables, and tomatoes make great leathers. Just purée cooked vegetables, strain, spread on a tray lined with plastic wrap, and dry. Spices can be added for flavoring.

Mixed-Vegetable Leather

2 cups cored, cut-up tomatoes
1 small onion, chopped
1/4 cup chopped celery
Salt to taste

Combine all ingredients in a covered saucepan and cook over low heat 15 to 20 minutes. Purée or force through a sieve or colander. Return to saucepan and cook until thickened. Spread on a cookie sheet or tray lined with plastic wrap. Dry at 140°F.

Pumpkin Leather

2 cups canned pumpkin or 2 cups fresh pumpkin, cooked and puréed

½ cup honey

¼ tsp cinnamon

⅛ tsp nutmeg

⅛ tsp powdered cloves

Blend ingredients well. Spread on tray or cookie sheet lined with plastic wrap. Dry at 140°F.

Tomato Leather

Core ripe tomatoes and cut into quarters. Cook over low heat in a covered saucepan, 15 to 20 minutes. Purée or force through a sieve or colander and pour into electric fry pan or shallow pan. Add salt to taste and cook over low heat until thickened. Spread on a cookie sheet or tray lined with plastic wrap. Dry at 140°F.

Vine Drying

One method of drying outdoors is vine drying. To dry beans (navy, kidney, butter, great northern, lima, lentils, and soybeans) leave bean pods on the vine in the garden until the beans inside rattle. When the vines and pods are dry and shriveled, pick the beans and shell them. No pretreatment is necessary. If beans are still moist, the drying process is not complete and the beans will mold if not more thoroughly dried. If needed, drying can be completed in the sun, an oven, or a dehydrator.

How to Make a Woodstove Food Dehydrator

1. Collect pliable wire mesh or screens (available at hardware stores) and use wire cutters to trim to squares 12 to 16 inches on each side. The trays

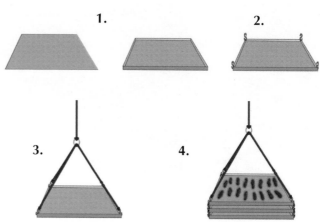

▲ Woodstove food dehydrator.

should be of the same size and shape. Bend up the edges of each square to create a half-inch lip.

2. Attach one S hook from the hardware store or a large paperclip to each side of each square (four clips per tray) to attach the trays together.

3. Cut four equal lengths of chain or twine that will reach from the ceiling to the level of the top tray. Use a wire or metal loop to attach the four pieces together at the top and secure to a hook in the ceiling above the woodstove. Attach the chain or twine to the hooks on the top tray.

4. To use, fill trays with food to dry, starting with the top tray. Link trays together using the S hooks or strong paperclips. When the foods are dried, remove the entire stack and disassemble. Remove the dried food and store.

Herbs

Drying is the easiest method of preserving herbs. Simply expose the leaves, flowers, or seeds to warm, dry air. Leave the herbs in a well-ventilated area until the moisture evaporates. Sun drying is not recommended because the herbs can lose flavor and color.

The best time to harvest most herbs for drying is just before the flowers first open when they are in the bursting, bud stage. Gather the herbs in the early

morning after the dew has evaporated to minimize wilting. Avoid bruising the leaves. They should not lie in the sun or unattended after harvesting. Rinse herbs in cool water and gently shake to remove excess moisture. Discard all bruised, soiled, or imperfect leaves and stems.

Dehydrator drying is another fast and easy way to dry high-quality herbs because temperature and air circulation can be controlled. Preheat dehydrator with the thermostat set to 95 to 115°F. In areas with higher humidity, temperatures as high as 125°F may be needed. After rinsing under cool, running water and shaking to remove excess moisture, place the herbs in a single layer on dehydrator trays. Drying times may vary from one to four hours. Check periodically. Herbs are dry when they crumble, and stems break when bent. Check your dehydrator instruction booklet for specific details.

Less-tender herbs—The more sturdy herbs, such as rosemary, sage, thyme, summer savory, and parsley, are the easiest to dry without a dehydrator. Tie them into small bundles and hang them to air dry. Air drying outdoors is often possible; however, better color and flavor retention usually results from drying indoors.

Tender-leaf herbs—Basil, oregano, tarragon, lemon balm, and the mints have a high moisture content and will mold if not dried quickly. Try hanging the tender-leaf herbs or those with seeds inside paper bags to dry. Tear or punch holes in the sides of the bag. Suspend a small bunch (large amounts will mold) of herbs in a bag and close the top with a rubber band. Place where air currents will circulate through the bag. Any leaves and seeds that fall off will be caught in the bottom of the bag.

Another method, especially nice for mint, sage, or bay leaf, is to dry the leaves separately. In areas of high humidity, it will work better than air drying whole stems. Remove the best leaves from the stems. Lay the leaves on a paper towel, without allowing leaves to touch. Cover with another towel and layer of leaves. Five layers may be dried at one time using this method. Dry in a very cool oven. The oven light of an electric range or the pilot light of a gas range furnishes enough heat for overnight drying. Leaves dry flat and retain a good color.

Microwave ovens are a fast way to dry herbs when only small quantities are to be prepared. Follow the directions that come with your microwave oven.

When the leaves are crispy, dry, and crumble easily between the fingers, they are ready to be packaged and stored. Dried leaves may be left whole and crumbled as used, or coarsely crumbled before storage. Husks can be removed from seeds by rubbing the seeds between the hands and blowing away the chaff. Place herbs in airtight containers and store in a cool, dry, dark area to protect color and fragrance.

Dried herbs are usually three to four times stronger than the fresh herbs. To substitute dried herbs in a recipe that calls for fresh herbs, use ¼ to ⅓ of the amount listed in the recipe.

Jerky

Jerky is great for hiking or camping because it supplies protein in a very lightweight form—not to mention the fact that it can be very tasty. A pound of meat or poultry weighs about four ounces after being made into jerky. In addition, because most of the moisture is removed, it can be stored for one to two months without refrigeration.

Jerky has been around since the ancient Egyptians began drying animal meat that was too big to eat all at once. Native Americans mixed ground dried meat with dried fruit or suet to make pemmican. *Biltong* is dried meat or game used in many African countries. The English word *jerky* came from the Spanish word *charque*, which means "dried, salted meat."

Drying is the world's oldest and most common method of food preservation. Enzymes require moisture in order to react with food. By removing the moisture, you prevent this biological action.

Jerky can be made from ground meat, which is often less expensive than strips of meat and allows you to combine different kinds of meat if desired. You can also make it into any shape you want! As with strips of meat, an internal temperature of 160°F is necessary to eliminate disease-causing bacteria such as *E. coli*, if present.

Food Safety

The USDA Meat and Poultry Hotline's current recommendation for making jerky safely is to heat meat to 160°F and poultry to 165°F before the dehydrating process. This ensures that any bacteria present are destroyed by heat. If your food dehydrator doesn't heat up to 160°F, it's important to cook meat slightly in the oven or by steaming before drying. After heating, maintain a constant dehydrator temperature of 130 to 140°F during the drying process.

According to the USDA, you should always:
- Wash hands thoroughly with soap and water before and after working with meat products.
- Use clean equipment and utensils.
- Keep meat and poultry refrigerated at 40°F or slightly below; use or freeze ground beef and poultry within two days, and whole red meats within three to five days.
- Defrost frozen meat in the refrigerator, not on the kitchen counter.
- Marinate meat in the refrigerator. Don't save marinade to re-use. Marinades are used to tenderize and flavor the jerky before dehydrating it.
- If your food dehydrator doesn't heat up to 160°F (or 165°F for poultry), steam or roast meat before dehydrating it.
- Dry meats in a food dehydrator that has an adjustable temperature dial and will maintain a temperature of at least 130 to 140°F throughout the drying process.

▲ Jerky makes a great snack to take along when hiking or camping.

Preparing the Meat

1. Partially freeze meat to make slicing easier. Slice meat across the grain ⅛ to ¼ inch thick. Trim and discard all fat, gristle, and membranes or connective tissue.
2. Marinate the meat in a combination of oil, salt, spices, vinegar, lemon juice, teriyaki, soy sauce, beer, or wine.

Marinated Jerky

¼ cup soy sauce
1 tbsp Worcestershire sauce
1 tsp brown sugar
¼ tsp black pepper
½ tsp fresh ginger, finely grated
1 tsp salt
1½ to 2 lbs of lean meat strips (beef, pork, or venison)

1. Combine all ingredients except the strips, and blend. Add meat, stir, cover, and refrigerate at least one hour.
2. If your food dehydrator doesn't heat up to 160°F, bring strips and marinade to a boil and cook for 5 minutes.
3. Drain meat in a colander and absorb extra moisture with clean, absorbent paper towels. Arrange strips in a single layer on dehydrator trays, or on cake racks placed on baking sheets for oven drying.
4. Place the racks in a dehydrator or oven preheated to 140°F, or 160°F if the meat wasn't precooked. Dry until a test piece cracks but does not break when it is bent (10 to 24 hours for samples not heated in marinade, 3 to 6 hours for preheated meat). Use a paper towel to pat off any excess oil from strips, and pack in sealed jars, plastic bags, or plastic containers.

Freezing Foods

Many foods preserve well in the freezer and can make preparing meals easy when you are short on time. If you make a big pot of soup, serve it for dinner, put a small container in the refrigerator for lunch the next day, and then stick the rest in the freezer. A few weeks later, you'll be ready to eat it again and it will only take a few minutes to thaw out and serve. Many fruits also freeze well and are perfect for use in smoothies and desserts, or served with yogurt for breakfast or dessert. Vegetables frozen shortly after harvesting keep many of the nutrients found in fresh vegetables and will taste delicious when cooked.

▲ Frozen fruit is perfect for making smoothies.　　▲ Plastic containers with lids are ideal for freezing food.

Containers for Freezing

The best packaging materials for freezing include rigid containers such as jars, bottles, or Tupperware, and freezer bags or aluminum foil. Sturdy containers with rigid sides are especially good for liquids such as soup or juice because they make the frozen contents much easier to get out. They are also generally reusable and make it easier to stack foods in the refrigerator. When using rigid containers, be sure to leave headspace so that the container won't explode when the contents expand with freezing. Covers for rigid containers should fit tightly. If they do not, reinforce the seal with freezer tape. Freezer tape is specially designed to stick at freezing temperatures. Freezer bags or aluminum foil are good for meats, breads and baked goods, or fruits and vegetables that don't contain much liquid. Be sure to remove as much air as possible from bags before closing.

Headspace to Allow Between Packed Food and Closure

Headspace is the amount of empty air left between the food and the lid. Headspace is necessary because foods expand when frozen.

Type of Pack	Container with Wide Opening		Container with Narrow Opening	
	Pint	Quart	Pint	Quart
Liquid pack*	½ inch	1 inch	¾ inch	1½ inches
Dry pack**	½ inch	½ inch	½ inch	½ inch
Juices	½ inch	1 inch	1½ inches	1½ inches

*Fruit packed in juice, sugar syrup, or water; crushed or puréed fruit
**Fruit or vegetable packed without added sugar or liquid

Foods That Do Not Freeze Well

Food	Usual Use	Condition After Thawing
Cabbage*, celery, cress, cucumbers*, endive, lettuce, parsley, radishes	As raw salad	Limp, waterlogged; quickly develops oxidized color, aroma, and flavor
Irish potatoes, baked or boiled	In soups, salads, sauces, or with butter	Soft, crumbly, waterlogged, mealy
Cooked macaroni, spaghetti, or rice	When frozen alone for later use	Mushy, tastes warmed over
Egg whites, cooked	In salads, creamed foods, sandwiches, sauces, gravy, or desserts	Soft, tough, rubbery, spongy
Meringue	In desserts	Soft, tough, rubbery, spongy
Icings made from egg whites	Cakes, cookies	Frothy, weeps
Cream or custard fillings	Pies, baked goods	Separates, watery, lumpy
Milk sauces	For casseroles or gravies	May curdle or separate
Sour cream	As topping, in salads	Separates, watery
Cheese or crumb toppings	On casseroles	Soggy
Mayonnaise or salad dressing	On sandwiches (not in salads)	Separates
Gelatin	In salads or desserts	Weeps
Fruit jelly	Sandwiches	May soak bread
Fried foods	All except French fried potatoes and onion rings	Lose crispness, become soggy

* Cucumbers and cabbage can be frozen as marinated products such as "freezer slaw" or "freezer pickles." These do not have the same texture as regular slaw or pickles.

Effect of Freezing on Spices and Seasonings

- Pepper, cloves, garlic, green pepper, imitation vanilla, and some herbs tend to get strong and bitter.
- Onion and paprika change flavor during freezing.
- Celery seasonings become stronger.
- Curry develops a musty off-flavor.
- Salt loses flavor and has the tendency to increase rancidity of any item containing fat.
- When using seasonings and spices, season lightly before freezing, and add additional seasonings when reheating or serving.

How to Freeze Vegetables

Because many vegetables contain enzymes that will cause them to lose color when frozen, you may want to blanche your vegetables before putting them in the freezer. To do this, first wash the vegetables thoroughly, peel if desired, and chop them into bite-size pieces. Then pour them into boiling water for a couple of minutes (or cook longer for very dense vegetables, such as beets), drain, and immediately dunk the vegetables in ice water to stop them from cooking further. Use a paper towel or cloth to absorb excess water from the vegetables, and then pack in resealable airtight bags or plastic containers.

Blanching Times for Vegetables

Artichokes	3–6 minutes
Asparagus	2–3 minutes
Beans	2–3 minutes
Beets	30–40 minutes
Broccoli	3 minutes
Brussels sprouts	4–5 minutes
Cabbage	3–4 minutes
Carrots	2–5 minutes
Cauliflower	6 minutes
Celery	3 minutes
Corn (off the cob)	2–3 minutes
Eggplant	4 minutes
Okra	3–4 minutes
Peas	1–2 minutes
Peppers	2–3 minutes
Squash	2–3 minutes
Turnips or Parsnips	2 minutes

▲ Frozen berries are perfect for use in pies, muffins, pancakes, or smoothies.

Some fruits have a tendency to turn brown when frozen. To prevent this, you can add ascorbic acid (crush a vitamin C in a little water), citrus juice, plain sugar, or a sweet syrup (1 part sugar and 2 parts water) to the fruit before freezing. Apples, pears, and bananas are best frozen with ascorbic acid or citrus juice, while berries, peaches, nectarines, apricots, pineapple, melons, and berries are better frozen with a sugary syrup.

How to Freeze Meat

Be sure your meat is fresh before freezing. Trim off excess fats and remove bones, if desired. Separate the meat into portions that will be easy to use when preparing meals and wrap in foil or place in resealable plastic bags or plastic containers. Refer to the chart to determine how long your meat will last at best quality in your freezer.

Meat	Months
Bacon and sausage	1 to 2
Ham, hotdogs, and lunchmeats	1 to 2
Meat, uncooked roasts	4 to 12
Meat, uncooked steaks or chops	4 to 12
Meat, uncooked ground	3 to 4
Meat, cooked	2 to 3
Poultry, uncooked whole	12
Poultry, uncooked parts	9
Poultry, uncooked giblets	3 to 4
Poultry, cooked	4
Wild game, uncooked	8 to 12

How to Freeze Fruits

Many fruits freeze easily and are perfect for use in baking, smoothies, or sauces. Wash, peel, and core fruit before freezing. To easily peel peaches, nectarines, or apricots, dip them in boiling water for 15 to 20 seconds to loosen the skins. Then chill and remove the skins and stones.

Berries should be frozen immediately after harvesting and can be frozen in a single layer on a paper towel-lined tray or cookie sheet to keep them from clumping together. Allow them to freeze until hard (about 3 hours) and then pour them into a resealable plastic bag for long-term storage.

▲ Hamburger freezes especially well. Thaw in the refrigerator before cooking.

Edible Wild Plants and Mushrooms

Wild Vegetables, Fruits, and Nuts

Agave

Description: Agave plants have large clusters of thick leaves that grow around one stalk. They grow close to the ground and only flower once before dying.

Location: Agave like dry, open areas and are found in the deserts of the American west.

Edible Parts and Preparing: Only agave flowers and buds are edible. Boil these before consuming. The juice can be collected from the flower stalk for drinking.

Other Uses: Most agave plants have thick needles on the tips of their leaves that can be used for sewing.

Asparagus

Description: When first growing, asparagus looks like a collection of green fingers. Once mature, the plant has fernlike foliage and red berries (which are toxic if eaten). The flowers are small and green and several species have sharp, thornlike projections.

Location: It can be found growing wild in fields and along fences. Asparagus is found in temperate areas in the United States.

Edible Parts and Preparing: It is best to eat the young stems, before any leaves grow. Steam or boil them for 10 to 15 minutes before consuming. The roots are a good source of starch, but don't eat any part of the plant raw, as it could cause nausea or diarrhea.

Beech

Description: Beech trees are large forest trees. They have smooth, light gray bark, very dark leaves, and clusters of prickly seedpods.

Location: Beech trees prefer to grow in moist, forested areas. These trees are found in the Temperate Zone in the eastern United States.

Edible Parts and Preparing: Eat mature beechnuts by breaking the thin shells with your fingers and removing the sweet, white kernel found inside. These nuts can also be used as a substitute for coffee by roasting them until the kernel turns hard and golden brown. Mash up the kernel and boil or steep in hot water.

Blackberry and Raspberry

Description: These plants have prickly stems that grow upright and then arch back toward the ground. They have alternating leaves and grow red or black fruit.

Location: Blackberry and raspberry plants prefer to grow in wide, sunny areas near woods, lakes, and roads. They grow in temperate areas.

Edible Parts and Preparing: Both the fruits and peeled young shoots can be eaten. The leaves can be used to make tea.

Burdock

Description: Burdock has wavy-edged, arrow-shaped leaves. Its flowers grow in burrlike clusters and are purple or pink. The roots are large and fleshy.

Location: This plant prefers to grow in open waste areas during the spring and summer. It can be found in the Temperate Zone in the north.

Edible Parts and Preparing: The tender leaves growing on the stalks can be eaten raw or cooked. The roots can be boiled or baked.

Cattail

Description: These plants are grasslike and have leaves shaped like straps. The male flowers grow above the female flowers; have abundant, bright yellow pollen; and die off quickly. The female flowers become the brown cattails.

Location: Cattails like to grow in full-sun areas near lakes, streams, rivers, and brackish water. They can be found all over the country.

Edible Parts and Preparing: The tender, young shoots can be eaten either raw or cooked. The rhizome (rootstalk) can be pounded and made into flour. When

the cattail is immature, the female flower can be harvested, boiled, and eaten like corn on the cob.

Other Uses: The cottony seeds of the cattail plant are great for stuffing pillows. Burning dried cattails helps repel insects.

Chicory

Description: This is quite a tall plant, with clusters of leaves at the base of the stem and very few leaves on the stem itself. The flowers are sky blue in color and open only on sunny days. It produces a milky juice.

Location: Chicory grows in fields, waste areas, and alongside roads. It grows primarily as a weed all throughout the country.

Edible Parts and Preparing: The entire plant is edible. The young leaves can be eaten in a salad. The leaves and roots may also be boiled as you would regular vegetables. Roast the roots until they are dark brown, mash them up, and use them as a substitute for coffee.

Cranberry

Description: The cranberry plant has tiny, alternating leaves. Its stems crawl along the ground and it produces red berry fruits.

Location: Cranberries only grow in open, sunny, wet areas. They thrive in the colder areas in the northern states.

Edible Parts and Preparing: The berries can be eaten raw, though they are best when cooked in a small amount of water, adding a little bit of sugar if desired.

Dandelion

Description: These plants have jagged leaves and grow close to the ground. They have bright yellow flowers.

Location: Dandelions grow in almost any open, sunny space in the United States.

Edible Parts and Preparing: All parts of this plant are edible. The leaves can be eaten raw or

cooked and the roots boiled. Roasted and ground roots can make a good substitute for coffee.

Other Uses: The white juice in the flower stem can be used as glue.

Elderberry

Description: This shrub has many stems containing opposite, compound leaves. Its flower is white, fragrant, and grows in large clusters. Its fruits are berry-shaped and are typically dark blue or black.

Location: Found in open, wet areas near rivers, ditches, and lakes, the elderberry grows mainly in the eastern states.

Edible Parts and Preparing: The flowers can be soaked in water for eight hours and then the liquid can be drunk. The fruit is also edible but don't eat any other parts of the plant—they are poisonous.

Hazelnut

Description: The nuts grow on bushes in very bristly husks.

Location: Hazelnut grows in dense thickets near streambeds and in open areas and can be found all over the United States.

Edible Parts and Preparing: In the autumn, the hazelnut ripens and can be cracked open and the kernel eaten. Eating dried nuts is also tasty.

Juniper

Description: Also known as cedar, this shrub has very small, scaly leaves that are densely crowded on the branches. Berrylike cones on the plant are usually blue and are covered with a whitish wax.

Location: They grow in open, dry, sunny places throughout the country.

Edible Parts and Preparing: Both berries and twigs are edible. The berries can be consumed raw or the seeds may be roasted to make a substitute for coffee. Dried and crushed berries are good to season meat. Twigs can be made into tea.

Lotus

Description: This plant has large, yellow flowers and leaves that float on or above the surface of the water. The lotus fruit has a distinct, flattened shape and possesses around 20 hard seeds.

Location: Found on fresh water in quiet areas, the lotus plant is native to North America.

Edible Parts and Preparing: All parts of the lotus plant are edible, raw or cooked. Bake or boil the fleshy parts that grow underwater and boil young leaves. The seeds are quite nutritious and can be eaten raw or they can be ground into flour.

Marsh Marigold

Description: Marsh marigold has round, dark green leaves and a short stem. It also has bright yellow flowers.

Location: The plant can be found in bogs and lakes in the northeastern states.

Edible Parts and Preparing: All parts can be boiled and eaten. Do not consume any portion raw.

Mulberry

Description: The mulberry tree has alternate, lobed leaves with rough surfaces and blue or black seeded fruits.

Location: These trees are found in forested areas and near roadsides in temperate and tropical regions of the United States.

Edible Parts and Preparing: The fruit can be consumed either raw or cooked and it can also be dried. Make sure the fruit is ripe or it can cause hallucinations and extreme nausea.

Nettle

Description: Nettle plants grow several feet high and have small flowers. The stems, leafstalks, and undersides of the leaves all contain fine, hairlike bristles that cause a stinging sensation on the skin.

Location: This plant grows in moist areas near streams or on the edges of forests. It can be found throughout the United States.

Edible Parts and Preparing: The young shoots and leaves are edible. To eat, boil the plant for 10 to 15 minutes.

Oak

Description: These trees have alternating leaves and acorns. Red oaks have bristly leaves and smooth bark on the upper part of the tree and their acorns need two years to reach maturity. White oaks have leaves with no bristles and rough bark on the upper part of the tree. Their acorns only take one year to mature.

Location: Found in various locations and habitats throughout the country.

Edible Parts and Preparing: All parts of the tree are edible, but most are very bitter. Shell the acorns and soak them in water for one or two days to remove their tannic acid. Boil the acorns to eat or grind them into flour for baking.

Palmetto Palm

Description: This is a tall tree with no branches and has a continual leaf base on the trunk. The leaves are large, simple, and lobed and it has dark blue or black fruits that contain a hard seed.

Location: This tree is found throughout the southeastern coast.

Edible Parts and Preparing: The palmetto palm fruit can be eaten raw. The seeds can also be ground into flour, and the heart of the palm is a nutritious source of food, but the top of the tree must be cut down in order to reach it.

Persimmon

Description: The persimmon tree has alternating, elliptical leaves that are dark green in color, and inconspicuous flowers. It has orange fruits that are very sticky and contain many seeds.

Location: Growing on the margins of forests, it resides in the eastern part of the country.

Edible Parts and Preparing: The leaves provide a good source of vitamin C and can be dried and soaked in hot water to make tea. The fruit can be consumed either baked or raw and the seeds may be eaten once roasted.

Pine

Description: Pine trees have needlelike leaves that are grouped into bundles of one to five needles. They have a very pungent, distinguishing odor.

Location: Pines grow best in sunny, open areas and are found all over the United States.

Edible Parts and Preparing: The seeds are completely edible and can be consumed either raw or cooked. Also, the young male cones can be boiled or baked and eaten. Peel the bark off of thin twigs and chew the juicy inner bark. The needles can be dried and brewed to make tea that's high in vitamin C.

Other Uses: Pine tree resin can be used to waterproof items. Collect the resin from the tree, put it in a container, heat it, and use it as glue or, when cool, rub it on items to waterproof them.

Plantain

Description: The broad-leafed plantain grows close to the ground and the flowers are situated on a spike that rises from the middle of the leaf cluster. The narrow-leaf species has leaves covered with hairs that form a rosette. The flowers are very small.

Location: Plantains grow in lawns and along the side of the road in the northern Temperate Zone.

Edible Parts and Preparing: Young, tender leaves can be eaten raw, and older leaves should be cooked before consumption. The seeds may also be eaten either raw or roasted. Tea can also be made by boiling 1 ounce of the plant leaves in a few cups of water.

Pokeweed

Description: A rather tall plant, pokeweed has elliptical leaves and produces many large clusters of purple fruits in the late spring.

Location: Pokeweed grows in open and sunny areas in fields and along roadsides in the eastern United States.

Edible Parts and Preparing: If cooked, the young leaves and stems are edible. Be sure to boil them twice and discard the water from the first boiling. The fruit is also edible if cooked. Never eat any part of this plant raw, as it is poisonous.

Reindeer Moss

Description: This is a low plant that does not flower. However, it does produce bright red structures used for reproduction.

Location: It grows in dry, open areas in much of the country.

Edible Parts and Preparing: While having a crunchy, brittle texture, the whole plant can be eaten. To remove some of the bitterness, soak it in water and then dry and crush it, adding it to milk or other foods.

Sassafras

Description: This shrub has different leaves—some have one lobe, others two lobes, and others have none at all. The flowers are small and yellow and appear in the early spring. The plant has dark blue fruit.

Location: Sassafras grows near roads and forests in sunny, open areas. It is common throughout the eastern states.

Edible Parts and Preparing: The young twigs and leaves can be eaten either fresh or dried—add them to soups. Dig out the underground portion of the shrub, peel off the bark, and dry it. Boil it in water to make tea.

Other Uses: Shredding the tender twigs will make a handy toothbrush.

Prickly Pear Cactus

Description: This plant has flat, pad-like green stems and round, furry dots that contain sharp-pointed hairs.

Location: Found in arid regions and in dry, sandy areas in wetter regions, it can be found throughout the United States.

Edible Parts and Preparing: All parts of this plant are edible. To eat the fruit, peel it or crush it to make a juice. The seeds can be roasted and ground into flour.

Spatterdock

Description: The leaves of this plant are quite long and have a triangular notch at the base. Spatterdock has yellow flowers that become bottle-shaped fruits, which are green when ripe.

Location: Spatterdock is found in fresh, shallow water throughout the country.

Edible Parts and Preparing: All parts of the plant are edible and the fruits have brown seeds that can be roasted and ground into flour. The rootstock can be dug out of the mud, peeled, and boiled.

Strawberry

Description: This is a small plant with a three-leaved pattern. Small, white flowers appear in the springtime and the fruit is red and very fleshy.

Location: These plants prefer sunny, open spaces, are commonly planted, and appear in the northern Temperate Zone.

Edible Parts and Preparing: The fruit can be eaten raw, cooked, or dried. The plant leaves may also be eaten or dried to make tea.

Edible Parts and Preparing: Peel the stalks, cut them into smaller sections, and boil them to consume. The root may be eaten raw or cooked.

Walnut

Description: Walnuts grow on large trees and have divided leaves. The walnut has a thick, outer husk that needs to be removed before getting to the hard, inner shell.

Location: The black walnut tree is common in the eastern states.

Edible Parts and Preparing: Nut kernels become ripe in the fall and the meat can be obtained by cracking the shell.

Thistle

Description: This plant may grow very high and has long-pointed, prickly leaves.

Location: Thistle grows in woods and fields all over the country.

Water Lily

Description: With large, triangular leaves that float on water, these plants have fragrant flowers that are white or red. They also have thick rhizomes that grow in the mud.

Location: Water lilies are found in many temperate areas.

Edible Parts and Preparing: The flowers, seeds, and rhizomes can be eaten either raw or cooked. Peel the corky rind off of the rhizome and eat it raw or slice it thinly, dry it, and grind into flour. The seeds can also be made into flour after drying, parching, and grinding.

Wild Grapevine

Description: This vine will climb on tendrils, and most of these plants produce deeply lobed leaves. The grapes grow in pyramidal bunches and are black-blue, amber, or white when ripe.

Location: Climbing over other vegetation on the edges of forested areas, they can be found in the eastern and southwestern parts of the United States.

Edible Parts and Preparing: Only the ripe grape can be eaten.

Wild Onion and Garlic

Description: These are recognized by their distinctive odors.

Location: They are found in open areas that get lots of sun throughout temperate areas.

Edible Parts and Preparing: The bulbs and young leaves are edible and can be consumed either raw or cooked.

Wild Rose

Description: This shrub has alternating leaves and sharp prickles. It has red, pink, or yellow flowers and fruit (rose hip) that remains on the shrub all year.

Location: These shrubs occur in dry fields throughout the country.

Edible Parts and Preparing: The flowers and buds are edible raw or boiled. Boil fresh, young leaves to make tea. The rose hips can be eaten once the flowers fall and they can be crushed once dried to make flour.

TIP

Violets can be candied and used to decorate cakes, cookies, or pastries. Pick the flowers with a tiny bit of stem, wash, and allow to dry thoroughly on a paper towel or a rack. Heat ½ cup water, 1 cup sugar, and ¼ teaspoon almond extract in a saucepan. Use tweezers to carefully dip each flower in the hot liquid. Set on wax paper and dust with sugar until every flower is thoroughly coated. If desired, snip off remaining stems with small scissors. Allow flowers to dry for a few hours in a warm, dry place.

Edible Wild Mushrooms

A walk through the woods will likely reveal several varieties of mushrooms, and chances are that some are the types that are edible. However, because some mushrooms are very poisonous, it is important never to try a mushroom of which you are unsure. Never eat a mushroom with gills, or, for that matter, any mushroom that you cannot positively identify as edible. Also, never eat mushrooms that appear wilted, damaged, or rotten.

Here are some common edible mushrooms that you can easily identify and enjoy.

▲ Chanterelles.

Chanterelles

These trumpet-shaped mushrooms have wavy edges and interconnected blunt-ridged gills under the caps. They are varied shades of yellow and have a fruity fragrance. They grow in summer and fall on the ground of hardwood forests. Because chanterelles tend to be tough, they are best when slowly sautéed or added to stews or soups.

Notes: Beware of Jack O'Lantern mushrooms, which look and smell similarly to chanterelles. Jack O'Lanterns have sharp, knifelike gills instead of the blunt gills of chanterelles, and generally grow in large clusters at the base of trees or on decaying wood.

Coral Fungi

These fungi are aptly named for their bunches of upward-facing branching stems, which look strikingly like coral. They are whitish, tan, yellowish, or sometimes pinkish or purple. They may reach 8 inches in height. They grow in the summer and fall in shady, wooded areas.

Notes: Avoid coral fungi that are bitter, have soft, gelatinous bases, or turn brown when you poke or squeeze them. These may have a laxative effect, though are not life-threatening.

▲ Coral fungi.

Morels

Morels are sometimes called sponge, pinecone, or honeycomb mushrooms because of the pattern of pits and ridges that appears on the caps. They can be anywhere from 2 to 12 inches tall. They may be yellow, brown, or black and grow in spring and early summer in wooded areas and on river bottoms. To cook, cut in half to check for insects, wash, and sauté, bake, or stew.

▲ Morels.

Notes: False morels can be poisonous and appear similar to morels because of their brainlike, irregularly shaped caps. However, they can be distinguished from true morels because false morel caps bulge inward instead of outward. The caps have lobes, folds, flaps, or wrinkles, but not pits and ridges like a true morel.

Puffballs

These round or pear-shaped mushrooms are often mistaken for golf balls or eggs. They are always whitish, tan, or gray and sometimes have a thick stem. Young puffballs tend to be white and older ones yellow or brown. Fully matured puffballs have dark spores scattered over the caps. Puffballs are generally found in late summer and fall on lawns, in the woods, or on old tree stumps. To eat, peel off the outer skin and eat raw or batter-fried.

▲ Puffballs.

WARNING!

Amanita mushrooms are very poisonous. Do not eat anything that resembles an amanita.

▲ Poisonous amanita mushroom.

Notes: Slice each puffball open before eating to be sure it is completely white inside. If there is any yellow, brown, or black, or **if there is a developing mushroom inside with a stalk, gills, and cap, do not eat!** Amanitas, which are very poisonous, can appear similar to puffballs when they are young. Do not eat if the mushroom gives off an unpleasant odor.

▲ Shaggy mane mushroom.

Shaggy Mane Mushrooms

This mushroom got its name from its cap, which is a white cylinder with shaggy, upturned, brownish scales. As the mushroom matures, the bottom outside circumference of the cap becomes black. Shaggy manes are generally 4 to 6 inches tall and grow in all the warm seasons in fields and on lawns.

Shaggy manes are tastiest eaten when young, but they're easiest to identify once the bottoms of the caps begin to turn black. They are delicious sautéed in butter or olive oil and lightly seasoned with salt, garlic, or nutmeg.

Make Your Own Foods

Make Your Own Butter

Making butter the old-fashioned way is incredibly simple and very gratifying. It's a great project to do with kids, too. All you need is a jar, a marble, some fresh cream, and about 20 minutes.

1. Start with about twice as much heavy whipping cream as you'll want butter. Pour it into the jar, drop in the marble, close the lid tightly, and start shaking.
2. Check the consistency of the cream every three to four minutes. The liquid will turn into whipped cream, and then eventually you'll see little clumps of butter forming in the jar. Keep shaking for another few minutes and then begin to strain out the liquid into another jar. This is buttermilk, which is great for use in making pancakes, waffles, biscuits, and muffins.

3. The butter is now ready, but it will store better if you wash and work it. Add ½ cup of ice-cold water and continue to shake for two or three minutes. Strain out the water and repeat. When the strained water is clear, mash the butter to extract the last of the water, and strain.
4. Scoop the butter into a ramekin, mold, or wax paper.

If desired, add salt or chopped fresh herbs to your butter just before storing or serving. Butter can also be made in a food processor or blender to speed up the processing time.

▲ Steps for making butter.

Make Your Own Yogurt

Yogurt is simple to make and is delicious on its own, as a dessert, in baked goods, or in place of sour cream. Yogurt is basically fermented milk. You can make it by adding the active cultures *Streptococcus thermophilus* and *Lactobacillus bulgaricus* to heated milk, which will produce lactic acid, creating yogurt's tart flavor and thick consistency.

Yogurt is thought to have originated many centuries ago among the nomadic tribes of Eastern Europe and Western Asia. Milk stored in animal skins would acidify and coagulate. The acid helped preserve the milk from further spoilage and from the growth of pathogens (disease-causing microorganisms).

Ingredients
Makes 4 to 5 cups of yogurt

- **1 quart milk** (cream, whole, low-fat, or skim)—In general the higher the milk fat level in the yogurt, the creamier and smoother it will taste. **Note:** If you use home-produced milk it *must* be pasteurized before preparing yogurt. See the center box for tips on pasteurizing milk.
- **Nonfat dry milk powder**—Use ⅓ cup powder when using whole or low-fat milk, or use ⅔ cup powder when using skim milk. The higher the milk solids, the firmer the yogurt will be. For even more firmness add gelatin (directions below).
- **Commercial, unflavored, cultured yogurt**—Use ¼ cup. Be sure the product label indicates that it contains a live culture. Also note the content of the culture. *L. bulgaricus* and *S. thermophilus* are required in yogurt, but some manufacturers may add *L. acidophilus* or *B. bifidum*. The latter two are used for slight variations in flavor, but more commonly for health reasons attributed to these organisms. All culture variations will make a successful yogurt.
- **2 to 4 tablespoons sugar or honey (optional)**
- **1 teaspoon unflavored gelatin (optional)**—For a thick, firm yogurt, swell 1 teaspoon gelatin in a little milk for 5 minutes. Add this to the milk and nonfat dry milk mixture before cooking.

Supplies
- **Double boiler or regular saucepan**—1 to 2 quarts in capacity larger than the volume of yogurt you wish to make.
- **Cooking or jelly thermometer**—A thermometer that can clip to the side of the saucepan and remain in the milk works best. Accurate temperatures are critical for successful processing.
- **Mixing spoon**
- **Yogurt containers**—cups with lids or canning jars with lids.
- **Incubator**—a yogurt-maker, oven, heating pad, or warm spot in your kitchen. To use your oven, place yogurt containers into deep pans of 110°F water. Water should come at least halfway up the containers. Set oven temperature at lowest point to maintain water temperature at 110°F.

Monitor temperature throughout incubation, making adjustments as necessary.

How to Pasteurize Raw Milk

If you are using fresh milk that hasn't been processed, you can pasteurize it yourself. Heat water in the bottom section of a double boiler and pour milk into the top section. Cover the milk and heat to 165°F while stirring constantly for uniform heating. Cool immediately by setting the top section of the double boiler in ice water or cold running water. Store milk in the refrigerator in clean containers until ready for making yogurt.

Processing

1. Combine ingredients and heat. Heating the milk is necessary to change the milk proteins so that they set together rather than form curds and whey. Do not substitute this heating step for pasteurization. Place cold, pasteurized milk in a double boiler and stir in nonfat, dry milk powder. Adding nonfat, dry milk to heated milk will cause some milk proteins to coagulate and form strings. Add sugar or honey if a sweeter, less tart yogurt is desired. Heat milk to 200°F, stirring gently and hold for 10 minutes for thinner yogurt, or hold 20 minutes for thicker yogurt. Do not boil. Be careful and stir constantly to avoid scorching if not using a double boiler.

2. Cool and inoculate. Place the top of the double boiler in cold water to cool milk rapidly to 112 to 115°F. Remove one cup of the warm milk and blend it with the yogurt starter culture. Add this to the rest of the warm milk. The temperature of the mixture should now be 110 to 112°F.

3. Incubate. Pour immediately into clean, warm containers; cover and place in prepared incubator. Close the incubator and incubate about 4 to 7 hours at 110°F, ± 5°F. Yogurt should set firm when the proper acid level is achieved (pH 4.6). Incubating yogurt for several hours past the time after the yogurt has set will produce more acidity. This will result in a more tart or acidic flavor and eventually cause the whey to separate.

4. Refrigerate. Rapid cooling stops the development of acid. Yogurt will keep for about 10 to 21 days if held in the refrigerator at 40°F or lower.

Yogurt Types

Set yogurt: A solid set where the yogurt firms in a container and is not disturbed.

Stirred yogurt: Yogurt made in a large container then spooned or otherwise dispensed into secondary serving containers. The consistency of the "set" is broken and the texture is less firm than set yogurt. This is the most popular form of commercial yogurt.

Drinking yogurt: Stirred yogurt into which additional milk and flavors are mixed. Add fruit or fruit syrups to taste. Mix in milk to achieve the desired thickness. The shelf life of this product is four to 10 days, since the pH is raised by the addition of fresh milk. Some whey separation will occur and is natural. Commercial products recommend a thorough shaking before consumption.

Fruit yogurt: Fruit, fruit syrups, or pie filling can be added to the yogurt. Place them on top, on bottom, or stir them into the yogurt.

Troubleshooting

- If milk forms some clumps or strings during the heating step, some milk proteins may have jelled. Take the solids out with a slotted spoon or, in difficult cases, after cooking pour the milk mixture through a clean colander or cheesecloth before inoculation.
- When yogurt fails to coagulate properly, it's because the pH is not low enough. Milk proteins will coagulate when the pH has dropped to 4.6. This is done by the culture growing and producing acids. Adding culture to very hot milk (+115°F) can kill bacteria. Use a thermometer to carefully control temperature.
- If yogurt takes too long to make, it may be because the temperature is off. Too hot or too cold of an incubation temperature can slow down culture growth. Use a thermometer to carefully control temperature.
- If yogurt just isn't working, it may be because the starter culture was of poor quality. Use a fresh, recently purchased culture from the grocery store each time you make yogurt.
- If yogurt tastes or smells bad, it's likely because the starter culture is contaminated. Obtain new culture for the next batch.
- If yogurt has over-set or incubated too long, refrigerate yogurt immediately after a firm coagulum has formed.

- If yogurt tastes a little odd, it could be due to overheating or boiling of the milk. Use a thermometer to carefully control temperature.
- When whey collects on the surface of the yogurt, it's called syneresis. Some syneresis is natural. Excessive separation of whey, however, can be caused by incubating yogurt too long or by agitating the yogurt while it is setting.

Storing Your Yogurt

- Always pasteurize milk or use commercially pasteurized milk to make yogurt.
- Discard batches that fail to set properly, especially those due to culture errors.
- Yogurt generally has a 10- to 21-day shelf life when made and stored properly in the refrigerator below 40°F.
- Always use clean and sanitized equipment and containers to ensure a long shelf life for your yogurt. Clean equipment and containers in hot water with detergent, then rinse well. Allow to air dry.

Make Your Own Cheese

There are endless varieties of cheese you can make, but they all fall into two main categories: soft and hard. Soft cheeses (like cream cheese) are easier to make because they don't require a cheese press. The curds in hard cheeses (like cheddar) are pressed together to form a solid block or wheel, which requires more time and effort, but hard cheeses will keep longer than soft cheeses, and generally have a much stronger flavor.

Cheese is basically curdled milk and is made by adding an enzyme (typically rennet) to milk, allowing curds to form, heating the mixture, straining out the whey, and finally pressing the curds together. Cheeses such

as *queso fresco* or *queso blanco* (traditionally eaten in Latin American countries) and *paneer* (traditionally eaten in India), are made with an acid such as vinegar or lemon juice instead of bacterial cultures or rennet.

You can use any kind of milk to make cheese, including cow's milk, goat's milk, sheep's milk, and even buffalo's milk (used for traditional mozzarella). For the richest flavor, try to get raw milk from a local farmer. If you don't know of one near you, visit realmilk.com/where.html for a listing of raw milk suppliers in your state. You can use homogenized milk, but it will produce weaker curds and a milder flavor. If your milk is pasteurized, you'll need to "ripen" it by heating it in a double boiler until it reaches 86°F and then adding 1 cup of unpasteurized, preservative-free, cultured buttermilk per gallon of milk and letting it stand 30 minutes to three hours (the longer you leave it, the sharper the flavor will be). If you cannot find unpasteurized buttermilk, diluting ⅛ teaspoon calcium chloride (available from online cheesemaker suppliers) in ¼ cup of water and adding it to your milk will create a similar effect.

Rennet (also called rennin or chymosin) is sold online at cheesemaking sites in tablet or liquid form. You may also be able to find Junket rennet tablets near the pudding and gelatin in your grocery store. One teaspoon of liquid rennet is the equivalent of one rennet tablet, which is enough to turn 5 gallons of milk into cheese (estimate four drops of liquid rennet per gallon of milk). Microbial rennet is a vegetarian alternative that is available for purchase online.

Preparation

It's important to keep your hands clean and all equipment sterile when making cheese.

1. Wash hands and all equipment with soapy detergent before and after use.
2. Rinse all equipment with clean water, removing all soapy residue.
3. Boil all cheesemaking equipment between uses.
4. For best-quality cheese, use new cheesecloth each time you make cheese. (Sterilize cheesecloth by first washing, then boiling.)
5. Squeaky clean is clean. If you can feel a residue on the equipment, it is not clean.

Yogurt Cheese

This soft cheese has a flavor similar to sour cream and a texture like cream cheese. A pint of yogurt will yield approximately ¼ pound of cheese. The yogurt cheese has a shelf life of approximately seven to 14 days when wrapped and placed in the refrigerator and kept at less than 40°F.

Ingredients
Plain, whole-milk yogurt

Directions

1. Line a large strainer or colander with cheesecloth.
2. Place the lined strainer over a bowl and pour in the yogurt. Do not use yogurt made with the addition of gelatin, as gelatin will inhibit whey separation.
3. Let yogurt drain overnight, covered with plastic wrap. Empty the whey from the bowl.
4. Fill a strong, plastic storage bag with some water, seal, and place over the cheese to weigh it down. Let the cheese stand another 8 hours and then enjoy!

Queso Blanco

Queso blanco is a white, semi-hard cheese made without culture or rennet. It is eaten fresh and may be flavored with peppers, herbs, and spices. It is considered a "frying cheese," meaning it does not melt and may be deep-fried or grilled. *Queso blanco* is best eaten fresh, so try this small recipe the first time you make it. If it disappears quickly, next time double or triple the recipe. This recipe will yield about ½ cup of cheese.

Ingredients

2 cups milk
4 tsp white vinegar
Salt
Minced jalapeño, black pepper, chives, or other herbs to taste

Directions

1. Heat milk to 176°F for 20 minutes.
2. Add vinegar slowly to the hot milk until the whey is semi-clear and the curd particles begin to form stretchy clumps. Stir for 5 to 10 minutes. When it's ready, you should be able to stretch a piece of curd about ⅓ inch before it breaks.
3. Allow to cool, and strain off the whey by filtering through a cheesecloth-lined colander or a cloth bag.
4. Work in salt and spices to taste.
5. Press the curd in a mold or simply leave in a ball.
6. *Queso blanco* may keep for several weeks if stored in a refrigerator, but is best eaten fresh.

Ricotta Cheese

Making ricotta is very similar to making *queso blanco*, though it takes a bit longer. Start the cheese in the morning for use at dinner, or make a day ahead. Use it in lasagna, in desserts, or all on its own.

Ingredients

1 gallon milk
⅓ cup plus 1 tsp white vinegar
¼ tsp salt

Directions

1. Pour milk into a large pot, add salt, and heat slowly while stirring until the milk reaches 180°F.
2. Remove from heat and add vinegar. Stir for one minute as curds begin to form.
3. Cover and allow to sit undisturbed for two hours.
4. Pour mixture into a colander lined with cheesecloth, and allow to drain for two or more hours.
5. Store in a sealed container for up to a week.

Mozzarella

This mild cheese will make your homemade pizza especially delicious. Or slice it and eat with fresh tomatoes and basil from the garden. Fresh cheese can be stored in saltwater but must be eaten within two days.

Ingredients

1 gallon 2 percent milk
¼ cup fresh, plain yogurt (see recipe on page 184)
One tablet rennet or 1 tsp liquid rennet dissolved in
    ½ cup tap water
Brine: use 2 pounds of salt per gallon of water

Directions

1. Heat milk to 90°F and add yogurt. Stir slowly for 15 minutes while keeping the temperature constant.
2. Add rennet mixture and stir for 3 to 5 minutes.
3. Cover, remove from heat, and allow to stand until coagulated, about 30 minutes.
4. Cut curd into ½-inch cubes. Allow to stand for 15 minutes with occasional stirring.
5. Return to heat and slowly increase temperature to 118°F over a period of 45 minutes. Hold this temperature for an additional 15 minutes.
6. Drain off the whey by transferring the mixture to a cheesecloth-lined colander. Use a spoon to press the liquid out of the curds. Transfer the mat of curd to a flat pan that can be kept warm in a low oven. Do not cut mat, but turn it over every 15 minutes for a 2-hour period. Mat should be tight when finished.
7. Cut the mat into long strips 1 to 2 inches wide and place in hot water (180°F). Using wooden spoons, tumble and stretch it under water until it becomes elastic, about 15 minutes.
8. Remove curd from hot water and shape it by hand into a ball or a loaf, kneading in the salt. Place cheese in cold water (40°F) for approximately 1 hour.
9. Store in a solution of 2 teaspoons salt to 1 cup water.

Cheddar Cheese

Cheddar is a New England and Wisconsin favorite. The longer you age it, the sharper the flavor will be. Try a slice with a wedge of homemade apple pie.

Ingredients

1 gallon milk
¼ cup buttermilk
1 tablet rennet, or 1 tsp liquid rennet
1½ tsp salt

Directions

1. Combine milk and buttermilk and allow the mixture to ripen overnight.
2. The next day, heat milk to 90°F in a double boiler and add rennet.

3. After about 45 minutes, cut curds into small cubes and let sit 15 minutes.
4. Heat very slowly to 100°F and cook for about an hour or until a cooled piece of curd will keep its shape when squeezed.
5. Drain curds and rinse out the double boiler.
6. Place a rack lined with cheesecloth inside the double boiler and spread the curds on the cloth. Cover and reheat at about 98°F for 30 to 40 minutes. The curds will become one solid mass.

7. Remove the curds, cut them into 1-inch wide strips, and return them to the pan. Turn the strips every 15 to 20 minutes for one hour.
8. Cut the strips into cubes and mix in salt.
9. Let the curds stand for 10 minutes, place them in cheesecloth, and press in a cheese press with 15 pounds for 10 minutes, then with 30 pounds for an hour.
10. Remove the cheese from the press, unwrap it, dip in warm water, and fill in any cracks.
11. Wrap again in cheesecloth and press with 40 pounds for 24 hours.
12. Remove from the press and let the cheese dry about five days in a cool, well-ventilated area, turning the cheese twice a day and wiping it with a clean cloth. When a hard skin has formed, rub with oil or seal with wax. You can eat the cheese after six weeks, but for the strongest flavor, allow cheese to age for six months or more.

Make Your Own Simple Cheese Press

1. Remove both ends of a large coffee can or thoroughly cleaned paint can, saving one end. Use an awl or a hammer and long nail to pierce the sides in several places, piercing from the inside out.
2. Place the can on a cooling rack inside a larger basin. Leave the bottom of the can in place.
3. Use a saw to cut a ¾-inch-thick circle of wood to create a "cheese follower." It should be small enough in diameter to fit easily in the can.
4. Place cheese curds in the can, and top with the cheese follower. Place several bricks wrapped in cloth or foil on top of the cheese follower to weigh down curds.
5. Once the cheese is fully pressed, remove the bricks and bottom of the can. Use the cheese follower to push the cheese out of the can.

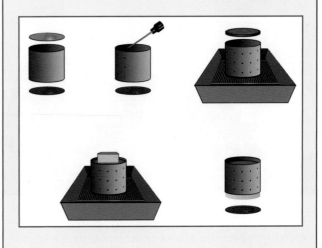

Make Your Own Ice Cream

Supplies
1-pound coffee can
3-pound coffee can
Duct tape
Ice
1 cup salt

Ingredients
2 cups half and half
½ cup sugar
1 tsp vanilla

Directions
1. Mix all the ingredients in the 1-pound coffee can. Cover the lid with duct tape to ensure it is tightly sealed.
2. Place the smaller can inside the larger can and fill the space between the two with ice and salt.

3. Cover the large can and seal with duct tape. Roll the can back and forth for 15 minutes. To reduce noise, place a towel on your working surface, or work on a rug.
4. Dump out ice and water. Stir contents of small can. Store ice cream in a glass or plastic container (if you leave it in the can it may take on a metallic flavor).

If desired, add cocoa powder, coffee granules, crushed peppermint sticks or other candy, or fruit.

Brew Your Own Beer

Making your own brew is not difficult, but be sure to use water that is not heavily chlorinated or that has a strong mineral flavor. The sweetness of malt (from barley) and the bitterness of hops (the female flower of the hop vine) balance each other to create beer's rich flavor. The fermentation is caused by the yeast consuming the sugar, which produces carbon dioxide and alcohol.

Malt is barley that has begun to germinate, which creates enzymes necessary for converting starch to sugar. When you're first experimenting with brewing beer, use store-bought malt and hops, as they will have more predictable results. If you want to make your own malt, let the barley grains sprout. Once the shoots are the same length as the kernels, stop the growth by heating the barley to between 185 and 230°F. At that point, the barley is malted and must be cracked and soaked in 150°F water for about six hours. Finally, strain the barley and use the liquid for your beer.

Supplies
10-gallon pail
Hydrometer
Siphon and clamp
12 2-liter bottles, sterilized

Ingredients
Water
40-oz can pre-hopped malt extract
6 to 7 cups white sugar or 8 to 9 cups corn sugar
1 tsp brewer's yeast
24 tsp white granulated sugar

Directions
1. Clean pail, hydrometer, and siphon with warm, soapy water and rinse thoroughly. Then sterilize by rinsing with a mix of 1 tablespoon household bleach and 1 gallon water. Rinse a final time with clean water.
2. Pour 2½ to 3 gallons cold water in the pail.

Make Your Own Wine

Supplies
Colander or strainer
Large bowl or pot
1-gallon container with a secure lid
Spoon
Potato masher
Funnel

Ingredients
1 qt fruit
2 cups sugar
1 gallon water, divided
1 package active yeast

3. Bring 7½ quarts of water to a boil in a large pot. Add malt extract very slowly, stirring, and then simmer uncovered for 20 minutes.
4. Add sugar and stir until dissolved.
5. Dump the hot mixture into the pail containing the cold water, splashing it in to increase the oxygen in the liquid (yeast needs oxygen to do its job).
6. Add ice water until mixture is about 70°F (water that is too hot can kill the yeast).
7. Add the yeast and stir well.
8. Cover loosely (if the lid is too tight, the pail could explode) and allow to sit in a moderate to cool place (around 62 to 68°F) for 6 to 10 days. Don't open the pail, tip it, or shake it for at least 6 days.
9. Place the hydrometer in the beer and give it a spin to release air bubbles. The hydrometer should read about 1.008 for dark beers and 1.010 to 1.105 for light beers.
10. When the beer is ready, place the bucket on a bench or sturdy table and place the sterilized bottles on the floor below. Add about 2 teaspoons of white granulated sugar to each bottle to help carbonate the beer.
11. Use the siphon and clamp to siphon the beer into the bottles, screw on the lids, give the bottles a quick shake, and store the bottles in a warm, dark area for a few days, and then move into cool, dark area. Store at least three weeks before drinking.

Directions
1. Thoroughly clean all your cooking utensils with warm, soapy water and rinse thoroughly. Then sterilize by rinsing with a mix of 1 tablespoon household bleach and 1 gallon water. Rinse a final time with clean water.
2. In a bowl, crush the fruit with a potato masher (or use a food processor) until smooth.
3. Dissolve the sugar in 1 cup of hot water. Allow to cool to room temperature and add to the fruit.
4. Dissolve the yeast in 2 cups of warm water and add to the fruit, along with the remaining water. Stir once every day for a week.
5. Strain through a colander into your 1-gallon container, close lid securely, and allow to rest in a cool, dark place for 6 weeks.
6. Strain the wine into your sterilized bottles (leaving one empty) and cork lightly. After three days, strain the wine from one bottle into the empty one, leaving about 1 inch headspace below the cork. Repeat until bottles are full.

Dandelion Wine

Ingredients

4 qts dandelion blossoms (use the full dandelion heads—not just the petals)

4 qts boiling water

2 oranges

2 lemons

4 lbs sugar

2 tbsp yeast

Directions

1. Wash dandelion blossoms and place them in a large pot. Pour 4 quarts of boiling water over them and let stand 24 hours.
2. Strain through cheesecloth and add grated rind and juice of two oranges and two lemons, four pounds of granulated sugar, and two tablespoonfuls yeast.
3. Let stand one week, then strain and fill bottles.

7. Soak new corks in warm water for about 2 hours, rinse several times, place securely in bottles, and seal with paraffin.

Sharing Your Bounty

Plant a Row for the Hungry (PAR) Program

One in ten households in the United States experience hunger or the risk of hunger every year. This is an astounding number of adults and children who are not receiving the proper foods, nutrients, and sustenance to maintain a healthy lifestyle. What can you do as a gardener to help provide fresh produce to the hungry in your community? Churches, schools, and other local organizations try to provide food for those who are hungry by giving to local food banks and shelters and by establishing soup kitchens and other programs. Often these food drives can only accept nonperishable items, but, recognizing the need for fresh fruits and vegetables in a healthy diet, many organizations are beginning to take produce on a conditional basis. If they can use the produce in their prepared meals or distribute them to needy families before the food begins to perish, they will accept it.

Started in 1995 in Anchorage, Alaska, by Jeff Lowenfels as a public service program of the Garden Writers Association (GWA) and Foundation, PAR is a way for those who garden and grow their own vegetables and fruit to help combat hunger and poverty in their local communities. PAR encourages local gardeners to plant one extra row of produce in their gardens and then to donate that harvest to neighbors or others in the community who struggle to feed themselves and their families. Donating excess vegetables and fruit to your local food bank, soup kitchen, shelter, or other food agency to help feed the hungry in your local area is a wonderful way to share your love of gardening and to be an active and important member of your community.

Anyone in the U.S. or Canada can participate in the PAR program, and members grow and donate over one million tons of food a year to help fight hunger in their local communities. Some people establish a community garden that solely grows food to give to local pantries and soup kitchens. Others simply grow additional crops and give individually to those in need.

If you want to become involved in the PAR program, it is best to call or e-mail the GWA to receive more information about PAR programs in your area. It is also beneficial to call or visit local food agencies and see what crops they need most or what types of fruits and vegetables they would like to provide for their customers. Most agencies seek out food that can be shelved for a few days if necessary and also foods that are high in nutritional value. They also accept fresh herbs that they can use when making foods such as soups. Flowers are also acceptable donations.

When thinking about growing excess vegetables and fruit in your garden for donation, it is good to select easily grown crops that will help to maximize your harvest and encourage enthusiasm about growing and tending the plants. Some easily grown and highly desirable plants are: beans, cucumbers, peas, radishes, summer squash, and tomatoes. Once your produce is ready for harvesting, gather up the excess and take it to a selected PAR drop-off site or, if acceptable, directly to the food agency.

There are some guidelines for growing fruits and vegetables that are acceptable for donation. Always be sure to contact your local food banks and soup kitchens for information on what they need in terms of fresh produce. Be sure to space your plantings apart so that your growing season and harvesting season are extended over a longer period of time. That way, you'll be able to donate longer. Choose to grow produce that lasts well and stays fresher longer. Pick your ripe produce promptly and be sure to clean it of any dirt (but don't wash it). And, of course, don't ever give away overripe or spoiled produce.

How to Start Your Own PAR Program

What if your local community does not yet have a PAR program? It is easy to establish your own program by contacting PAR (either by e-mail, by visiting the GWA website, or by calling toll free). This way, you will be able to gain access to information on creating a successful PAR program. Next, you should try to recruit volunteers (neighbors, community gardeners, garden clubs, garden centers, and nurseries) to be a part of the program. It is important to establish a local coordinator who can be a go-to person for any questions volunteers may have about the program, growing tips, and drop-off sites.

In addition to gathering volunteers, it is essential to find a food distribution agency partner who wants to collect the donated produce. This may be a food bank, food pantry, soup kitchen, or local shelter. It is also wise to find someone to market and publicize your local program. Getting the word out about the program will help gather support and more gardeners who want to help. There should also be someone appointed to help coordinate and oversee the drop-off sites and to take food to the designated area if need be.

For a PAR program to be a success, it is a good idea to reach out to your local extension services; community, church, and school gardens; businesses; and lo-

cal food agencies to see if a specific PAR garden can be established. It is also wise to ask farmers to donate their unsold produce from farmers' markets and trucks in the area. All of these various elements will help you to create a successful fresh food donation program in your area and will ensure that those who are hungry in your community will not be lacking in fresh produce.

For more information on Plant a Row for the Hungry, please call, e-mail, or visit the Garden Writers Association at:
1-877-GWAA-PAR
PAR@gwaa.org
www.gwaa.org
To find a local PAR contact in your area, please call the Foodchain at: 1-800-845-3008.

Dinner Parties

Inviting friends and family over for a feast is a wonderful way to share your garden's bounty. Whether you are celebrating a holiday or are just in the mood for some company, a dinner party is a chance to connect with others, experiment with exciting recipes, and showcase the fruits of your labor.

Plan your menu around the produce that is in season. For a spring celebration, serve an asparagus feta quiche with strawberry iced tea and rhubarb crisp for dessert. For a harvest feast, serve a hearty stew in a carved-out pumpkin and baked apples. Be creative with your place settings, utilizing dried berries, pinecones, gourds, and other natural decorations to set a welcoming table. Light a couple of homemade candles and your meal is sure to be a memorable treat.

Following are some possible menus, inspired by the seasons. If the ingredients used in these recipes are not available in-season in your area, get creative by substituting with local flavors.

Spring Menu

For spring menus, think light and fresh. Your garden is not likely to be in full bloom yet, but take advantage of early risers like artichokes, asparagus, rhubarb, and some berries. Pick fresh daffodils, tulips, or pussy willows, and arrange them in a vase for a centerpiece. Make the pie in the morning or a day ahead to free up your time closer to when guests arrive. The artichoke dip can also be made ahead and reheated before serving.

Hot Artichoke Dip with Homemade Crackers
Citrus Chicken
Steamed Asparagus with Tarragon Butter
Rhubarb Custard Pie

Hot Artichoke Dip with Homemade Crackers

Hot Artichoke Dip

1 pound cream cheese
1 chopped jalapeño
¼ cup grated Parmesan cheese

Crackers

1 cup flour, plus some for dusting the work surface (any flour will work; try mixing white, spelt, and rye)
½ tsp salt
2 to 3 tbsp butter or olive oil
4 to 6 tbsp water
Dried oregano, basil, garlic, or other herbs as desired

Directions

1. To make the artichoke dip, combine all ingredients in an ovenproof dish. Bake at 350°F until hot and bubbly.
2. To make the crackers, combine all dry ingredients. Add water slowly, mixing well until dough forms a stretchy ball. It should not be too sticky.
3. Roll dough to ¹/₈ inch thick on a lightly floured surface. Transfer to lightly floured baking sheet and bake at 400°F for 10 to 15 minutes.
4. Once crackers are lightly browned, remove from oven, cool, and break into pieces.

Citrus Chicken

Ingredients

3 to 4 pounds chicken thighs and legs with bones, trimmed of excess fat
Juice and zest from 1 large lemon

Juice and zest from 1 orange
1 to 2 cloves garlic, crushed
1 tbsp fresh, finely chopped thyme (or 1 tsp dried)
1 tbsp fresh, finely chopped rosemary (or 1 tsp dried)
2 tsp fresh, finely chopped parsley (or 1 tsp dried)
1 tsp sea salt
1 tsp black pepper

Directions

1. Cut ½-inch-deep slits into chicken pieces to allow the marinade to better soak into the meat. Combine all marinade ingredients in a bowl. Place chicken and marinade in a freezer bag or covered dish, place in refrigerator, and allow to marinate for 2 hours.
2. Remove the chicken from the marinade (reserving the marinade) and place in a single layer in a roasting pan or large baking dish. Bake at 425°F for 50 minutes, basting once or twice with reserved marinade. When the chicken is lightly browned and the insides are no longer pink, it's ready to serve.

Steamed Asparagus with Tarragon Butter

Ingredients

1 large bunch asparagus
Butter (see recipe on page 184) with finely chopped fresh or dried tarragon mixed in

Directions

1. Cut off the woody bottom part of the asparagus stems (usually about 1 inch)
2. Boil about 3 minutes, or until just tender
3. Serve with pats of tarragon butter

Rhubarb Custard Pie

Pie Crust
2 cups flour
1 tsp salt
1 tsp sugar
1¼ cups butter, chilled
¼ cup ice water

Custard Filling
1 cup sugar
2 tbsp flour
1 cup each milk and cream (or 2 cups half and half)
2 eggs, beaten
1 tbsp vanilla
½ tsp grated nutmeg
2 cups diced rhubarb

Directions

1. For the pie crust, combine flour, salt, and sugar.
2. Cut butter into dry mixture, crumbling with fingers or a pastry cutter until the mixture resembles small peas.
3. Add the water slowly, mixing until the dough holds together in a ball. Divide into two balls. Keep dough chilled if you don't use it immediately.

4. Flour a large cutting board, or cover board with wax paper. Roll the dough to about ⅛ inch thick.
5. For the custard filling, beat together all ingredients except the rhubarb. Add the rhubarb and pour into pastry-lined 9-inch pie plate. Bake at 425°F for about 10 minutes. Reduce heat and continue baking at 350°F until filling is set, about 24 to 30 minutes. Cool before slicing.

Summer Menu

Here's a menu that highlights summer's fresh flavors: tomatoes, herbs, berries, and more. Make the cookies ahead of time to ensure they have time to chill in the freezer and so you don't have to worry about baking them while the potatoes and Brussels sprouts are roasting. The pork medallions with blackberry cream sauce are a favorite recipe of Marie Lawrence, who picks the blackberries from her yard in Vermont. You can also pan-fry the pork medallions, and grill the potatoes and sprouts on an outdoor grill, if you'd prefer.

> Fresh Tomato, Basil, and Mozzarella Salad
> Pork Medallions with Blackberry Cream Sauce
> Roasted New Potatoes and Brussels sprouts
> Chipwiches with Homemade Peppermint Stick Ice Cream

Fresh Tomato, Basil, and Mozzarella Salad

Ingredients
4 medium-sized ripe tomatoes
About 4 oz of mozzarella (see recipe on page 188), thinly sliced
Leaves from several sprigs of fresh basil
1 to 2 shallots, finely diced
⅛ cup olive oil
⅛ cup balsamic vinegar
Salt and pepper to taste

Directions

1. Layer tomato, mozzarella, and basil in a shallow dish and sprinkle the chopped shallots over top.
2. Drizzle olive oil and balsamic vinegar over the salad and add salt and pepper to taste.
3. Serve immediately, or leave to chill in the refrigerator until ready to serve.

Pork Medallions with Blackberry Cream Sauce

Ingredients

¼ cup flour	¼ tsp ginger
¼ tsp salt	⅛ tsp white pepper
About 1 pound pork tenderloin	2 tbsp butter
	2 tbsp olive oil
1 cup chicken stock	

Fruit Sauce

3 tbsp blackberry jam

¼ cup fruity wine (try blackberry merlot or use your own homemade wine—see page 197)

1 cup fresh or frozen blackberries

¼ cup cream

Directions

1. Combine all dry ingredients, flatten medallions slightly, and dredge them in the flour mixture.
2. In a large frying pan, sear medallions on both sides in the butter and olive oil.
3. Once they are uniformly browned, add 1 cup chicken stock, cover, and cook about 5 minutes.
4. While the pork cooks, make the fruit sauce. Combine jam and wine in a small saucepan and bring to a boil, stirring until smooth. Add the blackberries and remove from heat.
5. Transfer the medallions to a serving platter. Add the cream to the frying pan containing the meat drippings, whisking and simmering over low heat for about a minute.
6. Pour cream sauce over the medallions and then top with the berry sauce.

Roasted New Potatoes and Brussels Sprouts

Ingredients

2 cups Brussels sprouts

2 cups new potatoes

⅓ cup olive oil

Several sprigs fresh rosemary, finely chopped

Sea salt and black pepper to taste

Directions

1. Preheat oven to 425°F. Place a roasting pan on the middle rack and allow it to warm up with the oven.
2. Clean Brussels sprouts thoroughly, remove dried or yellowed outer leaves, chop off brown stems, and cut sprouts in half. Wash potatoes and cut each one in half. Leave the peels on.
3. Mix all ingredients, place on a single layer in the roasting pan, and cook until vegetables are tender and lightly browned (20 to 30 minutes).

Chipwiches with Homemade Peppermint Stick Ice Cream

Ingredients

1¼ cups all-purpose flour

1 cup whole wheat flour

1 tsp baking soda

1 tsp salt

1 cup butter, softened

1 cup brown sugar

½ cup granulated sugar

2 tsp vanilla extract

2 eggs

2 cups semi-sweet chocolate chips

Peppermint stick ice cream (follow recipe on page 190, adding crushed peppermint sticks at the end)

Directions

1. Preheat oven to 375°F and grease two cookie sheets.
2. Combine dry ingredients in a small bowl. Beat butter, sugars, and vanilla in a mixing bowl until creamy.
3. Add eggs, one at a time, beating well after each addition. Add dry mixture gradually, beating continually until thoroughly mixed. Stir in chocolate chips.
4. Drop batter by spoonfuls onto prepared cookie sheets and bake. Check cookies after 9 minutes. They should still be slightly gooey in the centers when done. If the edges are still very soft, bake for another 2 minutes. Remove from oven and allow to cool for a few minutes before removing to a cookie rack.
5. Transfer cookies to freezer until ready to serve.
6. Just before serving, use a wide knife to spread the ice cream on half of the frozen cookies. Place the remaining cookies on top to make sandwiches. Serve immediately.

Fall Menu

With autumn come wonderful root vegetables that are fabulous for stews or for roasting, and you'll finally get to indulge in the produce of your fruit orchards. This sausage and apple stew is very easy to prepare. Just stick it in the slow cooker mid-morning and you'll have the rest of the day free to bake the oatmeal bread and to enjoy the crisp fresh air. Serving the stew in a hollowed-out pumpkin is a fun way to spruce up your table. Use colorful autumn leaves, bittersweet vines, or decorative gourds to decorate the place settings.

Sausage and Apple Stew in a Pumpkin Bowl
Oatmeal Bread
Poached Pears

Sausage and Apple Stew in a Pumpkin Bowl

Ingredients

1¼ pounds sausage, cut into 1-inch pieces
3 medium-sized apples, peeled, cored, and cut into chunks
1 medium onion, cut into rings
2 pounds red potatoes, quartered
1½ cups chicken stock
¼ cup apple cider
1 tsp dried rosemary
¼ tsp ground allspice
Salt and pepper to taste
1 pumpkin

Directions

1. Combine all ingredients except pumpkin and cook in a slow cooker on low for about 5 hours.
2. Cut out the top from a medium- to large-sized pumpkin, cutting out a circle that is 6 to 8 inches in diameter. Scoop out the flesh inside, retaining the seeds to bake on a cookie sheet for a later snack.
3. Serve the stew in the cleaned pumpkin.

Oatmeal Bread

Ingredients

2 cups very hot water
⅓ cup dry milk powder
1 cup oats
¼ cup honey or molasses
2 tsp salt
2 tbsp toasted wheat germ
¼ cup butter
2 tbsp dry yeast (2 packages)
¼ cup warm (not hot) water
5 to 6 cups bread flour

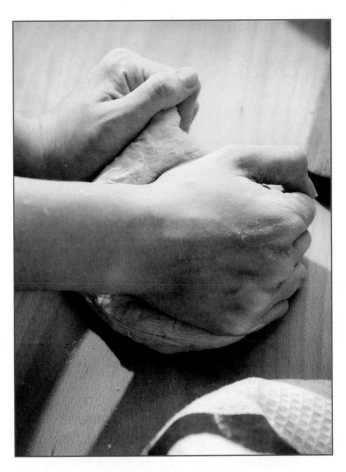

Directions

1. Preheat oven to 375°F.
2. Mix all ingredients (except for pears), crumbling the butter into the dry ingredients until it resembles coarse crumbs.
3. Grease a baking tray with a thin lip. Place pears cut side up on the pans. Fill the hollow of each pear (the area from which the seeds were removed) with the sugar mixture.
4. Bake for about 20 minutes. If desired, serve with ice cream or whipped cream.

Winter Menu

By winter all the gardening is done, all the food is harvested and stored, and it's time to enjoy more time in the warm kitchen. Draw from your stash of canned, frozen, and dried foods and experiment with warming spices such as garlic and ginger. Light candles or set the table near the fireplace for extra warmth and ambience. Evergreen branches, holly, and pinecones make lovely table decorations.

> Butternut Squash Soup
> Roasted Chicken and Root Vegetables
> Gingerbread with Pumpkin Cream Sauce

Directions

1. Combine water, milk powder, oats, honey or molasses, salt, wheat germ, and butter, stirring to melt the butter.
2. Dissolve the yeast in ¼ cup warm water and stir into the oatmeal mixture.
3. Add flour to make a stiff batter and let it rest for about 15 minutes. Stir in additional flour, using a wooden spoon, to make a soft dough. Knead dough until it is soft and elastic.
4. Place dough in a bowl and allow to rise in a warm place for about an hour. Turn out and shape into 2 to 3 loaves, depending on the size of the pans.
5. Place in greased pans and let rise until loaves double in size. Bake at 350°F until golden brown and hollow-sounding when tapped (about an hour). Remove from pans and allow to cool on racks.

Baked Pears

Ingredients

½ cup brown sugar
½ tsp cinnamon
⅛ tsp cloves
2 tbsp butter
1 tbsp crushed pecans or walnuts
3 pears, cut in half and remove seeds

Butternut Squash Soup

Ingredients
1 medium to large butternut squash
1 tbsp butter
1 shallot or small onion, finely chopped
1 clove garlic, crushed
1 cup chicken broth
½ tsp dried rosemary
½ tsp salt
⅛ tsp nutmeg
½ cup grated cheddar cheese
4 tbsp milk

Directions
1. Cut butternut squash in quarters, remove seeds, and boil until tender and skin can be easily removed (about 15 minutes). Remove and discard skin.
2. Melt butter in a medium saucepan over medium heat. Add shallot and garlic and sauté until shallot is tender (about 3 minutes).
3. Add squash and chicken broth and bring to a slow boil. Add the rosemary, salt, nutmeg, and cheese.
4. Transfer soup to a blender (or use an immersion blender) and blend until smooth and creamy.

Roast Chicken and Root Vegetables

Roast Chicken
One 2- to 3-pound whole chicken, entrails removed
About 1 tbsp kosher salt
About ½ tsp black pepper
1 tsp minced fresh or dried thyme

Roasted Root Vegetables
3 medium-sized potatoes, cut into 1-inch chunks
3 medium-sized carrots, cut into 1-inch chunks
2 apples or pears, quartered
1 clove garlic, crushed
½ cup olive oil
½ cup balsamic vinegar
1 tsp kosher salt
¼ tsp cinnamon

Directions
1. Preheat oven to 450°F.
2. Rinse the chicken thoroughly, inside and out, and sprinkle skin with salt, pepper, and thyme.
3. Mix all ingredients for roasted vegetables and place around the chicken in the roasting pan.
4. Roast for about an hour or until chicken skin is browned and flesh is no longer pink when cut.

Gingerbread with Pumpkin Cream Sauce

Gingerbread
¼ cup corn oil
¼ cup sugar
½ cup molasses
1 egg
1¼ cups all-purpose flour
1 tsp baking soda
½ tsp salt
½ tsp ginger
½ tsp cinnamon
¼ tsp nutmeg
¾ cup hot water

Pumpkin Cream Sauce
1 can sweetened condensed milk
¼ cup cooked, puréed pumpkin
½ tsp cinnamon

▲ Use warming spices like ginger and cinnamon in winter cooking.

Directions

1. Combine the oil, sugar, molasses, and egg in a medium bowl. Whisk together until well-blended.
2. Mix together dry ingredients and whisk into the wet mixture. Finally, whisk in the hot water (batter will be thin).
3. Pour into a greased and floured 8 x 8-inch cake pan. Bake for 25 to 30 minutes or until the top springs back when lightly pressed with your fingertip.
4. While the gingerbread is baking, combine sweetened condensed milk with cooked, puréed pumpkin in a saucepan. Simmer, stirring, until thick and smooth. Add ½ teaspoon cinnamon.
5. Serve gingerbread warm with a drizzle of pumpkin cream sauce.

Part Three

The Backyard Farm

"The greatness of a nation and its moral progress can be judged by the way its animals are treated."
—*Mahatma Gandhi*

The prospect of raising farm animals in your backyard does not need to be overwhelming. If you're concerned about not having enough land, keep in mind that a few chickens can be raised on less than an eighth of an acre; you may be able to have a beehive on your rooftop; and a couple of goats or sheep will be perfectly content on a quarter of an acre. Worried about the cost? With chickens, the small amount you will invest in buying chicks will quickly pay itself back in fresh eggs or meat, and since chicken feed is very inexpensive, the upkeep costs are minimal. If you shear your sheep or llamas, you can spin the wool and sell it at a local market or online to make a profit. However, if time is your concern, you should stop to think before purchasing animals or rescuing them from shelters. Any animal you bring onto your property deserves a portion of your time every day. You certainly don't have to spend every waking moment with your animals, but you will need to provide food, water, shelter, and a few other necessities. If you don't have the time for this on a regular basis, consider helping out at a local farm or shelter, or simply support other farmers by shopping at farmer's markets. If you do have the time to care properly for animals, very often you will find that they give you far more than you give them.

Chickens

Raising chickens in your yard will give you access to fresh eggs and meat, and because chickens are some of the easiest creatures to keep, even families in very urban areas are able to raise a few in a small backyard. Four or five chickens will supply your whole family with eggs on a regular basis.

Housing Your Chickens

You will need to have a structure for your chickens to live in to protect them from predators and inclement weather, and to allow the hens a safe place to lay their eggs. See "Poultry Houses" on page 255 to see several types of structures you can make for housing your chickens and other poultry.

Placing your henhouse close enough to your own home will remind you to visit it frequently to feed the chickens and to gather eggs. It is best to establish the house and yard in dry soil, away from areas in your yard that are frequently damp or moist, as this is the perfect breeding ground for poultry diseases. The henhouse should be well-ventilated, warm, protected from the cold and rain, have a few windows that allow the sunlight to shine in (especially if you live in a colder climate), and have a sound roof.

The perches in your henhouse should not be more than 2½ feet above the floor, and you should place a smooth platform under the perches to catch the droppings so they can easily be cleaned. Nesting boxes

▲ Building a chicken coop close to your house will make it easier to tend the chickens and gather eggs in inclement weather.

should be kept in a darker part of the house and should have ample space around them.

The perches in your henhouse can be relatively narrow and shouldn't be more than a few feet from the floor.

Selecting the Right Breed of Chicken

Take the time to select chickens that are well-suited for your needs. If you want chickens solely for their eggs, look for chickens that are good egg-layers. Mediterranean poultry are good for first-time chicken owners as they are easy to care for and only need the proper food to lay many eggs. If you are looking to slaughter and eat your chickens, you will want to have heavy-bodied fowl (Asiatic poultry) to get the most meat. For chickens that lay a good amount of

▲ A simple movable chicken coop can be constructed out of two-by-fours and two wheels. The floor of the coop should have open slats so that the manure will fall onto the ground and fertilize the soil. An even simpler method is to construct a pen that sits directly on the ground, providing a roof to offer the chickens suitable shade. The pen can be moved once the area is well-fertilized.

eggs and that can also be used for meat, invest in the Wyandottes or Plymouth Rock breeds. These chickens are good sources of both eggs and meat.

Wyandottes have seven distinct breeds: Silver, White, Buff, Golden, and Black are the most common. These breeds are hardy and are very popular in the United States. They are compactly built and lay excellent, dark brown eggs. They are good sitters and their meat is perfect for broiling or roasting.

Plymouth Rock chickens have three distinct breeds: Barred, White, and Buff. They are the most popular breeds in the United States and are hardy birds that grow to a medium size. These chickens are good for laying eggs, roost well, and also provide good meat.

Plymouth Rock chickens are good all-around farm chickens with their docile dispositions, hardiness, tendency to be very productive egg-layers, and good meat.

▲ Wyandottes originated in the United States and were first bred in the 1870s. This one is a golden laced Wyandott.

▲ A barred Plymouth Rock chicken.

Feeding Your Chickens

Chickens, like most creatures, need a balanced diet of protein, carbohydrates, vitamins, fats, minerals, and water. Chickens with plenty of access to grassy areas will find most of what they need on their own. However, if you don't have the space to allow your chickens to roam freely, commercial chicken feed is readily available in the form of mash, crumbles, pellets, or scratch. Or you can make your own feed out of a combination of grains, seeds, meat scraps or protein-rich legumes, and a gritty substance such as bone meal, limestone, oyster shell, or granite (to aid digestion, especially in winter). The correct ratio of food for a warm, secure chicken should be 1 part protein to 4 parts carbohydrates. Do not rely too heavily on corn as it can be overly fattening for hens; combine corn

▲ Chickens that are allowed to roam freely ("free-range" chickens) will be able to scavenge most of the food they need, as long as there is plenty of grass or other vegetation available.

with wheat or oats for the carbohydrate portion of the feed. Clover and other green foods are also beneficial to feed your chickens.

How much food your chickens need will depend on breed, age, the season, and how much room they have to exercise. Often it's easiest and best for the chickens to leave feed available at all times in several locations within the chickens' range. This will ensure that even

Chicken Feed

4 parts corn (or more in cold months)
3 parts oat groats
2 parts wheat
2 parts alfalfa meal or chopped hay
1 part meat scraps, fish meal, or soybean meal
2 to 3 parts dried split peas, lentils, or soybean meal
2 to 3 parts bone meal, crushed oyster shell, granite grit, or limestone
½ part cod-liver oil

You may also wish to add sunflower seeds, hulled barley, millet, kamut, amaranth seeds, quinoa, sesame seeds, flax seeds, or kelp granules. If you find that your eggs are thin-shelled, try adding more calcium to the feed (in the form of limestone or oystershell). Store feed in a covered bucket, barrel, or other container that will not allow rodents to get into it. A plastic or galvanized bucket is good, as it will also keep mold-causing moisture out of the feed.

the lowest chickens in the pecking order get the feed they need.

Hatching Chicks

If you want more chickens, or if you plan to sell chickens at the market, you may want your hens to lay eggs and hatch chicks. To hatch a chick, an egg must be incubated for a sufficient amount of time with the proper heat, moisture, and position. The period for incubation varies based on the species of chicken. The average incubation period is around 21 days for most common breeds.

If you are housing only a few chickens in your backyard, natural incubation is the easiest method with which to hatch chicks. Natural incubation is dependent upon the instinct of the mother hen and the breed of hen. Plymouth Rocks and Wyandottes are good hens to raise chicks. It is important to separate

the setting hen from the other chickens while she is nesting and to also keep the hen clean and free from lice. The nest should also be kept clean, and the hens should be fed grain food; grit; and clean, fresh water.

It is important, when you are considering hatching chicks, to make sure your hens are healthy, have plenty of exercise, and are fed a balanced diet. They need materials on which to scratch and should not be infested with lice and other parasites. Free-range chickens, which eat primarily natural foods and get lots of exercise, lay more fertile eggs than do tightly confined hens. The eggs selected for hatching should not be more than 12 days old and they should be clean.

You'll need to construct a nesting box for the roosting hen and the incubated eggs. The box should be roomy and deep enough to retain the nesting material. Treat

▲ A nesting box should have plenty of clean hay or straw for the hen to rest in.

the box with a disinfectant before use to keep out lice, mice, and other creatures that could infect the hen or the eggs. Make the nest of damp soil a few inches deep, placed in the bottom of the box, and then lay sweet hay or clean straw on top of that.

Place the nesting box in a quiet and secluded place away from the other chickens. If space permits, you can construct a smaller shed in which to house your nesting hen. A hen can generally sit on anywhere between 9 and 15 eggs. The hen should only be allowed to leave the nest to feed, drink water, and take a dust bath. When the hen does leave her box, check the eggs and dispose of any damaged ones. An older hen will generally be more careful and apt to roost than a younger female.

Once the chicks are hatched, they will need to stay warm and clean, get lots of exercise, and have access to food regularly. Make sure the feed is ground finely enough that the chicks can easily eat and digest it. They should also have clean, fresh water.

Bacteria Associated with Chicken Meat

- *Salmonella*—This is primarily found in the intestinal tract of poultry and can be found in raw meat and eggs.
- *Campylobacter jejuni*—This is one of the most common causes of diarrheal illness in humans and is spread by improper handling of raw chicken meat and not cooking the meat thoroughly.
- *Listeria monocytogenes*—This causes illness in humans and can be destroyed by keeping the meat refrigerated and by cooking it thoroughly.

Storing Eggs

Eggs are among the most nutritious foods on earth. Hens typically lay eggs every 25 hours, so you should have a fresh supply on a daily basis. Eggs, like any other animal byproduct, need to be handled safely and carefully to avoid rotting and spreading disease. Here are a few tips on how to best preserve your farm-fresh eggs:

1. Make sure your eggs come from hens that have not been running with male roosters. Infertile eggs last longer than those that have been fertilized.
2. Keep the fresh eggs together.
3. Choose eggs that are perfectly clean.
4. Make sure not to crack the shells, as this will taint the taste and make the egg rot much more quickly.
5. Place your eggs directly in the refrigerator where they will keep for several weeks.

▲ If an egg breaks, use it immediately or discard it. Once the egg is exposed to the air, it spoils much more quickly.

▲ Wash fresh eggs and then refrigerate them immediately.

Ducks

Ducks are slightly more difficult than chicks to raise, but they do provide wonderful eggs and meat. Ducks have pleasanter personalities than chickens and are generally prolific layers. The eggs taste similar to chicken eggs, but are usually larger and have a richer flavor. Ducks are happiest and healthiest when they have access to a pool or pond to paddle around in and when they have several other ducks to keep them company.

▲ Ducks are social birds—they are happiest in groups.

Breeds of Ducks

Below are some of the most common duck breeds, though there are many others to consider.

1. White Pekin—The most popular breed of duck, these are also the easiest to raise. These ducks are hardy and do well in close confinement. They are timid and must be handled carefully. Their large frame gives them lots of meat, and they are also prolific layers.
2. Indian Runner—Friendly and energetic, Indian Runners lay 150 to 200 eggs per year, which makes them almost as prolific as Pekins. They are excellent foragers and may be black, brown, gray, buff, or white.
3. Colored Rouens—These darkly plumed ducks are also quite popular and fatten easily for meat purposes.
4. Black Cayuga and Muscovy breeds—These are American breeds that are easily raised but are not as productive as White Pekins.

▲ White Pekins were originally bred from the Mallard in China and came to the United States in 1873.

▲ Ducks should have access to a lake, pond, or at least a small pool.

▲ A Black Cayuga (right) stands with two Saxony ducks.

Housing Ducks

You don't need a lot of space or a large body of water to raise ducks successfully, though they will be happier if you can provide at least a small pool of water for them to bathe and paddle around in. Housing for ducks is relatively simple. The houses do not have to be as warm or dry as for chickens but the ducks cannot be confined for as long periods as chickens can. They need more exercise out-of-doors to be healthy and to produce eggs. A house that is protected from dampness or excess rain water and that has straw or hay covering the floor is adequate for ducks. If you want to keep your ducks somewhat confined, a small fence about 2½ feet high will do the trick. Ducks don't require nesting boxes, as they lay their eggs on the floor of the house or in the yard around the house.

Feeding and Watering Ducks

Ducks require plenty of fresh water to drink, as they have to drink regularly while eating. Ducks eat both vegetable and animal foods. If allowed to roam freely and find their own foodstuff, ducks will eat grasses, small fish, and water insects (if streams or ponds are provided).

Ducks need their food to be soft and mushy in order for them to digest it. Ducklings should be fed equal parts cornmeal, wheat bran, and flour for the first week of life. For the next fifty days or so, the ducklings should be fed that mixture in addition to a little grit or sand and some green foods (green rye, oats, clover) all mixed together. After this time, ducks should be fed on a mixture of two parts cornmeal, one part wheat bran, one part flour, some coarse sand, and green foods.

Hatching Ducklings

The natural process of incubation (hatching ducklings underneath a hen) is the preferred method of hatching ducklings. It is important to take good care of the setting hen. Feed her whole corn mixed with green food, grit, and fresh water. Placing the feed and water just in front of the nest for the first few days will encourage the hen to eat and drink without leaving the nest. Hens will typically lay their eggs on the ground, in straw or hay that is provided for them. Clean the houses and pens often so the laying ducks have clean areas in which to incubate their eggs.

Caring for Ducklings

Young ducklings are very susceptible to atmospheric changes and must be kept warm. The ducklings are most vulnerable during the first three weeks of life; after that time, they are more likely to thrive to adulthood. Construct brooders for the young ducklings and keep them very warm by hanging strips of cloth over the door cracks. After three weeks in the warm brooder, move the ducklings to a cold brooder as they can now withstand fluctuating temperatures.

Common Diseases

On a whole, ducks are not as prone to the typical poultry diseases, and many of the diseases they do

▲ Ducklings should have warm, dry, clean environments, especially for the first three weeks of their lives.

contract can be prevented by making sure the ducks have a clean environment in which to live (by cleaning out their houses, providing fresh drinking water, and so on).

Two common ailments found in ducks are botulism and maggots. Botulism causes the duck's neck to go limp, making it difficult or even impossible for the duck to swallow. Maggots infest the ducks if they do not have clean water in which to bathe and are typically contracted in the hot summer months. Both of these conditions (as well as worms and mites) can be cured with the proper care, medications, and veterinary assistance.

Turkeys

Turkeys are generally raised for their meat (especially for holiday roasts) though their eggs can also be eaten. Turkeys are incredibly easy to manage and raise as they primarily subsist on bugs, grasshoppers, and wasted grain that they find while wandering around the yard. They are, in a sense, self-sustaining foragers.

To raise a turkey for Thanksgiving dinner, hatch the turkey chick in early spring, so that by November, it will be about 14 to 20 pounds.

▲ Bronze turkeys like this one are some of the most common in the United States.

Breeds of Turkeys

The largest breeds of turkeys found in the United States are the Bronze and Narragansett. Other breeds, though not as popular, include the White Holland, Black turkey, Slate turkey, and Bourbon Red.

Bronze breeds are most likely a cross between a wild North American turkey and domestic turkey, and they have beautiful rich plumage. This is the most common type of turkey to raise, as it is the largest, is very hardy, and is the most profitable. The White Holland and Bourbon Red, however, are said to be the most "domesticated" in their habits and are easier to keep in a smaller roaming area.

Housing Turkeys

Turkeys flourish when they can roost in the open. They thrive in the shelter of trees, though this can become problematic as they are more vulnerable to predators than if they are confined in a house. If you do build a house for them, it should be airy, roomy, and very clean.

It is important to allow turkeys freedom to roam; if you live in a more suburban or neighborhood area, raising turkeys may not be the best option for you, as your turkeys may wander into a neighboring yard, upsetting your neighbors. Turkeys need lots of exercise to be healthy and vigorous. When turkeys are confined for long periods of time, it is more difficult to regulate their feeding (turkeys are natural foragers and thrive best on natural foods), and they are more likely to contract disease than if they are allowed to range freely.

Feeding Turkeys

Turkeys gain most of their sustenance from foraging, either in lawns or in pastures. They typically eat green vegetation, berries, weed seeds, waste grain, nuts, and various kinds of acorns. In the summer months, turkeys especially like to eat grasshoppers. Due to their love of eating insects that can damage crops and gardens, turkeys are quite useful in keeping your growing produce free from harmful insects and parasites.

Turkeys may be fed grain (similar to a mixture given to chickens) if they are going to be slaughtered, in order to make them larger.

Hatching Turkey Chicks

Turkey hens lay eggs in the middle of March to the first of April. If you are looking to hatch and raise turkey chicks, it is vital to watch the hen closely for when she lays the eggs, and then gather them and keep the eggs warm until the weather is more stable. Turkey hens generally aim to hide their nests from predators. It is best, for the hen's sake, to provide her with a coop of some sort, which she can freely enter and leave. Or, if no coop is available, encourage the hen to lay her eggs in a nest close to your house (putting a large barrel on its side and heaping up brush near the house may entice the hen to nest there). This way, you can keep an eye on the eggs and hatchlings.

Hens are well-adapted to hatch all of the eggs that they lay. It takes 27 to 29 days for turkey eggs to hatch. While the hens are incubating the eggs, they should be given adequate food and water, placed close to their nest. Wheat and corn are the best food during the laying and incubation period.

Raising the Poults

Turkey chicks, also known as "poults," can be difficult to raise and require lots of care and attention for their first few weeks of life. In this sense, a turkey raiser must be "on call" to come to the aid of the hen and her poults at any time during the day for the first month or so. Many times, the hens can raise the poults well, but it is important that they receive enough food and warmth in the early weeks to allow them to grow healthy and strong. The poults should stay dry, as they become chilled easily. If you are able, encouraging the poults and their mother into a coop until the poults are stronger will aid their growth to adulthood.

Poults should be fed soft and easily digestible foods. Stale bread, dipped in milk and then dried until it crumbles, is an excellent source of food for the young turkeys.

Diseases

Turkeys are hardy birds but they are susceptible to a few debilitating or fatal diseases. It is a fact that the mortality rate among young turkeys, even if they are given all the care and exercise and food needed, is relatively high (usually due to environmental and predatory factors).

The most common disease in turkeys is blackhead. Blackhead typically infects young turkeys between 6 weeks and 4 months old. This disease will turn the head darker colored or even black and the bird will become very weak, will stop eating, and will have an insatiable thirst. Blackhead is usually fatal.

Another disease that turkeys occasionally contract is roup. Roup generally occurs when a turkey has been exposed to extreme dampness or cold drafts for long periods of time. Roup causes the turkey's head to swell around the eyes and is highly contagious to other turkeys. Nutritional roup is caused by a vitamin A deficiency, which can be alleviated by adding vitamin A to the turkey's drinking water. It is best to consult a veterinarian if your turkey seems to have this disease.

Slaughtering Poultry

If you are raising your own poultry, you may decide that you'd like to use them for consumption as well. Slaughtering your own poultry enables you to know exactly what is in the meat you and your family are consuming, and to ensure that the poultry is kept humanely before being slaughtered. Here are some guidelines for slaughtering poultry:

1. To prepare a fowl for slaughter, make sure the bird is secured well so it is unable to move (either hanging down from a pole or laid on a block that is used for chopping wood).

2. Killing the fowl can be done in two ways: one way is to hang the bird upside down and to cut the jugular vein with a sharp knife. It is a good idea to have a funnel or vessel available to collect the draining blood so it does not make a mess and can be disposed of easily. The other option is to place the bird's head on a chopping block and then, in one clean movement, chop its head off at the middle of the neck. Then, hang the bird upside down and let the blood drain as described earlier.

3. Once the bird has been thoroughly drained of blood, you can begin to pluck it. Have a pot of hot water (around 140°F) ready, in which to dip the bird. Holding the bird by the feet, dip it into the pot of hot water and leave it for about 45 seconds—you do not want the bird to begin to cook! Then, remove the bird from the pot and begin plucking immediately. The feathers should come off fairly easily, but this process takes time, so be patient. Discard the feathers.

4. Once the bird has been completely rid of feathers, slip back the skin from the neck and cut the neck off close to the base of the body. Remove the crop, trachea, and esophagus from the bird by loosening them and pulling them out through the hole created by chopping off the neck. Cut off the vent to release the main entrails (being careful not to puncture the intestines or bacteria could be released into the meat) and make a horizontal slit about an inch above it so you can insert two fingers. Remove the entrails, liver (carefully cutting off the gallbladder), gizzard, and heart from the bird and set the last three aside if you want to eat them later or make them into stuffing. If you are going to save the heart, slip off the membrane enclosing it and cut off the veins and arteries. Make sure to clean out the gizzard as well if you will be using it later.

5. Wash the bird thoroughly, inside and out, and wipe it dry.

6. Cut off the feet below the joints and then carefully pull out the tendons from the drumsticks.

7. Once the carcass is thoroughly dry and clean, store it in the refrigerator if it will be used that same day or the next. If you want to save the bird for later use, place it in a moisture-proof bag and set it in the freezer (along with any innards that you may have saved).

8. Make sure you clean and disinfect any surface you were working on to avoid the spread of bacteria and other diseases.

Beekeeping

Beekeeping (also known as apiculture) is one of the oldest human industries. For thousands of years, honey has been considered a highly desirable food. Beekeeping is a science and can be a very profitable occupation. It is also a wonderful hobby for many people. Keeping bees can be done almost anywhere—on a farm, in a rural or suburban area, and even in urban areas. Anywhere there are sufficient flowers from which to collect nectar, bees can thrive.

Apiculture relies heavily on the natural resources of a particular location and the knowledge of the beekeeper in order to be successful. Collecting and selling honey at your local farmers' market or just to family and friends can supply you with some extra cash if you are looking to make a profit from your apiary.

▲ Wearing a hat and veil will help to prevent stings to your face and head.

Why Raise Bees?

Bees are essential in the pollination and fertilization of many fruit and seed crops. If you have a garden with many flowers or fruit plants, having bees nearby will only help your garden flourish and grow year after year. Little is more satisfying than extracting your own honey for everyday use.

How to Avoid Getting Stung

Though it takes some skill, you can learn how to avoid being stung by the bees you keep. Here are some ways you can keep your bee stings to a minimum:

1. **Keep gentle bees.** Having bees that, by sheer nature, are not as aggressive will reduce the number of stings you are likely to receive. Carniolan bees are one of the gentlest species, and so are the Caucasian bees introduced from Russia.

2. **Obtain a good "smoker"** and use it whenever you'll be handling your bees. Pumping smoke of any kind into and around the beehive will render your bees less aggressive and less likely to sting you.

3. **Purchase and wear a veil.** This should be made out of black bobbinet and worn over your face. Also, rubber gloves help protect your hands from stings.

4. **Use a "bee escape."** This device is fitted into a slot made in a board the same size as the top of the hive. Slip the board into the hive before you open it to extract the honey, and it allows the worker bees to slip below it but not to return back up. So, by placing the "bee escape" into the hive the day before you want to gain access to the combs and honey, you will most likely trap all the bees under the board and leave you free to work with the honeycombs without fear of stings.

▲ A smoker will help to relax your bees and make them less aggressive.

What Type of Hive Should I Build?

Most beekeepers would agree that the best hives have suspended, movable frames where the bees make the honeycombs, which are easy to lift out. These frames, called Langstroth frames, are the most popular kind of frame used by apiculturists in the United States.

Whether you build your own beehive or purchase one, it should be built strongly and should contain accurate bee spaces and a close-fitting, rainproof roof. If you are looking to have honeycombs, you must have a hive that permits the insertion of up to eight combs.

Where Should the Hive Be Situated?

Hives and their stands should be placed in an enclosure where the bees will not be disturbed by other animals or humans and where it will be generally quiet. Hives should be placed on their own stands at least 3 feet from each other. Do not allow weeds to grow near the hives and keep the hives away from walls and fences. You, as the beekeeper, need to easily access your hive without fear of obstacles.

▲ Frame from a healthy beehive.

Swarming

Swarming is simply the migration of honeybees to a new hive and is led by the queen bee. During swarming season (the warm summer days), a beekeeper must remain very alert. If you see swarming above the hive, take great care and act calmly and quietly. You want to get the swarm into your hive, but this will be tricky. If they land on a nearby branch or in a basket, simply approach and then "pour" them into the hive. Keep in mind that bees will more likely inhabit a cool, shaded hive than one that is baking in the hot summer sun.

Sometimes it is beneficial to try to prevent swarming, such as if you already have completely full hives. Frequently removing the new honey from the hive before swarming begins will deter the bees from swarming. Shading the hives on warm days will also help keep the bees from swarming.

Bee Pastures

Bees will fly a great distance to gather food but you should try to contain them, as well as possible, to an area within 2 miles of the beehive. Make sure they have access to many honey-producing plants that you can grow in your garden. Alfalfa, asparagus, buckwheat, chestnut, clover, catnip, mustard, raspberry, roses, and sunflowers are some of the best honey-producing plants and trees. Also make sure that your bees always have access to pure, clean water.

Preparing Your Bees for Winter

If you live in a colder region, keeping your bees alive throughout the winter months is difficult. If your queen bee happens to die in the fall, before a young queen can be reared, your whole colony will die throughout the winter. However, the queen's death can be avoided by taking simple precautions and giving careful attention to your hive come autumn.

Colonies are usually lost in the winter months due to insufficient winter food storages, faulty hive construction, lack of protection from the cold and dampness, not enough or too much ventilation, or too many older bees and not enough young ones.

If you live in a region that gets a few weeks of severe weather, you may want to move your colony indoors, or at least to an area that is protected from the outside elements. But the essential components of having a colony survive through the winter season are

Beekeeping

▲ Bees thrive on sweet flowers, such as clover.

to have a good queen; a fair ratio of healthy, young, and old bees; and a plentiful supply of food. The hive needs to retain a liberal supply of ripened honey and a thick syrup made from white cane sugar (you should feed this to your bees early enough so they have time to take the syrup and seal it over before winter).

To make this syrup, dissolve 3 pounds of granulated sugar in 1 quart of boiling water and add 1 pound of pure extracted honey to this. If you live in an extremely cold area, you may need up to 30 pounds of this syrup, depending on how many bees and hives you have. You can either use a top feeder or a frame feeder, which fits inside the hive in the place of a frame. Fill the frame with the syrup and place sticks or grass in it to keep the bees from drowning.

▲ Raw honey is an anti-bacterial, anti-viral, and anti-fungal substance—besides being delicious.

Extracting Honey

To obtain the extracted honey, you'll need to keep the honeycombs in one area of the hive or packed one above the other. Before removing the filled combs, you should allow the bees ample time to ripen and cap the honey. To uncap the comb cells, simply use a sharp knife (apiary suppliers sell knives specifically for this purpose). Then put the combs in a machine called a honey extractor to extract the honey. The honey extractor whips the honey out of the cells and allows you to replace the fairly undamaged comb into the hive to be repaired and refilled.

The extracted honey runs into open buckets or vats and is left, covered with a tea towel or larger cloth, to stand for a week. It should be in a warm, dry room where no ants can reach it. Skim the honey each day until it is perfectly clear. Then you can put it into cans, jars, or bottles for selling or for your own personal use.

▲ Bees live off of the honey stored in the combs. In winter months they need a supply of ripe honey and benefit from extra sugary syrup.

Making Beeswax

Beeswax from the honeycomb can be used for making candles, can be added to lotions or lip balm, and can even be used in baking. Rendering wax in boiling water is especially simple when you only have a small apiary.

Collect the combs, break them into chunks, roll them into balls if you like, and put them in a muslin bag. Put the bag with the beeswax into a large stockpot and bring the water to a slow boil, making sure the bag doesn't rest on the bottom of the pot and burn. The muslin will act as a strainer for the wax. Use clean, sterilized tongs to occasionally squeeze the bag. After the wax is boiled out of the bag, remove the

pot from the heat and allow it to cool. Then, remove the wax from the top of the water and then re-melt it in another pot on very low heat, so it doesn't burn.

Pour the melted wax into molds lined with wax paper or plastic wrap and then cool it before using it to make other items or selling it at your local farmers' market.

▲ A beekeeper carefully removes a frame from the hive.

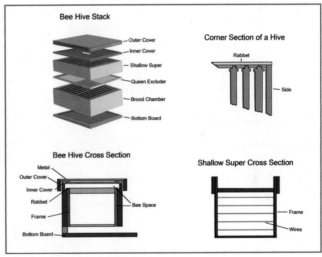

▲ A diagram of a simple beehive that you can easily construct in your backyard.

Extra Beekeeping Tips

General Tips

1. Clip the old queen's wings and go through the hives every 10 days to destroy queen cells to prevent swarming.
2. Always act and move calmly and quietly when handling bees.
3. Keep the hives cool and shaded. Bees won't enter a hot hive.

When Opening the Hive

1. Have a smoker ready to use if you desire.
2. Do not stand in front of the hive while the bees are entering and exiting.
3. Do not drop any tools into the hive while it's open.
4. Do not run if you become frightened.
5. If you are attacked, move away slowly and smoke the bees off yourself as you retreat.
6. Apply ammonia or a paste of baking soda and water immediately to any bee sting to relieve the pain. You can also scrape the area of the bee sting with your fingernail or the dull edge of a knife immediately after the sting.

When Feeding Your Bees

1. Keep a close watch over your bees during the entire season, to see if they are feeding well.
2. Feed the bees during the evening.
3. Make sure the bees have ample water near their hive, especially in the spring.

Making a Beehive

The most important parts of constructing a beehive are to make it simple and sturdy. Just a plain box with a few frames and a couple of other loose parts will make a successful beehive that will be easy to use and manipulate. It is crucial that your beehive be well-adapted to the nature of bees and also the climate in which you live. Framed hives usually suffice for the beginning beekeeper.

"Life is the flower for which love is the honey."
—Victor Hugo

Mackenzie Pierson *was born in San Francisco, California, and moved to Shelburne, Vermont when she was twelve. Now she is studying holistic medicine, art, dance, and environmental studies. She hopes to become an acupuncturist and use the bees for apitherapy treatments.*

I pull the white suit over my head, the sweet, musky smell enveloping me. I shove my feet into the cold rubber boots and stuff the matches in my pocket. Balancing the equipment on a wooden board, I waddle out into the field, the wet grass seeping through a hole in my boot. I zip the net over my head, and face the white boxes, awaiting today's lesson. The bees teach me, every day, that the nectar in life is achieved through intense focus, commitment, dedication to sustainable and nurturing communities, and the willingness to take risks.

I had never really thought about beekeeping until my sophomore year of high school when my history teacher, Bill Mares, brought a live queen bee to class in a small wooden box. I watched her small body through the mesh covering and wondered what her life must be like. I had not even seen a hive yet. So, what drew me to beekeeping? I guess it was the sweet-tasting golden joy that coated my oatmeal and toast. I had always loved honey, and now I loved it even more because of my respect for the bees. I looked down at my toast and thought of all the mystery that surrounded the hive. I wanted to be in the "in" group, to know where this sweet-tasting delight came from. However, it was more than that. In an ever-changing world, the bees are what hold us together. They are the most supportive structure in our lives, and they fly by unseen. Honeybees are responsible for approximately 80 percent of all fruit, vegetable, and seed crops in the United States, accounting for approximately every third bite of food one eats. They are the joy and the nectar in our lives.

I got my first hive on July 16, 2006. It was a generous gift from Russ Aceto, a published and two-year senior beekeeper in Fairfax, Vermont. It was a hot and humid day, and the bees hummed uncomfortably as we slid the covered nuc box [a box for transporting bees] into the trunk of my Subaru. I had never driven with bees in the back seat, and sweat dripped off the end of my nose. They were all boarded up with mesh netting that we had stapled down over their hive opening, but I still feared that an unexpected bump in the road would cause them to tip over and spill inside the car. I wondered if the bees minded the radio . . . anyway it calmed me down and drowned out the humming. Arriving home, we had to find the ideal site. It had to be somewhere away from or above the road, so the colonies would not be flooded or washed out. A northern windbreak (like a stand of trees, bushes, or a wood pile) would protect the hives from winter weather and keep them cool in the hot noon sun. They also needed fresh water and pesticide-free crops within their 2-mile range.

"A beautiful bee yard is a sacred place, often a cathedral of trees and plants nourished by years and relationships with generations of families that allow bees on a special place on their land," wrote Todd Hardie, founder of Honey Gardens Apiaries. Walking through our front yard, we found a perfect spot, tucked away next to a bush, but with plenty of morning sunlight available. We hauled the bees across the lawn and set them up on a stand (a piece of our old porch) so that the hive would not get damp. I had painted the hive boxes with house paint to make them weather-resistant, but the stand would keep the bottom from rotting. It also was necessary to prevent ants and other insects from directly entering the hive to steal honey.

All in all, the season went pretty smoothly, excluding getting a bloody nose the first time I wore the bee suit (with my mentor Mr. Mares watching) and the time I almost caught the hive on fire with the explosive smoker. As the days got colder, the bees started to slow down and bundle up together, creating a swarming mustache of moving bodies. Aceto showed me a new technique he had developed for "winterizing" the beehive so that there was no moisture buildup inside the boxes. The bees were all bundled up in the field by the first snow, but their summer's effort lingered sweetly in our mouths.

When we are in risky situations we often use force, but that does not work with the bees. Working with the bees has taught me that what the world really needs is compassion, respect, and awareness. I am willing to risk exploring the unknown so I can be a part of the solution and not react to the world from a place of fear. As I pull the white suit over my head, I realize I cannot pretend that social, environmental, or economic problems do not exist, but I can arm myself with knowledge, dreams, and hope. I can add my teaspoon of honey to the future.

Goats

Goats provide us with milk and wool and thrive in arid, semitropical, and mountainous environments. In the more temperate regions of the world, goats are raised as supplementary animals, providing milk and cheese for families and acting as natural weed killers.

Breeds of Goats

Some goat breeds are small (weighing roughly 50 pounds) and some are very large (weighing up to 250 pounds). Depending on the breed, goats may have horns that are corkscrew in shape, though many domestic goats are dehorned early on to lessen any potential injuries to humans or other goats. The hair of goats can also differ—various breeds have short hair, long hair, curly hair, silky hair, or coarse hair. Goats come in a variety of colors (solid black, white, brown, or spotted).

Six Major U.S. Goat Breeds

Alpine—Originally from Switzerland, these goats may have horns, are short haired, and are usually white and black in color. They are also good producers of milk.

◀ Alpine goat

Anglo-Nubian—A cross between native English goats and Indian and Nubian breeds, these goats have droopy ears, spiral horns, and short hair. They are quite tall and do best in warmer climates. They do not produce as much milk, though it is much higher in fat than other goats'. They are the most popular breed of goat in the United States.

◀ Anglo-Nubian goat

▲ La Mancha goat

▲ Toggenburg goat

LaMancha—A cross between Spanish Murciana and Swiss and Nubian breeds, these goats are extremely adaptable, have straight noses, short hair, may have horns, and have very short ear pinnae. They are not as good milk producers as the Saanen and Toggenburg breeds, and their milk fat content is much higher.

Pygmy—Originally from Africa and the Caribbean, these dwarfed goats thrive in hotter climates. For their size, they are relatively good producers of milk, though not usually considered a dairy breed.

Saanen—Originally from Switzerland, these goats are completely white, have short hair, and sometimes have horns. Goats of this breed are wonderful milk producers.

Toggenburg—Originally from Switzerland, these goats are brown with white facial, ear, and leg stripes; have straight noses; may have horns; and have short hair. This breed is very popular in the United States. These goats are good milk producers in the summer and winter seasons and survive well in both temperate and tropical climates.

▼ Saanen goat

▼ Pygmy goat

Feeding Goats

Goats can sustain themselves on bushes, trees, shrubs, woody plants, weeds, briars, and herbs. Pasture is the lowest-cost feed available for goats, and allowing goats to graze in the summer months is a wonderful and economic way to keep goats, even if your yard is small. Goats thrive best when eating alfalfa or a mixture of clover and timothy. If you have a lawn and a few goats, you don't need a lawn mower if you plant these types of plants for your goats to eat. The one drawback to this is that your goats (depending on how many you own) may quickly deplete these natural resources, which can cause weed growth and erosion. Supplementing pasture feed with other foodstuff, such as greenchop, root crops, and wet brewery grains will ensure that your yard does not become overgrazed and that your goats remain well-fed and healthy. It is also beneficial to supply your goats with unlimited access to hay while they are grazing. Make sure that your goats have easy access to shaded areas and fresh water, and offer a salt-and-mineral mix on occasion.

Dry forage is another good source of feed for your goats. It is relatively inexpensive to grow or buy and consists of good quality legume hay (alfalfa or clover). Legume hay is high in protein and has many essential minerals beneficial to your goats. To make sure your forages are highly nutritious, be sure that there are many leaves that provide protein and minerals and that the forage had an early cutting date, which will allow for easier digestion of the nutrients. If your forage is green in color, it most likely contains more vitamin A, which is good for promoting goat health.

▲ Goats enjoy having objects to climb on.

Goat Milk

Goat milk is a wonderful substitute for those who are unable to tolerate cow's milk, or for the elderly, babies, and those suffering from stomach ulcers. Milk from goats is also high in vitamin A and niacin but does not have the same amount of vitamins B6, B12, and C as cow's milk.

Lactating goats do need to be fed the best quality legume hay or green forage possible, as well as grain. Give the grain to the doe at a rate that equals ½ pound grain for every pound of milk she produces.

Common Diseases Affecting Goats

Goats tend to get more internal parasites than other herd animals. Some goats develop infectious arthritis, pneumonia, coccidiosis, scabies, liver fluke disease, and mastitis. It is advisable that you establish a relationship with a good veterinarian who specializes in small farm animals to periodically check your goats for various diseases.

Milking a Goat

Milking a goat takes some practice and patience, especially when you first begin. However, once you establish a routine and rhythm to the milking, the whole process should run relatively smoothly. The main thing to remember is to keep calm and never pull on the teat, as this will hurt the goat and she might upset the milk bucket. The goat will pick up on any anxiousness or nervousness on your part and it could affect how cooperative she is during the milking.

Supplies

- A grain bucket and grain for feeding the goat while milking is taking place
- Milking stand
- Metal bucket to collect the milk
- A stool to sit on (optional)
- A warm, sterilized wipe or cloth that has been boiled in water
- Teat dip solution (2 tbsp bleach, 1 quart water, one drop normal dish detergent mixed together)

Directions

1. Ready your milking stand by filling the grain bucket with enough grain to last throughout the entire milking. Then retrieve the goat, separating her from any other goats to avoid distractions and unsuccessful milking. Place the goat's head through the head hold of the milking stand so she can eat the grain and then close the lever so she cannot remove her head.

2. With the warm, sterilized wipe or cloth, clean the udder and teats to remove any dirt, manure, or bacteria that may be present. Then, place the metal bucket on the stand below the udder.

3. Wrap your thumb and forefinger around the base of one teat. This will help trap the milk in the teat so it can be squirted out. Then, starting with your middle finger, squeeze the three remaining fingers in one single, smooth motion to squirt the milk into the bucket. Be sure to keep a tight grip on the base of the teat so the milk stays there until extracted. Remember: The first squirt of milk from either teat should not be put into the bucket as it may contain dirt or bacteria that you don't want contaminating the milk.

4. Release the grip on the teat and allow it to refill with milk. While this is happening, you can repeat this process on the other teat and alternate between teats to speed up the milking process.

6. When the teats begin to look empty (they will be somewhat flat in appearance), massage the udder just a little bit to see if any more milk remains. If so, squeeze it out in the same manner as above until you cannot extract much more.

7. Remove the milk bucket from the stand and then, with your teat dip mixture in a disposable cup, dip each teat into the solution and allow to air dry. This will keep bacteria and infection from going into the teat and udder.

8. Remove the goat from the milk stand and return her to the pen.

Making Cheese from Goat Milk

Most varieties of cheese that can be made from cow's milk can also be successfully made using goats' milk. Goat milk cheese can easily be made at home. To make the cheese, however, at least one gallon of goat milk should be available. Make sure that all of your equipment is washed and sterilized (using heat is fine) before using it.

Cottage Cheese

1. Collect surplus milk that is free of strong odors. Cool it to around 40°F and keep it at that temperature until it is used.

2. Skim off any cream. Use the skim milk for cheese and the cream for cheese dressing.

3. If you wish to pasteurize your milk (which will allow it to hold better as a cheese) collect all the milk to be processed into a flat-bottomed, straight-sided pan and heat to 145°F on low heat. Hold it at this temperature for about 30 minutes and then cool to around 80°F. Use a dairy thermometer to measure the milk's temperature. Then, inoculate the cheese milk with a desirable lactic acid–fermenting bacterial culture (you can use commercial buttermilk for the initial source).

▲ Cottage cheese

Add about 7 ounces to 1 gallon of cheese milk, stir well, and let it sit undisturbed for about 10 to 16 hours, until a firm curd is formed.

4. When the curd is firm enough, cut the curd into uniform cubes no larger than ½ inch using a knife or spatula.

5. Allow the curd to sit undisturbed for a couple of minutes and then warm it slowly, stirring carefully, at a temperature no greater than 135°F. The curd should eventually become firm and free from whey.

6. When the curd is firm, remove from the heat and stop stirring. Siphon off the excess whey from the top of the pot. The curd should settle to the bottom of the container. If the curd is floating, bacteria that produces gas has been released and a new batch must be made.

7. Replace the whey with cold water, washing the curd and then draining the water. Wash again with ice-cold water to chill the curd. This will keep the flavor fresh.

8. Using a draining board, drain the excess water from the curd. Now your curd is complete.

9. To make the curd into a cottage cheese consistency, separate the curd as much as possible and mix with a milk or cream mixture containing salt to taste.

Domiati Cheese

This type of cheese is made throughout the Mediterranean region. It is eaten fresh or aged two to three months before consumption.

1. Cool a gallon of fresh, quality milk to around 105°F, adding 8 ounces of salt to the milk. Stir the salt until it is completely dissolved.

2. Pasteurize the milk as described in step 3 of the cottage cheese recipe.

3. This type of cheese is coagulated by adding a protease enzyme (rennet). This enzyme may be purchased at a local drug store, health food store, or a cheese maker in your area. Dissolve the concentrate in water, add it to the cheese milk, and stir for a few minutes. Use 1 milliliter of diluted rennet liquid in 40 milliliters of water for every 2½ gallons of cheese milk.

4. Set the milk at around 105°F. When the enzyme is completely dispersed in the cheese milk, allow the mix to sit undisturbed until it forms a firm curd.

5. When the desired firmness is reached, cut the curd into very small cubes. Allow for some whey separation. After 10 to 20 minutes, remove and reserve about one third the volume of salted whey.

6. Put the curd and remaining whey into cloth-lined molds (the best are rectangular stainless steel containers with perforated sides and bottom) with a cover. The molds should be between 7 and 10 inches in height. Fill the molds with the curd, fold the cloth over the top, allow the whey to drain, and discard the whey.

7. Once the curd is firm enough, apply added weight for 10 to 18 hours until it is as moist as you want.

8. Once the pressing is complete and the cheese is formed into a block, remove the molds and cut the blocks into 4-inch-thick pieces. Place the pieces in plastic containers with airtight seals. Fill the containers with reserved salted whey from step 5, covering the cheese by about an inch.

9. Place these containers at a temperature between 60°F and 65°F to cure for 1 to 4 months.

Feta Cheese

This type of cheese is very popular to make from goats' milk. The same process is used as the Domiati cheese except that salt is not added to the milk before coagulation. Feta cheese is aged in a brine solution after the cubes have been salted in a brine solution for at least 24 hours.

▲ Domiati cheese

▲ Feta cheese

Angora Goats

Angora goats may be the most efficient fiber producers in the world. The hair of these goats is made into mohair: a long, lustrous hair that is woven into fine garments. Angora goats are native to Turkey and were imported to the United States in the mid-1800s. Now, the United States is one of the two biggest produces of mohair on earth.

Angora goats are typically relaxed and docile. They are delicate creatures, easily strained by their year-round fleeces. Angora goats need extra attention and are more high-maintenance than other breeds of goat. While these goats can adapt to many temperate climates, they do particularly well in the arid environment of the southwestern states.

Angora goats can be sheared twice yearly, before breeding and before birthing. The hair of the goat will grow about ¾ inch per month and it should be sheared once it reaches 4 to 6 inches in length. During the shearing process, the goat is usually lying down on a clean floor with its legs tied. When the fleece is gathered (it should be sheared in one full piece), it should be bundled into a burlap bag and should be free of contaminants. Mark your name on the bag and make sure there is only one fleece per bag. For more thorough rules and regulations about selling mohair through the government's direct-payment program, contact the USDA Agricultural Stabilization and Conservation Service online or in one of their many offices.

Shearing can be accomplished with the use of a special goat comb, which leaves ¼ inch of stubble on the goat. It is important to keep the fleeces clean and to avoid injuring the animal. The shearing seasons are in the spring and fall. After a goat has been sheared, it will be more sensitive to changes in the weather for up to six weeks. Make sure you have proper warming huts for these goats in the winter and adequate shelter from rain and inclement weather.

Sheep

Sheep were possibly the first domesticated animals and are now found all over the world on farms and smaller plots of land. Almost all the breeds of sheep that are found in the United States have been brought here from Great Britain. Raising sheep is relatively easy, as they only need pasture to eat, shelter from bad weather, and protection from predators. Sheep's wool can be used to make yarn or other articles of clothing and their milk can be made into various types of cheeses and yogurt, though this is not normally done in the United States.

Sheep are naturally shy creatures and are extremely docile. If they are treated well, they will learn to be affectionate with their owner. If a sheep is comfortable with its owner, it will be much easier to manage and to corral into its pen if it's allowed to graze freely. Start with only one or two sheep; they are not difficult to manage but do require a lot of attention.

▲ Cotswold sheep

their wool. Six quality wool-producing breeds are as follows:

1. Cotswold Sheep—This breed is very docile and hardy and thrives well in pastures. It produces around 14 pounds of fleece per year, making it a very profitable breed for anyone wanting to sell wool.
2. Leicester sheep—This is a hardy, docile breed of sheep that is a very good grazer. This breed has 6-inch-long, coarse wool that is desirable for

Breeds of Sheep

There are many different breeds of sheep—some are used exclusively for their meat and others for

▲ Leicester sheep

Sheep

▲ Merino sheep

6. Southdown sheep—One of the oldest breeds of sheep, these sheep are popular for their good quality wool and are deemed the standard of excellence for many sheep owners. Docile, hardy, and good grazing on pastures, their coarse and light-colored wool is used to make flannel.

▲ Shropshire sheep

knitting. It is a very popular breed in the United States.

3. Merino sheep—Introduced to the United States in the early twentieth century, this small- to medium-sized sheep has lots of rolls and folds of fine white wool and produces a fleece anywhere between 10 and 20 pounds. It is considered a fine-wool specialist, and though its fleece appears dark in color, the wool is actually white or buff. It is a wonderful foraging sheep, is hardy, and has a gentle disposition, but is not a very good milk producer.

4. Oxford down sheep—A more recent breed, these dark-faced sheep have hardy constitutions and good fleece.

5. Shropshire sheep—This breed has longer, more open, and coarser fleece than other breeds. It is quite popular in the United States, especially in areas that are more moist and damp, as they seem to be better in these climates than other breeds of sheep.

▲ Oxford down sheep

▲ Southdown sheep

Housing Sheep

Sheep do not require much shelter—only a small shed that is open on one side (preferably to the south so it can stay warmer in the winter months) and is roughly 6 to 8 feet high. The shelter should be ventilated well to reduce any unpleasant smells and to keep the sheep cool in the summer. Feeding racks or mangers should be placed inside of the shed to hold the feed for the sheep. If you live in a colder region of the country, building a sturdier, warmer shed for the sheep to live in during the winter is recommended.

Straw should be used for the sheep's bedding and should be changed daily to make sure the sheep do not become ill from an unclean shelter. Especially for the winter months, a dry pen should be erected for the sheep to exercise in. The fences should be strong enough to keep out predators that may enter your yard and to keep the sheep from escaping.

What Do Sheep Eat?

Sheep generally eat grass and are wonderful grazers. They utilize rough and scanty pasturage better than other grazing animals and, due to this, they can actually be quite beneficial in cleaning up a yard that is overgrown with undesirable herbage. Allowing sheep to graze in your yard or in a small pasture field will provide them with sufficient food in the summer months. Sheep also eat a variety of weeds, briars, and shrubs. Fresh water should always be available for the sheep.

Especially during the winter months, when grass is scarce, sheep should be fed hay (alfalfa, legume, or clover hay) and small quantities of grain. Corn is also a good winter food for the sheep (it can also be mixed with wheat bran), and straw, salt, and roots can also be occasionally added to their diet. Good food during the winter season will help the sheep grow a healthier and thicker wool coat.

Shearing Sheep

Sheep are generally sheared in the spring or early summer before the weather gets too warm. To do your own shearing, invest in a quality hand shearer and a scale on which to weigh the fleece. An experienced shearer should be able to take the entire wool off in one piece.

You may want to wash the wool a few days to a week before shearing the sheep. To do so, corral the sheep into a pen on a warm spring day (make sure there isn't a cold breeze blowing and that there is a lot of sunshine so the sheep does not become chilled). Douse the sheep in warm water, scrub the wool, and rinse. Repeat this a few times until most of the dirt and debris is out of the wool. Diffuse some natural oil throughout the wool to make it softer and ready for shearing.

▲ Shear your sheep in the spring or early summer, before the weather gets hot.

The sheep should be completely dry before shearing and you should choose a warm—but not overly hot—day. If you are a beginner at shearing sheep, try to find an experienced sheep owner to show you how to properly hold and shear a sheep. This way, you won't cause undue harm to the sheep's skin and will get the best fleece possible. When you are hand-shearing a sheep, remember to keep the skin pulled taut on the part where you are shearing to decrease the potential of cutting the skin.

Once the wool is sheared, tag it and roll it up by itself, and then bind it with twine. Be sure not to fold it or bind it too tightly. Separate and remove any dirty or soiled parts of the fleece before binding, as these parts will not be able to be carded and used.

Carding and Spinning Wool

To make the sheared wool into yarn you will need only a few tools: a spinning wheel or drop spindle and wool-cards. Wool-cards are rectangular pieces of thin board that have many wire teeth attached to them (they look like coarse brushes that are sometimes used for dogs' hair). To begin, you must clean the wool fleece of any debris, feltings, or other imperfections before carding it; otherwise your yarn will not spin correctly. Also wash it to remove any additional sand or dirt embedded in the wool and then allow it to dry completely. Then, all you need is to gather your supplies and follow these simple instructions:

▲ Wool-cards are used to soften and clean the wool fibers.

Spinning Wool

1. Take one long roll of carded wool and wind the fibers around the spindle.
2. Move the wheel gently and hold the spindle to allow the wool to "draw," or start to pull together into a single thread.
3. Keep moving the wheel and allow the yarn to wind around the spindle or a separate spool, if you have a more complex spinning wheel.
4. Keep adding rolls of carded wool to the spindle until you have the desired amount of yarn.

▲ Spinning on a traditional spinning wheel.

Note: If you are unable to obtain a spinning wheel of any kind, you can spin your carded wool by hand, although this will not produce the same tightness in your yarn as regular spinning. All you need to do is take the carded wool, hold it with one hand, and pull and twist the fibers into one, continuous piece. Winding the end of the yarn around a stick, spindle, or spool and securing it in place at the end will help keep your fibers tight and your yarn twisted.

If you want your yarn to be different colors, try dying it with natural berry juices or with special wool dyes found in arts and crafts stores.

Carding Wool

1. Grease the wool with rape oil or olive oil, just enough to work into the fibers.
2. Take one wool-card in your left hand, rest it on your knee, gather a tuft of wool from the fleece, and place it onto the wool-card so it is caught between the wired teeth of the card.
3. Take the second wool-card in your right hand and bring it gently across the other card several times, making a brushing movement toward your body.
4. When the fibers are all brushed in the same direction and the wool is soft and fluffy to the touch, remove the wool by rolling it into a small, fleecy ball (roughly a foot or more in length and only 2 inches in width) and put it in a bag until it is used for spinning.

Note: Carded wool can also be used for felting, in which case no spinning is needed. To felt a small blanket, place large amounts of carded wool on either side of a burlap sack. Using felting needles, weave the wool into the burlap until it is tightly held by the jute or hemp fabrics of the burlap.

Milking Sheep

Sheep's milk is not typically used in the United States for drinking, making cheese, or other familiar dairy products. Sheep do not typically produce milk year-round, as cows do, so milk will only be produced if you bred your sheep and had a lamb produced. If you do have a sheep that has given birth and the lamb has been sold or taken away, it is important to know how to milk the ewe so her udders do not become caked. Some ewes will still have an abundance of milk even after their lambs have been weaned and this excess milk should be removed to keep the ewe healthy and her udder free from infection.

To milk an ewe, bring her rear up to a fence so she cannot step backwards and, placing two knees against her shoulders to prevent her from moving forward, reach under with both hands and squeeze the milk into a bucket. When the udder is still soft but the ewe has been partly milked out, set her loose and then milk her again a few days later. If there is still milk to be had, wait another three days and then milk her again. By milking the ewes in this manner, you can prevent their udders from becoming infected and the milk from spoiling.

Diseases

The main diseases to which sheep are susceptible are foot rot and scabs. These are contagious and both require proper treatment. Sheep may also acquire stomach worms if they eat hay that has gotten too damp or has been lying on the floor of their shelter. As always, it is best to establish a relationship with a veterinarian who is familiar with caring for sheep and have your flock regularly checked for any parasites or diseases that may arise.

▲ A basket of hand-spun yarn.

Llamas

Llamas make excellent pets and are a great source of wooly fiber (their wool can be spun into yarn). Llamas are being kept more and more by people in the United States as companion animals, sources of fiber, pack and light plow animals, therapy animals for the elderly, "guards" for other backyard animals, and good educational tools for children. Llamas have an even temperament and are very intelligent, which makes them easy to train, and their hardiness allows them to thrive well in both cold and warmer climates (although they can have heat stress in extremely hot and humid parts of the country).

Before you decide to purchase a llama or two for your yard, check your state requirements regarding livestock. In some places, your property must also be zoned for livestock.

Llamas come in many different colors and sizes. The average adult llama is between 5½ and 6 feet tall and weighs between 250 and 450 pounds. Llamas, being herd animals, like the company of other llamas, so it is advisable that you raise a pair to keep each other company. If you only want to care for one llama, then it would be best to also have a sheep, goat, or other animal that can be penned with the llama for camaraderie. Although llamas can be led well on a harness and lead, never tie one up as it could potentially break its own neck trying to break free.

Llamas tend to make their own communal dung heap in a particular part of their pen. This is quite convenient for cleanup and allows you to collect the manure, compost it, and use it as a fertilizer for your garden.

Much of the information here is adapted from www.autumnhillllamas.com and www.lostcreekllamas.com. Visit these sites for more on raising llamas and using their fibers.

Feeding Llamas

Llamas can subsist fairly well on grass, hay (an adult male will eat about one bale per week), shrubs, and trees, much like sheep and goats. If they are not receiving enough nutrients, they may be fed a mixture of rolled corn, oats, and barley, especially during the winter season when grazing is not necessarily available. Make sure not to overfeed your llamas, though, or they will become overweight and constipated. You can occasionally give cornstalks to your llamas as an added source of fiber, and many farmers add mineral supplements to the feed mixture or hay. Salt blocks are also acceptable to have in your llama pen, and a constant supply of fresh water is necessary. Nursing female llamas should receive a grain mixture until the cria (baby) is weaned.

Be sure to keep feed and hay off the ground. This will help ward off parasites that establish themselves in the feed and are then ingested by the llamas.

▲ Though alpacas are much smaller than llamas, they produce more fiber, making them increasingly popular among farmers. Alpacas are very intelligent and rarely bite, spit, or kick. They are raised similarly, though alpacas require less space due to their smaller size. Both require shelter, fencing, areas in which to forage, clean water, and often mineral supplements.

▲ Llamas enjoy hay, but you should keep it off the ground to help prevent your llamas from ingesting parasites.

Housing Your Llamas

Llamas may be sheltered in a small stable or even a converted garage. There should be enough room to store feed and hay, and the shelter should be able to be closed off during wet, windy, and cold weather. Llamas prefer light, open spaces in which to live, so make sure your shed or shelter has large doors and/or big windows. The feeders for the hay and grain mixture should be raised above the ground. Adding a place where a llama can be safely restrained for toenail clippings and vet checkups will help facilitate these processes but is not absolutely necessary.

The llamas should be able to enter and exit the shelter easily and it is a good idea to build a fence or pen around the shelter so they do not wander off. A fence about four feet tall should be enough to keep your llamas safe and enclosed. If you happen to have both a male and female llama, it is necessary to have separate enclosures for them to stave off unwanted pregnancies.

Toenail Trimming

Llamas need their toenails to be trimmed so they do not twist and fold under the toe, making it difficult for the llama to move around. Laying gravel in the area where your llamas frequently walk will help to keep the toenails naturally trimmed, but if you need to cut them, be careful not to cut too deeply or you may cause the tip of the toe to bleed and this could lead to an infection in the toe. Use shears designed for this purpose to cut the nails. Use one hand to hold the

llama's "ankle" just above where the foot bends. Hold the clippers in your other hand, cutting away from the foot toward the tip of the nail. The nail's are easiest to clip in the early morning or after a rain, since the wetness of the ground will soften them.

Shearing

It is important to groom and shear your llama, especially during hot weather. Brushing the llama's coat to remove dirt and keep it from matting will not only make your llamas look clean and healthy but it will also improve the quality of their coats. If you want to save the fibers for spinning into yarn, it is best to brush, comb, and use a hair dryer to remove any dust and debris from the llama's coat before you begin shearing.

Shearing is not necessarily difficult, but if you are a first-time llama owner, you should ask another llama farmer to teach you how to properly shear your llama. To shear your llama, you can purchase battery-operated shears to remove the fibers for sale or use. Different llamas will respond in different ways to shearing. Try holding the llama with a halter and lead in a smaller area to begin the shearing process.

Do not completely remove the llama from any other llamas you have, though, as their presence will help calm the llama you are shearing. It is best to have another person with you to aid in the shearing (to hold the llama, give it treats, and offer any other help). When shearing a llama, don't shear all the way down to the skin. Allowing a thin coating of hair to cover the llama's body will help protect it from the sun and from being scratched when it rolls in the dirt.

Start by shearing a flat top the length of the llama's back. Next, taking the shears in one hand, move them in a downward position to remove the coat. Shear a strip the length of the neck from the chin to the front legs about 3 inches wide to help cool the llama. Shearing can take a long time, so it may be necessary for both you and the llama to take a break. Take the llama for a quiet walk and allow it to go to the bathroom so it will not become antsy during the rest of the shearing process.

Collect the sheared fibers in a container and make sure you are working on a clean floor so you can collect any excess fibers and use them for spinning. Do not store the fiber in a plastic bag, as moisture can easily accumulate, ruining the fiber and making it unusable for spinning.

Caring for the Cria

Baby llamas require some additional care in their first few days of life. It is important for the cria to receive the colostrum milk from their mothers, but you may need to aid in this process. Approach the mother llama and pull gently on each teat to remove the waxy plugs covering the milk holes. Sometimes, you may need to guide the cria into position under its mother for it to start nursing.

▲ Baby llamas are called "crias."

Weigh the cria often (at least for the first month) to see that it's gaining weight and growing strong and healthy. A bathroom scale, hanging scale, or larger grain scale can be used for this.

If the cria seems to need extra nourishment, goat or cow milk can be substituted during times when the mother llama cannot produce enough milk for the cria. Feed this additional milk to the cria in small doses, several times a day, from a milking bottle.

Diseases

Llamas are prone to getting worms and should be checked often to make sure they do not have any of these parasites. There is special worming paste that can be mixed in with their food to prevent worms from infecting them. You should also establish a relationship with a good veterinarian who knows about caring for llamas and can determine if there are any other vaccinations necessary in order to keep your llamas healthy. Other diseases and pests that can affect llamas are tuberculosis, tetanus, ticks, mites, and lice.

Using Llama Fibers

Llama fiber is unique from other animal fibers, such as sheep's wool. It does not contain any lanolin (an oil found in sheep's wool); thus, it is hypoallergenic and not as greasy. How often you can shear your llama will depend on the variety of llama, its health, and environmental conditions. Typically, though, every year llamas grow a fleece that is 4 to 6 inches long and that weighs between 3 and 7 pounds. Llama fiber can be used like any other animal fiber or wool, making it the perfect substitute for all of your fabric and spinning needs.

▲ Llama fiber can be dyed and spun to be used for knitting.

Llamas

Llama fiber is made up of two parts: the undercoat (which provides warmth for the llama) and the guard hair (which protects the llama from rain and snow). The undercoat is the most desirable part to use due to its soft, downy texture, while the coarser guard hair is usually discarded.

Gathering llama hair is easy. To harvest the fiber, you must shear the llama. However, the steps involved in shearing when you are gathering the fiber are slightly different than when you are simply shearing to keep the llama cooler in the summer months. To shear a llama for fiber collection:

1. Clean the llama by blowing and brushing until the coat is free from dirt and debris.
2. Wash the llama. Be sure to rinse out all of the soap from the hair and let the llama air-dry.
3. You can use scissors or commercial clippers to shear the llama. Start at the top of the back, behind the head and neck, and work backwards. If using clippers, shear with long sweeping motions, not short jerky ones. If using scissors, always point

them downward. Leave about an inch of wool on the llama for protection against the sun and insect bites. You can shear just the area around the back and belly (in front of the hind legs and behind the front legs) if your main purpose is to offer the llama relief from the heat. Or you can shear the entire llama—from just below the head, down to the tail—to get the most wool. Once the shearing is complete, skirt the fleece by removing any little pieces or belly hair from the shorn fleece.

The fiber can be hand-processed or sent to a mill (though sending the fibers to a mill is much more expensive and is not necessary if you have only one or two llamas). Processing the fiber by hand is definitely more cost-effective but you will initially need to invest in some equipment (such as a spinning wheel, drop spindle, or felting needle).

To process the fiber by hand:

1. Pick out any remaining debris and unwanted (coarse) fibers.

▲ Llamas should be washed and allowed to air dry before shearing.

2. Card the fiber. This helps to separate the fiber and will make spinning much easier. To card the fiber, put a bit of fiber on one end of the cards (standard wool-cards do the trick nicely) and gently brush it until it separates. This will produce a rolag (log) of fiber.

3. Once the fiber is carded, you can use it in a few different ways:

   - Wet felting: To wet felt, lay the fiber out in a design between 2 pieces of material and soak it in hot, soapy water. Then, agitate the fiber by rubbing or rolling it. This will cause it to stick together. Rinse the fiber in cold water. When it dries, you will have produced a strong piece of felt that can be used in many crafting projects.

   - Needle felting: For this type of manipulation, you will need a felting needle (available at your local arts and crafts or fabric store). Lay out a piece of any material you want over a pillow or Styrofoam piece. Place the fiber on top of the material in any design of your choosing. Push the needle through the fiber and the bottom material and then gently draw it back out. Continue

this process until the fiber stays on the material of its own accord. This is a great way to make table runners or hanging cloths using your llama fiber.

   - Spinning: Spinning is a great way to turn your llama fiber into yarn. Spinning can be accomplished by using either a spinning wheel or drop spindle, and a piece of fiber that is either in a batt, rolag, or roving. A spinning wheel, while larger and more expensive, will easily help you to turn the fiber into yarn. A drop spindle is convenient because it is smaller and easier to transport, and if you have time and patience, it will do just as good a job as the spinning wheel. To make yarn, twist two or more pieces of spun wool together.

   - Other uses: carded wool can also be used to weave, knit, or crochet.

If you become comfortable using llama fiber to make clothing or other craft items, you may want to try to sell these crafts (or your llama fiber directly) to consumers. Fiber crafts may be particularly successful if sold at local craft markets or even at farmers' markets alongside your garden produce.

Part Four

Simple Structures for Your Land

"Regard it as just as desirable to build a chicken house as to build a cathedral."

—Frank Lloyd Wright

"Develop an infallible technique and then place yourself at the mercy of inspiration."

—Lao-Tzu

Even if you only have a small plot of land, it may be helpful to have a modest potting shed near your garden or a workshop where you can keep your tools. If you'll be raising animals, you'll need shelter for them—even a dog deserves a house it can call its own. Some of the projects in this chapter offer step-by-step instructions that will guide you through the entire building process. Others are meant to offer guidelines for a structure, which you can then alter to meet your own wants and needs. If you are new to woodworking, you may want to start off with one of the simpler projects, such as a birdhouse, and then progress to more complex structures as you build confidence. Follow the directions closely, measure materials carefully, and cross-reference with similar plans found online or in other books when needed. If you're an experienced builder, use the directions and illustrations here as inspiration to create your own unique masterpieces. Whatever your skill level, as with everything, try to enjoy the process as much as the end result.

Doghouses

Doghouses and kennels are easy to construct and are especially useful if you have dogs that primarily live outdoors. A dog kennel needs to protect the dog from harsh winds and heavy rains and should be spacious enough for the dog to move around in comfortably. Doghouses should be located near to your own house so you can have easy access to your pet, and should be situated on a side of your house that creates a natural barrier against the wind and weather. Dogs should not be left outside overnight in very cold weather, even with access to a doghouse. Below are a couple of doghouses and kennels that can be easily constructed for your outdoor pet.

Standard Dog Kennel

This kennel is constructed to be warm and windproof, to direct the rain away from the base by creating large roof overhangs, and to be easily cleaned.

Materials
- Matched boards for the sides, ends, and bottom (standard measurements for the kennel are 30 inches long, 20 inches wide, and 30 inches tall)
- Weather boards for the roof
- Strip of sheet metal
- Wooden beading

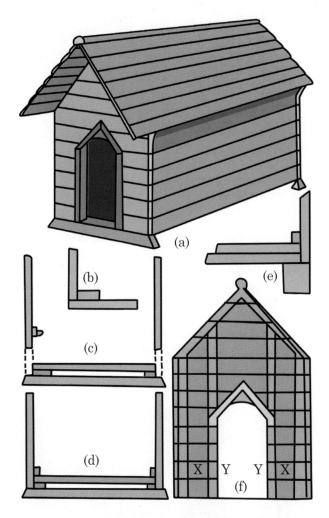

▲ Refer to this illustration when making the dog kennel. The kennel raised off the ground is shown by (c); (d) illustrates the parts in contact; (e) is a vertical section of the back end.

Directions
1. Make the ends first by nailing lengths of matching boards across uprights of 2 x 1-inch batten (f). At the top, halve the battens into the two roof pieces. Set the two outer uprights, X X, in about ¾ inch from the edges to allow the sides to be flush with the outside of the ends. Place these four uprights on the inside.
2. It is advisable to cut out the door—using a padsaw for the semicircular top—before nailing on Y Y, which should be a little nearer to one another than are the rough edges of the door. Two short verticals on the outside, also projecting beyond the edges, prevent the dog from injuring himself on them.
3. The battens may be omitted from the back end of the kennel, but they ultimately help strengthen the structure and so should be included.
4. When the ends are finished, the horizontal boards for the sides are nailed onto each end (b).

▲ Modify the dog kennel plans here to fit your dog if it is a larger breed.

Doghouses

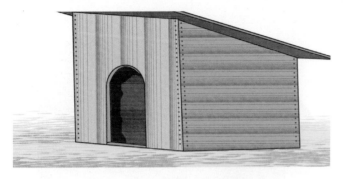

▲ This kennel has a floor that is 2 feet square, is 3 feet 4 inches high in front, and the roof has an overhang of 8 inches.

Begin at the bottom, arranging the lowest board with its tongue pointing upwards and add the upper boards one by one. The direction in which the tongue points is an important detail—if the boards are put on the wrong way, water will leak more easily into the kennel, rotting the boards and making your dog wet.

5. Battens (d) and (e) are nailed inside along the sides of the kennel and a third is nailed across the back, at a distance above the bottom edge equal to the thickness of the bottom boards and of the battens (b) and (c), to which they are attached. At each end a 2 x 2-inch deal, (f), is screwed to (b) and (c) to raise the bottom clear off the ground.

6. The roof weather boards must be long enough to project at least 6 inches beyond the door end, to prevent rain from coming through the entrance. The eaves overhang 3 inches and are supported, as shown in (a), by three brackets cut out of hard wood. Begin laying on the boards, starting at the eaves and finishing at the ridge, which is closed with a 6-inch strip of sheet metal placed on top of a wooden beading.

7. Stain all the exterior surfaces, including the bottom, and fill in the cracks with caulking to keep the water from seeping through.

The inside part of the kennel should be exposed to the sun occasionally by being turned on its end, and the bottom should be cleaned often.

▲ This doghouse is wider and has the door set off to one side, which allows for even more protection from the elements.

Birdhouses

If you are interested in attracting birds to your yard during the spring, summer, and fall months, in particular, you'll need to provide shelter for the birds. Birdhouses do not need to be very elaborate and they should be rather inconspicuous so birds can easily come and go without attracting predators to their house and nest. All that is really required of a birdhouse is a good hiding place, with an opening just large enough for the bird to fit through, and a strong roof that keeps out the rain.

Birdhouses can be made from a variety of materials—even an old hat tacked to the side of a shed with a hole cut in the top can suffice for a birdhouse. Other usable materials include tin cans, barrels, flowerpots, wooden buckets, and small boxes (preferably wooden or metal).

Most standard birdhouses are made of wood pieces nailed together to look like a miniature house. If you plan to have many birds nesting in your yard, you may want to build a few birdhouses during the winter so they can be ready for springtime, when birds are beginning to nest. To attract a particular kind of bird to your birdhouse, you must make the size of the hole appropriate for the type of bird. For wrens, make the hole about 1 inch; for bluebirds and tree-swallows, the hole should be 1½ inches; for martins, it should be 2½ inches. Below are a few examples of birdhouses you can easily make to attract beautiful birds to your yard.

▲ A bird ark birdhouse.

▲ Be creative with your birdhouse designs, and experiment with different shapes and materials.

Bird Ark Birdhouse

This birdhouse is constructed of three tin cans joined together. Both ends of the center can are removed, but the bottom is left on both end cans. To make the bird ark, simply:

1. Cut a hole into the side of the center can and another through the bottom of each can. Do not remove the pieces of tin but bend them out to serve as perches.
2. Cut the roof boards of the correct size to project over the ends and sides about 1 inch, nail them together, and fasten them in place by nailing the boards to the connecting blocks between the cans.
3. Fasten the ark between the blocks on a platform or board and then mount the platform on post supports and brace it with brackets, as seen in the picture above. Attach several sticks for perches.

Lean-to Birdhouse

This birdhouse is made out of an empty wooden box (or, if you want to put together your own box, just nail small pieces of wood together of any size you like). If you do make your own box, make sure that the top edges of the end pieces are cut at a slant to allow for a slanted roof. If you use an empty box, add triangular pieces to the edges to create a slant (a).

Cut the center partition, dividing the box into two compartments of equal size as the end pieces. The doorway can be cut with a jackknife—this is easily done if the ends are in two separate pieces because then half of the hole can be cut out of the edge of each

▲ Lean-to birdhouse.

piece. After the ends have been pieced out, nail a strip to the back, and then cut the roof board large enough so it will project out from the box about 1 inch.

The lean-to birdhouse can now be mounted on the side of a shed or on a tree and sticks can be fitted into the holes for perches. To mount the house, cut out and nail a wooden bracket to the shed wall and then nail the lean-to birdhouse into the wooden bracket.

Log Cabin Birdhouse

This birdhouse can be made out of any-sized box. Nail pieces together to form the roof, and then thatch the roofing itself to blend into the surrounding environment. The more sloped the roof, the easier the rain can fall off and not penetrate into the house. This house is slightly more elaborate in the sense that the support pole passes through the house to form a "chimney." The windows can be cut out and fake doors painted on for aesthetic purposes. Small branches should be cut to the proper lengths, split, and then nailed all over the exterior of the house to produce a "log cabin" look—this also helps the birdhouse to better blend into the surrounding trees and foliage in your yard.

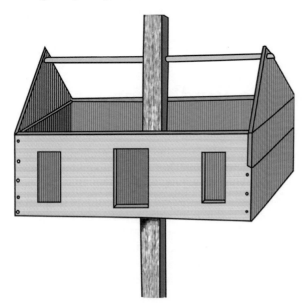

▲ Cross section of a log cabin birdhouse.

Temple Birdhouse

This is a small birdhouse, perfect for wrens. This birdhouse hangs from a tree branch.

Materials
- Large tin can
- Wooden board about 7 inches square
- Carpet or upholstery tacks
- Earthen flowerpot
- Small cork to plug up the flowerpot hole
- Eye screw
- Short stick
- Wire
- Small nails

Directions
1. Mark the doorway on the side of the can and cut the opening with a can opener.
2. Fasten the can to the square baseboard (A) by driving large carpet tacks through the bottom of the can into the board.

▲ Decorate your birdhouse with twigs and bark.

3. Invert the flowerpot to make the roof. Plug up the drain hole to make the house waterproof (use a cork or other means of stopping up the hole) (B).
4. Screw the eye screw into the top of the plug to attach the suspending wire. Drill a small hole through the lower end of the plug so that a short nail can be pushed through after the plug has been inserted to keep it from coming out.
5. Fasten the flowerpot over the can with wire, passing the loop of wire entirely around the pot and then running short wires from this wire down to small nails driven into the four corners of the base, (C).
6. Now the bird temple can be painted and hung on a tree.

Temple Birdhouse

This is a small birdhouse, perfect for wrens. This birdhouse hangs from a tree branch.

Materials
- Large tin can
- Wooden board about 7 inches square
- Carpet or upholstery tacks
- Earthen flowerpot
- Small cork to plug up the flowerpot hole
- Eye screw
- Short stick
- Wire
- Small nails

Directions
1. Mark the doorway on the side of the can and cut the opening with a can opener.
2. Fasten the can to the square baseboard (A) by driving large carpet tacks through the bottom of the can into the board.
3. Invert the flowerpot to make the roof. Plug up the drain hole to make the house waterproof (use a cork or other means of stopping up the hole) (B).
4. Screw the eye screw into the top of the plug to attach the suspending wire. Drill a small hole through the lower end of the plug so that a short nail can be pushed through after the plug has been inserted to keep it from coming out.
5. Fasten the flowerpot over the can with wire, passing the loop of wire entirely around the pot and then running short wires from this wire down to small nails driven into the four corners of the base, (C).
6. Now the bird temple can be painted and hung on a tree.

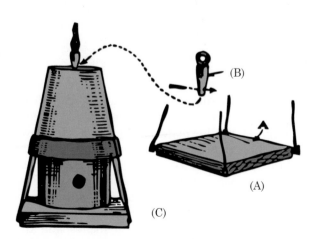

▲ Temple birdhouse.

Birdhouses for Specific Bird Species

Species	Floor of cavity (inches)	Depth of cavity (inches)	Entrance above floor (inches)	Diam. of entrance (inches)	Height above ground (feet)
Bluebird	5 x 5	8	6	1½	5 to 10
Robin	6 x 8	8	(a)	(a)	6 to 15
Chickadee	4 x 4	8 to 10	8	1⅛	6 to 15
Tufted titmouse	4 x 4	8 to 10	8	1¼	6 to 15
White-breasted nuthatch	4 x 4	8 to 10	8	1¼	12 to 20
House wren	4 x 4	6 to 8	1 to 6	⅞	6 to 10
Bewick wren	4 x 4	6 to 8	1 to 6	⅞	6 to 10
Carolina wren	4 x 4	6 to 8	1 to 6	1⅛	6 to 10
Dipper	6 x 6	6	1	3	1 to 3
Violet-green swallow	5 x 5	6	1 to 6	1½	10 to 15
Tree swallow	5 x 5	6	1 to 6	1½	10 to 15
Barn swallow	6 x 6	6	(a)	(a)	8 to 12
Martin	6 x 6	6	1	2½	15 to 20
Song sparrow	6 x 6	6	(b)	(b)	1 to 3
House finch	6 x 6	6	4	2	8 to 12
Phoebe	6 x 6	6	(a)	(a)	8 to 12
Crested flycatcher	6 x 6	8 to 10	8	2	8 to 20
Flicker	7 x 7	16 to 18	16	2½	6 to 20
Red-headed woodpecker	6 x 6	12 to 15	12	2	12 to 20
Golden-fronted woodpecker	6 x 6	12 to 15	12	2	12 to 20
Hairy woodpecker	6 x 6	12 to 15	12	2	12 to 20
Downy woodpecker	4 x 4	8 to 10	8	1¼	6 to 20
Screech owl	8 x 8	12 to 15	12	3	10 to 30
Sparrow hawk	8 x 8	12 to 15	12	3	10 to 30
Saw-whet owl	6 x 6	10 to 12	10	2½	12 to 20
Barn owl	10 x 18	15 to 18	4	6	12 to 18
Wood duck	10 x 18	10 to 15	3	6	4 to 20

(a) One or more sides open. (b) All sides open.

Simple Bird Shelters

Birds seek out dry places to nest and to escape from rain and wet leaves. Simple bird shelters can be constructed out of regular materials, some of which you may have lying about your house or garage.

The bird shelter in illustration (a) has a canvas or heavy muslin roof, supported on two uprights. Five perches are arranged from side to side, and this allows a few birds to rest and retreat from inclement weather. The uprights are 1½ x 3 inches and the strips forming the Y braces are 2 inches wide and ⅞ inch thick. The perches are ¾-inch dowels that are 3 feet long. You can find these at your local hardware store.

Make holes in the uprights to insert and secure the perches. Illustration (b) shows the inside of such a shelter. Make sure the canvas roof is waterproof and is tacked securely around all the edges of the house.

Bird shelters can also be made out of a barrel hoop, as shown in illustration (c). To make this house:

1. Cover a flat barrel hoop loosely with canvas or heavy muslin tacked around all the edges.
2. Drive a wooden peg into the top of a post. Cut a hole in the canvas and slip it over the post.

▲ If desired, paint your birdhouse or shelter after assembling.

3. Attach four wires to the hoop at equal distances apart. Pass the lower ends through staples or eye-screws driven into the post about a foot or two from the top.

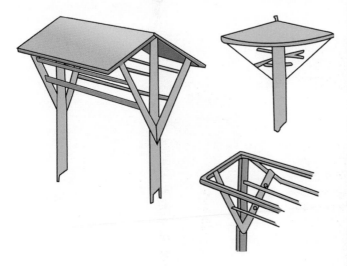

▲ Illustration (a) shows a shelter with a muslin or canvas roof. The inside of the shelter is drawn in illustration (b). Illustration (b) shows a shelter made out of a barrel hoop.

4. Make two or three holes in the post, and drive round perches through the holes for the birds to sit on.

Simple Stables

If you are raising larger livestock—sheep, goats, horses, or llamas, for example—you will need a small stable where they can go for protection during inclement weather and especially during the winter months in cooler regions. Building stables can be relatively easy and inexpensive, and doing it yourself means that you can customize the design to fit your and your animals' needs.

Stables should be built on relatively flat ground that does not become excessively wet or flooded during heavy rains. Laying down a thick bed of gravel or sand below the stable floor will help keep surface water drained. Also consider the positioning of the stable; try to find an area protected from strong winds but also near your own home so you don't have to go too far to tend the animals during bad weather. Facing the stable toward the south or west will help keep a nice breeze flowing through your stable while protecting it from harsh northerly winds. A place to store feed and hay for your animals is also a worthwhile addition when planning and building a simple stable.

General Stable Construction

When building a stable for your livestock, make sure that the interior walls are weatherproof and free of dampness. To keep moisture out of the stable, the building should be situated on slightly higher ground than that surrounding it. This will keep the ground from getting too damp, and vapors will not be as likely to rise through the floor and foundation walls. If possible, it is best to make the stable floor out of concrete between 4 and 6 inches thick.

The stable walls should be built solid. Brick and stone are preferable to wood, but wooden stables also do an adequate job of providing shelter and are much more common in the United States, due to the availability of wood. If you decide to build your stable using bricks, building the walls one brick (9 inches) thick should be suitable. Internal walls should be built solid, and the foundation must be deep and wide enough to give the whole structure stability. If one side of your stable gets

▲ The Dutch door on this stable can keep animals enclosed while allowing fresh air to circulate.

the brunt of driving rain or moisture, it is a good idea to cover it with an extra layer of concrete or stucco, or hang shingles to protect the wall.

The external angles of all of the doors and windows should be rounded. This can be done by using bull-nosed bricks. This way, horses and other livestock will not be injured by coming into contact with any sharp angles or ledges.

▼ A stable can be made out of a variety of materials, including brick and wood.

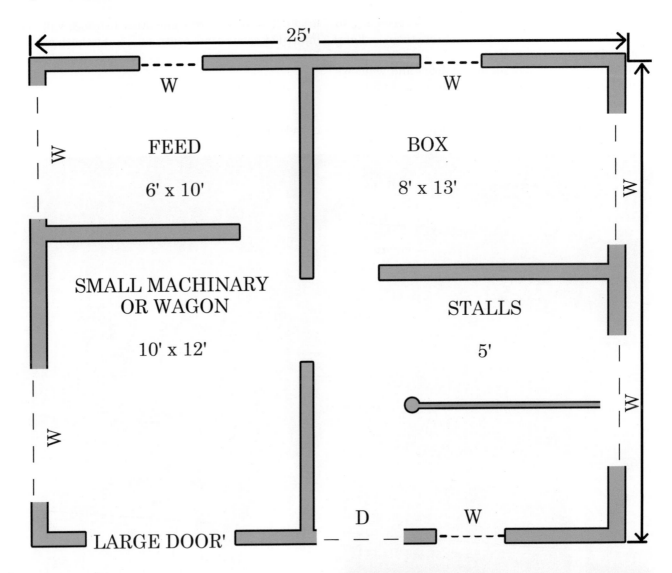

▲ Plans for a small stable.

A Small Stable for Horses, Llamas, or Sheep

This simple stable is inexpensive to build and has plenty of room for two horses, llamas, or sheep, along with feed and tack. Hay and grain can be kept in the loft. Place the windows as high up as possible and hinge them at the bottom so they'll open inwardly to permit the air to pass over the animals without blowing directly on them. Make the stable door a "Dutch door"; that is, a door divided horizontally in the middle so that the upper half may be opened and the lower half remain closed.

Poultry Houses

Poultry houses should be warm, dry, well-lighted, and ventilated shelters with convenient arrangements for roosts, feeding space, and nest boxes. In winter, if you're living in a cool climate, light and warmth are of the upmost importance. Fowl will stop laying eggs and their health will suffer when confined in cold, wet, and dark conditions. Windows facing the south or southeast, large enough to admit the sun freely, should be provided and made to slide open to increase circulation during the summer.

Beyond these few requirements, houses for your poultry can be made in a variety of ways and are, generally, relatively easy to construct. Below are many different types of poultry houses that can be used to keep your fowl warm, dry, and healthy.

Simplest Poultry House

While poultry can survive in this type of cheaply and simply built coop, it is best used in warmer climates, where the winter months do not become incredibly cold and not much, if any, snow falls. Also, this type of coop is best suited for only one or two chickens or ducks.

Materials
- Four pieces of 1 x 2-inch boards for the studs and rafters

- Strong nails
- Wire netting
- Tarred paper

1. Take two of the boards and nail them together in a T shape. Repeat with the other two. Set these apart from each other about 2 feet 10 inches on the centers, and cover them with tightly drawn wire netting (cut to size).
2. Cover the wire netting with tarred paper, creating a barrier between the outside winds and weather and the fowl inside.

Young Poultry Coops

Chicks need extra warmth and protection from predators. This coop, if it houses small chicks, should not hold the other fowl, as they may bully or even harm the young chicks.

▲ A pitched roof chicken coop.

This pitched roof chicken coop consists of a pitched roof mounted on three boards, 6 feet high. This coop is 3 feet wide and 2 feet deep. Nail slats across the front to prevent the hen from getting out but to allow the chicks to enter and exit freely into a small, fenced-in area surrounding the coop.

The coop pictured above is similar to the pitched roof chicken coop except that there is a canopy that keeps the rain out and shades the interior of the coop so it does not become too warm. This coop is 3 feet long, 2 feet wide, and 30 inches high at the front and 24 inches high in the back. The coop can be constructed from boards with matched edges and should be raised an inch or two above the ground to ensure the floor remains dry. Tack a piece of light canvas or muslin to the roof to serve as the awning.

▲ Chicken coop with canopy.

Practical Henhouse

This simple and efficient henhouse has a shed roof and, as most poultry houses should, faces toward the south. This house can be up to 10 feet wide and as long as you need to accommodate your chickens.

A scratching shed is in the center of the building and has windows that let sunlight in. The sleeping quarters should be kept warm. An open, wire-enclosed front for the scratching shed should be included, too. The roosts should be made movable, and fresh bedding should be kept on the floor of the henhouse.

The roof of the henhouse should project out 1 foot over the south, east, and west sides. It should also be 5 inches higher than the siding, allowing for free ventilation. Two large windows will admit light and warmth into the henhouse. A laying box should extend the entire length of the room and must be divided into compartments and covered with a hinged lid. This allows the eggs to be gathered simply by raising the lid from the outside. Make sure the floor is cleaned weekly to keep out disease. The inside of the walls should be whitewashed often to keep out moisture and pests.

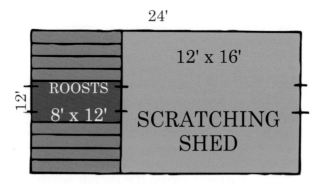

▲ Plan for a henhouse with a scratching shed.

This henhouse has a scratching shed, which allows the chickens ▶ access to the open air while still being protected from the elements.

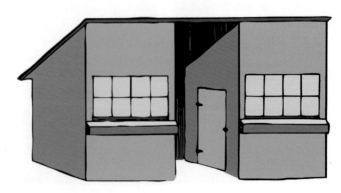

▲ You can build a simple ramp to give your chickens easy access to the coop.

Two-Room Henhouse

This two-room henhouse has a south-facing front to allow ample sunlight and warmth into the house. It can be made as large as 10 x 12 feet and should be constructed of wood or timber planks. It is divided into two rooms by a partition made out of wire netting. This henhouse can serve two separate yards. A fence constructed in the middle of the house yard should join the center of the front of the building (and at the back as well if you so desire). In this house, both hens and roosters can be kept and are easily separated while allowing each enough space and exercise.

The platform and perches should be constructed inside of each room. When the perches are in need of cleaning, they are raised up against the wall in the house, in a perpendicular position. To clean the trough, the perches and platform are raised perpendicular to the floor.

◄ A two-room henhouse with a south-facing front.

▲ These pictures show how the perches can be moved to allow for easy cleaning.

257

Duck Houses

Ducks, while they can survive rather well in any type of poultry house, are happiest when they have either a stream or pond in which to swim, bathe, and gather food. If you have a stream or pond on your property, situating a duck house nearby will help ensure that the duck eggs are safe and secure.

If you are raising a good number of ducks, your duck house should be about 30 feet long and 12 feet high. Doors should be situated in the front of the house and the house should have a few small windows that can be slid open to allow fresh air to circulate within the duck house. The rear of the house should hold the nests (boxes open at the front). A small door should be situated behind each nest so the eggs can be easily removed.

You can use a strip of wire netting to enclose a small, narrow yard in the front of the house. Do not use twine netting, however, as the ducks could get their heads twisted in it and strangle themselves.

▲ A simple duck house.

Easy, Creative Coops

If you don't have much space in your yard and only have a few chickens to keep, very good coops can be made at a very small cost from items found around your house, yard, or at rummage sales:

1. Barrel Coop
   a. First, drive shingle nails through the hoops on both sides of each stave and clinch them down on the inside.

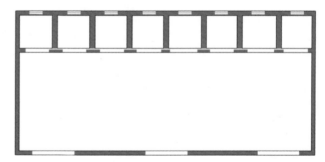

▲ Floor plan for the duck house.

▲ A barrel chicken coop.

▲ A simple box coop.

b. Divide the barrel in half, if it is big enough, by cutting through the hoops and the bottom.

c. Drive sticks into the ground to hold the coop in place, and drive a long stick at each side of the opened end just far enough from the coop to allow the front door to be slipped in and out.

d. The night door can be made from the head of the barrel or any solid board, and the slatted door, used to confine the hen, can be made by nailing upright strips of lath to a cross-lath at top and bottom.

2. Box Coop

a. Find a box that is roughly 2 to 2½ feet long, 16 inches deep, and 2 feet high and saw a hole, d, in one end.

b. Strengthen the box with narrow strips of wood, b, c, on each side of the hole. This acts as a groove for the door, a, to slide in. By doing so, you will have a sliding door that opens and shuts easily.

c. The front of the coop is enclosed with lath, or narrow strips, placed 2½ to 3 inches apart. The top should be covered with a good grade of roofing paper to make it completely waterproof.

3. Portable Coop—This type of coop will allow you to have a fresh yard for your chickens and other poultry to scrounge in and is easily transported to any place on your property.

a. The coop is built of ordinary material on a base frame and with a V-shaped roof and side frames. The preferred length of the coop is about 2 feet and the yard should be around 3 to 4 feet.

b. The ridge pole is extended, as shown at each end, to form a handle.

c. If desired, the hen may be allowed to freely roam the yard or can be contained within the coop by slats, as is pictured in the drawing.

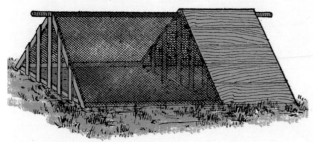

▲ A portable chicken coop.

Poultry House Aids and Other Considerations

Folding Chicken Roost

This roost is made of 3-inch boards cut to any desired length that will fit within your poultry house. A small bolt fastens the upright pieces at their top ends and the horizontal pieces are fastened on with nails. This roost can be kept at any angle and may be quickly taken out of the house when it is time to clean. This sort of roost will accommodate more fowl in the same space than the flat kind.

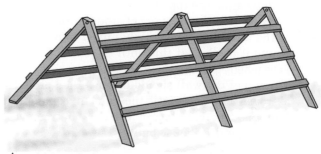

▲ A folding chicken roost.

Keeping Rats and Mice Out of the Poultry House

If you are building a permanent poultry house, you should try to make it as rodent-proof as possible. If rats and mice can easily enter your poultry house, they will not only steal eggs and spread diseases, but they could scare or even harm the fowl. Cheap and efficient walls can be made of small fieldstones in this way:

1. Dig trenches for the walls below the frost line.
2. Drive two rows of stakes into the trenches, one row at each side of the trench.
3. Set up boards in between the stakes. The boards will hold the stones and cement in place until the cement hardens. The top boards should have a straight upper edge and should be placed level to determine the top of the wall.
4. Place two or three layers of stone in the bottom of the trench, pour in thinly mixed cement, and pound it in. Repeat this until the desired height is reached.
5. The top of the wall should be smoothed off with a trowel and left until the cement completely hardens. The side boards can now be removed and the poultry house built.

Winter Care of Fowl

If chickens and other fowl are not kept warm in the winter, they will stop growing, cease laying eggs, and can become ill. There are several ways you can winterize chicken coops to ensure your birds' comfort and well-being.

Especially if you live in colder climates, having a house with hollow or double side walls will help keep your fowl warm during the winter season. Buildings with hollow side walls are warmer in the winter and are also cooler in the summer. They do not collect as much severe frost and result in less moisture seeping into the henhouse once the frost melts.

The outside walls of chicken coops can be plastered or lined with matched boards and the spaces between the boards filled with wood shavings, sawdust, or hay. The floor should be covered with several inches of dry sand, wood shavings, or straw, and the ventilating holes near the roof should be partly stopped up or shutters arranged to close most of them in very cold weather. You don't want to seal the place up completely, though. Nothing is more important to the health of fowl than pure air. Birds breathe with great rapidity and maintain a relatively high body temperature, so they need plenty of oxygen.

Constructing a solid, insulated roof for your poultry house for the winter is very important. A roof can be built either by sealing the inside with material to exclude draughts or by placing roof boards close together and covering them thoroughly with tarred paper before shingling. An ordinary shingled roof allows too much wind to come into the house and could cause your fowl to get frosted combs or wattles. If this happens, there will not be much, if any, egg production in the winter months.

Hanging curtains in front of the perches is also a great way to keep your fowl warm during the winter months. Make these curtains of burlap and hang them from the roof in such a way that the perches are enclosed in a little room. Make sure the curtains are long enough to touch the floor all around, and sew the edges of the burlap together, except at the corners. At night, the corners can be pinned together to keep the birds from leaving their sheltered perches. This pseudo–sleeping room allows air to move in without creating drafts and it also helps retain the birds' body heat. This maintains a comfortable temperature for the birds during cold, winter nights.

▼ A drinking fountain for your chickens can be made with a can or bucket and a tray. Cut out one end of the can and poke holes along the edge as shown. Fill with water, cover with a shallow tray, and turn the whole thing over quickly. Chicks will be able to drink water easily without risk of drowning.

Fences, Gates, and Pens

Whether you are looking to add a lovely fence and gate around your garden plants or you have poultry or other livestock to keep in check, you may need to build a fence, gate, or animal pen. These structures can be attractive if well-built and should be able to stand up to all kinds of weather and animals. Depending on your needs, here are some various fences, gates, and pens you can easily construct in your yard or on your property.

Fences

Fences are perfect for keeping animals or young children in a confined space or for drawing boundaries between yours and your neighbor's property lines—but check with your neighbors before you construct your fence to make sure they don't mind. Also call your local utility companies to make sure that you will not be digging up power or gas lines.

Wooden Fences

Wooden fences allow for good ventilation and an open, airy feel. They can provide protection for young shrubs and plants as well as keep animals and children safe within the yard or fenced-in space.

The most common type of wooden fence consists of horizontal rails nailed to posts or stakes that are placed vertically into the ground. These fences can be constructed with three or four horizontal rails made out of split wood, spruce, or pine wood planks. The posts are usually about 6 feet long and sharpened at the end that will be driven into the ground (to a depth

of roughly 8 inches). These posts should be spaced about 6 feet apart.

To keep the pointed, earth-bound ends from rotting, dip them in melted pitch before inserting them into the ground. To do this, boil linseed oil and stir in pulverized coal until it reaches the consistency of paint. Brush a coat of this on the wooden post. Make sure the posts are completely dry before painting them. If properly done, this should keep moisture from seeping into the buried parts of the posts and will keep your fence upright for many, many years.

To drive the posts into the ground, use a very good shovel or a heavy wooden mallet. For longer poles, use a post-hole borer. This saves lots of time and energy and will work with almost all types of soil.

To construct a basic wooden fence, you'll need:

▲ A simple wooden fence is enough to keep most animals in their pastures.

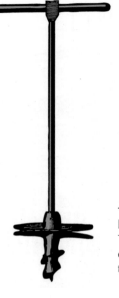

◀ A hole borer lifts the soil from the hole without having to use spades. These borers can be used by hand or electric models can be purchased for the same purpose.

Materials
- Post-hole diggers, a post-hole borer, or a shovel
- 4 x 4 wooden posts (wood that has been treated will last longer but is not necessary)
- 2 x 4 lumber (this too can be treated but does not need to be) or fence boards (which can be purchased at your local home and gardening center)
- Thick, long nails

Directions
1. Decide where the fence will be constructed and then lay a line of twine or string to mark out the border.
2. Decide how tall you want your fence to be. Take into consideration what the fence is being used for (if it's for larger animals, such as llamas, you may want a 6-foot-tall fence; if for decoration, a shorter fence may do the trick).
3. Dig holes for your end posts (in all four corners of your fence). Make sure the holes are deep enough to support the end posts. Fill in dirt around the posts and pack in the soil very well.
4. Start digging the remaining holes, keeping them aligned with the end posts.
5. Insert the remaining posts into the holes, piling in the dirt and packing it down as before.
6. Nail on your fence boards, leaving a little space in between. Paint or stain the finished fence if you wish.

Note: If you want a privacy fence, you can nail thicker boards horizontally or vertically between each post, leaving little space in between.

▲ You can nail wire mesh to the rails of a wooden fence for extra security or to allow vines or other climbing plants to grow up along the posts.

Fences, Gates, and Pens

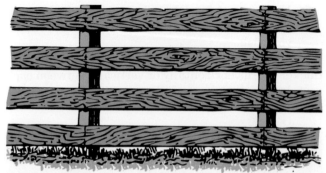

▲ A basic wooden fence.

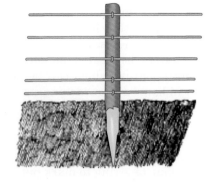

◀ Drive your fence poles far enough into the ground that they stand firmly upright even when moderate pressure is applied to one side.

◀ A picket fence is constructed by nailing two or more long boards to posts, and then nailing narrow vertical boards to the horizontal ones.

◀ A G-line wire fence consists of three-ply strands of wire.

▼ A very simple fence can be made by driving small tree trunks or branches into the ground in a tight row.

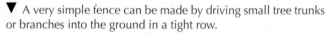

Wire Fences

Wire fences are both portable and durable, making them convenient and economical to build. Wire fences usually have a longer staying power than wooden fences since they are less prone to deterioration or rot.

The most common type of wire fence is one that has wire lines strung between wooden posts. The wires are fastened to the posts by galvanized wire staples. The wooden posts should be spaced roughly 6 feet apart and should use five single wires.

A more substantial wire fence can be made with G-line wires. Each line consists of a three-ply strand. Instead of the wires being fastened to the post by staples, holes are bored through the posts and the lines pass through. Straining eye bolts with nuts and washers are attached for tightening up the fence. This type of fence, however, is much more expensive to build and, unless you desire a fence that is incredibly strong, is probably not necessary.

Wire Netting Fence

Galvanized wire netting fences are used for enclosing root gardens and for poultry fences. The standard type of netting used when making this fence is 3-inch mesh netting that is 3 feet x 3 feet, and is rather inexpensive to buy.

A separate strip of 2-inch galvanized wire netting that is 6 inches wide can be laid flat on the ground on the side of the fence where the poultry are—this way they can not dig underneath, especially once grass and other natural materials hide the wire netting.

To dig in this type of fence, make a trench about 6 inches deep; drop the netting into it; and then fill the trench up with dirt, stones, or even concrete, depending on how permanent you want the fence to be.

Portable Fences

If you need a temporary fence or if you want to easily move your livestock fence to new grazing areas on your property, you may want to consider one of these easily made, movable fences. Below are a few types of portable fences that can be tailored to your specific needs.

Convenient and Portable Fence

Often it is helpful to have a fence that can be quickly erected and disassembled. This fence is very cheap, strong, and convenient to use. It is built out of pine (any other wood can be substituted, but pine is typically lighter and easier to move), 1 x 6 inches for the bottom rail and 1 x 4 inches for the top rails. The braces that hold it upright are 2 x 4 inches and the base (cross piece) is 2 x 6 inches. The base is notched 2 inches and the bottom boards are notched with holes.

The base piece, which is more susceptible to rot, could be made out of a stronger wood, such as oak. Make sure the panels aren't too long or they might warp out of shape. This fence can be put up very quickly and taken down again with ease if you want to move it to another part of your yard or get rid of it for a while.

Scotch Hurdle Fence

This movable fence consists of two posts, each 2 x 3 inches and 4½ feet long. The lower ends are long and pointed which allows them to easily enter the ground

▲ A wire netting fence.

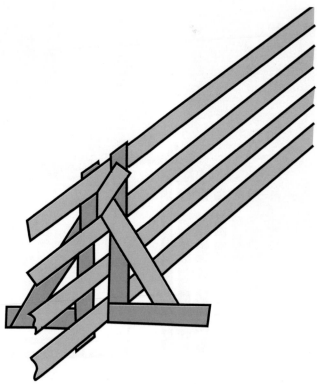

▲ A portable fence.

Fences, Gates, and Pens

▲ This Scotch hurdle fence is good for temporary use. If you live in a very windy area, however, this fence may not suit you well, as they do have a tendency to fall over in strong gales.

and prop up the fence. The brace and two diagonals are made of larch or fir wood. This fence is around 9 feet long and 4 feet high.

The Scotch hurdle fence is easy to set up. The incline should be facing away from any livestock you might have contained inside of it. A stay should be placed between every two hurdles to keep them in position. One wooden peg should be fastened to one end of the hurdle and another peg driven through the other end and into the ground.

English Hurdle Portable Fence

This movable fence is much lighter, cheaper, and more convenient than the Scotch hurdle fence. Usually made of split oak, this fence is tough and impenetrable. It consists of two upright end pieces that are joined by four or five mortised bars 7 to 9 feet long. These are strengthened by an upright bar in the middle and two or more diagonals. The end pieces are long and pointed for setting into the ground. To set these into the earth, use an iron crowbar to avoid splitting the top of the wooden piece.

These fences are set erect and no stay is needed. The two adjoining ends of the fences are connected with a band that is passed over them.

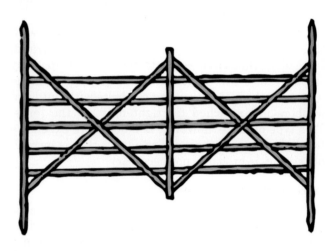

▲ An English hurdle portable fence.

▼ Gates can be useful for entrances to a yard or walkway, as well as for animal pens or pastures.

266

Gates

Gates are a necessary part of any fence or pen and they can be situated in the fence wherever they can be easily accessed. If you have a field, your gate should be roughly 10 feet wide to allow small machinery through.

Most gates are made of either wood or iron (though iron is obviously much more expensive and more complicated to work with). Wooden gates will suffice for most of your homesteading needs. The following are a few simple gates that can be used for your garden, your backyard fences, and your pens housing livestock.

Inexpensive, Simple Gate

A light, useful, and durable gate can be made of sassafras poles (or other tall grass poles) and wire. Dig and place a strong post 4 feet in the ground in the middle of the gateway and balance the gate on it. The lower rail is made of two forked sassafras poles securely nailed together so they can be coiled back over the post.

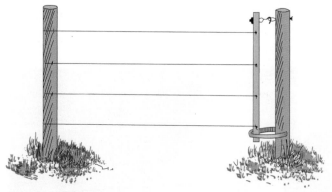

▲ A basic wire gate can be constructed when you need an opening in your fence.

Easily Opened Gate

To construct this simple gate, take an old wheel (possibly found at an antique store or rummage sale) and fasten it to make a gate that you will be opening frequently. The piece of board (A) drops between the spokes of the wheel and holds the gate either open or closed.

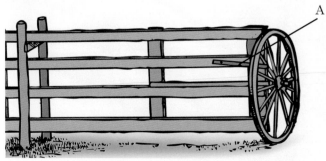

▲ An easily opened gate.

Rustic Garden Gate

If your garden is bordered with a fence, or if you have shrubs or hedges enclosing your backyard, you will want to install a homemade gate through which to enter the garden or yard.

This gate plan is made 6 feet square and 8 feet tall. Any type of timber can be used. To construct the gate:

▲ This rustic garden gate blends in well with natural surroundings.

1. Cut the closing and hinging sides 6 feet long, 6 inches wide, and 2½ inches thick. The three rails are of the same dimensions and can be halved to the stiles or wedged and braced.
2. Separate pieces are fixed on the center to support the gate and to make the frame, on which the boards will be attached.
3. Two gate hinges and hooks can be bolted on or secured from the back with square-headed coach screws.
4. Begin fixing the debarked twigs—they should be as straight as possible.
5. To make the joint ends, start by fixing the outside square then the two inner squares and finally the diagonal filling.
6. The posts should be 9 inches in diameter by 9 feet long (3 feet should be buried underground). Cut three mortises in the posts to insert the rails

▲ Closing stile for a garden gate.

▲ Either of these gates will work well with the rustic garden gate.

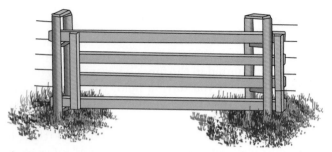

▲ A simple sliding gate can be made for any modern or wire fence.

for the side fencing. These rails are nailed flush to the secondary posts.

7. Dig holes for the posts and pack in the soil tightly (or fill in the holes with cement for a permanent fixture).

8. After a week or so (let the cement dry fully), the gate can be hung on the hinges and the latch positioned correctly.

▼ A bamboo fence or gate can be constructed by lashing the bamboo together with strong rope.

Simple Gate

This is a simple and appealing gate, especially for fences leading into pastures. The materials required to make this gate vary depending on what purpose the gate will serve.

For a paddock or pasture gate, make it out of seasoned boards, 1 x 6 inches and 12 to 14 feet long. The posts supporting the gate should be placed about 5 inches apart, the one on the inside being about 8 inches ahead of the other. These are joined together by cleats or rollers that support the gate and allow it to be pushed back and swing open. If rollers are not obtainable, cleats made of any hard wood are acceptable.

▲ This wire gate is hung on ordinary iron posts. The heel of the gate, made of angle iron, is fitted with winding brackets for tightening the wire bars.

▲ A simple wire swinging gate.

Pens

If you have built a simple stable to house your llamas, sheep, or other animals, it will be beneficial to build a small fence around it as an outdoor pen. A basic wooden fence or a simple wire fence will enclose most of your livestock in an area around the stable or shelter. If you have a llama or two, it is best to have at least a 4-foot fence so they cannot escape. If you have ample space, having a pathway into a larger grazing field or pasture from your pen will allow your animals to come and go as they please. Or, if you want to keep them confined in the pen, a simple gate will suffice for when the animals need to be removed or relocated.

▼ A pig peers over the edge of her pen.

Basic Bridges

If you have a river or brook on your property, you may want to construct a simple bridge. Building these bridges can be fairly easy, especially if you don't plan on transporting very heavy machinery or cars over them. Here are a few different ways to build basic bridges over streams, creeks, or other rather narrow waterways.

▲ A woodern footbridge.

Footbridge

This natural-looking footbridge can be built between 8 feet and 12 feet long.

Excavate the banks of the stream or creek to allow for the building of a small, low rubble or stonewall. The sleepers will rest on this wall. The girders are formed of wooden spars (four are used in this plan). The girders should be between 8 and 10 inches in diameter. Lay the girders down and bolt them together in pairs with six ¾-inch-diameter coach bolts. Wedge the posts to fit mortises in the girders.

The posts and top rails should be roughly 4½ to 5½ inches in diameter and the intermediate rails 3 inches in diameter. Finally, join the rails to the posts.

The bridge should be anchored well if it's in a place where flooding is frequent, as you don't want your footbridge floating away in the stream. To do so, drive four short piles into the soil on the inside of the girders, near their ends. Fasten the girders to the piles with coach bolts. The pile tops are hidden by the ends of the floor battens.

Now, if you want to decorate your footbridge, you can use small twigs and nails to make patterns on your bridge.

▼ Bridges can be fashioned in a range of shapes, styles, and sizes to meet your needs.

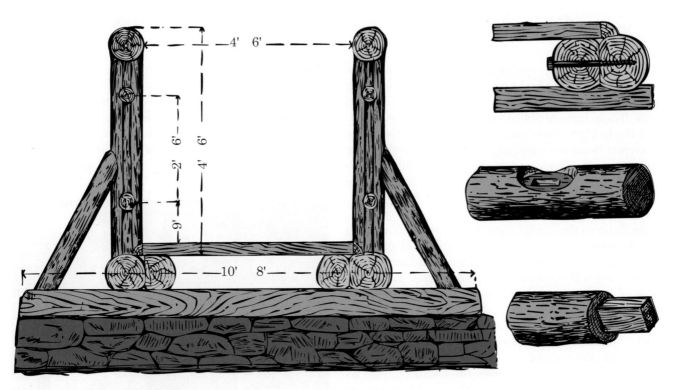

▲ A cross section of the footbridge.

▲ Join the rails of the footbridge to the posts as shown here.

Small Stream Bridge

If you have a small creek or stream on your property, you may want to construct a simple bridge for easy access to the other side. To build this bridge, you'll need lumber that is 6 inches wide and 2 inches thick, and additional lumber for the floor and four side braces.

Directions

1. Saw 11 pieces of wood the length required for the two sides.
2. Bore bolt holes 1½ inches from each end. Use ⁵⁄₈-inch bolts 8½ inches long for where four pieces come together, and use 6½-inch bolts where three pieces meet.
3. Bolt on the A-shaped supports and pieces for the approaches at one time, and then put on the side braces.
4. The sides of the bridge are made of triangles. The first triangle is made of pieces *a*, *b*, and *c*. The second triangle is made of pieces *b*, *d*, and *e*.
5. The piers for this bridge may be made of posts, stone, or even concrete, depending on how permanent you wish your small stream bridge to be.

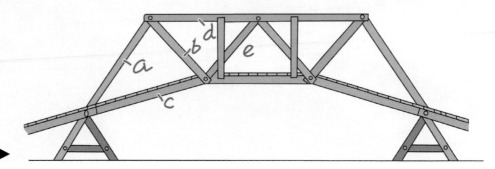

A bridge for a small stream. ▶

A Very Simple Bridge

Another very simple way of building a bridge across a creek or stream is to find a narrow part of the waterway and then find two logs that are longer than the creek is wide. These logs should be very sturdy (not rotted out) and thick. Place them across the creek, so they make a narrow beam over the water. Each log should have an extra foot at each end of the creek so they can be securely walked upon with no danger of slipping into the creek bed. Place the logs roughly two feet apart.

If the water comes up close to the bottom of the logs, raise them so the bridge does not get washed away in heavy storms or during the course of the stream rising. Raising the bridge will require a bit more work, as each log will need to be set into another log on the edge of the streambed or even into stone to make it more permanent.

After you have the two base logs secured, find some sticks that are long enough (and relatively thick) to lay across the tops of the two logs. Or, if you have extra plywood or other boards, those can be used as well. Just make sure to place the sticks or boards fairly close to one another, leaving only little gaps between them. Then, once all the sticks have been laid

down, secure these by tying twine or rope to them and the base logs.

If you'd like your bridge to last a little longer, you can pave it with clay or fine cement. Using a shovel, coat the bridge with the clay or cement until it's about 2 inches thick. Then shovel dirt onto the clay mixture, packing it down all over, and make the bridge as thick as you like. However, for just a simple bridge across a narrow stream or creek, the wooden sticks or boards will work just fine and won't require as much time and energy.

▲ Railings can be fashioned like wooden fences (see pages 260–262).

▼ For longer bridges, you will need supports underneath.

Tool Sheds and Workshops

Before building a tool shed, think about what you want to house in it. If you just need it for small tools, such as shovels, buckets, and a wheelbarrow, a smaller shed will be fine. However, if you plan to house machinery, such as a tractor, lawnmower, chainsaw, or rototiller, you'll need a larger shed and you may want to plan for a sliding garage door–style entrance. Will you want a workbench, space to pot plants, shelving, and drawers? Do you want electrical outlets for power tools and lights? Also consider location: It may be more convenient to have it close to your house, or you may prefer to have it nearer the garden. Here are a couple of examples of tool sheds that you can modify to meet your needs.

▲ Decide what you will store in your shed before you begin building so you know what size to make it.

Medium-sized Tool Shed and Workshop

This shed is large enough to easily store your basic farm machinery. The shed is basically a giant umbrella with posts 30 feet apart in one direction and 12 or 16 feet apart in the other. There are no sides to this shed at all (though you could modify this if you want to store other tools here). If you park your main machinery (tractor, lawnmower, and so on) in the innermost part of the shed, you should still have an overhang of 10 feet. This shed would be most beneficial if it were 10 feet high—that way, most any kind of machine you want to house under it will fit well. Boarding up one, two, or three sides will help prevent

snow from drifting in during the winter and rain from rusting your equipment. Making walls will also allow you to hang tools on the inside of the shed, such as clippers, weed whackers, or hoses.

The workshop described here will hold a lot of smaller tools and is a good place to mend harnesses, make repairs, and store grain. The workshop gives about a 30-foot clearance space for the shed below. The entire building is built together using the following materials:

- 2 x 8-inch posts
- Three pieces of 2 x 12-inch wood materials (space these 2 inches apart)
- 2 x 10-inch box plates
- 6 x 6-inch bridge truss
- 2 x 4-inch or 2 x 6-inch beams for the rafters (depending on how much weight they must hold)

The floor of your shed should be either hard dirt or cement and the posts should be anchored firmly into the ground or on stone pillars. A shingle roof will ensure your smaller workshop tools are kept safe from the rain and snow.

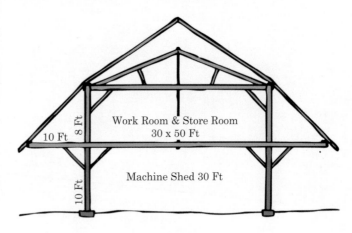

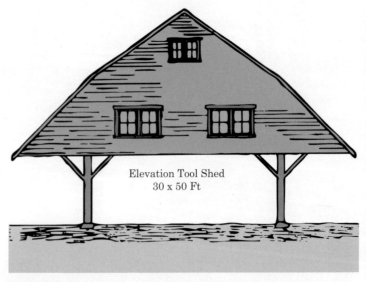

▲ Plans for a medium-sized tool shed and workshop.

▲ You may want to build a workbench in your shed for your woodworking projects.

▼ A finished small, rustic tool shed.

Small, Rustic Tool Shed

This small, rustic tool shed is made from "slabs" or "rough planks." If you are using trees from your own property to build the shed, you won't have to bother peeling the bark from the logs or cutting them as exactly. Slabs are cheap to buy (they can be found at saw mills and sometimes at home centers), and create an attractive, "woodsy" look. Although the boards are typically not uniform in size, you can position them in such a way to minimize the number of large cracks in your shed.

These boards may need to be straightened (especially the edges) with a saw or axe, and the interior of the tool shed should be lined with thin boards to cover up cracks and to keep out insects and animals.

When beginning construction on this type of shed, search for boards that lend themselves better to being end posts and those that are better-suited for the walls. The corners of the four main posts (4 inches square) construct a building roughly 7 x 5 feet. Dig holes 2 feet into the ground and fit in the end posts.

On the tops of these posts, rest the wall plates—these should be 3 inches deep. These boards will be at

Tool Sheds and Workshops

the back and sides of the shed only. The sides will also need cross rails that are around 2 to 3 inches thick with ends flush to the corner posts. Nail the side and back boards to these cross boards to secure them.

Place two door posts in the front of the shed. They should stand 2 feet 8 inches apart and should be about 3 inches square. They should rise about 6 feet or so to attach to the rafters. Fill in the space between the door and corner posts with extra boards.

The roof for this tool shed can be thatched or made of boards and shingles, whichever you prefer. Make rafters and laths out of regular boards, arranging them about 1 foot apart, and the laths should be placed 6 inches apart for thatching. The shed can also be cheaply roofed with galvanized iron or tin roofing.

The door of the tool shed has the slabs nailed to it on the outside only, to make it aesthetically consistent. Attach hinges and the door should be ready. Inside the shed, sets of shelves may be hung in which tools and other items can be stored (c). A wheelbarrow can

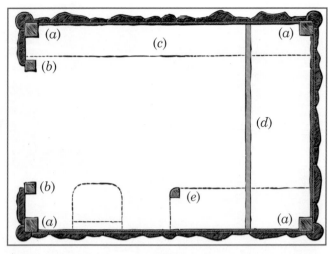

▲ Plans for the inside of a rustic tool shed.

be stored upright at the back (d) and tools hung from hooks coming down from the rafters. Gardening tools and rakes can be stored on the right-hand side (e) and a chair can sit near the front of the door (f).

▼ Sheds can be customized to meet your wants and needs.

276

Smokehouses

If you are slaughtering your own poultry or other livestock, or if you just like the taste of smoked meat, try making your own smokehouse. Smokehouses help expose meats to the action of creosote and empyreumatic vapors resulting from the imperfect combustion of wood. The peculiar taste of smoked meat is from the creosote—this also helps preserve the meat. Other flavors are also imparted onto the meat by the choice of wood that is burned in the smokehouse, such as hickory.

To make a smokehouse you'll need a space (anything from the size of a barrel to a barn-sized area will work) that can be filled with smoke and closed up tightly. You'll also need a way to hang the meat that needs to be cured. In common smokehouses, a fire is made on a stone slab in the middle of the floor. In other instances, a pit is dug about a foot deep into the ground and the fire is built within it. Sometimes a stone slab covers the fire like a standard table. The possibilities are many, depending on your space and needs. Below are a few examples of smokehouses that can be built and used for smoking your own meats.

▼ Smokehouses can be made out of stucco, brick, or wood.

Standard Smokehouse

This smokehouse diffuses the rising smoke and prevents the direct heat of the fire from affecting the meats that are hung directly above it. In the picture, a section of the smokehouse is shown.

This standard smokehouse is 8 feet square and built of bricks—making it a somewhat permanent structure in your yard. If you want to make it out of wood, be sure to plaster is completely on the inside. The chimney, (c), has an 8-inch flue and the fireplace, (b), is outside, below the level of the floor. From this point, a flue, (f), is carried underneath the chimney into the middle of the floor where it opens up under a stone table, (e).

To kindle the fire, a valve is drawn to directly draft up through the chimney. The woodchips are thrown onto the fire and the valve is then placed to direct the smoke into the brick smokehouse. There are openings, (g, g), in both the upper and lower parts of the chimney that are closed by valves (these can be manipulated from outside the smokehouse). The door of the smokehouse should be made to shut tightly and, when building the smokehouse, be sure that there are

Smokehouses

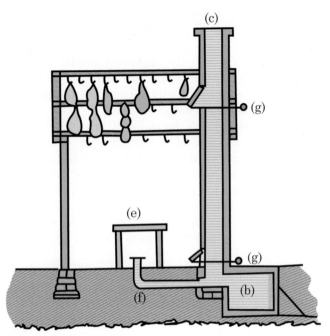

▲ Interior view of a standard smokehouse.

is for housing the fire and there is a door with steps leading up to it. A series of ventilating holes are situated above the lower bar and below the upper bar. These holes are meant to allow the smoke to escape from the house. By reinserting bricks into these holes, the smoke will stay mostly confined to the inside of the smokehouse.

The arch confines the fire and ashes, preventing any meat that might fall from being ruined or burned. The arch is made over a wooden frame of a few pieces of regular wood board, cut into an oval arch shape. Strips of wood are then nailed to this. When the brickwork is dry, the center is knocked out and removed. A small door can be fashioned to close up the arch when the fire is being kilned.

no cracks in the brick or mortar through which smoke can easily escape.

This type of smokehouse is convenient because the smoke cools before it is pumped into the chamber and no ashes rise with the smoke. Meat may be kept in this smokehouse all year without tasting too smoky.

Another Brick Smokehouse

A smokehouse of this kind, built 7 x 9 feet, will be sufficient for private use. The bottom of this smokehouse has a brick arch with bricks left out sporadically. This is to allow the extraction of smoke from the house.

Located above the arch are two series of iron rods that have hooks with grooved wheels. You can find these at most local hardware stores. The open archway

▼ This is a sectional view of a brick smokehouse that can be built to any size.

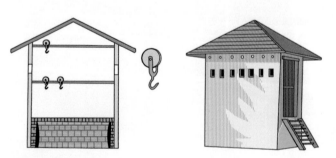

▲ The drawing shows a common smokehouse that is built on a brick wall and over a brick arch. There are a number of holes left in it for smoke to escape. The ash pit is located beneath the arch, and there is also a door that opens to this pit. To reach the meat room door, use a sturdy ladder.

A Simple Way to Smoke Meats

If you don't want to commit to building a permanent smokehouse in your yard but you would like to smoke meats occasionally, you can use a large cask or barrel as a smokehouse substitute.

To make the barrel into an effective smokehouse, just follow these steps:

1. Dig a small pit and place a flat stone or a brick across it. This is where the edge of the cask will rest.
2. Making sure that half of the pit is beneath the barrel and half is outside, remove the head and bottom of the barrel (or cut a hole into the bottom slightly larger than the portion of the pit beneath it).
3. Remove the top of the barrel and then hang the meat on cross-sticks. Rest these cross-sticks on crossbars that are made to fit into holes bored into the sides of the barrel, close to the top.
4. Put the lid on top of the barrel and cover it with a sack to confine the smoke inside.
5. Put coals into the pit outside of the cask, and then feed the fire with damp corncobs or a fine brush.
6. Cover the pit with a flat stone that will help regulate the fire and can be removed when more fuel is needed.

▲ A smoke barrel is a simple method for smoking meats.

▼ The interior of a smokehouse.

▲ Fish that are hung and ready to be smoked.

Root Cellars

While most modern houses have basements or crawl spaces in which to keep fresh vegetables and preserves cool and dry, you may want to construct an additional root cellar if you'll be storing significant amounts of these items. A root cellar should be located near your home and should be dry, well-ventilated, and frost-proof. Creating your own root cellar is not terribly expensive and will give your yard and property a true back-to-basics feel.

Root Cellar

A sloped area in your yard is the perfect place to make a root cellar. To construct the root cellar, follow these simple steps:

1. Make an excavation in the side of the hill, determining how large you'd like your root cellar to be.

▼ A root cellar can be built into the side of a hill using stone, bricks, or wood.

2. In the excavation, erect a sturdy frame of timber and planks, or even of logs. Put up planks to stand as side walls, and build a strong roof over the frame.
3. Throw the excavated earth over the structure until it is completely covered by at least 2 feet of soil.
4. On the exposed end, make a door that is large enough for you to enter without ducking. Or, if you like, you can make a "manhole" through which you can enter—this will actually protect your root cellar from frost much better than a full-sized door.

If the soil in the hill is composed of stiff clay, you may not even need to construct any side walls, and the roof can be fitted directly into the clay. Then build up the front of the cellar with planks, bricks, or stone, and create a door.

Root House

If you do not have a large hill on your property and would still like to construct a root cellar, find a knoll or other dry place and remove the soil over a space that is slightly larger than the size of the cellar (or root house if the structure is not built into a hill) and about 2 feet deep. To construct this root house:

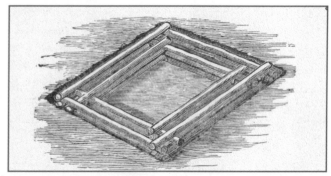

▲ The base of the root house.

▲ The finished root house.

1. Select poles or logs of two different sizes. The wider ones should be shorter than the other two.

2. Cut the ends of the logs very flat so they will fit closely together and make a very tight, pen-like structure.

3. Cut two logs in each layer long enough to pass through and fit into the outer pen. This will help fasten the two walls together.

4. Build the doorway up with short logs passing from one layer of poles to the other. These serve as supports to the ends of the wall poles.

5. Fill in the space between these two walls with soil. It is important that these are filled in fully (sod may also be used to pack in spaces between the logs) to protect the inside storage items from frost and to keep the whole structure cool. Pack up the soil as you construct the walls so you can more easily compact it as you build up.

6. When the walls are about 5 or 6 feet on one side and 2 or 3 feet on the other, put the roof on. The roof is made of poles placed close together, secured to the logs, and covered with sod, then 18 inches of soil. It is then finished off with sod once again.

Root cellars or houses are great for keeping vegetables like ▶ potatoes or carrots and for apples, which can keep for months in cool, dry storage.

Treehouses and Brush Houses

Treehouses and brush houses can be used as treetop forts and playhouses, or as relaxing spaces in which you can read and enjoy being surrounded by foliage and other treetop creatures. Building a treehouse requires a lot of work and some good planning. It is imperative that the house is built in trees that are large and sturdy. If you do not have such old trees in your yard, you can always modify these plans to build treetop havens on wooden platforms raised above ground, or construct a simpler brush house.

▼ Treehouses can be very simple or very elaborate, based on your resources and preferences.

Low Two-tree Treehouse

This treehouse can be constructed out of ordinary boards and timber. It does not sit up as high in the trees but is still elevated above the ground to give a good view of the yard and surrounding area.

Directions

1. Select a location between two trees that are roughly 6 to 8 feet apart. The trees should have fairly straight trunks and should be at least 15 inches in diameter. Make sure they are healthy and sturdy—not decaying in any way.

2. Using an axe, clear off the brush and small branches up to 20 feet on the tree trunks (or to the height of where the treehouse will be located).

3. Take four or five pieces of spruce (from a lumberyard or home center) that are 2 inches thick, 8 inches wide, and 16 feet long. Saw off and nail two of the pieces to the trunks of the trees 8 feet above the ground. First, cut away some of the bark and wood to make a flat surface on the trunk. You will need 16-inch steel-wire nails to anchor the boards to the trees.

4. Cut two timbers 6 feet long and the other two the length of distance between the tree trunks. In the 6-foot pieces, cut notches on the underside. The ends of the bracket timbers will fit into these notches.

5. Cut the ends of the timbers to form a square frame so that they dovetail. Spike in 6-foot timbers to the tree trunks so that they will rest on the first two timbers that were nailed to the trees (see top right image on page 283).

6. Place the remaining two timbers in position so that the ends fit into those fastened to the trees. Nail them well.

7. Support the first timbers that are spiked to the tree trunks with 15-inch blocks nailed below them. The cross timbers and last ones form the frame. Place the frame into the dovetailed joints at the ends.

8. Cut two more timbers and lay them across the supporting timbers nailed to the trees, so they will fit inside the front and back timbers, and secure them with long nails. The floor frame is now complete.

9. Construct a frame 7 feet high at the front and 6 feet high in the back out of 2 x 3-inch spruce. Spike the side timbers, forming the top, to the insides of the tree trunks (see bottom image on page 283). Mount the bottoms of the uprights on the corners of the floor frame and use four long nails to hold them in place.

10. Now, cut two timbers and arrange them in an upright position at the front, 30 inches apart. The door will be here. Halfway between the floor and the top of the framework, construct timber all around except between the door timbers. This will add strength and will allow the sheathing boards to be nailed. It will also make one more anchoring beam between the tree trunks.

11. Nail the side rails into the tree trunks in a corresponding way to the top (roof) strips.
12. Make the floor from lumber 4, 6, or 10 inches wide. The boards should be planed on both sides.
13. Construct the roof of the same boards. You can lay tarred paper over them and fasten it to the edges with nails. This will help waterproof the roof for at least one year. To make the roof last longer, you can shingle it.
14. Windows can also be made in the side and back walls. These should be about 24 inches square. The door can be constructed out of boards held together with battens. A lock can also be furnished to keep out unwanted visitors.

The treehouse will need a ladder for you to access it. This can either be purchased from a yard sale or can be made out of hickory poles and cross-sticks 20 inches wide. To keep the ladder from slipping while ascending and descending, affix loops to the top of the ladder; these will fit over large, sturdy nails driven into the doorsill, and the ladder will be relatively stable.

A flexible ladder can also be made out of ropes and hung much the same way as the wooden ladder. This type of ladder, though not as sturdy, can be drawn up when people are in the treehouse so no one else can enter.

Inside the treehouse, small chairs and other seats can be constructed and used for relaxing. Narrow

▲ Refer to these illustrations when constructing the low two-tree treehouse.

shelving can be made and fastened over the windows with brackets. Small things can then be housed on these shelves. A small table may also be housed in the treetop shelter.

High Treehouse in One Tree

If you have a tree large and strong enough (oaks are very good for this), a treehouse can be successfully built in its branches. For this plan, the treehouse will be 25 feet above the ground, and below it is a landing from which a rope ladder can be dropped to the ground. A more solid, wooden ladder connects the landing with the deck of the treehouse and it can be situated through a hole in the deck of the house.

Since every tree is different, it is difficult to give exact dimensions of the frame of this treehouse and how many floorboards should be used. But the construction of a single-tree treehouse is, in many ways, similar to that of the low two-tree treehouse. The trunk of the tree will have to project up through the treehouse and the out-spreading branches will need to support the lower parts of the floor frame. This treehouse can

▼ Plans for building a high treehouse in one tree.

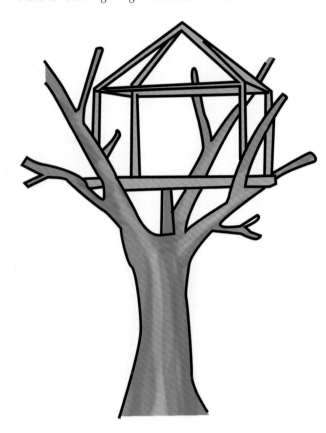

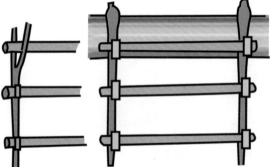

▲ You can construct a wooden ladder or a rope ladder for your treehouse.

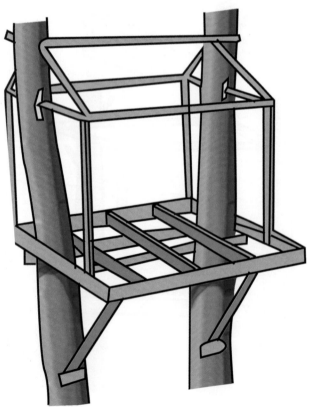

◄ A treehouse can also be built on two trees, as shown here.

have either a peaked or a flat roof, depending on the structure of the treehouse and the space allowed for a roof within the treetop.

Brace the floorboards well to the main trunk of the tree with long and short brackets or props. These will help make the house secure. Drive large spikes into the tree where the lower ends attach to the trunk. Nailing cleats or blocks under these will help to support and strengthen the structure.

Brush Houses

Brush houses also make wonderful outdoor escapes and can be great play structures for children. These too can be constructed from simple and inexpensive materials and look much like island huts. They are much easier to construct than treehouses and the materials can be found in most gardens or fields.

Simple Brush House

Brush houses can be made from any type of reed or tall garden or wild plant. Artichokes, cattail reeds, wild sunflowers, and some species of flag have long and strong stalks and reeds sufficient for making the sides and roof of a brush house. These plants sometimes grow up to 10 feet tall and have straight, uniform stalks that can be used for the house. To build a simple brush house, follow these steps:

1. Gather lots of tall reeds and stalks. Cut off the foliage at the top (if any) and other small under-branches and leaves. The goal is to leave a fairly straight shaft between 6 and 8 feet tall.
2. Take four sticks, each 8 feet long, and set them in the ground about 6 feet apart, forming a square. Sink each stick into the ground about 2 feet, and bind the upper ends together with rails 2 inches wide and an inch thick.

3. Give the roof a pitch by cutting off the rear posts 6 inches and leave 6 inches more on the front posts out of the ground. This will give you a pitch of 1 foot. While the slant is not necessary, it does add a different feel to the brush house than if the roof is left flat (though this works just as well).
4. Begin weaving the reeds as you would a basket (see above). Make three of the frames for the sides and back of the house. The front, above the doorway and at either side, should also have woven frames of reeds to cover up these spaces.
5. Bend the ends of the cross-reeds around the ends of the upright reeds (see illustration). Then

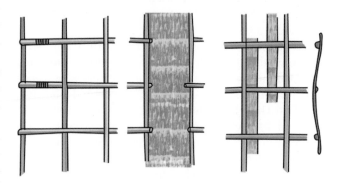

▲ Weaving and thatching steps for a brush house.

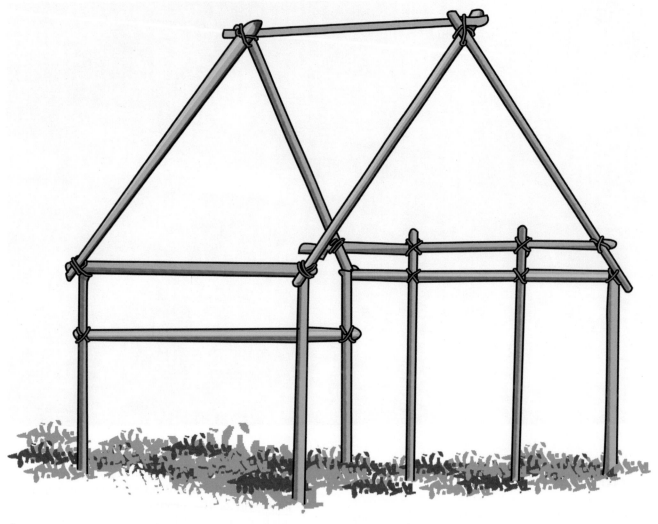

▲ Frame for a brush lean-to.

bind them with string or tie them tightly with long pieces of grass.

6. To make windows in the side walls, cut out a section of one or two upright reeds, and turning the cross-reeds back and tying them, you'll make a nice window.

7. To make the doorway, push two upright sticks into the ground on either side of the frame and nail a rail (another stick) to their upper ends. Front reeds can then be attached to the frame to make a door.

8. The house is now ready to be thatched with long, dry grass or dried cattail reeds. Thatching is done by interweaving long grasses or reeds between the cross-reeds in a vertical position. The thatching material should be between 18 and 24 inches long so that it can be easily woven between three cross-reeds. Straw can also be used to thatch the brush house.

9. Make sure that each side is lashed well to the corner posts with string or long grasses. The roof,

too, should be attached tightly to the top of the sides and front with long reeds or heavy string.

10. Weave the roof in the same way as the walls, but try to thatch it much tighter, to keep out the rain. Four inches of the roof should extend over the sides, front, and rear of the brush house.

Brush Lean-to

This extremely simple brush house can easily be made in less than an hour and is a wonderful place for children's imaginations to run wild. This lean-to can be constructed in almost the same way as the simple brush house and should be thatched with grass or reeds as well.

The corner posts for the brush lean-to are 3 feet high, the ridgepole is 7½ feet above the ground (a foot or so should be buried underground), and the hut should be from 5 to 8 feet square. Make the frame out of small trees and nail it together to stand strong against the wind. Lash the edges of the thatched framework to the sticks with strong string.

Trellises

A trellis can be a very attractive addition to any yard or garden. Creeping plants and vines can be planted and made to wind up the trellis, adding another element of green plant life to your garden.

Garden Trellis

If you want to build a substantial trellis in your yard or garden, the structure it leans against will need to be about 20 feet tall (of course, these dimensions can be easily altered to suit your needs and space). The trellis may be made out of any material (fir or other straight, debarked saplings or twigs work well). The trellis posts should be 12 feet long and the four posts for the arches should be roughly 4 inches in diameter. The rails of the trellis are 2½ inches in diameter and the twigs should be around 2 inches in diameter. If you want to incorporate seating into your trellis, make one seat roughly 6 feet long by 1 foot 4 inches wide.

The trellis shown below is complete with benches and a canopy. Place the shores 3½ feet above the ground line at a 50-degree angle. Dig the posts into the ground about 3 feet, to make them more secure. Pack the soil densely around the posts to make them stronger.

The archway may be constructed before being attached to the larger structure. Bevel the rail ends, notch them to the posts, and secure them with nails (see illustration). After the framework is erected and put into position, dig holes and bury the shores deep into the ground and nail the top ends to the upright pieces. Also firmly bury the shorter posts for the seats into the ground about a foot and a half. The end seat bearers should be nailed to the end posts and the center bearers should be nailed to the front and back center posts.

▼ This trellis is made from saplings and small branches.

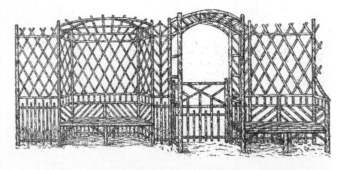

▲ Detail of the beveled and notched posts, secured with nails.

▲ This trellis is made of wooden latticework and painted white.

Trellises

▼ This simple trellis is ideal for the entrance to a yard or garden. The picket fence gate is an attractive addition.

Weathervanes

If you have just built one of the sheds or stables in this book, you could build a weathervane for the top of it. Weathervanes can be made in a variety of shapes and sizes, and many are made simply for decoration. Here are just a few examples of different weathervanes you can easily make.

Pinwheel Weathervane

This pinwheel weathervane is very simple to make. It consists of heavy-duty tin or sheet iron, a wooden shaft that is 20 inches long, and a fantail 12 inches long and 7 inches wide at the end. To construct this weathervane:

1. Punch a small hole in the center of the sheet of tin or iron no less than 10 inches square.
2. With a pencil compass (easily found at any office supply store), draw a circle 10 inches in diameter. Half an inch in from the circle's edge, draw another circle 9 inches in diameter. From the center, go out 1 inch and draw a third circle 2 inches in diameter. Then, divide the disk into eight equal parts.
3. With a small chisel or box cutter, cut on the lines and bend the metal ears so the corners can bend back an inch from the rim. With a pair of scissors, cut around the outside line and punch out the wheel from the sheet of metal.
4. At the front of the wheel, fasten a spool with steel wire nails driven through the metal wheel. This will act as a hub. Then, if you like, you can paint both with a coat of paint.
5. Make a wooden shaft one inch square and cut it in at one end about 10 inches. At the other end of the shaft, bind the wood for an inch or two with fine wire to prevent it from slipping and bore a hole in the end with an awl. Drive a flat-headed steel wire nail or a screw through the spool and disk, into the hole in the shaft to act as the pin on which the wheel can turn.
6. Cut a fantail out of a light piece of wood about $^3/_8$ inches thick and 7 inches wide at one end. Insert this into the cut on the shaft and secure it with small nails or screws.
7. Drill another hole near the top of the shaft and attach another spool to form a larger bearing. A vertical shaft or pin should pass through this hole to hold the vane steady and to prevent it from tilting forward or backward.
8. Place the weathervane on your shed or stable and watch it twist and turn in the wind.

▲ A pinwheel weathervane.

▲ A wind-speeder weathervane.

Wind-Speeder Weathervane

Wind-speeders may be constructed of metal or of wood.

Materials

- Two sticks (30 inches long and ¾ inch square)
- Four tin funnels with their ends stopped up
- A pole (drive a long iron pin into one end for the hub to revolve around)
- Small tubing
- Nails
- Large, flat washer
- Hub
- Paint (optional)

Directions

1. Cut the two sticks in the middle so they will overlap. With steel nails, attach them to a hub ¾ inch thick and 3 inches in diameter.
2. In the center of the hub, cut a hole ¼ inch in diameter.
3. Cut the end of each stick so a funnel can be inserted into it. Hold each funnel in place by fastening the neck to the top and bottom of the cross-sticks with a strap of tin or other binding device.
4. Punch a small hole with a sharp-pointed awl through the strap and neck and drive a long, slim steel nail through both ends into the end of the stick. This gives the funnels some additional hold.
5. Attach the washer to the wood to reduce friction and to prevent the wood from wearing away near the hub.
6. Before you slip the wind-speeder over the upright pin, place a short piece of small tubing over it so it will rest between the hub and the top of the pole.
7. Paint the wind-speeder whatever color you desire and mount it on a larger pole or shed roof.

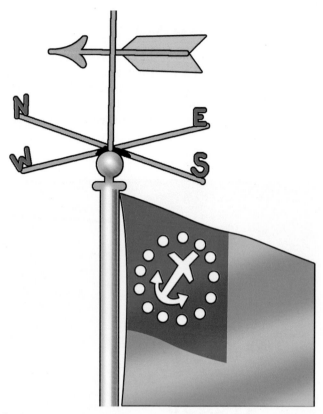

▲ An arrow weathervane.

Arrow Weathervane

The oldest and most recognized weathervane is the arrow weathervane. This universal model is simple to make and can be crafted out of many different types of material.

An arrow weathervane can be made of any length to suit the height and structure it will be placed on. For the roof of a stable or shed, however, it should be roughly 24 to 36 inches long, with a blade 5 to 6 inches wide.

This weathervane is made in three pieces: the point, the shaft, and the blade. The shaft is made from hard wood, ¾ inch square. Make cuts in the ends of the wood in for tin or sheet-metal points and blades to be inserted. Hold these blades in place with nails driven through the wood and clinched on the opposite side. Balance the arrow and make a hole in the shaft for the upright pin or rod to pass through.

Drive a ring or ferrule into the upright rod to hold the arrow in the correct place. Below it, place two rods at right angles. At the ends of these rods, attach the letters N, E, S, and W. These rods can be constructed of brass or wood. The letters should be made of tin or sheet metal and they should be inserted into slits made in the wood or brass and held in place with slim nails. Now your arrow weathervane is ready for use.

Wooden Weathervanes

You can make these decorative weathervanes with a scroll saw and jackknife or a compass saw and carving chisels. They can be any size and can be placed on any type of pole or building. To see the characters at the top, however, you may want to place them lower to the ground, in a garden or flower bed.

The fish weathervane is cut from wood that is ⅝ inch thick. The edges of the wood are beveled so as to give the fish a rounded look. Balance the fish on the edge of a piece of wood to determine where the rod should pass through it. Then, with a ¼-inch bit, carefully bore the hole from top to bottom. Make the compass point letters from sheet tin and support

▲ Wooden weathervanes.

them on two cross-sticks and a strong wire hoop, 12 to 15 inches in diameter.

The lady with the umbrella is cut from wood that is ½ inch thick. She should be around 15 inches high and ½ inches wide at the bottom of her skirt. Bore a ¼-inch hole from her shoes to her hat through her entire body. However, if this proves too difficult, you can put a large staple at the top and at the bottom and then insert the rod through these holes.

The squirrel is made in the same way as the lady and can be balanced on a rod that passes through the body or by means of staples. Put a ring and washer on the rod at the bottom of the weathervane so it can rest on them without any friction.

The bird is cut out and balanced in the same way as the fish. It may be carved in wood or painted to give shape and character to the weathervane. It should be mounted in the same way as the fish.

Part Five

Energy

"Energy conservation is the foundation of energy independence."

—Thomas H. Allen

With the extreme fluctuation in oil prices and ever-growing concerns about the state of our environment, it's no wonder that more and more people are turning to the natural elements for power. Sun, wind, water, and earth have provided for the basic needs of humanity since the beginning of time and it only makes sense to learn how to work with them more efficiently. The term "self-sufficiency," as it is commonly used, is something of a misnomer. We will never be able to meet all of our own needs alone. We don't create the natural world that supplies us with the light, heat, and other resources that we depend on. But we can learn how to make good use of those gifts. In these pages you will find both simple and advanced projects to do so, from fashioning and using solar cookers to building and installing wind turbines to utilizing geothermal systems. There's a lot here, but it's only a sampling of the methods available for harnessing natural energy. Look online or visit your library for more ideas, plans, and tips; you'll also find an extensive list of resources in the back of this book. Remember that the simplest and perhaps most effective way to be energy-efficient is to use less of it. The simple things, like turning off a light when you're not in the room—or even using candlelight in the evenings—can make a big difference. The more you understand about the process of turning the natural elements into usable energy, the more you'll appreciate the value of electricity and want to conserve it in any way you can.

Solar Energy

Solar energy is, in its simplest form, the sun's rays that reach the earth (also known as solar radiation). When you step outside on a hot, sunny summer day, you can feel the power of the sun's heat and light. Solar energy can be harnessed to do a variety of things in your home. These include:

- Heating your home through passive solar design or through active solar heating systems
- Generating electricity
- Heating water in your home
- Heating swimming pool water
- Lighting your home both inside and out
- Drying your clothes via a clothesline strung outside in direct sunlight

Solar energy can also be converted into thermal (heat) energy and used to heat water for use in homes, buildings, or swimming pools and also to heat spaces inside homes, greenhouses, and other buildings.

Photovoltaic energy is the conversion of sunlight directly into electricity. A photovoltaic cell, known as a solar or PV cell, is the technology used to convert solar energy into electrical power. A PV cell is a non-mechanical device made from silicon alloys. PV systems are often used in remote locations that are not connected to an electric grid. These systems are also used to power watches, calculators, and lighted road signs.

Advantages of Solar Energy

- It's free.
- Its supplies are unlimited.
- Solar heating systems reduce the amount of air pollution and greenhouse gases that result from using fossil fuels (oil, propane, and natural gas) for heating or generating electricity in your home.
- Solar heating systems reduce heating and fuel bills in the winter.
- It is most cost-effective when used for the entire year.

Disadvantages of Solar Energy

- The amount of sunlight that arrives at the earth's surface is not constant and depends on location, time of day and year, and weather conditions.
- A large surface area is required to collect the sun's energy at a useful rate.

Solar Thermal Energy

Solar thermal (heat) energy is used most often for heating swimming pools, heating water to be used in homes, and heating specific spaces in buildings. Solar space heating systems are either passive or active.

▼ PV system components.

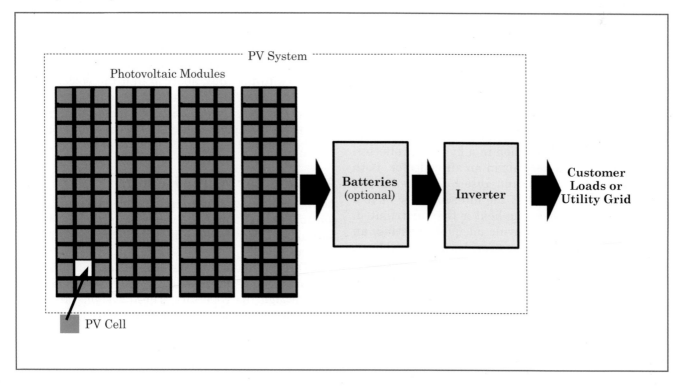

Passive Solar Space Heating

Passive space heating is what happens in a car on a sunny summer day—the car gets hot inside.In buildings, air is circulated past a solar heat surface and through the building by convection—less dense, warm air tends to rise while the denser, cooler air moves downward. No mechanical equipment is needed for passive solar heating.

Passive solar space heating takes advantage of the warmth from the sun through design features, such as large, south-facing windows and materials in the floors and/or walls that absorb warmth during the day and release it at night when the heat is needed most. Sunspaces and greenhouses are good examples of passive systems for solar space heating.

Passive solar systems usually have one of these designs:

1. Direct gain—This is the simplest system. It stores and slowly releases heat energy collected from the sun shining directly into the building and warming up the materials (tile or concrete). It is important that the space does not become overheated.
2. Indirect gain—This is similar to direct gain in that it uses materials to hold, store, and release heat. This material is generally located between the sun and the living space, usually in the wall.
3. Isolated gain—This collects solar energy separately from the primary living area (a sunroom attached to a house can collect warmer air that flows through the rest of the house).

Active Solar Space Heating

Active heating systems require a collector to absorb the solar radiation. Fans or pumps are used to circulate the heated air or the heat-absorbing fluid. These systems often include some type of energy storage system.

There are two basic types of active solar heating systems. These are categorized based on the type of fluid (liquid or air) that is heated in the energy collectors. The collector is the device in which the fluid is heated by the sun. Liquid-based systems heat water or an antifreeze solution in a hydronic collector. Air-based systems heat air in an air collector. Both of these systems collect and absorb solar radiation, transferring solar heat to the interior space or to a storage system, where the heat is then distributed. If the system cannot provide adequate heating, an auxiliary or backup system provides additional heat.

Liquid systems are used more often when storage is included and are well suited for radiant heating systems, boilers with hot water radiators, and absorption heat pumps and coolers. Both liquid and air systems can adequately supplement forced air systems.

Active solar space heating systems are comprised of collectors that absorb solar radiation combined with electric fans or pumps to distribute the solar heat. These systems also have an energy-storage system that provides heat when the sun is not shining.

Another type of active solar space heating system, the medium temperature solar collector, is generally used for solar space heating. These systems operate in much the same way as indirect solar water heating systems but have a larger collector area, larger storage units, and much more complex control systems. They are usually configured to provide solar water heating and can provide between 30 and 70 percent of residential heating requirements. All active solar space heating systems require more sophisticated design, installation, and maintenance techniques than passive systems.

Passive Solar Water Heaters

Passive solar water heaters rely on gravity and on water's natural tendency to circulate as it is heated. Since these heaters contain no electrical components, passive systems are more reliable, easier to maintain, and work longer than active systems. Two popular types of passive systems are:

1. Integral-collector storage systems—These consist of one or more storage tanks that are placed in an insulated box with a glazed side facing the sun. The solar collectors are best suited for areas where temperatures do not often fall below freezing. They work well in households with significant daytime and evening hot-water needs but they do not work as efficiently in households with only morning hot-water draws as they lose most of the collected energy overnight.
2. Thermospyhon systems—These are an economical and reliable choice particularly in newer homes. These systems rely on natural convection of warm water rising to circulate the water through the collectors and into the tank. As water in the collector heats, it becomes lighter and rises to the tank above it and the cooler water flows down the pipes to the bottom of the collector. In freeze-prone climates, indirect thermosyphons (using glycol fluid in the collector loop) can be installed only if the piping is protected.

Active Solar Water Heaters

Active solar water heaters rely on electric pumps and controllers to circulate the water (or other heat-transfer fluids). Two types of active solar water heating systems are:

1. Direct circulation systems—These use pumps to circulate pressurized potable water directly through the collectors. These systems are most appropriate for areas that do not have long freezes or hard/acidic water.
2. Indirect circulation systems—These pumps heat transfer fluids through the collectors. These heat

Installing a Passive Solar Space Heater

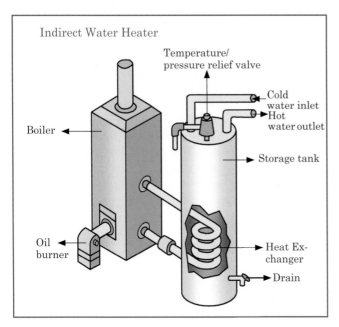

Indirect Water Heater

A combination of an indirect water heater and a highly efficient boiler can provide a very inexpensive method of water heating.

A passive solar space heater works when the sun shines through the solar panels to heat the air inside a box. As the air heats up in the box, it rises and moves into the house. Cool air moves into the box and out of the house—in this way, the house is heated without the use of a mechanized heating system. Using a passive solar heater works best if you have a house that faces south and has both basement and first floor windows on that side of the house. If your house meets these requirements (and there aren't too many obstructions that would impede the sun from shining on the heater), then you can begin construction.

The passive solar space heater is made up of a floor and two triangular end walls, all of which can be made simply out of plywood. In between the open space, insulation can be placed. A lid can also be added to cover the heater in the summer.

To build such a solar space heater, first decide where on the southern wall your collector will be located. If you can place the heater in between windows, that is the best option. You may need to cut through the wall near a window to allow for the proper ventilation but if you don't want to do this, you can also purchase a detachable plywood "chimney" to move the heated air into the house. Next, find the studs that will support the fiberglass panel and find a panel that will be of the appropriate size.

Next, make the base for your solar heating system. The base can be made of ⅜-inch plywood board. Nail the board to a 2 x 4 and level it. Next, add insulation

exchangers then transfer the heat from the fluid to potable water. Some of these indirect circulation systems have overheat protectors so the collector and glycol fluid do not become superheated. Common indirect systems include antifreeze, in which the heat transfer fluid is usually a glycol-water mixture, and drainback, in which pumps circulate the water through the collectors and then the water in the collector loop drains back into a reservoir tank when the pump stops.

▼ A passive solar space heater.

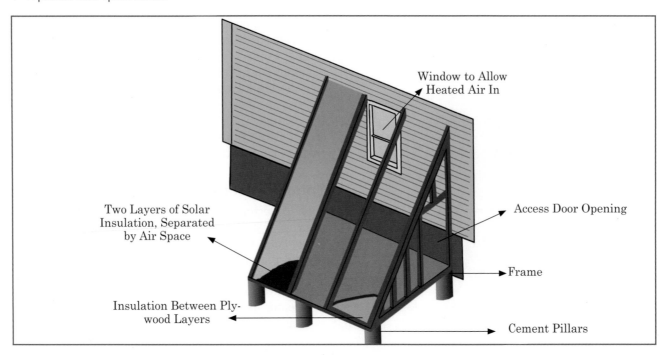

Window to Allow Heated Air In

Two Layers of Solar Insulation, Separated by Air Space

Insulation Between Plywood Layers

Access Door Opening

Frame

Cement Pillars

(the kind found on rolls is best), nailing it to the plywood. Then, nail the whole board to the side of the house. Make sloping supports out of 2 x 4s. Make sure the end wall studding is nailed in, and then attach the outside panel to it.

Under the shingles, install flashing or something else that will keep water out of the top of the solar heater. Then, install the fiberglass panels, making sure the edges are caulked so no water can come in. Enclose the edges of the fiberglass with small strips of plywood. Then, install the outer fiberglass panel so that it is flush with the top surface and caulk it. To finish up, paint the inside of the plywood surfaces black to absorb the heat. The inside of the cover panel should be painted white to reflect the light.

Building Your Own Solar Water Heater

This very simple and basic solar water heater is a low-pressure system and so should not be combined with your home plumbing system. This type of heater is perfect for camping trips or other smaller water heating uses. Find the supplies online or at a hardware store.

Supplies
- Corrugated, high-density polyethylene draining tube (4 inches is preferred)
- An EPDM rubber cap with clamp (available at hardware stores or online)
- Polyethylene terephthalate bottles (3-liter are preferred—soda bottles are fine)

▲ A solar water heater.

To construct the water heater, simply stretch the EPDM rubber cap over one end of the draining tube and make certain the clamp is tight. Cut the ends off the bottles and fit them over the other end of the drainage pipe. This will serve as the glazing to heat the water. Each bottle should be able to fit tightly over the other bottle if you cut a small hole in the bottom of each. Fill the tube with water, place it in the sun, and allow the water inside the bottles and drainage tube to heat up. Once it's warm (around 120°F is the maximum it will heat the water), it can be used to wash dishes or clothes, or for a small bath.

Heating a Room Using Collectors

Air collectors can be installed on a roof or an exterior, south-facing wall to facilitate the heating of one or more rooms in a house. Factory-built collectors can be used but you can also make and install your own air collector, though note that this is not always cost-efficient.

The air collector should have an airtight and insulated metal frame and a black metal plate. This will absorb the heat through the glazing on the front. The sun's rays heat the plate, which then heats the air in the collector. A fan or blower can pull the air from the room through to the collector and blow it into the room.

Room Air Heating with Collectors

Air collectors can be installed on a roof or an exterior (south facing) wall for heating one or more rooms. Although factory-built collectors for on-site installation are available, do-it-yourselfers may choose to build and install their own air collectors. A simple window air heat collector can be made for a few hundred dollars. Simple window box collector fans will fit in a window opening. These fans can be active or passive. A passive collector fan allows air to enter the bottom of the collector, rise as it heats, and enter the room. A damper keeps the room air from flowing back into the panel on overcast or cloudy days. Window box systems only provide a small amount of heat as the collectors are rather small.

Solar Collectors

Solar collectors are an essential part of active solar heating systems. These collectors harness the sun's energy and transform it into heat. Then, the heat is transferred to water, solar fluid, or air. Solar collectors can be one of two types:
1. Nonconcentrating collectors—These have a collector area that is the same size as the absorption area. The most common type is flat-plate

▲ Solar collectors on a roof.

collectors and these are used when temperatures below 200°F are sufficient for space heating.

2. Concentrating collectors—The area of these collectors gathering the solar radiation is much greater than the absorber area.

Solar thermal energy can be used for solar water heating systems, solar pool heaters, and solar space heating systems. There are many types of solar collectors, such as flat plate collectors, evacuated tube collectors, and integral collector storage systems.

Another Form of Solar Heating: Daylighting

Solar collector panels are not the only way in which the sun's heat can be harnessed for energy purposes. Daylighting uses windows and skylights to bring sunlight

Roof Area Needed in Square Feet (Shown in Bold Type)

PV module efficiency (¼)	PV capacity rating (watts)							
	100	250	500	1,000	2,000	4,000	10,000	100,000
4	30	75	150	300	600	1,200	3,000	30,000
8	15	38	75	150	300	600	1,500	15,000
12	10	25	50	100	200	400	1,000	10,000
16	8	20	40	80	160	320	800	8,000

▲ Although the efficiency (percent of sunlight converted to electricity) varies with the different types of PV modules available today, higher-efficiency modules typically cost more. So, a less-efficient system is not necessarily less cost-effective

Calculating Electricity Bill Savings for a Net-Metered PV System

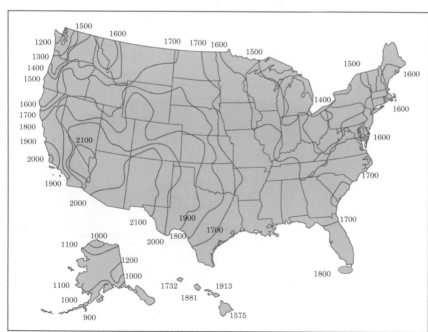

◀ First determine the system's size in kilowatts (kW). A reasonable range is 1 to 5 kW. This value is the "kW of PV" input in the equations. Next, based on your geographic location, select the energy production factor from the map below for the kWh/kW-year input for the equations.

Energy from the PV system = (kW of PV) x (kWh/kW-year) = kWh/year. (Divide this number by twelve if you want to determine your monthly energy reduction.)

Energy bills savings = (kWh/year) x (Residential Rate)/100 = $/year saved. (Residential Rate in this above equation should be in dollars per kWh; for example, a rate of 10 cents per kWh is input as $0.10/kWh.)

For example, a 2-kW system in Denver, CO, at a residential energy rate of $0.07/kWh will save about $266 per year (1,900 kWh/kW-year x $0.07/kWh x 2kW = $266/year).

▲ Including plenty of energy-efficient windows in your home will allow sunlight to warm your rooms naturally.

into your home. Using energy-efficient windows, as well as carefully thought-out lighting design, reduces the need for artificial lighting during the daytime. These windows also cut down on heating and cooling problems.

The effectiveness of daylighting in your home will depend on your climate and the design of your house. The sizes and locations of window and skylights should be based on the way in which the sun hits your home and not on the outward aesthetics of your house. Facing windows toward the south is most advantageous for daylighting and for moderating seasonal temperatures. Placing windows that face toward the south will allow more sunlight into your home during the winter months. North-facing windows are also useful for daylighting as they allow a relatively even, natural light into a room, produce little glare, and capture no undesirable summer heat.

Make Your Own Solar Cooking Oven

This type of simple, portable solar oven is perfect for camping trips or if you want to do an outdoor barbeque with additional cooked foods in the summer. This homemade solar oven can reach around 350°F when placed in direct sunlight.

Supplies
- A reflective car sunshade or any sturdy but flexible material (such as cardboard) covered with tin foil and cut to the notched shape of a car sunshade
- Velcro
- A bucket
- A cooking pot

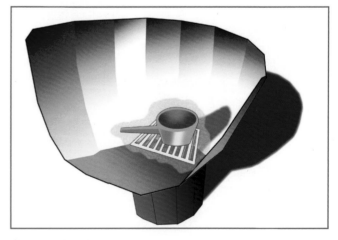

▲ A simple solar oven.

▲ Solar ovens can be fashioned in a variety of ways. The goal is to have as much surface area as possible reflecting the sun toward your food.

- A wire grill
- A baking bag

Directions

1. Place the car sunshade on the ground. Cut the Velcro into three separate pieces and stick on half of each piece onto the edge near the notch. Then, test the shade to see if the Velcro pieces, when brought together, form a funnel. Place the funnel atop the bucket.
2. Place the cooking pot on the wire grill. Put this all in the baking bag and put it inside the funnel. The rack should now be laying on top of the bucket. Now place the whole cooker in direct sunlight and angle the funnel in the direction of the sun. Adjust the angle as the sun moves.

Make Your Own Solar Panels

Making your own solar panels can be tricky and time-consuming, but with the right materials and lots of patience, you can certainly create an effective solar energy panel.

Supplies
- Pegboard

- Solar cells (quality will be determined on how much power you want to get from your solar panel)
- Contact wire
- Wire cutters
- Solder
- Soldering iron
- Bolts with washers and wingnuts
- Plexiglass
- Plywood board
- Aluminum framing
- Silicone caulking
- Screws

Directions

1. Apply silicone caulking in vertical strips between the rows of holes on the peg board. Place the solar cells face up along the caulking in straight rows, carefully aligning them so that the wires poke through the holes. The solar cells should completely cover the board.
2. Place a soft sheet or blanket on the ground or table (to prevent the cells from scratching) and carefully flip the board so that it is face down. Solder together the wires coming out to create one thick wire stemming from each hole. Then use connecting wire or metal strips to connect the wires along horizontal lines. Be sure to connect all positive wires together and all negative wires together, without mixing the two.
3. Drill two holes in the back of your panel and attach a positive and negative bolt, washer, and wingnut. Solder the positive wires to the positive bolt and the negative wires to the negative bolt.
4. Build a watertight frame to size, using aluminum framing for the sides, plywood for the backing, and a plexiglass face to allow the sunlight to shine through. Seal all cracks and edges with silicone sealant.

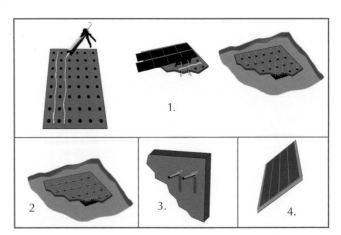

▲ Refer to these illustrations while constructing your own solar panel.

▲ The more surface area you cover with solar panels, the more power you'll get. It's best to install your panels on the south side of your home.

Installing Your Heat Collector

If possible, install your own solar heat collector on the south side of your house (the side that receives the most sunlight during the day). It can be placed in a window to help minimize your heating costs during the winter months.

▲ Solar panels can be placed in a field or other sunny area to collect energy, which is stored and then used as needed.

A solar heat collector can be made from heavy-duty foam insulation, window glass, sealant, aluminum foil, and heavy-duty tape. Paint the foam panel, or both sides of the aluminum sheets, black and then mount it on cubes that are cemented to the side of your house near a window. This will allow the air to come in on both sides of the heat collector.

All sides of the foam should be covered with aluminum foil and then adhered to the foam board. Then place and seal the glass panels over the foam, sealing it with the sealant and heavy-duty tape if needed. Another piece of foam can be utilized as a cover for the duct at night or during the warm, sunny summer months. Hinge this on with hinge brackets or clasps.

An Alternative Solar Heating Panel

This type of solar panel is different from the expensive, manufactured panels you can purchase and have installed on your roof or the side of your house. It is

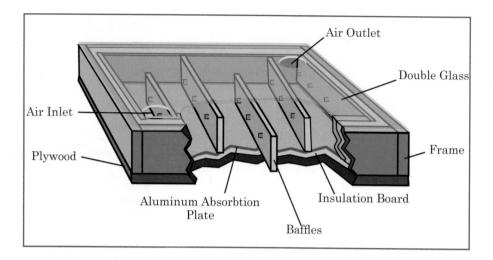

Air Outlet

Double Glass

Air Inlet

Plywood

Frame

Aluminum Absorbtion Plate

Insulation Board

Baffles

Alternate solar heating panel. ▶

great for heating air but cannot produce electricity. You can either situate this heater in a south-facing window of your home or place it on the outside, southern wall or on the roof. Heating panels that are on the outside of a house generally create more heat and are much more effective in heating a room or area of your home.

To start, you will need to purchase glass or Plexiglas for your solar heating panel. Either one should be double-paned to keep out moisture. To build the frame for your solar heating panel, use 2 x 4s and create a square or rectangle that will fit your pane of glass. Nail plywood to the back of the frame. Next, take a piece of insulation board and put it at the back of the panel. Heat absorption can be gained through aluminum flashing or copper. After this is inserted, screw down the window frame, if you are using one, and make sure it is caulked well to keep out water.

Add the interior boards that line the frame and the baffles to seal the top of the glass. Screw these interior boards to the sides of the panel to keep them secure. Then, cut out the air openings using a jigsaw. One circular opening should be in the lower left and the other in the upper right of your heating panel. Before hanging the panel up, you will need to determine where the studs are in the wall or, if you are installing it on your roof, where the roof rafters are located. It is also important that your openings do not fall on top of a stud or rafter as this will defeat their ability to direct airflow. Screw in boards along the studs or rafters, on which you will then mount the panel.

Once the panel is secured to the wall or roof, begin to install the air delivery system so the hot air can be circulated throughout your home. You may want to add a small fan (one used in a computer will be fine) to your heating panel so you can better circulate the air throughout the system, though this is not necessary to operate your heating panel effectively. If you do choose to use a fan, it must be able to fit inside the wall plate. You will need to drill a hole in your wall where the panel holes are situated on the outside. Cut the hole and add the connector to the ductwork, sliding it through the hole into the room, and seal off the edges of the hole.

Place the fan within the wall plate in the room, and place an electrical box near the fan to turn it on and off. If you aren't familiar with electrical work, you may want to ask an electrician to help you with connecting the electrical wiring. Next, mount the solar panel so it faces to the south, running a wire into the electrical box inside the room. This will save you money and energy while running your fan. Now turn on the fan and feel the warm air starting to blow through your room.

To finish your outside panel, simply paint the inside black to absorb more heat, add some weather stripping to seal the glass tightly, and screw the glass piece to the panel.

Regulations for Installing and Building Solar Heating Systems

Before you install a solar energy system, learn about the local building codes, zoning, and neighborhood covenants as they apply to these systems. You will most likely need to obtain a building permit to install a solar energy system onto an existing building. Common problems you may encounter as a homeowner in installing a solar energy system are: exceeding roof load, unacceptable heat exchangers, improper wiring, tampering with potable water supplies, obstructing property and yards, and placing the system too close to the street or lot lines. There are also local compliances that must be factored in before installing your system. Contact your local jurisdiction zoning and building enforcement divisions and any homeowner's, neighborhood, or community associations before building and installing any solar heating equipment.

Solar Greenhouse

Greenhouses collect solar energy on sunny days and then store the heat for use in the evening and on days when it is overcast. A solar greenhouse can be situated as a free-standing structure (like a shed or larger enclosure) or in an underground hole.

For gardeners who want to grow small amounts of produce, passive solar greenhouses are a good option and help extend the growing season. Active systems take supplemental energy sources to move the solar heated air from its storage facility to other parts of the greenhouse. Solar greenhouses can utilize many of the same features and installation techniques as passive solar heating systems used in homes to stay heated.

While standard greenhouses also rely on the sun's rays to heat their interiors, solar greenhouses are different because they have special glazing that absorbs large amounts of heat during the winter months and also use materials to store the heat. Solar greenhouses have a lot of insulation in areas with little sunlight to keep heat loss at a minimum.

Types of Solar Greenhouses

Two common types of solar greenhouses are the attached solar greenhouse and the freestanding solar greenhouse. Attached solar greenhouses are situated next to a house or shed and are typically lean-to structures. They are limited in the amount of produce they can grow and have passive solar heating systems.

Freestanding solar greenhouses are large structures that are best-suited for producing a large variety and quantity of produce, flowers, and herbs. They can be constructed in the form of either a shed structure or a hoop house. In a shed greenhouse, the south wall is glazed to maximize the heating potential and the north wall is extremely well-insulated. Hoop house greenhouses are rounded instead of shaped like an elongated shed. Solar energy is collected and stored

in earth thermal storage and in water. These systems, while common, are not as effective in utilizing solar energy as the shed and lean-to structures.

Sites for Solar Greenhouses

The glazing portion of the solar greenhouse should ideally face directly south to gain the maximum exposure to the sun's heat. Situating the solar greenhouse on a slight slope facing upward will maximize the amount of solar energy it can absorb.

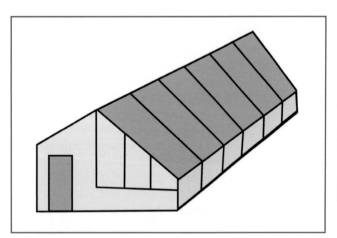

▲ A solar greenhouse.

▲ Both flowers and vegetables can thrive in greenhouses year-round.

Materials Used in Solar Greenhouse Construction

For a solar greenhouse to collect, circulate, and maintain the greatest amount of heat, it needs to be constructed out of the proper materials. Glazing materials need to allow photosynthetic radiation to get through so it can reach the plants. Clear glass allows direct light into the greenhouse and so should be used as a glazing material. It is also imperative that when the glazing materials are mounted on the greenhouse, there are no cracks or holes that can allow for heat to escape. Thus, glazing material should have high heat efficiency and be made of resistant material to hold up in inclement weather and hail.

Solar greenhouses also need to be able to store the heat that is collected for use on cloudy days or at night. The easiest method for storing heat is to situate rocks, concrete, and/or water in the path of the sunlight that is entering the greenhouse. These materials will absorb the heat during the day and release it during the evening hours. Pools of water, rocks, and concrete slabs or small walls should be large enough to absorb and emit enough heat to last for the night or for a few cloudy days.

Phase-change materials may also be used to effectively store heat in your solar greenhouse. These materials consist of paraffin, fatty acids, and Glauber's salt. These materials store heat as they change into liquid and release it as they turn back into a solid form. They are kept in sealed tubes and many are needed to provide enough heat.

All areas of the greenhouse that are not glazed need to be insulated to keep in the maximum amount of heat. Weather stripping is helpful in sealing doors and vents; foam insulation is helpful for walls. Place a polyethylene film between the insulation and the greenhouse walls to keep these materials dry—if they become too wet or saturated, they will be less effective and may start to mold. The floors of a solar greenhouse can also lose heat so they should be made out of brick or flagstone (with insulation foam underneath) to keep the heat in.

The solar greenhouse needs outdoor insulation as well, which can be attained by placing hay bales along the edges of the greenhouse, or the greenhouse can be situated slightly underground (a pit greenhouse). Of course, if a greenhouse is dug into the soil, it needs to be in an area that is above the water level to minimize leakage.

A solar greenhouse, like any other greenhouse, also needs proper ventilation for the warmer summer months. Vents in the sides of the greenhouse will help create air flow. Ridge vents in the roof will allow the hottest air to escape out of the top of the greenhouse as well. If a greenhouse needs more ventilation, a solar chimney can be hooked up to the passive solar collectors to release extra heat out into the air.

▲ Greenhouses can be made in a range of shapes and sizes and can be attached to or separate from your home.

Wind Energy

Wind energy is created naturally by circulation patterns in the Earth's atmosphere driven by the heat from the sun. These winds are caused by the uneven heating of the atmosphere by the sun, the irregularities of the earth's surface, and the rotation of the earth. Wind patterns are modified by the earth's terrain, bodies of water, and vegetation. Since the earth's surface is made of very different types of land and water, it absorbs the sun's heat at different rates. During the day, the air above the land heats up very quickly. The warm air over the land expands and rises and the heavier, cooler air rushes in to take its place, creating winds. At night, the winds are reversed as the air cools rapidly over land. This air flow is used for many purposes: sailing, flying kites, and generating electricity.

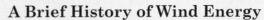

A Brief History of Wind Energy

People have been harnessing energy from the wind since ancient times. Wind was used to sail ships and windmills were build to help grind wheat, corn, and other grains. Windmills were also used to pump water and to cut wood at sawmills in the formative years of the American colonies. Even into the early twentieth century, windmills were being used to generate electricity in rural parts of America. The windmill again gained national attention in the early 1980s when wind energy was finally considered a renewable energy source. It continues to be a growing industry throughout the United States.

Small Wind Electric Systems

Small wind electric systems are one of the most cost-effective, home-based renewable energy systems. These systems are nonpolluting and are fairly easy to set up. A small wind electric system can effectively:

- Lower your electricity bills by 50 to 90 percent
- Help you avoid high costs of having utility power lines extended to a remote location
- Help uninterruptible power supplies ride through extended utility outages

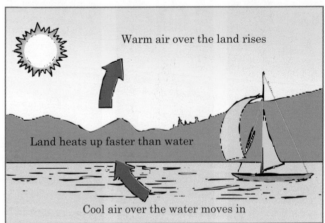

▲ Natural air flow cycle.

How Do Small Wind Electric Systems Work?

When the wind spins a wind turbine's blades, a rotor captures the kinetic energy of the wind, converting it into rotary motion to drive the generator. Most turbines have automatic overspeed-governing systems to keep the rotor from spinning out of control on very windy days.

A small wind system can be connected to an electric distribution system (grid-connected) or it can stand alone (off-grid). To capture and convert the wind's kinetic energy into electricity, a home wind energy system must generally be comprised of the following:

1. A wind turbine—This consists of blades attached to a rotor, a generator/alternator mounted on a frame, and a tail
2. A tower
3. Balance-of-system components—i.e., controllers, inverters, and/or batteries

A wind-electric turbine generator, more commonly known as a "wind turbine," converts kinetic energy in the wind into mechanical power. This power can be used directly for specific tasks, like grinding grains or pumping water. A generator can also convert this mechanical power into a high-value, highly flexible, and useful form of energy—electricity.

Wind turbines make electricity by working in the opposite way as a fan. Instead of using electricity to make wind, as a fan does, turbines use wind to make electricity. The wind turns the blades, spinning a shaft that connects to a generator, which makes electricity.

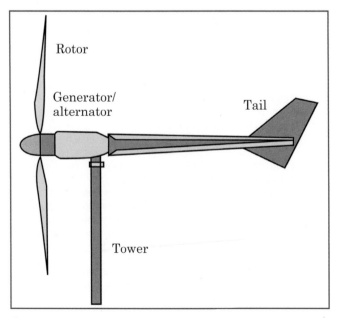

▲ The basic parts of a small wind electric system.

Installing a Small Electric Wind System

Small wind electric systems, with the proper installation and maintenance, can last over 20 years. Before installing your system, first find the best site, determine the appropriate size of your wind turbine, decide whether you want a grid-connected or off-grid system, and find out about your local zoning, permitting, and neighborhood covenant requirements.

Many people decide to install these systems on their own (though the manufacturer and/or dealer should also be able to help you install the small wind electric system). However, before you attempt to install the wind turbine, make sure you can answer these do-it-yourself questions:

1. Can I pour a proper cement foundation?
2. Do I have access to a lift, ladder, or another way to erect the tower safely?
3. Do I know the difference between alternating current (AC) and direct current (DC) wiring?
4. Do I know enough about electricity to safely wire my turbine?
5. Do I know how to safely handle and install batteries?

If the answer to any of these questions is "no," then you should have someone help you install the system (contact the manufacturer or your state energy office).

Evaluating a Potential Site for Your Small Wind Turbine

The site on which you choose to install your system should meet the following criteria:

- Your property has a good wind resource—good annual wind speeds and a prevailing direction for the wind.
- Your home is located on at least one acre of land in a rural area.
- Your local zoning codes and covenants do not prohibit construction of a wind turbine.
- Your average electricity bill is $150 per month or more.

If you live in an area that has complex terrain, be careful when selecting an installation site. If you place your wind turbine on the top of a hill or on an exceptionally windy side, you will have more access to

Wind Energy

prevailing winds than in a gully or on the sheltered side of a hill. Additionally, consider any existing obstacles—trees, houses, sheds—that may be in the way of the wind's path. You should also plan for future obstructions, such as new buildings or landscaping. Your turbine needs to be positioned upwind of any buildings and trees, and it needs to be 30 feet above anything within 300 feet of its site.

Inside a Wind Turbine

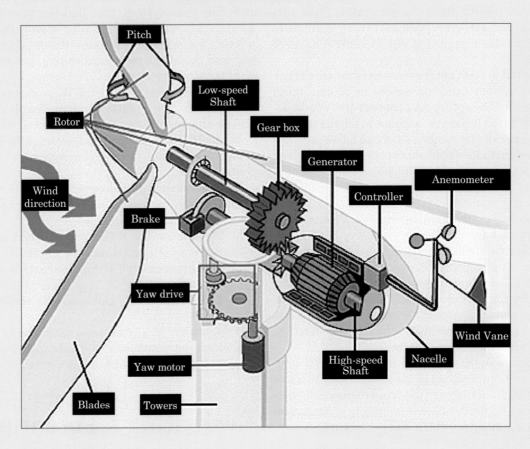

Parts of a wind turbine:

- Anemometer: measures the wind speed and transmits wind speed data to the controller.
- Blades: most turbines have either two or three blades and the wind blows over the blades, causing the blades to lift and rotate.
- Brake: a disc brake, applied mechanically, electrically, or hydraulically, and stops the rotor in emergencies.
- Controller: starts up the machine at wind speeds of about 8 to 16 mph and shuts off the machine at about 55 mph wind speeds. Turbines do not operate at wind speeds above 55 mph because they may be damaged.
- Gear box: gears connect the low-speed shaft to the high-speed shaft and increase the rotational speeds from about 30 to 60 rotations per minute (rpm) to about 1000 to 1800 rpm—the rotational speed required by most generators to produce electricity. The gear box is a costly and heavy part of the wind turbine.
- Generator: usually an off-the-shelf induction generator that produces 60-cycle AC electricity.
- High-speed shaft: drives the generator.

- Low-speed shaft: turned by the rotor at about 30 to 60 rpm.
- Nacelle: sits atop the tower and contains the gear box, low- and high-speed shafts, generator, controller, and brake. Some nacelles are large enough for a helicopter to land on.
- Pitch: Turns the blades out of the wind to control the rotor speed and keep the rotor from turning in winds that are too high or too low to produce electricity.
- Rotor: the blades and hub.
- Tower: made from tubular steel, concrete, or steel lattice. Since wind speed increases with height, taller towers enable turbines to capture more energy and generate more electricity.
- Wind direction: an "upwind" turbine operates facing into the wind while other turbines are designed to face "downwind" or away from the wind.
- Wind vane: measures wind direction and communicates with the yaw drive to orient the turbine properly with respect to the wind.
- Yaw drive: used to keep the rotor facing into the wind as the wind direction changes (not required for downwind turbines).
- Yaw motor: powers the yaw drive.

When determining the suitability of your site for a small electric wind system, estimate your site's wind resource. Wind resource can vary significantly over an area of just a few miles because of local terrain's influence on wind flow. Use the following methods to help estimate your wind resource before installing your small electric wind system:

1. Consult a wind resource map. This is used to estimate the wind resource in your area. You can find a specific map for your state at the U.S. Department of Energy's Wind Powering America Program Web site. A general U.S. map is shown in the figure.

2. Obtain wind speed data. The easiest way to quantify the wind resource in your area is by obtaining the average wind speed information from a local airport. Airport wind data are typically measured 20 to 33 feet above ground. Average wind speeds increase with height and may be as much as 15 to 25 percent greater at a usual wind turbine hub (80 feet high) than those measured at airports.

3. Watch vegetation flagging. Flagging is the effect of strong winds on an area of vegetation. For example, if a group of trees on flat ground is leaning significantly in one direction, chances are they've become that way due to strong winds.

4. Use a measurement system. Direct monitoring using a measurement system at a certain site provides the best picture of the available wind resource. These are very expensive, however, and so may not be practical to use.

5. Obtain data from a local small wind system—if there is a small wind turbine near your area, you may be able to obtain information on the annual output of the system, as well as wind speed data.

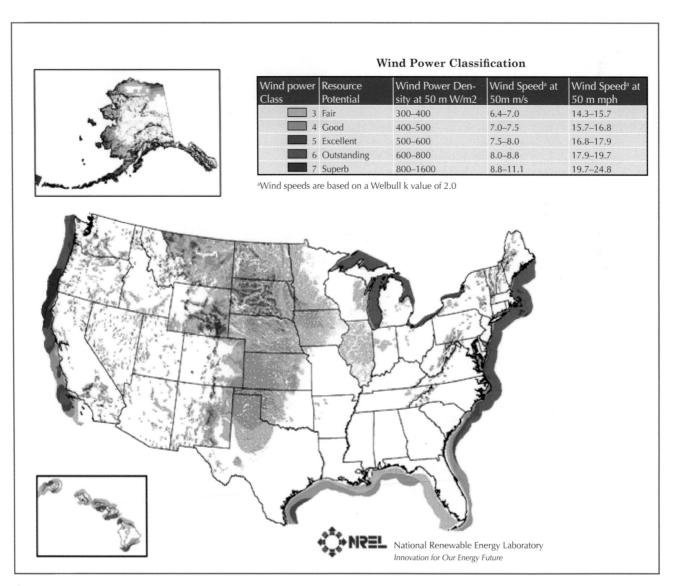

Wind Power Classification

Wind power Class	Resource Potential	Wind Power Density at 50 m W/m2	Wind Speed[a] at 50m m/s	Wind Speed[a] at 50 m mph
3	Fair	300–400	6.4–7.0	14.3–15.7
4	Good	400–500	7.0–7.5	15.7–16.8
5	Excellent	500–600	7.5–8.0	16.8–17.9
6	Outstanding	600–800	8.0–8.8	17.9–19.7
7	Superb	800–1600	8.8–11.1	19.7–24.8

[a]Wind speeds are based on a Welbull k value of 2.0

NREL National Renewable Energy Laboratory
Innovation for Our Energy Future

▲ This map shows the potential for wind energy in various parts of the United States.

Small Wind Turbines Used for Homes

Single, small, stand-alone turbines that are sized less than 100 kilowatts are used for homes, telecommunication dishes, and water pumping. Used in residential applications, these small wind turbines can range from 400 watts to 20 kilowatts. In addition to being used for generating electricity and pumping water, they can be used for charging batteries. Most U.S. manufacturers rate their small wind turbines by the amount of power they can safely produce at wind speeds between 24 and 36 mph.

An average home uses about 9,400 kilowatt-hours of electricity per year. Thus, a wind turbine rated in the 5- to 15-kilowatt range would make a significant contribution to this energy demand. Before deciding on a wind turbine you should:

1. Establish an energy budget. Try to reduce the electricity use in your home so you will only need a small turbine.
2. Determine an appropriate height for the wind turbine's tower so it will generate the maximum amount of energy.
3. Remember that a small home-sized wind machine has rotors that are between 8 and 25 feet in diameter and stand around 30 feet tall. If your property does not have enough space to accommodate this, you may not be able to have a powerful enough turbine to help significantly reduce your energy costs.

▲ Windmill blades can vary in shape but should always be angled to catch the most wind.

Maintaining Your Small Wind Turbine

To keep your turbine running smoothly and efficiently, do an annual check of the following:
- Check and tighten bolts and electrical connections as necessary.
- Check machines for corrosion.
- Check the guy wires for proper tension.
- Check for and replace any worn leading-edge tape on the turbine blades.
- Replace the turbine blades and/or bearings after 10 years.

Types of Wind Turbines

Modern wind turbines fall into two basic categories: horizontal-axis varieties and vertical-axis designs.

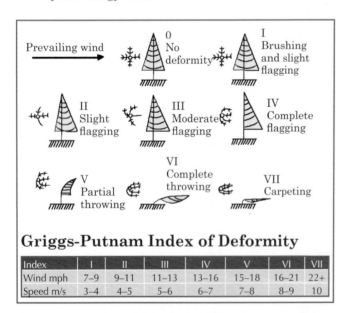

Griggs-Putnam Index of Deformity

Index	I	II	III	IV	V	VI	VII
Wind mph	7–9	9–11	11–13	13–16	15–18	16–21	22+
Speed m/s	3–4	4–5	5–6	6–7	7–8	8–9	10

▲ Vegetation flagging is the effect of strong winds on vegetation. It's a good indicator of how strong the winds are in that area.

Horizontal-axis Wind Turbines

Most wind machines used today fall into this category. Horizontal-axis wind machines have blades like an airplane propeller. A standard horizontal wind machine stands about 20 stories tall and has three blades spanning 200 feet across. These are the machines most readily found in large fields and on wind farms.

The majority of small wind turbines made today are of the horizontal-axis style. They have two or three blades made of composite material, such as fiberglass. The turbine's frame is a structure to which the rotor, generator, and tail are all attached. The diameter of the rotor will determine the amount of energy the turbine will produce. The tail helps keep the turbine facing into the wind. Mounted on a tower, the wind turbine has better access to stronger winds.

These machines also require balance-of-system components. These parts are required for water pumping systems and other residential uses of your wind turbine. These also vary based on the type of system you are using: either a grid-connected, stand-alone, or hybrid.

For example, if you have a residential grid-connected wind turbine system, your balance-of-systems parts will include:

- A controller
- Storage batteries
- A power conditioning unit (inverter)
- Wiring
- Electrical disconnect switch
- Grounding system
- Foundation for the tower

Vertical-axis Wind Turbines

These machines have blades that go from top to bottom. The most common type looks like a giant two-bladed egg beater. Vertical-axis wind machines are generally 100 feet tall and 50 feet wide. Though these wind turbines have the potential to produce a great deal of energy, they make up only a small percentage of the wind machines that are currently in use due to the cost and effort required to set them up. In addition, they produce a great deal of noise, can be unsightly, hurt the bird population, and require large roads and heavy-duty equipment to get them up and running.

▼ A horizontal-axis wind turbine.

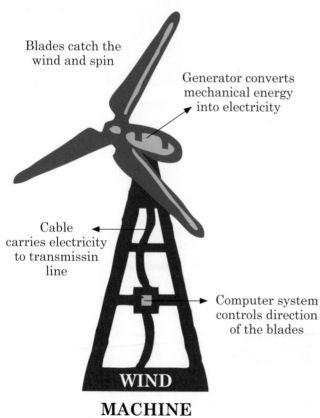

Blades catch the wind and spin

Generator converts mechanical energy into electricity

Cable carries electricity to transmissin line

Computer system controls direction of the blades

WIND

MACHINE

A hybrid wind and solar energy system.

Stand-Alone and Small Hybrid Systems

Wind power can also be used in off-grid systems. These are called stand-alone systems because they are not connected to an electric distribution grid. In these systems, small wind turbines can be used in combination with other components, such as small solar electric systems, to create a hybrid power system. Hybrid power systems provide reliable off-grid power for homes (and even for entire communities in certain instances) that are far from local utility lines.

A hybrid electric system may be a practical system for you if:
- You live in an area with average annual wind speed of at least nine mph.
- A grid connection is not available or can only be made through a very costly extension.
- You would like to become independent from your energy utility company.
- You would like to generate clean power.

Small hybrid systems that combine wind and solar technologies offer several advantages over either single system. In many parts of the United States, wind speeds are low in the summer when the sun shines the brightest and for the longest hours. Conversely, the wind is stronger in the winter when less sunlight is available. These hybrid systems, therefore, are more likely to produce power when you need it.

If there are times when neither the wind nor the solar systems are producing energy, most hybrid systems will then provide power through batteries or an engine generator powered by diesel fuel (which can also recharge the batteries if they run low).

▲ A solar and wind hybrid energy system.

Hybrid power ▶ systems combine multiple sources to deliver non-intermittent electric power.

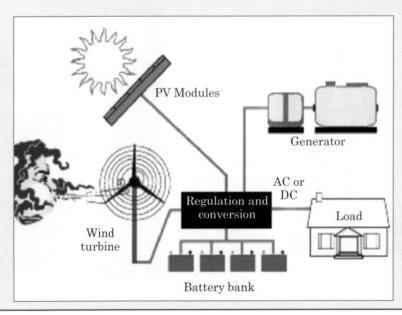

Grid-Connected Small Wind Electric Systems

Small wind energy systems can be connected to the electricity distribution system to become "grid-connected systems." These wind turbines can help reduce your consumption of utility-supplied electricity for appliances, electric heat, and lighting. The utility will make up the difference for any energy that your turbine cannot make. Any excess electricity that is produced by the system, and cannot be used by the household, can often be sent or sold to the utility. One drawback to this system, however, is that during power outages, the wind turbine is required to shut down for safety reasons.

Grid-connected systems are only practical if:

- You live in an area with average annual wind speeds of at least 10 mph.
- Utility-supplied electricity is expensive in your area.
- The utility's requirements for connecting your system to its grid are not exceedingly expensive.
- There are good incentives for the sale of excess electricity.

▼ A grid-connected small wind electric system.

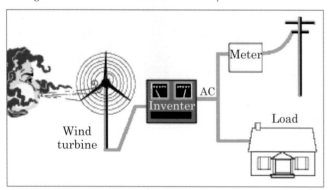

Mounting Your Small Wind Electric System on a Tower

Since wind speeds increase with height, it is essential that your small wind turbine be mounted on a tower. The higher the tower, the more power the wind system will be able to produce. To determine the best height for your tower, you will need to know the estimated annual energy output and the size of your turbine.

There are two types of towers: self-supporting (free-standing) and guyed. Most home wind power systems use a guyed tower as it is the least expensive. Guyed towers consist of these parts:

- Lattice sections
- Pipe
- Tubing (depending on the design)
- Supporting guy wires

These towers are easier to install but they do require lots of space—the radius of the tower must be ½ to ¾ of the tower height.

Tilt-down towers, while more expensive, offer an easy way to maintain smaller, lightweight turbines that are less than 10 kilowatts. These towers can be lowered to the ground during severe weather or unusually high winds.

Generally, it is a good idea to install a small wind turbine on a tower with the bottom of the rotor blades around 30 feet above any obstacle that is within 300 feet from the tower.

Windmills

Windmills are used for pumping water, milling, and operating light machinery all around the world. They are constructed in a variety of shapes and some are very picturesque. When set up properly, windmills cost nothing to operate and if the wheel is made well, it will last for many years without need for major repairs. To make a windmill requires a good understanding of carpentry and workmanship but it is not incredibly difficult or expensive to do.

Constructing a Windmill

Windmills can be of all sizes, though the larger the windmill, the more power it can generate. This windmill and tower can be easily constructed out of wood, an old wheel, and a few iron fittings you may be able to find at a hardware store or home center. Constructing the windmill in sections is the easiest way to create this structure. Simply follow these directions to make your own energy-producing windmill:

Wind Energy

The Tower

1. The tower is the first part to be built and should be constructed out of four spruce sticks that are 16 feet long and 4 inches square, in a configuration that measures 30 inches square at the top and 72 inches square at the base.

2. The deck should be 36 inches square and should project 2 inches over the top rails.

3. The rails and cross braces can be spruce or pine strips and should measure 4 inches wide and ⅛ inch thick. Attach these to the corner posts with steel-wire nails.

4. Embed the corner posts 2 feet into the ground, leaving 14 feet above the surface. The rail at the bottom, which is attached to the four posts, should measure 3 feet above the ground. Midway between this and the top rail of the deck, run a middle rail around the post. Make sure that where your wheel will be attached, this point rises at least 2 feet above any obstructions (buildings, trees, etc.) so it can have access to the blowing wind.

5. The cross braces should be beveled at the ends so they fit snugly against the corner.

6. The posts, rails, and braces should be planed so they present a nice appearance at the end of the building. A ladder can also be constructed at one side of the tower to allow easy access to the mill.

7. Nail a board across two of the rails halfway up the tower. Secure the lower end of a trunk tightly here if you are constructing a pumping mill. However, if a wooden mill is what you are after, you can use an old wheel from a wagon and six blades of wood.

▲ Beveled cross braces fit snugly against the corners.

The Turntable

1. The turntable (d, e, and f) holds the wheel and tail. It should be built of 2½ x 2-inch timber and 2-inch galvanized wrought iron "water" tube and flanges.

2. The upper flange (g and h) supports the timber framing. It should be countersunk, using a half-round file, and screwed tightly onto the tube as far as possible. The end of the tube should project just slightly beyond the face of the flange so that it can be riveted over to fill the countersink.

3. Bolt the two loose flanges to the framework of the tower. Use them with 2-inch pipe with the thread filed away so they may slide freely onto the tube. The upper loose flange should form a footstep bearing and the lower flange a guide for the turntable.

4. Now mount the turntable on the ball bearing to make sure the mill head can turn freely. Screw on two back nuts to guard against any possibility of the turntable being lifted out of place by a strong wind.

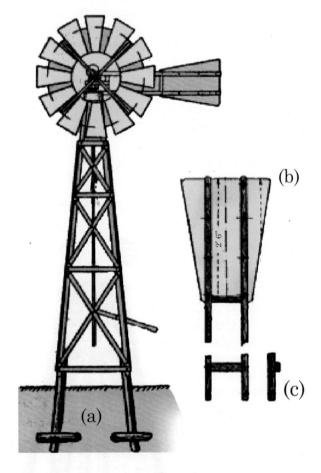

(b)

(c)

(a)

▲ Details of the windmill. Figure (a) shows a general view with the tail turned to "off" position. Figure (b) shows details of the tail, and (c) shows a cross-piece of the tail.

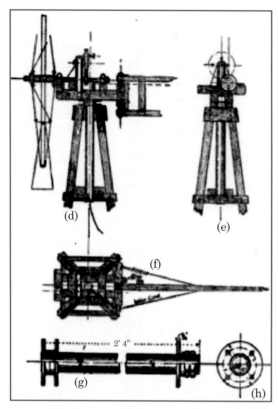

(d)

(e)

(f)

(g) 2' 4"

(h)

▲ The windmill turntable (d, e, and f) holds the wheel and tail. The upper flange (detailed drawings g and h) forms a support for the timber framing.

The Head

1. This is the part that will carry the wheel spindle.
2. Notch the joints and secure them with 2-inch bolts.
3. The upright, which carries a bolt or pin for the spur-wheel to revolve upon, is kept in place in the front and at the sides by a piece of hoop iron.
4. The tail vane swivel is a piece of 5-inch bore tube with back nuts and washers. Pass an iron bolt or other piece of iron through this, screw it to each end, and fit it with four nuts and washers.

The Wheel Shaft

1. Use wrought-iron tubing and flanges to create the wheel shaft. The bore of the tube is at least 5 inches, and the outside diameter should be roughly 1½ inches. Both the tube and the fittings should be of good quality and a thick gauge (steam quality is preferred).
2. If lathe is available, lightly skim it over the tubing. However, if it's not, a careful filing will do just as well to smooth down the edges.
3. Screw the tube higher up on one end to receive the flanges forming the hub. Screw these on and secure them on one side with back nuts and on the other with a distance piece made out of a 1½-inch

bore tube. Fit a cap to close the open front end of the tube.
4. Grease two plummer blocks with some form of lubrication. These will be the bearings for the shaft.
5. A pinion is needed of at least 2½ inches in diameter at the pitch circle. Bore it to fit the wheel shaft. A spur wheel of 7 inches in diameter should follow that (gear wheels from a lawn mower can be used if available).

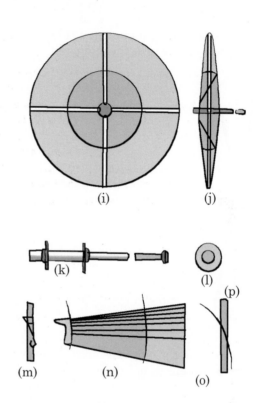

(i)

(j)

(k)

(l)

(p)

(m)

(n)

(o)

▲ Details of the wheel shaft frame (i, j); front and side views, (k, l); axle of wheel (m); attachment of inner end of vane to inner ring of frame (n); vane on rings (o); attachment of vane to outer brackets by bracket (p).

The Wheel

1. The wheel should be at least 5 feet in diameter to produce a good amount of energy. The framing consists of an inner and outer ring and four double arms with cross stays and diagonals (a regular wooden wheel will be sufficient, or you can find one made of galvanized steel).
2. Cut each spoke at an angle on one side so that the blades will have the necessary pitch to make the wind turn them.
3. The blades should be 18 inches long, 12 inches wide at the outer ends, and 6 inches wide next to the hub. Each blade should be only ¾ inch thick. Attach them to the spokes with simple screws.

4. If you desire, you can string a wire between the outer end of each blade to the end of the next spoke. This will help steady the blades.

The Tail

1. Run a fine saw cut up about 2 feet 6 inches from the outer end to receive the vane (optional).
2. Pass a cord over two pulleys and down the turntable tube. It is necessary to attach the end of the cord to a short cylinder of hard wood or metal (about 2 to 3 inches in diameter). This revolves with the turntable but can be slid up or down.
3. If you plan on using a pump, cut a hole through the axis of the cylinder to fit the pump rod.

◄ Each spoke should be cut at an angle so that the blades will have the pitch to make the wind turn them.

4. Cut a groove in the circumference of the cylinder, and bend two pieces of iron into shape and place them into the grooves. Now take the cords from the two bolts, untying the straps. Join these two cords to another cord, which acts as a reel or lever at the base of the tower. In this way, the position of the tail can be regulated from a stationary point.

Total Lift	Gallons per Hour	Bore of Pump	Approximate Stroke
26 ft	100	2 in.	3½ in.
60 ft	50	2 in.	1½ in.
100 ft	25	1½ in.	1½ in.

Adding Pumps to Your Windmill

If you want to use this windmill to pump water, then you may need to do some experimenting with different lengths of pump stroke. Below is a table indicating what should be expected from the pump, and also providing the size of the single-action pump suitable for a given lift (using a ratio of 1 to 3).

Make sure that your pump is not too large; otherwise, it may not start in a light wind or breeze.

The pump is driven by a pin screwed into the side of the spur wheel and is secured with a lock nut. Drill and tap three or four holes at different distances from the center of the wheel so the length of the stroke can be adjusted. If the spokes on the wheel are too thin for drilling, you can use a clamp with a projecting pin instead.

A pump rod—a continuous wooden rod about 1 inch square and thicker at the top end—can be used in connecting the bottom end (by bolting) to the "bow" supplied with the pump. Intermediate joints, if needed, can be fashioned with 1 x ½-inch fish plates roughly 6 inches long. If the pump is no more than 12 feet below the crank pin, one guide will be adequate. The pump rod must be able to revolve with the head and will be need to be thickened up in a circular section where it passes through the guide. Make the guide in two halves and screw or bolt it to a bar running across the tower.

Final Touches

When construction is finished, paint all of the woodwork any color that complements your yard or property and, if desired, lacquer it to protect the wood from rain and snow. A windmill of this size will create at least a one-quarter horsepower in a 15-mph wind.

Building a Small Wind Motor

This small wind motor can easily be made to generate energy for small machines, tool shed lightbulbs, and other small mechanics. The foundation for this windwheel can be made out of the front wheel of an old

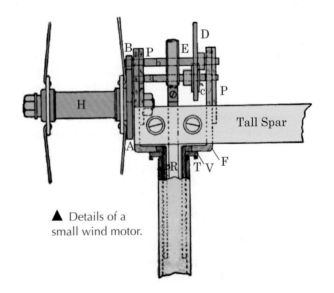

▲ Details of a small wind motor.

bicycle with the front spindle and cones completely intact.

Attach eight to 12 vanes of stout sheet tin to the rim. These sheets should be around 8 inches long and 4 to 6 inches wide and should lie at a 30-degree angle to the plane of the rim. The vanes will be much more efficient if they are curved in a circular arc about the same radius as the wheel. The concave side should be positioned to face toward the wind.

On the back of each vane, rivet a rib of strip iron ½ inch thick. This strip should project about ½ inch beyond the tip and 1½ inches at the other end. There, twist and bend it to make a bracket and then bolt the vane to the center line of the rim.

The illustration above shows a side view of the motor with its gearing and supports. *A* is the rim and part of the spokes of a toothed wheel that are attached at several points to the spokes of the bicycle wheel. It is loosely fixed and adjusted until it runs well when the wheel is moved. It should not wobble. *A* drives a smaller cog, *B*, mounted on the same spindle, *a*. This spindle revolves around two plates, *PP*, screwed to *F*. *c* drives a large cog, *D*, and an eccentric, *E*, which moves the eccentric rod, *R*, up and down. This works the small pump at the foot of the mast that supports the windmill. *E* can be quickly made out of a thick disc

with two larger discs soldered to it. *R* is a piece of stout brass strip bent around *E* and closed with a screw.

When all of the vanes are in position, connect the tips of the ribs and vanes together with rings of stout wire and solder them on at all the contact points. Screw one of the spindle nuts tightly against its cone. The other end of the spindle should pass through one arm of the stirrup (*F*) made out of ½-inch iron 1½ inches wide. This is then secured by a washer and nut on the inside. The stirrup and circular plate (*V*) are bored to accommodate the end of the iron pipe (*T*).

Close off the top of the hole (*F*) and heat the top of the pipe to expand it to fit into the chamber. Clean these parts well and weld them together. It is important that the *T* is square with the stirrup. Then, cut the pipe off 9 inches below *V*. Solder a small ring to the underside of *V* to prevent moisture from working its way along *T* and ruining your motor.

The tail spar is a wooden bar 1½ x 2½ inches wide and 40 inches long. It is notched to fit the stirrup and tapered off toward the tail. A sheet of sturdy iron, 15 x 12 inches, is then fitted into the saw cut. Two bolts clip the wings of the forked end tightly against the sides of the stirrup. The tail should be able to balance the wheel on the vertical pivot to avoid stressing the joint at the top of *T*.

Wind Energy

A wind-wheel this size will spin effectively in a blustery wind but will probably only generate enough energy to power a small pump. This will do nicely to fill a watering can for your garden or for powering other light machinery.

▲ A pumping windmill.

Zoning, Permitting, and Covenant Requirements

Before you invest in or make your own small wind energy system, you should research any zoning and neighborhood covenant issues that may deter your installing a wind turbine system. You can find out about local zoning restrictions by contacting a local building inspector, board of supervisors, or planning board. They will inform you whether or not you'll need a building permit and will provide you with a list of other requirements. Further, your neighbors or homeowners' association may object to a wind machine that will block their view or a system that will be too noisy

A Pumping Windmill

A pumping windmill can help you pump water from a well or other underground reservoir into a suction-pump. This windmill has a simple wheel with spokes and sails. It consists of a hub, six spokes, a fan tail, and a trunk or pole for attaching the wheel.

The hub is a hexagon 6 x 6 inches. One spoke can be driven into a hole made on either side (Fig. 1). The spokes should be 3 feet long, 3 x 1½ inches at the hub end, and 1 x 1½ inches on the outer end. The spokes are driven into the holes in the hub and pinned to hold them in place.

The hub should be made of hard wood and the holes may be cut with a mortise chisel and mallet. Make sure the holes are spaced evenly so the spokes will light up properly.

Attach triangular pieces of twilled muslin sheeting to the face of each spoke. The loose corner of each can be attached to the next spoke end with a piece of string. This creates an outlet between the leech and the spoke of each space between the spoke so that the wind can pass through. This, in effect, makes the wheel turn.

The wheel should be held in place at the top of the supporting post by a shaft passing through the hub and bolted to the front of the wheel with a nut. Fig. 2 is a good example of what this should look like. The shaft should be about 1 inch square where it passes through the hub. At the front end, it should be tightened with a nut and washer. The square part, A, where the end of the hub will be, should be welded at B to hold the hub in the proper place. About an inch beyond the square

shoulder, another one, C, should be welded to the shaft. This helps balance the wheel.

Now a crank can be formed, 2 inches wide and 3 inches out from the shaft. Another collar, C, C, should be welded onto the crank and then, beyond this point, the shaft should stick out about 6 inches.

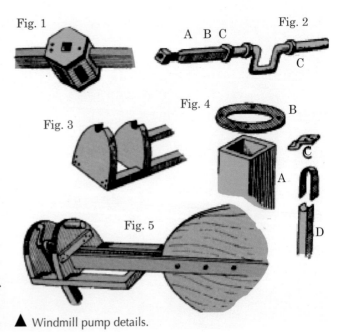

▲ Windmill pump details.

The total length of the shaft is 15 inches, and the whole device can be painted. To attach the fan tail, a head made out of two blocks of wood should be attached and fastened 5 inches apart on the lower rails (Fig. 3). The upper ends of the blocks should be cut so as to allow the shaft to enter them. The collars, *C* and *C*, *C*, are placed at the inside of the blocks. To hold the shaft in place, small iron straps can be screwed tightly over the top of each block.

This head rests on the top of a hollow square post through which the rod passes, connecting the crank with the piston-rod of the pump (Fig. 4 A). A flat iron collar, *B*, should be screwed tightly at the top. To keep the head properly secured, four iron cleats (Fig. 4 C) should be screwed tightly under the corners of the head to help grip the projecting edge of the collar. This will hold the head rigid while allowing it to move about with the force of the wind.

Apply a little bit of grease or Vaseline to the top of the collar so the head will move easily. The top of the connecting rod should be attached to the crank and bolted to the top of the hard wood rod (Fig. 4 D).

The tail, which is 33 inches long and 24 inches wide at the end, is made of boards that are ¾ inch thick. The tail should be attached to the head (Fig. 5).

To place the windmill over a pump, build a platform that is braced with pieces of wood (see the illustration). Wires can also be run from the upper part of the trunk down to pegs driven into the ground. This will add additional support and steadiness to the upright shaft.

To start the wheel, snap the ends of the sheets to the spoke ends. To stop the wheel, unsnap the ends and furl the sails around the spokes, tying them securely with a piece of yarn or a cotton cord.

What would happen if we used more wind energy?

According to the American Wind Energy Association, if we increase our nation's wind energy capacity to 20 percent by 2030, it would have the following effects:

- *Reduce Greenhouse Gas Emission:* A cumulative total of 7,600 million tons of CO_2 would be avoided by 2030, and more than 15,000 million tons of CO_2 would be avoided by 2050.
- *Conserve Water:* Reduce cumulative water consumption in the electric sector by 8 percent or 4 trillion gallons from 2007 through 2030.
- *Lower Natural Gas Prices:* Significantly reduce natural gas demand and reduce natural gas prices by 12 percent, saving consumers approximately $130 billion.
- *Expand Manufacturing:* To produce enough turbines and components for the 20 percent wind scenario, the industry would require more than 30,000 direct manufacturing jobs across the nation (assuming that 30 to 80 percent of major turbine components would be manufactured domestically by 2030).
- *Generate Local Revenues:* Lease payments for wind turbines would generate well over $600 million for landowners in rural areas and generate additional local tax revenues exceeding $1.5 billion annually by 2030. From 2007 through 2030, cumulative economic activity would exceed $1 trillion or more than $440 billion in net present value terms.

▼ The use of large scale windmills is often controversial. They can provide a significant amount of clean energy, but they also clutter ridgelines, produce a lot of noise, and hurt the bird population.

Hydropower

Water is constantly moving through a vast global cycle, evaporating from lakes and oceans, forming clouds, precipitating, and then flowing back into the ocean. The energy of this water cycle, which is mainly driven by the sun, can be tapped to produce electricity or to power machines—a process called hydropower. Hydropower uses water as a type of fuel that is neither reduced nor used up in the process. Since the water cycle is endless and will constantly recharge the system, hydropower is considered a renewable energy.

Hydropower (also known as hydroelectric power) is made when flowing water is captured and turned into electricity. There are many types of hydroelectric facilities that are all powered by the kinetic energy derived from flowing water as it moves downstream. Generators and turbines convert this energy into electricity. This is then fed into the electrical grid for use in homes, businesses, and other industries.

A Brief History of Hydropower

Humans have been using water to help them perform work for thousands of years. Water wheels have been employed for grinding grains into flour, to saw wood, and to power textile mills. The technology to use running water to create hydroelectricity has been around for over a hundred years. The modern hydropower turbine was created in the middle of the eighteenth century and developed into direct current technology. Today, an alternating current is in use and came about when the electric generator was combined with the turbine. The first hydroelectric plant in the United States was built in Appleton, Wisconsin in 1882.

▼ Diagram of a hydropower plant.

Types of Hydropower Plants

There are three types of hydropower plants:

1. Impoundment—Impoundment facilities are the most common type of hydroelectric power plants. This facility, typically a large hydropower system, uses a dam to store river water in a reservoir. Water that is released from the reservoir flows through a turbine, spinning it. This activates a generator to produce electricity. The water may be released either to meet the changing electricity needs or to maintain a constant reservoir level.
2. Diversion—A diversion facility, sometimes referred to as a run-of-river facility, channels a portion of a river through a canal or penstock. This does not always require the use of a dam.
3. Pumped storage—A pumped storage facility stores energy by pumping water from a lower reservoir to

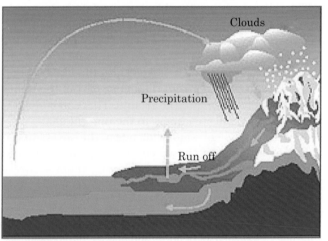

▲ Water's never ending cycle.

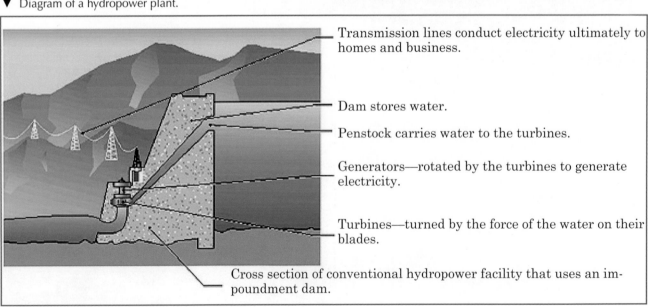

Transmission lines conduct electricity ultimately to homes and business.

Dam stores water.

Penstock carries water to the turbines.

Generators—rotated by the turbines to generate electricity.

Turbines—turned by the force of the water on their blades.

Cross section of conventional hydropower facility that uses an impoundment dam.

an upper reservoir when electricity demands are low. During times when electrical demands are high, water is then released back into the lower reservoir to generate electricity.

Some hydropower plants use dams and others do not. Many dams were originally built for other purposes and then hydropower was added at a later date. In the United States, only 2,400 of the 80,000 dams produce power—the rest are used for recreation, farm ponds, flood control, water supply, and irrigation.

enough electricity for a home, farm, or even a small village.

Hydropower Turbines

There are two main types of hydropower turbines: impulse and reaction. The type of turbine selected for a

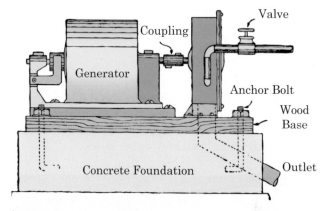

▲ Diagram of a hydroelectric motor.

Size of Hydropower Plants

Hydropower plants range in size from small and micro systems, which are operated for individual needs or to sell the power to utilities, to larger projects that produce electricity for utilities, supplying many consumers with electricity.

Micro hydropower plants have a capacity of up to 100 kilowatts. Small hydropower plants have a capacity between 100 kilowatts and 30 megawatts. Large hydropower plants have a capacity of more than 30 megawatts. The small and micro systems can produce

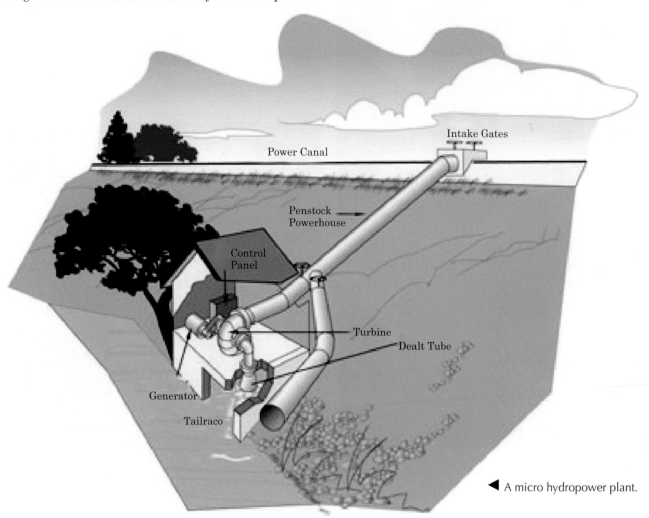

◀ A micro hydropower plant.

project is based on the height of the standing water (the "head") and the flow (volume) of the water at a particular site. It is also determined by how deep the turbine must be set, its efficiency, and its cost.

Impulse Turbine

An impulse turbine typically uses the velocity of water to move the runner and discharges to atmospheric pressure. The water stream then hits each bucket on the runner. The water flows out of the bottom of the turbine after hitting the runner. These turbines are suitable for high head, low flow applications.

Reaction Turbine

A reaction turbine generates power by the combined action of pressure and moving water. The runner is placed in the water stream, which flows over the blades instead of striking each one separately. These turbines are used for sites with lower head and higher flows.

Even a small waterfall can provide a lot of power.

Advantages of Hydropower

- It is fueled by water, making it a clean energy source.
- It does not pollute the air since it does not burn any fossil fuels.
- It is a domestic energy source.
- It relies on the water cycle and is a renewable energy source.
- It is usually available as needed.
- The water flow can be controlled through the turbine to produce energy on demand.
- The plants provide reservoirs for recreation (fishing, swimming, boating), water supply, and food control.

Disadvantages of Hydropower

- It can negatively impact fish populations by hampering fish migration upstream past dams, though there are ways to allow for passage both up- and downstream.
- It can impact the quality and flow of water, causing low dissolved oxygen levels that can negatively impact the riverbank habitats.
- The plants can be impacted by drought, and if they are not receiving adequate water, they cannot produce electricity.
- The plants compete for land use and can cause humans, plants, and animals to lose their natural habitat.

Geothermal Energy

Geothermal energy (the heat from the earth) is accessible as an alternative source of heat and power. Geothermal energy can be accessed by drilling water or steam wells using a process much like drilling for oil. This resource is enormous but is sadly underused as an energy source. When it is employed, though, it proves to be clean (emitting little or no greenhouse gases), reliable, economical, and domestically found (geothermal energy can be harnessed from almost anywhere and thus makes countries less dependent on foreign oil).

Wells a mile or more deep can be drilled into underground reservoirs to tap steam and very hot water. This can then be brought to the surface and used in a variety of ways—such as to drive turbines and electricity generators. In the United States, most geothermal reservoirs are located in the western states, in Alaska, and in Hawaii. People in more than 120 locations in the United States are using geothermal energy for space and district heating.

Geothermal resources can range from shallow ground water to hot water found in rocks several miles below the surface of the earth. It can even be harnessed, in some cases, from magma (hot molten rock near the earth's core). Geothermal reservoirs of low to moderate temperature (roughly 68 to 302°F) can be used to heat homes, offices, and greenhouses. Curiously, the dehydration of onions and garlic comprises the largest industrial use of geothermal energy in the United States.

Additional Resources

The U.S. Department of Energy, in conjunction with the Geo-Heat Center, conducts research, provides technical support, and distributes information on a wide range of geothermal direct-use applications. Some information that is provided revolves around greenhouse informational packages, cost comparisons of heat pumps, low temperature resource assessments, cost analysis for homeowners, and information directed to aquaculture developers.

The greenhouse informational package provides information for people who are looking to develop geothermal greenhouses. This package includes crop market prices for vegetables and flowers, operating costs, heating system specifications, greenhouse heating equipment selection spreadsheets, and vendor information.

Groundwater heat pumps have also been identified as offering substantial savings over other types of pump systems. Informational packets about heat pump systems are provided to answer frequently asked questions concerning the application and usage of geothermal heat pumps.

The Geo-Heat Center examined the costs associated with the installation of district heating systems in single-family residential sectors. They discovered that cost-saving areas included installation in unpaved areas, using non-insulated return lines, and installation in areas that are unencumbered by existing buried utility lines.

▼ A geothermal power plant in action.

Three Main Uses of Geothermal Energy

Some types of geothermal energy usage draw from the earth's temperatures closer to the surface and others require, as noted above, drilling miles into the earth. The three main uses of geothermal energy are:

1. Direct Use and District Heating Systems—These use hot water from springs and reservoirs near the earth's surface.
2. Electricity Generation—Typically found in power plants, this type of energy requires high-temperature water and steam (generally between 300 and 700°F). Geothermal power plants are built where reservoirs are positioned only a mile or two from the earth's surface.
3. Geothermal Heat Pumps—These use stable ground or water temperatures near the earth's surface to control building temperatures above the ground.

Direct Use Geothermal Energy

Since ancient times, people have been directly using hot water as a source of energy. The Chinese, Native Americans, and Romans used hot mineral springs for bathing, cooking, and heating purposes. Currently, a number of hot springs are still used for bathing and many people believe these hot, mineral-rich waters possess natural healing powers.

Besides bathing, the most common direct use of geothermal energy is for heating buildings. This is through district heating systems—these types of systems provide heat for roughly 95 percent of the buildings in Reykjavik, Iceland. District heating systems pipe hot water near the earth's surface directly into buildings to provide adequate heat.

Direct use of geothermal resources is a proven, economic, and clean energy option. Geothermal heat can be piped directly into facilities and used to heat

▼ You can combine solar and geothermal energy to produce more consistent power in your home.

buildings, grow greenhouse plants, heat water for fish farming, and even pasteurize milk. Some northern U.S. cities pipe hot water under roads and sidewalks to melt the snow.

Geothermal Heat Pumps

Even though temperatures above the surface of the earth change daily and seasonally, in general, temperatures in the top 10 feet of the earth's surface stay fairly constant at around 50 to 60°F. This means that, in most places, soil temperatures are typically warmer than air temperatures in the winter and cooler in the summer. Geothermal heat pumps (GHPs) use this constant temperature to heat and cool buildings. These pumps transfer heat from the ground (or underground water sources) into buildings during the winter and do the reverse process in the summer months.

Geothermal heat pumps, according to the U.S. Environmental Protection Agency (EPA), are the most energy-efficient, environmentally clean, and cost-effective systems for maintaining a consistent temperature control. These pumps are becoming more popular, even though most homes still use furnaces and air conditioners. Sometimes referred to as earth-coupled, ground-source, or water-source heat pumps, GHPs use the constant temperature of the earth as the exchange medium (using ground heat exchangers) instead of the outdoor air temperature. In this way, the system can be very efficient on cold winter nights in comparison to air-source heat pumps.

Geothermal heat pumps can heat, cool, and, in some cases, even supply hot water to a house. These pumps are relatively quiet, long-lasting, need little to no maintenance, and do not rely on outside temperatures to function effectively. While geothermal systems are initially more expensive to install, these costs are quickly returned in energy savings in about five to 10 years. Systems have a life-span of roughly 25 years for inside components and more than 50 years for ground loop systems. Each year, about 50,000 geothermal heat pumps are installed in the United States.

Types of Geothermal Heat Pump Systems

There are four basic types of ground loop heat pump systems: horizontal, vertical, pond/lake, and open-loop systems. The first three are closed-loop systems while the fourth is, as its name suggests, open-loop. The type of system used is generally determined based on the climate, soil conditions, land availability, and local installation costs of the site for the pump. All four types of geothermal heat pump systems can be used for both residential and commercial building applications.

Horizontal Heat Pump System

This closed-loop installation is extremely cost-effective for residential heat pumps and is well suited for new construction where adequate land is available for the system. Horizontal heat pump systems need 4-foot trenches to be installed. These systems are typically laid out using two pipes—one buried 6 feet and the other buried 4 feet below the ground—or by placing two pipes side by side at 5 feet underground in a 2-foot-wide trench.

▼ A horizontal closed-loop heat pump system.

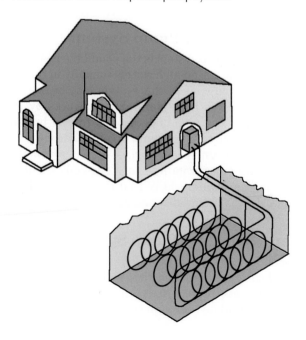

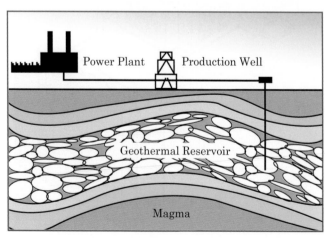

▲ A geothermal power plant.

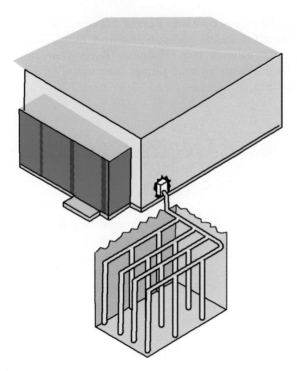

▲ A vertical closed-loop heat pump system.

Vertical Heat Pump System

Schools and larger commercial buildings use vertical heat pump systems because they require less land to be effectively used. These systems are best used where the soil is too shallow for trenching. They also minimize any disturbance to established landscaping. To install a vertical system, holes that are roughly 4 inches in diameter are drilled about 20 feet apart and 100 to 400 feet deep. Two pipes are inserted into these holes and are connected at the bottom with a U-bend, forming a loop. The vertical loops are then connected with a horizontal pipe, placed in the trenches, and connected to the heat pump in the building.

Pond/Lake Heat Pump System

Another closed-loop system is the pond/lake heat pump system. If a site has enough water—usually in the form of a pond or even a lake—this system may be the most cost-effective. This heat pump system works by running a supply line pipe underground from a building to the water source. The piping is coiled into circles no less than 8 feet under the surface—this prevents the water in the pipes from freezing. The coils should be placed only in a water source that meets the minimum volume, depth, and quality criteria.

Open-Loop Heat Pump System

An open-loop system uses well or surface body water as the heat exchange fluid that will circulate directly through the geothermal heat pump system. Once this water has circulated through the system, it is returned

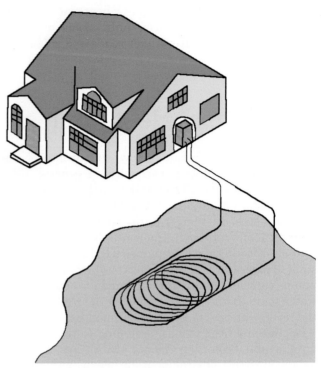

▲ A closed-loop pond/lake heat pump system.

to the ground through a recharge well or as surface discharge. The system is really only practical where there is a sufficient supply of clean water. Local codes and regulations for proper groundwater discharge must also be met in order for the heat pump system to be utilized.

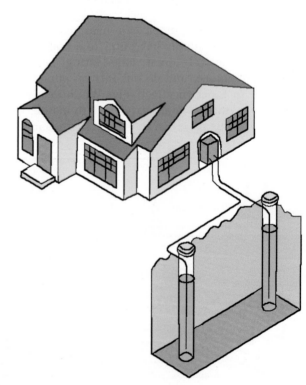

▲ An open-loop heat pump system.

Selecting and Installing a Geothermal Heat Pump System in Your Home

The heating efficiency of commercial ground-source and water-source heat pumps is indicated by their coefficient of performance (COP)—the ratio of heat provided in Btu per Btu of energy input. The cooling efficiency is measured by the energy efficiency ratio (EER)—the ratio of heat removed to the electricity required (in watts) to run the unit. Many geothermal heat pump systems are approved by the U.S. Department of Energy as being energy efficient products and so, if you are thinking of purchasing and installing this type of system, you may want to check to see if there is any special financing or incentives for purchasing energy efficient systems.

Evaluating Your Site

Before installing a geothermal heat pump, consider the site that will house the system. The presence of hot geothermal fluid containing low mineral and gas content, shallow aquifers for producing the fluid, space availability on your property, proximity to existing transmission lines, and availability of make-up water for evaporative cooling are all factors that will determine if your site is good for geothermal electric development. As a rule of thumb, geothermal fluid temperature should be no less than 300°F.

In the western United States, Alaska, and Hawaii, hydrothermal resources (reservoirs of steam or hot water) are more readily available than the rest of the country. However, this does not mean that geothermal heat cannot be used throughout the country. Shallow ground temperatures are relatively constant throughout the United States and this means that energy can be tapped almost anywhere in the country by using geothermal heat pumps and direct-use systems.

To determine the best type of ground loop systems for your site, you must assess the geological, hydrological, and spatial characteristics of your land to choose the best, most effective heat pump system to heat and cool your home:

1. Geology—This includes the soil and rock composition and properties on your site. These can affect the transfer rates of heat in your particular system. If you have soil with good heat transfer properties, your system will require less piping to obtain a good amount of heat from the soil. Furthermore, the amount of soil that is available also contributes to which system you will choose. For example, areas that have hard rock or shallow soil will most likely benefit from a vertical heat pump system instead of a system requiring large and deep trenches, such as the horizontal heat pump system.

2. Hydrology—This refers to the availability of ground or surface water, which will affect the type of system to be installed. Factors such as depth, volume, and water quality will help determine if surface water bodies can be used as a source of water for an open-loop heat pump system or if they would work best with a pond/lake system. Before installing an open-loop system, however, it is best to determine your site's hydrology so potential problems (such as aquifer depletion or groundwater contamination) can be avoided.

3. Available land—The acreage and layout of your land, as well as your landscaping and the location of underground utilities, also play an important part in the type of heat pump system you choose. If you are building a new home, horizontal ground loops are an economical system to install. If you have an existing home and want to convert your heat and cooling to geothermal energy, vertical heat pump systems are best to minimize the disturbance to your existing landscaping and yard.

Installing the Heat Pumps

Geothermal heat pump systems are somewhat difficult to install on your own—though it can certainly be done. Before you begin any digging, contact your local utility company to avoid digging into gas pipes or electrical wires.

The ground heat exchanger in a geothermal heat pump system is made up of closed- or open-loop pipe—depending on which type of system you've determined

▼ A vertical closed-loop system.

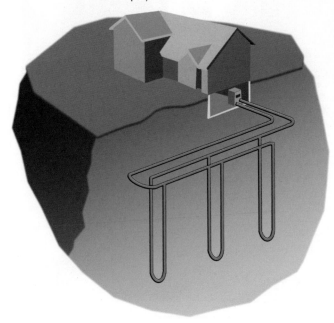

is best suited for your site. Since most systems employed are closed-loop systems, high density polyethylene pipe is used and buried horizontally at 4 to 6 feet deep or vertically at 100 to 400 feet deep. These pipes are filled with an environmentally friendly antifreeze/water solution that acts as a heat exchanger. You can find this at your local home store or contact a contractor to see where it is distributed. This solution works in the winter by extracting heat from the earth and carrying it into the building. In the summertime,

the system reverses, taking heat from the building and depositing it into the ground.

Air delivery ductwork will distribute the hot or cold air throughout the house's ductwork like traditional, conventional systems. An air handler—a box that contains the indoor coil and fan—should be installed to move the house air through the heat pump system. The air handler contains a large blower and a filter, just like standard air conditioning units.

Cost-Efficiency of Geothermal Heat Pump Systems

By installing and using a geothermal heat pump system, you will save on the costs of operating and maintaining your heating and cooling system. While these systems are generally a bit pricier to install, they prove to be more efficient and thus save you money on a monthly and yearly basis. Especially in the colder winter months, geothermal heat pump systems can reduce your heating costs by about half. Annual energy savings by using a geothermal heat pump system range from 30 to 60 percent.

▼ The hot springs at Yellowstone are a natural example of geothermal heating.

Benefits of Using Geothermal Energy

- It is clean energy. Geothermal energy does not require the burning of fossil fuels (coal, gas, or oil) to produce energy.
- Geothermal fields produce only about ⅙th of the carbon dioxide that natural gas-fueled power plants do. They also produce little to no sulfur-bearing gases, which reduces the amount of acid rain.
- It is available at any time of day, all year-round.
- Geothermal power is homegrown, which reduces dependence on foreign oil.
- It is a renewable source of energy. Geothermal energy derives its source from an almost unlimited amount of heat generated by the earth. And even if energy is limited in an area, the volume

taken out can be reinjected, making it a sustainable source of energy.

- Geothermal heat pump systems use 25 to 50 percent less electricity than conventional heating and cooling systems. They reduce energy consumption and emissions between 44 and 72 percent and improve humidity control by maintaining about 50 percent relative humidity indoors (GHPs are very effective for humid parts of the country).
- Heat pump systems can be "zoned" to allow different parts of your home to be heated and cooled to different temperatures without much added cost or extra space required.
- Geothermal heat pump systems are durable and reliable. Underground piping can last for 25 to 50 years and the heat pumps tend to last at least 20 years.
- Heat pump systems reduce noise pollution since they have no outside condensing unit (like air conditioners).

Alternate "Geothermal" Cooling System

True geothermal energy systems can be very expensive to install and you may not be able to use one in your home at this time. However, here is a fun alternative way to use the concepts of geothermal systems to keep your house cooler in the summer and your air conditioning bills lower. All you need are a basement, small window fan, and dehumidifier.

Your basement is a wonderful example of how the top layers of earth tend to remain at a stable temperature throughout the year. In the winter, your basement may feel somewhat warm; in the summer, it's nice and refreshingly cool. This is due to the temperature of the soil permeating through the basement walls. And this cool basement air can be used to effectively reduce the temperature in your home by up to five degrees during the summer months. Here are the steps to your alternative "geothermal" cooling system:

1. Run the dehumidifier in your basement during the night, bringing the humidity down to about 60 percent.
2. Keep your blinds and curtains closed in the sunniest rooms in your home.
3. In the morning, when the temperature inside the house reaches about 77°F, open a small window in your basement, just a crack, and open one of the upstairs windows, placing a small fan in it and directing the room air out of the window.
4. With all other windows and outside doors closed, the fan will suck the cool basement air through your home and out the open window. Doing this for about an hour will bring down the temperature inside your home, buying you a couple of hours of reprieve before switching on the AC.

▲ Composting toilets are being used more frequently in parks around the world.

Composting Toilets

Toilets come in three common varieties: siphon-jet flush valve toilets (common in most homes), pressurized tank toilets, and gravity flow. These toilets, generally speaking, use up large amounts of water and the waste is flushed into a sewer system and then dumped in a variety of locations. Composting toilets require little to no water, which provides a solution to sanitation and environmental problems in areas that are rural, without sewers, and in the suburbs throughout the world. Although composting toilets are rare in private homes—they are generally found in park facilities and small highway rest stops—these waterless toilets can be utilized by the regular homeowner.

It is astonishing that Americans flush about 4.8 billion gallons of water down toilets every day, according to the U.S. Environmental Protection Agency. Just replacing all existing U.S. toilets with 1.6-gallon-per-flush, ultra-low-flow (ULF) models would save about 5,500 gallons of water per person per year! So, if you are unable to install a composting toilet in your home or on your property, you may choose to install ULF models in your home to help conserve water usage.

▲ Diagram of a composting toilet.

The Basics of the Composting Toilet

Composting (or biological) toilet systems contain and process excrement, toilet paper, carbon additive, and, at times, food wastes. These systems rely on unsaturated conditions where aerobic bacteria break down waste—unlike septic systems—much like a compost heap for your gardening necessities. The resulting soil-like material—humus—must be buried or removed. It's a good idea to check state and local regulations regarding proper handling methods.

In many parts of the country, public health officials are realizing that there is a definite need for environmentally sound human waste treatment and recycling methods, and compost toilets are an easy way to work toward these needs. Because they don't require any water, composting toilets are ideal for remote areas and places that have high water tables, shallow soil, and rough terrain. These systems save water and allow for valuable plant nutrients to be recycled in the process.

There are a few key components for establishing a composting toilet:
- Composting reactor that is connected to a micro-flush toilet
- Screened air inlet and exhaust system to remove odors and heat, plus CO_2 and other decomposition byproducts
- Mechanism to provide proper ventilation that will help aerobic organisms in the compost heap
- Process controls
- Access door for the removal of the end product

It is important that the composting toilet separates the solid from the liquid waste and produces a humus-like material with less than 200 MPN per gram of fecal coliform. The compost chamber can be solar or electrically heated to maintain the right temperature for year-round use and bacterial decomposition.

Main Objective of the Composting Toilet

These systems are designed to contain, immobilize, and destroy pathogens. This reduces the risk of human infection and ensures that the toilets do not pollute the environment. If done correctly, the composted material can be handled with little to no risk of harming the individual working with it.

A composting toilet consists of a well-ventilated container that breeds a good environment for unsaturated, moist human excrement that can be decomposed under sanitary conditions. A composting toilet can be large or small, depending on the space and its use. Organic matter is transformed into a humus-like product through the natural breaking down from bacteria and fungi. Most systems like this use the process of continuous composting, which includes a single chamber where the excrement is added to the top and the end product is taken from the bottom.

Advantages of Using a Composting Toilet

Composting toilets can be used practically anywhere a flush toilet can be. They are most likely to be used in homes in rural areas, seasonal cabins, recreation areas, and other places where flush toilets are either unnecessary or impractical. They are more cost-effective than establishing a central sewage system and there is no water wasted. These systems—since they aren't using copious amounts of water—also reduce the quantity of wastewater that is disposed of on a daily basis. These toilets can also be used to recycle and compost food wastes, thus reducing the amount of household garbage that is dumped every day. Finally, these toilet systems are beneficial to the environment as they divert nutrient and pathogen-containing effluent from the soil, surface water, and the groundwater.

Disadvantages of Using a Composting Toilet

Composting toilets are a big responsibility; the owner of a composting toilet must be committed to maintaining the system. Removing the compost can be unpleasant if the toilet is not properly set up and they could end up having odor issues.

Successful Management of the Composting Toilet

Composting toilets do not require highly trained people to deal with the sewage as it is relatively harmless to handle. But be sure to maintain your composting toilet so it can be effective and safe. Some composting toilets may need organic bulking agents added to aid

Factors That Affect the Rate of Composting

1. Microorganisms—A mix of bacteria and fungi need to be present in order for the excrement to turn into composted material.
2. Moisture—This helps the microorganisms to make simpler compounds before they are metabolized. Moisture should be kept between 40 and 70 percent.
3. pH—The best pH for the composting toilet material should be between 6.5 and 7.5.
4. Carbon to nitrogen ratio—It is important to balance out the nitrogen found in urine with added carbon in your composting toilet.
5. Proper care—Managing your composting toilet well will help keep it efficient and productive.

the composting process. Adding grass clippings, sawdust, and leaves to your composting toilet reservoir will help aid the process. The end product should be removed every three months for smaller systems and, if composted correctly, should not smell and should not be toxic to humans or animals. Be sure to dispose of the waste materials in accordance with your particular state and local regulations.

Making Your Own Composting Toilet

Building your own composting toilet can be inexpensive and takes only a short amount of time to assemble. To construct a composting toilet, you will need the following materials:
- Two or three 5-gallon buckets with lids
- A standard toilet seat (a used one will work just fine) with lid
- ¾ x 3 x 18-inch plywood sheets
- Boards to be cut and used for the sides of the toilet box and for the legs
- Two hinges
- Screws
- Saw and measuring tape
- Bag of sawdust, to be used for soaking up excess moisture in the composting bucket

To begin, cut a hole in one of the pieces of plywood so that it fits the size of the bucket. Then, attach the pieces of plywood together using the hinges. Build a box with the boards and then screw in the solid piece of plywood to the box, allowing for the part

Composting Toilets

with the hole to remain on the top. Attach legs to the box, allowing the bucket to lift just slightly above the hole cut in the top piece of plywood. Then, attach the toilet seat to the plywood top, fitting it securely over the rim of the bucket. Finally, stain or paint the entire composting toilet so it will last longer and match the décor of your bathroom.

Before using your homemade composting toilet, sprinkle 1 to 2 inches of sawdust into the bottom of the bucket. This will help absorb extra moisture and will also add a necessary carbon element that is useful in composting. Sprinkle sawdust into the toilet after each use to facilitate the composting process and to minimize odors. When the first bucket is full, remove and cover (allowing the composting process to continue), insert another bucket, and continue use. When both buckets are full, remove them to your composting pile in your yard. Make a small indent in the center of your composting pile and dump the new compost into the depression, laying old compost and other organic materials on top of the new addition. If used properly, your composting toilet will be odorless and your compost will be rich and ready for use in your garden.

▲ Compost will enrich the soil in your garden to help grow healthier plants.

Greywater

Greywater is just wastewater. Greywater, however, does not include toilet wastewater, which is known as blackwater. These two different kinds of water should not be mixed together for basic health reasons. The main differences between greywater and blackwater are:

- Greywater contains less nitrogen than blackwater (and about half of the nitrogen that is found in greywater is organic nitrogen that can be filtered out and used by plants).
- Greywater contains fewer pathogens than blackwater and thus is not as likely to spread organisms that could be potentially harmful to humans.
- Greywater decomposes faster than blackwater and is less likely to cause water pollution because of this factor.

Greywater is not necessarily sewage to begin with, but if left untreated for a couple of days, it will become like blackwater and thus will be unusable. Therefore, it is important to know how best to treat and manage greywater so it can be successfully and safely reused. Much of the material in this section is adapted from Carl R. Lindstrom's excellent site, www.greywater.com.

What is Greywater?

Simply speaking, greywater is wash water—bath, dish, and laundry water that is free from toilet waste and garbage disposal remnants. Greywater, when it is managed properly, can be useful for growing things in your garden or yard. Greywater, in effect, is an excellent source of nutrients for plants when used properly.

Greywater Irrigation Systems

The practice of irrigating with greywater is common in areas where the water supply is short. To have effective greywater irrigation that successfully utilizes the nutrients in the greywater, take precautions before using it in irrigation.

Planning a greywater system requires either an assumption that the system is right for you and your family or an understanding that the system is needed for the house independent of who lives in it.

To assess whether your household could benefit from a greywater system, take inventory of all the sources of greywater in the house. Look at how many gallons of water you use, per person, per day, when doing the laundry, running the dishwasher, and taking a bath or shower, and then add up these numbers. Remember that the typical washing machine uses 30 gallons of water per cycle, a dishwasher uses between 3 and 5 gallons per cycle, and simply washing your hands and brushing your teeth daily wastes about 1 to 5 gallons of water per day. If you were able to recycle and reuse all of that wasted water, you can effectively reduce the amount of water consumption your family has every day and every year.

Once you've decided to use your greywater, check with your local authorities to see if there are any state or local regulations for greywater usage in your area. Once you have the go-ahead to proceed, you can begin reusing your greywater to the benefit of your garden and household.

Aerobic Pretreatment

This type of greywater treatment is suitable for shower, hand-washing, and laundry water. Aerobic pretreatment is a stretch filter technique that removes large particles and fibers to protect the pipes from clogging and transfers the greywater into a biologically active, aerobic soil-zone environment. Here, microorganisms can survive and flourish. Stretch filters retain fibers and large particles and allow the rest of the materials to travel to the next processing stage. The filter is good for sinks and showers at public water facilities.

Anaerobic to Aerobic Pretreatment

If you have food waste entering the water system from dishwashers and kitchen sinks, this is the better option

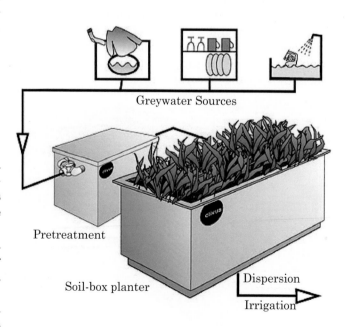

Greywater Sources

Pretreatment

Soil-box planter

Dispersion

Irrigation

▲ Greywater irrigation.

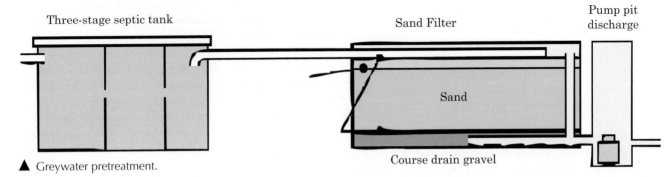

▲ Greywater pretreatment.

for treating your greywater. This system should have a three-stage septic tank to separate the sludge and grease from the water. This waste can then be removed easily. The outgoing water will be anaerobic and will need a sand filter to restore the aerobic conditions to the greywater. The final treatment leads the purified water to be treated in a planter bed. The system, while not inexpensive, is effective and is simple to maintain. A plan for this system can be seen above.

Planter Soil Box

Since 1975, soil boxes have been used to purify greywater. When using a soil box, however, it is vital that the planter bed be well drained to prevent water-logged zones from forming. Therefore, the bottom of the soil box should contain a layer of polyethylene pea gravel to provide for effective drainage. A layer of plastic mosquito netting should be placed over the gravel to prevent the layer of coarse sand from falling through. Atop the coarse sand should be a layer of concrete-mix sand and the top 2 feet should consist of humus-rich topsoil. Clay soils should not be used in soil boxes as they do not effectively allow water to pass through and drain.

Pressure infiltration pipes should be designed to allow for the even distribution of water in both level and uneven terrain. These pipes are easy to clean and should be placed on the soil surface after planting. Then, they should be covered by a 2- to 4-inch layer of

wood chip mulch. The pressure infiltration pipes consist of two concentric pipes that expand slightly due to the water pressure when the system is turned on. This causes the water to run out along the slot at the bottom of the soil box. When the water pressure is turned off, this causes the sleeve to close and prevents worms, insects, and roots from entering and clogging the pipe.

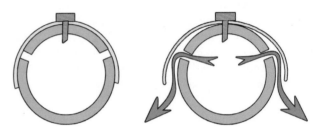

▲ Piping can usually be found in 5-foot sections.

Gravity/Pressure Leaching Chambers

Leaching chambers can be successful in loading and receiving 2.4 gallons per square foot per day of greywater from a three-bedroom home. Using half of a PVC pipe that is 6 inches in diameter, this leaching chamber can be placed within a trench on a 1- to 2-inch mesh plastic netting to prevent the walls from sinking into the soil. No pre-filtration is used in these chambers. All that

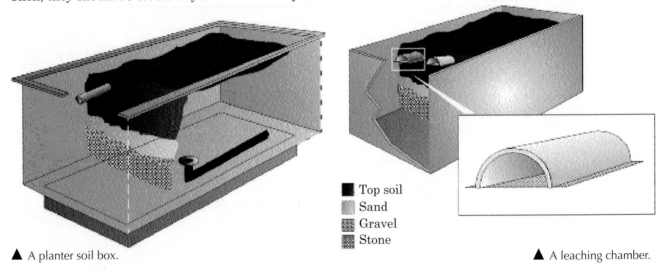

■ Top soil
  Sand
  Gravel
  Stone

▲ A planter soil box.

▲ A leaching chamber.

is required is a dosing pump chamber to pump every eight hours. The trench should have a minimum surface area of about 100 square feet—this will allow for a loading rate of around 2 to 2½ gallons per square foot per day for an average-sized home.

Gravity and Automatic Switch

The illustration below shows an example of an automatic switch system from a shallow leach chamber to one that is below the frost line—an important feature of any greywater system in the northern United States. If a shallow trench freezes and becomes clogged with ice, the water will back up and spill over into the pipe to the deeper, below-the-frost-line trench. It is worth noting that greywater is typically warmer than combined sewage and that the shallow leach zones that are operating in your system tend to stay freer of ice for longer periods of time than in places with combined waste water.

Automatic switching using pump pressure is different from gravity pressure switching. In an automatic switch system, a loop must be arranged indoors where the pressure needed for the shallow infiltration is normally lower than the pressure required to force the

water up to the top of the loop. The top of the loop must, then, be no higher than the shut-off head of the pump. About 3 feet of water is a good margin for this system. The system can also be designed to be switched manually by the opening and closing of the valves that feed the different zones and levels of the greywater box.

Options for Using Greywater in Cold Weather

Throughout New England, there are several greywater-irrigated greenhouses that feature a combination of automatically irrigated and fertilized growing beds that provide effective greywater treatment. Since these greenhouses are found in colder, northern states, it is important that these soil beds be deeper to store heat from both the sun and the greywater.

The greenhouse shown here provides enough salad greens for a family of four to six people throughout the long, cold northeastern winters. Growing broccoli, spinach, lettuce, mustard greens, and sorrel in these colder-climate greywater systems can be effective and profitable. To facilitate better distribution of greywater

▼ An active cooling/passive heating greywater irrigated greenhouse.

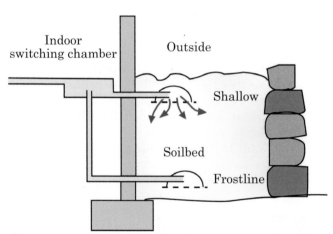

▲ An automatic switch system.

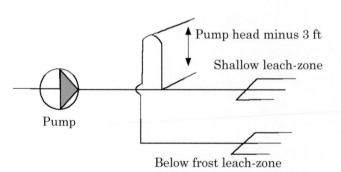

▲ About 3 feet of water is a good margin for this automatic switch system.

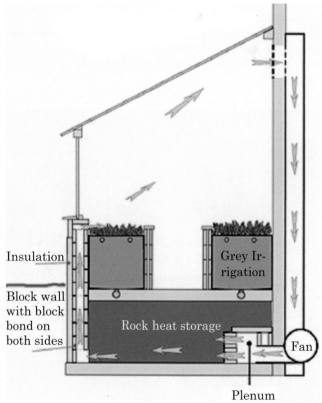

in the soil bed, a pipe-loop system can also be simply constructed to feed the bed from both sides.

Outdoor Planters

There are many variations of outdoor raised soil beds that are effective in replacing the soil needed for successful leach field treatment of greywater. Houses on ledges or in very sandy soils can be fitted with masonry soil boxes that serve to build up the site's soil profile. Such a strategy has been used in mounds or evapo-transpiration beds (a name derived from the assumption that all of the water will evaporate to the atmosphere even in wet and cold climates).

In parts of the country where construction density makes it very difficult to build a large mound or to locate planters for treating a significant volume of greywater, two adjacent neighbors can agree to build property dividers and plant hedges in their leaching area. This alternative combines privacy, landscaping aesthetics, and good environmental protection. Greywater gardens offer the added benefit of being able to garden at a higher elevation and in a raised garden bed.

Outdoor planters will have a less effective treatment during the winter seasons and during deep freezes. Yet, when relatively warm greywater is injected into the soil, increased biological activity as well as warming of the soil tends to keep the injection area unfrozen for longer periods of time than the surrounding area. Raised beds or planters can also be ideal for compost bins in the fall. The decomposing leaves and grasses act as an insulator as well as a composting fuel source that further insures that the soil beneath does not go into a deep freeze.

From greywater filter

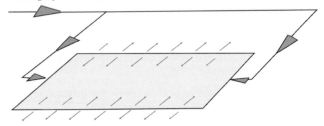

▲ An injector pipe fork in the soil bed. Use 1-inch piping and drill ¼-inch holes on each side. Cover with canvas and a layer of soil to hide the pipe arrangement.

Shallow Subsoil Irrigation

This type of irrigation (2 to 6 inches below the soil level) is preferable to surface irrigation when these factors are in play:

- The water used is "grey" (neither clean nor free of salts)
- The irrigation system is located in a high evaporation locale with water shortages
- It is desired to produce leaf or garden waste compost quickly
- Selective irrigation is needed (for a flower border, shrub, bush, tree, etc.)
- You want to automatically irrigate a drained planter indoors or outdoors

◀ Greywater is especially useful in areas that are very dry.

Part Six

Crafts

"Crafts make us feel rooted, give us a sense of belonging, and connect us with our history. Our ancestors used to create these crafts out of necessity, and now we do them for fun, to make money and to express ourselves."

—*Phyllis George*

"The artist must create a spark before he can make a fire and before art is born, the artist must be ready to be consumed by the fire of his own creation."

—*Auguste Rodin*

Many people think of arts and crafts as something involving markers and construction paper that the kids do at summer camp. Certainly, the creativity that children express with scissors, tape, colored pencils, or clay is at the heart of crafting, but there's more to it than that. Most craft projects done for pleasure now were once done out of necessity—making candles, soaps, or baskets, for example—and many are still useful today. Beyond that, making things with your hands can be soothing, stimulating, or even enlightening, depending on the project and your frame of mind. Many people find knitting especially relaxing, and potters often discover within their art philosophical principles of intentionality, change, flexibility, and acceptance. In addition, crafting can become a lucrative and fulfilling business; handmade items are sought-after gifts and can be sold for significantly more than their factory-produced counterparts. In these pages you'll find an introduction to several diverse forms of crafting, from making soap and candles to kites and boomerangs. Use the directions, descriptions, and images as a jumping-off point for your own creative endeavors, altering the projects as you're inspired to create one-of-a-kind pieces to use, give away, or sell . . . or just because they're fun to do.

3. In a large pot, start to boil water. Before putting the dipping container full of wax into the larger pot, place a small trivet, rack, or other elevating device into the bottom of the larger pot. This will keep the dipping container from touching the bottom of the larger pot and will prevent the wax from burning and possibly combusting.

4. Put the dipping container into the pot and start to melt the wax, keeping a thermometer in the wax at all times. The wax should be heated and melted between 150 and 165°F. Stir frequently to keep the chunks of paraffin from burning and to ensure all the wax is thoroughly melted. (If you want to add fragrance or dye, do so when the wax is completely melted and stir until the additives are dissolved.)

5. Once your wax is completely melted, it's time to start the dipping process. Removing the container from the stove, take your wick that's tied

onto a stick and dip it into the wax, leaving it there for a few minutes. Continue to lower the wick in and out of the dipping container, and by the eighth or ninth dip, cut off the weight from the bottom of the wick—the candle should be heavy enough now to dip well on its own.

6. To speed up the cooling process—and to help the wax continue to adhere and build up on the wick—blow on the hot wax each time you lift the candle out of the dipping pot.

7. When the candle is at the desired length and thickness, you may want to lay it down on a very smooth surface (such as a countertop) and gently roll it into shape.

8. On a drying rack (which can be made from a box long enough so the candles do not touch the bottom or from another device), carefully hang your taper candle to dry for a good 24 hours.

9. Once the candle is completely hardened, trim the wick to just above the wax.

Jarred Soy Candles

Soy candles are environmentally friendly and easy candles to make. You can find most of the ingredients

Handmade Candles

and materials needed to make soy candles at your local arts and crafts store—or even in your own kitchen!

Materials
1 lb soy wax (either in bars or flakes)
1 ounce essential oil (for fragrance)
Natural dye (try using dried and powdered beets for red, turmeric for yellow, or blueberries for blue)

Supplies
Stove
Pan to heat wax (a double boiler is best)
Spoon
Glass thermometer
Candle wick (you can find this at your local arts and crafts store)
Metal washers
Pencils or chopsticks
Heatproof cup to pour your melted wax into the jar(s)
Jar to hold the candle (jelly jars or other glass jars work well)

Directions
1. Put the wax in a pan or a double boiler and heat it slowly over medium heat. Heat the wax to 130 to 140°F or until it's completely melted.
2. Remove the wax from the heat. Add the essential oil and dye (optional) and stir into the melted wax until completely dissolved.
3. Allow the wax to cool slightly, until it becomes cloudy.
4. While the wax is cooling, prepare your wick in the glass container. It is best to have a wick with a metal disk on the end—this will help stabilize it while the candle is hardening. If your wick does not already have a metal disk at the end, you can easily attach a thin metal washer to the end of the wick, tying a knot until the wick can no longer pass through the washer. Position the wick in the glass container and, using a pencil or chopstick, wrap the excess wick around the middle and then, laying the pencil or chopstick on the rim of the container, position the wick so it falls in the center.
5. Using a heatproof cup or the container from the double boiler, carefully pour the cloudy wax into the glass container, being careful not to disturb the wick from the center.
6. Allow the candle to dry for at least 24 hours before cutting off the excess wick and using.

▲ Jelly jars work well for poured candles.

Making Your Own Soap

Making your own soap can be a very rewarding process. It does, however, require a good amount of time, patience, and caution, because you'll be using some caustic and potentially dangerous ingredients—the main one being lye (sodium hydroxide). It is important, whenever you are making soap, that you are careful to avoid coming into direct contact with the lye. Wear goggles, rubber gloves, and long sleeves, and work in a well-ventilated area. Be sure, as well, that you never breathe in the fumes produced by the lye and water mixture.

Soap is made up of three main ingredients: water, lye, and fats or oils. While lard and tallow were once used exclusively for making soaps, it is perfectly acceptable to use a combination of pure oils for the "fat" needed to make soap. For these ingredients to become soap, they must go through a process called saponification, in which the mixture becomes completely blended and the chemical reactions between the lye and the oils, over time, turn the mixture into a hardened bar of usable soap.

Once you've become comfortable with the basic soap-making process, you can experiment with adding different colored dyes, essential oils, and other ingredients to make a personalized and interesting bar of soap—perfect for your own use or for giving as a gift.

Basic Recipe for Cold-Pressed Soap

Ingredients
6.9 ounces lye (sodium hydroxide)
2 cups distilled water, cold (from the refrigerator is the best)
2 cups canola oil
2 cups coconut oil
2 cups palm oil

Supplies
Goggles, gloves, and mask to wear while making the soap
Mold for the soap (a cake or bread loaf pan will work just fine; you can also find flexible plastic molds at your local arts and crafts store)
Plastic wrap or wax paper to line the molds
Glass bowl to mix the lye and water
Wooden spoon for mixing
2 thermometers (one for the lye and water mixture and one for the oil mixture)
Stainless steel or cast iron pot for heating oils and mixing in lye mixture
Handheld stick blender (optional)

Directions
1. Put on the goggles and gloves and make sure you are working in a well-ventilated room.

Making Your Own Soap

2. Ready your mold(s) by lining with plastic wrap or wax paper. Set them aside.

3. Add the lye to the cold, distilled water in a glass bowl (*never* add the water to the lye) and stir continually for at least a minute, or until the lye is completely dissolved. Place one thermometer into the glass bowl and allow the mixture to cool to around 110°F (the chemical reaction of the lye mixing with the water will cause it to heat up quickly at first).

4. While the lye is cooling, combine the oils in a pot on medium heat and stir well until they are melted together. Place a thermometer into the pot and allow the mixture to cool to 110°F.

5. Carefully pour the lye mixture into the oil mixture (make sure you pour the lye solution in a small, steady stream), stirring continuously so that the lye and oils mix properly. Continue stirring, either by hand (which can take a very long time) or with a handheld stick blender, until the mixture traces (has the consistency of thin pudding). This may take anywhere from 30 to 60 minutes or more, so just be patient. It is well worth the time invested to make sure your mixture traces.

▲ You can pour your soap into molds, use stamps, or carve the finished bars to make them unique.

If it doesn't trace all the way, it will not saponify correctly and your soap will be ruined.

6. Once your mixture has traced, pour carefully into the mold(s) and let sit for a few hours. Then, when the mixture is still soft but congealed enough not to melt back into itself, cut the soap with a table knife into bars. Let sit for a few days, then take the bars out of the mold(s) and place on brown paper (grocery bags are perfect) in a dark area. Allow the bars to cure for another 4 weeks or so before using.

If you want your soap to be colored, add special soap-coloring dyes (you can find these at the local arts and crafts store) after the mixture has traced, stirring them in. Or try making your own dyes using herbs, flowers, or spices.

To make a yummy-smelling bar of soap, add a few drops of your favorite essential oils (such as lavender, lemon, or rose) after the tracing of the mixture and stir in. You can also add aloe and vitamin E at this point to make your soap softer and more moisturizing.

To add texture and exfoliating properties to your soap, you can stir some oats into the traced mixture, along with some almond essential oil or a dab of honey.

This will not only give your soap a nice, pumice-like quality but it will also smell wonderful. Try adding bits of lavender, rose petals, or citrus peel to your soap for variety.

To make soap in different shapes, pour your mixture into molds instead of making them into bars. For round soaps, you can take a few bars of soap you've just made, place them into a resealable plastic bag, and warm them by putting the bag into hot water (120°F) for 30 minutes. Then, cut the bars up and roll them into balls. These soaps should set in about an hour or so.

Natural Dyes for Soap or Candles

Light/Dark Brown	Cinnamon, ground cloves, allspice, nutmeg, coffee
Yellow	Turmeric, saffron, calendula petals
Green	Liquid chlrophyll, alfalfa, cucumber, sage, nettles
Red	Annatto extract, beets, grapeskin extract
Blue	Red cabbage
Purple	Alkanet root

Potpourri From Your Garden

Rose petals and sweet geranium leaves are the primary ingredients in most potpourri. Other additions to potpourri include lavender, sweet verbena leaves, bay leaves, rosemary, dried orange peels, and orrisroot powder. You can also experiment by adding spices to give your potpourri an extra "punch" (such as cinnamon or pine needles for Christmas potpourri batches).

Types of Potpourri

There are two types of potpourri: dry and moist. Dry potpourri is much easier to make: simply combine fully dried flowers and a fixative such as orrisroot, spices or seeds for fragrance, and essential oils as desired. Moist potpourri is a bit more difficult to make, as the ingredients must be made limp and leathery but not too wet or too dry, but the result will be a much more fragrant potpourri. Trial and error is really the only way to get the ingredients to the perfect consistency for moist potpourri. When you do have the ingredients at the perfect state of moistness, pack them tightly into jars and add a bit of salt to retain the right amount of dampness and to preserve the potpourri from any mold or decomposition.

▲ Dried apple slices and cinnamon sticks make a festive potpourri.

Preparing Ingredients for Moist Potpourri

Rose Petals

Rose petals should be in full bloom when picked, not faded or marred in any way, and should be thoroughly dried out. Roses tend to hold water well, so it's best to harvest the rose petals on a warm, sunny, dry day.

Cut a handful of roses (or buy a few at your garden center or farmers' market). Lay out the roses on a cloth in a dry, shady place and begin to pluck off the petals, separating any that tend to stick together.

Leave the separated petals on the cloth for two to three days so they lose their moisture and begin to dry out. Once they are shriveled to about half their size, they are ready to be jarred. A cylinder-shaped jar is best, as the petals need to be pressed and laid out flat, one on top of another. Once two handfuls or so of petals are in the jar, sprinkle a mixture of sea salt and kitchen salt (equal parts of each) over the petals. Continue adding handfuls of petals into the jar and sprinkling with the salt mixture. When all the petals are in the jar, place a heavy object (a heavy washer or rock) on top of the petals and close the jar. Now your petals can wait until you are ready to combine them with other fragrant petals and spices into a jar of potpourri.

Sweet Geranium Petals

Follow the same process as for preparing rose petals for potpourri, except be sure to take the petals off their stalks before they are dried and tear each large petal into three or four smaller pieces. Lay the petals out to dry as with the rose petals, and then pack them into a small jar with a mixture of salt as well.

Sweet Verbena, Bay Leaves, and Rosemary

Sweet verbena, bay leaves, and rosemary all dry extremely quickly, so they can be jarred immediately after being picked. Remember to layer the leaves and sprinkle with the salt mixture and press each kind as you would for rose petals.

Orange Peels

Remove peel from the orange and cut it into pieces half an inch wide and two inches long. Poke holes into these pieces and stick a shaft of clove into each, so the clove heads are nearly touching one another. Pack these strips into a jar and sprinkle the salt mixture over each layer and on the top.

Once your various ingredients are in jars, it is best to leave them there for a little while, even for a few months if you want. The petals, leaves, and orange peels will retain their fragrance and will even become more pungent the longer you leave them in the jars.

Adding Spices and Orrisroot to Your Potpourri

To enhance the fragrance of your potpourri, add spices and orrisroot (if available) to your final mixture. Gather violet powder (this will enhance the smell of the orrisroot but is not necessary), ground allspice, ground cloves, ground mixed spice, ground mace, whole mace, and/or whole cloves. How much potpourri you intend to make will determine how much of the spices you use—but experiment and see what works best.

Mixing Together Your Potpourri

Gather all of your various jars of petals, leaves, and orange peels and any spice mixtures you've created and clear a large spot on your counter or a tabletop.

▲ Display your potpourri in a pretty bowl or a pen jar.

Once you have all your ingredients, dump handfuls of each item and spices onto the countertop or table and mix them together by hand. Depending on how much potpourri you intend to place in a box, jar, or sachet, you will combine as many of the ingredients as needed on the mixing surface to make your potpourri. Be sure to wait until the very end to distribute the orange peel slices, as they are rather pungent and only a few need to be added to each bag or jar of potpourri.

If you want a more fragrant and pungent smell to your potpourri, store the mixture in a crock with a tight-fitting lid or a lidded jar for a few weeks or even months before using or distributing as gifts. As the mixture sits, the fragrance tends to become much richer. When you feel that your potpourri is finally ready for use, dish a small amount into a glass jar or bowl to freshen up a room or scoop some into a sachet and place in a drawer to give a nice fragrance to your clothing or linens.

"You Choose" Potpourri Recipe

Potpourri can be comprised of a mix of flowers, leaves, and herbs—depending on which of these are available to you. The ingredients in this recipe are interchangeable and can all be used together or you can pick and choose which you want to use in making your own potpourri.

Essential Ingredients
1 ounce orrisroot
1 ounce allspice
1 ounce bay salt
1 ounce cloves

Assorted Ingredients (to add as you like)
Rose petals	Lavender
Lemon plant	Verbena
Myrtle	Rosemary
Bay leaf	Violets
Thyme	Mint
Essence of lemon	Essence of lavender

Mix the orrisroot, allspice, bay salt, and cloves together. Combine this with about 12 handfuls of the dried petals and leaves and store in an airtight jar or bowl. A small quantity of essence of lemon and/or lavender may be added but these are not necessary. Let the mixture stand for a few weeks. If it becomes too moist, add additional powdered orrisroot. Once the potpourri is dry and very fragrant, parcel it into bowls to set around the house or give as gifts in jars or sachets.

Rose Potpourri
Ingredients
1 lb rose petals (already pressed and from a jar)
Dried lavender (any proportion you like)

Lemon verbena leaves (any proportion you like)
A dash of orange thyme
A dash of bergamot
1 dozen young bay leaves (dried and broken up)
A pinch of musk
2 ounces orrisroot, crushed
1 ounce cloves, crushed
1 ounce allspice, crushed
½ ounce nutmeg, crushed
½ ounce cinnamon, crushed

Combine all the ingredients together in a large crock, jar, or bowl with a lid. Seal and allow it to sit for a few weeks, until the aroma is to your liking. Parcel into small bowls to fragrance rooms or give as gifts.

A Simple Recipe for Sachet Potpourri

If you are unable to procure large amounts of petals and leaves, here is a simple recipe, using oils as substitutes, that makes fine potpourri sachets.

Ingredients

2 grams alcohol
10 drops bergamot
20 drops eucalyptus oil
4 drops oil of roses
½ tsp cloves
1 ounce orrisroot
¼ tsp cinnamon
½ tsp mace
1 ounce rose sachet powder

Throughly mix these ingredients together in a large stone crock or in a large glass bowl. Store the potpourri in small wooden boxes or sachets and place them around the house. This potpourri gives off a pleasing fragrance to any room or drawer.

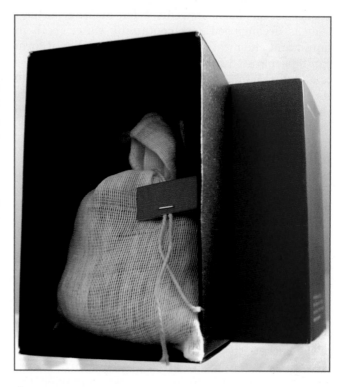

▲ Sachets make special gifts for wedding showers or other occations.

◀ Be creative with materials and ribbons for your sachets.

Pottery Basics

Pottery is enjoyable to make because of its flexibility and simplicity as a means of art expression, its utility, and its timelessness.

Clay is the basic ingredient for making pottery. Clay is decomposed rock containing water (both in liquid and chemical forms). Water in its liquid form can be separated from the clay by heating the mass to a boiling point—a process that restores the clay to its original condition once dried. The water in the clay that is found in chemical forms can also be removed by ignition—a process commonly referred to as "firing." After being fired, clay cannot be restored to any state of plasticity—this is what we term "pottery." Some clay requires greater heat to be fired, and these are known as "hard clays." These types of clay must be subjected to a "hard-firing" process. However, in the making of simple pottery, soft clay is generally used and is fired in an over-glaze (soft glaze) kiln.

Pottery clays can either be found in certain soils or bought from craft stores. If you have clay soil available on your property, the process of separating the clay from the other soil materials is simple. Put the earthen clay into a large bucket of water to wash the soil away. Any rocks or other heavy matter will sink to the bottom of the bucket. The milky fluid that remains—which is essentially water mixed with clay—may then be drawn off and allowed to settle in a separate container, the clear water eventually collecting on the top. Remove the excess water by using a siphon. Repeating this process will refine the clay and make it ready for use.

▼ Making pottery takes patience and practice, but the process can be very enjoyable.

▲ A potter carefully forms a bowl that will eventually be glazed and fired in a kiln.

You can also purchase clay at your local craft store. Usually, clay sold in these stores will be in a dry form (a grayish or yellowish powder), so you will need to prepare it before using it in your pottery. To prepare it for use, you must mix the powder with water. If there are directions on your clay packet, then follow those closely to make your clay. In general, though, you can make your clay by mixing equal parts of clay powder and water in a bowl and allowing the mixture to soak for 10 to 12 hours. After it has soaked, knead the mixture thoroughly to disperse the water evenly throughout the clay and pop any air bubbles. Air bubbles, if left in the clay, could be detrimental to your pottery once kilned, because the bubbles would generate steam and possibly crack your creation. However, be careful not to knead your clay mixture too much, or you may increase the chance of air bubbles becoming trapped in the mixture.

If, after kneading, you find that the clay is too wet to work with (test the wetness of the clay on your hands and if it slips around your palm very easily, it is probably too wet), the excess water can be removed by squeezing or blotting out with a dry towel or dry board.

▲ Sticks and other tools can be used to help you form and decorate your pottery.

The main tools needed for making pottery are simply your fingers. There are wooden tools that can be used for adding finer detail or decoration, but typically, all you really need are your own two hands. A loop tool (a piece of fine, curved wire) may also be used for scraping off excess clay where it is too thick. Another tool has ragged edges and this can be used to help regulate the contour of the pottery. Remember that homemade pottery will not always be symmetrical, and that is what makes it so special.

Basic Vase or Urn

Try making this simple vase or urn to get used to working with clay.

1. Take a lump of clay. The clay should be about the size of a small orange and should be elastic feeling. Then, begin to mold the base of your object—let's say it is either a bowl or a vase.
2. Continue molding your base. By now, you'll have a rather heavy and thick model, hollowed to look a little like a bird's nest. Now, using this base as support, start adding pieces of clay in a spiral shape. Press the clay together firmly with your fingers. Make sure that your model has a uniform thickness all around.
3. Continue molding your clay and making it grow. As you work with the clay, your hands will become more accustomed to its texture and the way it molds, and you will have less difficulty making it do what you want. As you start to elongate and lengthen the model, remember to keep the walls of the piece substantial and not too thin—it is easier to remove extra thickness than it is to add it.
4. Don't become frustrated if your first model fails. Even if you are being extra careful to make your bowl or vase sturdy, there is always the instance when a nearly complete vase will fall over. This usually happens when one side of the structure becomes too thin or the clay is too wet. To keep this from happening, it is sometimes helpful to keep one hand inside the structure and the other outside. If you are building a vase, you can extract one finger at a time as you reach closer and closer to the top of the model.
5. The clay should be moist throughout the entire molding process. If you need to stop molding for an extended period of time, cover the item with a moist cloth to keep it from drying out.
6. When your model has reached the size you want, you may turn it upside down and smooth and refine the contours of the object. You can also make the base much more detailed and shaped to a more pleasing design.
7. Allow your model to air dry.

Embellishing Your Clay Models

You may eventually want to make something that requires a handle or a spout, such as a cup or teapot. Adding handles and spouts can be tricky, but only if you don't remember some simple rules. Spouts can be modeled around a straw or any other material that is stiff enough to support the clay and light enough to burn out in the firing. In the designing of spouts and handles, it is still important to keep them solid and thick. Also, keeping them closer to the body of your model is more practical, as handles and spouts that are elongated are harder to keep firm and can also break off easily. Although more time-consuming and difficult to manage, handles and spouts can add a nice aesthetic to your finished pottery.

The simplest way to decorate your pottery is by making line incisions. Line incision designs are best made with wooden, finger-shaped tools. It is completely up to you as to how deep the lines are and into what pattern they are made.

Wheel-working and Firing Pottery

If you want to take your pottery-making one step further, you can experiment with using a potters' wheel and also glazing and firing your model to create beautiful pottery. Look online or at your local craft store for potters' wheels. Firing can leave your pottery looking two different ways, depending on whether you decide to leave the clay natural (so it maintains a dull and porous look) or to give it a color glaze.

Colored glazes come in the form of powder and are generally metallic oxides, such as iron oxides, cobalt oxide, chromium oxide, copper oxide, and copper carbonate. The colors these compounds become will vary depending on the atmosphere and temperature of the kiln. Glazes often come in the form of powder and need to be combined with water to be applied to the clay. Only

▲ Keep spouts and handles thick so they will not crack or break off. Use a stick or dowel to create line incisions like these shown here.

apply glaze to dried pottery because it won't adhere well to wet clay. Use a brush, sponge, or putty knife to apply the glaze. Your pottery is then ready to be fired.

There are various different kinds of kilns in which to fire your pottery. An over-glaze kiln is sufficient for all processes discussed here, and you can probably find a kiln in your surrounding area (check online and in your telephone book for places that have kilns open to the public). For schools that have pottery classes, over-glaze kilns may be installed there. It is important, whenever you are using a kiln, that you are with a skilled pottery maker who knows how to properly operate a kiln.

After the pottery has been colored and fired, a simple design may be made on the pottery by scraping off the surface color so as to expose the original or creamy-white tint of the clay.

Unglazed pottery may be worked with after firing by rubbing floor wax on the outer surface. This fills up the pores and gives a more uniform quality to the whole piece.

Pottery offers so many opportunities for personal experimentation and enjoyment; there are no set rules as to how to make a piece of pottery. Keep a journal about the different things you try while making pottery so you can remember what works best and

▲ Using different glazes will give your pottery variances in color and texture.

what should be avoided in the future. Note the kind of clay you used and its consistency, the types of colors that have worked well, and the temperature and positioning within the kiln, if you use firing. Above all, enjoy making unique pieces of pottery!

Making Jars, Candlesticks, and Bowls

Making pottery at home is simple and easy, and is a great way for you to make personalized, unique gifts for family and friends. Clay can be purchased at local arts and crafts stores. Clay must always be kneaded before you model with it because it contains air that, if left in the clay, would form air bubbles in your pottery and spoil it. Work out this air by kneading it the same way that you knead bread. Also guard against making the clay too moist, because that causes the pottery to sag, and sagging, of course, spoils the shape.

To make your own pottery, you need modeling clay, a board on which you can work, a pie tin on which to build, a knife, a short stick (one side should be pointed), and a ruler.

Jars

To start a jar, put a handful of clay on the board, pat it out with your hand until it is an inch thick, and smooth off the surface. Then, take a coffee cup, invert it upon the base, and, with your stick, trim the clay outside the rim.

To build up the walls, put a handful of clay on the board and use a knife to smooth it out into a long piece, ¼ inch thick. With the knife and a ruler, trim off one edge of the piece and cut a number of strips ¾ inch wide. Take one strip, stand it on top of the base, and rub its edge into the base on both sides of the strip. Take another strip and add it to the top of the first one, and continue building in this way, placing one strip on another, joining each to the one beneath it, and smoothing over the joints as you build. Keep doing this until the walls are as high as you want them to be. Remember to keep one hand inside the jar while you build, for extra support. Fill uneven places with bits of clay and smooth out rough spots with your fingers, having moistened your fingers with water first. When you are finished, you may also add decorations, or ornaments, to your jar.

Candlestick

Making a pottery candlestick requires a round base ½ inch thick and 4 inches in diameter. After preparing the base, put a lump of clay in the center, work it into the base, place another lump on top, work it into the piece, and continue in this way until the candlestick has been built as high as you want it. Then, force a candle into the moist clay, twisting it around until it has made a socket deep enough to place a candle into.

A cardboard "templet," with one edge trimmed to the proper shape, will make it easy to keep the walls of the candlestick symmetrical and the projecting cap on the top equal on all sides. Run the edge of the templet around the walls as you work, and it will show you exactly where and how much to fill out, trim, and straighten the clay.

If you want to make a candlestick with a handle, make a base just as described earlier. Then cut strips of clay and build up the wall as if building a jar, leaving a center hole just large enough to hold a candle. When the desired height for the wall has been reached, cut a strip of clay ½ inch wide and ½ inch thick, and lay it around the top of the wall with a projection of ¼ inch over the wall. Smooth this piece on top, inside, and outside with your modeling stick and fingers. For the handle, prepare a strip 1 inch wide and ³⁄₈ inch thick, and join one end to the top band and the other end to the base. Use a small lump of clay for filling around where you join the piece, and smooth off the piece on all sides.

When the candlestick is finished, run a round stick the same size as the candle down into the hole, and let it stay put until the clay is dry, to keep the candlestick straight.

Bowls

Bowls are fairly easy to make. Starting with a base, lay strips of clay around the base, building upon each strip as you did when making a jar. Once the bowl reaches its desired height and width, allow it to dry.

Glazing and Firing

Most pottery that you buy is glazed and then fired in a pottery kiln, but firing is not necessary to make beautiful, sturdy pottery. The clay will dry hard enough, naturally, to keep its shape, and the only thing you must provide for is waterproofing (if the pottery will be holding liquids). To do this, you can take bathtub enamel and apply it to the inside (and outside, if desired) of the pottery to seal off any cracks and keep the item from leaking.

If you do want to try glazing and firing your own pottery, you will need a kiln. Below are instructions for making your own.

Sawdust Kiln

This small, homemade kiln can be used to bake and fire most small pottery projects. It will only get up to about 1,200 degrees Fahrenheit, which is not hot enough to fire porcelain or stonewear. However, it will suffice for clay pinch pots and other decorative pieces.

You will need:

- Sawdust
- 20–30 red or orange bricks
- Chicken wire
- Sheet metal
- Newspaper and kindling

1. Choose a spot outdoors that is protected from strong winds. Clear away any dried branches or other flammables from the immediate area. A concrete patio or paved area makes an ideal base, but you can also place bricks or stones on the ground.
2. Stack bricks in a square shape, building each wall up at least four bricks high. Fill the kiln with sawdust.
3. Place the chicken wire on top of the bricks and add another layer or two of bricks. Carefully place your pottery in the center of the mesh, spacing the pieces at least ½ inch apart. Cover the pottery with sawdust.
4. Add another piece of chicken wire, add bricks and pottery, and cover with sawdust. Repeat until your kiln is the desired height.
5. Light the top layer of sawdust on fire, using kindling and newspaper if needed. Cover with the sheet metal, using another layer of bricks to hold it in place.
6. Once the kiln stops smoking, leave it alone until it completely cools down. Then carefully remove the sheet metal lid.

Permanent Homemade Pottery Kiln

As you continue to create pottery, you may find that you enjoy the art enough that you would like to continue

▲ Pottery may be ornamented by scratching a design on it with the end of a modeling stick. You can do a simple, straight-line design by using a ruler to guide the stick.

this craft for years to come. In that case, and if you have enough space in your yard, you may think about constructing a permanent kiln for all of your pottery needs. This kiln requires some intense construction, but having your own wood-burning pottery kiln will make firing your creations easier and more effective.

The essentials of this kiln are: a fire box, an oven, and a chimney. The kiln works by allowing the fire to pass up from the fire box through the oven floor, between the bricks (spaced about 1½ inches apart), and out through the chimney at the top of the oven.

The Construction of the Kiln

1. Begin by laying out a space for the foundation of the kiln. This should be on solid, dry ground. It is advisable to make an excavation a few inches below the surface and fill it in with cinders or broken brick. The place you choose for your kiln should also allow water to run off and not collect underneath.

2. Build the walls of the kiln three bricks deep on each of the sides and the back. Leave the front of the kiln open for the fire mouths.

3. Halfway between the two side walls, build a thin, central support, made of three courses of brick on the edge. This will leave a narrow ledge where the grates of the fire boxes can rest. Build the other edge of each grate into the side wall. The size of the kiln will be dependent on the amount of bricks you lay. Lay bricks endwise to make a stronger wall.

4 Make the mortar of common clay (or you can buy it if you desire). Mix the clay with water into a mortar. You can add some regular sand to give the mortar better working qualities, and this will also help prevent shrinkage.

5. Spread the mortar over the cinder foundation and start to lay the bricks. In building the walls and central support, make the joints between the bricks as tight and thin as possible. Tap the

▲ Red fire bricks are best for making a kiln.

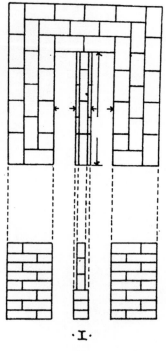

·I·

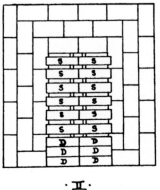

·II·

◄ The top illustrations shows plan and front view of the kiln foundation up to the oven floor. The walls are three bricks thick on each side and the front is left open. The bottom illustration shows the bricks that rest on the side walls and on the central support. These should be made of fire bricks, since they'll be subjected to the most extreme heat.

bricks into place so there will be no settling of the wall later on.

6. Build the walls and central support up to the point where the oven floor will be. To make the oven floor, arrange the bricks on their edges about 1½ inches apart from the front to the back of the kiln. These bricks should rest on the side walls and central support. Since this oven floor is going to be subjected to high heat, use fire bricks. Also be sure to project the bricks out in the front for the oven door to sit on.

7. Continue to build the side and back walls up nine more bricks. Then, you can start to taper the bricks into a chimney formation. Lay the next two levels of bricks (on the side walls only) in toward the center of the kiln about 1½ inches or so. The space between the walls at the top should not be more than 9 inches. Bridge the opening at the top across the front and back of the kiln, leaving an opening in the center just large enough for the chimney (about 8 or 9

inches square). You can do this by using large pieces of terra cotta flue lining (purchased at any hardware or home center store). The size of the flue lining should be about 2 feet x 8 inches x 6 inches.

8. Carefully cut lines in the flue lining from end to end, until the side falls away. Cut this in two and use the two halves for closing in the top of the kiln. Put these bricks in place with plenty of mortar and finish out the rest of the bricking over the walls with other pieces of flue lining, making them level.

9. Build two more levels of brick all around, leaving the chimney opening 9 inches by 9 inches.

10. Now build the chimney straight up with a single layer of bricks (or two bricks to each layer, if you desire). The inside diameter of the chimney should not be less than 7 inches by 7 inches.

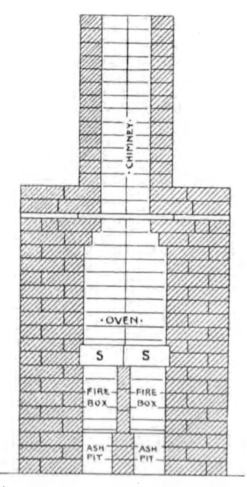

▲ Cross section of the finished kiln. The space between the walls at the top should not be more than nine inches.

When complete, the chimney should be about 3 feet high.

11. You can also build the chimney 1 foot high and then let one brick on each side project into the chimney cavity about 2 inches. Then, fit ordinary stovepipe with a square end to rest on these projections inside the chimney. This is a lighter method than building brick all the way up.

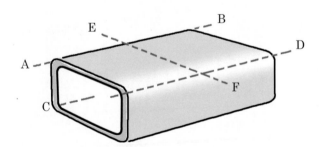

▲ Cut lines in the flue lining from end to end at AB and CD. Then cut in two at EF and use the two halves for closing in the top of the kiln.

12. Install grates to produce a better and cleared fire. You can find grates at your local hardware store or use old stove grates. Build these grates into the walls of the fire box and central support. Leave the front end of the oven open.

13. Place pottery in the oven. Brick up the front of the oven without any mortar and fill in the joints with wet sand.

14. The kiln will now need to be heated with wood. You should begin with a very simple fire lasting about an hour or two. This is extremely important, as the flame comes into contact with the raw clay, which, unless it is heated very gradually, could crack and split apart. After thoroughly warming the kiln, increase the heat more rapidly. After the firing is well underway (three or so hours later), close the doors of the fire boxes with pieces of sheet iron or bricks piled up in front. Only allow air in through the grates. Only remove the temporary doors to add fuel to the fire.

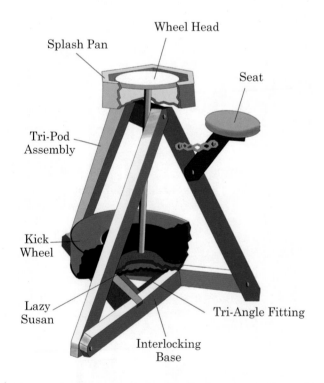

▲ You can make your own pottery wheel using wood, an old lazy susan, and a tire. Place bags of sand inside the tire to give your wheel a sturdier base.

Handmade Jewelry

Making jewelry can be as simple or as intricate as you like. Start with a simple, single-strand beaded bracelet and work your way up to multi-strand necklaces and experiment with different beads, shells, and knots. Jewelry makes wonderful gifts, and every piece you make will be unique.

Beaded Jewelry

Bead-weaving is a traditional way of making jewelry and possesses a distinct, artistic value. Small spots of pure color—where light can play—are juxtaposed in simple patterns, giving an effect unlike that of any other material. Beaded jewelry is perfect for necklaces, bracelets, earrings, small pouches, and belts.

Materials
Strong thread
Needle
Beads of any size and color

◀ A beaded bracelet.

A simple strand of beads. ▶

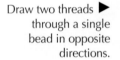

◀ Guide both threads through three beads at the center for this necklace.

Beginning Your Beadwork

To make a simple strand of beads, take two needles (No. 12 bead needles will work well), string them with thread, and fasten the end of each thread securely to a bead. On each, thread five beads, more if the beads are small, and then guide both threads through a bead. Again, take the same number of beads on each thread and guide the threads through a single bead, and so on, repeating the process until a necklace or bracelet of the desired length is completed. You can alter this type of beading by guiding both threads through three beads at the center. This will change the pattern and the look of the beadwork.

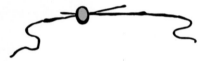

Draw two threads ▶ through a single bead in opposite directions.

To make a different kind of necklace or bracelet, use two threads drawn through a single bead in opposite directions. Next, string a bead onto each thread, both threads again through a single bead from opposite sides, and so on. In this design use two colors, a light and a dark, making an X pattern.

There is another beaded weave that is made up of diagonals and requires no loom. Fasten a bead to the end of the thread and, counting it as one, string the required number of beads—in this case, eight. String a bead and, carrying the needle through the seventh bead, draw the thread tight. String another bead and

▼ String a bead onto each thread, then draw both threads through a single bead again.

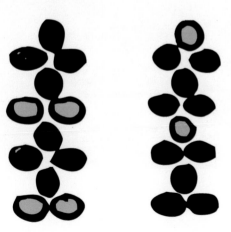

▲ A simple beaded weave.

pass the needle through the fifth one. Continue in this way, stringing a bead each time before passing the needle through the next bead, until the end of the line is reached. When you turn the work over, string a bead and pass the needle through the next bead but not the one at the edge. Repeat this process until the entire length is woven. With large beads, you can use fine wire instead of thread, especially if you desire a strong chain.

Cornstarch Jewelry

Beads for necklaces, pendants, bracelets, and all kinds of jewelry, large and small, can be made from cornstarch. Cornstarch jewelry is especially fun for children but, if done carefully and thoughtfully, these pieces can look exquisite.

Materials
1 tbsp cornstarch
2 tbsp table salt
1 tbsp cold water
Food coloring, natural dye, or watercolors

◀ A cross pendant.

Handmade Jewelry

Preparing the Cornstarch Mixture

Make the cornstarch, salt, and water into a mixture by combining all ingredients and stirring. If desired, add food coloring, natural dye from plants or spices, or watercolors to the mixture.

Two Types of Cornstarch Jewelry

1. Bracelets—Roll the cornstarch mixture between the palms of your hands until perfectly round balls are formed. Then, pierce holes through the balls before they harden so they can be easily strung. When you've strung enough beads to make the bracelet of your chosen size, knot the ends of the string tightly.
2. Pendants—Use a small bobby pin extending from the top down through the center of the cornstarch pendant, with just enough of the loop left exposed at the top to form a ring, through which you can pass a necklace chain.

▲ Dye cornstarch beads with natural dyes such as beet juice or coffee, or with a few drops of food coloring. Alternate your beads with bits of shell or sea glass for variety.

360

Handcrafted Paper

Instead of throwing away your old newspapers, office paper, or wrapping paper, use it to make your own, unique paper! The paper will be much thicker and rougher than regular paper, but it makes great stationery, gift cards, and gift wrap.

Materials
Newspaper (without any color pictures or ads if possible), scrap paper, or wrapping paper (non-shiny paper is preferable)

2 cups hot water for every ½ cup shredded paper

2 tsp instant starch (optional)

Supplies
Blender or egg beater

Mixing bowl

Flat dish or pan (a 9 x 13-inch or larger pan will do nicely)

Rolling pin

8 x 12-inch piece of non-rust screen

4 pieces of cloth or felt to use as blotting paper, or at least 1 sheet of Formica

10 pieces of newspaper for blotting

Directions
1. Tear the newspaper, scrap paper, or wrapping paper into small scraps. Add hot water to the scraps in a blender or large mixing bowl.
2. Beat the paper and water in a blender or with an egg beater in a large bowl. If you want, mix in the instant starch (this will make the paper ready for ink). The paper pulp should be the consistency of a creamy soup when it is complete.
3. Pour the pulp into the flat pan or dish. Slide the screen into the bottom of the pan. Move the screen around in the pulp until it is evenly covered.
4. Carefully lift the screen out of the pan. Hold it level and let the excess water drip out of the pulp for a minute or two.
5. With the pulp side up, put the screen on a blotter (felt) that is situated on top of some newspaper. Put another blotter on the top of the pulp and put more newspaper on top of that.
6. Using the rolling pin, gently roll the pin over the blotters to squeeze out the excess water. If you find that the newspaper on the top and bottom is becoming completely saturated, add more (carefully) and keep rolling.
7. Remove the top level of newspaper. Gently flip the blotter and the screen over. Very carefully, pull the screen off of the paper. Leave the paper to dry on the blotter for at least 12 to 24 hours. Once dry, peel the paper off the blotter.

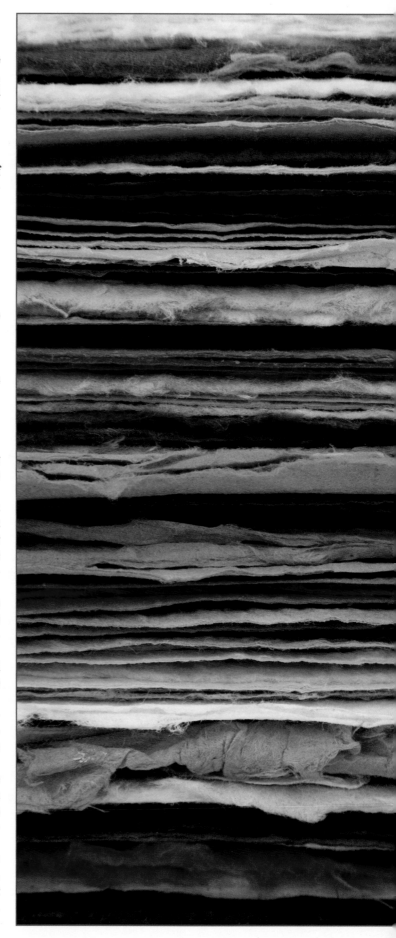

Handcrafted Paper

To add variety to your homemade paper

- If you would like to have colored paper, add a little bit of food coloring or natural dye to the pulp while mixing in the blender or with the egg beater.
- Try adding dried flowers (the smoother and flatter, the better) and leaves or glitter to the pulp.
- To make unique bookmarks, add some small seeds to your pulp (hardy plant seeds are ideal), make the paper as in the directions, and then dry your paper quickly using a hairdryer. When the paper is completely dry, cut out bookmark shapes and give to your friends and family. After they are finished using the bookmarks, they can plant them and watch the seeds sprout.

▼ Dried flowers and leaves can be added to your paper. Choose flat flowers for best results.

Knitting

The art of knitting was supposedly invented by the Spanish nobility as a means of relaxation for noble women in the country. The Scottish also claim to have developed knitting, and King Henry VII was the first to wear knitted stockings in England. Queen Elizabeth also wore knitted silk stockings made by Mistress Montegue.

Whenever and wherever knitting was first "discovered," it is useful, relaxing, and can be done while enjoying a good conversation with a friend.

Knitting Basics

Stitches

Knitting can be done in rows of plain or purl stitches or by incorporating a variety of stitches and knitting techniques in one project. However, the simpler stitches are better when first starting to knit. Just be sure not to pull the thread too tight or keep it too loose—as you continue to knit, you will learn the proper amount of tension to apply to your string so you create a perfect, knitted item.

General Tip for Beginning Knitters

Hold the needles loosely in your hands and close to the points. To knit easily and quickly, your hands should neither move too much nor should you make large gestures with the needles.

Tools Needed for Knitting

1. **Gauge**—This measures the knitting needles. Most needles already have their gauge listed on them, but if your needles do not, you should find this measuring tool at your local arts and crafts store.
2. **Knitting needles**—These are made of steel, wood, or plastic and are used to knit your material together.
3. **Knitting shields**—Although these are not a necessary tool for knitting, you may find that you want these so the material does not slip off of your needle.
4. **Material to be knitted**—Beginners should use thicker yarn in their knitted items. When you have become more proficient in knitting, you can

experiment with different types of threads and materials to create your various knitted items.

Knitting Terminology

To bring the thread forward—This means to pass the thread between the needles toward the knitter's body.

To cast off—You do this by knitting two stitches, passing the first over the second, and proceeding in this manner until the last stitch, which is secured by passing the thread through it.

To cast on the loops or stitches—Take the material in your right hand and twist it around the little finger, bringing it under the next two fingers, and passing it over the pointer finger. Then, take the end of the material in your left hand (holding the needle with your right), wrap it around the little finger, and then bring it over the thumb and around the second and third fingers. By doing so, you will have formed a loop. Now, bring the needle under the lower thread of the material and above the material that is over the right-hand pointer finger under the needle. The thread in the left hand should be pulled tightly, completing this step. You can repeat this process as many times as needed until you've cast the amount of stitches you want.

To cast over—This means to bring the material around the needle (bringing it forward).

To fasten on—This refers to fastening the end of the material when it's needed during the process of knitting. The best way to fasten on is to place the two ends in opposite directions and knit a few stitches with both.

Knitting stitch—In this stitch, the needle must be put through the cast-on stitch and the material should be turned over. This will be taken up and under the loop (or stitch) and then let off. This is also known as a plain stitch and will be continued until an entire round is complete.

A loop stitch—This is made by passing the thread before the needle.

Narrowing—This is to decrease the number of stitches by knitting two together, so you only form one loop.

Purl stitch—This is also known as a seam, ribbed, or turn stitch. It is formed by knitting with the material before the needle and instead of bringing the needle over the upper thread, the material is brought under it. This is the opposite of a knitting stitch.

Raising—This is to increase the number of stitches and is made by knitting one stitch in the usual way and then omitting to slip out the left-hand needle.

▲ Wrap the loose strand of yarn over and behind the right needle. For a purl stitch, wrap the yarn behind first and then over the needle. Slip the loop off of the left needle to finish the stitch.

Then, the material is passed forward, and a second stitch is formed by pulling the needle under the stitch. The material must be put back to its normal place when the extra stitch is completed.

To rib—To alternately knit plain and purled stitches (three plain then three purl, etc.).

A round—This is all of the stitches on two, three, or more needles.

A row—This refers to the stitches from one end of the needle to the other.

To seam—To knit a purl stitch every alternate row.

A slip stitch—This is made by passing the thread from one needle to another without knitting.

To turn—To change the type of stitch.

Welts—These are alternating plain and ribbed stitches and are used for anything that you don't want to twist or curl up.

▲ Hold the needles loosely in your hands with the loose yarn wrapped around your pointer finger.

How to Knit

1. To cast on, hold the two needles loosely in your hands. Pass a loop over the left-hand needle near the end of the yarn and hold the right-hand needle loosely. Put the right-hand needle into the loop, passing it from left to right and keeping the right-hand needle under the left needle. Pass the string over this needle—between it and the left-hand needle—and pull the loop up toward the right. Now, bring the right needle up and pass the stitch on it to the left needle by putting the left needle through the left side of the loop, keeping the right needle in the loop. It is ready to begin the next stitch. Repeat.

▲ Slip the right needle into the top loop on the left needle, keeping the left needle above the right needle. To do a purl stitch, the right needle would go on top of the left needle.

▼ Rows of knit stitches.

▼ Alternating rows of knit and purl stitches.

2. Knitting stitch: After you have made the correct number of stitches, hold the needle that has the stitches on it in your left hand and pass the right needle into the first stitch from left to right. Put the yarn between the two needles, pull the loop through the other loop on the left needle, and slip that loop off the left needle. Repeat.

3. Purling stitch: Keep the yarn in the front of the work and put the right needle into a stitch from right to left, passing it upward through the front loop of the stitch. The right needle should be resting on the left. Pass the yarn around the front of the needle and bring it back between the two needles. Pull the right needle slightly back, so as to secure the loop on the right needle and then draw off the loop on the left needle. Repeat. Note: This is basically the knitting stitch, only backwards.

4. Slipping a stitch: This is done by passing a stitch from one needle to another without knitting it at the beginning of a row. This should always been done when using two needles at the beginning of each row, so the rows remain even.

5. Casting (binding) off: Knit two stitches, passing the first stitch over the second, and then knit a third stitch, passing the second over the third. Continue in this way until all the stitches are off the needle.

Simple Knitting Patterns

1. Patent Knitting, or Brioche Knitting
Cast on any number of stitches divisible by three. Yarn forward, slip one, knit two together. Work every row in the same way.

2. Cane-work Pattern
Cast on any number of stitches divisible by four.

First Row: make one, knit one, make one, knit three. Repeat.
Second Row: purl.
Third Row: knit three, make one, slip one, knit two together, pass the slip-stitch over the two knitted together, make one. Repeat.
Fourth Row: purl.
Fifth Row: make one, slip one, knit two together, pass the slip-stitch over, make one, knit three. Repeat.

Sixth Row: purl.

Seventh Row: repeat the third row.

Eighth Row: purl.

Ninth Row: make one, slip one, knit two together, pass the slip-stitch over, make one, knit three. Repeat.

Tenth Row: purl.

Repeat from the third row until the item is complete.

Simple Scarf

Materials

Mid-weight or 4-ply yarn of any color (use at least one full bundle of yarn)

Knitting needles (size 8 to 10.5 are best for knitting scarves)

Directions

1. Decide how wide you want your scarf to be (26 to 35 stitches are the standard width for a scarf).
2. First row: knit 26 to 36 stitches.
3. Second row: knit 26 to 35 stitches (if you want something a little more intricate, purl this row instead).
4. Continue knitting (or knitting and purling alternately) until you reach the desired length (60 inches is a good length for a scarf).

5. At the end, cast (bind) off the stitches.

Hat

Materials

Yarn of a medium-heavy weight, any color of your choosing

Knitting needles (depending on the head size for the hat, use No. 6 or No. 8 needles)

Directions

1. Cast on 72 stitches.
2. First row: knit 72 stitches.
3. Second row: purl 72 stitches.
4. Continue in this fashion until your hat is about 9 inches tall.
5. To begin to cast (bind) off your hat, follow this pattern:
   a. Knit five stitches, knit two together, and continue to the end of the row.
   b. Purl the next row.
   c. Knit four stitches, knit two together, and continue to the end of the row.
   d. Purl the next row.
   e. Knit three stitches, knit two together, and continue to the end of the row.
   f. Purl the next row.
   g. Knit two stitches, knit two together, and continue to the end of the row.
   h. Purl the next row.
   i. Knit every two stitches together.
7. Take the excess yarn, pull it through the last stitches, and cut off so only about an inch and a half remains. Sew a seam, put the remaining yarn through the loops, and fold your hat inside out.

Knitting

▲ This hat shows the "knit one row, purl one row" pattern. You can also follow this pattern for six or eight rows and then switch to just knitting to give your hat a differentiated band around the bottom. If desired, use round needles (two knitting needles that are attached by a plastic or rubber cord) to avoid having to sew a seam at the end.

Fingerless Mittens

Fingerless mittens are wonderful to use if your hands are cold but you still need to have complete access to things, such as typing on a computer or making a meal. They make wonderful gifts for friends and family members.

▲ You can easily modify the pattern described here to include these individual finger openings and the finger "hood." Simply follow the steps to make the thumb hole (steps 8–10) for each of the additional finger openings. For the "hood," follow the directions for making a hat (only make it much smaller) and sew it onto the mitten above the knuckles.

Materials

150 yards of worsted-weight yarn or wool/yarn blend
Double-pointed knitting needles, No. 8

Directions

1. To make the cuff, cast on 28 stitches, making sure these stitches are even. Then, begin to knit in the round. Do not twist the stitches. Use the yarn tail to keep track of the round ends. Knit three rounds. Switching to the twisted rib pattern, knit one stitch through the back loop to twist it. Purl one, and repeat this pattern until the cuff measures roughly 2½ inches.
2. Using a stocking stitch, begin the hand and thumb portion of the mitten.
3. First row: knit one, purl one, make one (increase the stitch), knit one, make one, purl one, knit until the end of the round.
4. Second row: knit one, purl one, knit until you reach the next purl stitch in the row above, purl one, knit until the end of the round.
5. Third row: knit one, purl one, make one, knit until the next purl, make one, purl one, knit until the end of the round.
6. Repeat the second and third rows until you have nine stitches between the purls. The glove should now measure about 5½ inches from the edge of the cast-off point.
7. Place two purl and nine thumb gore stitches on a piece of scrap yarn. Cast off three stitches and knit four rounds of stocking stitch. Change to twisted rib stitch and make six rounds. Bind this off very loosely.
8. To make the thumb, put 11 stitches on hold for the thumb onto an extra knitting needle. Pick up three stitches at the base of the thumb and make 14 stitches.
9. Knit one round of only 12 stitches.
10. Using the twisted rib stitch, make six more rounds and bind off loosely.
11. To finish up, weave in the yarn ends and, if necessary, sew closed any holes at the sides of the thumb base.

Knitted Square Blanket

Materials

Thick yarn, any color you like (if you want a multicolored blanket, feel free to use different-colored yarn for each individual square)
Knitting needles, No. 6

Directions

1. Begin by making smaller squares that will be sewn together to form a larger blanket.

▲ If knitting your blanket for a baby, be sure to use soft yarn that will not irritate a baby's sensitive skin.

2. Cast on any number of stitches divisible by three. For a square of 6 inches, you'll need 45 stitches.
3. First row: Slip one, knit two. Turn the yarn around the needle and bring it again in front. Then, slip one, knit two together. Purl the last two stitches.
4. Second row: Turn the yarn around the needle, bringing it to the front. Slip one, knit two together. Knit the last two stitches in the row.
5. Continue the pattern in step 4 (alternating purled and knitted last two stitches) until you reach the end and cast off your square.
6. Continue making as many squares as you want to get the desired size of your blanket.
7. When you have all your knitted squares, take a knitting needle and sew each square together.

▲ Keeping your yarn in neat balls will make knitting easier and faster.

Bookbinding

Simple Homemade Book Covers

If you have loose papers that you want bound together, there is an easy way to make a book cover:

1. Take two pieces of heavy cardboard that are slightly larger than the pages of the book you wish to assemble. Make three holes near the edges of each cardboard piece with a hole-punch. Then, punch three holes (the same distance from each other as the cardboard pieces) in the papers that are to be in the interior of the book.
2. String a narrow ribbon through these holes and tie the ribbons in knots or bows. If the leaves of your book are thin, you can punch more than three holes into the paper and cardboard, and

then lace strong string or cord between the holes, like shoelaces.
3. To decorate your covers, you can paint them with watercolors or you can simply use colored cardboard. You can also take some fabric, cut it so the fabric folds just over the inside edges of the cardboard pieces, and then hot glue (or use a special paste—read on) the fabric to the cardboard. Or, you can glue on photographs or cutouts from magazines and protect the cover with laminating paper.

To Make Flour Paste for Your Book Covers

Mix ½ cup of flour with enough cold water to make a very thin batter. This must be smooth and free of lumps. Put the batter on top of the stove in a tin saucepan and stir it continually until it boils. Remove the pan from the stove, add three drops of clove oil, and pour the paste into a cup or tumbler and cover.

Bind Your Own Book

Making your own book or journal takes careful measuring, folding, and gluing, but the end product will be something unique that you'll treasure for ages. You can also rebind old, worn-out books that you'd like to preserve for more years to come.

Before binding anything very special, try to bind a "dummy" book, or a book full of blank pages—you could use this blank book as a journal if it comes out fairly well, so your efforts will not be wasted. To make a blank book, you need to plan out what you'll need—how thick the book will be, what the dimensions are, the quality of the paper being used (at least a medium-grade paper in white or cream), and so on. Carefully fold and cut the paper to the appropriate size.

Supplies
White or cream-colored paper (at least 32 sheets) or the pages you wish to rebind
Decorative paper (2 sheets)
Stiff cardboard
Cloth or leather
Silk or cloth cord
Glue
Scissors (or a metal ruler and Exacto knife)

1. Make 4 stacks of 8 sheets of paper. These stacks, once folded, are called "folios," Four stacks will

make a 64-page book. If you wish to make it longer or shorter you can do more or fewer stacks of 8 sheets. Carefully fold each stack in half.

2. Unfold the stacks and staple or sew along the crease. If stapling, only use two staples: one at the top of the fold and one at the bottom.

3. Refold all the stacks and pile them on top of each other. Use binder clips or a vice to hold them together. Cut a rectangular piece of fabric that is the same length as the spine of your book and about five times as wide. So if your stack of folded papers is 8 ½ inches long and 1 inch high, your fabric should be 8 ½ inches long and 5 inches wide.

4. Using a hot glue gun or regular white glue, cover the spine with glue and stick on the fabric. The fabric should hang off either side of the spine.

5. For the cover, cut two pieces of sturdy cardboard that are the same size as the pages of your book. Using a metal ruler and an Exacto knife will help you make the cuts straight and smooth. Place one piece of cardboard at the bottom of your stack of papers and another on the top. Cut another piece of cardboard of same height and width as the book's spine, including the pages and both covers.

6. Select a piece of fabric (or leather) to cover your book and lay it flat on a table. Place the three pieces of cardboard on the fabric with the spine between the two cover pieces. Use a ruler to measure and mark a rectangle on the fabric that is one inch larger on all sides than the combined pieces of cardboard. Remove the cardboard pieces and cut out the rectangle.

7. Lay the fabric on the table face down. Cover one side of the cardboard pieces with white glue or rubber cement. If using white glue, use a stiff brush, putty knife, or scrap piece of cardboard to spread the glue in an even, thin layer so there are no lumps. Place the cardboard glue-side-down on the fabric so that all three pieces are aligned with the spine between the two covers. Leave a gap of about twice the thickness of the cardboard between the spine and the two covers.

8. Smear glue on the top and bottom edges of the cardboard pieces and fold over the fabric. Repeat with the outside edges.

9. Smear glue on the inside edges of the cover boards. Don't glue the spine. Place the stack of pages spine-side-down on top of the boards. The extra material hanging off of the spine should adhere to the glue on the cover boards. Place two solid bookends, rocks, or jars of food on either side of the papers to hold them upright until they dry thoroughly.

10. Select a decorative piece of paper to use for endpapers. This will cover the inside front and back covers so that you won't see the folded material and cardboard. It can be a solid color or patterned, according to your preference. Cut it to be slightly wider than the pages you started with (before being folded) and not quite as tall.

11. Open your book and cover the inside front cover and first page with glue or rubber cement. Fold your endpaper in half to create a crease, open it back up, and then stick it to the inside cover and first page, making sure the crease slides into the space between the spine and front cover slightly. Allow to dry and then repeat at the back of the book.

12. Cut two pieces of thin cord for the head and tail band, which will cover the top and bottom of the spine. They should be the same length as the width of the spine. Use a hot glue gun or white glue to adhere them to the top and bottom of the spine, where the pages are gathered together.

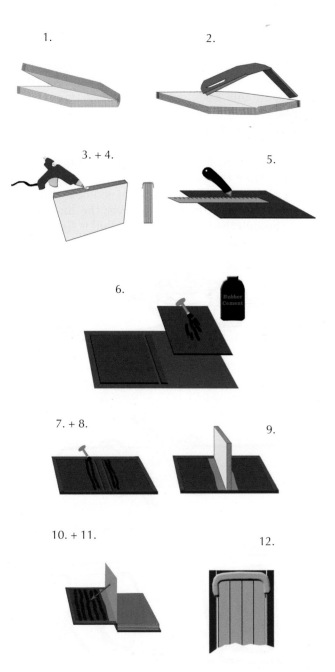

1.

2.

3. + 4.

5.

6.

7. + 8.

9.

10. + 11.

12.

Tying Knots

Knowing how to tie different types of knots is a useful skill to have, especially if you are involved in boating, rock climbing, fishing, or other outdoor activities.

Strong knots are typically those that are neat in appearance and are not bulky. If a knot is tied properly, it will almost never loosen and will still be easy to untie when necessary.

Three Parts of a Rope
1. **The standing part:** this is the long, unused part of the rope.
2. **The bight:** this is the loop formed whenever the rope is turned back.
3. **The end:** this is the part used in leading.

The best way to learn how to tie knots effectively is to sit down and practice with a piece of cord or rope. Practice, in this case, definitely makes tying knots much faster and easier. Listed below are a few common knots that are useful to know:

- **Bowline knot:** Fasten one end of the line to some object. After the loop is made, hold it in position with your left hand and pass the end of the line up through the loop, behind and over the line above, and through the loop once again. Pull it tightly and the knot is now complete.

- **Clove hitch:** This knot is particularly useful if you need the length of the running end to be adjustable.

- **Halter:** If you need to create a halter to lead a horse or pony, try this knot.

Qualities of a Good Knot
1. It can be tied quickly.
2. It will hold tightly.
3. It can be untied easily.

- **Sheepshank knot:** This is used for shortening ropes. Gather up the amount to be shortened and then make a half hitch around each of the bends.

- **Slip knot:** Slip knots are adjustable, so that you can tighten them around an object after they're tied.

- **Timber hitch:** If you need to secure a rope to a tree, this is the knot to use. It is easy to untie, too.

- **Two half hitches:** Use this knot to secure a rope to a pole, boat mooring, washer, tire, or similar object.

- **Square/reef knot:** This is the most common knot for tying two ropes together.

Kites

Flying kites is a wonderful way to spend a breezy summer day. Making your own kites is easy and fun and adds to the enjoyment and satisfaction of kite flying. Here are a few examples of kites that can easily be made and are particularly fun for children.

How to Paste Tissue Paper to Your Kite Frame

Make a good paste out of flour and water by boiling it until it reaches the consistency of starch. Put the paste on with a bristle brush, make the seams hardly more than ¼-inch wide, and press them together with a soft rag.

To adhere tissue paper to your frame, place the tissue paper on the ground and lay the frame over it, holding the frame down with heavy books. Cut the paper around the frame, leaving a ½-inch edge, and make a slit in the edge every 6 or 7 inches and at the angles. With your brush, coat the edge with paste, one section at a time, turn the sections over, and press down with the rag.

Frog Kite

Materials

Two 2-foot-long sticks (with the thinner part bent to form knees)

1-foot, 7-inch-long stick (for the spine)

2-foot, 5-inch-long piece of rattan (to make the body of the frog)

1. Place the two leg sticks one above the other and then place the spine stick on top of them. The tops of all three sticks should be perfectly even. Eight inches from the top, drive a pin through all three sticks and carefully clamp it on the other side where the point comes through.

2. For the body, bend the piece of rattan to form a circle (allow the ends of overlap about an inch or so—this will help in the binding of the ends to make a joint). The circle, when complete, should be about 8 inches in diameter.

3. Take the three sticks that are pinned together, lay them on the floor, and spread them apart to form an irregular star. The top of the spine should be just about halfway between the tops

▲ Frog kite.

Kites

of the legs (5 inches from each). Place the rattan circle over the sticks, with the intersection of the sticks in the middle of the circle.

4. With pins and thread, fasten the frame together. The lower limbs will be spread wide apart and they must be carefully drawn together and held in position by a string that is tied near the termination of each leg stick.

5. Cross-sticks for hands and feet may now be added and the strings attached to various points. Cover the kite with green tissue paper and decorate it to look like a frog.

Butterfly Kite

1. Make a thin, straight stick out of a piece of elastic wood or split rattan. At the top of this, attach a piece of thread or string.

2. Bend the stick as you would a bow until it forms an arc or half circle. Holding the stick in this position, tie the other end of the string to a point a few inches above the bottom end of the stick. At a point on the stick about one-quarter the distance from the top, tie another string, draw it taut, and fasten it to the bottom end of the bow.

3. Take another stick of exactly the same length and thickness as the first and go through the same process, making a frame that is exactly the same as the first. Fasten the two frames

together, allowing the arcs to overlap several inches, and bind the joints securely with thread.

4. Make the head of the insect by attaching two pipe cleaners to the top part of the wings where they are joined together. The straws must be crossed and the projecting ends can serve as the antennae.

5. Select a piece of yellow or blue tissue paper, place your frame over it, cut it to the correct measurements, and paste. After the kite is dry, draw some markings on the wings with black paint or cut out markings in dark-colored paper and paste them on.

Fish Kite

1. Cut two straight pine sticks and shave them down until they are thin enough to bend easily. They should be exactly the same length and roughly the same weight. Fasten the top ends together by driving a pin through them.

2. Bend each stick to form a bow and hold them in this position until you have secured a third stick across them at right angles about one-third the way down from the top. The kite should now be half as broad as it is long.

3. Let the lower ends of the side, or bow, sticks cross each other far enough up to form a tail for the fish and fasten the sticks together at their intersection.

4. Before stringing the frame, see that the cross-stick protrudes an equal distance from each side of the fish.

5. To make the tail, tie a string across the bottom from the end of one cross-stick to the end of the other and tie another string to this string in the middle. Pass the string up to the base of the tail, draw it taut, and fasten it there at the intersection of the side-sticks. This will make a natural look for the caudal fin.

6. The remainder of the strings can be put on. Take care that the dorsal and back fin are made exactly

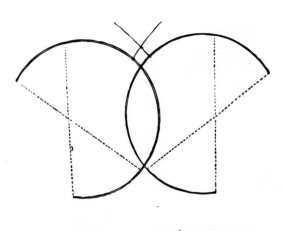

▲ Butterfly kite.

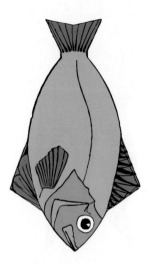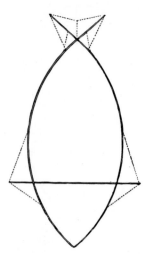

▲ Fish kite.

the same size. Choose yellow, red, or green tissue paper to cover the kite and decorate as you see fit.

7. Tie the strings of the breast-band to the side-sticks near the head and tail, and let them cross each other as in a common kite. Attach the tail-band to the tail of the fish.

Shield Kite

1. Make the frame of four sticks: two straight cross-sticks and two bent side-sticks.
2. Cover it with red, white, and blue tissue paper (making it look like a flag) or use any color of your choosing. Make sure to cut the paper so it looks like a shield.

Square Kite

1. This kite is not actually perfectly square. It is rectangular and made with a framework of very thin bamboo or cane sticks, bound together.
2. The frame should be covered with rice paper and all sides of the paper should be glued down well.
3. The kite should be bent backwards, making it slightly convex in the front. To hold the kite in this

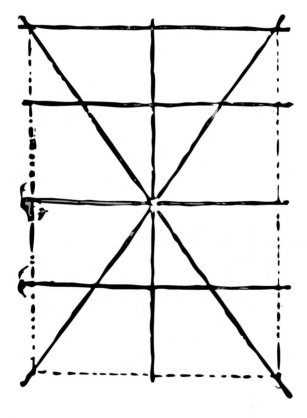

▲ Square kite.

 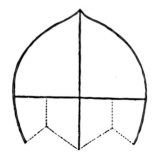

▲ Shield kite.

position, use strings that are tied from end to end of the cross-sticks at the back. The breast-band may be attached like any other six-sided kite.

4. Instead of a tail band, with a single tail attached, this kite carries two tails, one tied at each side to the protruding ends of he diagonal sticks at the bottom of the kite.

Boomerangs

To make a boomerang, scald a piece of well-seasoned elm, ash, or hickory plank (free from any knots) in a pot of boiling water. Leave the wood in the water until it becomes pliable enough to bend into a slight V-shaped form. When the wood has assumed the proper shape, nail on the side pieces to hold the wood in position until it is thoroughly dry. After the plank is completely dry, the side pieces can be removed—the wood will keep the curved shape.

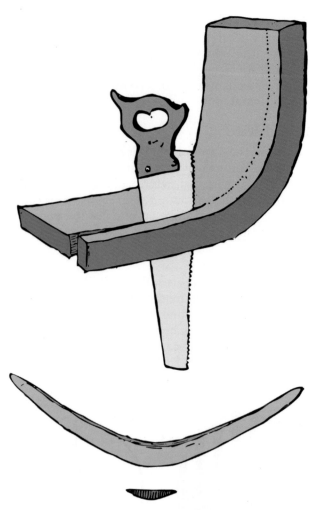

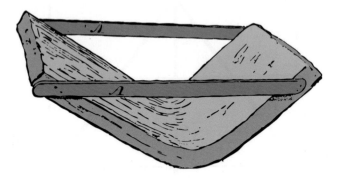

▲ Nail on side pieces to hold the bent wood in place.

Saw the wood into as many pieces as it will allow and each piece will become a boomerang. If the edges are very rough, trim them with a pocketknife and scrape them smooth. You can use a large file to help shape the boomerang. The efficiency of your boomerang (how well it soars and returns to you) will vary in each piece, depending on the curvature.

▲ Once the wood is dry, saw the wood into several boomerangs.

▼ Sand and finish your boomerang for best results.

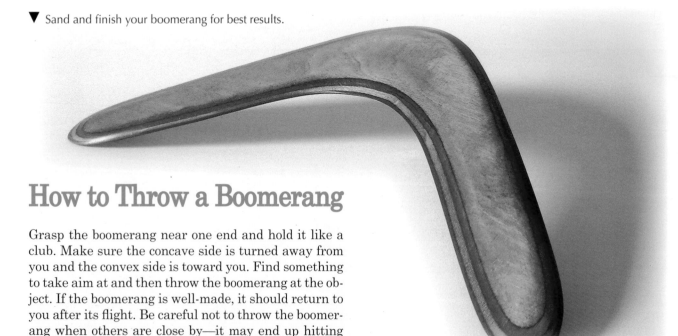

How to Throw a Boomerang

Grasp the boomerang near one end and hold it like a club. Make sure the concave side is turned away from you and the convex side is toward you. Find something to take aim at and then throw the boomerang at the object. If the boomerang is well-made, it should return to you after its flight. Be careful not to throw the boomerang when others are close by—it may end up hitting them and it can leave a bad welt. It is best to throw your boomerang in a large, open field by yourself.

Toboggans

Toboggans can fit several people on them, thus making the sledding experience all the more fun. Toboggans are suitable for deep snow and heavy drifts, due to their broad, smooth bottoms, enabling the sled to glide well over crusted snow.

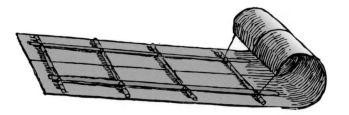

To make a toboggan, you will need two pieces of quarter-inch pine lumber that are either 8 or 10 feet long and 1 foot wide. Place the two boards side by side and join them together by means of round cross-sticks. Bind the cross-sticks to the lumber via thongs that pass through holes in the bottom boards on each side of the cross-stick and are held tightly by hammock hitches. Where the thongs pass underneath, cut grooves in the bottom board deep enough to prevent the cord from sticking out. These grooves are necessary as any cords that would be sticking out from the toboggan would not only slow down the sled but would eventually wear out, causing the toboggan to fall apart.

On top of the cross-sticks, lash together two side bars. Curl over the front ends of the boards and hold them in place by two thongs that are tied tightly onto the ends. Then you can take your handmade toboggan out during the first big snow and give it a test ride.

Preserving Flowers

Pressed Flowers and Leaves

Pressed flowers can be used to decorate stationery, handmade boxes, bookmarks, scrapbooks, or picture frames. Although these types of preserved flowers are perfectly flat, they seldom fade.

1. Have a large book or a quantity of old newspapers and blotting paper, and several weights ready.
2. Use the newspapers for leaves and ferns. Blotting paper is best for the flowers. Both the flowers and leaves should be fresh and without moisture. Place them as nearly as possible in their natural positions in the book or papers, and press, allowing several thicknesses of paper between each layer.
3. Remove the flowers and leaves onto dry papers each day until they are perfectly dried.

Some flowers must be immersed—all but the flower head—in boiling water for a few minutes before pressing, to prevent them from turning black. Orchids are the prime example of a flower that needs boiling before pressing.

To preserve your flowers forever, get a blank book or just pieces of stiff, white paper on which to mount your preserved flowers and leaves. Glue them down

▲ To preserve a whole plant, grasp it at the base of the stem and pull it out of the soil gently. Shake off excess dirt before pressing.

378

to the paper with hot glue or regular Elmer's glue. The sooner you mount the specimens, the better. Place them carefully on the paper and, beneath each flower or leaf, write the name of the plant, where it was found, and the date.

Natural Wax Flowers

To make wax flowers, dip the fresh buds and blossoms in paraffin that is just hot enough to be liquefied. First dip the stems of the flowers. When these have cooled

▲ For leaves, ferns, or flat flowers, you can place the plant between two sheets of wax paper and run a hot iron over the paper. Allow the paper to cool slightly and then carefully remove it.

and hardened, dip the flowers or sprays. Be sure to hold them by the stalks and move them gently. When they are completely covered, remove the flowers from the wax and shake them lightly to throw off the excess wax. Allow the flowers to dry completely. The flowers will keep their beautiful coloring, natural forms, and even their fragrance for a short while.

▼ Preserve beautiful flowers by dipping them in paraffin.

Cornhusk Dolls

This old-fashioned doll makes a wonderful gift for young children and also a unique, decorative, home-made item for your home or for sale at a craft fair. Cornhusk dolls are easy to make if you just follow these simple steps:

1. Gather husks from several large ears of corn (you may have these from your garden, if you grow corn, or you might find them at a garden center or a farmers' market in the fall). Select the soft, white husks that grow closest to the ear.

▲ Once you have the basics down, try adding skirts, costumes, or other details to your dolls.

2. Place the stiff ends of two husks together, fold one of the long, soft husks in a strip lengthwise, and wrap it around the ends.

3. Choose the softest and widest husk you can find, fold it across the center, and place a piece of strong thread or string around it and tie it tightly in a knot.

4. Bring this down over the al-ready-wound husks and tie it with a thread underneath. This will form the head and neck of the doll.

5. To make the arms, divide the husk below the neck into two equal parts. Fold two or three husks together and insert them in the space you've made by the division. Hold the arms in place with one hand, and use your other hand to fold several layers of husk over each shoulder, allow-ing them to extend down the back of the figure.

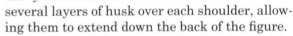

6. When the figure seems substantial enough, use your best husks for the topmost layers and wrap the waist with strong thread, tying it tightly.

7. Divide the husks below the waist band and make the legs by neatly wrapping each portion with thread. Trim the husks off evenly for the feet.

10 . If you want your doll to have clothing or a specific "costume," you can make these from any kind of material and in any way you wish.

For a variation on a traditional corn husk doll, try the following:

1. Gather a young ear of corn (whose silk has not yet browned), a crab apple for the head, and a leaf from the cob for a dress.

2. Cut off the bottom of the ear of corn where the husks are puckered and carefully take the silk from the other end, making sure not to disturb the closely wrapped husks remaining.

3. Roll part of the leaf for the arms and fasten the crab apple to the leaf arms with a small stick. Stick the other end of the twig into the small end of the corncob.

4. Now you can dress the doll. The hat for the doll can be made from a leaf (just where it joins the stalk. This can be fastened to the doll's head with a small twig or thorn. Make sure the silk is placed on the head to form hair before securing the hat.

5. Make a scarf by folding a leaf around the shoulders and securing it with small pins or thorns.

6. Stick tiny thorns into the crab apple to make eyes and a nose.

8. Twist the arms once or twice, tie them, and trim them evenly for the hands.

9. You can draw a face on the doll with a pen or marker, or you can glue tiny natural items on the head to make a face.

▼ Save corn husks and silk for making cornhusk dolls.

Basketweaving

Basketweaving is one of the oldest, most common, and useful crafts. The materials used in making baskets are primarily reed or rattan, raffia, corn husks, splints, and natural grasses. Rattan grows in tropical forests, where it twines about the trees in great lengths. It is numbered according to its thickness, and numbers 2, 3, and 4 are the best sizes for small baskets. Rattan should be thoroughly soaked before using. Raffia is the outer cuticle of a palm, and comes from Madagascar. Cattail reeds are excellent for baskets and may be more readily available, as they frequently grow near ponds or swampy areas. Most basket-making materials can also be found at local craft stores.

Small Reed Basket

Most reed baskets have at least sixteen spokes, and for small baskets and where small reeds are used, these spokes are often woven in pairs. You can vary the look of your reed basket by combining and interweaving two different-colored reeds.

Materials Needed
Sixteen 16-inch spokes, No. 2 reed
Five weavers of No. 2 brown reed

Directions

1. Separate the sixteen spokes into groups of four. Mark the centers and lay the first group on the table in a vertical position. Across the center of this group place the second group horizontally. Place the third group diagonally across these, having the upper ends at the right of the vertical spokes. Lay the fourth group diagonally with the upper ends at the left of the vertical spokes.

2. Soak the reeds well and then start the basket by laying the weaver's end over the group to the left of the vertical group, just above the center; then bring it under the vertical group, over the horizontal and then under, and so on until it reaches the vertical group again. Repeat this weave three or four times.

3. Separate the spokes into twos and bring the weaver over the pair at the left of the upper vertical group, and so on, over and under until it comes around again. At the beginning of each new row, the weaver passes under two groups of spokes, always under the last of the two under which it went before and the group at the right of it.

4. Continue weaving until your basket is the desired height. Weave the bottom until it is 4 inches in diameter; then wet and turn the spokes

▲ There are endless variations of basket weaves to experiment with.

gradually up and weave 1 inch. After that, turn the spokes in sharply and draw them in with at least three rows of weaving.

5. Trim the top of your basket, leaving about 3 inches of the spokes sticking up. Turn your basket upside down in a basin of water and soak until the spokes become pliable. Gently bend down each spoke, skipping the reed next to it, and tucking it into the basketweave. Continue all the way around.

Coiled Basket

Sweet grass, corn husks, or any pliable grasses can be used for this type of basket. Useful colorful raffia to add interest.

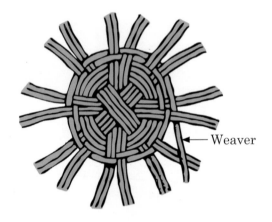

Weaver

▲ Start of a small reed basket.

Materials
A bunch of grasses
A bunch of raffia

Directions
1. Gather a bunch of long grasses and twist them together into one long cord. Thread the raffia through a needle and use the needle to help you wrap the cord from top to bottom with the raffia.

2. Begin to coil the wrapped cord, sewing the coils together as you go. To change color or start a new cord, tuck the ends into the weave and start up with the new piece where you left off with the old one.
3. When the base of the basket is as large as you want, begin the sides by raising each coil up slightly higher than the one below it, continuing to sew the coils together as before.
4. To finish, tuck the end of the coil into the weave and sew securely in place

▲ A variety of baskets are used to display goods at a farmers' market.

385

Birch Bark Basket

Birch bark baskets are a wonderful way to display dried wildflowers and make nice gifts. Making a basket in the shape of a canoe works very well with the bark. Gather bark strips (do not string directly from the tree; try to find these either on cut wood or from a craft or lumber store) that are 6½ inches long and 4 inches wide. Sew the ends of the bark together with a thick thread, leaving one side of each strip unstitched. Sew a ribbon on each end of the canoe—these will serve as handles. Now the basket may be filled with dried wildflowers or other things from nature (such as pinecones) and hung on the wall for display.

▼ Birch bark tends to peel easily from the tree trunks.

Marketing Your Skills

If you are serious about making crafts or would just like to make a little extra money by selling your homemade candles, soaps, baskets, pottery, jewelry, or other items, you may want to consider finding ways to make your creations visible in the marketplace. Keep in mind that if you do begin to sell your homemade crafts, and if you develop a market for them, you may need to begin making more of them to meet customer demands.

To start, find out what other similar products are available and what prices they're going for. Do some market research: Go into stores that sell homemade items like yours and look online as well—eBay is a great place to see what people are willing to pay for homemade crafts—and price your items accordingly. Also think about the amount of money you spend on supplies and how much time you spend making your craft item. If you are investing large amounts of money and time into making just one item, you most likely will not be able to make a good profit from it.

Advertising is key to selling your items. Print up flyers that you can distribute to people or hang on community bulletin boards. Make business cards, directing your potential customers to any Web site or blog you have about your crafts, along with a good way to reach you if they want to buy. Getting the word out there is key when you are first starting to sell your homemade items. Don't be afraid to tell friends and family members about your new business, and ask them to share it with their friends as well.

If you set up a table or booth at a local market, be sure it is attractive and inviting to your potential buyers. Elevate your items so they are easily seen and arrange some in baskets to add a "homey" feel. Have flyers and/or business cards available and always be friendly to anyone who approaches your table. Remember that word of mouth is a wonderful way to find people who want to buy your specific craft item.

Ways to Sell Your Homemade Crafts

Sell to Your Family and Friends

The best way to begin making money on your homemade products is to reach out to your family and friends and see if they are interested in buying your wares. You may also want to market your goods to your coworkers. Putting up flyers in your office (get permission first, of course) or sending out catalogs or postcards to friends, family, and neighbors advertising your crafts is not a bad way to start getting the word out.

Sell at a Garage Sale

Garage and yard sales are perfect places to sell your homemade items—especially if you do not have enough to sell at a local market or store. You might ask a

▲ Displaying your goods creatively will attract potential buyers to your table.

neighbor or two about hosting a combined garage sale or see if your neighborhood holds an annual garage sale weekend and then set up a small table on the side of the road. Again, display your items well and be sure to let your shoppers know that they are homemade.

Sell at Your Local Farmers' or Flea Market

Visit your local farmers' market or area flea market and see if they have a consignment table where you can sell your crafts. Find out how much it would cost to rent a space to set up a table. Local markets are wonderful ways to present your craft items to the community and many people visiting these types of markets are looking for locally produced products and good bargains.

Sell Your Crafts on Consignment

Perhaps there is a local shop you frequently visit that sells homemade products, or a hotel or airport gift shop nearby. Some stores are more than happy to sell local goods (especially if they complement the items the shop already sells) on consignment. Before you walk into a store with your goods, be sure you have a sales pitch ready. Dress professionally and make sure you have information, prices, and samples of your product to show them. Tell the owner or manager how your product is different or better than others available, and why their customers will want it. Always have a business card handy as well—just in case. If you and the store do come into agreement about selling your crafts, you probably want to draw up a contract stating how much profit the store will take from selling your items and what other terms and conditions may apply.

Some stores that may be interested in selling homemade items on consignment are: craft stores, airport and hotel gift shops, tourist stores, food co-ops, beauty shops and hair salons, flower shops, local antique stores, and other specialty stores.

Sell Online

More and more, consumers are choosing to shop online instead of in stores, so marketing your goods in an online capacity (even if you have items in stores as well) is a great way to sell your crafts. Check out eBay to see what other crafts are selling and for how much, or try to sell your crafts at sites such as www.etsy.com (an online craft website that sells certain homemade items). You will have to pay a small fee for an online "booth," but etsy.com will help market your wares, making it easy for you to sell them. Also search for online farmers' markets and see how to begin to sell your crafts in that capacity. Or, if you are really ambitious and tech-savvy, you can create your own Web site and sell direct to customers.

▲ Wrap your soap in a bit of handmade paper or tie with a simple string to make them attractive to potential customers.

Part Seven

Well-Being

"Health is a state of complete harmony of the body, mind, and spirit. When one is free from physical disabilities and mental distractions, the gates of the soul open."

—*B. K. S. Iyengar*

On some level, we all know what we need for optimum health. Our bodies are built to give us clues, from simple ones—if we're tired, we probably need rest—to ones that require a little more attention to discern, such as a headache or stomachache, which can stem from a wide range of issues. Many of us consistently ignore the clues, masking exhaustion with caffeine or popping an aspirin every time a pain begins to surface without even considering the cause. Well-being begins with taking the time to listen to ourselves, being honest about what needs healing or improvement, and nurturing the desire to reach a healthier level of being. Once the desire for health is strong, you will find a myriad of channels for achieving it. This section offers suggestions for finding well-being through natural means, from herbal medicine to natural spa products to massage techniques. You'll also find information on how to prepare your home for natural disasters, and instructions for basic first aid. There are times when the best thing to do is to go straight to a doctor, whether a doctor of Western medicine, a homeopath, or another type of medical practitioner. But part of leading a self-sufficient life is learning to recognize and meet your own needs, even in the areas of health and safety. From there, you can begin to help those around you, too. So start paying attention to your physical, mental, and spiritual state, and find out what you can do to be the best version of who you already are.

Herbal Medicine

An herb is a plant or plant part used for its scent, flavor, or therapeutic properties. For centuries herbs have been used in various forms for their health benefits. Many are now sold as tablets, capsules, powders, teas, extracts, and fresh or dried plants. However, some have side effects and may interact with other drugs you are taking.

To use an herbal product as safely as possible:

- Consult your doctor first.
- Do not take a bigger dose than the label recommends.
- Take it under the guidance of a trained medical professional.
- Be especially cautious if you are pregnant or nursing.

Herbal supplements are sold in many forms: as fresh or dried products; liquid or solid extracts; and tablets, capsules, powders, and tea bags. For example, fresh ginger root is often found in the produce section of food stores; dried ginger root is sold packaged in tea bags, capsules, or tablets; and liquid preparations made from ginger root are also sold. A particular group of chemicals or a single chemical may be isolated from a botanical and sold as a dietary supplement, usually in tablet or capsule form. Common preparations include teas, decoctions, tinctures, and extracts.

A *tea*, also known as an *infusion*, is made by adding boiling water to fresh or dried botanicals and steeping them. The tea may be drunk either hot or cold.

Some roots, bark, and berries require more forceful treatment to extract their desired ingredients. They are simmered in boiling water for longer periods than teas, making a *decoction*, which also may be drunk hot or cold.

A *tincture* is made by soaking a botanical in a solution of alcohol and water. Tinctures are sold as liquids and are used for concentrating and preserving a botanical. They are made in different strengths that are expressed as botanical-to-extract ratios (i.e., ratios of the weight of the dried botanical to the volume or weight of the finished product).

An *extract* is made by soaking the botanical in a liquid that removes specific types of chemicals. The liquid can be used as is or evaporated to make a dry extract for use in capsules or tablets.

▲ Herbs can be utilized medicinally in the form of teas, tinctures, extracts, or as an addition to soaps, lotions, or salves.

that have the health benefits, and use only those parts.

2. Coarsely chop the plant parts. Flowers can be left whole.
3. Clean and dry a small glass jar with an airtight lid and put the herbs inside. Fill the jar with 100-proof vodka or warm cider vinegar until plant parts are fully immersed. Screw the lid on securely and label the jar.
4. Store for 6 to 8 weeks, gently shaking a few times a week.
5. Strain out the herbs and store the liquid tincture in a clean, dry bottle. Be sure to label the jar with the ingredients, and date and store it in a safe place away from children's reach.

Make Your Own Herbal Tincture

Tinctures help concentrate and preserve the health benefits of your herbs. To use, mix 1 teaspoon of tincture with juice, tea, or water and drink no more than three times a day.

1. Pick the fresh herbs, removing any dirty, wilted, or damaged parts. Do not wash. Be sure you know whether it is the stems, leaves, roots, or flowers

Common Herbal Remedies

Here is a list of common herbs that can be used to cure or alleviate the symptoms of conditions ranging from cancer to acne to the common cold. If you are taking any other medications or supplements, check with your doctor before trying any herbs. As with any medication, every body is unique and certain herbs can have adverse side effects for certain people, so pay attention to your body and cease taking any herbs that make you feel worse in any way. It's a good idea to try one herb at a time per condition and to keep a journal documenting what you take, when, and how

▲ Add several drops of your tincture to tea or juice to receive the healing benefits without the strong flavor.

▲ Aloe vera can be used topically to treat and soothe a variety of skin irritations.

you feel. This way you'll be able to tell more easily what effects the herbs are having.

Aloe Vera

Uses: The clear gel in aloe is used topically to treat osteoarthritis, burns, and sunburn. The green part can be made into a juice or dried and taken orally to treat a variety of conditions, such as diabetes, asthma, epilepsy, and osteoarthritis.

Cautions: Using aloe vera on surgical wounds may inhibit their healing. If taken orally, aloe vera can produce abdominal cramps and diarrhea, which can decrease the absorption of many drugs.

If you have diabetes and take glucose-lowering medication, you should be careful of taking aloe orally, as studies suggest that aloe may decrease blood glucose levels.

Astragalus

Uses: Astragalus was traditionally used in Chinese medicine in combination with other herbs to help boost the immune system. It is still used widely in China for chronic hepatitis and as an additional cancer therapy. Astragalus is commonly used to boost the immune system to help colds and upper respiratory infections and has also been used to fight heart disease. The astragalus plant root is used in soups, teas, extracts, and capsules and is generally used with other herbs, like ginseng, angelica, and licorice.

Cautions: Astragalus may interact with medications that suppress the immune system (such as those taken by cancer patients or organ transplant recipients).

Bilberry

Uses: Bilberry fruit is used to treat diarrhea, menstrual cramps, eye problems, varicose veins, and circulatory problems. The leaf of a bilberry is used to treat diabetes. It's claimed that bilberry fruit also helps improve night vision, but this is not clinically

▼ Bilberries are a close relative of blueberries and can be eaten whole or made into an extract.

▲ Chamomile flowers can be used to make a relaxing tea.

proven. The bilberry fruit can be eaten or made into an extract. Likewise, its leaves can be used in tea or made into an extract.

Cautions: Though bilberry fruit is considered safe, high doses of the leaf or leaf extract may have possible toxic side effects.

Chamomile

Uses: Chamomile has a calming effect and is often used to counteract sleeplessness and anxiety, as well as diarrhea and gastrointestinal conditions. Topically, chamomile is used in the treatment of skin conditions and for mouth ulcers (particularly due to cancer treatment). The chamomile plant has flowering tops, which are used to make teas, extracts, capsules, and tablets. It can also be applied as a skin cream or ointment or even be used as a mouth rinse.

Cautions: Some people have developed rare allergic reactions from eating or coming into contact with chamomile. These reactions include skin rashes, swelling of the throat, shortness of breath, and anaphylaxis. People allergic to related plants, such as daisies, ragweed, or marigolds, should be careful when coming into contact with chamomile.

Cranberry

Uses: Cranberry fruit and leaves are used in healing many conditions, including wounds, urinary disorders, diarrhea, diabetes, and stomach and liver problems. Cranberries are often used in treating urinary tract infections and stomach ulcers. They may also be useful in preventing dental plaque and in preventing *E.coli* bacteria from adhering to cells along the urinary tract wall. Cranberry fruit can be eaten straight, made into juice, or used in the form of extracts, tea, or tablets and taken as a dietary supplement.

Cautions: Drinking copious amounts of cranberry juice can cause an upset stomach and diarrhea.

Dandelion

Uses: Dandelions, throughout history, have been most commonly used to treat liver and kidney diseases and spleen problems. Dandelions are sometimes used in liver and kidney tonics, as a diuretic, and for simple digestive issues. The dandelion's leaves and roots (and sometimes the entire plant) are used in teas, capsules, and extracts. The leaves are used in salads or are cooked, and the flowers are used to make wine.

Cautions: While using dandelions is typically safe, there are a few instances of upset stomach and diarrhea caused by the plant, as well as allergic reactions. If your gallbladder is inflamed or infected, you should avoid using dandelion products.

Echinacea

Uses: Traditionally, echinacea has been used to boost the immune system to help prevent colds, flu, and various infections. Echinacea can also be used for wounds, acne, and boils. The roots and exposed plant are used, either fresh or dried, for teas, juice, extracts, or in preparations for external use.

Cautions: Echinacea, taken orally, generally does not cause any problems. Some people do have allergic reactions (rashes, increased asthma, anaphylaxis),

▲ Echinacea is beautiful as well as useful medicinally. It grows well in moderately dry soil.

but typically only gastrointestinal problems are experienced. If you are allergic to any plants in the daisy family, it may be best to steer clear of echinacea.

Evening Primrose Oil

Uses: Since the 1930s, evening primrose oil has been used to fight eczema and recently, it has been used for other inflammatory conditions. Evening primrose oil is also used in the treatment of breast pain during the menstrual cycle, symptoms of menopause, and premenstrual issues. It may also relieve pain associated with rheumatoid arthritis.

The oil is extracted from the evening primrose seeds. You'll find it in capsule form at many health food stores.

Cautions: There may be some mild side effects, such as gastrointestinal upset or headache.

Flaxseed and Flaxseed Oil

Uses: Flaxseed is typically used as a laxative and to alleviate hot flashes. Flaxseed oil is used for treating arthritis pain. Both herbs are used to fight high cholesterol and can be beneficial for those with heart disease. Flaxseed, in either its whole or crushed form, may be mixed with water or juice and ingested. It is also available as a powder. Flaxseed oil can be taken in either a liquid or capsule form.

Cautions: It is essential to take flaxseed with lots of water, or constipation could worsen. Further, flaxseed fiber may decrease the body's ability to absorb other oral medications and so should not be taken together.

Garlic

Uses: Garlic is typically used as a dietary supplement for those with high cholesterol, heart disease, and high blood pressure. It may help decrease the hardening of the arteries and is also used in the prevention of stomach and colon cancer. It is also used topically or orally to heal some infections, including ear infections. Garlic cloves may be eaten either raw or cooked, or they may be dried or powdered and used in capsules. Oil and other extracts can be obtained from garlic cloves.

Cautions: Some common side effects of garlic are breath and body odor, heartburn, upset stomach, and allergic reactions. Garlic can also thin blood and so should not be used before surgeries or dental work, especially if you have a bleeding disorder. It also has an adverse effect on drugs used to fight HIV.

Ginger

Uses: Ginger is commonly used in Asian medicines to treat stomachaches, nausea, and diarrhea. Many U.S. dietary supplements containing ginger are used to help fight cold and flu and can be used to relieve

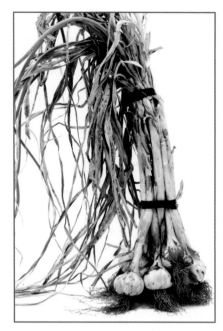

Garlic grows best ▶ in soil that is pH 6.5 to 7.0.

post-surgery nausea or nausea related to pregnancy. It has also been used for arthritis and other joint and muscle pain. Ginger root can be found fresh or dried, in tablets, capsules, extracts, and teas.

Cautions: Side effects are rare but can include gas, bloating, heartburn, and, for some people, nausea.

Ginkgo

Uses: Traditionally, extract from ginkgo leaves has been used in the treatment of illnesses such as asthma, bronchitis, fatigue, and tinnitus. People use gingko leaf extract in the hopes that it will help

Ginkgo leaves ▶ can be made into an extract and ingested for a wide range of health benefits.

improve their memory (especially in the treatment of Alzheimer's disease and dementia). It is also taken to treat sexual dysfunction, multiple sclerosis, and other health issues. Ginkgo leaf extracts are made into tablets, capsules, or teas. Sometimes the extracts can also be found in skin care products.

Cautions: Some common side effects are headache, nausea, gastrointestinal upset, diarrhea, dizziness, or skin irritations. Ginkgo may also increase bleeding risks, so those having surgery or with bleeding disorders should consult a doctor before using any ginkgo products. Uncooked ginkgo seeds are toxic and can cause seizures.

Ginseng (Asian)

Uses: Ginseng is used to help boost the immune system and contribute to the overall health of an individual. It has been used traditionally and currently for improving those who are recovering from illnesses, increasing stamina and mental and physical performance, treating erectile dysfunction and symptoms of menopause, and lowering blood glucose levels and blood pressure. In some studies, ginseng has been proven to lower blood glucose levels and boost immune systems. The ginseng root is dried and made into tablets, capsules, extracts, and teas. It can also be made into creams for external use.

Cautions: Limiting ginseng intake to three months at a time will most likely reduce any potential side effects. The most common side effects are headaches and sleep issues, along with some allergic reactions. If you have diabetes and are taking blood-sugar lowering medications, it is advisable not to use ginseng, as it too lowers blood sugar.

Grape Seed Extract

Uses: Grape seed extract is used for treating heart and blood vessel conditions, such as high blood pressure, high cholesterol, and low circulation. It is also used for those struggling with complications from diabetes, such as nerve and eye damage. Grape seed extract is also used in treating vision problems, reducing swelling after surgery, and cancer prevention. Extracted from grape seeds, it is readily available in tablets and capsules.

Cautions: Common side effects of prolonged grape seed oil use are headaches, dry, itchy scalp, dizziness, and nausea.

Green Tea

Uses: Green tea and its extracts have been used in preventing and treating breast, stomach, and skin cancers, as well as improving mental alertness, aiding weight loss, lowering cholesterol, and preventing the sun from damaging the skin. Green tea is typically brewed and drunk. Extracts can be taken in capsule form and sometimes green tea can be found in skin care products.

Cautions: While green tea is generally safe for most adults, there have been a few reports of liver problems occurring in those who take green tea extracts. Thus, these extracts should always be taken with food and should not be taken at all by those with liver disorders. Green tea also contains caffeine and can cause insomnia, anxiety, irritability, nausea, diarrhea, or frequent urination.

Lavender

Uses: Lavender, in the past, has been used as an antiseptic and to help with mental health issues. Now it is more commonly taken for anxiety, restlessness, insomnia, and depression, and can also be used to fight headaches, upset stomach, and hair loss.

Most commonly used in aromatherapy, lavender essential oil can also be diluted with other oils and rubbed on the skin. When dried, lavender flowers can be made into teas or liquid extracts and ingested.

Cautions: Lavender oil applied to the skin may cause some irritation and is poisonous if ingested. Lavender tea may cause headache, appetite change, and constipation. If used with sedatives, it may increase drowsiness.

▲ Lavender has a soothing, relaxing aroma. It can also be ingested in the form of tea or extracts, or even in baked goods.

Licorice Root

Uses: Traditionally, licorice root is used as a dietary supplement for the treatment of stomach ulcers, bronchitis, and sore throat. It is also used to help cure infections caused by viruses. When licorice root is peeled, it can be dried and made into powder. It is available in capsules, tablets, and extracts.

Cautions: If taken in large doses, licorice root can cause high blood pressure, water retention, and low potassium levels, leading to heart conditions. Taken with diuretics, it could cause the body's potassium levels to fall to dangerously low levels. If you have heart disease or high blood pressure, you should practice caution when taking licorice root. Large doses of licorice root may cause preterm labor in pregnant women.

Milk Thistle

Uses: Milk thistle is used as a protective measure for liver problems and in the treatment of liver cirrhosis, chronic hepatitis, and gallbladder diseases. It is also used to lower cholesterol, reduce insulin resistance in those with type 2 diabetes, and reduce the growth of cancerous cells in the breast, cervix, or prostate. Milk thistle seeds are used to make capsules, extracts, and strong teas.

Cautions: Occasionally, milk thistle may cause diarrhea, upset stomach, or bloating. It may also cause allergic reactions, especially in those with allergies to the daisy family.

▲ Milk thistle grows in a wide range of soil types and will thrive in sunny or partly shady areas.

Mistletoe

Uses: For hundreds of years, mistletoe has been used to treat seizures and headaches. In Europe, mistletoe is used to treat cancer and to boost the immune system. The shoots and berries of mistletoe are used in oral extracts. In Europe, these extracts are prescription drugs, available only by injection.

Cautions: Eating raw and unprocessed mistletoe may cause vomiting, seizures, a slowing of the heart rate, and even death. American mistletoe cannot be used for medical purposes. Injected mistletoe extract can irritate the skin and produce low-grade fevers or flu-like symptoms. There is also a slight risk for severe allergic reactions that could cause breathing difficulty.

Peppermint Oil

Uses: Usually, peppermint oil is used to treat nausea, indigestion, and cold symptoms and it can also be used to allay headaches, muscle and nerve pain, and irritable bowel syndrome. Peppermint essential oil can be taken orally in small doses. It can also be diluted with other oils and applied to the skin.

Cautions: Common side effects include allergic reactions and heartburn, though peppermint oil is relatively safe in small doses.

Red Clover

Uses: Red clover has been used for treating cancer, whooping cough, asthma, and indigestion. It is also used to allay menopausal symptoms, breast pain, high cholesterol, osteoporosis, and enlarged prostate. The red clover flower is used in preparing extracts in tablets and capsules as well as teas.

Cautions: No serious side effects have been reported, though it is unclear if it is safe for use by pregnant women, women who are breastfeeding, or women with breast or other hormonal cancer. The estrogen in red clover may also increase a woman's chance of contracting cancer in the uterus.

Soy

Uses: Soy products are typically used for treating high cholesterol, menopausal symptoms, osteoporosis, problems with memory, breast and prostate cancer, and high blood pressure. Available in dietary supplements, soy can be found in tablet or capsule form. Soybeans may be cooked and eaten, or made into tofu, soy milk, and other foods.

Cautions: Using soy supplements or eating soy products can create minor stomach and bowel problems, and in rare cases, allergic reactions causing breathing difficulties and rashes. While there is no conclusive evidence linking soy with increased risk of breast cancer, women who have or are at risk of getting breast cancer should consult a doctor about using soy products.

St. John's Wort

Uses: St. John's wort has been used for hundreds of years to treat mental illness and nerve pain. It has also been used as a sedative, in malaria treatment, and as a balm for wounds, burns, and insect bites. It is commonly used to treat depression, anxiety, and sleep disorders. The flowers are used, in extract form, for tea and capsules.

Cautions: A possible side effect of using St. John's wort is increased light sensitivity. Other common side effects are anxiety, dry mouth, dizziness, gastrointestinal symptoms, fatigue, headache, and sexual dysfunction. St. John's wort also interacts with drugs and may interfere with the way the body breaks down those drugs. It may affect antidepressants, birth control pills, cyclosporine, digoxin, indinavir and other HIV drugs, irinotecan and other cancer drugs, and anticoagulants.

If you are taking antidepressants, be careful if also taking St. John's wort, as it may increase the likelihood of nausea, anxiety, headache, and confusion.

Turmeric

Uses: Traditionally used in Chinese medicine, turmeric was supposed to aid digestion and liver function and to relieve arthritis pain. It was also taken to regulate the menstrual cycle. Applied directly to the skin, it was used to treat eczema and wounds. Now, turmeric is used in the treatment of heartburn, stomach ulcers, and gallstones. Turmeric is also used to reduce inflammation and in the prevention and treatment of certain cancers.

The underground stems of the turmeric plant are dried and taken orally in capsules, teas, or liquid extracts. It can also be made into a paste to be used on the skin.

Cautions: Considered safe for most adults, long-term use of turmeric may cause indigestion. Those with gallbladder problems should avoid turmeric, however, as it may worsen the condition.

▲ Make St. John's wort flowers into tea and drink to boost your mood and ease tension.

Valerian

Uses: For many years, valerian has been used for sleep disorders and to treat anxiety. Valerian has also been used to alleviate headaches, depression, irregular heartbeat, and trembling. The roots and underground stems of the valerian plant are usually made into supplements in capsule, tablet, or liquid extract form. It can also sometimes be made into teas.

Cautions: Valerian is typically safe to use for short periods of time (no more than six weeks) but there is no proof about its long-term effectiveness. Some common side effects of valerian use are headaches, dizziness, upset stomach, and grogginess the morning after use.

Homemade Herbal Teas

Herbal teas can be very tasty and deliver between 50 and 90 percent of the medicinal qualities of the herbs used. Teas you make yourself will be more potent and flavorful than those you can buy at the store, and much less expensive. Try experimenting with different herbal combinations, but be careful to avoid any plants you cannot confidently identify as edible, or any plants sprayed with pesticides. If using dried herbs, you can store your tea mixes in sealed containers for months. Be sure to label each container with the name of the tea.

Use 1 to 2 teaspoons of dried herbs per cup of hot water or 3 teaspoons of fresh herbs per pint of water. Steep the herbs for about 10 minutes and then strain. The following plants can all be safely used in teas:

Flowers

Alliums, bee balm, carnations, echinacea (roots and flowers), hibiscus, hollyhocks, honeysuckle (avoid the poisonous berries), lavender, marshmallow (use the roots), nasturtiums, red clover, roses (flowers or hips), violets.

Herbs

Basil, chamomile flowers, chives, dill, eucalyptus, ginger root, lemon balm, lemongrass, linden leaves,

marjoram, mint, oregano, parsley, peppermint, rosemary, sage, thyme, valerian root, verbena.

Bushes and Trees

Birch leaves, blackberry leaves, citrus blossoms, elderberry flowers, gardenia, pine needles, raspberry leaves.

Weeds

Chickweed, chicory, dandelions, goldenrod, stinging nettle.

Tea for the Common Cold

Combine the following herbs in any proportion you like. Boil for 10 minutes, strain, and add honey to taste.

- Marshmallow root (eases body aches, reduces inflammation)
- Peppermint (reduces congestion, eases headaches, soothes stomach)
- Echinacea roots and flowers (boosts the immune system)

- Thyme (reduces chest and nasal congestion, increases circulation)
- Cinnamon (reduces inflammation and fights infection)
- Rosehips, finely chopped (full of vitamin C, which boosts the immune system and energizes)
- Ginger root, peeled and finely chopped (warms from the inside out)
- Lavender, crushed (eases migraines)
- Lemon peel, finely grated (full of vitamin C)

Calming Tea

Combine the following calming herbs, using about ¼ as much valerian as the other herbs (valerian can be very potent). Boil for 10 minutes, strain, and add honey to taste.

- Lemon balm leaves
- Chamomile flowers
- Valerian root, crushed
- Ginger root, peeled and finely chopped

▲ Red clover blossoms promote estrogen and nourish the uterus.

Fertility Tea

Drink one cup of fertility tea a day to help balance your hormones and to get nutrients that can aid in becoming pregnant. Combine the herbs in equal proportion, boil for 10 minutes, strain, and add honey to taste.

- Red clover blossoms (nourishes the uterus, promotes estrogen, rich in magnesium and calcium)
- Nettle leaves (rich in calcium, potassium, phosphorous, iron, and sulfur)
- Red raspberry leaves (aids the fertilized egg in attaching to the uterine lining, rich in minerals, helps to tone muscles in the pelvic region)
- Peppermint (aids in absorption of red raspberry leaf nutrients)

Cleansing Tea

The herbs in this tea will improve your digestion, help your body in its natural detoxification process, and give you more energy. Combine the herbs in any proportion (go easy on the cayenne), boil for 10 minutes, strain, and add honey if desired.

- Peppermint leaves
- Dandelion root

▲ Herbal teas are also delicious served cold in the summer months.

- Whole allspice berries
- Ginger root, peeled and finely chopped
- Licorice root, crushed
- Cayenne pepper

▼ Dried peppermint leaves.

Natural Cosmetics

HOMEMADE LIP GLOSS

You only need a few ingredients to make your own lip gloss, though once you understand the basic recipe you can begin to experiment by adding different essential oils, aloes, and food products to create your own, unique type of gloss.

Homemade lip gloss containers can be any small glass jar or tin, or you can reuse an old lip gloss con-

tainer (just make sure all the old gloss is out of the container). To sterilize the container, wash with soap and hot water, dunk the container in a jar of rubbing alcohol, rinse clean, and then allow the container to completely dry before pouring in your melted gloss. Allow the gloss mixture to cool completely before using (you can speed up this process by placing the container of gloss into the refrigerator for a few hours).

Honey Lip Gloss

Ingredients
1 tsp beeswax (you can find this at a craft store or at your local farmers' market)
½ tsp honey
2 tsp almond oil (optional)
Vitamin E oil from a capsule (optional)

Directions
1. Melt the beeswax and honey in a heat-proof jar in the microwave or use a double boiler method.
2. When the wax and honey are just melted, remove from the heat source and whisk in the almond oil and vitamin E oil, if you so desire. To remove the vitamin E oil from the capsule, simply prick the end of the capsule with a safety pin and squeeze it out.

3. Pour the mixture into the containers and allow to cool fully before using.

Note: If you want to add a citrus flavoring to this lip gloss, you can add a few drops of lemon or lime essential oil during the whisking stage.

Tinted Lip Balm

If you have leftover make-up (such as blush, lipstick, or shimmering eye shadow), don't let it go to waste. You can use it in this "recycled" lip balm.

Ingredients
Petroleum jelly
Blush, mineral eye shadow with shimmer, lipstick (only use one or two of these for your balm)
Essential oil for flavoring (optional)

Directions
1. Mix together the petroleum jelly and either the blush (add a little at a time until the desired color is attained), eye shadow, or the last remnants of any lipstick. Add essential oil and mix thoroughly.
2. Scoop the mixture into containers and put in the refrigerator to harden.

Note: You can also experiment by melting the jelly with some beeswax and then adding in the leftover makeup. The possibilities are endless.

HOMEMADE BATH PRODUCTS

Lavender Bath Salt

Pour several tablespoons of this into your bath as it fills for an extra-soothing, relaxing, and cleansing experience. You can also add powdered milk or finely ground old-fashioned oatmeal to make your skin especially soft. Toss in a few lavender buds if you have them.

Ingredients
2 cups coarse sea salt
½ cup Epsom salts
½ cup baking soda
4 to 6 drops lavender essential oil
Red and blue food coloring, if desired (use more red than blue to achieve a lavender color)

Mix all ingredients thoroughly and store in a glass jar or other airtight container.

Citrus Scrub

Use this invigorating scrub to wake up your senses in the morning. The vitamin C in oranges serves as an astringent, making it especially good for oily skin.

Ingredients
½ orange or grapefruit
3 tbsp cornmeal
2 tbsp Epsom salts or coarse sea salt

Squeeze citrus juice and pulp into a bowl and add cornmeal and salts to form a paste. Rub gently over entire body and then rinse.

Healing Bath Soak

This bath soak will relax tired muscles, help to calm nerves, and leave skin soft and fragrant. You may also wish to add blackberry, raspberry, or violet leaves. Dried or fresh herbs can be used.

Ingredients
2 tbsp comfrey leaves
1 tbsp lavender
1 tbsp evening primrose flowers
1 tsp orange peel, thinly sliced or grated
2 tbsp oatmeal

Combine herbs and tie up in a small muslin or cheesecloth sack. Leave under faucet as the tub fills with hot water. If desired, empty herbs into the bathwater once the tub is full.

▲ Citrus scrub.

Rosemary Peppermint Foot Scrub

Use this foot scrub to remove calluses, soften skin, and leave your feet feeling and smelling wonderful.

Ingredients
1 cup coarse sea salt
¼ cup sweet almond or olive oil

2 to 3 drops peppermint essential oil

1 to 2 drops rosemary essential oil

2 sprigs fresh rosemary, crushed, or ½ tsp dried rosemary

Combine all ingredients and massage into feet and ankles. Rinse with warm water and follow with a moisturizer.

Minty Cucumber Facial Mask

Ingredients

1 tbsp powdered milk

1 tsp plain yogurt (whole milk yogurt is best)

1 tsp honey

1 tsp fresh mint leaves

½ cucumber, peeled

Blend ingredients thoroughly, using a food processor or blender if available. Apply to face, avoiding eyes. Leave on for 10 to 15 minutes, then rinse.

After-Sun Comfrey Lotion

Comfrey root soothes skin and minimizes inflammation. Apply this lotion to sunburned skin for immediate relief and faster healing.

Ingredients

3 tbsp fresh comfrey root

1 cup water

1 tbsp beeswax, unrefined

¾ cup sweet almond oil or light cooking oil

¼ cup cocoa butter

4 vitamin E capsules

¼ cup aloe vera gel

1 tsp borax powder

12 to 16 drops essential oil (peppermint, lavender, or sandalwood are all good choices)

Directions

1. Place the comfrey root and water in a small pot and bring to a boil, simmering for about 30 minutes. Strain, retaining the water. Discard the root.

2. In a double boiler, combine beeswax, oil, and cocoa butter, stirring over low heat until melted. Remove from heat. Pierce the vitamin E capsules and add the oil from inside, stirring to combine.

3. In a separate saucepan, combine the comfrey water, aloe vera gel, and borax powder, stirring over low heat until the borax is fully dissolved. Allow to cool.

4. Once both mixtures are cooled to room temperature, pour the beeswax and oil mixture in a thin stream into the comfrey water mixture, whisking vigorously to combine (or use a food processor). Add the essential oils and continue mixing until thoroughly combined.

5. Cover and store in a cool, dark place.

Herbs for Your Hair

Herbs for dry hair	Burdock root, comfrey, elderflowers, lavender, marshmallow, parsley, sage, stinging nettle
Herbs for oily hair	Calendula, horsetail, lemon juice, lemon balm, mints, rosemary, witch hazel, yarrow
Herbs to combat dandruff	Burdock root, garlic, onion, parsley, rosemary, stinging nettle, thyme
Herbs for body and luster	Calendula, catnip, horsetail, licorice, lime flowers, nasturtium, parsley, rosemary, sage, stinging nettle, watercress
Herbs for shine	Horsetail, parsley, nettle, rosemary, sage, calendula
Herbs for hair growth	Aloe, arnica, birch, burdock, catmint, chamomile, horsetail, licorice, marigold, nettles, parsley, rosemary, sage, stinging nettle
Herbs for coloring	Brown: henna (reddish brown), walnut hulls, sage Blonde: calendula, chamomile, lemon, saffron, turmeric, rhubarb root

Shampoo

Cleaning your hair can be as simple as making a baking soda and water paste, scrubbing it into your hair, and rinsing well. However, if you enjoy the feel of a sudsy, soapy, scented shampoo, try this recipe. You can substitute homemade soap flakes for the castile soap, if desired.

Ingredients
4 ounces liquid castile soap
3 tbsp fresh or dried herbs of your choice, boiled for 30 minutes in 2 cups water and strained

Pour the soap and herbal water into a jar, cover, and shake until well-combined.

Hair Conditioner

This conditioner will add softness and volume to your hair. Avocado, bananas, and egg yolks are also great hair conditioners. Apply conditioner, allow to sit in hair a minimum of five minutes (longer for a deeper conditioning), and then rinse well. You may wish to shampoo a second time after using this conditioner.

Ingredients
1 cup olive oil
1 tsp lemon juice
1 tsp cider vinegar
2 tsp honey
6 to 10 drops essential oils, if desired

Whisk all ingredients together or blend in a food processor. Store in an airtight container.

Fruits and Vegetables for Your Skin

These fruits and vegetables can be applied directly to your face or blended together to make a mask. Leave on skin for 20 to 30 minutes and then rinse thoroughly with clean water.

Beneficial for Oily Skin	Beneficial for Normal Skin	Beneficial for Dry Skin
Lemons, grapes, limes, strawberries, grapefruits, apples	Peaches, papayas, tomatoes, apricots, bananas, persimmons, bell peppers, cucumbers, kiwi, pumpkins, watermelons	Carrots, iceberg lettuce, honeydew melons, avocados, cantaloupes

Tropical Face Cleanser

The vitamin C in kiwi has enzymatic and cleansing properties, and the apricot oil serves as a moisturizer. The ground almonds act as an exfoliant to remove dead skin cells. Yogurt has cleansing and moisturizing properties.

   1 kiwi

   ¾ cup avocado, banana, apricot, peach, strawberry, or papaya (or some of each)

   2 tbsp plain yogurt (whole milk is best)

   1 tbsp apricot oil (almond oil also works well)

   1 tbsp honey

   1 tsp finely ground almonds

Purée all ingredients together. Massage into face and neck and rinse thoroughly with cool water. Store excess in refrigerator for one to two days.

▲ Papaya is ofen used in face creams for its anti-aging and anti-acne properties.

Natural Disasters

▲ Hurricanes occur more frequently in coastal areas, but they can happen anywhere.

It is impossible to predict exactly when a storm will come your way, or how severe it will be. However, you can be prepared. There are many steps you can take to help ensure your safety, as well as that of your family, pets, and property.

Hurricanes

If you live in an area particularly prone to hurricanes, taking precautions is especially important. However, hurricanes can form anywhere, so don't assume that just because you're not in the tropics, you're not at risk. Thinking ahead will, at the very least, give you greater peace of mind.

What to Do Before a Hurricane

If you live in a hurricane-prone area, you may want to take the following precautions:

- Install permanent shutters to protect your windows. Or you can board up windows with $5/8$-inch marine plywood. Have the plywood cut to fit and ready to install.
- Install straps or additional clips to fasten your roof securely to the frame structure. This will reduce roof damage.
- Be sure trees and shrubs around your home are well-trimmed.
- Clear loose and clogged rain gutters and downspouts.
- Determine how and where to secure your boat, if you have one.

▲ If there's time before a storm hits, remember to moor your boat securely.

▼ Shutters will help to protect your windows during wind storms.

If you are aware of a hurricane approaching, you should:

- Listen to the radio or TV for information.
- Secure your home, close storm shutters, and secure outdoor objects or bring them indoors.
- Turn off utilities if instructed to do so. If you leave the electricity on, turn the refrigerator thermostat to its coldest setting and keep its

doors closed so the food will stay colder longer if the electricity goes out.

- Turn off propane tanks. Avoid using the phone, except for serious emergencies.
- Moor your boat if time permits.
- Draw fresh water in jugs or in your bathtub or sink for use in drinking, bathing, and flushing toilets if the electricity goes out.

What to Do During a Hurricane

You should evacuate if:

- You are directed by local authorities to do so. Be sure to follow their instructions.
- You live in a mobile home or temporary structure—such shelters are particularly hazardous during hurricanes no matter how well-fastened to the ground.
- You live in a high-rise building—hurricane winds are stronger at higher elevations.
- You live on the coast, on a floodplain, near a river, or on an inland waterway.
- You feel you are in danger.

If you are unable to evacuate, go to a basement or underground shelter. If you do not have one, follow these guidelines:

- Stay indoors during the hurricane and away from windows and glass doors.
- Close all interior doors—secure and brace external doors.
- Keep curtains and blinds closed. Do not be fooled if there is a lull; it could be the eye of the storm—winds will pick up again.
- Take refuge in a small interior room, closet, or hallway on the lowest level.
- Lie on the floor under a table or another sturdy object.

▲ Watch the sky for warning signs of a serious storm approaching.

Floods

Floods are one of the most common hazards in the United States. However, not all floods are alike. Some floods develop slowly, sometimes over a period of days. Flash floods can develop quickly, sometimes in just a few minutes and without any visible signs of rain. Flash floods often have a dangerous wall of roaring water that carries rocks, mud, and other debris and can sweep away most things in its path. Overland flooding occurs outside a defined river or stream, such as when a levee is breached, but still can be destructive. Flooding can also occur when a dam breaks, producing effects similar to flash floods.

Be aware of flood hazards no matter where you live, but especially if you live in a low-lying area, near water, or downstream from a dam. Even very small streams, gullies, creeks, culverts, dry streambeds, or low-lying ground that appears harmless in dry weather can flood. Every state is at risk of this hazard.

What to Do Before a Flood

To prepare for a flood, you should:

- Avoid building in a flood-prone area unless you elevate and reinforce your home.
- Elevate the furnace, water heater, and electric panel if susceptible to flooding.
- Install "check valves" in sewer traps to prevent floodwater from backing up into the drains of your home.
- Contact community officials to find out if they are planning to construct barriers (levees, beams, or floodwalls) to stop floodwater from entering the homes in your area.
- Seal the walls in your basement with water-proofing compounds to avoid seepage.

If a flood is likely in your area, you should:

- Listen to the radio or television for information.

▲ If your home is by a river, lake, or canal, you are at a higher risk for flooding.

- Be aware that flash flooding can occur. If there is any possibility of a flash flood, move immediately to higher ground. Do not wait for instructions to move.

▲ In some areas particularly prone to flooding, homes are built on stilts.

- Be aware of streams, drainage channels, canyons, and other areas known to flood suddenly. Flash floods can occur in these areas with or without such typical warnings as rain clouds or heavy rain.

What to Do During a Flood

If you must prepare to evacuate, you should do the following:

- Secure your home. If you have time, bring in outdoor furniture. Move essential items to an upper floor.
- Turn off utilities at the main switches or valves if instructed to do so. Disconnect electrical appliances. Do not touch electrical equipment if you are wet or standing in water.

> **TIP** The following are important points to remember when driving in flood conditions:
> - Six inches of water will reach the bottom of most passenger cars, causing loss of control and possible stalling.
> - A foot of water will float many vehicles.
> - Two feet of rushing water can carry away most vehicles, including sport utility vehicles and pickup trucks.

If you have to leave your home, remember these evacuation tips:

- Do not walk through moving water. Six inches of moving water can make you fall. If you have to walk in water, walk where the water is not moving. Use a stick to check the firmness of the ground in front of you.
- Do not drive into flooded areas. If floodwaters rise around your car, abandon the car and move to higher ground if you can do so safely. You and the vehicle can be quickly swept away.

What to Do After a Flood

After a flood, you should:

- Listen for news reports to learn whether the community's water supply is safe to drink.
- Avoid floodwaters; water may be contaminated by oil, gasoline, or raw sewage. Water may also be electrically charged from underground or downed power lines.
- Avoid moving water.
- Be aware of areas where floodwaters have receded. Roads may have weakened and could collapse under the weight of a car.
- Stay away from downed power lines, and report them to the power company.
- Return home only when authorities indicate it is safe.
- Stay out of any building if it is surrounded by floodwaters.
- Use extreme caution when entering buildings; there may be hidden damage, particularly in foundations.
- Service damaged septic tanks, cesspools, pits, and leaching systems as soon as possible. Damaged sewage systems are serious health hazards.
- Clean and disinfect everything that got wet. Mud left from floodwater can contain sewage and chemicals.

> **TIP** Familiarize yourself with these terms to help identify a flood hazard:
> **Flood Watch:** Flooding is possible. Tune in to NOAA Weather Radio, commercial radio, or television for information.
> **Flash Flood Watch:** Flash flooding is possible. Be prepared to move to higher ground; listen to NOAA Weather Radio, commercial radio, or television for information.
> **Flood Warning:** Flooding is occurring or will occur soon; if advised to evacuate, do so immediately.
> **Flash Flood Warning:** A flash flood is occurring; seek higher ground on foot immediately.

Wildfires

The threat of wildfires for people living near wildland areas or using recreational facilities in wilderness areas is real. Dry conditions at various times of the year and in various parts of the United States greatly increase the potential for wildfires.

▲ Dry grass or other vegetation will encourage fire to spread quickly.

▲ Stucco homes are less vulnerable to fire than homes made of wood.

Advance planning and knowing how to protect buildings can lessen the devastation of a wildfire. There are several safety precautions that you can take to reduce the risk of fire losses. Protecting your home from wildfires is your responsibility. To reduce the risk, you'll need to consider the fire resistance of your home, the topography of your property, and the nature of the vegetation close by.

If you are considering moving to a home or buying land in an area prone to wildfires, consider having a professional inspect the property and offer recommendations for reducing the wildfire risk. Determine the community's ability to respond to wildfires. Are roads leading to your property clearly marked? Are the roads wide enough to allow firefighting equipment to get through?

Learn and Teach Safe Fire Practices

- Build fires away from nearby trees or bushes.
- Always have a way to extinguish the fire quickly and completely.
- Install smoke detectors on every level of your home and near sleeping areas.
- Never leave a fire—even a cigarette—burning unattended.
- Avoid open burning completely, especially during dry season.

What to Do Before a Wildfire

To prepare your home for a wildfire you should:

- **Create a 30-foot safety zone around the house.** Keep the volume of vegetation in this zone to a minimum. If you live on a hill, extend the zone on the downhill side. Fire spreads rapidly uphill. The steeper the slope, the more open space you will need to protect your home. Swimming pools and patios can be a safety zone and stonewalls can act as heat shields and deflect flames.
- Remove vines from the walls of the house and move shrubs and other landscaping away from the sides of the house. You should also prune branches and shrubs within 15 feet of chimneys and stovepipes, remove tree limbs within 15 feet of the ground, and thin a 15-foot space between tree crowns.
- Replace highly flammable vegetation such as pine, eucalyptus, junipers, and fir trees with lower growing, less-flammable species within the 30-foot safety zone. Check with your local fire department or garden store for suggestions. Also replace vegetation that has living or dead branches from the ground level up (these act as ladder

▲ Do not attempt to go back inside a house that is already burning.

fuels for the approaching fire). Cut the lawn often, keeping the grass at a maximum of 2 inches. Watch grass and other vegetation near the driveway, a source of ignition from automobile exhaust systems. Finally, clear the area of leaves, brush, evergreen cones, dead limbs, and fallen trees.

- **Create a second zone at least 100 feet around the house.** This zone should begin about 30 feet from the house and extend to at least 100 feet. In this zone, reduce or replace as much of the most flammable vegetation as possible. If you live on a hill, you may need to extend the zone for several hundred feet to provide the appropriate level of safety.

- **Remove debris from under sun decks and porches.** Any porch, balcony, or overhang with exposed space underneath is fuel for an approaching fire. Overhangs ignite easily by flying embers and by the heat and fire that get trapped underneath. If vegetation is allowed to grow underneath or if the space is used for storage, the hazard is increased significantly. Clear leaves, trash, and other combustible materials away from underneath sun decks and porches. Extend a ½-inch mesh screen from all overhangs down to the ground. Enclose wooden stilts with non-combustible material such as concrete, brick, rock, stucco, or metal. Use non-combustible patio furniture and covers. If you're planning a porch or sun deck, use non-combustible or fire-resistant materials. If possible, build the structure close to the ground so that there is no space underneath.

- **Enclose eaves and overhangs.** Like porches and balconies, eaves trap the heat rising along the exterior siding. Enclose all eaves to reduce the hazard.

- **Cover house vents with wire mesh.** Any attic vent, soffit vent, louver, or other opening can allow embers and flaming debris to enter a home and ignite it. Cover all openings with ¼ inch or smaller corrosion-resistant wire mesh. If you're

designing louvers, place them in the vertical wall rather than the soffit of the overhang.

- **Install spark arrestors in chimneys and stovepipes.** Chimneys create a hazard when embers escape through the top. To prevent this, install spark arrestors on all chimneys, stovepipes, and vents for fuel-burning heaters. Use spark arrestors made of 12-gauge welded or woven wire mesh screen with openings ½ inch across. Ask your fire department for exact specifications. If you're building a chimney, use non-combustible materials and make sure the top of the chimney is at least 2 feet higher than any obstruction within 10 feet of the chimney. Keep the chimney clean.

- **Use fire-resistant siding** such as stucco, metal, brick, cement shingles, concrete, or rock. You can treat wood siding with UL-approved fire retardant chemicals, but the treatment and protection are not permanent.

- **Choose safety glass for windows and sliding glass doors.** Windows allow radiated heat to pass through and ignite combustible materials inside. The larger the pane of glass, the more vulnerable it is to fire. Dual- or triple-pane thermal glass and fire-resistant shutters or drapes help reduce the wildfire risk. You can also install non-combustible awnings to shield windows and use shatter-resistant glazing such as tempered or wire glass.

- **Prepare for water storage; develop an external water supply such as a small pond, well, or pool.**

- **Always be ready for an emergency evacuation.** Evacuation may be the only way to protect your family in a wildfire. Know where to go and what to bring with you. You should plan several escape routes in case roads are blocked by a wildfire.

Handling Combustibles

- Install electrical lines underground, if possible.
- Ask the power company to clear branches from power lines.
- Avoid using bark and wood chip mulch.
- Stack firewood 100 feet away and uphill from any structure.
- Store combustible or flammable materials in approved safety containers and keep them away from the house.
- Keep the gas grill and propane tank at least 15 feet from any structure. Clear an area 15 feet around the grill. Place a ¼-inch mesh screen over the grill. Always use the grill cautiously and refrain from using it at all during high-risk times.

Safety Measures for New Construction or Remodeling

- Choose locations wisely; canyon and slope locations increase the risk of exposure to wildfires.
- Use fire-resistant materials when building, renovating, or retrofitting structures.
- Avoid designs that include wooden decks and patios.
- Use non-combustible materials for the roof.
- The roof is especially vulnerable in a wildfire. Embers and flaming debris can travel great distances, land on your roof, and start a new fire. Avoid flammable roofing materials such as wood, shake, and shingle. Materials that are more fire-resistant include single-ply membranes, fiberglass shingles, slate, metal, clay, and concrete tile. Clear gutters of leaves and debris.

What to Do if a Wildfire is Approaching

- Evacuate your pets and all family members who are not essential to preparing the home. Anyone with medical or physical limitations and the young and the elderly should be evacuated immediately.
- Wear protective clothing.
- Remove combustibles. Clear items that will burn from around the house, including woodpiles, lawn furniture, barbecue grills, tarp coverings, and so on. Move them outside of your defensible space.
- Close outside attic, eave, and basement vents, and windows, doors, and pet doors. Remove

Survival in a Vehicle

- This is dangerous and should only be done in an emergency, but you can survive the firestorm if you stay in your car. It is much less dangerous than trying to run from a fire on foot.
- Roll up windows and close air vents. Drive slowly with headlights on. Watch for other vehicles and pedestrians. Do not drive through heavy smoke.
- If you have to stop, park away from the heaviest trees and brush. Turn headlights on and ignition off. Roll up windows and close air vents.
- Get on the floor and cover up with a blanket or coat.
- Stay in the vehicle until the main fire passes.
- Stay in the car. Do not run! The engine may stall and not restart. Air currents may rock the car. Some smoke and sparks may enter the vehicle. Temperature inside will increase. Metal gas tanks and containers rarely explode.

If Caught in the Open

- The best temporary shelter is in a sparse fuel area. On a steep mountainside, the back side is safer. Avoid canyons, natural "chimneys," and saddles.
- If a road is nearby, lie face down along the road cut or in the ditch on the uphill side. Cover yourself with anything that will shield you from the fire's heat.
- If hiking in the back country, seek a depression with sparse fuel. Clear fuel away from the area while the fire is approaching and then lie face down in the depression and cover yourself. Stay down until after the fire passes!

flammable drapes and curtains. Close all shutters, blinds, or heavy non-combustible window coverings to reduce radiant heat.
- Close inside doors and open damper. Close all doors inside the house to prevent draft. Open the damper on your fireplace, but close the fireplace screen.
- Shut off any natural gas, propane, or fuel oil supplies at the source.
- Connect garden hoses and fill any pools, hot tubs, garbage cans, tubs, or other large containers with water.
- If you have gas-powered pumps for water, make sure they are fueled and ready.
- Place a ladder against the house in clear view.
- Back your car into the driveway and roll up the windows.
- Disconnect any automatic garage door openers so that doors can still be opened by hand if the power goes out. Close all garage doors.
- Place valuable papers, mementos, and anything you "can't live without" inside the car, ready for quick departure. Any pets still with you should also be put in the car.
- Just before evacuating, turn on outside lights and leave a light on in every room to make the house more visible in heavy smoke.
- Leave doors and windows closed but unlocked. It may be necessary for firefighters to gain quick entry into your home. The entire area will be isolated and patrolled by police.

What to Do After a Wildfire

- Check the roof immediately. Put out any roof fires, sparks, or embers. Check the attic for hidden burning sparks.
- If you have a fire, get your neighbors to help fight it.

- The water you put into your pool or hot tub and other containers will come in handy now. If the power is out, try connecting a hose to the outlet on your water heater.
- For several hours after the fire, maintain a "fire watch." Re-check for smoke and sparks throughout the house.

Earthquakes

One of the most frightening and destructive phenomena of nature is a severe earthquake and its terrible aftereffects. Earthquakes strike suddenly, violently, and without warning at any time of the day or night. If an earthquake occurs in a populated area, it may cause many deaths and injuries and extensive property damage.

Although there are no guarantees of safety during an earthquake, identifying potential hazards ahead of time and planning appropriately can save lives and significantly reduce injuries and property damage.

What to Do Before an Earthquake

- **Check for hazards in the home.** Fasten shelves securely to walls, place large or heavy objects on lower shelves, and store breakable items such as bottled foods, glass, and china in low, closed cabinets with latches. Hang heavy items such as pictures and mirrors away from beds, couches, and anywhere people sit. Brace overhead light fixtures. Repair defective electrical wiring and leaky gas connections and secure a water heater by strapping it to the wall studs and bolting it to the floor. Repair any deep cracks in ceilings or foundations, getting expert advice if there are signs of structural defects. Store weed killers, pesticides, and flammable products securely in closed cabinets with latches and on bottom shelves.
- **Identify safe places indoors and outdoors.** Safe places include under sturdy furniture such as a heavy desk or table; against an inside wall; away from where glass could shatter around windows, mirrors, pictures, or where heavy bookcases or other heavy furniture could fall over; or in the open, away from buildings, trees, telephone and electrical lines, overpasses, or elevated expressways.
- **Educate yourself and family members.** Contact your local emergency management office or American Red Cross chapter for more information on earthquakes. Teach children how and when to call 911, police, or fire department and which radio station to tune to for emergency information. Teach all family members how and when to turn off gas, electricity, and water.

▲ Even a relatively minor earthquake can leave a home in shambles.

▲ It is best to store china and other breakables in closed, latched cabinets.

- **Have disaster supplies on hand**, including a flashlight and extra batteries, portable battery-operated radio and extra batteries, first aid kit and manual, emergency food and water, non-electric can opener, essential medicines, and sturdy shoes.
- **Develop an emergency communication plan**. In case family members are separated from one another during an earthquake, develop a plan for reuniting after the disaster. Ask an out-of-state relative or friend to serve as the "family contact." After a disaster, it's often easier to call long distance. Make sure everyone in the family knows the name, address, and phone number of the contact person.

What to Do During an Earthquake

Be aware that some earthquakes are actually foreshocks and a larger earthquake might occur. Minimize your movements to a few steps to a nearby safe place and stay indoors until the shaking has stopped and you are sure exiting is safe.

If indoors:
- Drop to the ground, take cover by getting under a sturdy table or other piece of furniture, and hold on until the shaking stops. If there isn't a table or desk near you, cover your face and head with your arms and crouch in an inside corner of the building.
- Stay away from glass, windows, outside doors and walls, and anything that could fall, such as lighting fixtures or furniture.
- Stay in bed if you are there when the earthquake strikes. Hold on and protect your head with a pillow, unless you are under a heavy light fixture that could fall. In that case, move to the nearest safe place.

- Use a doorway for shelter only if it is in close proximity to you and if you know it is a strongly supported, load-bearing doorway.
- Stay inside until shaking stops and it is safe to go outside. Research has shown that most injuries occur when people inside buildings attempt to move to a different location inside the building or try to leave.
- Be aware that the electricity may go out or the sprinkler systems or fire alarms may turn on.

If outdoors:
- Stay outside.
- Move away from buildings, streetlights, and utility wires.
- Once in the open, stay there until the shaking stops. The greatest danger exists directly outside buildings, at exits, and alongside exterior walls. Many of the 120 fatalities from the 1933 Long Beach earthquake occurred when people ran outside of buildings only to be killed by falling debris from collapsing walls. Ground movement during an earthquake is seldom the direct cause of death or injury. Most earthquake-related casualties result from collapsing walls, flying glass, and falling objects.

If in a moving vehicle:
- Stop as quickly as safety permits and stay in the vehicle. Avoid stopping near or under buildings, trees, overpasses, and utility wires.
- Proceed cautiously once the earthquake has stopped. Avoid roads, bridges, or ramps that might have been damaged by the earthquake.

If trapped under debris:
- Do not light a match.
- Do not move about or kick up dust.
- Cover your mouth with a handkerchief or clothing.
- Tap on a pipe or wall so rescuers can locate you. Use a whistle if one is available. Shout only as a last resort. Shouting can cause you to inhale dangerous amounts of dust.

What to Do After an Earthquake

- **Expect aftershocks.** These secondary shockwaves are usually less violent than the main quake but can be strong enough to do additional damage to weakened structures and can occur in the first hours, days, weeks, or even months after the quake.
- **Listen to a battery-operated radio or television.** Listen for the latest emergency information.
- **Open cabinets cautiously.** Beware of objects that can fall off shelves.

▲ Inspect your utilities after an earthquake to be sure there are no leaks or other damage.

- **Stay away from damaged areas** unless your assistance has been specifically requested by police, fire, or relief organizations. Return home only when authorities say it is safe.
- **Be aware of possible tsunamis if you live in coastal areas.** These are also known as seismic sea waves (mistakenly called "tidal waves"). When local authorities issue a tsunami warning, assume that a series of dangerous waves is on the way. Stay away from the beach.
- **Help injured or trapped persons.** Remember to help your neighbors who may require special assistance, such as infants, the elderly, and people with disabilities. Give first aid where appropriate. Do not move seriously injured persons unless they are in immediate danger of further injury. Call for help.
- **Clean up spilled medicines, bleaches, gasoline, or other flammable liquids immediately.** Leave the area if you smell gas or fumes from other chemicals.
- **Inspect the entire length of chimneys for damage.** Unnoticed damage could lead to a fire.
- **Inspect utilities. Check for gas leaks.** If you smell gas or hear a blowing or hissing noise, open a window and quickly leave the building. Turn off the gas at the outside main valve if you can and call the gas company from a neighbor's

home. If you turn off the gas for any reason, it must be turned back on by a professional. Second, **look for electrical system damage.** If you see sparks or broken or frayed wires, or if you smell hot insulation, turn off the electricity at the main fuse box or circuit breaker. If you have to step in water to get to the fuse box or circuit breaker, call an electrician first for advice. Finally, **check for sewage and water line damage.** If you suspect sewage lines are damaged, avoid using the toilets and call a plumber. If water pipes are damaged, contact the water company and avoid using water from the tap. You can obtain safe water by melting ice cubes.

▲ An excavator cleans up debris after an earthquake.

First Aid

It's impossible to predict when an accident will occur, but the more you educate yourself ahead of time, the better you'll be able to help should the need arise. The first step in an emergency situation should always be to call for help, but there are many things you can do to help the victim while you're waiting for assistance to arrive. The most important procedures are described in this section.

▼ Keep a buoy nearby whenever spending time in or near the water.

Drowning

1. As soon as the patient is in a safe place, loosen the clothing, if any.
2. Empty the lungs of water by laying the body breastdown and lifting it by the middle, with the head hanging down. Hold for a few seconds until the water drains out.
3. Turn the patient on his breast, face downward.
4. Give artificial respiration: Press the lower ribs down and forward toward the head, then release. Repeat about twelve times to the minute.
5. Apply warmth and friction to extremities, rubbing toward the heart.
6. Don't give up! Persons have been saved after hours of steady effort, and after being underwater for more than twenty minutes.
7. When natural breathing is reestablished, put the patient into a warm bed, with hot-water bottles, warm drinks, fresh air, and quiet.

Sunstroke

1. Move the patient to a cool place, or set up a structure around the patient to produce shade.
2. Loosen or remove any clothing around the neck and upper body.
3. Apply cold water or ice to the head and body, or wrap the patient in cold, damp cloths.
4. Encourage the patient to drink lots of water.

Burns and Scalds

1. Cover the burn with a thin paste of baking soda, starch, flour, petroleum jelly, olive oil, linseed oil, castor oil, cream, or cold cream.
2. Cover the burn first with the paste, then with a soft rag soaked in the paste.
3. Shock always accompanies severe burns, and must be treated.

Shock or Nervous Collapse

A person suffering from shock has a pale face, cold skin, feeble breathing, and a rapid, feeble pulse, and will appear listless.

1. Place the patient on his back with head low.
2. Give stimulants, such as hot tea or coffee.

▼ A simple hand bandage can be made from any square cloth or handkerchief.

417

3. Cover the patient with blankets.
4. Rub the limbs and place hot-water bottles around the body.

Cuts and Wounds

1. After making sure that no dirt or foreign substance is in the wound, apply a tight bandage to stop the bleeding.
2. Raise the wound above the heart to slow the bleeding.
3. If the blood comes out in spurts, it means an artery has been cut. For this, apply a tourniquet: Make a big knot in a handkerchief, tie it around the limb, with the knot just above the wound, and twist it until the flow is stopped.

How to Make a Tourniquet

The tourniquet is an appliance used to check severe bleeding. It consists of a bandage twisted more or less lightly around the affected part. The bandage—a cloth, strap, belt, necktie, neckerchief or towel—should be long enough to go around the arm or leg affected. It can then be twisted by inserting the hand, and the blood stopped.

If a stick is used, there is danger of twisting too tightly.

The tourniquet should not be used if bleeding can be stopped without it. When used it should be carefully loosened every 15 to 20 minutes to avoid permanent damage to tissues.

Hemorrhage or Internal Bleeding

Internal bleeding usually comes from the lungs or stomach. If from the lungs, the blood is bright red and frothy, and is coughed up; if from the stomach, it is dark, and is vomited.

1. Help the patient to lie down, with head lower than body.
2. Encourage the patient to swallow small pieces of ice, and apply ice bags, snow, or cold water to the place where the bleeding is coming from.
3. Hot applications may be applied to the hands, arms, feet, and legs, but avoid stimulants, unless the patient is very weak.

Fainting

Fainting is caused by a lack of blood supply to the brain and is cured by getting the heart to correct the lack.

1. Have the person lie down with the head lower than the body.
2. Loosen the clothing. Give fresh air. Rub the limbs. Use smelling salts.
3. Do not let the person get up until fully recovered.

Snake Bite

1. Put a tight cord or bandage around the limb between the wound and the heart. This should be loose enough to slip a finger under it.
2. Keep the wound lower than the heart. Try to keep the patient calm, as the faster the heart beats, the faster the venom will spread.
3. If you cannot get to a doctor quickly, suck the wound many times with your mouth or use a poison suction kit, if available.

Insect Stings

1. Wash with oil, weak ammonia, or very salty water, or paint with iodine.
2. A paste of baking soda and water also soothes stings.

Poison

1. First, get the victim away from the poison. If the poison is in solid form, such as pills, remove it from the victim's mouth using a clean cloth wrapped around your finger. Don't try this with infants because it could force the poison further down their throat.
2. If the poison is corrosive to the skin, remove the clothing from the affected area and flush with water for 30 minutes.
3. If the poison is in contact with the eyes, flush the victim's eyes for a minimum of 15 minutes with clean water.

How to Put Out Burning Clothing

1. If your clothing should catch fire, do not run for help, as this will fan the flames.
2. Lie down and roll up as tightly as possible in an overcoat, blanket, rug, or any woolen article—or lie down and roll over slowly, at the same time beating the fire with your hands. Smother the fire with a coat, blanket, or rug. Remember that woolen material is much less flammable than cotton.

Ice Rescue

1. Always have a rope nearby if you're working or playing on ice. This way, if someone falls through, you can tie one end to yourself and one to a tree or other secure anchor onshore before you attempt to rescue the person.
2. You could also throw one end to the victim if his head is above water.
3. Do not attempt to walk out to victim. Push out to him or crawl out on a long board or rail or tree trunk.
4. The person in the water should never try to crawl up on the broken ice, but should try merely to support himself and wait for help, if it is at hand.

For elbow, arm, or wrist ▶ injuries, a simple sling can be made out of a piece of cloth or clothing.

Broken Bone

A simple fracture is one in which the bone is broken but does not break the skin. In a compound fracture, the bone is broken and the skin and tissue are punctured or torn. A simple fracture may be converted into

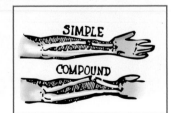

A compound fracture ▶ is one that breaks through the flesh.

a compound fracture by careless handling, as a broken bone usually has sharp, saw-tooth edges, and just a little twist may push it through the skin.

1. Do not move the patient without supporting broken member by splints.
2. In a compound fracture, bleeding must be checked—by bandage over compress, if possible, or by tourniquet in extreme cases. Then splints may be applied.
3. Where skin is broken, infection is the great danger, so exercise care that compress or dressing is sterile and clean.

Dislocation

A dislocation is an injury where the head of a bone has slipped out of its socket at a joint.

1. Do not attempt to replace the joint. Even thumb and finger dislocations are more serious than usually realized.
2. Cover the joint with cloths wrung out in very hot or very cold water. For the shoulder—apply padding and make a sling for the arm.
3. Seek medical assistance.

Grip to form basket seat

Two-handed chair carry

Chair carry

"Three bearers' position for lift"

"Three bearers' lift"

Arm carry

Horseback carry

▲ There are many ways to carry someone with an injury. If neck or spine injury is suspected, do not attempt to move the victim if you can get help to come to the victim instead. If the victim must be moved, the head and neck must first be carefully stabilized.

First Aid Checklist

To administer effective first aid, it is important to maintain adequate supplies in each first aid kit. A first aid kit should include:

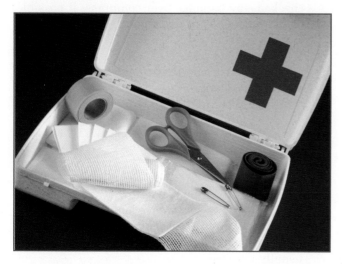

- Adhesive bandages: These are available in a large range of sizes for minor cuts, abrasions, and puncture wounds.
- Butterfly closures: These hold wound edges firmly together.
- Rolled gauze: These allow freedom of movement and are recommended for securing a wound dressing and/or pads. These are especially good for hard-to-bandage wounds.

Nature's First Aid

Antiseptic or *wound-wash*: A handful of salt in a quart of hot water.

Balm for wounds: Balsam fir. The gum can be used as healing salve, usually spread on a piece of linen and laid over the wound for a dressing.

Cough remedy: Slippery elm or black cherry inner bark boiled, a pound to the gallon, boiled down to a pint, and given a teaspoonful every hour.

Linseed can be used the same way; add honey if desired. Or boil down the sap of the sweet birch tree and drink it on its own or mixed with the other remedies.

Diuretic: A decoction of the inner bark of elder is a powerful diuretic.

Inflammation of the eyes or skin: Wash with a strong tea made of the bark of witch hazel.

Lung balm: Infusion of black cherry bark and root is a powerful tonic for lungs and bowels. Good also as a skin wash for sores.

Poison ivy: Wash every hour or two with hot soapy water, then with hot salt water.

- Nonstick sterile pads: These are soft, super-absorbent pads that provide a good environment for wound healing. These are recommended for bleeding and draining wounds, burns, or infections.
- First aid tapes: Various types of tapes should be included in each kit. These include adhesive, which is waterproof and extra strong for times when rigid strapping is needed; clear, which stretches with the body's movement and is good for visible wounds; cloth, recommended for most first aid taping needs, including taping heavy dressings (less irritating than adhesive); and paper, which is recommended for sensitive skin and is used for light and frequently changed dressings.
- Items that can also be included in each kit are tweezers, first aid cream, thermometer, an analgesic or equivalent, and an ice pack.

▲ Witch hazel bark can be brewed and used to soothe irritated skin or eyes.

Managing and Reducing Stress

Stress is the body's natural response to what it perceives as a threatening condition, and in and of itself it is not a bad thing. Stress can trigger the release of adrenaline in your system to help you get through difficult or dangerous situations, and studies have shown that brief stressful experiences can actually boost your immune system. However, prolonged periods of stress can take a serious toll on your mental and physical health.

Stress can cause our bodies to react in a number of physical ways, including tightening of muscles and rapid breathing—resulting in rapid blood flow, which spreads the increased oxygen throughout the body—and nausea may set in, and thinking processes become chaotic. Once the stress is alleviated, our body then slips into a weakened state as it recovers from the adrenaline surge. Although life would be dull without some stress, finding yourself in a constant state of stress can impair the immune system, making it less able to resist viruses, and can lead to a constant sense of exhaustion and loss of energy.

Symptoms of Stress

Stress can manifest itself in a variety of ways and can be easily confused with symptoms of other problems. If it is not managed properly, stress may cause problems that can reduce our overall ability to function effectively.

Common symptoms of stress also include:
- Constipation, diarrhea, or problems with urination

▲ Spending even a few minutes outdoors in natural light can help relieve stress, boost your mood, and increase productivity.

- Difficulty concentrating
- Fatigue
- Feelings of inadequacy
- Feelings of irritability or hostility
- Feelings of nervousness or anxiety
- Frequent headaches
- Increased use of alcohol or drugs
- Withdrawal from family and friends
- Increased appetite

Myths About Stress

There are many myths about stress, including how stress affects us and what causes it. Listed below are the most common.
- Myth: Stress is the same for everyone.

Truth: Stress is different for each of us and what is stressful for one person may or may not be for another. There's no way to say that one thing that causes stress is "bad" or "stressful," because everyone is different.

Managing and Reducing Stress

• Myth: Stress is always bad for you.

Truth: Stress can overwhelm you or it can add zest to life. The determining factor is how well you manage your stress. If effectively managed, stress can result in increased productivity and happiness, while poorly managed stress can have the opposite effect.

• Myth: Stress is everywhere and is unavoidable.

Truth: Stress is everywhere, but this is a negative outlook. You can take control of your life and plan so that stress does not overwhelm you. Learning to delegate and prioritize can help you manage stress. As a wise person once said, "Managing stress is like weeding your garden; you can never get rid of [the weeds] completely, but you can keep them under control."

Strategies for Stress Management

Stress management is the way we respond and react to the everyday pressures and demands of life. Developing effective stress management skills is crucial for controlling stress.

Balance work and recreation. Take time out for yourself and do something you enjoy, letting yourself relax and recharge. Consider scheduling a break into your busy day, taking five or 10 minutes to stop working and do something you enjoy. Work on a crossword puzzle, take a quick walk, step outside for a breath of fresh air, sing, call a friend to schedule a lunch date, or simply stare out the window. If you're at home and start to feel stressed, turn off the TV or music, find a place by yourself that is quiet, and let yourself relax.

Once a month, schedule a few hours or even an entire day that is just for you. Remember that this time should be special and not rushed. During this time, do what makes you feel happy and relaxed, whether that is taking a walk or driving somewhere, sleeping in, or reading a new book. Learning to integrate joyful moments into your daily life will go a long way toward alleviating and preventing stress.

Deep breathing, when done properly, will relax the body even as it confronts high levels of stress or panic. It is physically impossible for your muscles to remain tense when you take deep, relaxing breaths. When you feel the tension mounting, stop, close your eyes, and take a few long, deep breaths. Breathe through your diaphragm and not your chest. Feel the breath coming in through your nostrils and into your belly—your belly will actually rise—and allow the breath to expel through your mouth as your belly contracts. This pause only lasts a minute or so, but it can clear your mind and allow you to refocus your energy on the task at hand. If you can, try closing your eyes, letting yourself become conscious of the sounds and smells in your surroundings. While your eyes are closed, relax the muscles of your body, starting with the small muscles around your eyes, your cheeks, and

▲ With its focus on breath, yoga helps to strengthen and heal the body and to discipline the mind.

▲ Take at least a few minutes every day to be still.

▲ Journaling can be a healthy way to process stressful situations.

your neck, then progressing to the larger ones in your shoulders and arms, back, and legs and feet.

Consider the source. Figuring out what is causing your body to feel stressed is the first step toward resolving the problem. Speaking with your boss about difficulties at work or talking with your neighbor about his dog's constant barking can reduce your stress simply because you've had the chance to express your feelings on the matter. Remember that not all stress is bad, and effective stress management means changing how you respond to difficult situations. You can't control all the outside events in your life, but you can change how you handle them emotionally and psychologically.

Get enough rest and sleep. Although not everyone has the same requirements for rest and sleep, the majority of us need at least seven to eight hours per night. Try to develop a regular sleep schedule, going to bed and getting up at about the same time every day. Avoid alcohol, caffeine, nicotine, and exercise prior to bedtime. You may also want to develop a bedtime routine, like showering, soaking in a warm tub, reading, or listening to soft music, prior to falling asleep.

Learn to laugh! Research has shown that laughter helps the body relax, enhances the immune system, and increases problem-solving abilities. Think about how good you feel after a good laugh: You are breathing more deeply, your face and neck are more relaxed, and you feel happier. Making a special effort to look for humor, noticing the lighter side of things, and learning to laugh at yourself and with others will go a long way in reducing your stress.

Moving your body is an excellent way to dissipate stress. You can develop a formal exercise plan, but a less formal approach will work equally well. Taking daily walks can go a long way toward reducing stress

and increasing your energy level. When you feel too tired to move, get up and dance, walk, or just jump in place. Doing any of these actions will increase the flow of blood through the body and the brain, reinvigorating you for the tasks ahead.

Organize and manage time effectively. Trying to do too much in too little time is a stress trap. Since you cannot make more time, managing the time you have is vital. The three Ps of effective time management that can assist you are as follows:

- Plan: Schedule and set realistic time lines.
- Prioritize: Set goals for important things.
- Protect: Learn to say "no" to unwanted demands and avoid time wasters.

Seek out support. Having a network of supportive friends and acquaintances is a vital resource in coping with stress. Sharing and confiding can buffer the stress connected with life's daily hassles. It is important to remember that you are not alone and that others can understand and empathize.

Stress-Management Techniques

- Try to have an ending and beginning to each task. This definition will program progress. Take at least a minute-long break between each task.
- Throughout the day, take several small breaks of just a couple of minutes each (up to five minutes). Using this time to oxygenate the lungs—fill your lungs to capacity by inhaling slowly, then exhale slowly, pursing your lips as if exhaling through a straw.
- Occasionally, close your eyes and become conscious of the sounds and smells in your surroundings. While your eyes are closed, relax the muscles of your body, starting with the small muscles around your eyes, your cheeks, your neck, your shoulders and arms, your back, legs, and feet.
- Take a walk for pleasure.
- Go to the forest or a stream and sit, relax, read, or just sleep.
- Once a month, schedule a few hours or a day, especially for you. Write it down like an appointment with your doctor. During this time, take a walk or drive, sleep, write, draw, meet a new person, or read a new book.
- Remember to care for your body with natural remedies and supplements.

Seek professional assistance. Stress is a fact of life that may require permanent life style changes to manage. It gets easier with practice, but you must be constantly aware of the symptoms and avoid slipping back into your old habits. If you continue to have problems managing your stress, you may want to seek professional help. If you take that route, find a caring, knowledgable, and non-judgmental person to assist you. Consider seeing a psychologist, psychiatrist, doctor, minister, social worker, or counselor. If you do seek professional assistance, be prepared with a list of the things in your life that are currently causing you to feel stressed.

Stress is a reality of modern society. Everyone confronts it daily and must decide for themselves how they will live with it. Recognizing the symptoms of stress will allow you to address the source before the physical or emotional consequences become overwhelming. Learning to slow down, breathe deeply, and see the humor in life will promote health and well-being.

Massage

Massage therapy (and, in general, the laying on of hands for health purposes) dates back thousands of years. References to massage have been found in ancient writings from many cultures, including those of Ancient Greece, Ancient Rome, Japan, China, Egypt, and the Indian subcontinent.

In the United States, massage therapy first became popular and was promoted for a variety of health purposes starting in the mid-1800s. In the 1930s and 1940s, however, massage fell out of favor, mostly because of scientific and technological advances in

medical treatments. Massage has been gaining in popularity since the '70s, as more and more people recognize its ability to rehabilitate sports injuries, reduce stress, increase relaxation, address feelings of anxiety and depression, and aid general wellness.

There are more than 80 types of massage therapy. In all of them, therapists press, rub, and otherwise manipulate the muscles and other soft tissues of the body, often varying pressure and movement. They most often use their hands and fingers, but may use their forearms, elbows, or feet. Typically, the intent is to relax the soft tissues, increase delivery of blood and oxygen to the massaged areas, warm them, and decrease pain.

A few popular forms of massage are:

Aromatherapy massage: This is similar to Swedish massage but incorporates strong-scented plant oils that contribute to a sense of relaxation and well-being. Aromatherapy has helped to cure a range of conditions, even including acne and whooping cough.

Deep tissue massage: The therapist uses patterns of strokes and deep finger pressure on parts of the body where muscles are tight or knotted, focusing on layers of muscle deep under the skin.

Shiatsu massage: The therapist applies varying, rhythmic pressure from the fingers on parts of the body that are believed to be important for the flow of a vital energy called *qi* (pronounced "chee"). In traditional Chinese medicine, *qi* is the vital energy or life force proposed to regulate a person's spiritual, emotional, mental, and physical health and to be influenced by the opposing forces of yin and yang.

Swedish massage: The therapist uses long strokes, kneading, and friction on the muscles and moves the joints to aid flexibility.

Trigger point massage (also called pressure point massage): The therapist uses a variety of strokes but applies deeper, more focused pressure on myofascial trigger points. These "knots" that can form in the muscles are painful when pressed, and cause symptoms elsewhere in the body as well.

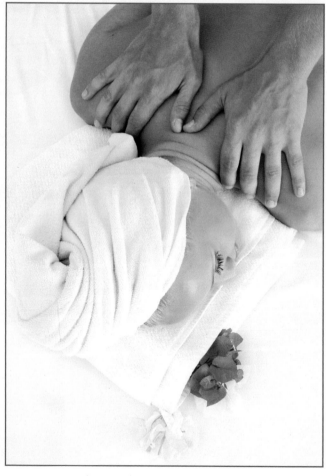

Massage is particularly powerful because it works on the physical, psychological, and often emotional and spiritual levels. When done with love, care, and skill, it soothes and stimulates the skin, muscles, organs, mind, emotions, and spirit, all of which are connected more than we often consider. We can observe this in some obvious ways; if you are stressed, for example, your shoulders and neck tense up and the muscles can constrict and form knots. Likewise, when you have a bad headache, you're more likely to be irritable or emotional, which can then lead to stomach upset. Massage, when it is most effective, helps to heal the body, emotions, and spirit.

Preparation

A massage can be as simple as squeezing the top of your own shoulder while you stand in line at the grocery store or gently rubbing your child's back in a circular motion to soothe her to sleep. However, if you wish to give a friend or loved one a more complete massage, you may want to do a little setting up.

Choose a draft-free, quiet room where there will be few distractions. Be sure it is warm enough that the person receiving the massage will not get cold while lying still for a length of time. Lighting should be soft and, if desired, have soothing music playing in the background. The surface where the recipient will be lying should be comfortable but firm; a futon covered with a clean sheet or several blankets layered on the floor will work.

If you plan to use massage oils or lotion to ease the friction on the skin, have these close at hand. You may also want to light scented candles or burn incense, depending on the recipient's needs and desires. Finally, be sure your hands are clean before beginning a massage, and tie back your hair if it's likely to get in your way.

Basic Strokes and Principles

Always make the massage recipient's needs your priority. Pay attention to the recipient's reactions to your strokes and ask occasionally whether she would prefer a lighter or firmer touch, or if what you're doing feels good. It is normal to experience slight pain or discomfort when pressure is applied to tense muscles, but if the recipient experiences sharp jolts of pain, nausea, or ripping or tearing sensations, ease off the pressure or move your touch to a different location. The recipient should always have the final say as to what is most beneficial in his or her massage.

For a basic full-body massage, the recipient should begin lying on her stomach with elbows at a right angle and hands on either side of the head. A small pillow can be placed under the chest or head if desired.

Do not massage areas where there is bruised or broken skin, infected areas, unusual swelling or inflammation, or where there are varicose veins present. Do not massage anyone who has a fever or high temperature.

Do massage toward the heart to improve blood circulation and lymph return, stay focused throughout the massage, respect the recipient's needs and desires, and start with a light touch, gradually using the leverage of your body weight to increase pressure as the recipient desires.

Long, gentle, flowing strokes using consistent light pressure on the full surface of the hands should be used to begin and end a massage. Use both hands, moving up and down the length of the back and then in sweeping motions across the width of the back. This stimulates the skin, gives the recipient a chance to adjust to your touch, and allows you a few moments to sense the recipient's needs. At the end of the massage, it will leave the recipient with a sense of being calmed and nurtured.

Muscle kneading involves picking up the muscles with one hand and squeezing with the other, from the spinal column outward, following the course of the trapezius and latissimus muscles, first on one side of the back, then on the other. This is also effective moving from the shoulders down to the elbow and from the tops of the thighs to just above the knees. This increases circulation and the action of the nerves and helps to relax tired muscles.

◄ Use gentle pressure in small circles on the temples and along the eyebrows and jawline for a relaxing face massage.

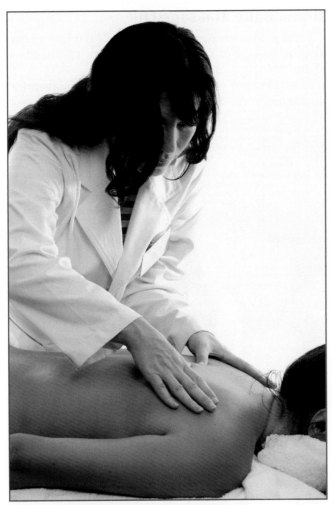

▲ When using the circular kneading technique, pause and do a few extra circles in any area where you can feel knots or extra tension.

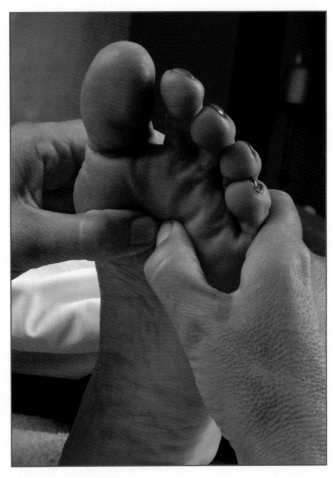

▲ When massaging feet, start at the center just below the ball of the foot and work down toward the heel. Then gently squeeze each toe from the base to the tip. Finally, use your thumbs to press along the arch, sliding them from just above the heel up toward the base of the big toe.

Circular kneading involves using the middle three fingers or thumb of each hand, beginning at the neck on each side of the spine and applying the circular kneading outward, then beginning a little lower and working outward, one hand on each side, and so on to the end of the spine. This technique can also be used along the arms and legs. It increases blood flow, which will loosen and soothe muscles.

Muscle rolling involves putting both hands side by side on one of the recipient's shoulders and making an alternating, very rapid pushing and pulling motion with the hands, gradually moving downward to the buttocks. The hands must be firmly on the patient so as to move his muscles from side to side, thereby causing a quick stretching and a vibration of them. First roll the muscles of one side of the back three to five times, then the other side. This helps to increase circulation, which will help muscles to loosen and improve the skin.

Vibration involves putting both hands, with the fingers spread out, one on each side of the patient's

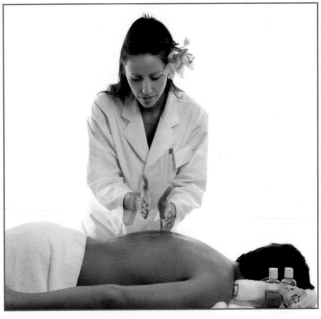

▲ Percussion massage is great for stimulating nerve centers and increasing blood flow.

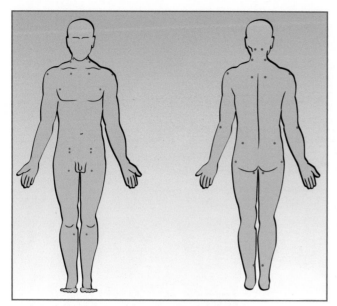

▲ Gently massaging pressure points can help to relieve pain and promote healing.

back at the shoulders. Pull downward with a firm pressure and a rapid vibration of hands and fingers. Repeat three to five times to stimulate the nerves.

Spinal nerve compression involves pressing with the middle and index fingers on each side of the spinal column from the neck to the end of the spine. The pressure should be made a little inward and upward and firmly, without jerking, in a slow and quiet way. Repeat two to four times to relieve backache and to stimulate nerve centers.

Percussion is applied with the edges of both hands and fingers alternately and very quickly from the neck downward on both sides of the spinal column. On the upper part of the back, from the shoulders to the lower end of the lungs, the percussion may also be applied outward to the sides. This technique can also be applied to the fleshy parts of the arms and legs, but avoid elbows, knees, the underside of the arms, and any other sensitive areas. This has a very stimulating and strengthening effect on the nerve centers.

Homemade Massage Oil

1 cup jojoba, grape seed, or almond oil (olive oil can also be used, but can cause breakouts on sensitive skin)

12 to 15 drops essential oil of your choice (lavender, jasmine, myrrh, orange, or mint are all good choices)

Interior Design

Making the Most of Your Space

The space that you live in will have an effect on how you feel. Taking the time to make your space pleasant will help you to feel more productive, peaceful, and creative. Even in small apartments or houses, you can arrange your furniture and belongings and decorate in a way that will make your space feel open and airy.

The majority of rooms are square and the walls are broken up by doors and windows. Finding enough shelving or even room for bookcases can be difficult when you are dealing with smaller rooms. Since shelving is necessary in most homes (and in confined spaces), here are some simple ideas of how to add shelving to make the most of your small space:

1. Shelves can be placed above sofas or tables. These can house books, picture frames, games, candles, and, if in the kitchen, spices and other small foodstuffs.
2. Windowsills can be extended and made into shelves as well. These are great places to keep plants and books, as long as the rain does not come in and ruin them.
3. If you have a fireplace with a mantelpiece, use the mantel for storing books and other items and you can also build bookcases around the mantel to store trinkets, magazines, DVDs, etc.
4. Shelves can also be built around the trim of doors or even above the door frame. These can

▼ Shelves can be built directly onto a wall to conserve floor space.

house books and other items, and pieces of pottery or wicker baskets can be placed above the doorframe to add a cozy and interesting effect to the room.

If you are trying to arrange a room that has very little wall space, place any furniture at right-angles to the wall. For example, your couch can be situated at a right angle to the fireplace or television. This way, you'll have extra wall space in which to situate bookshelves and other means of storing things. And, if you need to incorporate a table for eating in your living room, reserve one corner of the room for the table to be pushed up against. Then, at meal time, if you need to you can pull it away from the wall before using.

If you need to incorporate a desk into your small space, choose one with a drop front so it takes up less room when closed. If the desk does not have any shelves or drawers underneath, get a stool instead of a chair to sit on at the desk. This way, you can push the stool completely under when the desk is not in use. Another great way to utilize space is to make your own desk using filing cabinets or low, narrow bookshelves and a larger piece of finished or stained wood as a top. This way, you can store papers or books underneath your homemade desk.

In smaller houses or apartments, oftentimes hallways are long and narrow. Placing a small, narrow bench in the hallway can be useful—especially if it can be drawn into the main room for added seating. Or, if you need a place to store all your shoes, place a small shelf of medium height in the hallway where you can place them as soon as you come in. That way, they won't take up needed space in your closets and you won't track in all the dirt from outside into your home.

If your rooms are long and narrow, they can be made to appear wider by placing larger pieces of furniture, such as beds and couches, crosswise to make the room look wider. Mirrors placed on the longer walls will also give the room the illusion of being larger than it is.

Built-in furniture is also well-suited for small houses, though this might not be feasible for rented apartments. Building in bookcases, shelving units, kitchen pantries, and wardrobes can save you lots of precious floor space and also add a nice touch to any room.

If there is a door in one of your rooms that doesn't allow for furniture to be placed behind it, think about splitting it in two so that it opens in the middle. Or, consider installing a folding (accordion like) door or, if the door is not even really needed, remove it altogether and hang a curtain or beads to partition off the room.

If you are able, paint the walls of your smaller rooms light, bright colors. This will make the rooms appear larger than they are and give a sense of brightness and airiness to your living space. Light gray, buff, and white walls are best for apartments, as they give an expansive appearance to the room and reflect the greatest amount of light. Furniture should be opposite—the darker the furniture, the smaller it looks and the larger the space appears. If you have a narrow hallway leading into your apartment, be sure that it too is painted with a light color to make it feel less constricting. You can also place a mirror (if possible) facing the doorway to make the hallway appear larger than it is.

For rooms that are full of dark, heavy-looking furniture, you can make them seem more "grounded" and less gigantic by placing a darker carpet or rug in the center of the room. This will "hold down" the heavier pieces of furniture and also add a nice focal point to the room. And, as in any small space, keep the amount of furniture at a minimum so the room does not start to feel overcrowded and stuffy. Larger pieces of furniture should never be placed in the middle of the room and if the room is exceedingly small, no furniture should be placed in the middle of the room at all.

If you have a few windows in your room, cover them with curtains that are the same color as your walls and woodwork. This way, you will make the rooms look larger. Lighter curtains, made of fine fabric, allow more light to enter the room and create a sense of space when opened. Hanging curtains all the way to the floor will make the room appear taller.

▲ Vibrant colors can make a small space feel bigger and brighter.

Making the Most of Your Studio Apartment

The best way to arrange a studio (one room) apartment in the city is to place the bed in one corner, away from the "living" area of the room. Make sure the bedding complements the color of the furniture (white bedding goes with everything and gives an fresh feel to the space). Avoid using dark colors in the room as it will make it seem much smaller than it is. A small couch can be used, and a small dresser can be kept in the corner of the room near the bed. A flat writing desk can serve also as a table. A few chairs that can be folded up will add additional seating without taking up space.

In the kitchen area, hang the cooking utensils over the stove. Shelves can be put on the walls to hold bowls and other cookware, and plates can also be stored with hangers on the walls. Hooks on which to hang mugs can be screwed in below the cabinets.

Stenciling

Stenciling on walls, trim, and even wooden furniture adds interest to any room in your home. The wonderful thing about stenciling is that it's relatively easy to do and you can choose whichever pattern and colors best fit your home and the decorations in each room.

Stenciling is by no means an exact science. It is supposed to be unique, imaginative, and creative. You can easily stencil anything by buying pre-made stencils at a local arts and crafts store or, if you are artistically inclined, you can create your own stencils by drawing a pattern on a piece of thick plastic or paper, cutting it out, and using it in your design.

Although stenciling is subjective and individual, here are a few guidelines to follow to help you get started:

▲ Choose patterns and colors that fit your home décor.

1. The first step to consider is the room you want to embellish with stenciling. Consider the size and shape of the room, the windows and their placement, the trim, any wall art, rugs, and furniture. This will help you decide what you'd like the room to look like and which parts should be decorated with stenciling (will you stencil a border around the top of the room or just embellish corners or window sills with stencil art?).
2. Next, select a stencil design and color scheme that will harmonize with the room and its furnishings. Some suggestions are:

   a. Rooms that have high ceilings or fancy wood paneling need simple, dignified stenciling that can be used around baseboards or corners of door frames or where there is dark, heavy woodwork.
   b. Small hallways, entryways, or rooms with lower ceilings should have small, conventional stenciling that runs underneath the crown molding at the top or just below where the ceiling meets the wall.
   c. Rooms containing dark, rich-colored furniture should have stenciling with delicate designs to reduce the bulkiness of the furniture. In rooms such as these, the stenciling will help accent and complement the richness of the furniture.
   d. Dining rooms tend to work well with rich, deep colors and stenciling should be done along any trip or rails to add a pop of color.

3. Stenciling should always be applied in a straight line along the wall or the effect will be ruined. Haphazardly stenciled areas make a room look sloppy instead of accentuating its design and furnishings.
4. Stenciling should be done with a good stencil brush of any size needed. A brush with smooth, pliable bristles is recommended.
5. Always study the stencil before beginning to paint. Stencil patterns can sometimes be delicate and so great care needs to be taken to keep the stencil intact until you've finished using it. You may want to buy a few sheets of the same stencil so you can keep the pattern consistent if one stencil gets ruined.
6. When you are using the brush, tie the bristles halfway down so they will not creep and spread underneath the stencil, ruining your design. Be careful not to overload the brush with paint. Apply the paint by stippling (to paint with small dots or brushstrokes), tapping the brush lightly in the confines of the stencil. Never rush the painting and always work carefully around the more intricate parts of the stencil pattern. Always brush from the edges of the stencil to the center.
7. Always wipe off your stencil after each use and before you begin your next design. Wipe off both the front and the back of the stencil so no paint collects there and ruins your artwork.

▲ Use a different pattern along the base of the wall for more variety.

Supplies Needed For Stenciling:
- 2 tubes of oil paint
- 2 brushes (10 inches each)
- 2 sheets blotting paper (10 inches each)
- Yard stencil paper (15 inches)
- Thumbtacks (5 inches each)
- Turpentine

Making Your Own Stencil Designs

While stencil patterns can be bought at arts and crafts stores, you can also make your own stencil design. A design can be geometrical, conventional, or realistic (this will require shading and is not for the beginner stenciler). If you aren't good at drawing, you can follow any sort of pattern (e.g., wallpaper designs, designs on tea towels, etc.). Geometric designs can be easily made by folding a slip of paper and cutting it with a pair of sharp scissors. In this way you can make triangles and squares that are symmetrical.

After you've found a good design, trace it with a sharp pencil onto a stencil board (found at arts and crafts stores). If you cannot find special stencil paper, tough paperboard, foil, thin copper sheets, vellum, parchment, or a manila envelope shellacked on both sides make good substitutes. The stencil paper should be roughly two inches larger on all sides than your design. This extra paper aids in handling and avoids getting paint on the wall outside of the design. If you have a smaller design, you may want to make a few identical patterns on one piece of stencil paper in order to make the painting go more quickly.

Once the design has been drawn, you will need to cut it out. This can be difficult, especially if your design is very intricate. To cut out the stencil, lay the board on a piece of glass or a smooth cutting surface and use a sharp penknife or X-Acto knife to cut the design out. Punch out the design and you have a stencil ready for use!

▲ You can stencil light switch covers or other small objects to hang on your walls, rather than stenciling the whole wall.

Simple Stencil Ideas

Stenciling is often used for mural decoration. In many cases, small, tilelike borders are stenciled around door and window trims. This is a simple design and allows for all types of motifs: various flowers, fruits, trees, ships, birds, mountains, animals, and people. The appropriateness of the design should be considered before stenciling, however. If you have no decorations with fruit in them in your living room, it is probably silly to stencil a bunch of grapes around your doorframe in that room.

Fruit motifs work well for dining rooms and kitchens. Grapes, pineapples, and oranges lend themselves very well to stenciling and give good decoration. Flower motifs are very appropriate for the bedroom. Poppies, roses, lilies, etc., add a bright and dainty feel to the room. Nautical designs—sailboats, water lilies, crabs, fish, shells—are great for cottages and sea-themed dens. If you have a music room, stenciling staffs, clefs, notes, and instruments are a fun way to bring out the theme and atmosphere of the room.

Types of Stencils

There are three general classes of stencils:
1. Single stencil—the entire design is cut on one sheet.
2. Double stencil—half of the design is cut on one sheet and the other half on another sheet.
3. Parti-colored stencil—cut in sets so that different colors may be used for the stencil without bleeding into one another.

Spacing Off a Design

Some stencil designs are continuous and some are detached. The continuous stencil is achieved by measuring the space that is to be stenciled and seeing if your pattern will align just right. If not, you will need to figure in what type of spacing is necessary in order for your first stencil and your last stencil to meet up in just the right manner.

When you are using a detached design, decide how many designs your space will require and then measure so you will have equal space between each design. Don't place any of these "running" designs in the corner of your room. It will be too difficult to paint.

To ensure that your design runs on a straight line, provide two notches in your stencil pattern and then draw a faint chalk line on your wall with a level, making sure it is even. Lay your stencil pattern on top of the chalk line, matching up the line with the notches on the stencil. If you do this every time, your stencil design will follow a straight line.

One thing to remember when stenciling designs: Stenciling is used primarily for ornamentation, so avoid overcrowding or overdoing the design.

Applying Color

1. Fix the stencil pattern in position with a few pins or double-sided tape.
2. Use a little color on the brush and dab it squarely against the plate. Don't draw the brush along the design as it may slip or seep underneath.
3. Lift the pattern away from the wall carefully and avoid sliding it.
4. Wipe the back of the plate after each application to prevent smearing.
5. If using two or more colors, allow one to dry thoroughly before applying another.

▲ You can also stencil fabric for curtains or upholstery.

Wallpapering

Wallpaper has the power to create a mood in any room and harmonize the objects in the room by serving as a common background. Its color should be chosen in relation to the general tone and color of the room. Like the curtains and furniture, it must either complement or contrast with the carpet. A safe way to choose a complementary color is to work with varying shades of one main color, such as the color of the carpet or a central piece of furniture.

The pattern of your wallpaper is also important to consider. This choice is a bit more difficult because the design in the paper will have an effect on the entire look of the room. Small designs are good for smaller rooms as wallpaper with larger designs tend to make small rooms look even smaller. Larger designs are tricky to work with as each strip of paper needs to be carefully cut and fitted so the seams are not apparent due to mismatched images. As a general rule, wallpaper with larger designs serves as its own form of decoration and should only be used in rooms where no other items will be hung on the walls.

The furniture in the room (and the style of the furniture) should also be taken into consideration when choosing wallpaper. If your furniture if dark, such as mahogany, then the wallpaper should have a softer, lighter feel so as not to make the room dark and enclosed. If you have period furniture or antiques, choosing a wallpaper pattern that complements those pieces will give a wonderful, rich feeling to the entire room.

Buying Wallpaper

Wallpaper comes in various sizes and thicknesses. Lighter-weighted wallpaper will dry faster, but it is sometimes harder to work with than a slightly thicker-weighted paper. Before buying wallpaper, you should examine it in bright light and also, if possible, in the light of the room in which it will hang. The colors in paper take on different hues depending on the light, and you want to make sure that you'll like how the paper looks in the room before you spend time and energy hanging it.

Remember to measure the size of the room that will be wallpapered and then figure out the dimensions of the roll of paper you choose. Make sure you have enough paper to overlap any larger patterns at the seams to keep the image consistent around the room.

▲ Wallpaper can give your rooms an old-fashioned feel.

▲ Wallpapering only one wall can add interest to your room.

Prepping the Walls

Before hanging the wallpaper on fresh walls, make sure that any plaster or caulking (if you've filled in nail holes, for example) is completely dry, otherwise the paper will wrinkle at these points. If you are re-papering a room, it is best to remove the old paper first and then hang the new paper (instead of laying one sheet over another). Old seams may show through and the new paper may also sag off of the walls when the room gets warmer, as in the summer. If your rooms are painted, the walls must be washed and completely dried before you can begin to hang any wallpaper.

If you are hanging wallpaper on new walls (that have never had paper on them before), it is a good idea to size the walls before papering. Sizing consists of "painting" the walls with a mixture of a half pound of glue dissolved into water.

Making Your Own Wallpaper Paste
Rather than buying wallpaper glue, you can make your own paste at home. To do so, just follow these simple instructions:

1. Boil a gallon of water in a two-gallon pot, adding a rounded tablespoon of salt.
2. Mix in two rounded teaspoons of flour gradually with enough cold water to make it a little thicker than cream.
3. When the water boils, pour in the flour mixture, stirring constantly to ensure a smooth texture.
4. Drop in a lump of tallow (walnut-sized), cook for five minutes, and then add an ounce of alum that has been previously dissolved in a cup of boiling water.
5. If there are any lumps, strain them out before using the paste. Adding a few drops of clove oil will keep the paste fresher longer.

Tools Needed for Hanging Wallpaper

- sheets of wallpaper (enough to cover the entire room)
- apron to cover your clothes
- a stiff brush (wallpaper brushes can be sold at your home store)
- a clean rag
- wallpaper roller (sold at home centers)
- scissors
- trimming knife
- straight edge (a ruler is perfect)
- tape measure
- wallpaper paste (store-bought or home-made)

Hanging the Paper

With patterned paper, begin hanging at the top of the wall and measure to the baseboard, but before cutting it, look at the pattern. If the bottom of your pattern at the baseboard does not match the pattern at the top, raise the top of the paper until it matches, with one half on the top of the wall and the other half at the bottom. By doing this you will ensure your pattern remains consistent throughout the room. Cut a dozen or so lengths, matching up the patterns, and make sure that the pattern will run straight across the wall. Arrange the cut sheets of wallpaper on a ladder or table. Apply the paste to the paper with a flat, broad brush, evenly distributing paste over all parts of the paper. Brush down the middle of the piece of wallpaper first and then sweep the brush diagonally from the edges. When the strip is pasted, fold both ends toward the center and assess whether not the paper is even. Now you can go and paste a few more strips of paper before hanging.

To begin papering a room, it is best to begin at a protruding edge or next to a door or window frame. Using a stepladder, unfold the upper half of the strip and apply it firmly to the wall. Then, carefully spread it smooth and press the upper half firmly in place. Step off the ladder and affix the lower half of the strip. With a soft cloth or roller, gently wipe the whole length of the paper, starting from the middle and moving to the edges. Continue hanging strips of paper in this manner, making sure the edges match up perfectly so the seams are hardly noticeable. When you come to a door or window frame, try to cut the paper exactly to fit against the straight edge. Then, with a box cutter or other small, fine knife, carefully cut around the sills or door frame, allowing a little bit of paper to rest on the frame if necessary. This can always be trimmed later.

Removing Paper

To remove paper from walls, you can first attempt to pull strips off dry; however, you may need to wet down the paper before it starts coming off. Apply hot water with a cloth, brush, or sponge. If it is varnished or enameled paper, you can dissolve a handful of washing soda in a quart of hot water. You may also need to make scratches and holes in the paper so that the water can get in. When the paper is thoroughly wet, you will most likely be able to peel it off in large strips and scrape off the remainder with an ordinary steel scraper.

Wallpapering

▲ To remove wallpaper, you may need to dampen the walls before scraping or peeling them.

Lighting

The feeling of a room is influenced greatly by the amount, type, and distribution of light—both natural and artificial.

Rooms can be lit in a number of ways, including:

▲ Creative lighting can make a plain room come alive.

- A central chandelier—this only works in large rooms with high ceilings. Though ornate and beautiful, one of a chandelier's biggest faults

▲ Chandeliers are great in rooms with high ceilings.

is that unless everything is concentrated in the center of the room, it is impossible to produce pleasing effects and adequate lighting throughout the space.

- Side bracket lighting (sconces)—this is a nice way to light a small room and also works well as accent lights in a hallway, under kitchen cabinets, or in a dining room.
- Lamps and fixtures—these are the typical means by which rooms are lit. Table and overhead lamps can produce very pleasing, warm light throughout the room.

The size of the room and its function will largely determine the number of lamps you need and where they should be situated. Placing lamps in areas where you will be reading, working at a desk, or where you want to highlight a piece of furniture or a decorative object (such as a painting over a fireplace) will help give the room a sense of purpose and functionality.

Rooms are best lighted by table lamps and floor lamps that are placed throughout the space. The table lamps should be placed near chairs and couches where light is needed in the evenings to read. Standing, or floor, lamps should be arranged so they fit in with the surrounding décor or, if they are especially elaborate, to call attention to themselves as an artistic piece in the room.

Knowing where to place your floor and table lamps is important to not only make the room look attractive but to also benefit from the best use of the incandescent light. If you have an area rug, you can run the cords of your table and floor lamps underneath the rug so no one will trip over them and you won't have unsightly cords hanging about.

Floor lamps work well for reading lights since they can be easily moved about and even their height can be adjusted depending on the type of lamp you have. Floor lamps fit perfectly into corners where placing furniture is awkward.

Lampshades and Bases

After deciding where your lamps should go, you'll need to consider what styles of lamps and what shades should be used to both maximize the amount of light emitted and to complement the décor. Lampshades that are made of soft, neutral tones (yellows, light oranges, greens, and blue-greens) are preferable in the way they emit light. The texture of the lampshades should match the textures in the room. The shades should also be lined with white to help concentrate the light on objects or areas you wish to highlight.

Different rooms and different uses require different colors of light to be given off by the lamp. For reading

▲ A darker-colored lampshade will allow less light to show through, creating a more romantic, subdued ambience.

and sewing, having a lampshade that disperses a soft green color is restful and easy on the eyes. Faint, yellow light is also good for this purpose.

Lamp bases and the styles of the fixtures are also important in maintaining the consistency of the room's atmosphere and decoration. If you have a room that is full of antiques and older furniture, try to find lamp bases or hanging fixtures from that same time period, with shades that complement the furniture. If you want a small accent light in a room, try finding a candlestick and attach a simple, candle-shaped bulb to it. Placing this kind of light in the corner of a dining room or in a bathroom will add a subtle yet inviting glow to the room. As a rule, if you have large, bulky furniture, lamps and fixtures that are daintier, made

of metal or even streamlined wood will help accent the furniture pieces without making the room feel overbearing.

Making Lampshades

If you can't find the perfect lampshade for your table or floor lamp, try making your own. You can salvage an old lampshade frame from a garage sale, second-hand store, or even from an old lampshade in your basement or you can make your own (though this is more difficult and takes some time and skill). However, a simple wire frame, twisted into shape with pliers, and topped with a hole and balled screw to attach the shade to the base will make a perfectly usable lampshade skeleton.

figures (or bright-colored tissue paper cut in floral designs) between two layers of gold silk gauze. This will give the shade an interesting depth and appearance.

A cretonne lampshade can be transformed by applying several coats of shellac. The shellac fills in the pores, making the surface very smooth, hard, and translucent. This is particularly good for lamps that will be situated on an indoor porch, as they are also waterproof.

Hand-painted vellum shades are also very charming. A shade combined with vellum and chintz can be made by fastening the cutout chintz figures to a watercolor paper and lacquering it onto the shade. This is inexpensive and can be made by anyone. Plastic or stiff fabric shades may also be stenciled to tie them into a particular theme or room décor.

For an interesting accent lamp, make a shade of your painting tin or tin that has a design punched into it with tiny awl holes. This will not give off much light but will be an interesting addition to smaller rooms or bathrooms. Painting the inside white will also help more light reflect out from the shade and into the room.

Lampshades can be made out of a variety of fabrics. It's important, however, to choose fabrics that are thick enough to be stretched over the frame. For the beginner, you can buy an inexpensive, white lampshade frame and then cover it with your own fabric. However, if you are making this completely from scratch, inserting plastic forms into the interior of the shade will also help keep the shades secure and the form intact.

Silk shades can be made six-sided with the light-colored silk fabric of your choosing drawn over the top to hide the bulb and the wire frame. With a covered top, the silk throws a softened shadow upward but reduces the amount of light emitted from the lamp. The bottom of the shade may be edged with a narrow, silk fringe or finished with a ruffle or chiffon band. At the top edge, the fringe may be cut away, leaving only the heading. At the center of the top of the shade, a small rosette may be made on the fringe. Silk shades that are striped with darker colors lend themselves well to offices and dens while striped taffetas in pastel shades are best for bedrooms. Several combinations of silk produce a nice, attractive coloring and light for homes. Champagne lined with pink, yellow, rose, or orange gives a warm, cheery glow. Gray lined with pink, yellow, or orange also give a nice hue to the room.

Especially for children's rooms, figured cretonne or silk may be overlaid with plain, silk gauze to highlight the figures and to give off an interesting pattern. The figures could be black silhouettes of fairies, trucks, or animals. To make this shade, insert these

Sconces

Lighting fixtures tend to be a main point of focus in almost every room. When you enter a room, wall fixtures usually catch your attention, and this is especially true at night when they are illuminating the home. Since these fixtures (hanging lamps and sconces) are partially permanent, it is important to pay careful attention to the style and placement of these fixtures in a room so they complement the color scheme and the overall design.

Sconces are a pleasant, convenient, and useful way to illuminate a room. These light each side of the room and, if you put them on a dimmer switch, they can help set the mood for parties, dinner, or for everyday living. Rooms that require a great deal of light (such as larger living rooms or entryways) will benefit more from a center fixture hanging from the ceiling than from wall sconces.

The placement of outlets needs to be taken into consideration before hanging your sconces. The average height for the outlet is six feet above the floor. However, if the sconce has arms inverted downward, the outlet may be a little higher than six feet. Also, the height of the ceiling will play a role in how high your sconces will be placed. If you have a 9-foot ceiling, the outlet should not be higher than 5 ½ feet from the floor.

Feng Shui

Feng shui is a Chinese observance of beliefs and practices tied into nature—a type of geomancy. It has been noted that feng shui—a "wind and water" system—is just like these two elements: wind, in the sense that it cannot be comprehended and water, because it cannot be grasped. Despite this somewhat cryptic explanation of feng shui, Putting its principles into practices need not be difficult.

Feng shui is guided and controlled by four divisions:

1. *It*, the general order of nature
2. *Shu*, It's numerical proportion (this includes the 5 elements of nature: earth, fire, metal, water, and wood)
3. *Ch'i*, the vital breath and subtle energies, and
4. *Hsing*, the form and outward aspect.

These four divisions should be blended harmoniously to create a perfect feng shui.

There are also three principles that underlie this blending. These principles are:

1. Heaven rules Earth.
2. Both Heaven and Earth influence all living beings and humans have the power to use this influence for their highest good.
3. The fortunes of the living depend also on the goodwill and influence of the dead.

In the principle of feng shui, the soul of a human is twofold—the *hun* and the *p'o* and the *animus* (breath of Heaven) and *anima* (quasi-material returning to Earth). Within this idea, the dead are thought of as being chained to the tomb by the quasi-material soul while the spiritual nature hovers around the old home. Thus, if the corpse is in a good place (has good feng shui), then the earthly soul is complacent and will bring prosperity to the house of the living through unseen influence.

According to feng shui, a home should have a specific balance and order that is in touch with the five elements of nature.

Feng Shui in Your Home

Your home has an energy of its own, and this energy channels in positive forces from the outside world and helps to create a happier life for you and your family. Therefore, having a home with good feng shui will help create a better energy and more restful environment in which you can live.

Feng shui design helps to give a purpose to every item in a particular room or in the house as a whole. These items have their own energies that play a significant role in your life. When designing a plan for your home to make it more harmonious, here are a few things to consider:

- Chi enters through your front door and flows throughout your home. Check the paths in your home for the chi to flow, and redecorate or reposition your furniture to allow it to move better and create better energy.
- Pick up clutter throughout your home. This will help improve the energy.

- Open windows for a few minutes each day to allow new chi to enter and the stale chi to escape.
- Beds should be placed against solid walls to ground you; no TVs should reside in the bedroom, and no mirrors should be placed in the bedrooms either (especially not across from the bed) as they will create negative energy as you sleep.
- If at all possible, install a small, indoor water fountain for relaxation and to improve the flow of the chi.
- As fire and water clash, stoves should not be placed opposite of refrigerators or sinks.

Certain objects and colors in your home help represent the five elements of feng shui and can harness their positive energies:

- Earth—this symbolizes stability and permanence and so placing flower pots with soil in your room will help harness this energy. Earth is also represented in the colors beige and light yellow.
- Fire—this is a symbol of passion and is found in red, orange, bright yellow, and purple. It is

powerful and so should only be placed sparingly throughout your home.

- Metal—this is a conductor of energy and promotes health. Copper is an especially powerful energy source and so metal should be used sparingly to not over-energize your home. Metal comes through in grays and whites.
- Water—water helps increase communication and can symbolize wealth. Small fountains in your home with running water or fish tanks will promote better communication between family members and monetary prosperity. Blue and black help channel the energy of water.
- Wood—symbolizing development and creativity, wooden objects (also items that are brown or green) placed in rooms in your home will draw this positive energy.

Creating a Feng shui Room

Designing your room to have feng shui elements is relatively simple. When looking at the room you want to apply feng shui to sketch a floor plan of the room as it is now and then think about how you can place items and harness the five elements to help balance the energy in your room and to allow the chi to move freely and positively throughout.

Looking at your sketch, the left-hand corner of the room should harness knowledge. Placing objects that promote wisdom and learning, such as books, in this part of your room will help direct this energy. In the bottom center of the room, you want to place objects, such as trophies or prior workplace accomplishments, that will help boost your career. The bottom right-hand corner of the room represents travel and people we connect with every day. Highlighting travel souvenirs or hanging pictures of people who inspire you will increase your positive energy toward those in your daily life.

The top right-hand corner of the room should contain items that remind you of love and relationships to foster positive energy in this area. The top middle part of the room is focused on harboring a good reputation in life and with others. Bright light and objects you are proud of should be in this area. The top left-hand corner should be kept tidy in order to promote wealth and good finances.

The center parts of the room are focused more on your family's health, wellness, and prosperity. The middle left section of the room is a place to improve your relationships. Placing pictures of family members and friends here will help you treasure those around you. The middle right section is the "child" or creativity part of the room and instruments and artwork should be placed here to improve your creative mind. The center of the room—probably the most important part—is reserved for the "self." This is your personal well-being and positive state of mind—all the other parts of the room flow their energy toward the center. This part of the room should be about "you"—your style, your likes, and all the things that mean the most to you in your life.

After you've sketched a plan of your room, think about where the five elements of feng shui come into play. Water generally stays in the career area of the room and so putting water fountains here will help balance that energy. Fire can be found opposite water (perhaps in the form of candles). The family section contains wood. Perhaps your family photos can be placed on a wooden bookshelf here. Metals resides in the creativity area and can be harnessed in metal frames or other circular metal designs. In the center of the room is earth; living plants should be placed here to bring good energy to this area of the room.

The most important thing to remember is that feng shui in your home will translate into more positive energy, happiness, and harmony in your own life. While it's not a cure for everyday problems, having a home in which you feel relaxed and at peace helps make the hardships and annoyances in daily life easier to accept and deal with.

▼ Fill your space with colors and objects that make you feel peaceful, happy, and energized.

Intentional Communities

The challenges of a self-sufficient lifestyle can become overwhelming, especially if you are trying to do it alone, or even with just your family. Gardening, raising animals, preparing and preserving food, maintaining your energy-producing systems, and perhaps selling your produce or crafts all take a great deal of time and energy. Some people find that living together with a group of other like-minded individuals or families can ease these burdens and offer many additional benefits.

Intentional communities are groups of people who choose to live together because of common ideals, spirituality, or political views, or simply to accomplish a common purpose. Intentional communities differ in purpose, legal structure, location, financial resources, and demographics. Ecovillages in particular focus on creating self-sufficient, sustainable lifestyles, while other communities may exist to support families with mentally disabled children, or to intensify a particular spiritual walk. In some cases, all the members live and work within the community, possibly even pooling all financial resources. In other cases, people may hold regular outside jobs and contribute to the community life in the evenings or on weekends. Remember, when considering location, to consider the zoning laws in that area and how they relate to your vision. Some places may have restrictions on the number of people who can live in a particular area, whether you can subdivide a property, or whether you can have a business there. Whether the intentional community shares a city apartment building or an organic farm, whether they're a group of artists or yogis, the goal is to create an environment where the common goal can more likely be achieved.

Many intentional communities fail, mainly due to financial constraints or interpersonal conflict. If you are interested in starting an intentional community, there are several things you should do to set a firm foundation for your endeavors:

1. **Create a clear vision.** Know specifically why you want to form a community and put it in writing. First, dream of what your "utopia"

would be, and then outline clear, realistic goals to move toward that environment. No community is perfect, but you should at least know what perfection would look like for you, and have ideas of how you can come closer to that vision. Giving your community a name can help to create a clearer identity and make it easier to explain to others.

2. **Determine how people can become members and what members' roles will be.** At first, this may be as simple as getting a few friends excited about the community and asking them to join. However, the most successful communities are generally those that take the time to consider what kind of people should become members, and how they'll be involved. You may want someone to keep records, someone to run meetings, and someone to oversee the chores. Or maybe everyone will share all the responsibilities. Be very clear about what sort of time, financial, or even emotional commitment is expected of members. An application process can be helpful in determining who becomes a member.

3. **Figure out finances.** You may need a substantial amount of money to buy land, rent an apartment, or otherwise prepare a location for your community. Determine how much your startup costs will be and where that money will come from. Then decide how members will contribute financially to the community (whether they'll pay monthly dues, or share a percentage of their income, etc.). Some communities are almost entirely self-sustaining, but you'll probably at least need money for taxes or rent.

4. **Lay down the law.** It's important to determine early on how decisions within the community will be made—who can vote on group decisions, whether decisions must be unanimous or whether the majority rules, and so on. Generally, the more that people are involved in decisions that will affect the community, the less conflict and resentment there will be. Be sure to write these bylaws down.

5. **Be honest and open.** Don't try to hide anything from members, potential members, or those outside your intentional community. Doing so will only create problems, build tension, and threaten your vision. If there's a financial problem, share it with the other members. If your vision for the community begins to shift, talk about it. Being genuine and communicating freely with those within and around your community may be the biggest factor in your success.

Even with the best planning and preparation, once your community is up and running, you are bound to run into interpersonal conflict. Personalities may clash, or practical problems such as a noisy dog, an unruly child, or a lazy worker will pop up. Expect problems to arise, and you won't feel so overwhelmed when they actually do. Here are a few tips for dealing with interpersonal conflict:

- When a disagreement between community members arises, determine whether the conflict is about the facts pertaining to a situation, or how they feel about the facts. If they are disagreeing about the facts, some research or questioning of other members may be helpful. If, however, they agree on the facts but are reacting differently to them, simply helping them to communicate their feelings adequately may be enough to settle the dispute.

- When a member feels very strongly about an issue, ask that person why she feels the way she does. Understanding each member's underlying values, beliefs, and assumptions will help to create harmony within the group.

- Play devil's advocate. Agree to argue the opposite side of a dispute for 15 minutes, and see if you discover some validity in the other person's argument.

- Stop discussions before they become explosions. If an argument is getting too heated, call a time out. Return to the discussion after 15 minutes, or once emotions have settled.

- Practice active listening. Listen to what someone has said, paraphrase it back to them, and ask relevant questions. This will facilitate clearer and deeper communication.

- Understand that everyone has a different way of perceiving and navigating the world. Another's worldview may seem threatening at first, but if you take the time to understand it, you may find your own worldview sharpened.

- Know when to let go. Some conflicts need immediate resolution and some do not. In some cases, it's best to give the issue a rest and revisit it in a week or a month. By then, circumstances or perceptions may have shifted.

Appendix:
Trees, Stars, and Birds

Becoming Acquainted with Trees

From *Trees, Stars, and Birds: A Book of Outdoor Science* by Edwin Lincoln Moseley, 1919

Trees have a fascination for us that abides as long as we live. The coming of the leaves on the bare branches is one of the most pleasing signs of spring; the deep green of the summer foliage is restful to the eyes; the red and gold of the autumn woods is one of the most splendid sights of nature; and even in winter the play of shadows and colors in a woodland is beautiful to behold. In the early history of our country trees were so plentiful that they were destroyed to get them out of the way. Now millions of them are planted every year. We like them about us because they are pleasing to our eyes and afford a source of interest and healthful enjoyment to our minds.

But trees are useful as well as beautiful. They shade us from the summer's sun and help to break the force of the winter winds. Their fruits and seeds are a most important source of food for men and animals, and, above all, they furnish us wood, without which civilized life would not be possible. Much of the material for our houses and vehicles is wood; the paper of the book you are reading is made from wood; your pencil, chair, and desk are mostly wood; and it is probable that in any household fifty different articles could be found that are made wholly or in part from the products of trees. Millions of persons are engaged in making these articles and in procuring and preparing the necessary materials. A knowledge of trees and woods is, therefore, not only satisfying to our minds, but useful in every kind of manual work. Few subjects that we study have more practical value than trees and the woods that come from them.

▲ Fig. 2. A sugar maple in summer.

Jesse E. Hyde

Studying trees by seeing and thinking. The following pages will help you to become acquainted with some of the trees that are common over large parts of the United States and with others that are especially useful to us. But reading a book about trees is of little use, if you do not observe the trees themselves. Notice the buds, blossoms, and fruit, the shape of the tree and arrangement of its branches, the color of the bark, the peculiarities of the leaves, and whether any of these parts has a characteristic odor or taste. Try to answer the questions you will find in the various chapters by making the necessary observations yourself or by reflecting on what you have already observed or read. Perhaps some one at home will be interested in discussing these questions with you. If not, do the best you can in answering them alone. When they come up in class, you will learn what others think about them, but knowing this will be of little use to you unless you have thought about them yourself. Other questions as interesting and important as any of those in the book may suggest themselves to your mind. Try to answer these, too, for yourself before asking any one else about them.

▲ Fig. 3. The same tree in winter.

How to make a collection. To learn to know the trees, their names, peculiarities, and uses, do not merely read about them, but look at them and take leaves and other parts to keep for further examination and for comparison with other trees. In gathering leaves for your collection, select those that have not been eaten by insects or damaged in other ways. Unless the leaves are very large, cut off a twig with several typical leaves attached. If you cannot press your specimens at once, you may prevent withering by keeping them inclosed in a box or laying them in a large magazine.

For pressing leaves, use absorbent paper like large sheets of blotting paper, or the soft felt paper that is used under carpets. If you cannot get either of these kinds of paper, place several thicknesses of newspapers between each two specimens. Spread out the leaves on a sheet of the absorbent paper in such a way that each leaf will lie flat and will not cover other leaves. It may be necessary to trim off some of them. Let at least one leaf of each specimen show its under side. Cover the first specimen with absorbent paper and upon this paper spread out another specimen, continuing in this way until you have put into the press all the good specimens you have collected. With each specimen place a strip of paper telling where you found it, the date, and the name of the tree, if you know it. Then put the pile of papers and specimens where it will not be in the way and cover it with a board on which is placed a stone or some other convenient weight. For a few delicate specimens a weight of 15 or 20 pounds will suffice. Ordinarily a heavier weight will be better.

The day after you put the specimens in the press, change the drying sheets. If you use felt paper, one or two changes at intervals of a day or two will probably suffice for the leaves of most trees. If newspapers are used for "driers," they should be changed each day until the specimens are dry. In pressing delicate plant specimens it is easier to handle them if you lay each one in a folded sheet of thin paper before putting it into the press. You need not remove it from this thin paper when you change the drying sheets, or before you find time to mount the dry specimen.

The slat press. If you have the tools and materials, you can make a slat press, to which pressure is applied by means of a cord or by straps. Such a press is convenient to handle at home and may be carried to the woods. It makes better-looking specimens than a board press, because it is somewhat flexible and applies pressure along the edges as well as in the middle and thus keeps the tips of all the leaves flat.

Mounting specimens. To preserve the pressed spedmens so that they can be examined without risk of breaking, mount them on sheets of unruled stiff white paper. You can fasten them to the paper with glue, but you will find strips of gummed paper or linen more satisfactory for this purpose. These may be purchased from a botanical supply

▲ Figs. 4-5. A slat press for drying specimens of leaves and flowers.

house or possibly at a printing office or stationer's. A neat label may be attached to the sheet. It should give the name of the tree, the place where it grows, the date when the specimen was collected, and the collector's name. Do not mount leaves from more than one kind of tree on the same sheet, as that would interfere with a systematic arrangement of the specimens. If the bark of the tree is peculiar and a thin piece can easily be obtained, attach it to the same sheet as the leaves.

All the sheets of closely related specimens, e.g., the different kinds of maples or oaks, should be placed together in a folder made of a larger sheet of strong manila paper, or a large-paged blank book may be used for mounting the specimens. A bookbinder will prepare suitable books at a small cost for each pupil, if enough of them can be ordered at one time; it is best to have the sheets removable, so as to make possible the insertion of specimens in their proper order. If a suitable book cannot be obtained, a pasteboard box may be used to hold the sheets, or they may be perforated and fastened together in book form by tying them with a shoestring or ribbons.

Fruit collections. The term "fruit" as used in botany means the part of the plant that contains the seed. It may be fleshy or dry, edible or quite unfit for food. From what part of the blossom does it develop? Frequently a tree can be most easily identified by its fruit, and when possible specimens of the fruit should be collected with the leaves. Fruits that are dry and thin may be attached to the same sheets as the leaves.

Have also a collection of fruits in a box. A strong paper box 3 or 4 inches deep and a foot or so in length may be divided into a score or more of compartments by partitions running both ways. It is best to have the partitions not more than half as high as the box; they are merely to keep the specimens from the same tree together, and apart from those of different trees. Some compartments should be larger than others, to accommodate cones and other large specimens. More than one box may well be used for the fruit collection; or, instead of using a box with partitions, you may sew the fruit specimens to a card or to the inside of a pasteboard box—say a suit box—that can be closed and put away.

Arrangement of specimens. Whatever method is used for keeping the specimens of leaves and fruit in place, they should be arranged according to some plan. Usually they are arranged according to their natural classification. Specimens from different kinds of oak, for instance, will be placed near each other, preceded or followed by beech and chestnut, which belong to the same family as the oak; likewise walnut and the different kinds of hickory will be associated.

School collections. The directions given above refer to individual collections. For use in the schoolroom, large cardboards can be prepared, with specimens of leaves or other parts or products of trees mounted on them. They should be arranged, not with a view to making a design or picture, but to facilitate a comparison of things that are related.

If you wish to preserve for a time the autumnal tints of the foliage, gather leaves that are free from blemishes and ragged edges, and press them for a day or so between blotters. Then dip them in barely melted paraffin and press them between papers with a hot iron. Leaves prepared in this way look very pretty mounted on green cardboard.

Collections of woods. In Europe so few kinds of wood are in common use that woodworkers soon learn to recognize the different kinds. But the number of woods in use in America is so large that even lumbermen, carpenters, and cabinet makers rarely are able to distinguish closely related kinds. They know red oak from white oak, but do not distinguish the various species that are sold under the name of red oak or of white oak.

To learn to recognize a dozen or more kinds of wood is easy. The best way to do this is to get samples from persons who know what they are, label them, and then find articles that are made of these different kinds of wood. Every pupil should have, either at home or in the schoolroom, a collection of this kind, and the school should have a larger collection. The samples can be obtained from various sources, some of which will be suggested by the uses of the wood given for the different species in this book. At a woodworking shop it is often possible to obtain small pieces of a dozen kinds, some of them in sufficient quantity for a class. By visiting more than one such shop quite a variety can be procured without any expense. If the manager is willing to have the whole class visit the factory at one time, much can be learned. You may send any specimens of wood concerning which you are doubtful to the United States Forest Products Laboratory, Madison, Wisconsin, for identification. A study of Chapter Six and the key beginning on page 147 may help you to identify some common kinds of wood.

Many useful tree products besides wood and fruit are mentioned in the following chapters. A collection of them might be so arranged as to make an instructive exhibit in a schoolroom. Of course there are many trees not mentioned in this book that are just as interesting to those who live where they grow as any that are included here.

The Structure of a Tree

From *Trees, Stars, and Birds: A Book of Outdoor Science* by Edwin Lincoln Moseley, 1919

We are awed by the grandeur of a great tree; it is the largest and the oldest of living things. Its roots penetrate deep into the earth to anchor the tree in its place and to gather water and food materials from the soil. Its trunk and branches hold the crown of leaves up to the light. It is a living being like ourselves and also a structure that, like a tall building, must carry a great weight and withstand the force of the winds. And so well is this structure planned and built that generations of men and animals may come and go and even nations may rise and fall while a tree lives on and on. In nearly every part of the United States there are trees still standing that Indian children may have played under before the white man came, and some of the trees that are still growing in the Western states had already reached a large size before Julius Cæsar or Hannibal was born. One way in which a tree differs from a person is that some of its parts are always young; for unlike ourselves, trees grow as long as they live.

Only part of a living tree alive. The outer bark of an old tree is dead and a great part of the wood is dead. But just as the dead mineral material that is found in the bones of men and animals is useful in supporting them, so the dead wood of a tree forms a skeleton and holds the tree in place; and as the dead outer layers of our skin protect the living tissues beneath, so the dead outer bark of a tree protects the living parts within. The dead parts, of course, do not grow, but they form a skeleton that is useful in supporting and protecting the tree. Each year a new set of leaves, twigs, and small roots are produced, and the part that has changed to wood and died is buried within the tree to aid in its support. You have seen trees with hollow trunks whose crowns remained thrifty. In such trees it is not the living part but the dead wood in the heart that has decayed; but a tree in this condition is more likely to be blown down than one whose trunk is sound throughout.

The living material of a tree. The living parts of a tree, like the living parts of every other plant and animal, are composed of *cells*. In the young growing parts the cells are shaped like little boxes fitted together in an irregular manner. Each cell has a wall about it, and the inside of the cell is composed of living material called *protoplasm*, which in appearance is something like raw white of egg. Besides the protoplasm there is usually watery sap and often starch or other food material stored in a plant cell, but only the protoplasm is alive. Although most cells are too small to be seen with the naked eye, the cells in such material as the thin leaf of a moss or the skin from the bulb of an onion may easily be seen with a compound microscope. A tree, therefore, though it appears to be but a single thing, is in reality made of many small parts. A leaf is like a great structure built up of many hundreds of little boxes, and aU the other living parts of a tree are, in the same way, built of many parts.

How the wood is formed in a tree. The cells in the tip of a growing shoot or root of a tree are all alike, but as they grow older great changes take place in many of them. Some of them grow wider and at the same time become greatly elongated. Then the cell walls are thickened by woody material being laid down on the inside of them. Finally, the end walls are absorbed, so that each cell is connected with the one above and below to form a long tube. The living matter in the cells then dies, leaving long, empty vessels, sometimes several inches or even several feet in length, made of cells joined end to end within the plant. These vessels are called *tracheæ* (singular, *trachea*). Through them water flows up to the leaves. In the cut end of a grapevine, in the root of a willow, and in many woods these large vessels are

◀ Fig. 6. The "Boone Tree" near Jonesboro, Tennessee. On it was carved: "D. Boon cilied a Bar on the tree in year 1760." The tree was blown down in 1916. It was a beech about 90 feet tall.

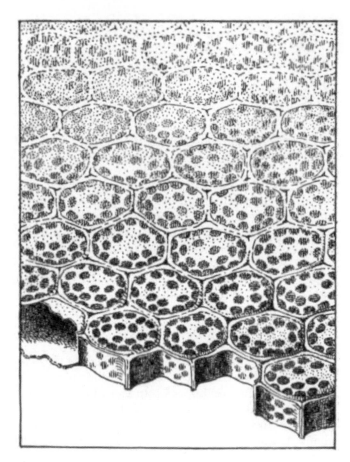

▲ Fig. 7. Cells from a moss leaf.

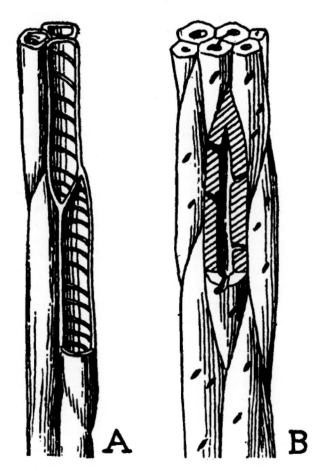

▲ Fig. 8. Tracheids from a basswood tree (A), and wood fibers from a hard maple (B).

plainly visible as open pores. Is it possible to draw air through them?

Others of the cells become changed into *tracheids.* These have thicker walls than the tracheæ, and the end walls are not absorbed. They do not, therefore, form long open vessels in the tree, and the water makes its way from tracheid to tracheid by passing through thin places in the walls. The tracheids conduct water more slowly than do the much larger tracheæ that have no cross walls, but they give more strength to the wood.

A third element that is prominent in wood, especially in hard woods, is the *wood fibers.* These are formed by groups of cells elongating and forming slender fibers with pointed ends and thick walls. These fibers are much like the tracheids, but they are smaller and have walls so thick that the spaces within them are sometimes almost closed. They do not conduct water, but when the protoplasm in them dies they stand in a tree like bundles of little, tightly sealed tubes filled with air. The function of the wood fibers is to give strength to the wood; their thick walls make it difficult to crush or break them. Oak wood has in it dense bundles of these fibers, and other hard and heavy woods also are richly supplied with them.

It should be understood also that in all woods many of the cells do not change into vessels or fibers, but retain their thin walls, and except in the older wood remain alive. They are called *parenchyma* cells. The pith of a tree is composed of cells of this kind, and in a freshly cut stump or log strands of these cells, called *medullary rays,* or pith rays, may be seen running out from the center to the bark. Cells of this kind may also be scattered through the wood; or they may lie in groups or run in chains, crosswise or up and down, in the wood, making connections with each other and with the living portions of the bark. These living cells are found in the wood of the roots as well as in the trunks and branches of trees. They make up a considerable part of many woods, sometimes as much as a quarter of the whole, and along with the tracheæ are the weakest elements in the wood. If the bark were hewed from a pine, it is estimated that the ends of 15,000 fine rays would be exposed on each square inch of surface. In oaks some of the rays are an inch, and in some species of oak even 4 or 5 inches, in height, and may be seen as light-colored bands running through the wood

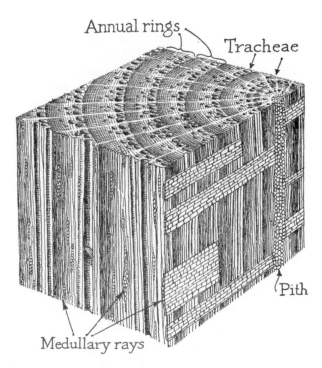

▲ Fig. 9. The structure of wood (diagrammatic).

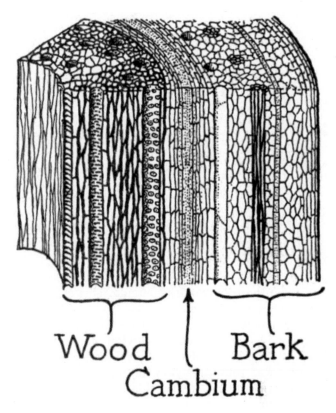

Wood Bark
Cambium

▲ Fig. 10. The cambium is a growing layer between the wood and the bark.

(page 103); but for each large ray that you see in a piece of oak there are perhaps one hundred too small to be seen without a lens.

These four elements are found arranged in various ways and in different proportions in all our hard woods (page 109). The woods of pines, cedars, firs, and other evergreens are composed of tracheids and parenchyma cells. They lack the large open vessels and the dense bundles of wood fibers and are therefore very even in texture.

How a tree grows in height. In the tip of a tender root or shoot each cell is growing; it increases in size by taking in food and out of this food building up more protoplasm. After the cell reaches a certain size, a partition is built across it which divides it into two cells. In like manner the two may become four, and so on until a large number of cells have been formed. This multiplication of cells and the increase in size of the cells as they become old cause growth.[1] The trunk of a tree is built upward, and the branches and roots increase in length in this way. New material is built on the top of the trunk, and added to the tips of the branches and roots by the multiplication of the cells in these parts.

Proof of where the trunk lengthens. It is said that if two nails are driven into a living tree trunk, one 6

feet above the other, they will remain 6 feet apart, no matter how long the tree grows. Driving nails into a trunk is not good for the tree or for the saw that may sometime cut it into lumber. Without driving in nails or waiting for years to see the result, you can decide about the lengthening of a trunk by examining trees that have been used as posts for a wire fence. You may find some in which the wire and staples have been covered by years of growth. Are the wires farther apart and higher above the ground than where they were fastened to dead posts? How do you account for the fact that on old trees the distance from the ground to the lowest limbs is so much greater than on young trees? Where is the growth in a tree, that causes the trunk to become longer?

Mark off with ink the first foot of the end of a rapidly growing vine or other shoot into inch spaces. Watch the plant for a number of days. Where do the marks become separated most widely?

How a tree grows in diameter. A tree increases in diameter through the growth of the *cambium*. This is a layer of growing cells just inside the bark. Each year the cells of the cambium multiply; during the growing season they are constantly being divided by longitudinal partitions which cut off layers of cells on both the inside and outside of the cambium. On the outside this forms a thin layer of tissues in the inner part of the bark; inside the cambium a new layer of wood is laid down. Thus each year a sheet of wood is

---

[1] In older plant cells there is usually in the center of the cell a large amount of water ("cell sap") in which mineral matter and certain food materials are dissolved. The taking in of this water stretches the cell and greatly enlarges it,—sometimes to several hundred times the size it has before the absorbing of the water begins. It is this pumping of water into the young shoots that causes the young branches of trees to push out so rapidly in the spring.

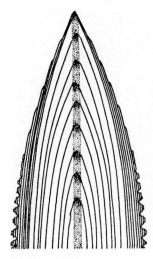

◀ Fig. 11. Diagram showing the structure of a tree. The dotted part in the center represents the pith. The diagram is of course much wider in proportion to its length than is the trunk of a tree.

laid upon the tree from the outside. This causes the tree to increase in diameter.

If you could remove from a tree the layer of wood that is added in a single year, what shape would it have? Do the layers of wood that were formed when the tree was young reach to the top of the tree? Do you understand that if you could begin with the outermost and remove the layers of wood one by one from the trunk of an unbranched tree, you would take off a series of thin-walled hollow columns which taper to a point above and which in the tree fit over one another? The column which grew last year incloses the one that grew the year before, and the columns that will grow in the years to come will be fitted about those that are now standing in place.

Springwood and summerwood. When a pine tree begins its growth in the spring, comparatively large vessels with thin walls are formed. Later in the summer, as growth becomes slower, the vessels formed are smaller and have thicker walls; the openings in them are much smaller than the openings in the springwood. We have in the tree, therefore, alternating layers of light springwood and of denser summerwood. This causes the appearance of rings in the wood, which you have often seen. In different kinds of trees there are often differences in the springwood and summerwood; these will be discussed in a later chapter (page 43).

The bark of a tree. The inner cells of the bark of a tree are alive, and as the tree increases in size the bark grows by the multiplication of these cells. Thus the bark increases in thickness year by year, unless at the same time the outer layers are scaling off and falling away. Why are the outer layers of bark on an old oak or elm furrowed and broken? Why is the bark of an oak or elm rougher than the bark of a sycamore **or** birch of the same size?

Cork and how it is formed. In the bark of trees the outer cells become changed into cork. This is done by thickening the cell walls with a waxlike material, after

which the protoplasm in the cells dies. The corky layer of cells thus formed protects the tree from drying and also keeps out fungi that would otherwise attack the tree and cause decay. An idea of the great usefulness of the cork may be gained by noting what happens to an Irish potato when the thin, corky layer on its surface is broken or removed. When this is injured, decay very readily sets in, and a peeled potato loses water sixty times as fast as one that has its protective coat. In the cork oak the corky layer is of great thickness and is removed from the tree in large slabs. Examine the stoppers of bottles and see if you can find evidences of annual rings in them. Can you explain why a cork does not become water-soaked as a piece of wood does?

Vessels and fibers in the bark. The inner part of the bark is a layer of tissues consisting of vessels for conducting food, cells in which food is stored, and long, slender, and strong fibers. The latter are called *bast fibers* and are very abundant in some trees (page 59). Why do beetles and borers often feed on this layer of tissues in a tree? Will the roots of a tree die if the bark on the trunk is cut all around it? Why?

Telling the age of trees. On the top of a stump or the end of a log you can often count the rings. To determine the age of the tree, do you count the spring-

Dryden

▲ Fig. 12. The monarch oak, the patriarch of the trees, Shoots rising up, and spreads by slow degrees. Three centuries he grows, and there he stays Supreme in state; and in three more decays.

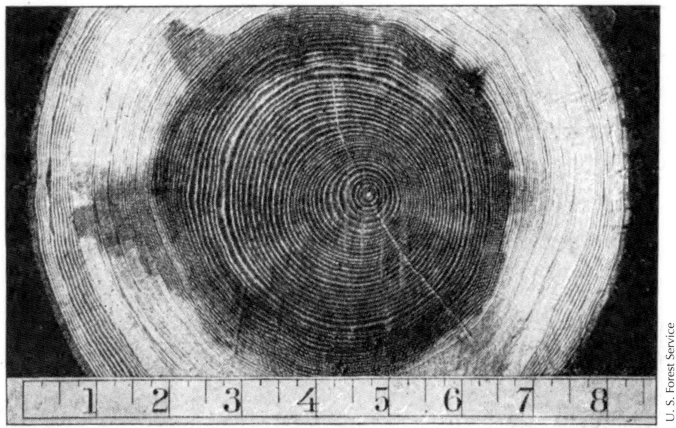

U. S. Forest Service

U. S. Forest Service

▲ Fig. 13. Section through a white ash almost 100 years old. It grew in a thick forest, but 12 years before it was cut some of the trees about it were blown down by a severe storm. Study the rings and see what you can learn of the life of the tree from them. (See also Figure 61, page 99, and Figure 87, page 131.)

wood and summerwood as representing two years or one? In exceptional cases, as when a drought divides the growing season into two parts, two fairly distinct rings may form in one year, but generally you can tell the age of a tree quite closely by counting the number of rings. If the section whose rings you are counting was not made near the ground, you must make allowance for the time it took for the tree to attain that height.

Are the annual rings all of equal thickness in the same stump? Are there places where you can count twice as many to the inch as in other places? What may have caused the tree to grow more in some years than in others? Can you think of a way to test the correctness of your explanation? How could you find out, without asking any one to tell you and without reading about it, whether a certain kind of tree

grows fast or slowly? On the stump or other section of a tree or of a branch, is the same ring uniform in thickness all the way round? How do you account for this? Frequently disputes about the ownership of land have been decided by the age of trees and by counting the rings to find how many years ago a certain mark was placed on a tree by a surveyor.

You will find it interesting to fix as nearly as possible the date when some large tree first began to grow. If you are careful, you will probably come near the actual date. Having done this, try to form a mental picture or give a description of the surrounding country when this tree was a young sapling. Regarding the tree as an individual which has suffered and enjoyed many experiences, you might write a story of its life, an imaginary autobiography, telling what it has seen and done.

Identifying Trees

From *Trees, Stars, and Birds: A Book of Outdoor Science* by Edwin Lincoln Moseley, 1919

Maples

Maple trees may be found in most parts of the United States and southern Canada. The larger kinds are widely planted for shade, and smaller varieties with cut leaves or richly colored foliage are often used for ornamental purposes in parks and on lawns. Some maples produce wood that is hard and handsome, and the leaves of many kinds show beautiful autumn coloration.

The blossoms of the maple are small, but they abound in honey and are very attractive to bees. In spring or early summer the peculiar key fruit is produced (Fig. 17). Among children, who like to eat them, these are known as "chickens." At the base of each wing is a seed. Have you ever noticed it? Are the leaves on one branch sometimes more highly colored than those on the rest of the tree? Will this branch show the same peculiarity year after year?

Making maple sugar. You have eaten maple sugar or maple sirup. It is made usually from sap of the sugar maple, occasionally from that of other maples. Good sugar may be obtained also from hickory or birch sap.

The first warm days in February or March start the sap flowing. Then the tree is tapped—that is, a hole is bored through the bark into the wood—and a spile, or little spout, is inserted so that the sap will flow along it and be caught in a bucket instead of trickling down the trunk of the tree. The rise of the sap in early spring is due partly to freezing and thawing; therefore a succession of warm days and cold nights is necessary for a continuous flow. Later in the spring the sap becomes watery and bitter and is not suitable for sugar making. From 25 to 50 pounds of maple sap must be boiled down to obtain 1 pound of sugar.

A group, or orchard, of sugar maples is called a "sugar bush." The place where the sugar is made is called a "sugar camp." Oftentimes one or more sheds are built in the woods to accommodate those who gather the sap and keep up the fires under the kettle or great pans that are used in evaporating the water from the sap. Boys enjoy the work of sugar making and often stay in the camps at night. Nevertheless, much labor is required to produce a gallon of sirup or a few pounds of sugar. Can you think of three reasons why genuine maple sugar is expensive?

The maple-sugar industry has become so important in some of the Northern states and Canada that those who engage in it make use of improved evaporators. These are broad, shallow pans with a number of partitions that do not reach entirely across the pan. The openings left between these partitions and the sides of the pan alternate, so that the sap in flowing around the partitions goes from one side of the evaporator to the other. As wa-

▲ Fig. 14. Tapping the tree.

▲ Fig. 15. Collection the sap.

U. S. Forest Service

U. S. Forest Service

▲ Fig. 16. Silver map in winter.

ter is continually being driven off by the fire under the pan, what was at first thin sap has become thick sirup by the time it reaches the farther end of the evaporator. This sirup may be converted into sugar by driving off still more water. To test the boiled sap, a small amount is stirred and cooled in a saucer. If it granulates and adheres to the spoon and saucer, evaporation has gone on long enough, and the hot sirup is poured into molds to form cakes of sugar of the desired shape.

Maple sugar, like that made from sugar cane, is darker than ordinary brown sugar, unless the impurities are removed. To do this milk or beaten eggs are stirred into the boiling maple sap. This causes most of the coloring matter to rise to the top and mingle with the froth, which is then skimmed off. Those who live near sugar bushes enjoy making and eating maple wax. This is formed by letting the hot sirup fall upon snow or ice.

The sugar made by the leaves of the trees. The leaves are the food-making organs of a plant, and the sugar that is obtained from maple sap in the spring was made the summer before by the leaves of the tree. As the sugar is manufactured it passes down from the leaves into the trunk and roots of the tree, and is stored in the living cells of these parts in the form of starch. Then when food is needed in the spring to enable the buds to grow and expand into blossoms and leaves, and to produce the seeds, the starch is changed back to sugar, which is dissolved out of the storage cells and carried upward in the sap.

The sugar that is manufactured by the leaves is made from water, which is absorbed by the roots and passed up through the vessels of the wood, and from carbon dioxid, a gas that is taken in from the air. In the leaves these are united to form sugar. Leaves cannot do this work without light; when the sun shines on them it supplies the energy for the process.

Uses of the wood of the maple. The sugar maple is called also "hard maple." Try to cut a piece across the grain with a knife or saw and see whether it is the hardest wood you have. Hardwood floors are often made of maple, the pieces of which have been planed and matched with tongue and groove. Maple wood is used for this purpose because it has no soft places to wear away and leave the floor uneven or splintered (page 152).

▲ Fig. 17. Leaves and fruit of silver maple (A) and red maple (B).

"Bird's-eye maple" is an ornamental wood obtained from certain sugar-maple trees of the same species as those whose wood is straight-grained. "Curly maple" is found in this species as well as in the soft maples.

Until a tree is cut it is seldom possible to tell whether its wood will show these peculiarities.

Have you seen maple furniture? Try to find examples of bird's-eye maple and of curly maple. Tool handles, rulers, butcher's blocks, piano actions, and the backs and sides of violins often are made of hard maple. This wood is used also for shoe lasts and pegs, croquet balls and mallets, for various implements, and in the construction of machinery, cars, and automobiles. It has a fine and even grain, polishes well, and is heavy, hard, strong, and elastic. Which of these properties are most needed in a wood used for each of the purposes mentioned?

The sugar maple as a shade tree. The sugar maple is one of the very best of our shade trees. It

▲ Fig. 18. Leaves and fruit of silver maple (C) and Norway maple (D).

is well shaped, affords dense shade in summer, and in autumn becomes beautiful because of the rich and varied colors of its foliage. In the spring its blossoms unfold with the leaves. It grows more slowly than the soft maples, but it requires less moisture and is more useful and durable.

Red and silver maples. The red maple and silver maple are both soft maples. They are extensively planted for shade, but like the sugar maple they grow wild also in all our Eastern states, and in southeastern Canada, and as far west as Kansas. You will not find it easy to distinguish these maples at all times from each other or from other maples. In autumn the leaves of the red maple turn crimson, and where this species abounds it adds much to the beauty of the woods at that season. Its blossoms, which are red, open before the leaves.

The silver maple, also called "white maple," grows larger than the red maple. It is one of the most common of shade trees, although not always known by its correct name. The leaves are pale underneath, but not so white as those of the white poplar. Its blossoms open in advance of its leaves, before most kinds of trees show signs of life.

Experience has shown that the silver maple, in spite of its rapid growth, is a poor tree for street planting. Many kinds of insects eat the foliage or bore into the trunk. The breaking of its limbs causes much trouble. In the living tree the wood is quite subject to decay. When the tree is cut down, even the wood that is still sound is not very valuable, but both silver maple and red maple are now used for woodenware and flooring.

The Norway maple. Of late years the Norway maple has been planted in many cities in the United States. Its flowers are greenish yellow; its leaves are large and remain green until late in autumn. The leafstalks contain a milky juice. This tree is remarkably free from insects and has proved a very satisfactory shade tree.

Maple leaves and their arrangement. Notice that the leaves of different kinds of maples differ a little in shape. All have, however, the main veins diverging from the leafstalk, whereas elm leaves have a midrib with veins coming off on each side (page 38). The former arrangement is called *palmate* (palmlike); the latter is *pinnate* (featherlike). Find other examples of palmate and of pinnate leaves. Which is wider in comparison with its length, a palmate or a pinnate leaf?

The maples have the leaves and twigs *opposite* each other on the stem, as contrasted with the *alternate* leaves and twigs of the elm (Fig. 23). Find other examples of opposite and alternate leaves.

The ash-leaved maple. This tree, more commonly called the "box elder," is a maple, as its fruit shows. It differs from the other maples, however, in having *compound* instead of *simple* leaves; that is, its leaves are cut into a number of leaflets instead of being all in one piece. In ordinary locations it is not so desirable a shade tree as some of the other maples, but it grows rapidly and may be planted in sandy or gravelly soil, where most other trees do not thrive. The box elder is distinguished from other trees with opposite leaves by the green bark of the young shoots. This tree is rare east of the Appalachians, but can be found in most parts of the United States with the exception of the states in the northwestern portion.

▲ Fig. 19. Leaves and fruit of the ash-leaved maple or "box elder." This maple, unlike the other members of the family, has compound leaves.

The maple family. Nearly one hundred species of maples are known in the wild state, most of them growing in the north temperate zone. Some are found on mountains, others on ground that is low and wet. Most species thrive best in rich, moist soil. They differ greatly in size; some of the Japanese species, which are cultivated in this country on account of the rich colors of the finely divided foliage, seem like dwarfs when compared with our great sugar maples, which tower to a height of 100 feet.

Considering their wide distribution, the great number that have been planted, and the variety of uses made of them, we may well give maples a prominent place among important trees.

Maple seeds dispersed by the wind. Out of doors, when the wind is blowing, drop a maple seed from a height of several yards and see whether it falls straight down. Does it acquire a whirling motion? Does this retard its descent? Is it better for the seeds of a maple to fall close to the tree or to be carried to distant places? Why? Are seeds more likely to get loose from the tree on still days or windy days? How far do you suppose the wind carries them? Name different kinds of trees with winged fruits; name some kinds whose seeds have cottonlike appendages that enable them to be carried through the air. Have you seen young maples pushing up in lawns or along fences?

Leaves and light. Examine Figure 18. The stalk of one leaf has lengthened and pushed the leaf out to the light, past the other leaves on the tip of the branch. Almost any maple tree will show this interesting leaf arrangement on dozens of its twigs.

Study the plants that are growing about you and note that leaves always seek the light. When a vine grows on a wall, each leaf fits itself into its space as best it can to receive the light. Note the arrangement of the leaves on a plantain or a dandelion. Do the upper leaves grow so that they will not cover the lower ones, or must the lower leaves take care of themselves? Does each leaf on a tree grow as it pleases, or is there some outside directing force that causes each one to take its proper place?

Birches

Because of their grace and beauty birches are a favorite subject for landscape artists and photographers, and they are frequently planted in parks and on lawns. The white and the paper birch are the species of birch most frequently planted for ornamental purposes. They are especially effective when placed among evergreens, because of the contrast in colors. Many of the white birches have slender, drooping branchlets with deeply cut leaves that might be taken for those of some varieties of maples. White birch grows wild in Europe and Canada and to some extent in our Northern states, but with us the paper birch is more common. Where a forest of spruce or of certain species of pine—as white pine—has been burned, paper birch and aspens spring up. In the abundant sunlight of the open spaces these trees grow more rapidly than seedlings of the spruce or pine, and a forest of birch and aspen grows up in place of the evergreen forest.

▲ Fig. 20. White birches.

▲ Fig. 21. River birches.

Birch bark. The yellow birch has yellowish or silver-gray bark which has an aromatic odor. The bark of the white birch and paper birch is creamy or pinkish white and splits into paperlike layers. From birch bark the Indians made canoes, as well as boxes, buckets, baskets, kettles, and dishes. In making their canoes, they stitched together large plates of birch bark with the fibrous roots of white spruce, coating the seams with resin obtained from spruce and pine trees. If you can get a piece of the bark, see into how many layers you can split it.

In parts of northern Europe the bark of the white birch is used for shingles. Boats made from it are used on the Volga River. From it are made birch oil and birch tar. Russia leather has an aromatic odor due to the oil of birch bark used in tanning it. As the odor repels insects, this leather is valuable for binding books. A few such bindings in a bookcase are a safeguard against insect enemies, and this oil is said also to prevent damage to the books by mildew.

Birch wood. The wood of the white birch is used as a fuel for smoking hams and herrings, because of the flavor which it imparts. Being light colored, soft, and easily worked, it is used for making spoons, ladles, bowls, and fish casks. Spools, wooden shoes, ox yokes, chairs, and tables also are made of it. Charcoal made from it is burned in forges, and soot made from birch fires is used for making printer's ink.

The wood of the paper birch is used for fuel, shoe pegs, spools, and toys. The yellow birch and sweet birch yield wood that makes fine furniture and a good interior finish for houses. It is often stained dark red and varnished. It is then said to have a "mahogany finish." Few trees are useful for so many purposes as is the birch.

Birches in the far north. The paper birch grows in Newfoundland, in Labrador, about Great Slave Lake, and along the valley of the Yukon. Dwarf birches, which are mere shrubs, grow even farther north. They are common in Greenland and in the arctic barrens of America and Asia, beyond the northern limit of trees. In these frigid regions the birches have for companions several kinds of willows, only a few inches tall, crowberry, bearberry, and a number of other low shrubs, besides lichens, mosses, and, during the short summer season, many herbs with brightly colored blossoms.

Size of branches and size of leaves. Have you ever thought of any connection between the size of a tree's leaves and the coarseness or slenderness of its branches? Even in winter birch trees look quite different from ash or hickory, not merely in color but in the appearance of the branchlets. Can you explain the difference? Name several trees with slender branchlets and others with thick branchlets.

The function of the branches is to hold the leaves up to the light, and the number of branches required depends on the size of the leaves. Trees with small leaves, like birch, elm, and willow, have very numerous branchlets. Those with large leaves, like ash and hickory, do not require so many branchlets. The leaves themselves reach out to the light and fill up the spaces in the crown of the tree. Most palm trees, of which there are a thousand kinds in the tropics, do not branch at all, but they have immense leaves with long stalks to reach out to the light.

Breathing pores in the bark of small branches. On the twigs or small branches of a tree look for small oblong and elevated places on the bark. These are called *lenticels*. They are breathing pores through which the air can enter to reach the living inner portion of the bark and from which water vapor escapes. On birch and cherry trees the lenticels may be seen not only on the branches but even on the trunk. Here they have become elongated by the growth of the bark. Does their long axis extend across the tree, or up and down?

Lenticels are to be found on all trees. Where the bark is very thick, as it is on old oaks, they are at the bottom of the deep cracks.

Elms

In the wild state elms are common throughout most of the country. In many cities they are planted for shade more generally than any other kind of tree, for in deep soil they grow fast and make large, well-shaped trees. The elm is one of the first trees to show signs of life in the spring, and at this season it has a peculiarly graceful and airy appearance. The flowers do not attract much attention, although they appear before the leaves. The winged fruits soon develop and are blown away by the wind, some falling where the seed may grow into another great tree.

▲ Fig. 22. Elm at Northampton, Massachusetts. It is 75 feet high, 18 feet in circumference, and has a spread of 125 feet.

Journal of Heredity

The American elm. Without the flowers or fruit, or even the leaves, an American elm may be distinguished from other trees. Its bark is dark and rough, with deep fissures. The trunk is short and divides into large branches before reaching the upper parts of the tree. The small branches or twigs are slender and the outer ones drooping, giving it a graceful appearance by which you can tell it at a considerable distance even in winter.

American Forestry

▲ Fig. 23. Leaves, flowers, and fruits of American elm.

In the woods the American elm sometimes grows to be more than 100 feet tall, and in open places a large tree spreads over a wide area. There have been wellknown trees of this kind in the older cities of the Eastern states, such as the famous elm at Cambridge, Massachusetts, under which Washington took command of the Continental army, and the one at Philadelphia, under which William Penn signed a treaty with the Indians.

Notice the buttresses that are found at the bases of many large elms. What purpose do these serve, and why are they especially needed by the elm?

The wood of the elm. Elm wood is less prized than many other kinds of wood. It is heavy and solid, but difficult to work because it is very hard to split. This is because, as the wood fibers grow, the ends push past each other and become interlaced. Because of its toughness, however, elm wood is useful for some purposes. The hubs of wheels and the handles and bands of baskets are made of it, and much elm is used for barrel hoops and crating.

Elm trees are subject to decay, and many of the old elms that were formerly so common in the woods contained large hollows high up in the trunk, or even in the limbs. These afforded nesting places for owls and homes for raccoons, porcupines, and squirrels. Many of the "bee trees," which were cut down simply to get the stores of honey the bees had placed in them, were elms.

The early settlers chopped down elms for still another purpose. Knowing that the buds and twigs are nutritious, they gave their cattle a chance to eat them, when other feed was scarce. The cattle would leave their barn feed to browse on the elm.

The slippery elm. The red elm, or slippery elm, has a fragrant and mucilaginous inner bark which children like to chew. Its leaves are larger and rougher than those of the American elm, and its wood, in contrast with that of the latter, is easy to split. Because it wears well and is pliable when steamed, it is sometimes used for making sleigh runners. It is also used for parts of agricultural implements. It is sometimes used locally for the framing of buildings. The slippery elm grows in deep, fertile soil on the banks of streams and on rich, rocky hillsides, throughout most of the eastern half of the United States.

Objections to elms as shade trees. The principal objection to the elm for planting is that its foliage is attacked by many kinds of insects. Caterpillars of the gypsy moth and tussock moth as well as the larvae of the elm-leaf beetle eat the leaves. In the streets of Eastern cities many elms have been ruined by insects. On this account it would be better not to plant so many elms. They should not be planted at all along ordinary city streets where houses are close to the sidewalk, for they need space to grow into their full beauty. Nor should they be planted where large quantities of soft coal are burned, for their rough leaves catch the soot, which, sticking fast, chokes up the breathing pores and in time kills the tree.

What beautiful bird selects the swaying branches of the elm from which to hang its nest? Why is the nest built so far out from the trunk of the tree?

Shapes of trees. The trunks of some kinds of trees divide into so many branches that in the upper part of the tree no trunk can be distinguished. Such trees are called *deliquescent*. In other kinds of trees the trunk extends to the top of the tree. These trees are called *excurrent*. The pine (page 129) is an example of a tree of this kind.

Examine an elm tree. Is it of the deliquescent or excurrent type? Note that the lower branches are drooping, those midway up the tree are horizontal, and those in the top of the tree ascending. By this arrangement all the leaves are exposed to the light.

Position of leaves in the crown of a tree. If you stand under a young Norway maple or other tree that has a dense head of foliage, and look up, you may be surprised to see how scanty the foliage is except near the outside of the head. Such trees have a dense layer of leaves on the outer branches, and these cut off the light from the bases of the branches so that few or no leaves are found in the inner part of the crown. Other

▲ Fig. 24. American elm near Mumford, New York.

▲ Fig. 30. Leaves and fruit of the white ash.

kinds of trees have open crowns; the outer branches stand apart so that the sunlight penetrates to the heart of the crown. Such trees have leaves near the trunk and on twigs springing from the bases of the large branches. To which of these types of trees does the elm belong?

The Ash

The ash belongs to the olive family. It is common in the wild state and is often planted for shade; yet many persons fail to recognize ash trees when they see them. The leaves of the ash are large and compound and bear some resemblance to the leaves of the walnut and hickory, but the leaves of these latter trees are arranged alternately on the branchlets, while those of the ash are opposite. Since young branches come from buds at the bases of leaves, the branches of the ash are also opposite, while those of the walnut and hickory are alternate. The fruit of the ash is winged and identifies the tree at once (Fig. 30).

To support the long and heavy leaves of the ash the branchlets must be large and strong. This gives to the ash in winter a stiff and naked appearance, very different from the graceful elm with its many slender, drooping twigs. The bark on the branches of most kinds of ash is somewhat tinged with red.

Species of ash. Black ash may be distinguished from other native species by its *sessile* leaflets; that is, each leaflet is attached to the common leafstalk without even a short stalk of its own. Blue ash may

Fig. 31. Ash trees in a ▶ North Carolina forest.

U. S. Forest Service

be recognized by its square branchlets. The branchlets and leafstalks of red ash are downy, those of the white ash smooth. Where only these four kinds grow, they can be distinguished in this way; but four other kinds grow in the eastern half of the United States, and several others farther west. The following points may prove helpful in recognizing the different kinds:

The inner bark of the blue ash will give a blue color to water. The bark on the branches of the red ash has a more decidedly reddish brown color than the bark of other species. Black ash has very dark-colored buds. White-ash leaves are usually whitish underneath. Green-ash leaves are brighter green than the leaves of other species. Pumpkin ash, which grows in the South, often has the base of the trunk bulging so that it is of a much greater diameter at a height of 4 feet than at a height of 12 feet. Water ash grows in Southern swamps. The Biltmore ash is found from Pennsylvania to Georgia, but was first distinguished from other kinds of ash at Biltmore, North Carolina.

The best kinds of ash for planting. The European ash is an attractive shade tree. A tree of this kind was set out in Sandusky, Ohio, after the Civil War, where a quarry had been filled with earth. It now spreads about 80 feet and is the finest tree in the city. How did its location favor its rapid growth?

White ash also is a desirable tree for planting, though it does not give so dense a shade as some other trees. It grows fast, is straight and symmetrical, and has no serious insect enemies. Blue ash, which is much less common, also is recommended for planting, but it is more likely to be damaged by insects.

◀ Fig. 32. A white ash that grew in a forest. The other trees have only recently been cut away from around it.

Properties and uses of ash wood. Since ash is strong, elastic, and not very heavy, it is a valuable wood for oars, bats, handles of hoes, rakes, and pitchforks, and for various parts of wagons, railway-car frames, and agricultural implements. White ash and blue ash produce the best timber, when a high degree of strength and elasticity is required. By the elasticity of a wood is meant its power to spring back after it has been bent.

▲ Fig. 33. A white ash that grew in the open. Note the difference in the trunk of this tree and that of the tree shown in Figure 32.

For ball bats and some other purposes second-growth trees are valued much more than those which formed part of the original forest. Which do you think grew faster? Contrary to what you might think, the more rapidly growing trees produce the tougher wood. This is because the wood is ring-porous, and the faster the tree grows the thicker the layers of firm summerwood will be and the farther apart the rings of weak, porous springwood will be placed.

The mountain ash. The foliage of the mountain ash somewhat resembles that of the true ash; but, as is shown by the flowers and fruit, it belongs to the family of the rose and apple and is not a relative of the ash. The streets of Toronto, Canada, are beautified by these trees, and they should be planted more frequently in the United States. They are found growing wild only where the climate is cool. Their scarlet

▲ Fig. 43. Leaves and catkins of aspen (left) and leaves of cottonwood (right).

duce seed. The small seeds are provided with tufts of fine white hairs. These are blown about by the wind, sometimes for long distances.

The cottonwood. The cottonwood, or necklace poplar, is found from Quebec to Florida and west to the Rocky Mountains. It produces as fruit little capsules strung along a curved stem like beads in a necklace. They mature and split open in the spring, and the seeds with their cottonlike tufts of hairs are scattered by the wind. They do not wait till the next spring to sprout, but like some maple seeds germinate at once.

As the cottonwood will grow where other trees do not thrive, it is very widely distributed. On recently formed sand spits in rivers and lakes the soil is too poor for any trees except cottonwood and willows, for it contains no humus, or vegetable mold, such as you can find in any woods where trees have grown and shed their leaves year after year.

American Museum of Natural History

▲ Fig. 34. The mountain ash Decked with autumnal berries that outshine spring's richest blossoms, Yields a splendid show amid the leafy woods.Wordsworth

fruits, which attract birds, make them ornamental all winter, and their foliage is admired in summer. The mountain ash has one serious disadvantage: it suffers much from the scale insects which attack members of the apple family.

Growth affected by light. Have you observed how a plant, when placed in a window, grows toward the source of light? Notice trees that are growing in open places, along streams, in the edge of a forest, and in a forest surrounded by other trees. Do the branches grow in such a way as to bring the leaves to the light? Why do forest trees have longer trunks than trees of the same kind that grow in the open (pages 53 and 54)?

Poplars

The leaves of poplars, especially those called aspens, quake in even a slight breeze. The sound they make has been compared to the patter of rain. Secure a leaf from a poplar and examine the leafstalk just below the blade of the leaf. Do you understand why the leaves of a poplar are stirred by even a light breeze?

The flowers of the poplar are borne in long, drooping *catkins* which appear in early spring. The staminate flowers are borne on one tree and the pistillate flowers on another tree; thus only certain trees pro-

Fig. 44. Giant cotton ▶ wood near Shakopee, Minnesota. It is over 9 feet in diameter and 130′feet tall. Note the man near the base.

H. B. Ayer

468

Generally speaking, the cottonwood is likely to be short lived, but some cottonwood trees are more than a century old and are among the largest trees east of the Rocky Mountains.

The wood. Cotton-woods abound along streams in the plains where other trees are scarce. In such places people use the wood for fuel and for other purposes. Boards made of it warp badly, especially when exposed to moisture, and are inferior in both strength and durability to boards made from most other woods. The tree is a very rapid grower, sometimes increasing in diameter 10 inches in as many years. The wood is soft and light colored and is much used for paper pulp.

Objections to the cottonwood as a shade tree. The leaves of the cottonwood, being smooth, do not catch soot and dust like those of the elm. On this account and because of its rapid growth, this tree (especially the variety known as the Carolina poplar) has been planted along many city streets. Like many other things that are cheap, the cottonwood usually proves unsatisfactory. It is attacked by several kinds of insects and is likely to be short lived. It is not ornamental, and its capsules and cottony seeds—and in summer its leaves and twigs—litter the ground. Its roots, sometimes more than 100 feet long, in their search for water send their rootlets into drains and obstruct the drainage; they have been known even to break through the cement linings of cisterns. Some cities have passed ordinances forbidding the planting of this tree.

▲ Fig. 45. Leaves of Lombardy poplar (left) and silver poplar (right).

Aspens. The American aspen is a small species of poplar with light-colored bark and soft, light wood. It is found through the cool portions of North America and grows in poor soil, often springing up extensively where woods have been burned. Beavers cut it down with their strong, sharp incisor teeth, using it to build their dams and lodges and eating for food the bark and water-soaked wood. Its wood, like that of other poplars, is much used for making paper. A similar species of aspen grows in Europe.

Lombardy poplar. The tree that is best known under the name of "poplar" is one which is not a native of this country but has been brought from Europe. It is called the *Lombardy poplar.* Its branches are ascending, so that the tree is like a spire and becomes very tall without spreading out. This variety is often prominent in French and Italian landscapes. Driveways that lead back from main thoroughfares to country mansions are often bordered by Lombardy poplars.

Silver poplar. The white or silver-leaf poplar, also from Europe, has quite a different habit from the Lombardy poplar, for its branches are spreading. Its leaf-stalks are only slightly flattened, and its leaves are cottony white on the under side. Some people incorrectly call it the "silver maple." It spreads by means of the roots, the sprouts which it sends up forming within a few years extensive thickets that are difficult to eradicate. On this account it is not a desirable tree to plant.

Root systems. The root system of poplars and most other trees is composed of many slender branches of nearly equal length. Such a system of roots is called a *fibrous root system.* On the other hand, an oak, a pine, or a walnut or other nut-bearing tree has a *tap root;* that is, it has one large root going down deep into the ground, with smaller roots branching off from the side. The radish and dandelion are examples of herbs with tap roots. Grasses, corn, and other grains have fibrous root systems.

▲ Fig. 46. A cottonwood seedling less than 1 year old. The roots have reached a length of from 3 to 4 feet.

The combined length of all the roots of so small a plant as a wheat plant has been found to be more than 1800 feet. It would be difficult to tell how far all the roots of a big cottonwood tree would reach if placed end to end. Figure 46 shows the roots of a cottonwood tree less than one year old. This tree grew in sandy soil. In arid parts of the Southwest the mesquite has been known to send its roots to a depth of 60 feet in search of

◀ Fig. 47. Young Lombardy poplars.

▲ Fig. 55. Leaves and acorns of the white oak (A) and of the bur oak (B).

water. In ordinary soils the roots of trees must remain nearer the surface, where they can get air as well as water. If the soil is not drained and water completely fills the spaces between the soil partides, the roots of most trees will die for lack of oxygen.

Functions of roots. The roots of most trees do not serve, like those of the silver poplar, to reproduce the tree, but they have other very important functions. They anchor the tree in its place, and they gather from the soil and supply to the tree the water and mineral materials that it needs. Roots excrete substances which help to dissolve limestone and other mineral materials in the soil. In this way they secure more mineral matter for the tree. If the ground on one side of a tree is well watered and on the other side dry, the roots grow toward the water.

Oaks

Oaks are among the most common and useful of trees. Nearly three hundred kinds of oak are known, of which about fifty grow wild in the United States. There are probably few areas of the size of a county that contain more than ten species of oak, though in one piece of woodland thirteen different species have been found growing wild. Because of their abundance and the many valuable properties of their woods, oaks are the most important of all the hardwood trees of our forests.

Oak leaves. A collection of the leaves of the different oaks that grow near your home is easily made and will help you to know the trees. The leaves of most species are lobed, but the shape of the lobes is different in the different species. Look at Figures 55 and 56 or at specimens, and tell how a white-oak leaf differs from a red-oak leaf. Which species of oak have leaves

that closely resemble each other? How can you tell them apart? Does any species of oak retain its leaves long after they have lost their green color?

Acorns. The acorns as well as the leaves of different kinds of oaks differ and should also be collected. Pin oaks have small and nearly hemispherical acorns, which in many cases are striped. Bur oaks have large acorns with deep, shaggy cups or cupules, and are therefore also called "mossy-cup" oaks. Red oaks have large acorns with shallow, saucerlike cupules. Which kinds of oaks have acorns that are good to eat? What birds eat them?

When the crop of acorns is abundant in parts of our Southern states, the hogs that run in the woods fatten on them. Cattle, deer, and squirrels also eat them. The Indians esteemed them as an article of food; in southern Europe the people boil and eat them, and we too should do this if we were not well supplied with better food.

Uses of oak bark and wood. In the bark of some kinds of oak a dark-colored substance called *tannin* is deposited very abundantly. This is used in tanning hides to make leather. Why are untanned hides less

▲ Fig. 56. Leaves and, acorns of the red oak (C) and of the pin oak (D). The lobes in the leaves of the red oak point forward. In its near relative, the black oak, they point to the side.

Journal of Heredity

◀ Fig. 57. Giant white oak near Amelia, Virginia. It has a height of 118 feet and a spread of 128 feet.

Pan American Union

▲ Fig. 59. Live oak near Sutherland Springs, Texas. The branches are draped with Spanish moss.

U. S. Forest Service

▲ Fig. 60. Young pin oaks on Pennsylvania Avenue, Washington, D. C.

useful than leather for making shoes, harness, and other articles? Have you ever seen a piece of raw hide? Corks are made from the bark of an oak that grows in Spain and in northern Africa.

Oak wood is heavy, hard, and strong; it has wide pith rays that give many of the boards a mottled appearance, and many of the species are very durable. For fuel how does oak compare with other kinds of wood? What properties of oak adapt it for floors? for the making of furniture? of wagons? of ships? What other things are made from it? Why? Verify by actual test all the properties of oak that you have named.

Galls. On some oak leaves and branches you will find peculiar growths which you might suppose to be fruits, if you did not know that the fruit of the oak is an acorn. These peculiar growths are **galls.** Some twenty-five kinds of galls have been found on white oaks alone. Open a gall and look for a tiny, wormlike creature. It is not a real worm, for, if you had not disturbed it, it would in time have developed into a gall-fly. Indeed, it came from an egg laid by a gallfly and is the young of the fly. Like the caterpillar and grub, it is the larva stage,—the stage which follows the egg of an insect and during which it eats a great deal and grows fast. The little gallfly lays an egg beneath the

skin of the leaf or twig, and when this egg hatches, the larva feeds on the juices contained in the leaf or twig. The abnormal growth (the gall) which the plant makes around the larva serves to protect the young insect from other insects and from birds.

Some galls are quite pretty. A collection of a dozen or more kinds would form an interesting exhibit in a schoolroom. Black ink is made from copperas and certain oak galls called "nutgalls," combined with a little dextrin or gum arabic, which is added to make it adhere to the pen. In Hungary and the Balkan States certain oak galls are gathered and sold for tanning, and pyrogallic acid, which is used in photography, is made from them.

Oaks as shade trees. Besides the usefulness of their wood, bark, acorns, and galls, oaks are desirable as shade and ornamental trees. Oaks from the original forest, left standing after the land has become the site of a town or city, are often highly prized. The red oak is considered one of the best of all our shade trees. It is suitable for planting along broad streets. This species and the scarlet and pin oaks grow more rap-

◀ Fig. 58. Trunk of the same tree. The circumference is more than 15 feet at a height of 6 feet from the ground.

Journal of Heredity

idly than most of the other oaks. They are desirable as shade trees on account of their durability, symmetry, beauty of foliage, and comparative freedom from injury by insects or fungi.

Have you seen many large oak trees? How old do you suppose they are? How do live oaks get their name? Where do they grow? Which kind of oak do you consider the most valuable? Why?

Relatives of the oak. To the same family as the oak belong the beech and chestnut. All these trees produce staminate and pistillate flowers on the same tree. The flowers have no corolla, and the pistillate flowers are rarely noticed. They give rise to nuts which have no partition and contain but one seed. The seed or meat contains nourishment to start the growth of a new tree. Beechnuts, chestnuts, and acorns constitute a large part of the food of many birds and mammals.

Evergreens

The trees that we have studied up to this time are *deciduous;* that is, they shed their leaves in the autumn. But in many parts of the United States and Canada *evergreens* are more common than the trees that lose their leaves with the coming of the cold months. Each type of tree is best suited for life under certain conditions, and whether evergreens or deciduous trees are more common in any given region depends on the prevailing conditions of soil and climate.

Definition of an evergreen. While any plant that remains green throughout the winter is an evergreen, and while in many parts of the United States we have broad-leaved evergreen trees and shrubs like the magnolia, holly, and rhododendron, yet we commonly mean by an evergreen a tree or shrub with needle-shaped, awl-shaped, or scaly leaves. The pine, spruce, cedar, and fir are trees that belong to this group. They do not, however, retain the same leaves as long as they live. Under a pine or cedar tree the ground may be covered with fallen leaves, but they fall a few at a time and not all in a single season or year.

The deciduous tree. In the spring a deciduous tree spreads out a vast number of broad, thin leaves to the light. All leaves give off water, and it is estimated that a large birch tree must draw from the earth 100 gallons of water each day to prevent its leaves from withering and drying in the hot sun. The delicate, thin leaves of such a tree cannot endure cold, and in winter it is possible for the roots of a tree to secure only very small amounts of water from the frozen soil; so trees with broad, thin leaves drop them before the cold season comes. During the months when the air is warm and water is abundant they run a great food factory and store in their branches, stems, and roots the surplus food which they make. On this surplus they live through the winter, and from it they build in the spring their flowers, leaves, and young twigs. The working season of most deciduous trees is even

shorter than we think, for the delicate leaves cannot appear until after the season of frost is over, and they fall from many trees as soon as the first frosts of autumn come.

On the other hand, the leaves on most evergreen trees are small, and they are tough and leathery so that they resist cold and drying. A tree of this kind does not have the great spread of leaf surface that a deciduous tree has. At no time can it manufacture food as rapidly as a deciduous tree does when it is in full leaf; yet the leaves of evergreens are able to build some food for the tree during the greater part of the year, whereas the trees that lose their leaves at the end of summer cannot add to their stock of nourishment until the following spring. In some locations the slower and steadier method of the evergreen succeeds better than the plan of rapid work for a shorter part of the year followed by the deciduous tree.

Where the deciduous and evergreen types succeed. In most parts of the temperate zone where the soil is deep and moist, as in rich river bottoms, and where the growing season is long and the air moist, the deciduous tree grows better than the evergreen. The abundant water supply and the low rate of evaporation from the leaves enable it to support a great crown of leaves, and the long growing season allows it to keep these leaves for so long a time that in the course of a summer it can manufacture more food than an evergreen can, even though it keeps its leaves during the whole year.

The evergreen, on the other hand, succeeds where the water supply is not so great, where evaporation

▲ Fig. 68. Cones from six different evergreens: (I) Blue spruce, (II) Norway spruce, (III) White spruce, (IV) Douglas fir, (V) Big Tree, (VI) Austrian pine.

is more intense, or where the winters are long and cold. In sandy soils and on steep and rocky mountain slopes; where the air is dry; and in the far north, it is the prevailing type of tree. Its small, tough leaves demand only a small amount of water, and by working through a longer season they make more food for the tree than the leaves of a deciduous tree can produce in dry locations or during short summers. Do you think evergreens are not found in deep, moist soils because they will not grow in these locations, or because in such places the deciduous trees grow more rapidly and crowd them out?

In the moist tropics where there are no cold seasons the trees do not need to shed their leaves and are all evergreens. But these evergreens have broad leaves like our deciduous trees and differ in type from the evergreens of dry and cold regions. Just why the trees in many swamps are evergreens has not been fully explained, but one reason probably lies in the fact that under swamp conditions only a feeble root system can be developed.

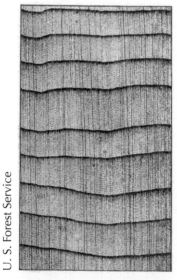

U. S. Forest Service

◀ Fig. 69. Wood of arbor vitæ as seen through a microscope. The wood is light and, like that of other evergreens, is non-porous and uniform in texture.

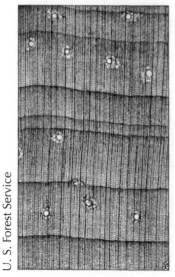

U. S. Forest Service

◀ Fig. 70. Wood of the piñon, a species of western pine. In the pine there are resin ducts which appear as openings in the wood.

Conifers. Most of our evergreens produce cones and hence are called *conifers* or cone bearers. The cone *is* the fruit. The seeds are protected by the scales of *the* cone but are not inclosed in an ovary. Pollen from other flowers falls directly upon the ovules. The pollen is produced in great abundance and is carried by *the* wind. If the tree is surrounded by others of the same species, its chance of receiving pollen for its many ovules *is* greater. For this reason evergreen trees are not often found scattered in small numbers over a large area. You might travel a hundred miles without seeing a pine, spruce, or hemlock, excepting such as have been planted, but when you come to one you will probably see near it many others of the same species.

U. S. Forest Service

▲ Fig. 71. Paper leaving the mill for a metropolitan daily. The paper in this photograph represents about one half the amount used by the newspaper each day. Much paper is made from spruce and other evergreens.

The coniferous trees of the United States and Canada all belong to the pine family. Among lumbermen their wood is spoken of as "soft wood," although that of the Georgia pine and some other kinds is hard. The wood of deciduous trees is called "hardwood," although that of some kinds of deciduous trees is soft. In the four chapters that follow will be found descriptions of our most important conifers. The wood that is furnished by these trees is a most important source of lumber. It is fine grained and easily worked, is light, and for its weight strong, and shrinks evenly when it is dried. The habit which these trees have of growing in large numbers together is also valuable to the lumberman. It enables him to get out a large amount of lumber of the same kind at one time.

Spruce and Fir

Spruce and fir resemble pines in having the branches arranged in whorls; that is, several branches grow in a circle at the same level. They differ from pines in having the leaves scattered on the branchlets instead of being arranged in clusters. They grow as forest trees in the northern parts of the United States and in our Western mountains, but spruce trees have been extensively planted in cemeteries and near dwellings in other parts of the country. Besides affording dense shade, these trees are ornamental and break the force of the wind. Many thousands of young spruce and fir trees are sold each year as Christmas trees. At the holiday season children who live hundreds of miles from the forests where these trees grow become familiar with them.

Kinds of spruce. The blue spruce from Colorado has foliage of a bluish color. From the main branches the longer branchlets droop. When not trimmed, the lowest branches are near the ground and the tree is shaped like a cone.

The Norway spruce sometimes grows two or three feet in one season and is the species most commonly found in cultivation. Its branches extend out almost horizontally from the trunk, curving up a little toward the ends. By its larger cones it is readily distinguished from the white, red, and black spruces, all of which grow in Canada and the Northern states. Other large species of spruce are found in the mountains of the West.

The cones and seeds of the spruce. The cones of both spruces and firs have much thinner scales than the cones of the pines. The cones of the spruce are drooping. In what part of the tree do they hang in greatest numbers? If you can get a full-grown cone which has not yet lost its seed, take it home or to the schoolroom. After a time the scales will spread apart so that the winged seeds can drop out. When thrown in the air, do the seeds fall straight down? Why?

The wood of the spruce. In Europe masts and spars are often made from the tall, straight trunks of the Norway spruce. On account of its uniform grain the wood of this and other species of spruce is used for the sounding boards of musical instruments. The lumber is soft, white, and straight grained and, in proportion to its weight, has great strength. It is

U. S. Forest Service

Fig. 81. Alpine fir, ▶ Blackfeet National Forest, Montana.

used for many purposes, and of recent years has come into great prominence because of the large amounts of it needed for the manufacture of airplanes. Much of the paper used in books and newspapers is made of spruce wood.

Firs. Different species of pine and spruce are often called "firs"; but the name "fir" is properly applied to evergreens that resemble spruces in general appearance, but have erect instead of drooping cones, and leaves that are not jointed at the base. The only true fir native to the northeastern part of the United States is the balsam fir, which grows also over much of Canada and in the mountains as far south as Virginia.

The leaves on this fir are blunt and flat, and not foursided like those of a spruce. On the horizontal branches they appear to be two-ranked instead of standing out all around the branch, as do the leaves of the spruce. Persons camping where fir trees are growing often make a bed of the boughs; but they avoid the spruce because its leaves (needles) are sharp and stand out all around the stem. The leaves of the fir last a long time; if undisturbed, they persist on the tree for 8 years.

R. E. Horsey

◀ Fig. 80. Blue spruce in Highland Park, Rochester, New York.

R. E. Horsey

Fig. 82. Douglas fir, ▶ Highland Park, Rochester, New York.

◀ Fig. 83. Red fir forest on Mount Shasta at an elevation of 5000 feet.

Young balsam firs and Norway spruces look so much alike that it is difficult to tell them apart at a distance. But the bark of the fir, except on old trunks, is quite smooth, and on its surface are numerous blisters of a resinous substance called "balsam." These blisters distinguish the true firs from all other trees. The balsam which is obtained from the balsam fir is called "Canada balsam." It is used in fixing delicate specimens on glass slides for examination through a compound microscope. "Pine pillows," filled with the leaves of this tree, keep their fragrance for 2 or 3 years.

In the mountains of Tennessee, North Carolina, and Virginia a different species called "Fraser's fir" is found, and other large species of fir from which valuable lumber is obtained grow in the mountains of our Western states. Although abundant in the woods in cold regions, firs are not seen in cultivation as often as spruces.

The Douglas fir. The Douglas fir is also called "Douglas spruce," though it is neither a fir nor a spruce, but only a close relative of these trees. It is one of the most valuable trees of the whole country. It is widely distributed in the mountains of the West and along the coast of Oregon, Washington, and British Columbia, where it grows taller than any tree in the Eastern forests. In the interior of the continent it is not a remarkably large tree, but on the Pacific coast it frequently exceeds 250 feet in height and 10 feet in diameter. Ladders used by fire departments are made from its wood, for it is light, straight grained, and free from knots. Large quantities of this wood are used for building and other purposes. Many masts and flagpoles are made of it.

When the Douglas fir grows in open places, the lowest branches, like those of various spruces, touch the ground. It grows rapidly and is a handsome tree. In the moist, mild atmosphere of England it was found to thrive as soon as introduced, but in our Northeastern states the climate is too severe for it. It has been

found recently that stock from the mountains of Colorado is perfectly hardy, so that the tree may now be successfully planted in various parts of this country.

The Pine

More of our lumber comes from the pine than from any other one tree, yet many people do not know a pine when they see one. Some think that all evergreens are pines.

Pine trees have slender leaves, called "needles," growing in clusters. When young, each cluster has a sheath of papery scales at its base. The cone scales of the pine are thicker than those of spruce or fir. Pines, like spruces and most other conifers, are excurrent trees. Many species have trunks that extend to a height of more than 100 feet, and some species to a height of more than 200 feet. They often grow in *pure stands;* that is, to the exclusion of other kinds of trees.

▲ Fig. 84. Long-leaf pine forest near Ocilla, Georgia. Turpentine and rosin are being collected from the trees.

Products of pine trees. Tar, turpentine, and rosin are obtained from several species of pine. These materials have long been called "naval stores," but they are now used more extensively on land than in connection with ships. Pieces of pine stumps and roots are heated in retorts, ovens, or kilns, and the turpentine thus driven off as a vapor is condensed by cooling it and afterwards separated from the acids, wood alcohol, and other products that come from wood when it is heated without air. Tar requires more heat to change it to vapor, so that it collects in another part of the distilling apparatus. What is pine tar used for? What other kind of tar is there and how is it used?

When a small cavity is made in the trunk of a Georgia pine or of a western yellow pine, crude turpentine flows out. By distillation in large copper stills, oil or spirit of turpentine is derived from this. Rosin is left in the still. This is used in making the cheaper kinds

Fig. 85. White pine trees about 120 years old, St. Louis County, Minnesota. The trees are still growing in height.

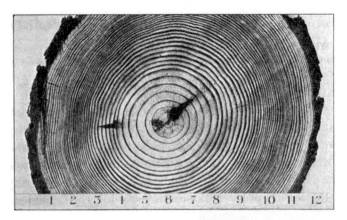

Fig. 87. Section from a 52-year-old short-leaf pine. The tree grew in a forest near Glenville, Arkansas, and was of average size.

of soap and varnish, and also in sealing wax and shoemaker's wax. What other uses has rosin? Turpentine is used largely in varnish and paint. What other uses has it?

Most frame houses are built chiefly of pine. Can you name other uses for the wood? What are the properties of the wood? How do these properties adapt it to its various uses? Do pines furnish any food?

What other uses have pine trees besides those already mentioned?

Species of pines. In the United States there are about thirty-six species of pines growing wild. The white pine formerly grew abundantly in parts of the Northern states from Maine to Minnesota and in southern Canada. It furnished a vast amount of good lumber, but the supply is now nearly exhausted, so that white pine of good grade brings a high price. Southern yellow pine has taken its place for many uses. It is a harder and heavier wood than white pine, and contains more resin, but it is likely to split along the annual rings when it is nailed. Test the cleavability of a piece of yellow pine by driving a nail through it near the end.

In California, the sugar pine grows 200 feet tall and produces cones that may be 18 inches or more in length. Its seed or nut,

Fig. 86. Spray of Scotch pine, showing leaves and cone (A). Leaves of the white pine are shown at the left (B) and of the Georgia or long-leaf pine at the right (C).

the size of a navy bean, is edible, as are the seeds of several smaller species of pine, called "piñons," that grow in the Southwest. Another important pine is the western yellow pine, which is a valuable source of both lumber and turpentine.

Cones of the pine. By comparing the cones of such pines as grow in your vicinity you will find differences in form and size. The Scotch pine, which is often planted in this country, has cones about 2 inches long, while the cones of the white pine are usually from 4 to 6 inches in length and may reach a length of 11 inches. The cones of pines require 2 years for their development, while those of the spruce and fir require but 1 year. When the winged seeds at the base of the scales are mature, the scales spread apart enough to allow the seeds to fall out and be borne away by the wind. The seeds of these and other evergreens are not inclosed in an ovary, but grow at the base of the cone scales. See if you can find them.

Pine needles. The needles of the valuable Georgia pine, which is one species of yellow pine, are sometimes as much as 18 inches long and grow in clusters of three; those of the white pine are very slender, but shorter, and grow in fives; those of the Scotch pine are still shorter and are in twos, as are those of many of the native species.

Examine the leaves of a young pine seedling. Are they needle leaves or ordinary leaves, and are they on the ends of dwarf branches or attached to the sides of the stem? What inference can you draw as to the leaves of the ancestor of the pine?

Pollen of the pine. In spring the yellow pollen from the pine trees falls in such quantity that it is sometimes spoken of as a shower of sulfur. For seed production some of this pollen must fall on the young cones. You can see an advantage to these trees from growing in pure stands. Will a cornstalk growing by itself produce much grain?

Knowledge of the Star

From *Trees, Stars, and Birds: A Book of Outdoor Science* by Edwin Lincoln Moseley, 1919

Can you remember looking up into the sky when you were a little child and wondering about the stars? And did you learn to recite the familiar lines:

> Twinkle, twinkle, little star,
> How I wonder what you are!
> Up above the world so high,
> Like a diamond in the sky.

Are you now too old to wonder about the stars or to wander in imagination among the celestial spheres? Should you like to know where shooting stars come from, what they are, and what becomes of them? Are the other stars like them? Do people live on the stars? If they do, can they see the earth, and what would the earth look like from the stars?

The science of astronomy. The science which treats of the heavenly bodies is called *astronomy*. It is interesting to study because it satisfies the spirit of wonder within us, our desire to know, which is the foundation of all science. It is also a most useful science. It enables us to determine directions and to keep accurate time. For thousands of years men have guided their course across the seas and over desert wastes by the stars, and by the use of astronomy explorers have found their way over unknown regions

▲ Fig. 109. Yerkes Astronomical Observatory, Lake Geneva, Wisconsin.

of the earth. Maps and surveys are based on observations on the stars. The surveyor who marks out the line of a railroad or the boundaries of a farm is using knowledge gained from study of the heavenly bodies.

Time measured by the movements of the heavenly bodies. If your clock gained 5 minutes a day, would it matter, provided that every other clock and watch did the same? People could keep appointments because their timepieces would agree. School would begin each morning when the clock pointed to nine o'clock. But after a few weeks a clock gaining 5 minutes a day would point to nine o'clock before sunrise. A little reflection will show that the length of a day is not determined by our clocks and watches, but that our timepieces must be made to conform to the actual length that the day has. Likewise the length of a year does not depend on any human law or decree. We might agree to call 360 days a year. If we did, after a while Christmas would come in summer and the Fourth of July in winter. Like the day, the year has its own length. What determines the length of a day and of a year?

Fitting the calendar to the year. In the early history of the world much confusion arose because of the lack of a calendar, but before the beginning of the Christian era, Julius Cæsar, by the advice of the astronomer Sosigenes, decreed that the calendar year should be 365¼ days, every fourth year containing 366 days and the others 365 days. The actual length of a year is almost 365¼ days, but in 16 centuries the difference between the true length and 365¼ days caused the seasons to shift in reference to the calendar 10 days. To remedy this, Pope Gregory in 1582 decreed that the day following October 4 should that year be called October 15, thus making up the 10 days. He further decreed that the last year of each century should not be a leap year unless divisible by 400. Thus 1700, 1800, and 1900 were not leap years, although they are divisible by 4, but the year 2000 will be a leap year. This arrangement so nearly approximates the length of the real year that in 4000 years the seasons will shift not more than 1 day.

Astronomy the oldest of the sciences. When the ancient Assyrians and Egyptians went on a journey, they often traveled at night, for the day was hot. They did not ride on a railroad train or along a highway with a fence on either side, but guided their courses by the stars. They had no electric or gas lights or such lamps as ours, and so the light of the moon was more important to them than it is to us. Whether on a journey or at home, they often spent much of the night with no roof over them but the great vault of heaven, and clouds or mist rarely obscured the stars. These ancient peoples, therefore, had many opportunities for observing the heavenly bodies, and although they possessed no telescopes they learned more about astronomy than most persons nowadays know. They knew what bright stars and what groups of stars could be seen in the east at a certain season. They could compute when the moon would rise, when there would be a new moon, and when an eclipse. They knew the polestar and that it is always in the north, and from their knowledge of astronomy they knew the directions and how to guide themselves across uncharted wastes.

How to know the heavenly bodies. Some fields of study are too wide to be passed over in a short time. They are rich enough for us to visit again and again. Only in this way can we see and appreciate the treasures that are there stored. We cannot become well acquainted with more than a few kinds of trees or birds in a single month. We may come to know them better as long as we have health to enjoy life. The same is true of the stars. The student might read the chapters in this book on the stars in an hour or two. It would be more profitable for him to read them a little at a time. The stars cannot all be seen to advantage at any one season. To study them most conveniently one should look at them night after night through the different months of the year.

It would be well to begin the study of the stars and constellations sometime in the fall, when a clear sky permits them to be well seen, and to take them up again every week or two for several months and perhaps again the next year. In this way, little by little you will acquire an acquaintance with some of the brightest stars and most conspicuous constellations, and this will continue to be a source of pleasure to you in after years.

Reasoning as well as observation required in astronomy. By looking through a telescope you could see many stars too faint to be seen with the naked eye, but even the brightest stars would appear as points of light, just as they do when seen without a telescope. How, then, do we know that some of them are very large? Science has revealed to us many wonderful things in the heavens which the ancients did not know. Telescopes and other instruments are very useful to the astronomers, but what is seen by means of them would not afford much knowledge about the heavenly bodies if the astronomers did not reason correctly from the facts that they gather. The scientific method requires not only careful observations but also careful reasoning.

The questions that are asked in the chapters that treat of the heavenly bodies are intended to guide you in your thinking. Many of them may seem difficult to young pupils. Older students, even, will be puzzled to find correct answers to some of them. It would be well to give some attention to them early in your study, so that, as opportunity occurs for observing the heavens, some of them at least may be answered without the aid of teachers or of books.

The Universe and Solar System

From Trees, Stars, and Birds: A Book of Outdoor Science by Edwin Lincoln Moseley, 1919

Lying with your back upon the earth and looking up into the blue sky, did you ever wonder what there might be far away in space? Is there a wall that bounds it all? If there is, what is beyond that wall? If not, how far does space extend? Are there other suns, larger, hotter, and more brilliant than our own? Are there great heavenly bodies, thousands of times as large as the earth, which no one on the earth has ever seen? Far out in space are there other worlds like ours on which beings like ourselves could live?

The earth, with everything on it, and all the heavenly bodies, seen and unseen, make up the *universe*. In every direction it stretches away through limitless space, a vast collection of giant bodies that the imagination can hardly picture. When we stand forth under the sky at night and think of

> Clusters and beds of worlds and beelike swarms
> Of stars and starry streams,

sweeping on and on through space, we are awed by the majesty of the spectacle before our eyes.

The stars. What are the twinkling points of light which our eyes behold in whatever direction we look on a clear night? They are great blazing suns, set here and there at vast distances through space. We do not see that they are farther from us than the clouds, except when a drifting cloud hides them from our view. Yet the clouds are only a short distance from us, floating in the air above us, while the stars are out in space so far away that even were we able to fly with the swiftness of a nighthawk we could not reach them in a thousand years. The sun is a star, no larger or brighter than thousands of others; but it is much nearer to us, and that is why it gives us so much more heat and light and seems so much larger than the other stars.

The solar system. The earth and seven other worlds or planets, some smaller than the earth, others larger, revolve around the sun (Fig. 108). These are the *major* planets. The sun controls the motion of several hundred *minor* planets, which are of much smaller size also, as well as the movements of various comets and a host of meteors. Some of the major planets are attended by satellites that revolve around them as they themselves revolve around the sun. The moon is the earth's satellite, and some other planets have several moons or satellites.

The sun and all the bodies that revolve around it—the planets with their satellites, the minor planets, and the comets and meteors—constitute the *solar system;* that is, the system of the sun. Whether, like the sun, the other stars have smaller bodies revolving about them we cannot tell. They are so far away that at such distances bodies like our earth would be invisible to us. Yet it would seem reasonable to believe that each star is the controlling center of a great system of worlds like our own.

The vastness of the universe. The earth on which we live is so large that none of us will ever see more than a small part of its surface, and the vast mass of matter that lies deep in the earth's interior has never been seen by human eye. Yet the earth is but a small member of our solar system, and our entire solar system is so small a part of the whole universe that blotting it out of existence would be only like wiping a speck of star dust from the sky. Well has the poet Emerson said: "If the stars should appear one night in a thousand years, how would men believe and adore; and preserve for many generations the remembrance of the city of God which had been shown."

The work of astronomers. In the vast voids of space between the heavenly bodies there is no air, and across them no sounds can pass. In them all is darkness and silence, and there the cold is of an intensity not known on earth. Nothing comes to us across this space except waves of light and heat and the mysterious force of gravitation, which all material bodies exert on each other. Yet from the information gained from these sources, astronomers have measured the distances to some of the stars, learned that certain of them are young and others old, and calculated the weights of the sun, moon, and many other heavenly bodies. By countless observations and by careful thought and long computations they have learned the secrets of the universe and have built them into a system so wonderful and so complete that of it the philosopher Laplace has said: "Contemplated as one grand whole, astronomy is the most beautiful monument of the human mind, the noblest record of its intelligence."

Determining the Distances to the Heavenly Bodies

From *Trees, Stars, and Birds: A Book of Outdoor Science* by Edwin Lincoln Moseley, 1919

A baby reaches for the moon and a dog barks at it. Apparently they think it is near them. Can you tell merely by looking at it whether it is near or far away? Have you ever mistaken a town clock at night or some other artificial light for the moon and are you sure that the moon is farther away than objects on the earth? Doubtless you have read about the great distances of the sun, moon, and other heavenly bodies from the earth, and perhaps you have wondered how it is possible to learn the distance to an object that no one has ever been able to reach. Astronomers and surveyors do this in a rather simple way.

Determining distances without measuring them. A surveyor can find the distance to a tree on the other side of a river without crossing the river. On his own side of the river he drives two stakes and then carefully measures the distance between them. Then with his instruments he sights at the tree from each stake, measuring the angles that lines from each stake to the tree make with a line connecting the two stakes. The two stakes and the tree form a triangle of which he knows the length of one side and the size of two angles. By his knowledge of trigonometry he is then able to calculate the length of the other sides of the triangle and thus find the distance from either of the stakes to the tree. By ex amining Figure no you will note that the farther away the tree is the larger are the angles at the two stakes.

Finding the distances to the heavenly bodies. Astronomers use the method of the surveyor in finding the distances to the heavenly bodies. Two observers can sight their instruments on the moon

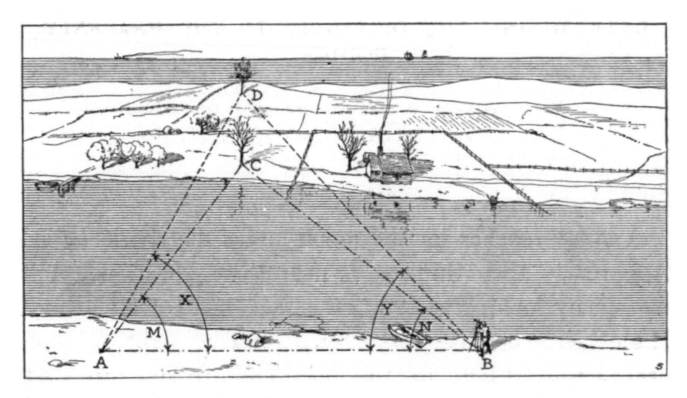

▲ Fig. 110. Determining distances to objects without measuring them.

480

from different points on the earth's surface and find the angles which the lines to the moon make with a line connecting the two points on the surface of the earth. They know the distance apart of the observers on the surface of the earth, and they can then calculate the length of the lines which extend to the moon (Fig. 111).

In measuring the distance to fixed stars, which are very distant from us, astronomers take observations at different times of the year and use the distance of the earth from the sun as one side of the triangle. Figure 112 will help to make clear how this is done.

Distances to some heavenly bodies. Suppose that Romulus and Remus, the traditional founders of Rome, had started from Italy in 753 B.C. in an airplane that would carry them 125 miles an hour. In 2 days they might have reached North America, and on the third they would have crossed the continent and reached the Pacific Ocean. Keeping on around the world they would have arrived at their native land in about a week from the time they started. Suppose them to start again on a journey, this time to the moon, traveling at the same high rate of speed. The journey would have required about 80 days, and if they had started back to the earth at once it would have been more than 5 months before they reached their home again.

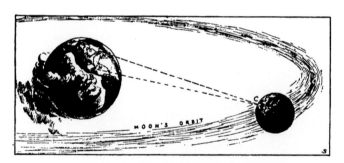

▲ Fig. 111. How the distance to the moon is measured. If the astronomer knows the length of the line AB and the size of the angles M and N, he can compute the distance to the point C.

Suppose they had then set out for the sun. They would have taken 85 years to reach it and would have grown quite old before they arrived. If, not content with seeing so much of the universe, they had kept on through space, directing their swift flight toward the great planet Jupiter, the journey from the sun to Jupiter would have required 441 years; for Jupiter is more than 5 times as far from the sun as we are.

If they had arrived at Jupiter in 227 B.C., and that same year had directed their course toward the orbit of Neptune, the most distant of all the worlds that revolve around the sun, they would not have reached the path of that planet until the year 1879.

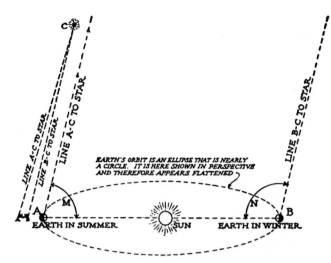

▲ Fig. 112. How the distance to a star is measured.

Suppose Neptune in 1879 to have been on the opposite side of his orbit from the point where Romulus and Remus arrived, and that they had set out to meet him, traveling still at the rate of 125 miles an hour, or 3000 miles a day. Neptune is the slowest of all the planets; nevertheless, he moves along his path at a speed of about 200 miles a minute, which is farther than Romulus and Remus are flying in an hour. Although Neptune and our voyagers through space were moving toward each other with such high speed, yet some 80 years would elapse before they would meet.

Within your lifetime let Romulus and Remus bid adieu to Neptune and set out for Alpha Centauri, the star that is nearest to our solar system. Their journeys made among the planets have occupied nearly 27 centuries. 7000 times 27 centuries would be required to reach Alpha Centauri, the nearest star. Many of the stars are hundreds of times as far away as Alpha Centauri. Only a few of them are within 400 trillion miles of the earth. Most of them are many times this distance from us, but it is believed that none are so far away as 1000 times this distance.

Some problems to be explained. Riding along a straight road in the country at night, did you ever notice a light in some house to your right or left, and, after riding for some minutes more, notice that it was still in nearly the same direction? Was the house near the road or far from it? Did you ever go along a city street and notice when you came to a cross street that the moon was right down that street? Going on another block, you saw the moon again right over another cross street, and so on, block after block. Was the moon following you? What other explanation can you give?

Birds

From *Trees, Stars, and Birds: A Book of Outdoor Science* by Edwin Lincoln Moseley, 1919

Birds and insects come to our notice oftener than most other creatures. Their rapid movements and bright colors or the sounds they make attract our attention. Some of our common insects spread diseases among us, and many of them destroy our crops; in the United States they take each year one tenth of all the farmer's produce and cause a loss of more than a billion dollars. Birds are the natural enemies of the insect world,—the balance nature has provided to hold insects in check. Almost all birds feed their young on bugs, flies, and worms, and many birds throughout their whole lives eat little other food. Indeed, if it were not for the work of the birds, insects would overrun the earth; in the stomach of one martin nearly 2000 mosquitoes were found. Whether birds are harmful or beneficial you can judge after you have watched the feeding habits of a score or more of different kinds.

Birds may be studied both in town and country; in some city parks more than a hundred kinds have been seen. Wherever you find a variety of trees and shrubs you are likely to find a number of birds, if they are safe from enemies there. Look for them in orchards, pastures, and along the borders of ponds and brooks. You will find them at all seasons, but the best time to see them is when the leaves are developing on the trees.

To get a good view of a bird, take such a position that you can watch it without having to face the sun. If it is easily frightened, do not go straight toward it, but walk steadily as if you were going past. When looking for birds in the woods, walk quietly, notice the motion of twigs or leaves, and listen to the various sounds. A windy day is unfavorable for bird study.

Finley & Bohlman

▲ Fig. 158. Birds are the natural enemies of insects.

▲ Fig. 159. Small birds rear their young almost entirely on insect food. The illustration shows a black-throated gray warbler feeding its young.

Finley & Bohlman

In a good locality for birds you may succeed in observing them if you sit down and allow the birds to come to you. If you have opera or field glasses, practice using them so as to bring a bird quickly into clear view. Try mimicking some of the birds you hear; you may succeed in calling them to you.

When you see an unfamiliar bird, make notes that will help you to identify it in a museum or by the use of a bird book. Compare its size with that of some common bird. Notice whether its bill is slender and straight, whether its wings and tail are short, any color markings you are able to see, and how it is getting food. Do not stop to make notes until you have watched the bird for some minutes or have lost track of it.

A notebook will be useful also in keeping a list of the birds you see and various things you notice about their habits. Record the date, weather, locality where found, and any observations that interest you. If the notes you make outside are written up more carefully after you return home and before you go on another trip, they will be interesting and useful to you at various times, perhaps for years to come.

The birds described in the following pages are those that are most likely to be seen in the eastern and, middle parts of the United States and Canada. However, not many of them may be seen at all seasons, and it is better to study each kind when it can be observed than to follow invariably the order in the book, where they are arranged according to their relationships to one another. It is not important to study every bird that is mentioned in the book. If you answer half the questions by means of your own observation, you will have acquired some real knowledge of birds.

Finley & Bohlman

▲ Fig. 160. A call for insect food.

Making Grounds Attractive to Birds

From *Trees, Stars, and Birds: A Book of Outdoor Science* by Edwin Lincoln Moseley, 1919

Within the last few years appreciation of birds has led to efforts to protect them and enable them to increase in number. The United States Government has given the birds about seventy islands, lakes, and other bird reserves, for their exclusive use, so that they may rear their young unmolested, and the National Association of Audubon Societies guards with paid agents over one hundred of the most important breeding colonies of birds in the United States. In addition, private citizens have appropriated large tracts of land for the use of wild birds, and the grounds about thousands of homes have been made more pleasant by making them attractive to the feathered songsters.

Houses, food, drink, and safety for birds. even in small yards, boxes or houses can be put up for birds to occupy, sheltered feeding places can be provided and stocked with food in winter, and water supplied in dry seasons. A fountain with a shallow bowl where birds may drink and bathe will attract a great many,

Joseph H. Dodson

▲ Fig. 242. Grounds that are attractive to birds.

R. E. Horsey

▲ Fig. 243. A robin in a bird bath.

R. E. Horsey

▲ Fig. 244. Making birdhouses.

which may then be watched while they are having a good time. However, none of these things will be of much use if the birds are allowed to be killed by cats or driven off by English sparrows. Families that are unwilling to dispense with cats sometimes provide them with collar and bell to give the birds warning of the enemy's approach.

Planting trees and shrubs for birds. Where room permits, grounds may be beautified and at the same time made more attractive to birds by planting a variety of trees, shrubs, and vines. Smoothly trimmed hedges and stiff trees of a formal garden are not so attractive to them as untrained bushes and tangled thickets. Seclusion from real or imaginary foes, protection from wind and storm, as well as a supply of food and water, are advantages the birds derive from trees and shrubbery of the right sort.

The choice of the trees and shrubs to be planted must be determined partly by the climate. There are wild plants in every part of America whose fruit is relished by birds as much as is the fruit of cultivated varieties.

The planting of some of these wild varieties on the borders of orchards and vineyards oftentimes serves to protect the cultivated fruit. If selected for this purpose, the wild fruit should ripen at the same time as that which is to be saved. For the sake of the birds, various plants can be grown whose fruit ripens at different seasons. A number of kinds are useful to supply food in winter.

Of plants that retain their fruit a long time, some of the best are the juniper, sumach, mountain ash, frost grape, roses, and in the South, the magnolia, chinaberry, and holly. The mulberries, service berries, redberried elder, European bird cherry, and mahaleb cherry ripen in the spring or early in the sum-mer. Some of the best of the fruits that ripen later are the elder, wild cherry, chokecherry, the flowering dogwood and other cornels, the black haw and other viburnums, the Virginia creeper, and the climbing bittersweet. Some foreign species that may be obtained from nurseries are very fine for birds. Among these are honeysuckles of different kinds, especially the Tartarian, honeysuckle, the hawthorn, the larch, the Japanese rose, and the Japanese flowering crab. Old apple trees, cherry trees, and blackberry, raspberry, currant, and other bushes whose fruit we prize are of use to the birds.

Dimensions of Nesting Boxes

As given in Farmers' Bulletin 609, U. S. Department of Agriculture

Species	Floor of Cavity	Depth of Cavity	Entrance Above Floor	Diameter of Entrance B	Height Above Ground
	Inches	Inches	Inches	Inches	Feet
Bluebird	5 by 5	8	6	1½	5 to 10
Robin	6 by 8	8	*	*	6 to 15
Chickadee	4 by 4	8 to 10	8	1⅛	6 to 15
Tufted titmouse	4 by 4	8 to 10	8	1¼	6 to 15
White-breasted nuthatch	4 by 4	8 to 10	8	1¼	12 to 20
House wren	4 by 4	6 to 8	1 to 6	⅞	6 to 10
Bewick wren	4 by 4	6 to 8	1 to 6	1	6 to 10
Carolina wren	4 by 4	6 to 8	1 to 6	1⅛	6 to 10
Dipper	6 by 6	6	1	3	1 to 3
Violet-green swallow	5 by 5	6	1 to 6	1½	10 to 15
Tree swallow	5 by 5	6	1 to 6	1½	10 to 15
Barn swallow	6 by 6	6	*	*	8 to 12
Martin	6 by 6	6	1	2½	15 to 20
Song sparrow	6 by 6	6	†	†	1 to 3
House finch	6 by 6	6	4	2	8 to 12
Phœbe	6 by 6	6	–	*	8 to 12
Crested flycatcher	6 by 6	8 to 10	8	2	8 to 20
Flicker	7 by 7	16 to 18	16	2½	6 to 20
Red-headed woodpecker	6 by 6	12 to 15	12	2	12 to 20
Golden-fronted woodpecker	6 by 6	12 to 15	12	2	12 to 20
Hairy woodpecker	6 by 6	12 to 15	12	1½	12 to 20
Downy woodpecker	4 by 4	8 to 10	8	1¼	6 to 20
Screech owl	8 by 8	12 to 15	12	3	10 to 30
Sparrow hawk	8 by 8	12 to 15	12	3	10 to 30
Saw-whet owl	6 by 6	10 to 12	10	2½	12 to 20
Bam owl	10 by 18	15 to 18	4	6	12 to 18
Wood duck	10 by 18	10 to 15	3	6	4 to 20

*One or more sides open.

†All sides open.

Identifying Common Birds

From *Fifty Common Birds of Farm and Orchard* by Henry W. Henshaw, 1913

Bluebird (Sialia sialis)

Length,*about 6½ inches.
Range: Breeds in the United States (west to Arizona, Colorado, Wyoming, and Montana), southern Canada, Mexico, and Guatemala; winters in the southern half of the eastern United States and south to Guatemala.

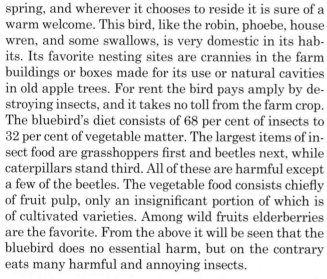

Habits and economic status: The bluebird is one of the most familiar tenants of the farm and dooryard. Everywhere it is hailed as the harbinger of spring, and wherever it chooses to reside it is sure of a warm welcome. This bird, like the robin, phoebe, house wren, and some swallows, is very domestic in its habits. Its favorite nesting sites are crannies in the farm buildings or boxes made for its use or natural cavities in old apple trees. For rent the bird pays amply by destroying insects, and it takes no toll from the farm crop. The bluebird's diet consists of 68 per cent of insects to 32 per cent of vegetable matter. The largest items of insect food are grasshoppers first and beetles next, while caterpillars stand third. All of these are harmful except a few of the beetles. The vegetable food consists chiefly of fruit pulp, only an insignificant portion of which is of cultivated varieties. Among wild fruits elderberries are the favorite. From the above it will be seen that the bluebird does no essential harm, but on the contrary eats many harmful and annoying insects.

Robin (Planesticus migratorius)

Length, 10 inches.
Range: Breeds in the United States (except the Gulf States), Canada, Alaska, and Mexico; winters in most of the United States and south to Guatemala.

Habits and economic status: In the North and some parts of the West the robin is among the most cherished of our native birds. Should it ever become rare where now common, its joyous summer song and familiar presence will be sadly missed in many a homestead. The robin is an omnivorous feeder, and its food includes many orders of insects, with no very pronounced preference for any. It is very fond of earthworms, but its real economic status is determined by the vegetable food, which amounts to about 58 per cent of all. The principal item is fruit, which forms more than 51 per cent of the total food. The fact that in the examination of over 1,200 stomachs the percent-

age of wild fruit was found to be 5 times that of the cultivated varieties suggests that berry-bearing shrubs, if planted near the orchard, will serve to protect more valuable fruits. In California in certain years it has been possible to save the olive crop from hungry robins only by the most strenuous exertions and considerable expense. The bird's general usefulness is such, however, that all reasonable means of protecting orchard fruit should be tried before killing the birds.

Russet-Backed Thrush (Hylocichla ustulata)

Length, 7¼ inches.
Among thrushes having the top of head and tail nearly the same color . as the back, this one is distinguished by its tawny eye-ring and cheeks. The Pacific coast subspecies is russet brown above, while the other subspecies is the olive-backed thrush. The remarks below apply to the species as a whole.

Range: Breeds in the forested parts of Alaska and Canada and south to California, Colorado, Michigan, New York, West Virginia (mountains), and Maine; winters from Mexico to South America.

Habits and economic status: This is one of a small group of thrushes the members of which are by many ranked first among American songbirds. The several members resemble one another in size, plumage, and habits. While this thrush is very fond of fruit, its partiality for the neighborhood of streams keeps it from frequenting orchards far from water. It is most troublesome during the cherry season, when the young are in the nest. From this it might be inferred that the young are fed on fruit, but such is not the case. The adults eat fruit, but the nestlings, as usual, are fed mostly upon insects. Beetles constitute the largest item of animal food, and ants come next. Many caterpillars also are eaten. The great bulk of vegetable food consists of fruit, of which two-fifths is of cultivated varieties. Where these birds live in or near gardens or orchards, they may do considerable damage, but they are too valuable as insect destroyers to be killed if the fruit can be protected in any other way. (See Biol. Surv. Bul. 30, pp. 86–92.)

Ruby-Crowned Kinglet (Regulus calendula)

Length, about 4¼ inches. Olive green above, soiled whitish below, concealed feathers on head (crest) bright red.

Range: Breeds in southern Canada, southern Alaska, and the higher mountains of the western United States; winters in much of the United States and south to Guatemala.

Habits and economic status: In habits and haunts this tiny sprite resembles a chickadee. It is an active, nervous little creature, flitting hither and yon in search of food, and in spring stopping only long enough to utter its beautiful song, surprisingly loud for the size of the musician. Three-fourths of its food consists of wasps, bugs, and flies. Beetles are the only other item of importance (12 per cent). The bugs eaten by the kinglet are mostly small, but, happily, they are the most harmful kinds. Treehoppers, leafhoppers, and jumping plant lice are pests and often do great harm to trees and smaller plants, while plant lice and scale insects are the worst scourges of the fruit grower—in fact, the prevalence of the latter has almost risen to the magnitude of a national peril. It is these small and seemingly insignificant birds that most successfully attack and hold in check these insidious foes of horticulture. The vegetable food consists of seeds of poison ivy, or poison oak, a few weed seeds, and a few small fruits, mostly elderberries. (See Biol. Surv. Bul. 30, pp. 81–84.)

Chickadee (Penthestes atricapillus)

Length, about 5¼ inches.

Range: Resident in the United States (except the southern half east of the plains), Canada, and Alaska.

Habits and economic status: Because of its delightful notes, its confiding ways, and its fearlessness, the chickadee is one of our best-known birds. It responds to encouragement, and by hanging within its reach a constant supply of suet the chickadee can be made a regular visitor to the garden and orchard. Though insignificant in size, titmice are feu: from being so from the economic standpoint, owing to their numbers and activity. While one locality is being scrutinized for food by a larger bird, 10 are being searched by the smaller species. The chickadee's food is made up of insects and vegetable matter in the proportion of 7 of the former to 3 of the latter. Moths and caterpillars are favorites and form about one-third of the whole. Beetles, ants, wasps, bugs, flies, grasshoppers, and spiders make up the rest. The vegetable food is composed of seeds, largely those of pines, with a few of the poison ivy and some weeds. There are few more useful birds than the chickadees.

White-Breasted Nuthatch (Sitta carolinensis)

Length, 6 inches. White below, above gray, with a black head.

Range: Resident in the United States, southern Canada, and Mexico.

Habits and economic status: This bird might readily be mistaken by a careless observer for a small woodpecker, but its note, an oft-repeated *yank,* is very unwoodpecker-like, and, unlike either woodpeckers or creepers, it climbs downward as easily as upward and seems to set the laws of gravity at defiance. The name was suggested by the habit of wedging nuts, especially beechnuts, in the crevices of bark so as to break them open by blows from the sharp, strong bill. The nuthatch gets its living from the trunks and branches of trees, over

which it creeps from daylight to dark. Insects and spiders constitute a little more than 50 per cent of its food. The largest items of these are beetles, moths, and caterpillars, with ants and wasps. The animal food is all in the bird's favor except a few ladybird beetles. More than half of the vegetable food consists of mast, i.e., acorns and other nuts or large seeds. One-tenth of the food is grain, mostly waste corn. The nuthatch does no injury, so far as known, and much good.

Brown Creeper (Certhia familiaris americana and other subspecies)

Length, 5½ inches.

Range: Breeds from Nebraska, Indiana, North Carolina (mountains), and Massachusetts north to southern Canada, also in the mountains of the western United States, north to Alaska, south to Nicaragua; winters over most of its range.

Habits and economic status: Rarely indeed is the creeper seen at rest. It appears to spend its life in an incessant scramble over the trunks and branches of trees, from which it gets all its food. It is protectively colored so as to be practically invisible to its enemies and, though delicately built, possesses amazingly strong claws and feet. Its tiny eyes are sharp enough to detect insects so small that most other species pass them by, and altogether the creeper fills a unique place in the ranks of our insect destroyers. The food consists of minute insects and insects' eggs, also cocoons of tineid moths, small wasps, ants, and bugs, especially scales and plant lice, with some small caterpillars. As the creeper remains in the United States throughout the year, it naturally secures hibernating insects and insects' eggs, as well as spiders and spiders' eggs, that are missed by the summer birds. On its bill of fare we find no product of husbandry nor any useful insects.

House Wren (Troglodytes aëdon)

Length, 4f inches. The only one of our wrens with wholly whitish under-parts that lacks a light line over the eye.

Range: Breeds throughout the United States (except the South Atlantic and Gulf States) and southern Canada; winters in the southern United States and Mexico.

Habits and economic status: The rich, bubbling song of the familiar little house wren is one of the sweetest associations connected with country and suburban life.

Its tiny body, long bill, sharp eyes, and strong feet peculiarly adapt it for creeping into all sorts of nooks and crannies where lurk the insects it feeds on. A cavity in a fence post, a hole in a tree, or a box will be welcomed alike by this busybody as a nesting site; but since the advent of the quarrelsome English sparrow such domiciles are at a premium and the wren's eggs and family are safe only in cavities having entrances too small to admit the sparrow. Hence it behooves the farmer's boy to provide boxes the entrances to which are about an inch in diameter, nailing these under gables of bams and outhouses or in orchard trees. In this way the numbers of this useful bird can be increased, greatly to the advantage of the farmer. Grasshoppers, beetles, caterpillars, bugs, and spiders are the principal elements of its food. Cutworms, weevils, ticks, and plant lice are among the injurious forms eaten. The nestlings of house wrens consume great quantities of insects. (See Yearbook U. S. Dept. Agric. 1895, pp. 416–418, and Biol. Survey Bul. 30, pp. 60–62.)

Brown Thrasher (Toxostoma rufum)

Length, about 11 inches. Brownish red above, heavily streaked with black below.

Range: Breeds from the Gulf States to southern Canada and west to Colorado, Wyoming, and Montana; winters in the southern half of the eastern United States.

Habits and economic status: The brown thrasher is more retiring than either the mocking bird or catbird, but like them is a splendid singer. Not infrequently, indeed, its song is taken for that of its more famed cousin, the mocking bird. It is partial to thickets and gets much of its food from the ground. Its search for this is usually accompanied by much scratching and scattering of leaves; whence its common name. Its call note is a sharp sound like the smacking of lips, which is useful in identifying this long-tailed, thicket-haunting bird, which does not much relish close scrutiny. The brown thrasher is not so fond of fruit as the catbird and mocker, but devours a much larger percentage of animal food. Beetles form one-half of the animal food, grasshoppers and crickets one-fifth, caterpillars, including cutworms, somewhat less than one-fifth, and bugs, spiders, and millipede comprise most of the remainder. The brown thrasher feeds on such coleopterous pests as wire-worms, May beetles, rice weevils, rose beetles, and figeaters. By its destruction of these and other insects, which constitute more than 60 per cent of its food, the thrasher much more than compensates for that portion (about one-tenth) of its diet derived from cultivated crops. (See Yearbook U. S. Dept. Agric. 1895, pp. 411–415.)

Catbird (Dumetella carolinensis)

Length, about 9 inches. The slaty gray plumage and black cap and tail are distinctive.

Range: Breeds throughout the United States west to New Mexico, Utah, Oregon, and Washington, and in southern Canada; winters from the Gulf States to Panama.

Habits and economic status: In many localities the catbird is one of the commonest birds. Tangled growths are its favorite nesting places and retreats, but berry patches and ornamental shrubbery are not disdained. Hence the bird is a familiar dooryard visitor. The bird has a fine song, unfortunately marred by occasional cat calls. With habits similar to those of the mocking bird and a song almost as varied, the catbird has never secured a similar place in popular favor. Half of its food consists of fruit, and the cultivated crops

most often injured are cherries, strawberries, raspberries, and blackberries. Beetles, ants, crickets, and grasshoppers are the most important element of its animal food. The bird is known to attack a few pests, as cutworms, leaf beetles, clover-root curculio, and the periodical cicada, but the good it does in this way probably does not pay for the fruit it steals. The extent to which it should be protected may perhaps be left to the individual cultivator; that is, it should be made lawful to destroy catbirds that are doing manifest damage to crops. (See Yearbook U. S. Dept. Agric. 1895, pp. 406–411.)

Mocking Bird (Mimua polyglottos)

Length, 10 inches. Most easily distinguished from the similarly colored loggerhead shrike (see p. 16) by the absence of a conspicuous black stripe through the eye.

Range: Resident from southern Mexico north to California, Wyoming, Iowa, Ohio, and Maryland; casual farther north.

Habits and economic status: Because of its incomparable medleys and imitative powers, the mocking bird is the most renowned singer of the Western Hemisphere. Even in confinement it is a masterly performer, and formerly thousands were trapped and sold for cage birds, but this reprehensible practice has been largely stopped by protective laws. It is not surprising, therefore, that the mocking bird should receive protection principally because of its ability as a songster and its preference for the vicinity of dwellings. Its place in the affections of the South is similar to that occupied by the robin in the North. It is well that this is true, for the bird appears not to earn protection from a strictly economic standpoint. About half of its diet consists of fruit, and many cultivated varieties are attacked, such as oranges, grapes, figs, strawberries, blackberries, and raspberries. Somewhat less than a fourth of the food is animal matter, and grasshoppers are the largest single element. The bird is fond of cotton worms, and is known to feed also on the chinch bug; rice weevil, and boll worm. It is unfortunate that it does not feed on injurious insects to an extent sufficient to offset its depredations on fruit. (See Yearbook U. S. Dept. Agric. 1895, pp. 415–416, and Biol. Survey Bul. 30, pp. 52–56.)

Myrtle Warbler (Dendroica coronate)

Length, 5½ inches. The similarly colored Audubon's warbler has a yellow throat instead of a white one.

Range: Breeds throughout most of the forested area of Canada and south to Minnesota, Michigan, New York, and Massachusetts; winters in the southern two-thirds of the United States and south to Panama.

Habits and economic status: This member of our beautiful wood warbler family, a family peculiar to America, has the characteristic voice, coloration, and habits of its kind. Trim of form and graceful of motion, when seeking food it combines the methods of the wrens, creepers, and flycatchers. It breeds only in the northern parts of the east-

ern United States, but in migration it occurs in every patch of woodland and is so numerous that it is familiar to every observer. Its place is taken in the West by Audubon's warbler. More than three-fourths of the food of the myrtle warbler consists of insects, practically all of them harmful. It is made up of small beetles, including some weevils, with many ants and wasps. This bird is so small and nimble that it successfully attacks insects too minute to be prey for larger birds. Scales and plant lice form a very considerable part of its diet. Flies are the largest item of food; in fact, only a few flycatchers and swallows eat as many flies as this bird. The vegetable food (22 per cent) is made up of fruit and the seeds of poison oak or ivy, also the seeds of pine and of the bayberry.

Loggerhead Shrike (Lanius ludovicianus)

Length, about 9 inches. A gray, black, and white bird, distinguished from the somewhat similarly colored mocking bird by the black stripe on side of head.

Range: Breeds throughout the United States, Mexico, and southern Canada; winters in the southern half of the United States and in Mexico.

Habits and economic status: The loggerhead shrike, or southern butcher bird, is common throughout its ranee and is sometimes called "French mocking bird" from a superficial resemblance and not from its notes, which are harsh and unmusical. The shrike is naturally an insectivorous bird which has extended its hill of fare to include small mammals, birds. and reptiles. Its hooked beak is well adapted to tearing its prey, while to make amends for the lack of talons it has hit upon the plan of forcing its victim, if too large to swallow, into the fork of a bush or tree, where it can tear it asunder. Insects, especially grasshoppers, constitute the larger part of its food, though beetles, moths, caterpillars, ants, wasps, and a few spiders also are taken. While the butcher bird occasionally catches small birds, its principal vertebrate food is small mammals, as field mice, shrews, and moles, and when possible it obtains lizards. It habitually impales its surplus prey on a thorn, sharp twig, or barb of a wire fence. (See Biol. Survey Bul. 9, pp. 20–24, and Bul. 30, pp. 33–38.)

Barn Swallow (Hirundo erythrogastra)

Length, about 7 inches. Distinguished among our swallows by deeply forked tail.

Range: Breeds throughout the United States (except the South Atlantic and Gulf States) and most of Canada; winters in South America.

Habits and economic status: This is one of the most familiar birds of the farm and one of the greatest insect destroyers. From daylight todark on tireless wings it seeks its prey, and the insects destroyed are countless. Its favorite nesting site is a barn rafter, upon which it sticks its mud basket. Most modern barns are so tightly constructed that swallows can not gain entrance, and in New England and some other parts of the country barn swallows are much less numerous than formerly. Farmers can easily provide for the entrance and exit of the birds and so add materially to their numbers. It may be well to add that the parasites that sometimes infest the nests of swallows are not the ones the careful housewife dreads, and no fear need be felt of the infestation spreading to the houses. Insects taken on the wing constitute the almost exclusive diet of the barn swallow. More than one-third of the whole consists of flies, including unfortunately some useful parasitic species. Beetles stand next in order and consist of a few weevils and many of the small dung beetles of the May beetle family that swarm over the pastures in the late afternoon. Ants amount to more than one-fifth of the whole food, while wasps and bees are well represented.

Purple Martin (Progne subis)

Length, about 8 inches.

Range: Breeds throughout the United States and southern Canada, south to central Mexico; winters in South America.

Habits and economic status: This is the largest as it is one of the most beautiful of the swallow tribe. It formerly built its nests in cavities of trees, as it still does in wild districts, but learning that man was a friend it soon adopted domestic habits. Its presence about the farm can often be secured by erecting houses suitable for nesting sites and protecting them from usurpation by the English sparrow, and every effort should be made to increase the number of colonies of this very useful bird. The boxes should be at a reasonable height, say

15 feet from the ground, and made inaccessible to cats. A colony of these birds on a farm makes great inroads upon the insect population, as the birds not only themselves feed upon insects but rear their young upon the same diet. Fifty years ago in New England it was not uncommon to see colonies of 50 pairs of martins, but most of them have now vanished for no apparent reason except that the martin houses have decayed and have not been renewed. More than three-fourths of this bird's food consists of wasps, bugs, and beetles, their importance being in the order given. The beetles include several species or harmful weevils, as the clover-leaf weevils and the nut weevils. Besides these are many crane flies, moths, May flies, and dragonflies.

Black-Headed Grosbeak (Zamelodia melanocephala)

Length, about 8¼ inches.

Range: Breeds from the Pacific coast to Nebraska and the Dakotas, and from southern Canada to southern Mexico; winters in Mexico.

Habits and economic status: The black-headed grosbeak takes the place in the West of the rosebreast in the East, and like it is a fine songster. Like it also the blackhead readily resorts to orchards and gardens and is common in agricultural districts. The bird has a very powerful bill and easily crushes or cuts into the firmest fruit. It feeds upon cherries, apricots, and other fruits, and also does some damage to green peas and beans, but it is so active a foe of certain horticultural pests that we can afford to overlook its faults. Several kinds of scale insects are freely

eaten, and one, the black olive scale, constitutes a fifth of the total food. In May many cankerworms and codling moths are consumed, and almost a sixth of the bird's seasonal food consists of flower beetles, which do incalculable damage to cultivated flowers and to ripe fruit. For each quart of fruit consumed by the black-headed grosbeak it destroys in actual bulk more than 1½ quarts of black olive scales and 1 quart of flower beetles, besides a generous quantity of codling-moth pupae and cankerworms. It is obvious that such work as this pays many times over for the fruit destroyed. (See Biol. Survey Bul. 32, pp. 60–77.)

Rose-Breasted Grosbeak (Zamelodia ludoviciana)

Length, 8 inches.

Range: Breeds from Kansas, Ohio, Georgia (mountains), and New Jersey, north to southern Canada; winters from Mexico to South America.

Habits and economic status: This beautiful grosbeak is noted for its clear, melodious notes, which are poured forth in generous measure. The rosebreast sings even at midday during summer, when the intense heat has silenced almost every other songster. Its beautiful plumage and sweet song are not its sole claim on our favor, for few birds are more beneficial to agriculture. The rosebreast eats some green peas and does some damage to fruit. But this mischief is much

more than balanced by the destruction of insect pests. The bird is so fond of the Colorado potato beetle that it has earned the name of "potato-bug bird," and no less than a tenth of the total food of the rosebreasts examined consists of potato beetles—evidence that the bird is one of the most important enemies of the pest. It vigorously attacks cucumber beetles and many of the scale insects. It proved an active enemy of the Rocky Mountain locust during that insect's ruinous invasions, and among the other pests it consumes are the spring and fall cankerworms, orchard and forest tent caterpillars, tussock, gipsy, and brown-tail moths, plum curculio, army worm, and chinch bug. In fact, not one of our birds has a better record. (See Biol. Survey Bul. 32, pp. 33–59.)

Song Sparrow (Melospiza melodia)

Length, about 6¼ inches. The heavily spotted breast with heavy central blotch is characteristic.

Range: Breeds in the United States (except the South Atlantic and Gulf States), southern Canada, southern Alaska, and Mexico; winters in Alaska and most of the United States southward.

Habits and economic status: Like the familiar little "chippy," the song sparrow is one of our most domestic species, and builds its nest in hedges or in garden shrubbery close to houses, whenever it is reasonably safe from the house cat, which, however, takes heavy toll of the nestlings. It is a true harbinger of spring, and its delightful little song is trilled forth from the top of some green shrub in early March and April, before most of our other songsters have thought of leaving the sunny south. Song' sparrows vary much in habits, as well as in size and coloration. Some forms live along streams bordered by deserts, others in swamps among bulrushes and tules, others in timbered regions, others on rocky barren hillsides, and still others in rich, fertile valleys. With such a variety of habitat, the food of the species naturally varies considerably. About three-fourths of its diet consists of the seeds of noxious weeds and one-fourth of insects. Of these, beetles, especially weevils, constitute the major portion. Ants, wasps, bugs (including the black olive scale), and caterpillars are also eaten. Grasshoppers are taken by the eastern birds, but not by the western ones. (See Biol. Survey Bul. 15, pp. 82–86.)

Chipping Sparrow (Spizella passerina)

Length, about 5¼ inches. Distinguished by the chestnut crown, black line through eye, and black bill.

Range: Breeds throughout the United States, south to Nicaragua, and north to southern Canada; winters in the southern United States and southward.

Habits and economic status: The chipping sparrow is very friendly and domestic, and often builds its nest in gardens and orchards or in the shrubbery close to dwellings. Its gentle and confiding ways endear it to all bird lovers. It is one of the most insectivorous of all the sparrows.

Its diet consists of about 42 per cent of insects and spiders and 58 per cent of vegetable matter. The animal food consists largely of caterpillars, of which it feeds a great many to its young. Besides these, it eats beetles, including many weevils, of which one stomach contained 30. It also eats ants, wasps, and bugs. Among the latter are plant lice and black olive scales. The vegetable food is practically all weed seed. A nest with 4 young of this species was watched at different hours on 4 days. In the 7 hours of observation 119 feedings were noted, or an average of 17 feedings per hour, or 4¼ feedings per hour to each nestling. This would give for a day of 14 hours at least 238 insects eaten by the brood. (See Biol. Survey Bul. 15, pp. 76–78.)

White-Crowned Sparrow (Zonotrichia leucophrys)

Length, 7 inches. The only similar sparrow, the whitethroat, has a yellow spot in front of eye.

Range: Breeds in Canada, the mountains of New Mexico, Colorado, Wyoming, and Montana, and thence to the Pacific coast; winters in the southern half of the United States and in northern Mexico.

Habits and economic status: This beautiful sparrow is much more numerous in the western than in the eastern States, where, indeed, it is rather rare. In the East it is shy and retiring, but it is much bolder and more conspicuous in the far West and there often frequents gardens and parks. Like most . of its family it is a seed eater by preference, and insects comprise very little more than 7 per cent of its diet. Caterpillars are the largest item, with some beetles, a few ants and wasps, and some bugs, among which are black olive scales. The great bulk of the food, however, consists of weed seeds, which amount to 74 per cent of the whole. In California this bird is accused of eating the buds and blossoms of fruit trees, but buds or blossoms were found in only 30 out of 516 stomachs, and probably it is only under exceptional circumstances that it does any damage in this way. Evidently neither the farmer nor the fruit grower has much to fear from the whitecrowned sparrow. The little fruit it eats is mostly wild, and the grain eaten is waste or volunteer. (See Biol. Survey Bul. 34, pp. 75–77.)

English Sparrow (Passer domesticus)

Length, about 6¼ inches. Its incessant chattering, quarrelsome disposition, and abundance and familiarity about human habitations distinguish it from our native sparrows.

Range: Resident throughout the United States and southern Canada.

Habits and economic status: Almost universally condemned since its introduction into the United States, the English sparrow has not only held its own, but has ever increased in numbers and extended its range in spite of all opposition. Its habit of driving out or even killing more beneficial species and the defiling of buildings by its droppings and by its own unsightly structures, are serious objections to

this sparrow. ' Moreover, in rural districts, it is destructive to grain, fruit, peas, beans, and other vegetables. On the other hand, the bird feeds to some extent on a large number of insect pests, and this fact points to the need of a new investigation of the present economic status of the species, especially as it promises to be of service in holding in check the newly introduced alfalfa weevil, which threatens the alfalfa industry in Utah and neighboring States. In cities most of the food of the English sparrow is waste material secured from the streets.

Crow Blackbird (Quiscalus quiscula)

Length, 12 inches. Shorter by at least 3 inches than the other grackles with trough-shaped tails. Black, with purplish, bluish, and bronze reflections.

Range: Breeds throughout the United States west to Texas, Colorado, and Montana, and in southern Canada; winters in the southern half of the breeding range.

Habits and economic status: This blackbird is a beautiful species, and is well known from its habit of congregating in city parks and nesting there year after year. Like other species which habitually assemble in great flocks, it is capable of inflicting much damage on any crop it attacks, and where it is harmful a judicious reduction of numbers is probably sound policy.

It shares with the crow and blue jay the evil habit of pillaging the nests of small birds of eggs and young. Nevertheless it does much good by destroying insect pests, especially white grubs, weevils, grasshoppers, and caterpillars. Among the caterpillars are army worms and other cutworms. When blackbirds gather in large flocks, as in the Mississippi Valley, they may greatly damage grain, either when first sown or when in the milk. In winter they subsist mostly on weed seed and waste grain. (See Biol. Surv. Bul. 13, pp. 53–70.)

Brewer's Blackbird (Euphagus cyanocephalus)

Length, 10 inches. Its glossy purplish head distinguishes it from other blackbirds that do not show in flight a trough-shaped tail.

Range: Breeds in the West, east to Texas, Kansas, and Minnesota, and north to southern Canada; winters over most of the United States breeding range, south to Guatemala.

Habits and economic status: Very numerous in the West and in fall gathers in immense flocks, especially about barnyards and corrals. During the cherry season in California Brewer's blackbird is much, in the orchards. In one case they were seen to eat freely of cherries, but when a neighboring fruit raiser began to plow his orchard almost every blackbird in the vicinity was upon the newly opened ground and close at the plowman's heels in its eagerness to get the insects exposed by the plow. Caterpillars and pupæ form the largest item of animal food (about 12 per cent). Many of these are cutworms, and cotton bollworms or corn earworms were found in 10 stomachs and codling-moth pupae in 11. Beetles constitute over 11 per cent of the food. The vegetable food is practically contained in three items—grain, fruit, and weed seeds. Grain, mostly oats, amounts to 54 per cent; fruit, largely cherries, 4 per cent; and weed seeds, not quite 9 per cent. The grain is probably mostly wild, volunteer, or waste, so that the bird does most damage by eating fruit. (See Biol. Surv. Bul. 34, pp. 59–65.)

Bullock's Oriole (Icterus bullocki)

Length, about 8 inches. Our only oriole with top of head and throat black and cheeks orange.

Range: Breeds from South Dakota, Nebraska, and Kansas to the Pacific Ocean and from southern Canada to northern Mexico; winters in Mexico.

Habits and economic status: In the West this bird takes the place occupied in the East by the Baltimore oriole. In food, nesting habits, and song the birds are similar. Both are migratory and remain on their summer range only some five or six months. They take kindly to orchards, gardens, and the vicinity of farm buildings and often live in villages and city parks. Then* diet is largely made up of insects that infest orchards and gardens. When fruit trees are in bloom they are constantly busy among the blossoms and save many of them from destruction. In the food of Bullock's oriole beetles amount to 35 per cent and nearly all are harmful. Many of these are weevils, some of which live upon acorns and other nuts. Ants and wasps amount to 15 per cent of the diet. The black olive scale was found in 45 of the 162 stomachs examined. Caterpillars, with a few moths and pupae, are the largest item of food and amount to over 41 per cent. Among these were codling-moth larvae. The vegetable food is practically all fruit (19 per cent) and in cherry season consists largely of that fruit. Eating small fruits is the bird's worst trait, but it will do harm in this way only when very numerous. (See Biol. Surv. Bul. 34, pp. 68–71.)

Meadowlarks (Sturnella magna and Sturnella neglecta)

Length, about 10¾ inches.

Range: Breed generally in the United States, southern Canada, and Mexico to Costa Rica: winter from the Ohio and Potomac Valleys and British Columbia southward.

Habits and economic status: Our two meadow-larks, though differing much in song, resemble each other closely in plumage and habits. Grassy plains and uplands covered with a thick growth of grass or weeds, with near-by water, furnish the conditions best suited to the meadowlark's taste. The song of the western bird is loud, clear, and melodious. That of its eastern relative is feebler and loses much by comparison. In many localities the meadowlark is classed and shot as a game bird. From the farmer's standpoint this is a mistake, since its value as an insect eater is far greater than as an object of pursuit by the sportsman. Both the boll weevil, the foe of the cotton grower, and the alfalfa weevil are among the beetles it habitually eats. Twenty-five per cent of the diet of this bird is beetles, half of which are predaceous ground beetles, accounted useful insects, and one-fifth are destructive weevils. Caterpillars form 11 per cent of the food and are eaten in every month in the year. Among these are many cutworms and the well-known army worm. Grasshoppers are favorite food and are eaten in every month and almost every day. The vegetable food (24 per cent of the whole) consists of grain and weed seeds. (See Yearbook U. S. Dept. Agr. 1895, pp. 420–426.)

Red-Winged Blackbird (Agelaius phœniceus)

Length, about 9¼ inches.

Range: Breeds in Mexico and North America south of the Barren Grounds; winters in southern half of United States and south to Costa Rica.

Habits and economic status: The prairies of the upper Mississippi Valley, with their numerous sloughs and ponds, furnish ideal nesting places for redwings, and consequently this region has become the great breeding ground for the species. These prairies pour forth the vast flocks that play havoc with grain-fields. East of the Appalachian Range, marshes on the shores of lakes, rivers, and estuaries are the only available breeding sites and, as these are comparatively few and small, the species is much less abundant than in the West. Redwings are eminently gregarious, living in flocks and breeding in communities. The food of the redwing consists of 27 per cent animal matter and 73 per cent vegetable. Insects constitute practically one-fourth of the food. Beetles (largely weevils, a most harmful group) amount to 10 per cent. Grasshoppers are eaten in every month and amount to about 5 per cent. Caterpillars (among them the injurious army worm) are eaten at all seasons and aggregate 6 per cent. Ante, wasps, bugs, flies, dragonflies, ana spiders also are eaten. The vegetable food consists of seeds, including grain, of which oats is the favorite, and some small fruits. When in large flocks this bird is capable of doing great harm to grain. (See Biol. Survey Bul. 13, pp. 33–34.)

Bobolink (Dolichonyx oryzivorus)

Length, about 7 inches.

Range: Breeds from Ohio northeast to Nova Scotia, north to Manitoba, and northwest to British Columbia; winters in South America.

Habits and economic status: When American writers awoke to the beauty and attractiveness of our native birds, among the first to be enshrined in song and story was the bobolink. Few species show such striking contrasts in the color of the sexes, and few have songs more unique and whimsical. In its northern home the bird is loved for its beauty and its rich melody; in the South it earns deserved hatred by its destructiveness. Bobolinks reach the southeastern coast of the United States the last half of April just as rice is sprouting and at once begin to pull up and devour the sprouting kernels. Soon they move on to their northern breeding grounds, where they feed upon insects, weed seeds, and a little grain. When the young are well on the wing, they gather in flocks with the parent birds and gradually move southward, being then generally known as reed birds. They reach the rice fields of the Carolinas about August 20, when the rice is in the milk. Then until the birds depart for South America planters and birds fight for the crop, and in spite of constant watchfulness and innumerable devices for scaring the birds a loss of 10 per cent of the rice is the usual result. (See Biol. Survey Bul. 13, pp. 12–22.)

Common Crow (Corvus brachyrhynchos)

Length, 19 inches.

Range: Breeds throughout the United States and most of Canada; winters generally in the United States.

Habits and economic status: The general habits of the crow are universally known. Its ability to commit such misdeeds as pulling corn and stealing eggs and fruit and to get away unscathed is lime short of marvelous. Much of the crow's success in life is due to cooperation, and the social instinct of the species has its highest expression in the winter roosts, which are sometimes frequented by hundreds of thousands of crows. From these roosts daily flights of many miles

are made in search of food. Injury to sprouting corn is the most frequent complaint against this species, but by coating the seed grain with coal tar most of this damage may be prevented. Losses of poultry and eggs may be averted by proper housing and the judicious use of wire netting. The insect food of the crow includes wireworms, cutworms, white grubs, and grasshoppers, and during outbreaks of these insects the crow renders good service. The bird is also an efficient scavenger. But chiefly because of its destruction of beneficial wild birds and their eggs the crow must be classed as a criminal, and a reduction in its numbers in localities where it is seriously destructive is justifiable.

California Jay (Aphelocoma californica)

Length, 12 inches. Distinguished from other jays within its range by its decidedly whitish underparts and brown patch on the back.

Range: Resident in California, north to southern Washington, and south to southern Lower California.

Habits and economic status: This jay has the same general traits of character as the eastern blue jay. He is the same noisy, rollicking fellow and occupies a corresponding position in bird society. Robbing the nests of smaller birds is a favorite pastime, and he is a persistent spy upon domestic fowls and well knows the meaning of the cackle of a hen. Not only does he steal eggs but he kills young chicks. The insect food of this jay constitutes about one-tenth of its annual sustenance. The inclusion of grasshoppers and caterpillars makes this part of the bird's

food in its favor. But the remainder of its animal diet includes altogether too large a proportion of beneficial birds and their eggs, and in this respect it appears to be worse than its eastern relative, the blue jay. While its vegetable food is composed largely of mast, at times its liking for cultivated fruit and grain makes it a most unwelcome visitor to the orchard and farm. In conclusion it may be said that over much of its range this jay is too abundant for the best interests of agriculture and horticulture. (See Biol. Survey Bul. 34, pp. 50–56.)

Blue Jay (Cyanocitta Cristata)

Length, 11½ inches. The brilliant blue of the wings and tail combined with the black crescent of the upper breast and the crested head distinguish this species.

Range: Resident in the eastern United States and southern Canada, west to the Dakotas, Colorado, and Texas.

Habits and economic status: The blue jay is of a dual nature. Cautious and silent in the vicinity of its nest, away from it it is bold and noisy. Sly in the commission of mischief, it is ever ready to scream "thief" at the slightest disturbance. As usual in such cases, its remarks are applicable to none more than itself, a fact neighboring nest holders know to their sorrow, for during the breeding season the jay lays heavy toll upon the eggs and young of other birds, and in doing so deprives us of the services of species more beneficial than itself. Approximately three-fourths of the annual food of the blue jay is vegetable matter, the greater part of which is composed of mast, i. e., acorns, chestnuts, beechnuts, and the like. Corn is the principal cultivated crop upon which this bird feeds, but stomach analysis indicates that most of the corn taken

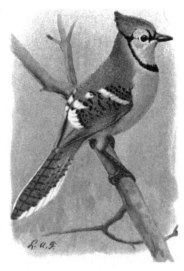

is waste grain. Such noxious insects as wood-boring beetles, grasshoppers, eggs of various caterpillars, and scale insects constitute about one-fifth of its food.

Horned Lark (Otocoris alpestris)

Length, about 7¾ inches. The black mark across the breast and the small, pointed tufts of dark feathers above and behind the eyes distinguish the bird.

Range: Breeds throughout the United States (except the South Atlantic and Gulf States) and Canada; winters in all the United States except Florida.

Habits and economic status: Horned larks frequent the open country, especially the plains and deserts. They associate m large flocks, are hardy, apparently delighting in exposed situations in winter, and often nest before snow disappears. The flight is irregular and hesitating, but in the breeding season the males ascend high in air, singing as they go, and pitch to the

ground in one thrilling dive. The preference of horned larks is for vegetable food, and about one-sixth of this is grain, chiefly waste. Some sprouting grain is nulled, but drilled grain is safe from injury. California horned larks take much more grain than the eastern birds, specializing on oats, but this is accounted for by the fact that oats grow wild over much of the State. Weed seeds are the largest single element of food. The insect food, about 20 per cent of the whole, includes such pests as May beetles and their larvæ (white grubs), leaf beetles, clover-leaf and clover-root weevils, the po-

tato-stalk borer, nut Weevils, billbugs, and the chinch bug. Grasshoppers are a favorite food, and cutworms are freely eaten. The horned larks, on the whole, may be considered useful birds. (See Biol. Survey Bui. 23.)

Arkansas Kingbird (Tyrannus verticalis)

Length, 9 inches. The white edge of the feather on each side of the tail distinguishes this from all other flycatchers except the gray and salmon-colored scissortail of Texas.

Range: Breeds from Minnesota, Kansas, and Texas to the Pacific Ocean and from northern Mexico to southern Canada; winters from Mexico to Guatemala.

Habits and economic status: The Arkansas kingbird is not so domestic as its eastern relative and seems to prefer the hill country with scattered oaks rather than the orchard or the vicinity of ranch buildings, but it sometimes places its rude and conspicuous nest in trees on village streets. The bird's yearly food is composed of 87 per cent animal matter and 13 per cent vegetable. The animal food is composed almost entirely of insects. Like the eastern species, it has been accused of destroying honeybees to a harmful extent, and remains of honeybees were found to constitute 5 per cent of the food of the individuals examined, but nearly all those eaten were drones. Bees and wasps, in general, are the biggest item of food (38 per cent), grasshoppers and crickets stand next (20 per cent), and beetles, mostly of noxious species, constitute 14 per cent of the food. The vegetable food consists mostly of fruit, such as the elder and other berries, with a few seeds. This bird should be strictly preserved. (See Biol. Survey Bul. 34, pp. 32–34, and Bul. 44, pp. 19–22.)

Kingbird (Tyrannus tyrannus)

Length, about 8½ inches. The white lower surface and white-tipped tail distinguish this flycatcher.

Range: Breeds throughout the United States (except the southwestern part) and southern Canada; winters from Mexico to South America.

Habits and economic status: The kingbird is a pronounced enemy of hawks and crows, which it vigorously attacks at every opportunity, thereby affording efficient protection to near-by poultry yards and young chickens at large. It loves the open country and is especially fond of orchards and trees about farm buildings. No less than 85 per cent of its food consists of insects, mostly of a harmful nature. It eats the common rose chafer or rose bug, and more remarkable still it devours blister beetles freely. The bird has been accused of eating honeybees to an injurious extent, but there is little ground for the accusation, as appears from the fact that examination of 634 stomachs showed only 61 bees in 22 stomachs.

Of these 51 were useless drones. On the other hand, it devours robber flies, which catch and destroy honeybees. Grasshoppers and crickets, with a few bugs and some cutworms, and a few other insects, make up the rest of the animal food. The vegetable food consists of fruit and a few seeds. The kingbird deserves full protection. (See Biol. Surv. Bul. 44, pp. 11–19.)

Nighthawk (Chordeiles virginianus)

Length, 10 inches. Not to be confused with the whippoorwill. The latter lives in woodland and is chiefly nocturnal. The nighthawk often flies by day, when the white bar across the wing and its nasal cry are distinguishing.

Range: Breeds throughout most of the United States and Canada; winters in South America.

Habits and economic status: The skillful evolutions of a company of night-hawks as the birds gracefully cleave the air in intersecting circles is a sight to be remembered. So expert are they on the wing that no insect is safe from them, even the swift dragonfly being captured with ease.

Unfortunately their erratic flight tempts men to use them for targets, and this inexcusable practice is seriously diminishing their numbers, which is deplorable, since no birds are more useful. This species makes no nest, but lays its two spotted eggs on the bare ground, sometimes on the gravel roof of the city house. The night-hawk is a voracious feeder and is almost exclusively insectivorous. Some stomachs contained from 30 to 50 different kinds of insects, and more than 600 kinds have been identified from the stomachs thus far examined. From 500 to 1,000 ants are often found in a stomach. Several species of mosquitoes, including *Anopheles,* the transmitter of malaria, are eaten. Other well-known pests destroyed by the nighthawk are the Colorado potato beetle, cucumber beetles, chestnut, rice, clover-leaf and cotton-boll weevils, billbugs, bark beetles, squash bugs, and moths of the cotton worm.

Flicker (Colaptes auratus)

Length, 13 inches. The yellow under surface of the wing, yellow tail shafts, and white rump are characteristic.

Range: Breeds in the eastern United States west to the plains and in the forested parts of Canada and Alaska; winters in most of the eastern United States.

Habits and economic status: The flicker inhabits the open country rather than the forest and delights in park-like regions where trees are numerous and scattered. It nests in any large cavity in a tree and readily appropriates an artificial box. It is possible, therefore, to insure the presence of this useful bird about the farm and

to increase its numbers. It is the most terrestrial of our woodpeckers and procures much of its food from the ground. The largest item of animal food is ants, of which the flicker eats more than any other common bird. Ants were found in 524 of the 684 stomachs examined and 98 stomachs contained no other food. One stomach contained over 5,000 and two others held over 3,000 each. While bugs are not largely eaten by the flicker, one stomach contained 17 chinch bugs. Wild fruits are next to ants in importance in the flicker's dietary. Of these sour gum and wild black cherry stand at the head. The food habits of this bird are such as to recommend it to complete protection. (See Biol. Survey Bul. 37, pp. 52–58.)

Yellow-Bellied Sapsucker (Sphyrapicus varius)

Length, about 8½ inches. Only woodpecker having top of head from base of bill red, combined with a black patch on breast.

Range: Breeds in northern half of the United States and southern half of Canada; winters in most of the States and south to Costa Rica.

Habits and economic status: The yellow-bellied sapsucker is rather silent and suspicious and generally manages to have a tree between himself and the observer. Hence the bird is much better known by its works than its appearance. The regular girdles of holes made by this bird are common on a great variety of trees; in all about 250 kinds are known to be attacked. Occasionally young trees are killed outright, but more loss is caused by stains and other blemishes in the wood which result from sapsucker punctures. These blemishes, which are known as bird pecks, are especially numerous in hickory, oak, cypress, and yellow poplar. Defects due to sapsucker work cause an annual

loss to the lumber industry estimated at $1,250,000. The food of the yellow-bellied sapsucker is about half animal and half vegetable. Its fondness for ants counts slightly in its favor. It eats also wasps, beetles (including, however, very-few wood-boring species), bugs, and spiders. The two principal components of the vegetable food are wild fruits of no importance and cambium (the layer just beneath the bark of trees). In securing the cambium the bird does the damage above described. The yellow-bellied sapsucker, unlike other woodpeckers, thus does comparatively little good and much harm. (See Biol. Survey Bul. 39.)

Downy Woodpecker (Dryobates pobescens)

Length, 6 inches. Our smallest woodpecker; spotted with black and white. Dark bars on the outer tail feathers distinguish it from the similarly colored but larger hairy woodpecker.

Range: Resident in the United States and the forested parts of Canada and Alaska.

Habits and economic status: This woodpecker is commonly distributed, living in woodland tracts, orchards, and gardens. The bird has

several characteristic notes, and, like the hairy woodpecker, is fond of beating on a dry resonant tree branch

a tattoo which to appreciative ears has the quality of woodland music. In a hole excavated in a dead branch the downy woodpecker lays four to six eggs. This and the hairy woodpecker are among our most valuable allies, their food consisting of some of the worst foes of orchard and woodland, which the woodpeckers are especially equipped to dig out of dead and living wood. In the examination of 723 stomachs of this bird, animal food, mostly insects, was found to constitute 76 per cent of the diet and vegetable matter 24 per cent. The animal food consists largely of beetles that bore into timber or burrow under the bark. Caterpillars amount to 16 per cent of the food and include many especially harmful species. Grasshopper eggs are freely eaten. The vegetable food of the downy woodpecker consists of small fruit and seeds, mostly of wild species. It distributes seeds of poison ivy, or poison oak, which is about the only fault of this very useful bird. (See Biol. Survey Bul. 37, pp. 17–22.)

Yellow-Billed Cuckoo (Coccyzus americanus)

Length, about 12 inches. The yellow lower part of the bill distinguishes this bird from its near relative, the black-billed cuckoo.

Range: Breeds generally in the United States and southern Canada; winters in South America.

Habits and economic status: This bird lives on the edges of woodland, in groves, orchards, parks, and even in shaded village streets. It is sometimes known as rain crow, because its very characteristic notes are supposed to foretell rain. The cuckoo has sly, furtive ways as it moves among the bushes or flits from tree to tree, and is much more often seen than heard. Unlike its European rela-

tive, it does not lay its eggs in other birds' nests, but builds a nest of its own. This is, however, a rather crude and shabby affair—hardly more than a platform of twigs sufficient to hold the greenish eggs. The cuckoo is extremely useful because of its insectivorous habits, especially as it shows a marked preference for the hairy caterpillars, which few birds eat. One stomach that was examined contained 250 American tent caterpillars; another, 217 fall webworms. In places where tent caterpillars are abundant they seem to constitute a large portion of the food of this and the black-billed cuckoo.

Screech Owl (Otus asio)

Length, about 8 inches. Our smallest owl with ear tufts. There are two distinct phases of plumage, one grayish and the other bright rufous.

Range: Resident throughout the United States, southern Canada, and northern Mexico.

Habits and economic status: The little screech owl inhabits orchards, groves, and thickets, and hunts for its prey in such places as well as along hedgerows and in the open. During warm shells in winter it  forages quite extensively and stores up in some hollow tree considerable quantities of food for use during inclement weather. Such larders frequently contain enough mice or other prey to bridge over a period of a week or more. With the exception of the burrowing owl it is probably the most insectivorous of the nocturnal birds of prey. It feeds also upon small mammals, birds, reptiles, batrachians, fish, spiders, crawfish, scorpions, and earthworms. Grasshoppers, crickets, ground-dwelling beetles, and caterpillars are its favorites among insects, as are field mice among mammals and sparrows among birds. Out of 324 stomachs examined, 169 were found to contain insects; 142, small mammals; 56, birds; and 15, crawfish. The screech owl should be encouraged to stay near barns and outhouses, as it will keep in check house mice and wood mice, which frequent such places. (See Biol. Survey Bul. 3, pp. 163–173.)

Barn Owl (Aluco pratincola)

Length, about 17 inches. Facial disk not circular as in our other owls; plumage above, pale yellow; beneath, varying from silky white to pale bright tawny.

Range: Resident in Mexico, in the southern United States, and north to New York, Ohio, Nebraska, and California.

Habits and economic status: The barn owl, often called monkey-faced owl, is one of the most beneficial of the birds of prey, since it feeds almost exclusively on small mammals that injure farm produce, nursery, and orchard stock. It hunts principally in the open and consequently se-cures such mammals as pocket gophers, field mice, common rats, house mice, harvest mice, kangaroo rats, and cotton rats. It occasionally captures a few birds and insects. At least a half bushel of the remains of pocket gophers have been found in the nesting cavity of a pair of these birds. Remembering that a gopher has been known in a short time to girdle seven apricot trees worth $100 it is hard to overestimate the value of the service of a pair of barn owls. 1,247 pellets of the barn owl collected from the Smithsonian towers contained 3,100 skulls, of which 3,004, or 97 per cent, were of mammals; 92, or 3 per cent, of birds; and 4 were of frogs. The bulk consisted of 1,987 field mice, 656 house mice, and 210 common rats. The birds eaten were mainly sparrows and blackbirds. This valuable owl should be rigidly protected throughout its entire range. (See Biol. Survey Bul. 3, pp. 132–139.)

Sparrow Hawk (Falco sparverius)

Length, about 10 inches. This is one of the best known and handsomest, as well as the smallest, of North American hawks.

Range: Breeds throughout the United States, Canada, and northern Mexico; winters in the United States and south to Guatemala.

Habits and economic status: The sparrow hawk, which is a true falcon, lives in the more open country and builds its nest in hollow trees. It is abundant in many parts of the West, where telegraph poles afford it convenient perching and feeding places. Its food consists of insects, small mammals, birds, spiders, and reptiles. Grasshoppers, crick-  ets, and terrestrial beetles and caterpillars make up considerably more than half its subsistence, while field mice, house mice, and shrews cover fully 25 per cent of its annual supply. The balance of the food includes birds, reptiles, and spiders. Contrary to the usual habits of the species, some individuals during the breeding season capture nestling birds for food for their young and create considerable havoc among the songsters of the neighborhood. In agricultural districts when new ground is broken by the plow, they sometimes become very tame, even alighting for an instant under the horses in their endeavor to seize a worm or insect. Out of 410 stomachs examined, 314 were found to contain insects; 129, small mammals; and 70, small birds. This little falcon renders good service in destroying noxious insects and rodents and should be encouraged and protected. (See Biol. Survey Bul. 3, pp. 115–127.)

Red-Tailed Hawk (Buteo borealis)

Length, about 2 feet. One of our largest hawks; adults with tail reddish brown.

Range: Breeds in the United States, Mexico, Costa Rica, Canada, and Alaska; winters generally in the United States and south to Guatemala.

Habits and economic status: The red-tailed hawk, or "hen-hawk," as it is commonly called, is one of the best known of all our birds of prey, and is a widely distributed species of great economic importance. Its habit of sitting on some prominent limb or pole in the open, or flying with measured wing beat over  prairies and sparsely wooded areas on the lookout for its favorite prey, causes it to be noticed by the most indifferent observer. Although not as omnivorous as the red-shouldered hawk, it feeds on a variety of food, as small mammals, snakes, frogs, insects, birds, crawfish, centipedes, and even carrion. In regions where rattlesnakes abound it destroys considerable numbers of the reptiles. Although it feeds to a certain extent on poultry and birds, it is nevertheless entitled to general protection on account of the insistent warfare it wages against field mice and other small rodents and insects that are so destructive to young orchards, nursery stock, and farm produce. Out of 530 stomachs examined, 457, or 85 per cent, contained the remains of mammal pests such as field mice, pine mice, rabbits, several species of ground squirrels, pocket gophers, and cotton rats, and only 62 contained the remains of poultry or game birds. (See Biol. Survey Bul. 3, pp. 48–62.)

Cooper's Hawk (Accipiter cooperi)

Length, about 15 inches. Medium sized, with long tail and short wings, and without the white patch on rump which is characteristic of the marsh hawk.

Range: Breeds throughout most of the United States and southern Canada; winters from the United States to Costa Rica.

Habits and economic status: The Cooper's hawk, or "blue darter," as it is familiarly known throughout the South, is preeminently a poultry- and bird-eating species, and its destructiveness in this direction is surpassed only by that of its larger congener, the goshawk, which occasionally in autumn and winter enters the United States from the North in great numbers. The almost universal prejudice against birds of prey is largely due to the activities of

these two birds, assisted by a third, the sharp-shinned hawk, which in habits and appearance might well pass for a small Cooper's hawk. These birds usually approach under cover and drop upon unsuspecting victims, making great inroads upon poultry yards and game coverts favorably situated for this style of hunting. Out of 123 stomachs examined, 38 contained the remains of poultry and game birds, 66 the remains of other birds, and 12 the remains of mammals. Twenty-eight species of wild birds were identified in the above-mentioned material. This destructive hawk, together with its two near relatives, should be destroyed by every possible means. (See Biol. Survey Bul. 3, pp. 38–43.)

Mourning Dove (Zenaidura macroura)

Length, 12 inches. The dark spot on the side of the neck distinguishes this bird from all other native doves and pigeons except the white-winged dove. The latter has the upper third of wing white.

Range:, Breeds throughout the United States and in Mexico, Guatemala, and southern Canada; winters from the central United States to Panama.

Habits and economic status: The food of the mourning dove is practically all vegetable matter (over 99 per cent), principally seeds of plants, including grain. Wheat, oats, rye, corn, barley, and buckwheat were  found in 150 out of 237 stomachs, and constituted 32 per cent of the food. Three-fourths of this was waste grain picked up after harvest. The principal and almost constant diet is weed seeds, which are eaten throughout the year and constitute 64 per cent of the entire food. In one stomach were found 7,500 seeds of yellow wood sorrel, in another 6,400 seeds of barn grass or foxtail, and in a third 2,600 seeds of slender paspalum, 4,820 of orange hawk-weed, 950 of hoary vervain, 120 of Carolina cranesbill, 50 of yellow wood sorrel, 620 of panic grass, and 40 of various other weeds. None of these are useful, and most of them are troublesome weeds. The dove does not eat insects or other animal food. It should be protected in every possible way.

Ruffed Grouse (Bonasa umbellus)

Length, 17 inches. The broad black band near tip of tail distinguishes this from other grouse.

Range: Resident in the northern two-thirds of the United States and in the forested parts of Canada.

Habits and economic status: The ruffed grouse, the famed drum-mer and finest game bird of the northern woods, is usu-ally wild and wary and un-der reasonable protection well withstands the attacks of hunt-ers. Moreover,

when reduced in numbers, it responds to protection in a gratifying manner and has proved to be well adapted to propagation under artificial conditions. Wild fruits, mast, and browse make up the bulk of the vegetable food of this species. It is very fond of ha-zelnuts, beechnuts, chestnuts, and acorns, and it eats practically all kinds of wild berries and other fruits. Nearly 60 kinds of fruits have been identified from the stomach contents examined. Various weed seeds also are consumed. Slightly more than 10 per cent of the food consists of insects, about half being beetles. The most important pests devoured are the potato beetle, clover-root weevil, the pale-striped flea beetle, grapevine leaf-beetle, May beetles, grasshoppers, cot-ton worms, army worms, cutworms, the red-humped apple worm, and sawfly larvæ. While the economic record of the ruffed grouse is fairly commendable, it does not call for more stringent protection than is nec-essary* to maintain the species in reasonable num-bers. (See Biol. Survey Bul. 24, pp. 25–38.)

Bobwhite (Colinus virginianus)

Length, 10 inches. Known everywhere by the clear whistle that suggests its name.

Range: Resident in the United States east of the plains; introduced in many places m the West.

Habits and economic status: The bobwhite is loved by every dweller in the country and is better known to more hunters in the United States than any

other game bird. It is no less appreciated on the ta-ble than in the field, and in many States has unques-tionably been hunted too closely. Fortunately it seems to be practicable to propagate the bird in captivity, and much is to be hoped for in this direction. Half the food* of this quail consists of weed seeds, almost a fourth of grain, and about a tenth of wild fruits. Although thus eating grain, the bird gets most of it from stubble. Fifteen per cent of the bobwhite's food is composed of insects, including several of the most serious pests of agriculture. It feeds freely upon Col-orado potato beetles and chinch bugs; it devours also cucumber beetles, wire worms, billbugs, clover-leaf weevils, cotton-boll weevils, army worms, bollworms, cutworms, and Rocky Mountain locusts. Take it all in all, bobwhite is very useful to the farmer, and while it may not be necessary to remove it from the list of game birds every farmer should see that his own farm is not depleted by eager sportsmen. (See Biol. Survey Bul. 21, pp. 9–46.)

Killdeer (Oxyechus vociferus)

Length, 10 inches. Distinguished by its piercing and oftrepeated cry—*kildee.*

Range: Breeds throughout the United States and most of Canada; winters from central United States to South America.

Habits and eco-nomic status: The killdeer is one of the best known of the shorebird fam-ily. It often vis-its the farmyard and commonly nests in pastures or cornfields. It is

rather suspicious, however, and on being approached takes flight with loud cries. It is noisy and restless, but fortunately most of its activities result in bene-fit to man. The food is of the same general nature as that of the upland plover, but is more varied. The kill-deer feeds upon beetles, grasshoppers, caterpillars, ants, bugs, caddis flies, dragonflies, centipedes, spi-ders, ticks, oyster worms, earthworms, snails, crabs, and other crustacea. Among the beetles consumed are such pests as the alfalfa weevil, cotton-boll wee-vil, clover-root weevil, clover-leaf weevil, pine weevil, billbugs, white grubs, wireworms, and leaf beetles. The bird also devours cotton worms, cotton cutworms, horseflies, mosquitoes, cattle ticks, and crawfish. One stomach contained hundreds of larvæ of the salt-marsh mosquito, one of the most troublesome species. The killdeer preys extensively upon insects that are annoying to man and injurious to his stock and crops, and this should be enough to remove it from the list of game birds and insure its protection.

Upland Plover (Bartramia longicauda)

Length, 12 inches. The only plainly colored shorebird which occurs east of the plains and inhabits exclusively dry fields and hillsides.

Range: Breeds from Oregon, Utah, Oklahoma, Indiana, and Virginia, north to Alaska; winters in South America.

Habits and economic status: This, the most terrestrial of our waders, is shy and wary, but it has the one weakness of not fearing men on horseback or in a vehicle. One of these methods of approach, therefore, is nearly always used by the sportsman, and, since the bird is highly prized, as a table delicacy, it  has been minted to the verge of extermination. As the upland plover is strictly beneficial, it should no longer be classed as a game bird and allowed to be shot. Ninety-seven per cent of the food of this species consists of animal forms, chiefly of injurious and neutral species. The vegetable food is mainly weed seeds. Almost half of the total subsistence is made up of grasshoppers, crickets, and weevils. Among the weevils eaten are the cotton-boll weevil, greater and lesser clover-leaf weevils, cowpea weevils, and billbugs. This bird devours also leaf beetles, wireworms, white grubs, army worms, cotton worms, cotton cutworms, sawfly larvæ, horseflies, and cattle ticks. In brief, it injures no crop, but consumes a host of the worst enemies of agriculture.

Black Tern (Hydrochelidon nigra surinamensis)

Length, 10 inches. In autumn occurs as a migrant on the east coast of the United States, and then is in white and gray plumage. During the breeding season it is confined to the ulterior, is chiefly black, and is the only dark tern occurring inland.

Range: Breeds from California, Colorado, Missouri, and Ohio, north to central Canada; winters from Mexico to South America; migrant in the eastern United States.

Habits and economic status: This tern, unlike most of its relatives, passes much of its life on fresh-water lakes and marshes of the interior. Its nests are placed among the tules and weeds, on floating vegetation, or on muskrat houses. It lays from 2 to 4 eggs. Its food is more varied than that of any other tern. So far as known it preys upon no food fishes, but feeds extensively upon such enemies of fish as dragonfly nymphs, fish-eating beetles, and crawfishes. Unlike most of its family, it devours a great variety of insects, many of which it catches as it flies. Dragon-flies, May flies, grasshoppers, predaceous diving beetles, scarabæid beetles, leaf beetles, gnats, and other flies are the principal kinds preyed upon. Fishes of little economic value, chiefly minnows and mummichogs, were found to compose only a little more than 19 per cent of the contents of 145 stomachs. The great consumption of insects by the black tern places it among the beneficial species worthy of protection.

Franklin's Gull (Larus franklini)

Length, 15 inches. During its residence in the United States Franklin's gull is practically confined to the interior and is the only inland gull with, black head and red bill.

Range: Breeds in the Dakotas, Iowa, Minnesota, and the neighboring parts of southern Canada; winters from the Gulf Coast to South America.

Habits and economic status: Nearly all of our gulls are coast-loving species and spend comparatively little of their time in fresh water, but Franklin's is a true inland gull. Extensive marshes bordering shallow lakes are its chosen breeding grounds, and as many such areas are being reclaimed for agricultural purposes it behooves the tillers of the soil to protect this valuable species. When undisturbed this  gull becomes quite fearless and follows the plowman to gather the grubs and worms from the newly turned furrows. It lives almost exclusively upon insects, of which it consumes great quantities. Its hearty appetite is manifest from the contents of a few stomachs: A, 327 nymphs of dragonflies; B, 340 grasshoppers, 52 bugs, 3 beetles, 2 wasps, and 1 spider; C, 82 beetles, 87 bugs, 984 ants, 1 cricket, 1 grasshopper, and 2 spiders. About four-fifths of the total food is grasshoppers, a strong point m favor of this bird. Other injurious creatures eaten are billbugs, squash bugs, leaf-hoppers, click beetles (adults of wireworms), May beetles (adults of white grubs), and weevils. Franklin's gull is probably the most beneficial bird of its group.

Sources

Adams, Joseph H. *Harper's Outdoor Book for Boys*. New York: Harper & Brothers, 1907.

American Heart Association. *How Can I Manage Stress?*. http://americanheart.org/downloadable/heart/1196286112399ManageStress.pdf (accessed June 24, 2009).

American Wind Energy Association. *Wind Energy Fact Sheet*. http://www.awea.org/pubs/factsheets/HowWindWorks 2003.pdf (accessed June 22, 2009).

Andersen, Bruce and Malcolm Wells. *Passive Solar Energy Book*. Build It Solar (2005). http://www.builditsolar.com/Projects/SolarHomes/PasSolEnergyBk/PSEbook.htm (accessed June 23, 2009).

Anderson, Ruben. "Easy homemade soap." *Treehugger: A Discovery Company*. http://treehugger.com/files/2005/12/easy_homemade_s.php (accessed June 24, 2009).

Andress, Elizabeth L. and Judy A. Harrison, ed. *So Easy to Preserve, 5th ed*. Athens: The University of Georgia Cooperative Extension, 2006.

Autumn Hill Llamas & Fiber. "Llama Fiber Article." *Autumn Hill Llamas & Fiber*. http://autumnhillllamas.com/llama_fiber_article.htm (accessed June 24, 2009).

Bailey, Henry Turner, ed. *School Arts Book*, vol. 5. Worcester, MA: The Davis Press, 1906.

Beard, D.C. *The American Boy's Handy Book*. With Foreword by Noel Perrin. Jaffrey, NH: David R. Godine, Publisher, Inc., 1983.

Beard, Linda and Adelia Belle Beard. *The Original Girl's Handy Book*. New York: Black Dog & Leventhal Publishers Inc., 2007.

Bell, Mary T. *Food Drying with an Attitude*. New York: Skyhorse Publishing, Inc., 2008.

Bellows, Barbara. "Solar Greenhouse Resources." *ATTRA: National Sustainable Agriculture Information Service* (2009). http://attra.ncat.org/attra-pub/solar-gh.html (accessed June 24, 2009).

Ben. "My Inexpensive 'Do It Yourself' Geothermal Cooling System." *Trees Full of Money*, June 4, 2009. http://www.treesfullofmoney.com/?p=131 (accessed June 29, 2009).

Brooks, William P. *Agriculture vol. III: Animal Husbandry, including The Breeds of Live Stock, The General Principles of Breeding, Feeding Animals; including Discussion of Ensilage, Dairy Management on the Farm, and Poultry Farming*. Springfield, MA: The Home Correspondence School, 1901.

Bower, Mark. "Building an inexpensive solar heating panel." *Mobile Home Repair* (Aberdeen Home Repair, 2007). http://www.mobilehomerepair.com/article17c.htm (accessed June 22, 2009).

Boy Scouts of America. *Handbook for Boys*. New York: The Boy Scouts of America, 1916.

"Build a Solar Cooker." *The Solar Cooking Archive*. http://www.solarcooking.org/plans/default.htm (accessed June 22, 2009).

California Integrated Waste Management Board. "Compost—What Is It?" http://ciwmb.ca.gov/organics/CompostMulch/CompostIs.htm (accessed June 24, 2009).

California Integrated Waste Management Board. "Home Composting." http://ciwmb.ca.gov/Organics/HomeCompost (accessed June 24, 2009).

Call Ducks: Call Duck Association UK. http://callducks.net (accessed June 24, 2009).

"Candle making." *Lizzie Candles Soap*. http://lizziecandle.com/index.cfm/fa/home.page/pageid/12.htm (accessed June 24, 2009).

Comstock, Anna Botsford. *How to Keep Bees; A Handbook for the Use of Beginners*. Doubleday, Page & Co., 1905.

Cook, E.T., ed. *Garden: An Illustrated Weekly Journal of Horticulture in all its Branches*, vol. 64 (London: Hudson & Kearns, 1903).

Corie, Laren. "Building a Very Simple Solar Water Heater." *Energy Self Sufficiency Newsletter* (Rebel Wolf Energy Systems, September 2005). http://www.rebelwolf.com/essn/ESSN-Sep2005.pdf (accessed June 22, 2009).

"Craft instructions: how to make hemp jewelry." *Essortment*. http://essortment.com/hobbies/makehempjewelr_sjbg.htm (accessed June 24, 2009).

Dahl-Bredine, Kathy. "Windshield Shade Solar Cooker." *Wikia*. http://solarcooking.wikia.com/wiki/Windshield_shade_solar_funnel_cooker (accessed June 22, 2009).

Dairy Connection Inc. http://dairyconnection.com (accessed June 24, 2009).

Danlac Canada Inc. http://danlac.com (accessed June 24, 2009).

Davis, Michael. "How I built an electricity producing Solar Panel." *Welcome to Mike's World* (2009). http://www.md-pub.com/SolarPanel/index.html (accessed June 22, 2009).

Department of Energy. "Energy Kid's Page." *Energy Information Administration*, November 2007. http://www.eia.doe.gov/kids/energyfacts/sources/renewable/solar.html (accessed June 26, 2009).

Sources

Dickens, Charles, ed. *Household Worlds*, vol. 1 (London: Charles Dickens & Evans, 1881).

"DIY Home Solar PV Panels." *GreenTerraFirma* (2007). http://greenterrafirma.com/home-solar-panels.html (accessed June 23, 2009).

"Do-It-Yourself Wind Turbine Project." *GreenTerraFirma* (2007). http://greenterrafirma.com/DIY_Wind_Turbine. html (accessed June 23, 2009).

Druchunas, Donna. "Pattern: Fingerless Gloves for Hand Health." *Subversive Knitting*. http://sheeptoshawl.com (accessed June 24, 2009).

Subversive Knitting. http://sheeptoshawl.com (accessed June 24, 2009).

Earle, Alice M. *Home Life in Colonial Days*. New York: Macmillan Company, 1899.

"Easy Cold Process Soap Recipes for Beginners." *Teach-Soap.com: Cold Process Soap Recipes*. http://teachsoap. com/easycpsoap.html (accessed June 24, 2009).

Flach, F., ed. *Stress and Its Management*. New York: W.W. Norton & Co. 1989.

"Fun-Panel." *Wikia*. http://solarcooking.wikia.com/wiki/Fun-Panel (accessed June 22, 2009).

Gegner, Lance. "Llama and Alpaca Farming." *Appropriate Technology Transfer for Rural Areas (ATTRA)*, December 2000. http://attra.ncat.org/attra-pub/llamaalpaca.html (accessed June 24, 2009).

Glengarry Cheesemaking and Dairy Supply Ltd. http://glengarrycheesemaking.on.ca (accessed June 24, 2009).

"Guide to Herbal Remedies." *Natural Health and Longevity Resource Center*. http://all-natural.com/herbguid.html (accessed June 24, 2009).

Hall, A. Neely and Dorothy Perkins. *Handicraft for Handy Girls: Practical Plans for Work and Play*. Boston: Lothrop, Lee & Shepard Company, 1916.

Hill, Thomas E. *The Open Door to Independence: Making Money From the Soil*. Chicago: Hill Standard Book Company, 1915.

"Homemade Solar Panel." http://pyronet.50megs.com/Re-Power/Homemade%20Solar%20Panels.htm (accessed June 24, 2009).

"Homemade Teat Dip & Udder Wash Recipe." *Fias Co Farm*. http://fiascofarm.com/goats/teatdip-udderwash.html (accessed June 24, 2009).

"How to Build a Composting Toilet." *eHow, Inc.* (2009). http://www.ehow.com/how_2085439_build-composting-toilet.html (accessed June 28, 2009).

"How to Knit a Hat." *Knitting for Charity: Easy, Fun and Gratifying*. http://knittingforcharity.org/how_to_knit_a_hat.html (accessed June 24, 2009).

"How to Knit a Scarf for Beginners." *AOK Coral Craft and Gift Bazaar*. http://aokcorral.com/how2oct2003.htm (accessed June 24, 2009).

"How to Make Hemp Jewelry." *Beadage: All About Beading!* http://beadage.net/hemp/index.shtml (accessed June 24, 2009).

"How to make Taper candles?" *How To Make Candles. info*. http://howtomakecandles.info/cm_article.asp?ID=-CANDL0603 (accessed June 24, 2009).

"How to Milk a Goat." *Fias Co Farm*. http://fiascofarm.com/goats/how_to_milk_a_goat.htm (accessed June 24, 2009).

"How to Sell Your Crafts on eBay." *Craft Marketer: DIY Home Business Ideas*. http://craftmarketer.com/sell-your-crafts-on-ebay-article.htm (accessed June 24, 2009).

J.G. "The Fragrance of Potpourri." *Good Housekeeping*, January 1917. New York: Hearst Corp., 1916.

Junket: Making Fine Desserts Since 1874. http://junketdesserts.com (accessed June 24, 2009).

Kellogg, Scott and Stacy Pettigrew. *Toolbox for Sustainable City Living: A Do-It-Ourselves Guide*. Cambridge, MA: South End Press, 2008.

Kendall, P. and J. Sofos. "Drying Fruits." *Nutrition, Health & Food Safety*. Colorado State University Cooperative Extension: No. 9.309 (2003), http://uga.edu/nchfp/how/dry/csu_dry_fruits.pdf (accessed June 24, 2009).

Kleen, Emil, and Edward Mussey Hartwell. *Handbook of Massage*. Philadelphia: P. Blakiston Son & Co.,1892.

Kleinheinz, Frank. *Sheep Management: A Handbook for the Shepherd and Student, 2nd ed.* Madison, WI: Cantwell Printing Company, 1912.

Ladies' Work-Table Book, The: Containing Clear and Practical Instructions in Plain and Fancy Needlework, Embroidery, Knitting, Netting and Crochet. Philadelphia: G.B. Zeiber & Co., 1845.

Lambert, A. *My Knitting Book*. London: John Murray, 1843.

Lamon, Harry M. and Rob R. Slocum. *Turkey Raising*. New York: Orange Judd Publishing Company, 1922.

"Learn to Make Beeswax Candles." *MyCraftBook*. http://mycraftbook.com/Make_Beeswax_Candles.asp (accessed June 24, 2009).

Lindstrom, Carl. *Greywater* (2002). http://www.greywater. com/(accessed June 25, 2009).

Llucky Chucky Llamas. http://llamafarm.com/welcome. html (accessed June 24, 2009).

Lynch, Charles. *American Red Cross Abridged Text-book on First Aid: General Edition, A Manual of Instruction.* Philadelphia: P. Blakiston's Son & Co., 1910.

"Make Your Own Paper." *Environmental Education for Kids!* http://dnr.wi.gov/org/caer/ce/eek/cool/paper.htm (accessed June 24, 2009).

"Marketing your homemade crafts." *Essortment.* http:// essortment.com/all/craftsmarketing_mfm.htm (accessed June 24, 2009).

McGee-Cooper, Ann. *You Don't Have to Go Home From Work Exhausted!: The energy engineering approach.* Dallas, Texas: Bowen & Rogers, 1990.

Moore, Donna. "Shear Beauty." *International Lama Registry.* http://lamaregistry.com/ilreport/2005May/shear_beauty_may.html (accessed June 24, 2009).

Moorlands Cheesemakers: Suppliers of Farm and Household Dairy Equipment. http://cheesemaking.co.uk (accessed June 24, 2009).

Natural Skin and Body Care Products. http://natural-skinandbodycare.com (accessed June 24, 2009).

Morais, Joan. "Beeswax Candles." *Natural Skin and Body Care Products.* http://naturalskinandbodycare.com/2008/12/beeswax-candles.html

Murphy, Karen. "How to make beeswax candles." *SuperEco,* February 14, 2009. http://supereco.com/how-to/how-to-make-beeswax-candles/(accessed June 24, 2009).

N., Beth. "How to Make Taper Candles." *Associated Content,* September 3, 2007. http://associatedcontent.com/article/360786/how_to_make_taper_candles.html?cat=24 (accessed June 24, 2009).

National Ag Safety Database. "Basic First Aid: Script." *Agsafe.* http://nasdonline.org/docs/d000101-d000200/d000105/d000105.html (accessed June 24, 2009).

National Center for Complementary and Alternative Medicine. "Herbal Medicine." *MedlinePlus: Trusted Health Information for You.* http://nlm.nih.gov/medlineplus/herbalmedicine.html (accessed June 24, 2009).

National Center for Complementary and Alternative Medicine. *Herbs at a Glance.* http://nccam.nih.gov/health/herbs-ataglance.htm (accessed June 24, 2009).

National Center for Complementary and Alternative Medicine. *Massage Therapy: An Introduction.* http://nccam.nih.gov/health/massage/#1 (accessed June 24, 2009).

National Center for Home Food Preservation. "Drying: Herbs." http://uga.edu/nchfp/how/dry/herbs.html (accessed June 24, 2009).

National Center for Home Food Preservation. "General Freezing Information." http://uga.edu/nchfp/how/freeze/dont_freeze_foods.html (accessed June 24, 2009).

National Center for Home Food Preservation. "USDA Publications: USDA Complete Guide to Home Canning, 2006." http://uga.edu/nchfp/publications/publications_usda.html (accessed June 24, 2009).

National Institutes of Health: Office of Dietary Supplements. "Botanical Dietary Supplements: Background Information." *Office of Dietary Supplements.* http://ods.od.nih.gov/factsheets/BotanicalBackground.asp (accessed June 24, 2009).

National Renewable Energy Laboratory. "Wind Energy Basics." *Learning About Renewable Energy,* December 16, 2008. http://www.nrel.gov/learning/re_wind.html (accessed June 24, 2009).

New England Cheesemaking Supply Company. http://cheesemaking.com (accessed June 24, 2009).

Nissen, Hartvig. *Practical Massage in Twenty Lessons.* Philadelphia: F.A. Davis Company, 1905.

Nucho, A. O. *Stress Management: The Quest for Zest.* Illinois: Charles C. Thomas, 1988.

Nummer, Brian A. "Fermenting Yogurt at Home." National Center for Home Food Preservation: 2002. http://uga.edu/nchfp/publications/nchfp/factsheets/yogurt.html (accessed June 24,2009).

Ostrom, Kurre Wilhelm. *Massage and the Original Swedish Movements: their application to various diseases of the body.* 6th ed. Philadelphia: P. Blakiston's Son & Co., 1905.

Ponder, T. *How to Avoid Burnout.* California: Pacific Press Publishing Association, 1983.

Reyhle, Nicole. "Selling Your Homemade Goods." *Retail Minded,* January 23, 2009. http://retailminded.com/blog/2009/01/selling-your-homemade-goods (accessed June 24, 2009).

Retail Minded. http://retailminded.com/blog (accessed June 24, 2009).

Sanford, Frank G. *The Art Crafts for Beginners.* New York: The Century Co., 1906.

Sell, Randy. "Llama" *Alternative Agriculture* Series, no. 12 (August 1993). http://ag.ndsu.edu/pubs/alt-ag/llama.htm (accessed June 24, 2009).

Singleton, Esther. *The Shakespeare Garden.* New York: The Century Co., 1922.

Smith, Kimberly. "Where to Sell Your Homemade Crafts Offline." *Associated Content,* April 29, 2009. http://associatedcontent.com/article/1678550/where_to_sell_your_homemade_crafts.html (accessed June 24, 2009).

Sources

"Soap making – General Instructions." *Walton Feed, Inc.* http://waltonfeed.com/old/old/soap/soap.html (accessed June 24, 2009).

"Soy candle making." *Soya – Information about Soy and Soya Products.* http://soya.be/soy-candle-making.php (accessed June 24, 2009).

Swenson, Allan A. *Foods Jesus Ate and How to Grow Them.* New York: Skyhorse Publishing, Inc., 2008.

Szykitka, Walter. *The Big Book of Self-Reliant Living: Advice and Information on Just About Everything You Need to Know to Live on Planet Earth.* 2nd ed. Guilford, CT: The Lyons Press, 2004.

Taylor, George Herbert. *Massage: Principles and Practice of Remedial Treatment by Imparted Motion.* New York: John B. Alden, 1887.

Thompson, Nita Norphlet and Sue McKinney-Cull. "Soothing Those Jangled Nerves: Stress Management." *ARCH Factsheet,* no. 41 (September 1995, revised February 2002). http://archrespite.org/archfs41.htm (accessed June 24, 2009).

U.S. Department of Agriculture: Natural Resources Conservation Service. "Backyard Conservation: Composting." http://nrcs.usda.gov/feature/backyard/compost.html (accessed June 24, 2009).

U.S. Department of Agriculture: Natural Resources Conservation Service. "Backyard Conservation: Nutrient Management." http://nrcs.usda.gov/feature/backyard/nutmgt.html (accessed June 24, 2009).

U.S. Department of Agriculture: Natural Resources Conservation Service. "Composting in the Yard." http://nrcs.usda.gov/feature/backyard/compyrd.html (accessed June 24, 2009).

U.S. Department of Agriculture: Natural Resources Conservation Service. "Home and Garden Tips: Composting." http://nrcs.usda.gov/feature/highlights/homegarden/compost.html (accessed June 24, 2009).

U.S. Department of Agriculture: Natural Resources Conservation Service. "Home and Garden Tips: Lawn and Garden Care." http://nrcs.usda.gov/feature/highlights/homegarden/lawn.html (accessed June 24, 2009).

U.S. Department of Agriculture. *The Honey Bee: A Manual of Instruction in Apiculture.* Frank Benton. Washington: Government Printing Office, 1899.

U.S. Department of Agriculture: National Agricultural Library. "Organic Production." http://afsic.nal.usda.gov/nal_display/index.php?info_center= 2&tax_level=1&tax_subject=296 (accessed June 24, 2009).

U.S. Department of Agriculture: Food Safety and Inspection Service. *Fact Sheets: Egg Products Preparation.* http://fsis.usda.gov/Factsheets/Focus_On_Shell_Eggs/index.asp (accessed June 24, 2009).

U.S. Department of Agriculture: Food Safety and Inspection Service. *Fact Sheets: Poultry Preparation.* http://fsis.usda.gov/Fact_Sheets/Chicken_Food_Safety_Focus/index.asp (accessed June 24, 2009).

U.S. Department of Energy. "Active Solar Heating." *Energy Efficiency and Renewable Energy: Energy Savers,* March 29, 2009. http://www.energysavers.gov/your_home/space_heating_cooling/index.cfm/mytopic=12490 (accessed June 26, 2009).

U.S. Department of Energy. "Benefits of Geothermal Heat Pump Systems." *Energy Efficiency and Renewable Energy: Energy Savers,* December 30, 2008. http://www.energysavers.gov/your_home/space_heating_cooling/index.cfm/mytopic=12660 (accessed June 25, 2009).

U.S. Department of Energy. "Energy Efficiency and Renewable Energy." *Wind and Hydropower Technologies Program,* June 4, 2009. http://www1.eere.energy.gov/windandhydro/(accessed June 24, 2009).

U.S. Department of Energy. "Energy Technologies." *Efficiency and Renewable Energy: Solar Energy Technologies Program,* January 5, 2006. http://www1.eere.energy.gov/solar/want_pv.html (accessed June 26, 2009).

U.S. Department of Energy. "Geothermal Heat Pumps." *Energy Efficiency and Renewable Energy: Energy Savers,* February 24, 2009. http://www.energysavers.gov/your_home/space_heating_cooling/index.cfm/mytopic=12650 (accessed June 26, 2009).

U.S. Department of Energy. "Heat Pump Water Heaters." *Energy Efficiency and Renewable Energy: Energy Savers,* March 24, 2009. http://www.energysavers.gov/your_home/water_heating/index.cfm/mytopic=12840 (accessed June 26, 2009).

U.S. Department of Energy. "Hydropower Basics." *Energy Efficiency and Renewable Energy: Wind and Hydropower Technologies Program,* January 8, 2008. http://www1.eere.energy.gov/windandhydro/hydro_basics.html (accessed June 26, 2009).

U.S. Department of Energy. "Renewable Energy." *Energy Efficiency and Renewable Energy: Energy Savers,* April 3, 2009. http://www.energysavers.gov/renewable_energy/solar/index.cfm/mytopic=50011 (accessed June 26, 2009).

U.S. Department of Energy. "Selecting and Installing a Geothermal Heat Pump System." *Energy Efficiency and Renewable Energy: Energy Savers,* December 30, 2008. http://www.energysavers.gov/your_home/space_heating_cooling/index.cfm/mytopic=12670 (accessed June 25, 2009).

U.S. Department of Energy. "Technologies." *Energy Efficiency and Renewable Energy: Geothermal Technologies Program,* January 13, 2006. http://www1.eere.energy.gov/geothermal/faqs.html (accessed June 25, 2009).

U.S. Department of Energy. "Your Home." *Energy Efficiency and Renewable Energy: Energy Savers*, March 24, 2009. http://www.energysavers.gov/your_home/space_heating_cooling/index.cfm/mytopic=12300 (accessed June 26, 2009).

U.S. Department of Energy: National Renewable Energy Laboratory. "Direct Use of Geothermal Energy." *Office of Geothermal Technologies*, March 1998. http://www1.eere.energy.gov/geothermal/pdfs/directuse.pdf (accessed June 26, 2009).

U.S. Department of Energy: National Renewable Energy Laboratory. "Wind Energy Myths." *Wind Powering American Fact Sheet Series*, May 2005. http://www.nrel.gov/docs/fy05osti/37657.pdf (accessed June 26, 2009).

U.S. Department of Energy. "Solar." *Energy Sources*. http://www.energy.gov/energysources/solar.htm (accessed June 26, 2009).

U.S. Department of Energy. "Toilets and Urinals." *Greening Federal Facilities*, second edition, May 2001. http://www1.eere.energy.gov/femp/pdfs/29267-6.2.pdf (accessed June 29, 2009).

U.S. Environmental Protection Agency. "Composting Toilets." *Water Efficiency Technology Fact Sheet*, September 1999. http://www.epa.gov/owm/mtb/comp.pdf (accessed June 29, 2009).

U.S. House of Representatives. United States Department of Agriculture. *Report of the Commissioner of Patents for the Year 1831: Agriculture*. 37th congress, 2nd sess., 1861.

University of Maryland. *National Goat Handbook*. http://uwex.edu/ces/cty/richland/ag/documents/national_goat_handbook.pdf (accessed June 24, 2009).

"Where to sell crafts? Consider these often overlooked alternative markets..." *Craft Marketer: DIY Home Business Ideas*. http://craftmarketer.com/where_to_sell_crafts.htm (accessed June 24, 2009).

Whipple, J. R. "Solar Heater." *J. R. Whipple & Associates*. http://www.jrwhipple.com/sr/solheater.html (accessed June 23, 2009).

Williams, Archibald. *Things Worth Making*. New York: Thomas Nelson and Sons, Ltd., 1920.

"Wind Energy Basics." *Wind Energy Development Programmatic EIS*, http://windeis.anl.gov/guide/basics/index.cfm (accessed June 25, 2009).

Wolok, Rina. "How to Build a Composting Toilet." *Greeniacs*, June 15, 2009. http://greeniacs.com/GreeniacsGuides/How-to-Build-a-Composting-Toilet.html (accessed June 29, 2009).

Woods, Tom. "Homemade Solar Panels." *Forcefield* (2003). http://www.fieldlines.com/story/2005/1/5/51211/79555 (accessed June 24, 2009).

Woolman, Mary S. and Ellen B. McGowan. *Textiles: A Handbook for the Student and the Consumer*. New York: The Macmillan Company, 1921.

Worcester Polytechnic Institute. "A Passive Solar Space Heater for Home Use." *Solar Components Corporation* (2007). http://www.solar-components.com/SOLARKAL.HTM#doityourself (accessed June 22, 2009).

Young Ladies' Journal, The: Complete Guide to the Work-Table. London: E. Harrison, 1885.

Resources

THE HOME GARDEN

American Community Gardening Association
Start your garden in an urban area.
http://communitygarden.org/
American Community Gardening Association
1777 East Broad Street
Columbus OH 43203
info@communitygarden.org
1-877-ASK-ACGA
1-877-275-2242

Garden Village Web
A complete directory of garden organizations.
www.gardenweb.com

GardenWeb
Good site for discussion of various garden types
and gardening techniques, including directories
of garden retailers and local garden resources.
http://gardenweb.com/

Local Harvest
Find a farmer's market nearest to you!
http://localharvest.org/

Oasis NYC
A website covering urban gardening organizations in the New York City area.
http://oasisnyc.net/gardens/resources.htm

The Food Project
Building sustainable local food systems.
http://thefoodproject.org/
555 Dudley Street
Dorchester, MA 02125

PANTRY

Eating Well
Whole Living
Information and tips on eating and living well.
http://wholeliving.com
42 Pleasant Street
Watertown, MA 02472
617-926-0200
Fax: 617-926-5021

Food Co-ops
Coop Directory Service
Searchable listings of food co-ops across the US
and Canada.
http://coopdirectory.org/
1254 Etna Street, St. Paul, MN 55106
Phone and Fax: 651-774-9189
thegang@coopdirectory.org

Cooperative Grocer
Directory for food coops by Cooperative Grocer,
a food co-op magazine.
http://cooperativegrocer.coop/coops
2600 E. Franklin Avenue
Minneapolis, MN 55406
612/436-9182
Fax: 612/692-8563

Feeding America—Food Bank Results
Find food banks in your area.
http://feedingamerica.org/foodbank-results.aspx
35 East Wacker Drive, Suite 2000
Chicago, IL 60601
tel: 800.771.2303
fax: 312.263.5626

Canning, Drying, and Freezing
National Center for Home Food Preservation
Good source for other publications on food pres-
ervation methods.
http://uga.edu/nchfp
The University of Georgia
208 Hoke Smith Annex
Athens, GA 30602-4356
FAX: (706) 542-1979

PickYourOwn.org
Search to find pick-your-own farms near you.
Learn when to pick fruits and vegetables, and
how to can or dry them.
http://pickyourown.org
blacke2007@pickyourown.org

Edible Wild Plants and Mushrooms
What's Cooking America
Complete guide to edible plants and mushrooms.
http://whatscookingamerica.net

Make Your Own Food
Brownie Points
A blog full of fun, easy to follow recipes.
http://browniepointsblog.com

Sharing Your Bounty
Ample Harvest

Resources

Ample Harvest is a non-profit organization which helps food pantries and gardeners to share extra produce.
www.ampleharvest.org
info@AmpleHarvest.org

THE BACKYARD FARM

Chickens, Ducks, and Turkeys
American Poultry Association
http://amerpoultryassn.com
PO Box 306
Burgettstown, PA 15021
(724) 729-3459
danderson@keygroupinc.com

Poultry Pages
Information on types of poultry and how to build a chicken coop.
http://poultrypages.com

Beekeeping and Livestock
American Beekeeping Federation
List of Internet resources for beekeepers
http://abfnet.org/node/16
3525 Piedmont Rd. NE, Bldg. 5, Suite 300
Atlanta, GA 30305-1509
(404) 760-2875
Fax (404) 240-0998
info@abfnet.org

FarmIssues.com—Media Resource Center
Resource site for farming questions. Good information on livestock.
http://farmissues.com/mPortal/index.asp

The Better Barnyard
List of resources for raising small farms animals.
http://betterbarnyard.com/resources

STRUCTURES

50birds Birdhouses & Feeders
Lots of information on birdhouses including free printable birdhouse designs.
http://50birds.com/Default.htm

All About Dog Houses
How to build a dog house with links to free plans.
http://all-about-dog-houses.com

American Society of Interior Designers
A directory for green building.
http://asid.org/designknowledge/sustain/news

608 Massachusetts Ave., NE
Washington, DC 20002-6006
T: (202) 546-3480
F: (202) 546-3240

Buildeazy
Instructions for building nearly anything, with lots of free plans available.
http://buildeazy.com
Buildeazy.Com Ltd
P.O. Box 39-303 Howick.
Auckland. New Zealand 1730
buildeazy@gmail.com

Design Green
Blog devoted to discussing the newest development in green interior design.
http://interiordesign.net/blog/1860000586.html

Gateway Farm Alpacas—Farm Fencing
How to build a durable farm fence for livestock.
http://gatewayalpacas.com/alpaca-farming/fence-building.htm

Sustainable ABC
A directory of sustainable architecture products.
http://sustainableabc.com/products.html

Sustainable Style Foundation
An international, member-supported nonprofit organization created to provide information, resources, and innovative programs that promote sustainable living and sustainable design.
http://sustainablestyle.org
5113 Russell Ave NW, Studio 5
Seattle, WA 98107
telephone 206.324.4850
fax 206.324.4852
info@sustainablestyle.org

ENERGY

Composting Toilet World
A site dedicated to educating about composting toilets and promoting their use, including where to buy one and how to make your own.
http://compostingtoilet.org
info@compostingtoilet.org

Oasis Degins
Links for information on using greywater
http://oasisdesign.net/greywater/references.htm

SustainableABC.com
Provides links on sustainable building for eco-friendly communities as well as a directory for environmental and green building products.

http://sustainableabc.com/index.html
P.O. Box 30085
Santa Barbara, CA 93130

Solar Energy
USA non-profit organization whose mission is to help others use renewable energy and environmental building technologies through education.
www.solarenergy.org

The American Solar Energy Society
The nation's leading nonprofit association of solar professionals & grassroots advocates. Includes ways to get involved in promoting solar energy.
http://ases.org
2400 Central Ave, Suite A
Boulder, Colorado 80301
303.443.3130
Fax 303.443.3212
ases@ases.org

The Energy Bible
Articles on the use of renewable energy as well as links to organizations that support various types of renewable energy, from solar to geothermal.
http://energybible.com/default.html
11525 Piona Lane
Atascadero, CA 93422
editor@energybible.com

CRAFTS

Candles and Soap
Bramble Berry
An online retailer of soapmaking and candlemaking supplies.
Brambleberry.com.

Candle and Soap Making Techniques
A complete guide on how to make soap and candles at home.
http://candletech.com

How to Make Candles at Home
Offers tips, and teaches you what you need and how to make candles.
http://makecandlesathome.com/index.html

Snow Drift Farm
Online supplier of soapmaking, aromatherapy, and perfumery products.
www.snowdriftfarm.com

Soap Making Fun
Learn how to make all kinds of soaps!
http://soapmakingfun.com

Other Crafts
Basket Maker
Everything you need to know about making baskets.
http://basketmakers.com/topics/tips/tipsmenu.htm

Craft Site Directory
A directory, by topic, of useful online sites dedicated to arts and crafts. http://craftsitedirectory.com/index.html

Pottery Basics
A discussion group and a guide to where to find suppliers and workshops.
http://potterybasics.com

Marketing Your Skills
Craft Answers
Explains how to sell homemade wares based on the type of craft.
http://craftanswers.com

Craft Marketer
Discover ways to get homemade products out into the market.
http://craftmarketer.com
PO Box 75
Torreon, NM 87061
4jamesd@gmail.com

Etsy: The Storque
Esty's blog has great information on how to sell homemade crafts, specifically in their "Indiepreneur" sections.
http://etsy.com/storque
Etsy, Inc.
325 Gold St., 6th Floor
Brooklyn, NY 11201
support@etsy.com

Handmade Catalog
Another online forum to buy and sell handmade goods.
http://handmadecatalog.com
(800) 851-0183
pam@handmadecatalog.com

WELL-BEING

Herbal Medicine
Herbology
Online resource for herbal remedies with a blog for discussion.
http://herbology.com.au

MotherNature.com
Suggestions for herbal first-aid remedies.

Resources

http://mothernature.com
322 7th Avenue, 3rd Floor
New York, NY 10001

Natural Disasters and First-Aid

ASPCA – Disaster Preparedness
Disaster preparedness focused on keeping pets safe.
http://aspca.org/pet-care/disaster-preparedness
American Society for the Prevention of Cruelty to Animals (ASPCA)
424 E. 92nd St
New York, NY 10128-6804
(212) 876-7700

FEMA
www.fema.gov
Federal Emergency Management Agency (FEMA)
500 C Street S.W.
Washington, D.C. 20472
(202) 646-2500

Prepare.org
Disaster preparations from the American Red Cross.
http://prepare.org
prepare@usa.redcross.org.

Managing and Reducing Stress

Mind, Body, Spirit Directory
Listings on Conscious Living, Holistic Health, Natural Healing, Spirituality and Green Resources
http://bodymindspiritdirectory.org

The National Association for Holistic Aroma-therapy
Non-profit organization dedicated to educating the public on the benefits of aromatherapy.
http://naha.org
3327 W. Indian Trail Road PMB 144
Spokane, WA 99208
PH: (509)325-3419
FAX: (509) 325-3479
info@naha.org

Interior Design

Feng Shui World Magazine (Online)
Malaysia's magazine on the topic of feng shui.
A-17-1, 17th Floor, Northpoint Office,
Northpoint Mid Valley City,
No.1, Medan Syed Putra Utara,
59200, Kuala Lumpur, Malaysia.
+603-2080 3488

letters@wofs.com
http://fswmag.com

Lighting.com
A website full of lighting products for both outdoors and indoors.
231 North Avenue W #135
Westfield, NJ 07090
Phone: 908-233-1116
http://lighting.com

Primitive Designs Stencil Co.
Purchase antique designed stencils.
http://primitivestenciling.com/index.htm

Sims Stencils
Everything you need to do your own stenciling at home
http://stencilsource.com

World of Feng Shui
Online feng shui magazine.
http://wofs.com/index.php

Living in Community

FIC (Fellowship for Intentional Communities)
FIC nurtures connections and cooperation among communitarians and their friends. They provide publications, support services for co-housing groups, ecovillages, support organizations, and people seeking a home in a community.
http://ic.org

Twin Oaks Intentional Community
Located in Virginia, Twin Oaks shares their daily life through pictures, information about their way of living, and more.
http://twinoaks.org/index.html

RECYCLING

Earth 911
One-stop shop for all you need to know about reducing your impact, reusing what you've got, and recycling your trash.
14646 N. Kierland Blvd., Suite 100
Scottsdale, AZ 85254
(480) 337-3024
www.earth911.com

Grass Roots Recycling Network
Includes a directory of all US state recycling organizations.

http://grrn.org/resources/sros.html
PO Box 282
Cotati, CA 94931

Planet Green
Everything you wanted to know about living
green. Subjects include Fashion & Beauty, Food
& Health, Home & Garden, Tech & Transport,
Travel & Outdoors, and Work & Connect.
http://planetgreen.discovery.com/go-green/recycling

National Recycling Coalition
NRC is a national non-profit advocacy group.
http://nrc-recycle.org

National Center for Electronics Recycling
Non-profit organization for reclycling electronics.
Good directory for where to recycle electronics in
your area.
http://electronicsrecycling.org/Public/default.aspx
jlinnell@electronicsrecycling.org

Index

Index

Index

Index